OUTDOOR SCULPTURE IN BALTIMORE

OUTDOOR SCULPTURE IN BALTIMORE

A HISTORICAL GUIDE TO PUBLIC ART IN THE MONUMENTAL CITY

Cindy Kelly

Photographs by

EDWIN HARLAN REMSBERG

THE JOHNS HOPKINS UNIVERSITY PRESS

Baltimore

Violins Violence Silence, by Bruce Nauman, is reproduced on page 205 courtesy of the Baltimore Museum of Art (BMA 1984.2).

The Johns Hopkins University Press
2715 North Charles Street
Baltimore, Maryland 21218-4363
www.press.jhu.edu

Library of Congress Cataloging-in-Publication Data

Kelly, Cindy.
  Outdoor sculpture in Baltimore : a historical guide to public art / Cindy Kelly ;
photographs by Edwin Harlan Remsberg.
      p. cm.
  Includes bibliographical references and index.
  ISBN-13: 978-0-8018-9722-1 (hardcover : alk. paper)
  ISBN-10: 0-8018-9722-X (hardcover : alk. paper)
  1. Outdoor sculpture—Maryland—Baltimore—Guidebooks. 2. Public sculpture—Maryland—
Baltimore—Guidebooks. 3. Monuments—Maryland—Baltimore—Guidebooks. 4. Baltimore
(Md.)—Tours. I. Remsberg, Edwin Harlan. II. Title. III. Title: Cultural history of outdoor
sculpture in the monumental city.
  NB235.B35K45 2011
  730.9752'6dc22   2010017557

A catalog record for this book is available from the British Library.

Special discounts are available for bulk purchases of this book. For more information, please contact Special Sales at 410-516-6936 or specialsales@press.jhu.edu.

The Johns Hopkins University Press uses environmentally friendly book materials, including recycled text paper that is composed of at least 30 percent post-consumer waste, whenever possible. All of our book papers are acid-free, and our jackets and covers are printed on paper with recycled content.

Book design by Kimberly Glyder.

Contents

Preface

THIS GUIDE TO BALTIMORE'S OUTDOOR SCULPTURE is divided into eighteen walking and driving tours, all within the city limits. The eighteen tours include 246 entries. Some of the entries include multiple pieces of sculpture. For instance, there is one entry for each of the three sculpture gardens in Baltimore, the two at the Baltimore Museum of Art and one on the campus of the Johns Hopkins University, which together contain forty-six pieces of sculpture. These works of art, sited in every zip-code area of the city, are organized herein on the basis of geography.

The tours begin in the Inner Harbor, move north up Charles Street, and then span out east, west, and south. Each tour is identified by a letter, and the pieces of sculpture within a tour are numbered in order of appearance along the tour route. The section for each tour begins with a map showing the locations of all of the sculptures in the tour and a list giving the title of each sculpture and the page on which it is described.

The entry for each piece of sculpture begins with the title and date, location, sculptor, medium, and donor. The date is the year the sculpture was completed, not when it was commissioned. If a piece of sculpture was created over a period of years, the full span of years is given. If an architect conducted a competition to select the sculptor or designed an important element of the monument, the architect's name is included in this introductory material. The same is true for a landscape architect or carver. The donor is, of course, the person or organization or government entity that gave or commissioned the work of art to be sited in a public place, and that information reveals an interesting history of its own. The three sculpture gardens are treated a little differently, but the entries provide the history of their development and a list of the pieces they include.

In the essay for each sculpture, I try to relate the provenance to all the stories associated with that particular piece throughout its history, for those accumulated stories reveal the city's history in such a magical way. The stories of the Washington Monument and the sixteen bronzes in Mount Vernon Place reveal a huge slice of nineteenth-century Baltimore history, just as those about the sculpture in Charles Center and the Inner Harbor—who the donors were, what the donors and artists said at the public dedications, what the sculptors' choices say about the city—reveal just as much about the city's downtown renaissance. This guide strives to document the existence and history of all the publicly visible sculpture in the city; it is not meant to be a book of criticism.

Information for these essays comes from earlier guides, most notably the 1929 revised guide by William S. Rusk, *Art in Baltimore: Monuments and Memorials.* Another important publication on sculpture and monuments in Baltimore is *The Rinehart School of Sculpture 75th Anniversary Catalogue,* with an essay and listing of sculpture by Wilbur Harvey Hunter, then director of the Peale Museum. An essay by John Dorsey written as an introduction to *Public Monuments and Sculpture of Baltimore: An Introduction to the Collection,* a 1987 publication by the Maryland State Arts Council and the Writer's Center in Bethesda of Carolyn and Henry Naylor's list and photographs of public sculpture, presents a broad survey of the public art in the city as only Dorsey could do. Leslie Freudenheim's small publication *Baltimore's Public Art, 1960–1980,* has taken on added importance because it includes early images of several very important contemporary sculptures that are no longer on view. Baltimore newspapers, both the *Baltimore Sun* and the *News American,* printed hundreds of articles on the city's monuments that proved invaluable while I was writing their histories. Most important of all, though, have been my interviews with almost every contemporary sculptor who created a work of art on public display in the city. Their recollections have more often than not shed new light on their work, offering fresh insights never before recorded. I owe these sculptors a debt of gratitude, not only for making sculpture for the city but also for sharing memories of their experiences, sometimes from thirty years ago, for inclusion in this guide.

Included here are all the monuments and sculptures that can be found in large parks, pocket parks, and green spaces; that line the city streets and the city harbor and fill the city's plazas; that are sited in front of city, state, and federal buildings such as schools, fire stations, police stations, community health centers, recreation centers, housing projects, courthouses, office buildings, museums, city hall, the zoo, and even animal shelters, parking garages, and senior centers. Sculpture sited on private property, such as private schools and universities, is sometimes included, especially if the public has access to those places. As with public schools, visiting private schools and universities requires special consideration, as noted at the end of essays on sculpture on private property. Also included are pieces of sculpture on extended loan from artists that are expected to remain on public view indefinitely.

This guide does not include religious sculpture, with two exceptions. Reliefs at two churches are included because of their historical significance: Antonio Capellano's *Angel of Truth,* at the First Unitarian Church on Franklin Street, and his *Moses* and *Christ,* at St. Paul's Episcopal Church at Charles and Saratoga streets. Three other pieces of sculpture sited on church property are included—the statue of Cardinal Gibbons at the Basilica of the Assumption, the statue of Pope John Paul II in the nearby Prayer Garden, and the Children's Peace Memorial, sited at the Episcopal Cathedral of the Incarnation at University Parkway and N. Charles Street.

Ceramic murals are not included, although there are several around the city, mostly at city schools. There are no entries for monuments created only by architects, without sculpture, but without exception their history and significance are discussed in essays on related or nearby sculpture. They are also cross-referenced in the index. These architectural monuments include the Wells and McComas obelisk, on the corner of Monument and Aisquith streets; the Armistead Monument, on Federal Hill; and the earliest monument to Columbus, dating from 1792, an obelisk in Herring Run Park. Architects designed most of the city's fountains, and for that reason they are not included here.

Objects in the very lovely Monument Street Garden, at the entrance to the Maryland Historical Society, which today are displayed as sculpture, are not included in this guide, not because they do not offer valuable historical information about the city but because they were originally either architectural fragments or funerary sculpture, neither of which this guide covers. Nor is the sculpture in Greenmount Cemetery or in any other cemetery in the city included here. Those monuments are discussed in detail in *The Very Quiet Baltimoreans: A Guide to the Historic Cemeteries and Burial Sites of Baltimore,* by Jane B. Wilson and Barbara A. Treadaway, published in 1991. These were not easy decisions, but they were made to keep the focus on the sculptures and on the sculptors who created them.

This guide strives to avoid repetition. For instance, it includes only one biography for each sculptor who created a piece of outdoor sculpture that is currently on view in the city; it does not repeat the biography in an entry for a second or third sculpture by the same artist. The index cross-references artists and the tours in which their sculptures appear. If an entry on a piece of sculpture mentions a historical event in passing, the event has already been discussed in an earlier entry, which readers can locate by consulting the index. Inscriptions on the monuments are included only when they add to the cumulative story.

For a fuller appreciation of the history of sculpture in Baltimore, several appendixes are included. The most useful may be appendix 1, the time line, which lists sculptures created from 1817 to the beginning of 2009. The explosion of sculpture commissioned for the city beginning in 1964 as a result of new legislation setting aside 1 percent of the construction budget for city buildings is clearly evident. In appendix 2, the forty-nine pieces of sculpture that have been moved over the years, sometimes more than once, are listed. A sculpture loses a bit of its history when it is moved from its original site. The most successful relocation in Baltimore may be that of the Union Soldiers and Sailors Monument from Druid Hill Park to Wyman Park, and the most disappointing relocation may be that of the Fallsway Fountain, which originally stood at the 1915 terminus of The Fallsway and now stands at Guilford and Biddle streets. Both relocations occurred in 1959, necessitated by the development of the Jones Falls Expressway.

Sculptures that no longer grace the city's public spaces are listed in appendix 3. Just since 1993, nineteen pieces have been removed from view.

I encourage readers to visit as many of the city's public sculptures as possible, to see their settings, to sense their scale, to walk around them and see every purposeful detail in order to better appreciate the myriad decisions the artists had to make. The reward will be a richer awareness of Baltimore's history and a very special kind of connectedness to the city.

OUTDOOR SCULPTURE IN BALTIMORE

Introduction
MONUMENTAL BALTIMORE

DURING THE FIRST THREE DECADES OF the nineteenth century, from 1800 to 1830, Baltimore constructed the most impressive monuments in America. And when one looks at the monuments created in Baltimore in those first thirty years of the nineteenth century against the background of what was happening in the new field of public art in major cities such as New York, Philadelphia, and Washington, Baltimore's leadership becomes clear. Baltimore and these other cities shared similarities in monument making—from which artists were commissioned to what the monuments commemorated, to their neoclassical style, to how they were dedicated. But in those early years there was a noticeable difference in the timing and scale of Baltimore's monuments.

In the years after the Revolution, a path opened for the emergence of an *American* public art. A spirit of national honor, patriotism, and pride emerged. There was a dramatic shift from private to public life, and the arts found a special symbolic place in the expression of American unity. American's fondness for portraiture moved from a domestic context to the public domain and from painting to sculpture. American monuments and portraiture celebrated the nation's new heroes.

The earliest monuments in New York, Philadelphia, Baltimore, and Washington were created by European artists—primarily from Italy and France but also from England, Scotland, and Germany—in the first half of the century. Then, as the century unfolded, more and more American sculptors traveled to Paris, Rome, or both, to study. After 1876, more often American sculptors were chosen to make the country's monuments. In fact, all these cities, including Baltimore, erected most of their monuments and statues after the centennial, from 1876 to 1917, a period now known as the American Renaissance.

Monument making did not really begin in earnest in Washington or Philadelphia or even New York until after 1850. Even though New Yorkers wanted an equestrian monument to George Washington as early as 1802, they waited until 1851 to form a committee and did not manage to unveil the monument in Union Square until July 4, 1856. That equestrian monument, by Henry Kirk Brown, was New York's first outdoor bronze and the first major monument in the city.

Prior to 1830, larger than life-size figures intended for niches and pediments of buildings made up the majority of Philadelphia's sculpture. Philadelphians can lay claim to the first public monument in the new country: a slightly larger than life-size marble statue of Benjamin Franklin by the Italian artist Francesco Lazzarini, dating from 1789 and sited in a niche over the main entrance to The Library Company. As early as July 4, 1810, civic leaders in Philadelphia resolved to raise their own monument to George Washington, but their great equestrian statue by Rudolf Siemering did not appear until 1897. In Philadelphia as in New York, the majority of the city's important monuments appeared after mid-century.

I

During the early decades of the nineteenth century, officials directing construction of Washington, D.C., focused on building the Capitol and decorating its pediments and niches with sculptures. Benjamin Henry Latrobe, then the Architect of the Capitol, brought Italian sculptors to Washington for just that purpose, Enrico Causici and Antonio Capellano among them. Baltimore benefited greatly from its proximity to Washington, for these two sculptors accepted commissions in Baltimore as well. The architect Robert Mills held his own competition to choose a sculptor for the colossal statue of George Washington atop his Washington Monument, choosing Causici. Maximilian Godefroy hired Capellano to carve *Lady Baltimore,* the figure atop his Battle Monument, and the *Angel of Truth* for his Unitarian Church.

A very important early monument in Washington was the Tripoli Monument, dating from 1807. The first outdoor monument in the capital, it was privately commissioned by American naval officers to honor heroes of the Tripolitan War who had been killed in combat off the coast of North Africa. In 1831 Washingtonians moved this 30-foot-high piece from the Naval Yard to a site adjacent to the west front of the Capitol, and then in 1860 it was moved to Annapolis, where it can be seen today. Horatio Greenough sculpted the District of Columbia's earliest monument to George Washington, a portrait statue completed in the 1840s. Slightly earlier, in 1833, the Washington Monument Society raised private funds for its own major monument to the first president. Today this monument by Robert Mills is one of the most famous in the United States, though notably Baltimore completed its own Washington Monument, also by Mills, almost twenty years before work began on the one in the capital.

So before New York, Philadelphia, or Washington, D.C., Baltimoreans raised a monument to George Washington. Planning was under way in 1809, the cornerstone laid in July 1815, and Baltimoreans raised the statue of George Washington to complete the 178-foot monument on November 25, 1829. Nowhere else in the country was there a monument like this one, created publicly—from lottery proceeds, private contributions, and state appropriations—or on such a scale.

The third tour in this guide tells the fascinating story of the monument's creation, but first a few significant facts. Robert Mills, a 29-year-old native of Charleston, South Carolina, won the architectural competition despite the unrivaled costliness of his plan for an unfluted, colossal Doric column. The present site of the monument, in Mount Vernon Place, was not the site originally proposed. Mills intended the monument for Courthouse Square, but wealthy owners of land around the square became fearful that such a dangerously tall column might fall on their homes. They preferred the less lofty Battle Monument, which remains in Courthouse Square to this day. Mills' column eventually found a home on land donated by John Eager Howard, George Washington's former chief of staff in the Continental army.

On July 4, 1815, a crowd of twenty-five thousand people attended the cornerstone ceremony and celebration. Festivities included raising a painting of the monument and a painting of George Washington, followed by a thirty-nine-gun salute (the age of the country), strains of "Yankee Doodle," and finally a one-hundred-gun salute. That evening, fireworks exploded over Fort McHenry. Cornerstone and dedication celebrations like this one became common in the later part of the nineteenth century in New York,

Philadelphia, and Washington. Businesses closed, and thousands of people attended band concerts, parades, and marathon speeches. This celebration in Baltimore and the one that followed fourteen years later, when the city hoisted the colossal statue to the top of the column, were among the earliest.

In September 1815, a few months after the cornerstone ceremony for the Washington Monument, Baltimore's other great monument of the first quarter of the nineteenth century—the Battle Monument, designed by Maximilian Godefroy, a French émigré to the city—received its cornerstone. This monument too was unlike anything in any other American city, and it remains Baltimore's most unique monument today. Regarded by art historians as the first *public* American monument raised to those killed in battle, the Battle Monument was commissioned by civic leaders in Baltimore to celebrate the victory over the British and to remember the officers and enlisted men who died in the 1814 battle of Baltimore at Fort McHenry and at North Point.

Baltimoreans threw another very impressive cornerstone celebration on the first anniversary of the battle of North Point. Samuel Smith, major general of the militia in defense of Baltimore, along with Brig. Gen. John Stricker, commander of American forces at the battle of North Point, and Col. George Armistead, commander of Fort McHenry during the bombardment, took part in the ceremonies. A procession bearing a model of the monument arrived at Courthouse Square in a funeral car drawn by six white horses. The monument itself took twelve years to complete.

In 1827 Baltimore's legislature selected the Battle Monument to appear on the seal of the city. That year, President John Quincy Adams saw both the Washington Monument and the Battle Monument while visiting, and he proposed a toast to Baltimore, the "Monumental City." The designation is still in use today, although some have challenged its appropriateness, most strongly in 1959, when construction of the Jones Falls Expressway displaced more than a few monuments. Remembering that the city had also moved the Watson Monument from Mount Royal Avenue and Lanvale Street when its weight became a concern in the plans to extend Howard Street under that intersection, someone anonymously sent a letter to the *Baltimore Sun* accompanied by a simple drawing of a pickup truck carrying an obelisk. Perhaps Baltimore did not deserve to be called the "Monumental City," the letter suggested, if all the city was going to do was move its great monuments.

Between 1800 and 1830 more churches were built in Baltimore than in any other city, and sculptors turned their attention to decorating these new buildings, earning Baltimore the title "Athens of America." Italian artists contributed important relief sculptures. Capellano carved the *Moses* and *Christ* relief panels on Robert Cary Long Sr.'s St. Paul's Episcopal Church, on Charles Street at Saratoga Street, the oldest relief sculpture in the city today, slightly predating his pediment relief for Godefroy's Unitarian Church. Aside from an 1857 portrait statue of George Washington by Edward Sheffield Bartholomew for a niche on the Noah Walker Building on East Baltimore Street and an 1865 monument to Thomas Wildey, the founder of the Odd Fellows in America, the city did not add any other sculpture to its urban landscape until after the centennial in 1876.

New bridges over the Jones Falls in the 1880s elevated ornamental sculpture's position figuratively and literally. For the St. Paul Street Bridge, Herman D. A. Henning, a German-born sculptor who grew up in Baltimore and who has been called Baltimore's first sculptor, carved four seated ladies, two for each end of the bridge. In 1960 Baltimoreans tore down and rebuilt the bridge to make room for the Jones Falls Expressway, but the city wisely saved the four ladies. Four stone lions created similarly for opposite ends of the old Calvert Street Bridge are also attributed to Henning. They were removed in 1957 as part of the expressway project but reappeared rather magically in 1975 in Lanvale Street Park, a small area created by the development of new townhouses in Bolton Hill.

As in other American cities, important citizens and citizen societies established a practice that endures today: commissioning and donating significant works of art for permanent placement in public spaces. In Baltimore, William T. Walters offered the first great example of this kind of gift giving when in 1885 he presented the city with not one but six sculptures, which, not very surprisingly, were sited in the west square of Mount Vernon Place, right in front of the townhouse he had purchased for his family in 1871. This gift included four bronze sculptures by Antoine-Louis Barye, which today sit at the ends of the balustrades that parenthetically enclose the Washington Monument, as well as the majestic *Seated Lion,* by Barye, and its counterpoint at the west end of the square, *Military Courage,* by Paul Dubois. Two years later, in 1887, Walters gave the city a replica of the seated portrait statue of Roger B. Taney that William Henry Rinehart had created in 1872 for placement on the lawn of the State House in Annapolis.

In 1890 Robert Garrett, president of the Baltimore & Ohio Railroad, presented the city with his gift of sculpture, a seated portrait of George Peabody that rests, appropriately, across from the entrance to the institute that Peabody founded in 1857 and that today bears his name. This nineteenth-century statue commemorates the man, his work, and his legacy, for Peabody inspired Enoch Pratt to begin the Enoch Pratt Free Library, Johns Hopkins to found his university, and an interest in collecting art that certainly contributed to what evolved into the Walters Art Museum and the Baltimore Museum of Art (BMA).

The turn of the century saw an increase in sculptural activity in Baltimore, which paralleled developments in New York, Philadelphia, and Washington. The Municipal Art Society deserves credit for much of this heightened activity. Like its sister organizations—the Municipal Art Society that formed in New York in 1892 and the Fairmount Park Art Association that formed in Philadelphia in 1895—Baltimore's Municipal Art Society originated in 1899 "to provide adequately for sculpture and pictorial decoration for public buildings, streets and open spaces in the city of Baltimore and to help generally to beautify the city." The society decided to erect statues to men who had played an important part in Maryland history. As its first action, the society commissioned one of the leading nineteenth-century French sculptors, Emmanuel Frémiet, to create a monument to John Eager Howard, Maryland's most distinguished Revolutionary hero. Next, the society commissioned the French sculptor Laurent Honoré Marqueste to create a statue of Severn Teakle Wallis, one of the most prominent lawyers in Baltimore. Both monuments were erected in Mount Vernon Place.

The Rinehart School of Sculpture, which opened at the Maryland Institute for the Promotion of the Mechanic Arts in 1896, trained many of the artists working in the early decades of the new century, including Edward Berge, Hans Schuler, and J. Maxwell Miller. These sculptors studied in Europe, usually Paris or Rome, and returned to Baltimore to begin their careers. Other American artists who came to Baltimore to create monuments also received commissions in New York, Washington, and Philadelphia. But now these artists were being asked to create monuments honoring the men who had fought and died in America's wars. Chicago's A. L. Van den Bergen (Berghen) designed the heroic bronze *Goddess of Liberty* sculpture for the top of the Maryland Line Monument's graceful Ionic shaft as a memorial to all the young Maryland troops who served on land or sea during the Revolutionary War. The Maryland Society of the Sons of the American Revolution sponsored this monument and raised the necessary money. Another early monument was Edward Berge's statue of Lt. Col. William H. Watson, dedicated to Watson and his men, who fought and died in the Mexican War of 1846–48.

Almost every city erected monuments to commemorate the heroes and battles of the Civil War, but Baltimore may be the only city with monuments honoring the soldiers and sailors of both sides of the conflict. In 1903 the Daughters of the Confederacy commissioned the sculptor F. Wellington Ruckstuhl, a New Yorker who sympathized with the South, to create their monument on Mount Royal Avenue—a Confederate soldier breathing his last breath in the arms of Glory. At this time, less than fifty years after the end of the Civil War, many Baltimoreans who had fought for the Confederacy were still alive, as were their family members and the families of those who had died. These men marched to the sound of "Dixie" in a somber parade from the Washington Monument to the Mount Royal monument, prompting many tears along the way.

Later that same year, New York unveiled Augustus Saint-Gaudens' Sherman Monument. A celebratory parade through the city unfolded to the sounds of "Marching through Georgia," with many of Sherman's men participating. The stories of these two monuments reveal much about that time in the country's history, demonstrating how slowly the coals of civil strife die down. Six years later, in 1909, city officials in Baltimore unveiled near the Mount Royal Avenue entrance to Druid Hill Park a monument to the Union soldiers and sailors of Maryland. The state legislature paid for this Union monument, which was significantly larger in scale than the Confederate monument. Comparing these two Civil War monuments sheds light on how difficult it must have been to live in a border state at this time in history. William Walters' decision to take his family to Europe for the duration of the war seems all the more understandable.

The long list of war monuments in Baltimore includes the four monuments originally sited along Mount Royal Avenue—Maryland's Revolutionary War monument, the two Civil War monuments, and Berge's statue of Watson. Hans Schuler's huge relief tablet *To the Glory of Maryland*, commemorating the participation of the Fifth Regiment in World War I, was not far away. Joining the earlier monument dedicated to John Eager Howard, Andrew O'Connor's monument to Lafayette is surely one of the best in the city, and the equal of equestrian monuments anywhere. Commissioned in memory of those American soldiers who died on French soil during World War I, the monument honors the young Frenchman for his assistance to America during the Revolutionary War.

The monument's position in Mount Vernon Place caused the greatest controversy having to do with any piece of sculpture in Baltimore thus far, but it continued the grand tradition of war memorials. Its dedication in September 1924 continued the Baltimore tradition of great celebrations. President Coolidge spoke at the ceremony, which included many foreign dignitaries, two bands, and more than twenty thousand citizens.

So the first one hundred years of public art comes to an end where it began, in Mount Vernon Place. Just as in other cities during this century, the earlier portrait of Washington was created by an Italian, Enrico Causici, and the later one of Lafayette by an American, Andrew O'Connor. Both monuments commemorated great men and their worthy deeds. Whether a standing portrait figure or an equestrian monument, each celebrated the history of the country and signaled the preferred form for commemorative monuments in every city. After setting the standards in the new field of public art during the very first decades of the nineteenth century, Baltimore settled in and followed the national trends.

Fast forward to 1964, when Baltimoreans again stepped boldly forward into the field of public art as theirs became only the second city in the country, after Philadelphia, to pass legislation setting aside 1 percent of the city's budget for construction projects to assure that art would be created for either the interior or the exterior of those buildings. Soon thereafter, other cities across the country passed similar legislation.

It is true that Baltimore, like Philadelphia, New York, and Washington, D.C., had a history of thoughtfully integrating sculpture with major architectural projects rather than merely trimming pediments and friezes with relief carvings. In Baltimore as early as 1906, when the B&O Railroad rebuilt its office building after the Great Fire of 1904, the heroic figures of Mercury and Commerce seated on either side of a globe appeared over the entrance, designed by John Evans of Boston. In 1927 Laurence Hall Fowler, like Robert Mills before him, organized a competition to choose not only a sculptor but also the subject for the figures that grace the front entrance to his War Memorial Building. Fowler's jury chose a design by Edmond Romulus Amateis, who proposed sculpting two aquatic sea horses, one holding an osprey to represent the navy and one holding an eagle to represent the army. Two years later, John Russell Pope, the architect for the BMA, chose Adolph Alexander Weinman to design the pediment relief and lions that symbolically guard the museum's entrance. Then, interestingly, in 1940 the Baltimore sculptor Henry Berge received commissions from the chief of design at the Baltimore Housing Authority, Edward C. Minor, to create relief sculpture for two new housing projects. That same year, Reuben Kramer won a BMA competition to create a pair of reliefs as part of a third housing project.

Outdoor sculpture was planned as an integral part of two private architectural projects, both on the Johns Hopkins University campus: Shriver Hall, completed in 1956, and the Newton H. White, Jr. Athletic Center, which opened in 1965. But not until a few years after passage of the 1964 Percent for Art legislation, as it came to be called, would sculpture begin to be part of city-sponsored building projects, namely, schools, fire stations, recreations centers, community health centers, and libraries. No longer would chance decide whether new city buildings incorporated artwork; legislation guaranteed art's presence.

The first Percent for Art projects appeared in 1967, and a few more reached completion in 1968 and 1969, but the 1970s saw the largest number of Percent for Art commissions for outdoor sculptures. Forty pieces of sculpture appeared across the city during that decade, compared with fourteen during the 1960s and sixteen during the 1980s, with fewer completed in each of the succeeding decades, mostly abstract, made of steel, primarily by sculptors with studios in the city, many of whom had been trained at the Rinehart School of Sculpture or at the University of Maryland in College Park. The architects of these city buildings selected artists personally, and a few chose artists from farther away, most notably Harry Bertoia for Lake Clifton High School (today the Lake Clifton Campus), Joel Perlman for Southwestern High School (today the SEED School), Michio Ihara for Baybrook Elementary School, and David von Schlegell for Southern High School (today Digital Harbor High School).

Other publicly mandated art programs spurred the increase in publicly sited sculpture after 1964. The U.S. General Services Administration, which oversees the construction of courthouses and federal office buildings across the country, instituted a public art program for its buildings, setting aside one-half of 1 percent for art. Baltimore received five pieces of outdoor sculpture through this program, including the city's second most controversial piece, *Baltimore Federal*, by George Sugarman, at the Edward A. Garmatz Federal Building and U.S. Courthouse in 1978 and most recently Alice Aycock's 2004 piece *Swing Over* at the George H. Fallon Federal Building in Hopkins Plaza. In 1967 the National Endowment for the Arts established an Art in Public Places program, which provided matching grants for public art projects initiated by communities across the country. City developers applied for one of these grants to place a major work of sculpture in the Inner Harbor and won a grant in support of Mark di Suvero's *Under Sky/One Family*. More recently, Baltimore earned funds to support the Market Center Development Corporation's untitled bronze horse in its pedestal by Jeffrey Schiff, installed in Liberty Plaza in 1991 to link Market Center to Charles Center.

Redevelopment authorities across the country began including public art in their plans. Some cities, like Philadelphia, legislated percent programs for redeveloped properties too. In Baltimore, the practice of including art in redevelopment projects began with the installation of Francesco Somaini's *Energy* in Charles Center in 1970. Under the leadership of Robert Embry, who headed Baltimore City's Department of Housing and Community Development at the time, the Inner Harbor included four major sculptures: Kenneth Snelson's *Easy Landing*, on the Promenade, near the Science Center in 1977; Mary Ann Mears' *Red Buoyant*, in front of the new IBM Building in 1978; Reuben Kramer's portrait statue of Thurgood Marshall, near the Pratt Street entrance to the Edward A. Garmatz Federal Building and U.S. Courthouse, a site that doubled as the entrance to the Inner Harbor, in 1979; and Mark di Suvero's *Under Sky/One Family*, at the edge of the harbor just east of the World Trade Center in 1980. Subsequently, the city planned to include three major sculptures for the redeveloped Market Center. The Market Center Development Corporation commissioned David Gerlach's 1985 *John Eager Howard* for Howard's Park, at the northern end of Howard Street; Linda DePalma's 1988 *RedwoodArch* for the 400 block of Redwood Street; and the NEA-supported piece by Jeffrey Schiff, mentioned above, sited just outside the former Baltimore Gas &

Electric Company building. Even the Maryland Transit Administration instituted a public art program and commissioned art for its Metro stations above and below ground, including Jim Sanborn's *Cold Spring Outcrop* and Greg Moring's *Rogers Avenue*, both completed in 1983, when those stations opened.

Sculpture symposia in the city also nurtured the idea of public art. The city's 1976 symposium, proposed by Robert DuBourg, and the 1977 symposium, also sponsored by the city and administered by the Department of Housing and Community Development, drew attention to working sculptors and resulted in six pieces of sculpture for the city. The International Sculpture Symposium that DuBourg organized took place around the Shot Tower, where pieces by him and William Bennett remain today; Commerce Park, along Lombard Street, received two other pieces from that symposium. Gateway pieces by Jim Sanborn and Dominick Cea stand in Reedbird Park, at one of the southern entrances to the city, and in the median along Russell Street, respectively. An untitled piece by Greg Moring that he eventually gave to the city remains in place from a program sponsored by the Mayor's Advisory Committee on Art and Culture (MACAC), called Sculpture Spaces, which installed sculpture around the city in hopes that corporations might buy pieces and make them permanent. In 2007 the Baltimore Office of Promotion and The Arts, which replaced MACAC, began a similar program called the Baltimore Sculpture Project.

Throughout the 1980s, the 1990s, and the first decade of the twenty-first century, as the city's rate of new building projects declined, nongovernmental agencies took up the public art mantle, not unlike what happened during the latter half of the nineteenth century. The Municipal Art Society continued its gift giving, with Jonathan Silver's *Birth of Venus* in Hopkins Plaza in 1984, David Hess' *Working Point* at the Museum of Industry in 1997, and, most recently, Jonathan Borofsky's *Male/Female* at Penn Station in 2004 in celebration of the society's hundredth anniversary. Other societies and organizations joined in this activity, among them the Italian American Organization United of Maryland, which in 1984 gave the city a statue of Columbus for the Inner Harbor, just as the Italian United Society had done in 1892; the Maryland Zoological Society, which gave *Otter Rocks*, by Bart Walter, to the Maryland Zoo in Baltimore (formerly the Baltimore Zoo) in 1993; the Cuban American Foundation Pro José Martí Monument, Inc., which gave the city the José Martí Monument in 1998; the National Katyn Memorial Committee, formed by members of the Polish American community, which gave the city the National Katyn Memorial in 2000; and the Baltimore City Fraternal Order of Police, which gave the city the Policeman's Memorial, on President's Street, in 2003.

Individuals and families also stepped forward. Like William Walters, Robert Garrett, and William Wallace Spence, who gave the city the statue of William Wallace in Druid Hill Park in 1893, Janet and Alan Wurtzburger gave their collection of early twentieth-century sculpture to the BMA for a garden that opened in 1980, and Ryda H. and Robert H. Levi presented the same museum with their collection of late twentieth-century sculpture for a garden that opened in 1988. The Levis gave individual works of public sculpture before and after they made the eponymous garden possible. In 1975 they gave David Lee Brown's *Centennial* to Johns Hopkins University in celebration of its hundredth anniversary, and in 1984 they presented the Johns Hopkins Hospital with its own centennial piece of sculpture, *Great Ascension,* by Beverly Pepper. In 1995 Ryda Levi gave the American Visionary Art Museum the iconic *Whirligig,* by Vollis Simpson, in memory of her husband. Maureen and Louis Van Dyke commissioned David Hess to create an arbor for a new playground for children of the Mount Vernon–Belvedere neighborhood, and Emil "Buzzy" Budnitz made it possible for the Lacrosse Museum to commission Jud Hartmann in 1992 to create a sculpture of two Iroquois Indians playing lacrosse for the front of the building.

Artists themselves have given many pieces of their own sculpture directly to the city or to a school or museum where it would remain on public view, a practice virtually unheard of during the nineteenth century but one that became common starting about 1970. The only early gifts of sculpture by artists in Baltimore were the Lizette Woodworth Reese Monument, which Grace Turnbull gave to Eastern High School in 1939, and a sculpture of a gorilla named *John Daniel II,* given by Valerie Harrisse Walter to the Baltimore Zoo in 1948. Since 1970 many artists have given their work to be publicly sited permanently or placed on long-term loan. This is most noticeable around the Maryland Institute, along Mount Royal Avenue, and on the grounds behind the Commons, MICA's student apartment building on McMechen Street. In 1978 the Rinehart alum John Parker gave a large untitled yellow sculpture that looks like a prehistoric praying mantis, which today is sited in the median of Mount Royal at Lafayette. Since 1996, four sculptures originally commissioned as part of an Artscape exhibition celebrating the hundredth anniversary of the founding of the Rinehart School of Sculpture at the Maryland Institute have remained on loan. The four sculptures that have remained since 1996 include *The Pulse of Time Starts and Stops,* by Gregory Henry; *Time Flies,* a snail clock by Christy Rupp; an untitled sphere on top of the Fox Building, by Allyn Massey; and *Tenchi-Nage,* by Rodney Carroll. *Babette,* by Paul Daniel, a 1982 kinetic piece loaned to MICA in 1994, and *Catch the Wind If You Can,* a 1974 piece by Jeffrey Johnson, remain behind the Commons on long-term loan. The American Visionary Art Museum boasts another large collection of sculpture donated by artists. Ted Ludwiczak, Clyde Jones, and Dick Brown each gave work currently displayed on the museum grounds—Ludwiczak's *Fountain Heads,* Jones' *Critters,* and Brown's *Bluebird of Happiness.*

Corporate gifts have been important to the city since 1970 but have not been frequent. Following the earliest corporate gift of sculpture, by the Baltimore Gas & Electric Company (BG&E) for Charles Center in 1970, in 1978 the Chesapeake and Potomac (C&P) Telephone Company commissioned Michio Ihara to create a sculpture for the entrance to its new building at Light and Pratt streets, and the United States Fidelity & Guaranty Company (USF&G) purchased a sculpture by Henry Moore for the plaza area that wrapped around its new building in the Inner Harbor. British American Properties included Antoni Milkowski's sculpture *Diamond #II-III* in its proposal for an office building in Hopkins Plaza, becoming the city's first developer to incorporate a sculpture in its plans. In 1969 Milkowski's sculpture was installed in front of the new Mercantile-Safe Deposit & Trust Company. The few developers who followed its lead included the Rouse Company, which bought three pieces of sculpture by John Ferguson between 1968 and 1974 and most recently, in 1997, a piece by John Van Alstine, all for Cross Keys;

Samuel Himmelrich, who commissioned Rodney Carroll's *Subvator* for his new business park on Ostend Street in 1989; and most recently, David S. Brown Enterprises, which commissioned Rodney Carroll's *Firebird,* installed in 2005 at Symphony Center.

Conservation and maintenance must be included in any discussion of outdoor sculpture. Every city faces the challenges of pollution, vandalism, and neglect while struggling to determine the correct balance between preserving older sculpture and commissioning new works for the future. In Baltimore, in 1982 the Commission for Historical and Architectural Preservation (CHAP) initiated a conservation and maintenance program known today as the Bronze Project for the historic bronzes in the city. The program began with a general assessment by a professional conservator of the city's nineteenth- and early twentieth-century bronzes. The conservator then prescribed treatments and an annual maintenance program of cleaning followed by a protective coating of wax.

CHAP continues to employ the same professional conservator on an annual basis, even if not every bronze can receive maintenance annually due to financial considerations. To assist the city, in 2007 the Baltimore Community Foundation (BCF), in partnership with CHAP, established the Adopt-a-Monument City-Wide Partnership Fund to encourage private citizens, businesses, organizations, and institutions to adopt a particular monument for three to five years. This program is based on earlier successes with a more limited adoption program initiated by concerned residents living near the bronzes in Mount Vernon Place. A public-private partnership may offer the only sound approach to this increasingly demanding task as all the sculpture in the city ages. Currently, this Adopt-a-Monument fund primarily services the city's historic bronzes, although it does include some more contemporary bronzes, such as the Negro Soldier's Monument, by James E. Lewis, from 1971 and *Billie Holiday,* by James Earl Reid, from 1983, both of which are under the care of CHAP. New Percent for Art legislation passed by the city council in 2007 may begin to provide some funding for the conservation and maintenance so sorely lacking for Baltimore's contemporary sculpture. Those funds, however, will never be sufficient to care for the just under one hundred outdoor sculptures created since 1967, and it will only become more urgent for the private sector to join the city in this battle against acid rain, pollutants from car emissions, graffiti, and other kinds of vandalism to preserve the city's artistic inheritance. But first some agency of city government will have to step forward to take the lead in developing a conservation and maintenance program for the contemporary sculptures, and CHAP can serve as a good model.

Baltimore benefited from two very important periods of leadership in the field of public art—in the first three decades of the nineteenth century, when the most impressive monuments in the country went up in the city, and again in 1964, when Baltimore became only the second city in the country to pass legislation setting aside 1 percent of a city construction project's budget for the inclusion of art. Baltimoreans may be poised to open a third such period of leadership in this field as the city embarks on a new Percent for Art program guided by new legislation that incorporates many of the best practices in use nationally in the selection and commissioning processes. But Percent for Art programs have always provided only a partial answer to the challenging question how a city should approach its responsibility for ensuring that the urban landscape incorporates art and ultimately fosters a significant cultural legacy. Strong leadership and vocal advocacy are needed to once again inspire city officials, leaders of corporations, civic and private organizations, and individuals to become more involved in the public art process and to impress upon all citizens how important it is for the city to create public artworks that enrich, inspire, teach, surprise, challenge, and renew its citizens. This civic activity is the responsibility of many, and we will all reap the rewards.

TOURS

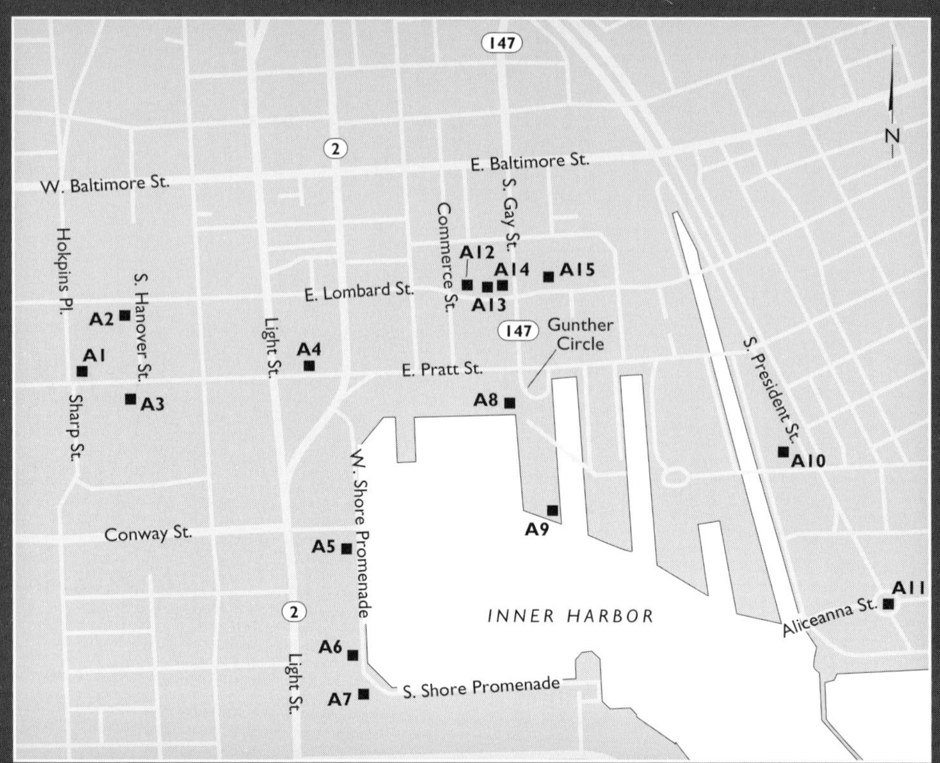

147
2
N
W. Baltimore St.
E. Baltimore St.
S. Gay St.
Commerce St.
Hokpins Pl.
S. Hanover St.
E. Lombard St.
A12
A14
A15
A13
A2
147
Gunther Circle
A1
Light St.
A4
Sharp St.
A3
E. Pratt St.
S. President St.
A8
A10
A9
Conway St.
W. Shore Promenade
A5
A11
Aliceanna St.
2
INNER HARBOR
Light St.
A6
A7
S. Shore Promenade

THE INNER HARBOR

Walking

A1

TITLE
Thurgood Marshall, 1979

LOCATION
Edward A. Garmatz Federal Building and
U.S. Courthouse, 101 W. Lombard Street

SCULPTOR
Reuben Kramer (1909–1999)

MEDIUM
Bronze

DONOR
Baltimore City Department of Housing
and Community Development

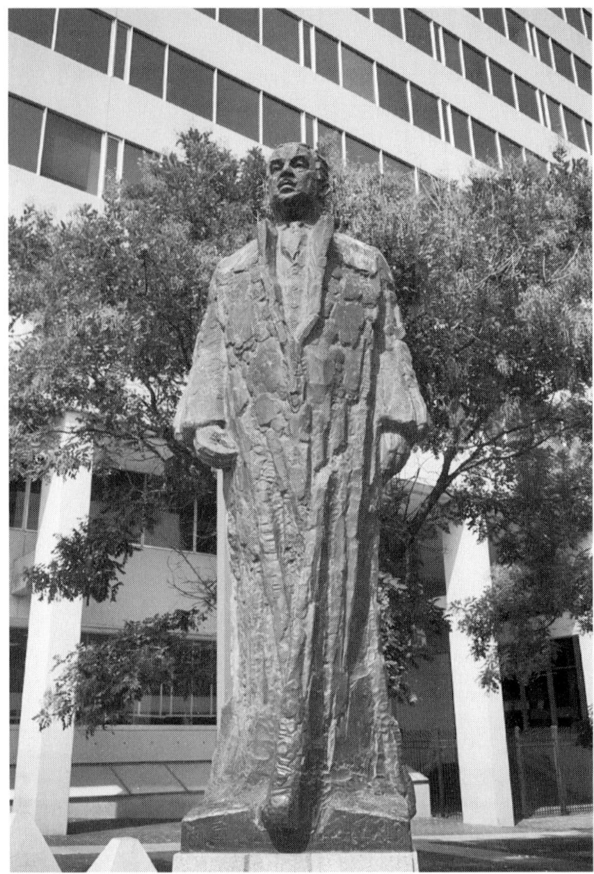

In 1977, after a national competition in which forty-two sculptors participated, Reuben Kramer was awarded the commission to create a statue of Supreme Court Justice Thurgood Marshall (1908–93). It was to be sited at the Pratt Street entrance to the new federal courthouse, a site that doubled as the entrance to the city's most important redevelopment project under way at the time. This commission was one of four offered by the Baltimore City Department of Housing and Community Development as part of Baltimore's Inner Harbor Redevelopment. (The other three commissions went to Mary Ann Mears, Kenneth Snelson, and Mark di Suvero.)

Kramer did not usually work on such a large scale. After being awarded the commission, he made many sketches and small models. He also made several portrait busts of Thurgood Marshall prior to sculpting the full standing portrait. One of these portrait busts is in the Langdell Reading Room of the Harvard Law School in Cambridge. Kramer also built a unique armature. To achieve the greatest accuracy and flexibility, he used electrical wire of different colors and thicknesses, which he wove so densely and with such detail that the armature itself looked like Marshall. The different colors aided in the weaving process. Kramer was so pleased with his armature that he kept it in his studio.

When Kramer was modeling the head, Thurgood Marshall was driven to Baltimore from Washington for four or five sittings. These were hour-long sessions to which Kramer would invite someone to visit with Justice Marshall so he would not be bored. Over the years, the two men, who were both 69 years old when work began on the commission, became friends, and Kramer visited Marshall in Washington several times. Kramer was pleased that a Baltimore sculptor had been given the opportunity to create a monument to Marshall, who was also a native son, and that the sculpture would remain in Baltimore.

Kramer designed the supporting pedestal as a continuation of the figure. Marshall is depicted in his court robes, standing straight and tall—the form not missed by anyone. The lines of his robe extend up from the lines of the base, illustrating and underscoring the artist's idea that Marshall, who had been raised in the slums of Baltimore and risen to the heights of the Supreme Court, was like a great oak tree, strong and powerful. Kramer was especially pleased with the head, which he thought made Marshall look like a lion, another reference to his strength.

Marshall had been nominated to the U.S. Supreme Court by President Lyndon B. Johnson. He was sworn in on October 2, 1967, the first African American and the second Marylander to serve on the Court. He had had a long career as chief legal counsel to the National Association for the Advancement of Colored People, during which time he won twenty-nine of the thirty-two cases he argued before the Supreme Court, including his victory in *Brown v. Topeka Board of Education,* which outlawed discrimination in public education. He retired from the Court in 1991 and died in 1993. His was a life dedicated to achieving racial equality and social justice. An editorial in the *Washington Afro-American* on the occasion of Marshall's death noted, "We make movies about Malcolm X, we get a holiday to honor Martin Luther King Jr., but every day we live with the legacy of Justice Thurgood Marshall."

Reuben Kramer was born and raised in Baltimore. His parents were Russian immigrants who had arrived there in 1896. Kramer attended City College High School and then the Maryland Institute. In 1929 he entered the Rinehart School of Sculpture for four years of study. J. Maxwell Miller was the director of the Rinehart then, and Kramer always said that he was greatly influenced by Miller, who imparted to his students a fundamental knowledge of anatomy and a respect for and love of the human figure. Those were the days when Rinehart students spent the mornings working on the human figure and the afternoons modeling portraits. Kramer was awarded two Rinehart Traveling Scholarships, one in 1931, when he traveled to London, Paris, Genoa, Florence, and Rome, and another in 1933, when he traveled to Paris. In 1934 he applied for and won the very prestigious Prix de Rome, which afforded him the opportunity of returning to Rome for two years. In 1938, after two more years in Europe, this time in London, Kramer returned to Baltimore, where he lived and worked as a sculptor until his death. In 1939, just after his return from abroad, he had his first of many one-man exhibitions at the Baltimore Museum of Art. During his sixty-five-year career, Kramer exhibited his work at the Corcoran Gallery of Art in Washington, the Philadelphia Museum of Art, the Pennsylvania Academy of Art in Philadelphia, and the American University. Kramer's one other public commission in Baltimore is a 1940 relief for the city's first housing project, the Frederick Douglass Homes (O8).

A2

TITLE
Baltimore Federal, 1977

LOCATION
Edward A. Garmatz Federal Building and
U.S. Courthouse, 101 W. Lombard Street

SCULPTOR
George Sugarman (1912–1999)

MEDIUM
Painted aluminum

DONOR
Art in Architecture Program, U.S. General
Services Administration

This large-scale, site-specific, abstract aluminum sculpture commissioned by the federal government for the plaza of Baltimore's new federal building and courthouse, which opened in November 1976, generated controversy even before it was completed. George Sugarman never intended the piece to be so controversial, but the nine sitting judges found the colorful, meandering work he suggested to lack the solemnity and gravitas they expected, and they asked the General Services Administration to rescind the commission.

In a letter to the administrator of the GSA, the judges cited their concern that the sculpture might "cause injury to children playing around it" and serve as a "haven for miscreants." After receiving letters in support of the judges written by several congressmen, from Maryland and elsewhere, the GSA administrator decided that Sugarman should suspend work on the piece. That was May 1, 1976, almost two years after the commission had been awarded. Then a very interesting thing happened: support for Sugarman began to grow across Baltimore and across the country. Editorials in the Baltimore and Washington papers suggesting that members of the federal bench did not have the authority to intervene in the established selection procedures of the GSA began to have an impact. After receiving a few letters from congressmen supporting the Sugarman piece, the GSA administrator decided to hold a hearing in Baltimore to resolve the controversy.

The hearing was held on September 8, 1976. The art community of Baltimore, along with civic leaders, lawyers, architects, and the lay public, showed up in force and spoke eloquently and passionately with one voice about the integrity and legitimacy of both the process for selecting the artist and the process for overseeing the project's development, supporting the notion that a challenge to either was baseless. After a six-month hiatus and this hearing, Sugarman was given permission to complete the commission as proposed. The piece was dedicated on May 1, 1978, almost four years after it was commissioned. The citizens of Baltimore had confirmed that art commissioned with public funds belongs to the people.

The sculpture was initially installed on the plaza immediately outside the Lombard Street entrance. After a reconfiguration of that entrance, however, the sculpture was relocated to a site further from the entrance on Hanover Street.

By the time Sugarman received this commission, he was considered one of the most talented and inventive artists working in the field of public art. Born in New York City, he attended City College, receiving a BA in 1934. After serving in the U.S. Navy from 1941 to 1945, he took evening classes at the Museum of Modern Art and subsequently studied art in Paris, Italy, and Spain. In 1955 he returned to New York and set up a studio, where he began making colorful wooden sculptures. From 1960 to 1970 Sugarman was an associate professor of sculpture at New York's Hunter College and a visiting professor at the Yale University Graduate School of Art and Architecture in 1967–68. He was a prolific artist, exhibiting in many one-person and group exhibitions all over the world. Today his work is in major collections in the United States and abroad, including those of the Museum of Modern Art, the Whitney Museum of American Art, and the Art Institute of Chicago. A pioneer in the use of color in sculpture, Sugarman was using painted aluminum for all his outdoor pieces by the 1970s.

It is ironic that Sugarman's *Baltimore Federal* was initially so misunderstood, for his intention had been to incorporate, at least metaphorically, the idea that the law was open and accessible to every citizen and

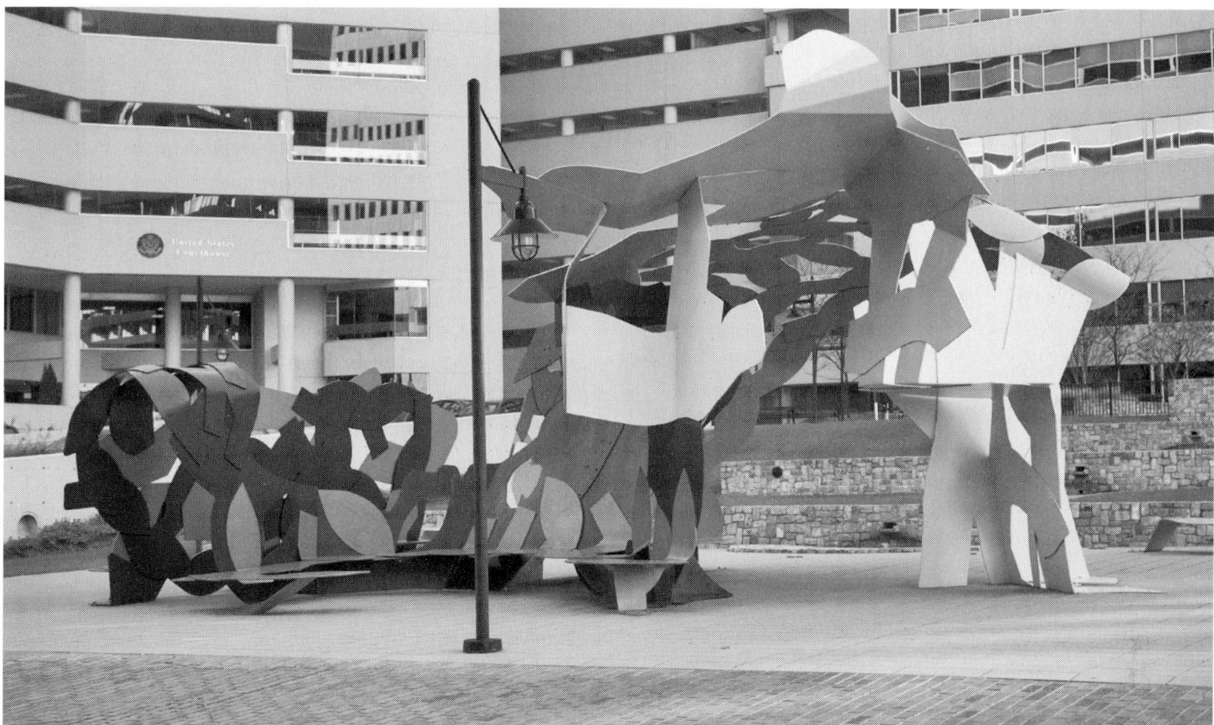

that legal precedent was built upon many laws over time. He tried to express these ideas in the design, by using the abstracted shapes of leaves welded together to create canopied areas under which people could sit on benches, sheltered and protected, just as they were meant to be by laws. The buildup of leaves against and on top of other leaves was meant to reflect the idea of legal precedent upon which the U.S. system of laws is based. In addition to its references to the law, Sugarman wanted his piece to "delight the eye" and "refresh the spirit." To achieve that goal he incorporated a certain degree of playfulness in the piece that inadvertently and unintentionally distracted some viewers from its seriousness of purpose.

A note about the GSA's Art in Architecture Program, through which the nation's leading artists are commissioned to create large-scale works of art for new federal buildings and renovation projects across the country: The GSA reserves at least one-half of 1 percent of the estimated construction costs to commission project artists. Artists are selected for GSA commissions by panels whose members are chosen from among museum professionals, members of university art faculties, artists, architects, and civic leaders who live and work in the community receiving the artwork. Since the program began in 1962, more than 325 artworks have been commissioned for federal buildings nationwide, 7 for the Baltimore area alone—this piece by George Sugarman; *Baltimore Project* by Richard Fleischner, an environmental artwork commissioned for the Social Security computer center in Woodlawn, just outside Baltimore; *Chorale,* by Isaac Witkin (E5), *Host of the Ellipse,* by Ronald Bladen (E6), and an untitled interior piece by Loren Madsen, all for Social Security Metro West; and, most recently, *Swing Over,* by Alice Aycock (B2), and *Dress Code,* an interior piece by Jean Shin, both for the George H. Fallon Federal Building in Hopkins Plaza.

A3

TITLE
Fan Figure, 1987

LOCATION
Convention Center, 1 W. Pratt Street

SCULPTOR
Greg Moring (b. 1949)

MEDIUM
Polished stainless steel

DONOR
Baltimore Development Corporation

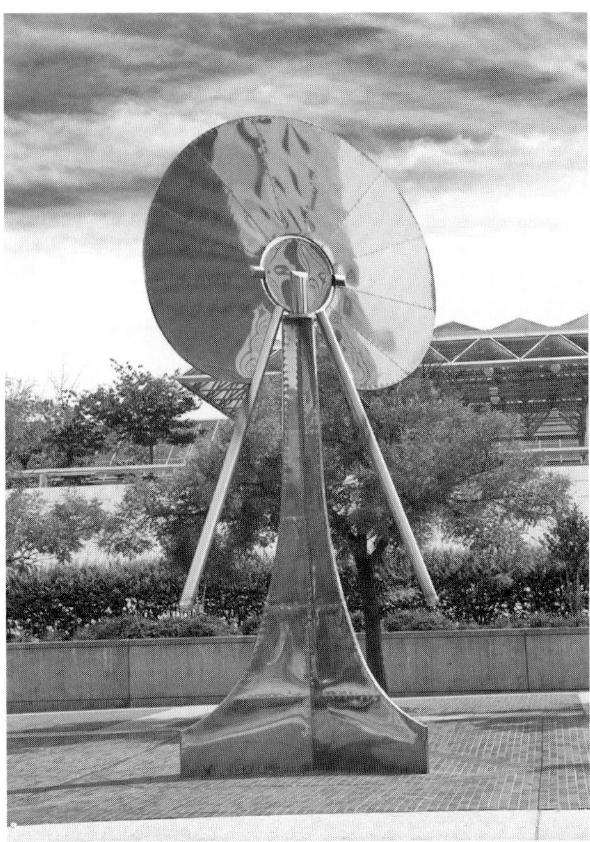

This 25-foot-high abstract sculpture has a fan-shaped element that rotates in the wind. Seated in a three-part shaft, the rotating fan of mirror-polished stainless steel reflects the city around it. Counterweights hang down on either side as the piece sweeps around, providing a strong visual statement in a visually crowded streetscape in front of the Convention Center.

This piece was originally commissioned for the plaza in front of the Brokerage, a development in the Inner Harbor in the early 1980s that had a rocky history. The private commission offered by the developer was almost complete when the project faltered. The Baltimore Development Corporation, which was overseeing the downtown development, took over the failing Brokerage project and made the final payment to the artist, accepting responsibility for the sculpture. When plans for the Brokerage plaza changed to include serving as a site for concerts and other performances, the Baltimore Development Corporation found a new site for the sculpture on Pratt Street at Liberty Road. The expansion of the Convention Center under way at the time changed the existing roadway and necessitated a second move of the sculpture, slightly eastward, to where it is sited today.

Greg Moring was born in Jamaica, Queens, in New York City. He received his MFA from the Maryland Institute College of Art's Rinehart School of Sculpture in 1975. Moring remained in Baltimore until 1996, when he took a faculty position at Youngstown State University in Ohio, where he is an associate professor and head of the sculpture department. In Ohio, he has continued to create large-scale, site-specific sculpture, most recently completing a decorative gateway to an addition to the university's Bliss Hall that depicts figures from Youngstown's steel industry.

Moring created several other outdoor sculptures for the city of Baltimore. In addition to an untitled piece in Commerce Street Park (A13), he completed a Percent for Art commission for Edmondson-Westside High School (Q6) and a commission from the Maryland Transit Administration for the Rogers Avenue Metro Station (N10). He also completed a private commission for a decorative fence at Roland Park Elementary and Middle School (L5). Moring's work is represented in public and private collections in the United States, including the collections of Towson University, the Baltimore Museum of Art, and the Butler Institute of American Art in Youngstown, Ohio.

A4

TITLE
Red Buoyant, 1978

LOCATION
IBM Building Plaza, 100 E. Pratt Street

SCULPTOR
Mary Ann Mears (b. 1946)

MEDIUM
Painted aluminum

DONOR
Baltimore City Department of Housing and
Community Development

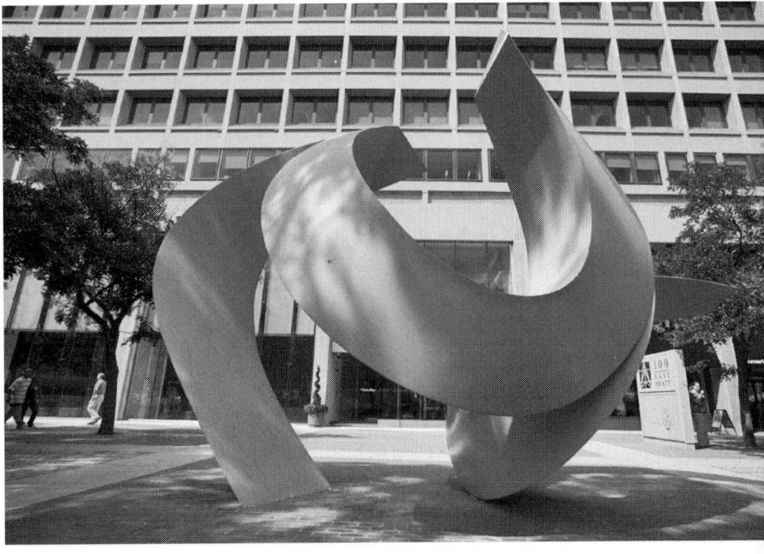

One of four artworks commissioned for the Inner Harbor Redevelopment—the other three commissions went to Reuben Kramer, Mark di Suvero, and Kenneth Snelson—this work by Mary Ann Mears was created for the plaza in front of the IBM Building, immediately across from Harborplace. Designed by Pietro Belluschi, one of the world's leading architects, who had served as dean of the School of Architecture and Planning at MIT, the IBM Building opened in 1976, the same year that the Maryland Science Center and the Harbor Campus of the Baltimore City Community College opened in the Inner Harbor.

Mears designed the sculpture to be a major focal point on Pratt Street. She intended the brightly colored, abstract, curvilinear piece to reflect the movement of people and traffic and to provide a sharp contrast to the very angular building behind it. The piece evokes the idea of a sweeping wave and reflects Mears' view of Baltimore as an alive and energetic city.

In 1983 the city of Baltimore commissioned a copy of *Red Buoyant*, which it sent as a gift to Kawasaki, its sister city in Japan, to commemorate the fifth anniversary of their affiliation as sister cities. Mears' sculpture was selected as a symbol of the revitalization shared by the two cities. The government of Kawasaki reciprocated with a large stone lantern, which was sited on the southern edge of the Inner Harbor Promenade, near the Science Center.

Born in Chatham, New Jersey, Mears graduated from Mount Holyoke College in 1968 and received her MFA from New York University in 1971. A position as an art instructor at the Baltimore City Community College brought her to Baltimore in 1970. Her large-scale, brightly colored sculptures can be found across the country as well as in Baltimore. She completed two commissions through Baltimore City's Percent for Art program (K16 and appendix 3) and one from the Maryland Transit Administration for its Owings Mills Metro Station. Other public sculptures by Mears can be found in nearby Bethesda and Washington, as well as in North Carolina, Michigan, New York, and Connecticut.

A5

TITLE
Triaxial Link, 2004

LOCATION
Baltimore Visitor Center, 401 Light Street

SCULPTOR
William J. Niebauer (b. 1974)

MEDIUM
Concrete

DONOR
Baltimore City Percent for Art program

Commissioned through the Baltimore City Percent for Art program, this work by William J. Niebauer is sited on the lawn of Baltimore's new Visitor Center, which opened in 2004. Made of cast concrete, the three geometric fragments spaced at equal distances from one another can be clearly envisioned as three parts of a circle that have been separated by some invisible force. Curvilinear and graceful, the sculptural elements quietly offer points of interest and complement the new building, with its curving bluestone-clad roof.

Niebauer received his BFA from the Rhode Island School of Design in 1997 and his MFA from the University of Maryland in 1999. Since 2001 he has been on the faculty of the Institute of Art Design and Interactive Media at the Community College of Baltimore County. He has exhibited his drawings, ceramics, and sculpture throughout the mid-Atlantic region. Most recently his work was included in the first annual Baltimore Sculpture Project, an outdoor sculpture exhibition of thirty artworks sited around the city by the Baltimore Office of Promotion and The Arts.

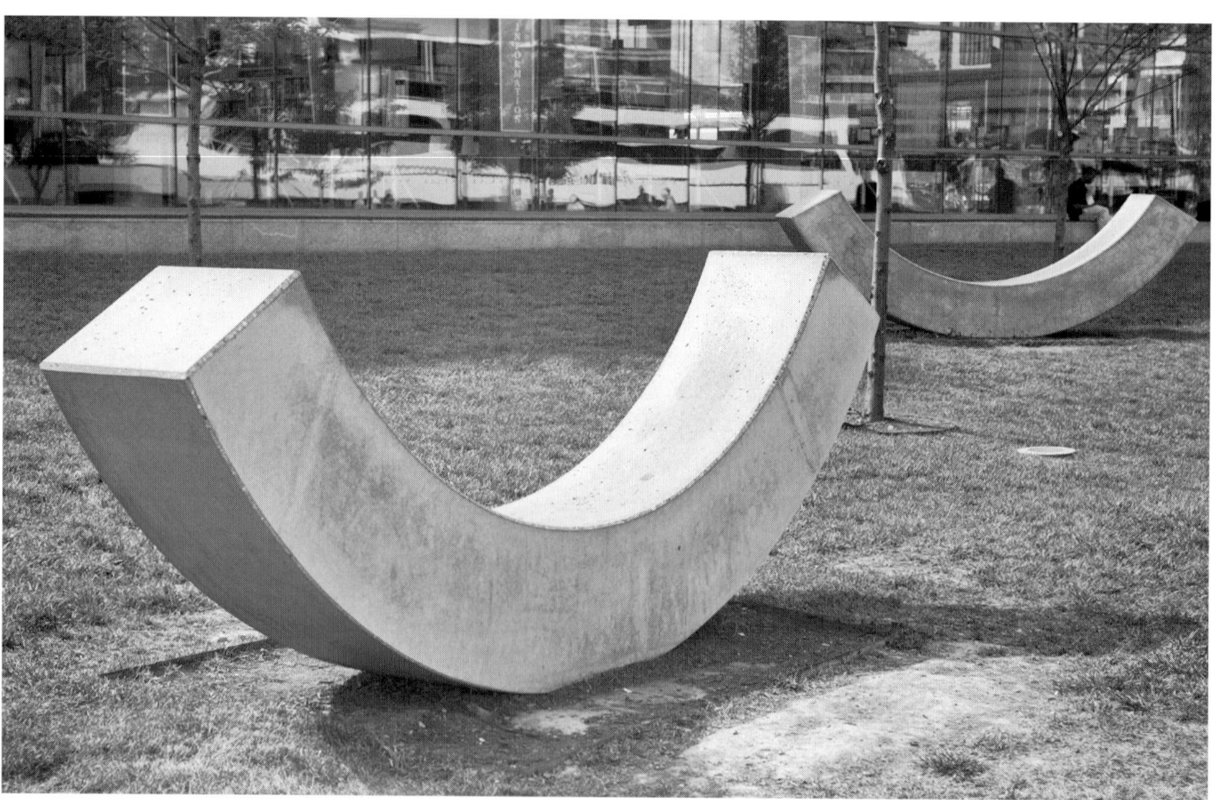

A6

TITLE
King Penguin, 1956

LOCATION
Inner Harbor Promenade, near Harbor Cruises,
561 Light Street

SCULPTOR
Grace Hill Turnbull (1880–1976)

MEDIUM
Marble

DONOR
Penguin Books

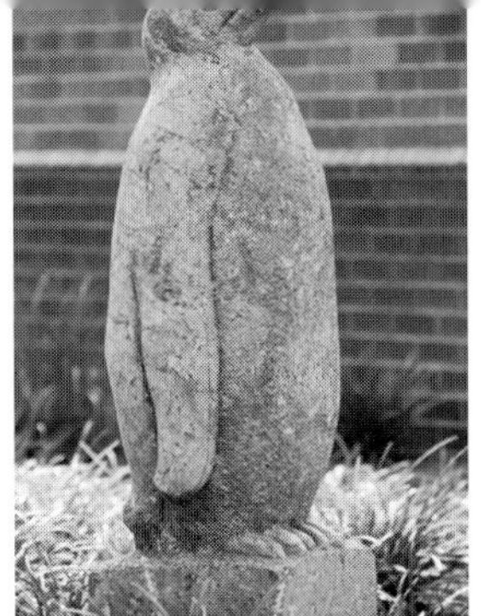

Penguin Books is a British publishing company founded in 1935 with the radical aim of producing inexpensive paperback editions of high-quality books. Hemingway's *A Farewell to Arms* was among the first of its publications. The company internationalized its operations in the United States, Canada, Australia, New Zealand, and India. By the end of World War II, Penguin was distributing a million books a month in the United States, with its headquarters in Baltimore.

For the sculpture commissioned by Penguin Books, Grace Turnbull chose Vermont green marble. King Penguins, which are found on many of the sub-Antarctic islands, are the second largest species of penguins, measuring about 3 feet tall and weighing 24–35 pounds. They have an orange-yellow patch on their chests, and their backs are grayish black. Turnbull's penguin appears to replicate the species' dimensions, if not their natural coloring. Turnbull's penguin is very blocklike and symmetrical. He looks straight ahead, with his beak slightly raised and his wings close to his sides. The surface features a small-tooled texture on the chest and a smooth finish on the wings, head, beak, and back.

The title of this sculpture may also refer to the King Penguin Editions, a highly acclaimed series of books first published in 1939. Written by noted experts, they were attractive and accessible books on subjects ranging from natural history to decorative arts, including such diverse titles as *Russian Icons, A Book of Spiders, Ballooning,* and *Woodcuts of Albrecht Dürer.* Each book had a beautifully designed cover that was, and still is, highly regarded as a fine achievement in design.

Grace Turnbull was born into a prominent and cultured Baltimore family. Her father, Lawrence, edited literary magazines, the *New Eclectic* and the *Southern Magazine,* in which he published new poems of Sidney Lanier, among other young poets, and her mother was a historical novelist. Turnbull herself was a painter, sculptor, and author. She received some formal training in painting at the Maryland Institute and then decided to study sculpture at the Rinehart School of Sculpture, from which she graduated in 1911. She had also studied in Rome with the American expatriate sculptor Moses Ezekiel, whose statue of Edgar Allan Poe sits on the plaza of the University of Baltimore School of Law (F3). She never married. Her architect brother designed a house for her on Chancery Road, for which she carved four wooden corner posts, all with religious themes. In 1953 she published her autobiography, *Chips from My Chisel.*

Turnbull's two best-known pieces of public sculpture in Baltimore are *Naïad,* in the east square of Mount Vernon Place (C13), and the Reese Monument (K3), at Johns Hopkins at Eastern, the former Eastern High School. Turnbull exhibited her work in the Salon des Beaux-Arts in Paris, at the Metropolitan Museum of Art in New York and the Corcoran Gallery in Washington, and in two one-person exhibitions at the Baltimore Museum of Art, in 1931 and 1946. Prizes included the Anna Hyatt Huntington Prize in 1942, an Honorable Mention at the Corcoran Gallery's Regional Sculpture Exhibition in 1948, and the American Institute of Architects Award from the Baltimore chapter in 1959. She was a Fellow of the National Sculpture Society.

TITLE

Easy Landing, 1977

LOCATION

Inner Harbor Promenade near the Maryland Science Center, 601 Light Street

SCULPTOR

Kenneth Snelson (b. 1927)

MEDIUM

Stainless steel

DONOR

Baltimore City Department of Housing and Community Development

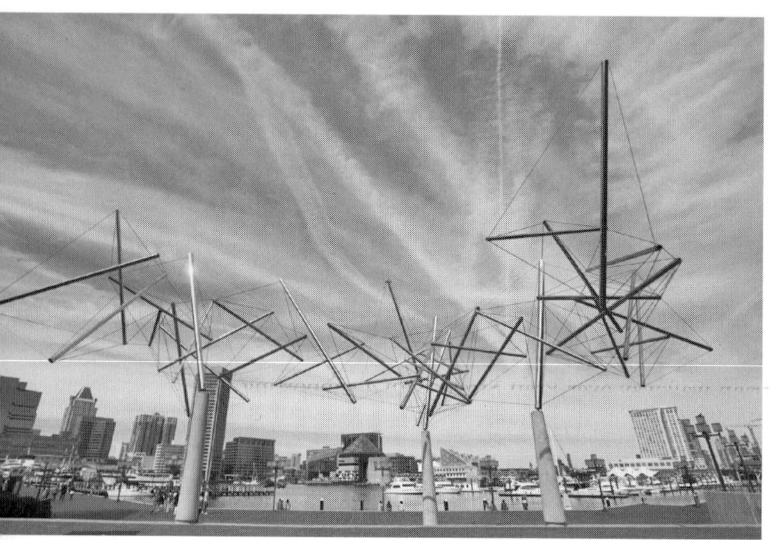

The first to be installed of the four artworks commissioned as an integral part of Baltimore's Inner Harbor, *Easy Landing*'s dedication on a very cold and blustery January day was celebrated by all.

Kenneth Snelson's abstract piece is constructed out of stainless steel tension cables and compression tubes. This mass of cantilevered cables and tubes held together by screw fastenings is perfectly balanced atop three concrete columns. The work extends 72 feet horizontally and 24 feet into the air. Flight or the movement of the sails of a boat is implied in the piece, even though it weighs 9,000 pounds!

The hundreds of individual pieces that make up the sculpture arrived in the Inner Harbor for assembly on site. Assembly began in the middle of the piece and spread outward in all directions over a twelve-day period in late December. Snelson said at the time that "every part that is necessary is there and every part that is there is necessary." Those who watched as the sculpture took shape were mesmerized. Snelson describes his works as organizations of forces in space, or "force diagrams in space." Until the sculpture is put together, the forces are not present; they are introduced as things are added, piece by piece. When the last cable is attached, the resulting closed system of forces is complete, and so is the work.

Snelson was a very well known and respected artist in 1977, and this is one of his signature pieces. For Snelson this approach to art was a long time evolving. Raised in Oregon, he attended the University of Oregon in Eugene. In 1948 and 1949, as a young art student, he attended the summer sessions at Black Mountain College, near Asheville, North Carolina, a major center for avant-garde art at the time. Buckminster Fuller, who was teaching there those summers, had a profound effect on Snelson's art. Snelson had arrived a painter, but he got interested in Buckminster Fuller's ideas about tension and compression and left making small wire sculptures that moved. As his work progressed and he began using stainless steel and aluminum with wire rope, the scale and mathematics became more complex. Today his work is in almost every major museum and collection in the United States and Europe. He lives and works in New York.

A8

TITLE
Under Sky/One Family, 1980

LOCATION
East of the World Trade Center, 401 E. Pratt Street

SCULPTOR
Mark di Suvero (b. 1933)

MEDIUM
Steel

DONOR
Baltimore City Department of Housing and
Community Development

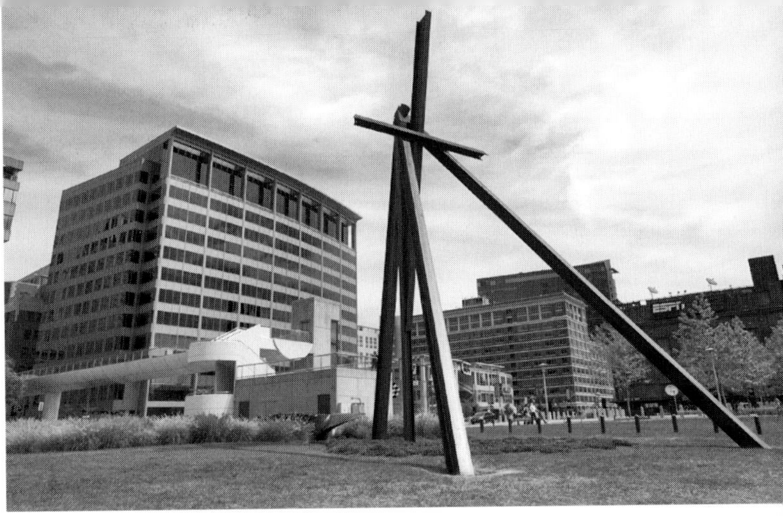

In 1977, when he received a commission to create a large, site-specific sculpture for Baltimore's Inner Harbor, Mark di Suvero was considered one of the nation's leading sculptors. Baltimore had applied for and was awarded a grant from the National Endowment for the Arts based solely on the location at the harbor's edge between the World Trade Center and the National Aquarium. Di Suvero was chosen soon thereafter, and the NEA grant was confirmed. The sculpture was dedicated in May 1980 by Mrs. Joan Mondale, the wife of Vice President Walter Mondale and a passionate supporter of the arts, with Mark di Suvero's participation.

Born in Shanghai, China, of Italian parents, di Suvero immigrated to California in 1941. He graduated in 1957 from the University of California at Berkeley, where he studied sculpture. He moved to New York immediately after graduating and had his first one-man gallery exhibition by 1960.

Di Suvero's focus on large-scale public works began in 1964. It was in that year that he began incorporating movement in his sculpture. All of the early designs for his Baltimore piece, as well as the model of the piece, involved movement. The sixteen early drawings on deposit at the Baltimore Museum of Art do not document how *Under Sky/One Family* developed into a stationary piece.

The title of the piece was taken from a Chinese saying di Suvero remembered from his childhood, but it also makes reference to Martin Luther King's belief in "one people, living together, working together, playing together," ideas di Suvero hoped his sculpture might also evoke. Other references in the work are to Baltimore's history as a maritime and steel center. The vertical steel elements and his dramatic arrangement of them conjure up the mast of a ship, and his inclusion of an actual propeller from a large ship, meant for children's play here, underscores Baltimore's seafaring history. In 1980 the sculpture was beautifully sited on an open, grassy knoll that was clearly visible from Pratt Street. At that time there was neither an entrance off Pratt Street to an underground parking garage nor an elevated pedestrian walkway over Pratt Street with a supporting pier just feet away from the piece.

In 1975, before he was awarded this commission, di Suvero had been the first living artist to have his work shown in the Tuileries Gardens in Paris. That same year he was given an exhibition at the Whitney Museum, in New York City, and his monumentally scaled sculptures were sited across the New York metropolitan area. In 2005, di Suvero achieved another first: he was given a third major exhibition at Storm King Art Center in Mountainville, New York, having exhibited there in 1985 and 1995. Today he has studios in Long Island City, in Petaluma, California, and in Chalon-sur-Saône, France, where he founded an atelier for emerging artists, and his distinctive monumental sculptures, like his piece for Baltimore fashioned from industrial materials and found objects, can be found in museums and outdoor settings across the country and around the world.

A9

TITLE
Family of Dolphins, 1991

LOCATION
Marine Mammal Pavilion, National Aquarium,
501 E. Pratt Street

SCULPTOR
Leonard Streckfus (b. 1951)

MEDIUM
Bronze

DONOR
National Aquarium

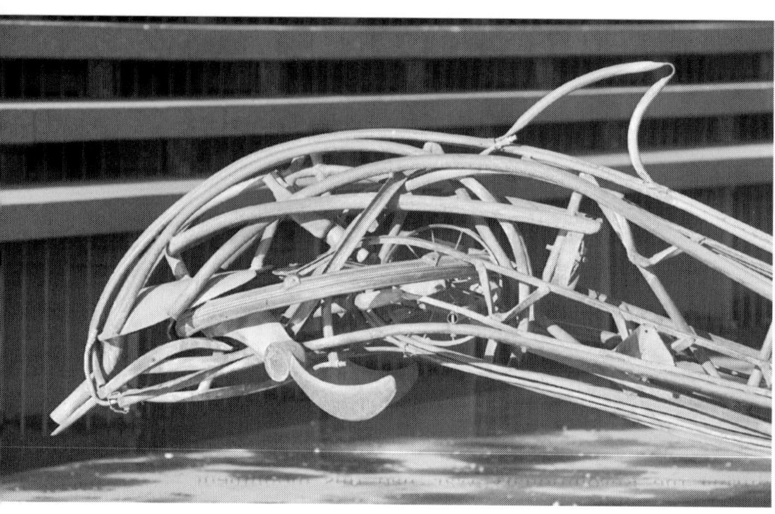

Leonard Streckfus' family of five dolphins of varying sizes—a father, a mother and three siblings, all constructed entirely of found objects cast in bronze—is installed in a triangular pool outside the Marine Mammal Pavilion at the National Aquarium in Baltimore. The pool in which the dolphins were to frolic originally looked like a small slice taken right out of the ocean, with waves that spread across the pool continually and a water-spraying feature near each dolphin that erupted at intervals as if created by the movement of the dolphins. The wave-making machine, designed by The Fountain People Inc., of San Marcos, Texas, worked well for a period of time, providing a very realistic environment for the dolphins. Unfortunately, the mechanism failed and has not been restored.

For this, Streckfus' first public commission, he collected hundreds of found objects, which he assembled with wit and ingenuity to create the five dolphins. He carefully documented each dolphin photographically before taking it apart to send the largest individual pieces to A.R.T. Research Enterprises Inc., in Lancaster, Pennsylvania, to be cast in bronze; he cast the smaller pieces himself. After receiving the cast bronze elements from the foundry, he reconstructed the dolphins and installed them in the pool. Easily seen are the bicycle parts and tractor seats, watering cans, a sled, shovels, and a croquet mallet. Less obvious is the big old fan Streckfus found in a cow barn, which he cut up to use for the dolphins' front fins. The smallest dolphin, the last in the group, is made primarily of a helmet and a golf bag, yet it is clearly understood to be a small dolphin. Deciphering what makes up the rest of each dolphin is an unexpected treat.

Leonard Streckfus was born in Baltimore and earned both his BFA and MFA degrees from the Maryland Institute College of Art. Today he lives and maintains a studio in Upperco, Maryland, just outside Baltimore. Originally trained as a painter, Streckfus has spent the last twenty-five years making sculpture out of what he calls "the flotsam and jetsam of modern life." Discarded Christmas tree stands, old chairs, bicycles and tricycles, golf bags, bird cages, shovels, shoe trees, motorcycle helmets, old tires—almost anything can find its way into his assembled animal sculptures. His horses, rhinoceroses, elephants, badgers, dogs, and antelopes have been exhibited nationally and internationally, including in a solo exhibition at the Galerie Françoise in Baltimore; in *Transformations,* an exhibition curated by Lloyd Herman, director emeritus at the Renwick Gallery of American Craft, at the Fuller Craft Museum in Brockton, Massachusetts; and in the Smithsonian Craft Show, all in 2004. Recent public commissions include *Family of Wolves* for the Meijer Gardens and Sculpture Park in Grand Rapids, Michigan, and *Grazing Horse, Resting Hiker* for the Heritage Trail in York County, Pennsylvania. He has won numerous awards for his work, including the 1999 Director's Choice Award at the Kentucky Derby Museum at Churchill Downs in Louisville.

A10

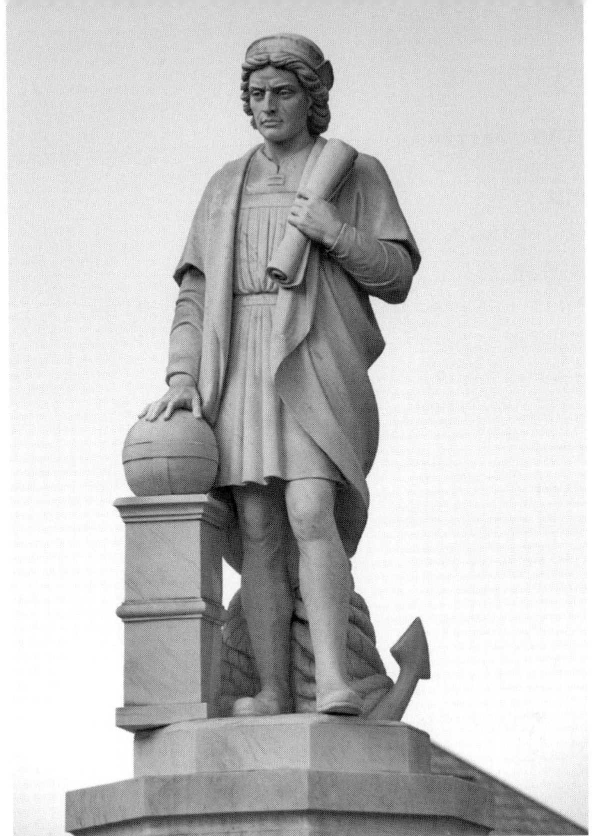

On October 8, 1984, Mayor William Donald Schaefer and President Ronald Reagan dedicated this statue of Christopher Columbus. Like almost every American monument to Columbus, this sculpture represents Columbus as a young man with shoulder-length hair wearing a short tabard, or sleeveless coat, one hand resting on a globe and one holding a rolled chart, with an anchor and rope nearby. Again, like most Columbus monuments in this country, this one was sponsored by an Italian American group and sculpted by an Italian sculptor working in Italy.

Columbus is shown standing on a tall base with six relief panels that depict his ships, the *Niña*, the *Pinta*, and the *Santa Maria;* his birthplace, Genoa; his landing; and his meeting with the Indians of the new land. Columbus looks eastward from the outskirts of Little Italy in a small green space named Columbus Piazza. Rising behind it to the west is another Baltimore monument to Columbus—the Columbus Center. Built in 1995, it is a national center for research and education in marine biotechnology and a division of the University of Maryland.

This is the third Columbus monument to be erected in Baltimore. Actually Baltimore is home to the oldest monument to Columbus in the country. That monument, which dates from 1792, is a 44-foot-high unadorned brick and cement obelisk, painted white, at Walther Avenue and Harford Road, in Herring Run Park. Charles François Adrian de Paulmier, Chevalier d'Anmour, the first French consul to the city, who was instrumental in securing French aid for the colonies during the Revolutionary War, had this monument built on his estate near what is today North Avenue and Harford Road. In 1963 it was moved to its current location to make room for the new Sears & Roebuck store, a building that today houses the Eastern District Court. The Columbus Obelisk is the oldest commemorative monument in the city. The city's second Columbus monument was erected in Druid Hill Park in 1892, when most Columbus monuments in the United States were commissioned to celebrate the four-hundredth anniversary of Columbus' first voyage (M10).

In 1999 a gigantic Columbus monument by the Russian artist Zurab Tsereteli was offered to Baltimore as a gift from Russia. However, Baltimore decided not to accept this gift, as the cost of installing the nearly 360-foot-high monument was prohibitive and Columbus was thought to be already well represented in the city.

A11

NATIONAL KATYN MEMORIAL, 2000

Katyn Circle at President and Aliceanna streets

Andrzej Pitynski (b. 1947)

Bronze

National Katyn Memorial Committee

On September 1, 1939, Nazi Germany invaded Poland from the west, and a couple of weeks later the Soviet Union, then an ally of the Nazis, invaded Poland from the east. Sandwiched in between the Nazis and the Soviets, Poland fought valiantly before falling to the invaders. The Soviets terrorized the people of Poland, and more than fifteen thousand Polish military officers, mostly reservists—intellectuals including priests, doctors, professors, schoolteachers, lawyers, judges, and civil servants—were sent to prison camps and later driven deep into remote areas of the Katyn Forest, not too far from Kiev, Ukraine, where they were bound, shot in the back of the head, and thrown into mass graves. Some had had sawdust stuffed into their mouths to keep them quiet. It is said that since this hideous crime, the birds in the Katyn Forest have stopped singing. The Soviet Union tried for years to blame this massacre on the Germans, but finally, in 1990, the Soviet Union admitted guilt, and in 1993 they apologized. The year that the Soviets admitted guilt, a group of Polish American residents of Baltimore decided to erect a monument to those who had died in the Katyn Forest. They formed a nonprofit organization called the Katyn Memorial Committee of Baltimore, which raised five hundred thousand dollars over the next eleven years. The city donated the circular site at the eastern edge of the Inner Harbor, into which President and Aliceanna streets feed.

Now that the committee had a site, it needed to select a sculptor. The Polish Embassy in Washington, D.C., recommended the Polish-born artist Andrzej Pitynski. Pitynski had earned his MA degree at the Academy of Fine Art in Krakow in 1974 and moved to the United States later that year to study at the Art Students League in New York City. He had become well known for his 1979 memorial titled *The Partisans,* which was sited in Boston Common in 1982 as part of the "Immigrant Heritage Trail." In that memorial, Pitynski depicted five horsemen with bayoneted rifles, gaunt and exhausted, and equally emaciated horses walking in a row, one behind the other. A very emotional work, it memorializes guerrilla freedom fighters everywhere in the name of the Poles, called Partisans, who spent years resisting first the Nazis and then the Polish Communists.

For the Katyn Memorial, Pitynski designed a large yellow-gold flame, a symbol of rebirth or transformation. In the center of this flame—a little hard to decipher—is an eagle, the symbol of Poland, rising from the flames of war. Also amid the flames are three statues representing the Katyn martyrs. Above and around them and also wrapped in the flame are statues of national heroes from Poland's history, including Boleslaw Chrobry, the first crowned king of Poland; King Jan III Sobieski, a seventeenth-century cavalryman who helped defeat the Turks; and two men who served under George Washington in the Continental army—Kazimierz Pulaski, "Father of the American Cavalry," and Tadeusz Kosciuszko, "Father of the American Artillery." In this monument the Katyn martyrs are raised spiritually into the pantheon of national heroes of Poland.

The monument was designed to be viewed in the round. Set on a circular base of black granite and cobblestone pavers, it rises impressively to a height of 44 feet. The sound and sight of water cascading over the pavers seems to offer some solace to those trying to remember and honor the victims of this tragedy. As stated on the plaques installed on the site—which tell the story of the Katyn Massacre and provide a guide for locating the Polish heroes represented on the monument—it is hoped that the experience of remembering this massacre will help ensure that another tragedy such as this never occurs.

After the monument was dedicated, the National Katyn Memorial Committee was disbanded. It was succeeded by the National Katyn Memorial Foundation, whose mission is to maintain the monument in perpetuity. The foundation will conduct annual Katyn remembrance ceremonies every April and continue to preserve the story of the Katyn Massacre so that future generations may learn from this tragic event.

A12

TITLE
Untitled, 1976

LOCATION
Commerce Street Park,
Lombard and Commerce streets

SCULPTOR
Hiroshi Mikami (b. 1944)

MEDIUM
Pink Tennessee marble

DONORS
International Sculpture Symposium of Baltimore and
City of Baltimore

In the fall of 1976, the first International Sculpture Symposium of Baltimore was held on the two-acre lot on which the Shot Tower stands, at E. Fayette Street and The Fallsway. From September 15 to October 30, 1976, four sculptors worked ten hours a day, seven days a week, to create four monumental sculptures. Robert DuBourg, a sculptor from Baltimore and Harpers Ferry, West Virginia, developed the idea for this stone-carving symposium. He had organized a similar symposium in Harpers Ferry the previous year with the same invited sculptors and hoped to make it an annual event in Baltimore. DuBourg received $16,500 from then Baltimore City Mayor William Donald Schaefer and the Board of Recreation and Parks. Each sculptor received a $2,000 honorarium for airfare, housing, meals, and a lot of hard work.

In addition to DuBourg, Hiroshi Mikami from London, Gerald Höweler from Amsterdam, and William Bennett from New York took part. During the symposium, people could visit the site, meet the artists, discuss the work, and follow their daily progress.

Although the symposium was to end in late October, none of the work was finished. Two of the artists returned in the spring to do some final grinding, sanding, and polishing; two remained on site to complete their work. Mikami remained a month longer to complete his piece.

The four stone sculptures carved on site that fall remained at the Shot Tower for many years and became an integral part of the new park. Subsequent development for the new Metro stop nearby in the 1990s necessitated relocating two of the pieces. The pieces by Mikami and Höweler were moved to Commerce Street Park and placed on either side of Greg Moring's sculpture, which had been on the site since 1982 (A13). Unfortunately, the 3-foot-high base of Tennessee marble that Mikami had designed for his piece was left behind; otherwise, the two pieces would not have appeared to be so similar.

Mikami was born in China and raised in Japan. He studied at the University of Tokyo before moving to London to attend St. Martin's School. Prior to this outdoor urban sculpture symposium, Mikami had participated in similar symposia in Austria, Yugoslavia, and the United States.

In the short term the symposium was a great success. There was a steady flow of shoppers, businessmen, children, mailmen, bus drivers, artists, and many others who stopped by to ask questions of the sculptors or to watch them work. A catalog documenting the work of the four sculptors was published with funding from the Maryland State Arts Council. Unfortunately, DuBourg could not secure city funding for another symposium in Baltimore, so he turned again to the state arts council, which awarded the International Sculpture Sympo-

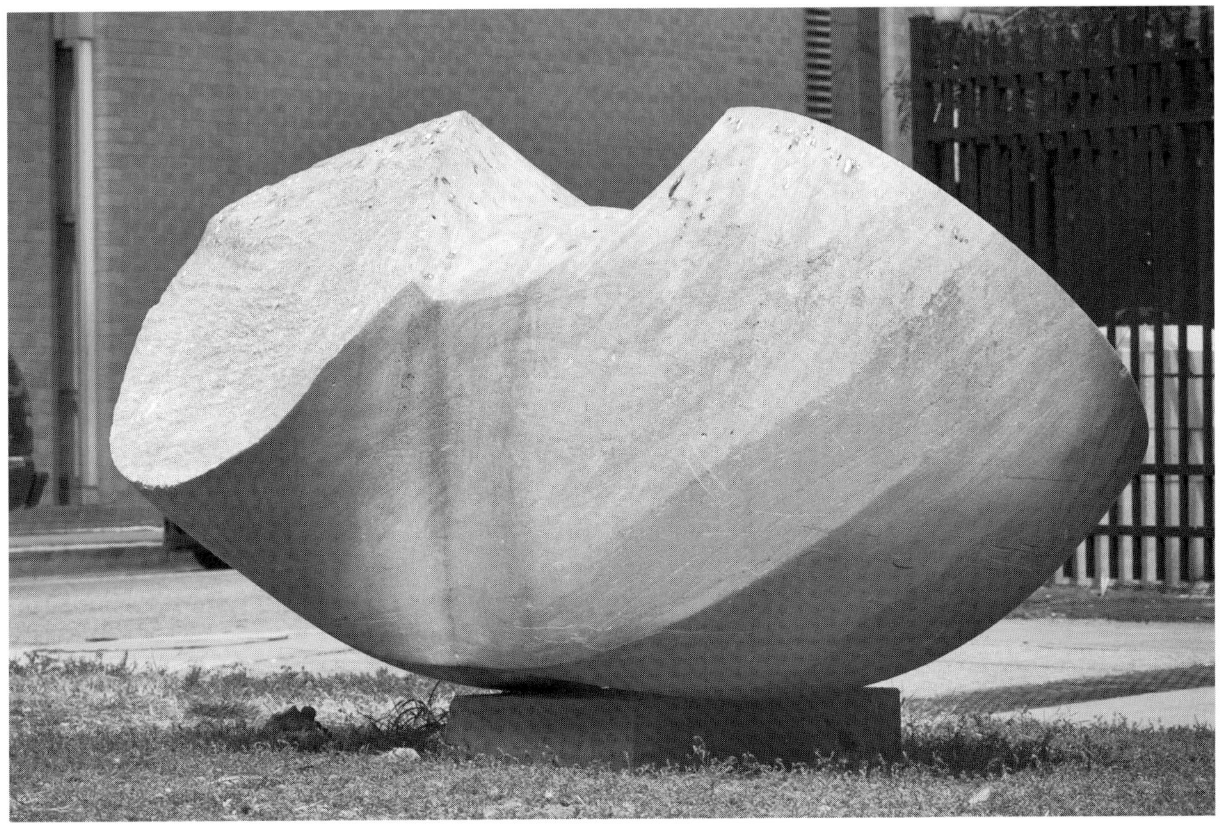

sium a $10,000 grant. With that grant and additional funds raised in Baltimore and West Virginia, DuBourg produced a second sculpture symposium in Baltimore in 1980, when three of the original sculptors from the 1975 and 1976 symposia—DuBourg, Mikami, and Höweler—were joined by William Hopen from West Virginia. They carved their sculptures in an open lot at Holliday and East Saratoga streets. No pieces from the 1980 symposium remain in the city.

Recognizing the benefits of having sculptors working to create large outdoor sculpture for sites around the city, the city's Department of Housing and Community Development organized a sculpture symposium of its own for the summer of 1977. Each of four sculptors was given a site and a small stipend to create a gateway piece. Two of these pieces remain from the 1977 symposium—*Patapsco River Project*, by Jim Sanborn (R4), and *Atlantic Blue Roller Column*, by Dominick Cea (H5). Another piece from the 1977 symposium, *Points on a Line*, by Greg Moring, remained on view on the grounds of City Hospital (today Johns Hopkins Bayview Medical Center) for years. The fourth piece, by James Adajian, was sited at Cold Spring Lane and Falls Road.

A13

TITLE
Untitled, 1982

LOCATION
Commerce Street Park,
Commerce and Lombard streets

SCULPTOR
Greg Moring (b. 1949)

MEDIUM
Painted steel

DONOR
Gift of the artist

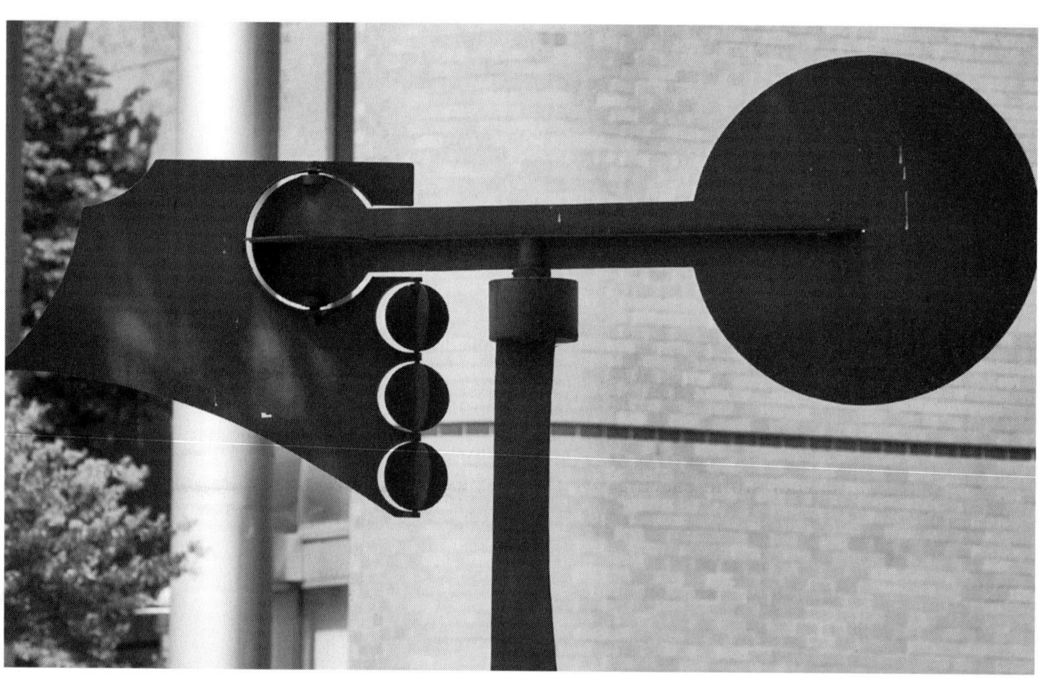

This painted steel sculpture by Greg Moring was sited in 1982 in a newly created green space at the corner of Lombard and Commerce streets as part of the city's new Sculpture Spaces program, sponsored by the Mayor's Committee on Art and Culture, MACAC (today the Baltimore Office of Promotion and The Arts). Eleven works of art by eight sculptors were selected for placement in three areas downtown for one year. A jury of local art experts chose the eight participating sculptors from among more than one hundred applicants. Moring's piece was the first to be installed. At the end of the year, Moring gave his piece to the city, and it has been on view ever since that time. When originally installed, the black, abstract piece was wind activated. The top, horizontal element turned freely in the wind.

The Sculpture Spaces program did not continue after that one year. MACAC had hoped that corporations might be encouraged to buy the artworks and give them to the city, but that did not happen. Moring's piece is the only one from that program that remains on public view.

A14

TITLE
Untitled, 1976

LOCATION
Commerce Street Park,
Commerce and Lombard streets

SCULPTOR
Gerard Höweler (b. 1940)

MEDIUM
Black Tennessee marble

DONORS
International Sculpture Symposium of Baltimore
and City of Baltimore

Gerard Höweler came to Baltimore from Amsterdam in the fall of 1976 to participate in Baltimore's first International Sculpture Symposium (discussed more fully in A12). The symposium was organized by Robert DuBourg, who the previous year had organized a similar stone-carving symposium in Harpers Ferry, West Virginia, in which Höweler had participated. For the Baltimore symposium, DuBourg invited the same sculptors who had joined him in Harpers Ferry—Höweler, Miroshi Mikami, and William Bennett.

Höweler had participated in earlier stone-carving symposia in Germany, Austria, Italy, and the United States. He valued the opportunity to work in direct contact with other sculptors from around the world, to exchange ideas, to create monumental sculptures with the same sense of freedom that he would have in his own studio, and to engage in a cultural exchange between artist and community. A collective activity in which artists shared tools, workspace, and living space remained the principal goal of the symposium.

Höweler, like his fellow sculptors, was interested in the relationship of rough (natural) and smooth (polished) surfaces. On site they carved and chiseled and polished the stone to create surfaces that were dramatically different even though they existed literally side by side. The juxtaposition serves as a subtle reminder of the hand of the sculptor and the sculptor's respect for strength and beauty of the natural material.

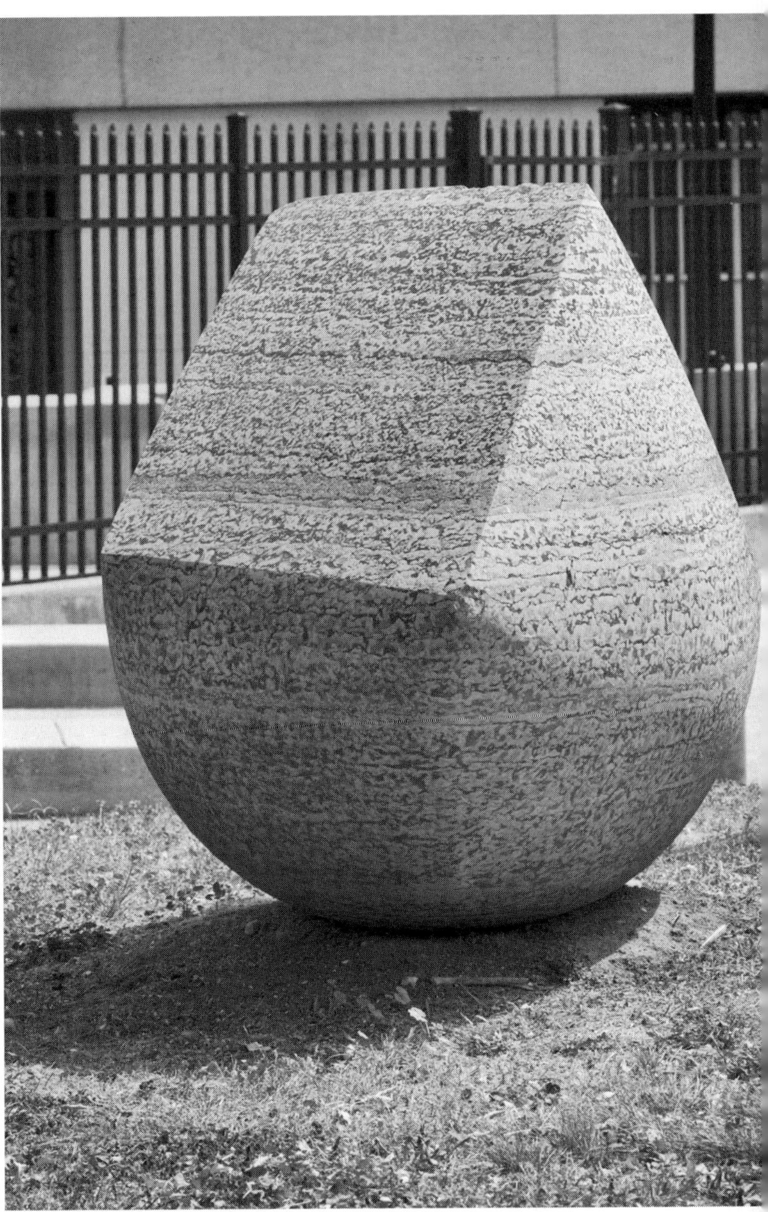

A15

TITLE
The Flame, 1987

LOCATION
Gay and Lombard streets

SCULPTOR
Joseph Sheppard (b. 1930)

MEDIUM
Bronze

DONORS
Jack and Jean Luskin and Jeanne and Melvin Berger

On November 6, 1988, Joseph Sheppard's sculpture was unveiled on the site of the city's Holocaust Memorial and dedicated as part of the ceremony to mark the fiftieth anniversary of Kristallnacht, the Night of Broken Glass. At thousands of Jewish homes throughout Germany and Austria that night in 1938, the horror of storm troopers breaking down front doors and smashing everything in sight was repeated over and over again. Synagogues were destroyed, Jewish shops were looted, and about thirty thousand Jews were arrested and sent to concentration camps. It marked the beginning of the implementation of the Nazis' final plan to eliminate all Jews from the Third Reich.

In 1980, Baltimore's Holocaust Memorial, designed by Donald Kann of Kann & Associates and Arthur D. Valk of Valk Design Associates, was installed on a lot at the intersection of Gay and Lombard streets. The memorial was a project of the Baltimore Jewish Council, which raised $300,000 to build it. It consisted primarily of two concrete monoliths representing boxcars used to transport Jews to Nazi death camps during World War II. Even before the memorial was completed, there was very strong opposition it; it was considered too architectural and uninspiring.

As sentiment against the memorial remained strong, Jack and Jean Luskin and Jeanne and Melvin Berger decided to commission a piece that would be more representative of the horror of the Holocaust. In response to the commission, Joseph Sheppard designed a sculpture that very dramatically depicted thin, emaciated concentration camp victims being consumed by fire. On the base he placed a quotation from George Santayana (1863–1952) that reads, "Those who cannot remember the past are condemned to repeat it."

Like Kann and Valk's Holocaust Memorial, Sheppard's work was also controversial. Many people were offended by the graphic nature of the piece and the explicitness of the nude bodies shown, including a child being held, presumably by a parent, as they were consumed by the fire together. Still other people were upset that the piece had been commissioned privately.

Also controversial was the fact that one memorial had been added to a completed memorial without any consideration for the integrity of the first. After a redesign of the Kann and Valk memorial in 1999, led by the architect Jonathan Fishman, of Cornbrooks, Gribble and Richter, these controversies died down, and the two memorials have coexisted peacefully.

Joseph Sheppard was born just outside Baltimore in Owings Mills. He attended the Maryland Institute College of Art on a four-year scholarship from 1948 to 1952. Soon after graduation, Sheppard was awarded a Guggenheim Fellowship to travel and study in Europe. Sheppard has received numerous awards, including bronze and silver medals of honor from the Allied Artists of America; the First Purchase Award from the

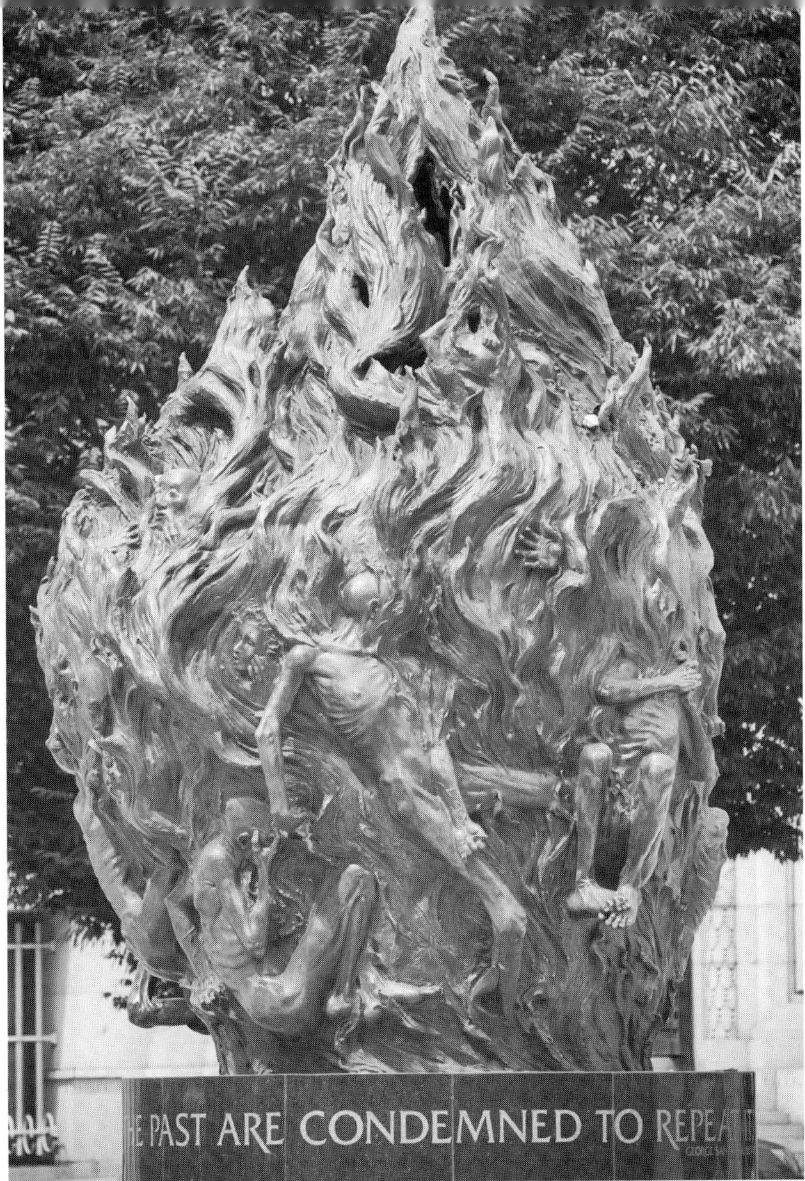

Butler Institute of American Art; and the Agapoff Gold Medal from the National Sculpture Society. In 2008 Sheppard was presented with the XVIII Premio Internazionale di Scultura in Pietrasanta, Italy. A collection of his paintings and sculpture is on permanent display in the Leroy Merritt Center for the Art of Joseph Sheppard, a new museum next to the Conference Center at the University of Maryland, University College, in College Park, that opened in April 2009. This museum has exhibition spaces for Sheppard's paintings and sculpture and a study center, which holds his collection of more than nine hundred books on art from the Greeks to the nineteenth century, as well as a collection of his anatomical drawings of the figure.

Sheppard divides his time between his native Baltimore and Pietrasanta, Italy, which is home to many sculptors, quarries, and bronze foundries. Sheppard's other commissions in Baltimore include the large interior murals at the Police Department headquarters, as well as sculpture, including a relief at the Oldtown firehouse (O4) and a statue of Pope John Paul II (B8).

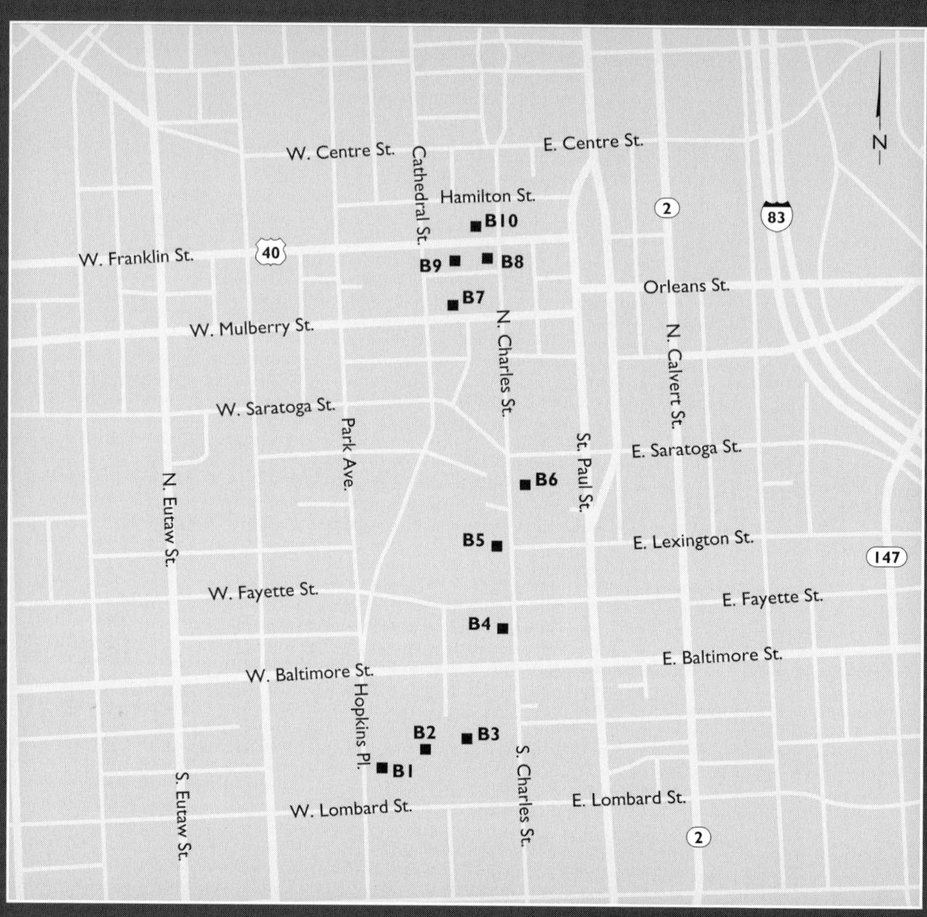

W. Centre St.
E. Centre St.
Cathedral St.
Hamilton St.
B10
2
83
W. Franklin St.
40
B9
B8
Orleans St.
B7
N. Charles St.
N. Calvert St.
W. Mulberry St.
W. Saratoga St.
Park Ave.
E. Saratoga St.
N. Eutaw St.
St. Paul St.
B6
B5
E. Lexington St.
147
W. Fayette St.
E. Fayette St.
B4
E. Baltimore St.
W. Baltimore St.
Hopkins Pl.
B2
B3
B1
S. Charles St.
S. Eutaw St.
W. Lombard St.
E. Lombard St.
2
N

CHARLES CENTER
TO MOUNT VERNON PLACE

Walking

B1

TITLE
Diamond #II-III, 1969

LOCATION
2 Hopkins Plaza

SCULPTOR
Antoni Milkowski (1935–2001)

MEDIUM
Cor-Ten steel

DONOR
British American Properties

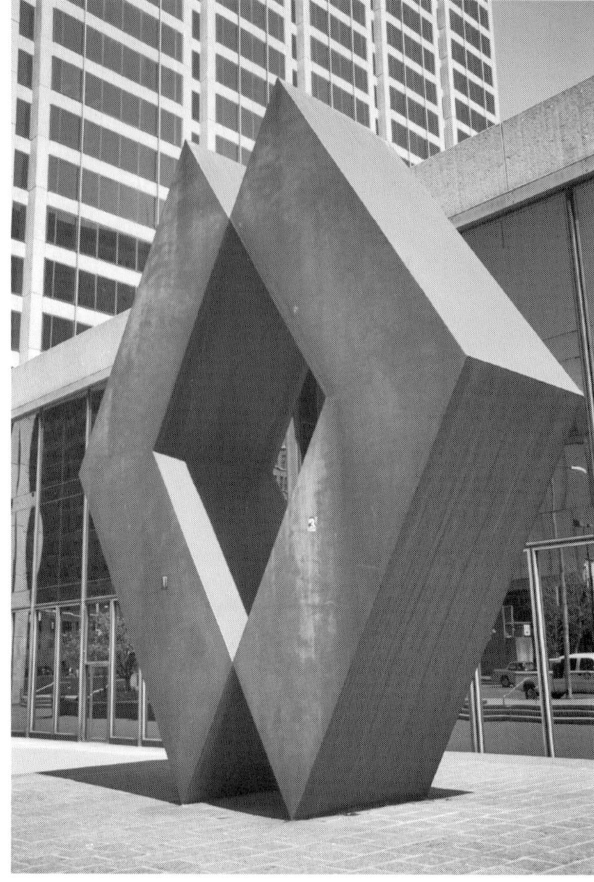

Antoni Milkowski was commissioned by British American Properties to design a large-scale outdoor sculpture for a new office building it hoped to build in Charles Center. British American Properties won the competition, based in part on the proposed inclusion of Milkowski's handsome geometric sculpture of Cor-Ten steel, which was subsequently created and installed on the west side of the building. The main tenant of architect Charles Brickbauer's handsome building for many years was the Mercantile-Safe Deposit & Trust Company.

Milkowski made three diamonds, assigning each a Roman numeral. *Diamond #I-III* (1967) was the result of his first public commission, for the Albright-Knox Art Gallery in Buffalo, New York, where it can be seen today. The second was for Baltimore, and the third he kept in his studio.

Milkowski grew up in New York and attended Kenyon College in Ohio. He considered medical school for a while before enlisting in the U.S. Marine Corps. While he was stationed in San Diego, in 1958–61, he began taking drawing and art history courses. By 1962 he had enrolled in a master's program at Hunter College in New York, where he studied with George Sugarman and Tony Smith, whose work influenced his. After two years on a Fulbright Scholarship, awarded in 1964 and spent in Warsaw, Milkowski joined the Hunter College faculty where he taught until his retirement in 1998. Like the piece shown here, his work was characterized by a precise geometry and an interest in both the interior and the exterior space of his compositions.

B2

TITLE
Swing Over, 2004

LOCATION
George H. Fallon Federal Building, 31 Hopkins Plaza

SCULPTOR
Alice Aycock (b. 1946)

MEDIUM
Aluminum

DONOR
Art in Architecture Program, U.S. General Services Administration

This surprising and lyrical new work of art by Alice Aycock, an artist of national and international acclaim, was dedicated in Baltimore by the General Services Administration in 2004. It is the sixth public artwork in the Baltimore area to be commissioned by the GSA. Not since 1981, when the federal government built the new Social Security complex along Greene Street, has a public artwork been commissioned for Baltimore through the GSA's Art in Architecture Program. Funding for this work by Aycock was generated from a $33 million renovation to the Fallon Building. The GSA also commissioned a second artwork, *Dress Code* by Jean Shin, for the newly refurbished lobby.

Aycock's work has always incorporated multiple references, focused sometimes on the specific environment, sometimes on the physical character of the building or the site, sometimes on the history of one or both. Just as often her pieces might include references to distant galaxies, as she creates some astronomical-looking machine that might capture messages from outer space. Always large and expansive, her sculpture is as complex structurally as it is intellectually and usually requires the collaboration of an engineer to help her preserve the artistic intent while ensuring a stable structure. All this is true of this piece.

One other interesting fact about Aycock's approach to each new piece is that she studies diagrams—of dance steps, airplane movement, atomic particles in motion, spiral galaxies merging—as a way of developing ideas for the curvilinear configuration of the work. For *Swing Over,* she used aerial diagrams of the courting patterns of hummingbirds in flight. She was less interested in the hummingbird itself, although she does have hummingbirds in her summer gardens, than in a dynamic event that is not constrained by gravity. Elements in this piece can be found in Aycock's 1995 roof installation for the East River Park Pavilion, *East River Roundabout,* in which a similar three-dimensional triangulated truss sweeps across the roof in a kind of aerial ballet, another example of Aycock's continuing fascination with patterns found in gravity-defying phenomena.

Aycock's sculpture at the Fallon Building consists primarily of two triangulated trusses that loop across the facade and through two rectangular openings in the entrance portico that spans the front of the building. The two large, central, hornlike structures, found in many of Aycock's pieces, serve as receivers that might be taking in astronomical information, energy, or both, which could travel throughout the rest of the piece. The sculpture is supported by a system of aluminum and steel tension cables, on which Aycock was advised by the Washington, D.C., office of the engineering firm Robert Silman Associates. To fabricate the sculpture, she hired Arrow Dynamics, in Clearfield, Utah, which builds amusement park rides, with which *Swing Over* shares certain characteristics requiring the same precision.

Responding to the formal qualities of the Fallon Building itself, Aycock did not want a perfect, balanced aesthetic but something asymmetrical and a little ungainly. She was keenly aware that the Mechanic Theatre was across the plaza and felt that its architecture made the space more animated. The dynamism of Aycock's sculpture in the plaza is compelling. One of the most beautiful aspects of this piece, contributing to its dynamism, is its reflection in the glass facade of the building's first floor, making it appear to extend physically into the lobby.

Aycock was born in Harrisburg, Pennsylvania. In 1968 she received her BA from Douglass College, in New Jersey, and in 1971 she completed her MA at Hunter College, in New York City, where she studied with Robert Morris. Just six years later, in 1977, she had a solo exhibition at the Museum of Modern Art in New York City. In 1983 a traveling survey of her work created between 1972 and 1983 was organized by the Württembergischer Kunstverein in Stuttgart, Germany. Today her work is included in the collections of MoMA and the Whitney Museum of American Art in New York, the National Gallery of Art in Washington, and Storm King Art Center in Mountainville, New York, where she was given a retrospective exhibition, Complex Visions, in 1990. Her site-specific public artworks can be found across the country—in New York, Philadelphia, San Francisco, Kansas City, Nashville, and now Baltimore. A monograph of the artist's work entitled *Alice Aycock, Sculpture and Projects,* was published in 2005 by the MIT Press.

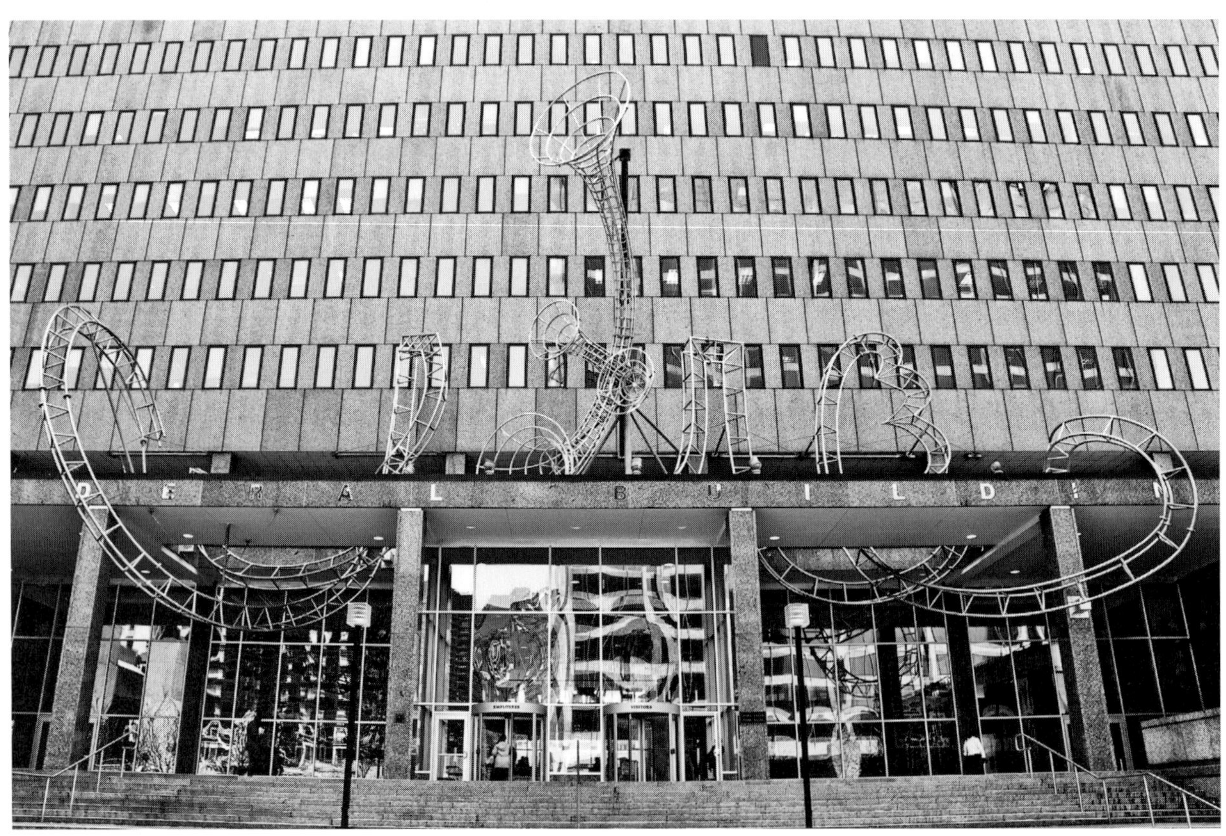

B3

TITLE
Birth of Venus, 1984

LOCATION
Hopkins Plaza

SCULPTOR
Jonathan Silver (1937–1992)

MEDIUM
Bronze

DONOR
Municipal Art Society of Baltimore City

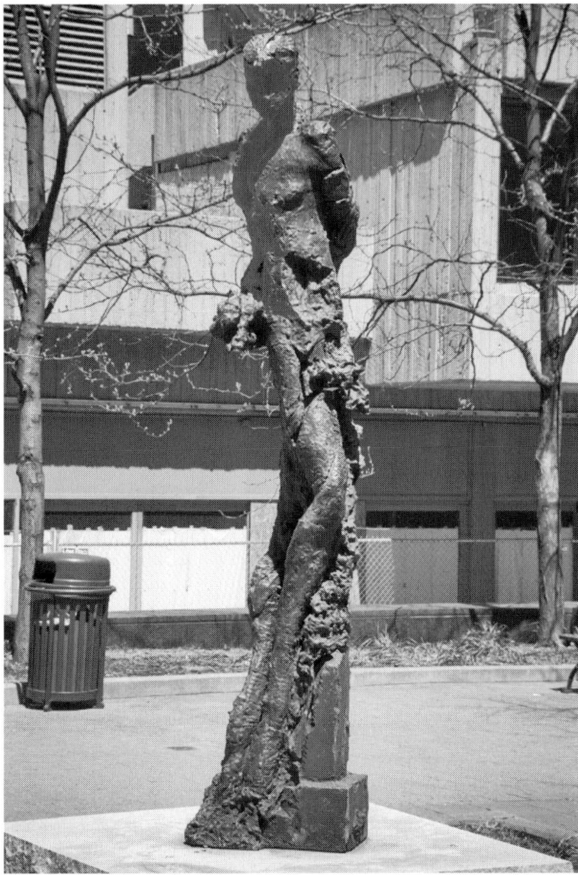

This work by Jonathan Silver is one of the Municipal Art Society's more recent gifts to the city. After an exhibition of Silver's work in 1987 at the C. Grimaldis Gallery in Baltimore, members of the society expressed a willingness to purchase a piece of his sculpture for the city if a suitable site could be found. The current site in Charles Center, in a quiet, tree-shaded area in the southeast corner of Hopkins Plaza, was chosen, and the piece was installed and dedicated on January 27, 1989.

The bronze piece, very typical of Silver's sculpture, is reminiscent of Alberto Giacometti, whose work Silver studied as an art history graduate student with Meyer Schapiro at Columbia University. The figure of Venus is attenuated yet elegant in its graceful form, which dissolves into pure material at many different points. The arms, the legs, and even the face are at once figurative and amorphous. This mysterious quality gives the piece a certain power, lending the rather slight figure its monumentality.

Jonathan Silver was a very well respected New York sculptor, even though he did not begin to exhibit his work until 1976, when he was nearly 40 years old. Throughout his career, he wrote and lectured on art and alternated between teaching art history and making art. His first one-man show was at the New York Studio School only eight years before his death. Then, in a very short period of time, his work was exhibited in New York at the Sculpture Center and at the Victoria Munroe Gallery in SoHo; at the Weatherspoon Gallery at the University of North Carolina in Greensboro, where he had taught in the 1960s; at the Comfort Gallery at Haverford College in Pennsylvania; at the Montclair Art Museum in New Jersey; and in Baltimore. At the time of his death he was teaching at both Montclair State College and the New York Studio School.

B4

TITLE
Mercury and Commerce, 1906

LOCATION
B&O Railroad Building, 2 N. Charles Street

SCULPTOR
John Evans (1847–1923)

MEDIUM
Granite

DONOR
B&O Railroad Company

The two heroic granite figures sit atop the main entrance to what was originally built as the general office building for the Baltimore & Ohio Railroad. Designed by the Boston office of the architectural firm Parker and Thomas and built in just over one year, it was one of the largest and most imposing railroad buildings in the country when it opened on September 12, 1906. For $3 million, Baltimore had gotten a luxury office building for the railroad's two thousand employees.

Uncertainty over the identification of at least one of the two figures has endured. It has always been clearly understood that the figure on the left is Mercury, the messenger of the gods in Greek mythology. He is shown here with his traditional winged cap and caduceus. The figure on the right was called Commerce in the only contemporary reference to the sculptural pair that has been found, in the *Baltimore Sun* on August 11, 1906, the day the figures were unveiled: "Mercury and the allegorical figure of Commerce are depicted guarding the American continent."

That reference should have ended any further speculation about the identity of "Mercury's friend," but it did not, for several reasons. For one thing, Mercury has traditionally been considered the protector of commerce and wayfarers, and therefore Mercury usually represents commerce as well. The attributes of the second figure added to the mystery, because not only are they difficult to see and decipher but one of them has

no basis in mythology. The figure holds what might be a torch in his left hand, and tucked under his right arm is a steam engine, which certainly was not an attribute of a Greek or a Roman god.

Every newspaper carried a story about the opening of the building because all five thousand lights were turned on at midnight on September 12, 1906. But there was no further mention of the two mythological figures over the entrance until June 1913, when they were identified in the *Monthly Journal of the Engineering Society of Baltimore* as Mercury and Progress. Given the contemporary practice of using traditional classical figures to personify modern concepts, it is conceivable that this figure, with its steam engine as an attribute, could have been meant to represent Progress—the progress of industry or the progress of the railroad industry specifically. The large globe between the two figures, showing both North and South America, underscores the idea of growth in the railroad industry, with transportation across great distances. The second figure seems never to have been definitively identified, perhaps in part because, by comparison, Mercury's identity is so clear.

The nude figures are beautifully and effectively draped with flowing fabric revealing their chests and their long muscular legs, which extend outward, helping to create an overall triangular composition over the arched doorway below.

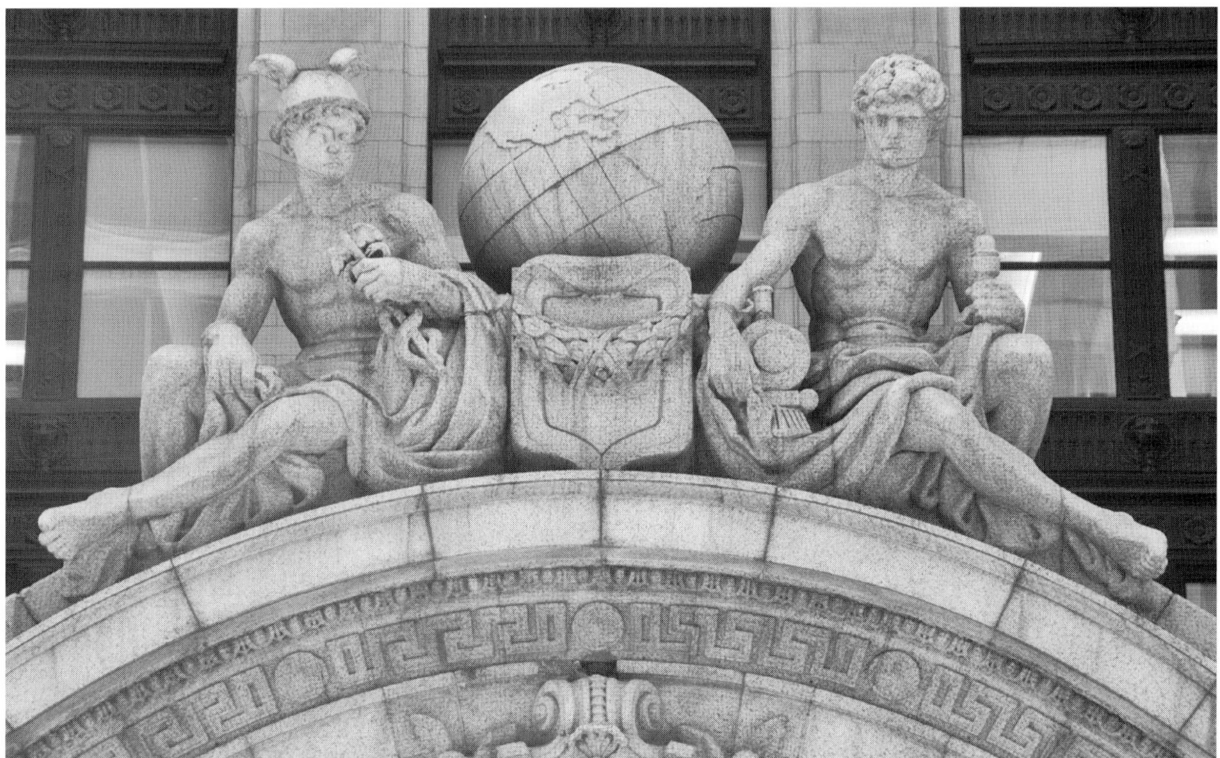

If the figures look blurry or out of focus, it is because the building has been bird proofed and the figures have been screened to prevent birds from sitting on or around them.

John Evans was born in North Wales. He apprenticed himself to his father, a noted architectural sculptor, before immigrating to New York in 1872. He moved to Chicago about a year later, before settling in Boston, where his early work dates from 1877. By 1891 he had established the John Evans Company of Boston, which modeled exterior stone decoration and interior woodwork for buildings. Evans described himself as an architectural sculptor. He worked with the leading architects of his day, most notably H. H. Richardson, McKim, Mead & White, Peabody and Stearns, and R. M. Hunt, on buildings in Boston, St. Louis, Pittsburgh, and New York. His obituary stated that many of the principal buildings erected in Boston during the previous forty years bore evidence of his taste and skill. Evans designed this figural pair and supervised the modeling of the figures by Italian workmen, who spent four months carving them out of New Hampshire granite.

B5

TITLE
Mayor Thomas D'Alesandro Jr., 1987

LOCATION
1 Charles Center Plaza

SCULPTOR
Lloyd Lillie (b. 1932)

MEDIUM
Bronze

DONORS
Friends of Thomas D'Alesandro Jr. and the citizens of Baltimore

Thomas "Tommy" D'Alesandro Jr. (1903–87) was the mayor of Baltimore from 1947 until 1959. He had served in the Maryland House of Delegates and on the Baltimore City Council prior to becoming mayor. While mayor, he envisioned the first major revitalization program for downtown Baltimore, which came to be known as Charles Center. His vision for the city and his strong leadership in the early 1950s ensured the success of the Charles Center Urban Renewal project, which in turn led the way for all the city's subsequent redevelopment projects.

This double portrait of D'Alesandro by Lloyd Lillie depicts the former mayor standing and sitting, in both cases looking out over Center Plaza, the middle plaza of Charles Center, with Hopkins Plaza to the south and Charles Plaza to the north. With an extremely good likeness, Lillie captured D'Alesandro twice, in very natural yet pensive poses. Standing, D'Alesandro is posed casually, with one hand in his pants pocket and the other on the railing overlooking the plaza below. Seated, he leans back comfortably, his arms resting on the top of the bench. Lillie signed the piece along the edge of D'Alesandro's jacket on his left side.

Lillie is professor emeritus at Boston University, where he began teaching in 1961. His public sculpture is sited around the country, from Massachusetts to Virginia and Colorado, but the piece most closely related to his D'Alesandro monument is one he completed in Boston in 1980 dedicated to Mayor James Michael Curley in which Curley is shown standing and seated on a park bench in Curley Mall at Faneuil Hall, across from City Hall. The original proposal for the monument to Curley was for a single life-size figure seated on a park bench, but after a city councilman commented that Curley had never sat on a park bench in his life, the standing figure was added. The Curley monument is one of the most popular in Boston, and that fact may have encouraged Lillie to use the same double-portrait approach in Baltimore.

In 2007 a new plaque appeared at this site commemorating the historic election of D'Alesandro's daughter, Nancy Pelosi, as Speaker of the U.S. House of Representatives. The plaque was added on the occasion of Pelosi's January 2 visit to Baltimore to lay a wreath at this monument to her father.

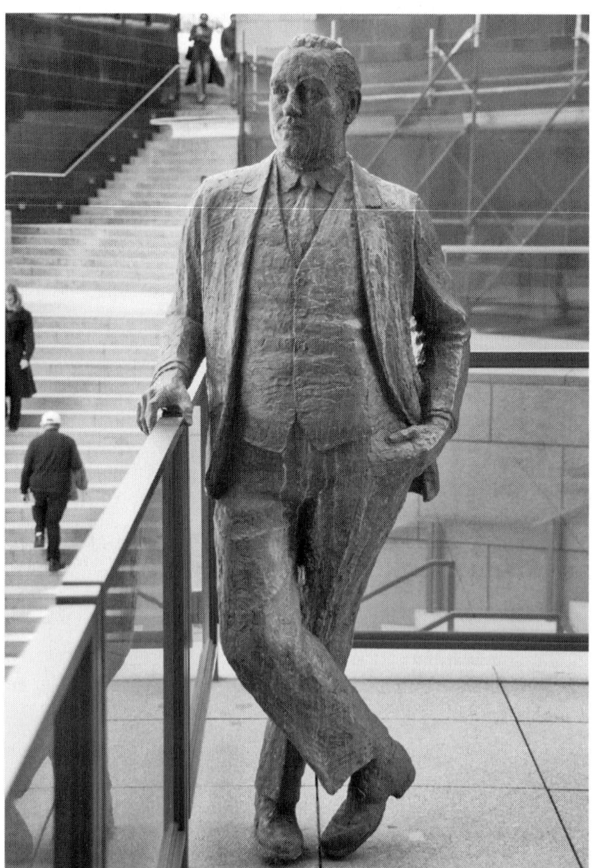

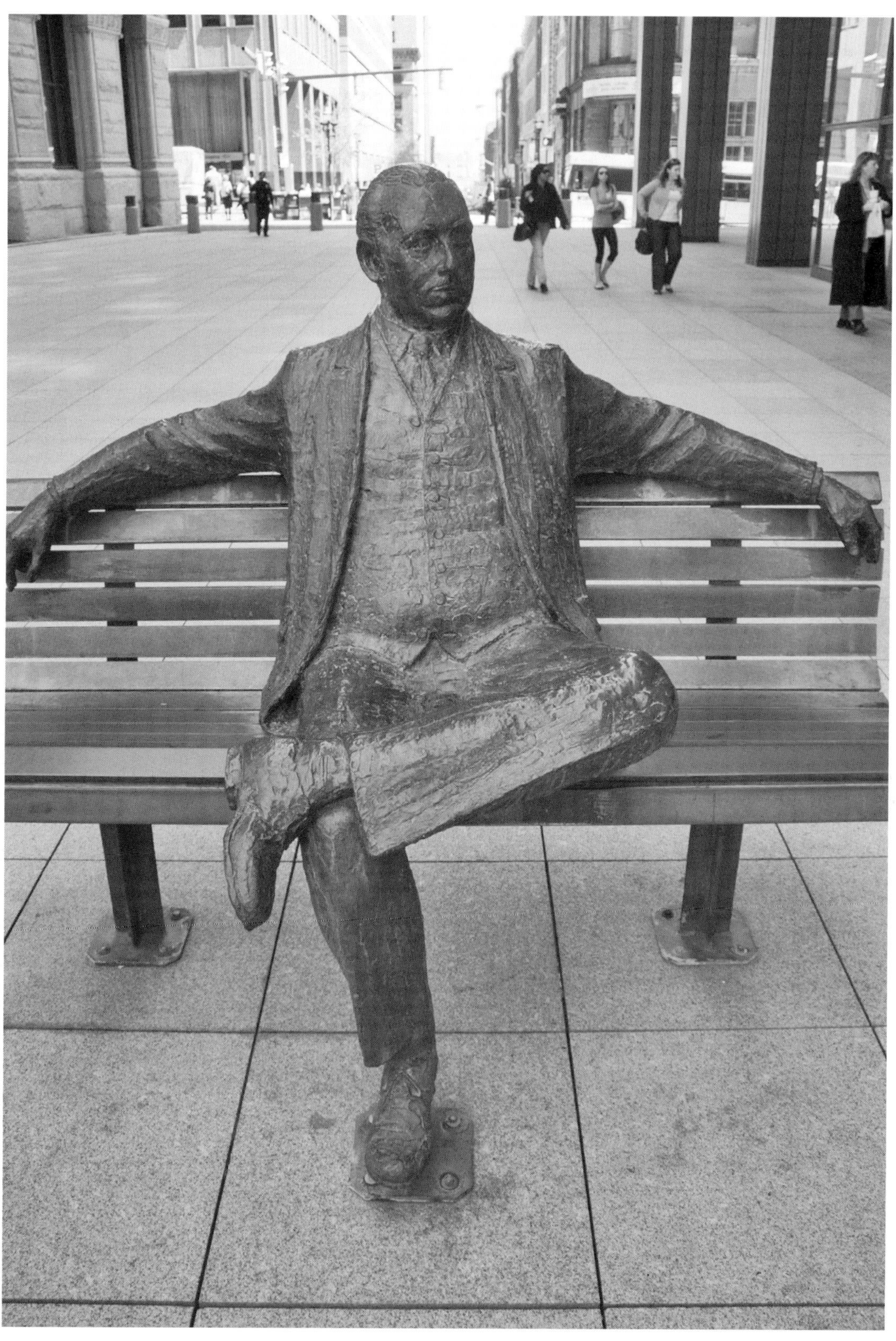

B6

TITLES
Moses and *Christ,* 1817

LOCATION
St. Paul's Episcopal Church, 233 N. Charles Street

SCULPTOR
Antonio Capellano (1780–1840)

MEDIUM
Marble

DONOR
St. Paul's Episcopal Church

The Italian sculptor Antonio Capellano, a pupil of the Venetian sculptor Antonio Canova's, was First Sculptor to the Napoleonic court in Madrid prior to coming to America. He is best known in Baltimore for his work on the Battle Monument (D1). He was selected by the French architect Maximilian Godefroy to sculpt the female figure, the eagles, and the two reliefs on that monument. Godefroy had asked Capellano to come from New York to Baltimore, but when Capellano arrived Godefroy was not in residence. Capellano became impatient and spoke of returning to New York.

A project was needed to occupy Capellano until Godefroy returned. It just so happened that Robert Cary Long Sr. (ca. 1770–1833), who was completing the building of St. Paul's Episcopal Church, had purchased two large blocks of stone to be used for carving the figures of Moses holding the Ten Commandments and Christ breaking bread, to appear on the facade of the upper story of the church. The painter Rembrandt Peale must have suggested this project as a way of keeping Capellano in Baltimore, for Peale paid one-half of the cost of the two small clay models Capellano was asked to create in order to determine his ability. The architect paid the rest.

One figure was nearly finished before Godefroy returned. Capellano completed this project, as well as another for Godefroy's First Unitarian Church (B10) and then his work on the Battle Monument, before

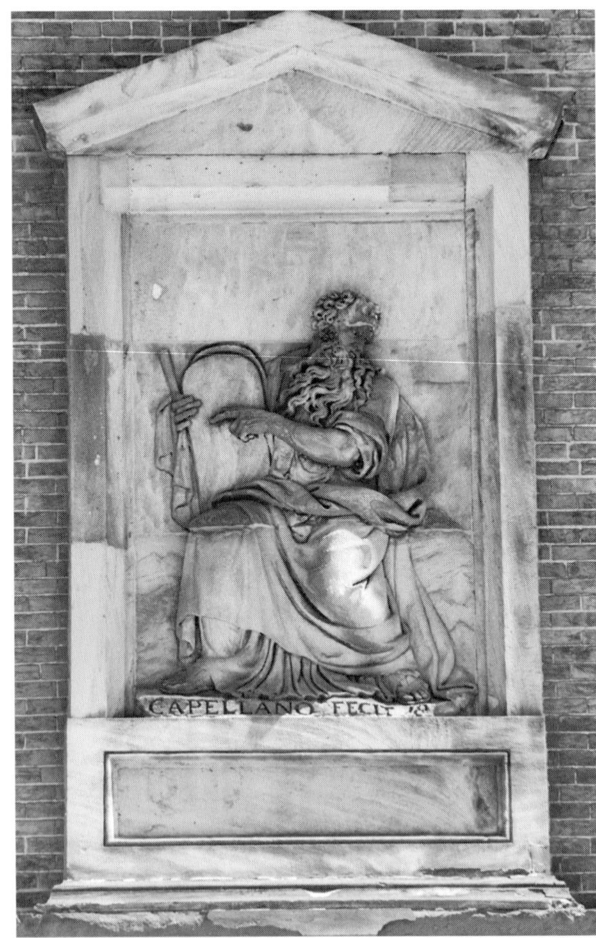

going to Washington, where he completed many architectural reliefs for the Capitol building.

The *Moses* and *Christ* reliefs were probably completed in 1817, the year given for completion of the church. They are thought to be the oldest architectural sculptures in the country. Long's 1817 church was destroyed by fire in 1854, but these panels were saved, to be installed on the facade of the new church designed by Richard Upjohn, completed in 1856. The new church and these panels later escaped the Great Fire of 1904.

In these reliefs both figures are seated and covered in expressive drapery. Moses turns his head to his left and points with his forefinger to a spot on one of the tablets he holds. The Christ figure, with rays of light around his head, looks toward heaven, holding the bread in his outstretched hands.

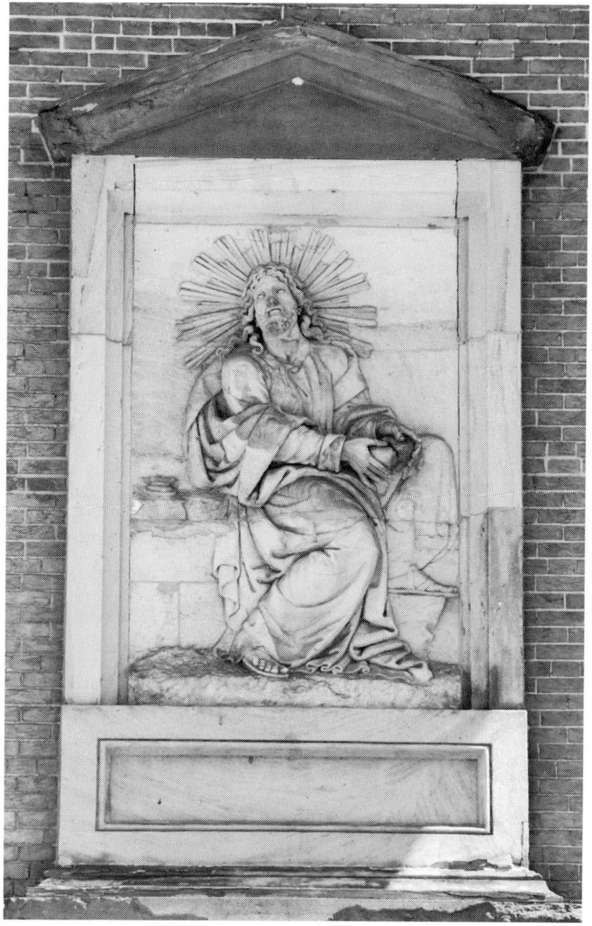

B7

TITLE
James Cardinal Gibbons, 1967

LOCATION
Basilica of the Assumption, 409 Cathedral Street

SCULPTOR
Betti Richard (b. 1916)

MEDIUM
Bronze

DONORS
Cardinal Gibbons Foundation and the
citizens of Baltimore

Money was raised privately and ecumenically to commission this statue of James Cardinal Gibbons (1834–1921), a native son. Ordained in 1861, he became archbishop of Baltimore in 1877 and a cardinal in 1886. The statue was a gift from Baltimore citizens of all religious faiths—Catholics, Protestants, and Jews. The chairman of the group that raised $40,000 for the monument was a Lutheran, and participating in the dedication ceremony were a rabbi, an Episcopal bishop, a Second Presbyterian minister, and a Catholic cardinal. Cardinal Gibbons was said to demonstrate the sense of ecumenism so important in religious life.

Cardinal Gibbons' influence reached into many areas of life beyond the sphere of the Catholic Church. He concerned himself with the problems of new immigrants and with defending the poor. His work was recognized by two presidents, William H. Taft and Theodore Roosevelt, who paid tribute to his devotion to his country and to his church. The inscription on the base of the monument says it all: "JAMES / CARDINAL GIBBONS / ARCHBISHOP OF BALTIMORE / DEVOTED CHURCHMAN / EXEMPLARY CITIZEN / FRIEND OF HUMANITY / JULY 23, 1834 / MARCH 24, 1921 / CITIZENS OF MANY FAITHS / HEREBY HONOR A GREAT AMERICAN."

Betti Richard, an internationally known sculptor living in New York, had been recommended "by people in the field of sculpture" and contacted through the National Sculpture Society in New York. She depicted a contemplative Cardinal Gibbons standing, wearing a skull cap and the simple cassock and short cape of a priest. In his right hand he holds his book, undoubtedly the famous *Faith of Our Fathers*, and his left hand is on the pectoral cross that hangs from a chain around his neck. Originally the sculptor had planned to depict Cardinal Gibbons seated on a throne, but it was decided that his dynamic spirit would be lost in such a high-backed chair and that a standing posture would better suit the man who was known for his walks through downtown Baltimore. For similar reasons, Richard chose not to show the cardinal in the grand robes of his office; he was best known as a man of the people.

During the early planning stages for the monument, it had been tentatively decided to place the statue somewhere in Charles Center. But some thought the tall buildings in that complex would dwarf the statue. After further study, it was decided to place the statue on the south lawn of the Basilica, where each year "the Cardinal's crocuses" signal that spring is soon to arrive in Baltimore.

Richard was known for her earlier commissions of religious statues, alters for religious houses and churches, as well as portrait busts. In 1957 she was commissioned by the friars of St. Francis Church in New York City to create a life-size statue of St. Francis. A reproduction of this statue stands on the campus of St. Bonaventure University, in western New York State.

In 1959 she was commissioned to create a likeness of the great horse Omaha, who had won the Triple Crown in 1935. The monument marks the horse's grave at the Ak-Sar-Ben Racetrack in Omaha, Nebraska. Richard had studied at the Art Students League with Paul Manship and was a member of the National Academy of Design (1947), the National Sculpture Society (1960), and the Pen and Brush Club (1951).

Cardinal Gibbons is buried in a crypt of the Basilica, the church in which he presided as the archbishop of Baltimore for forty-four years. There is also a bust of the cardinal inside the cathedral.

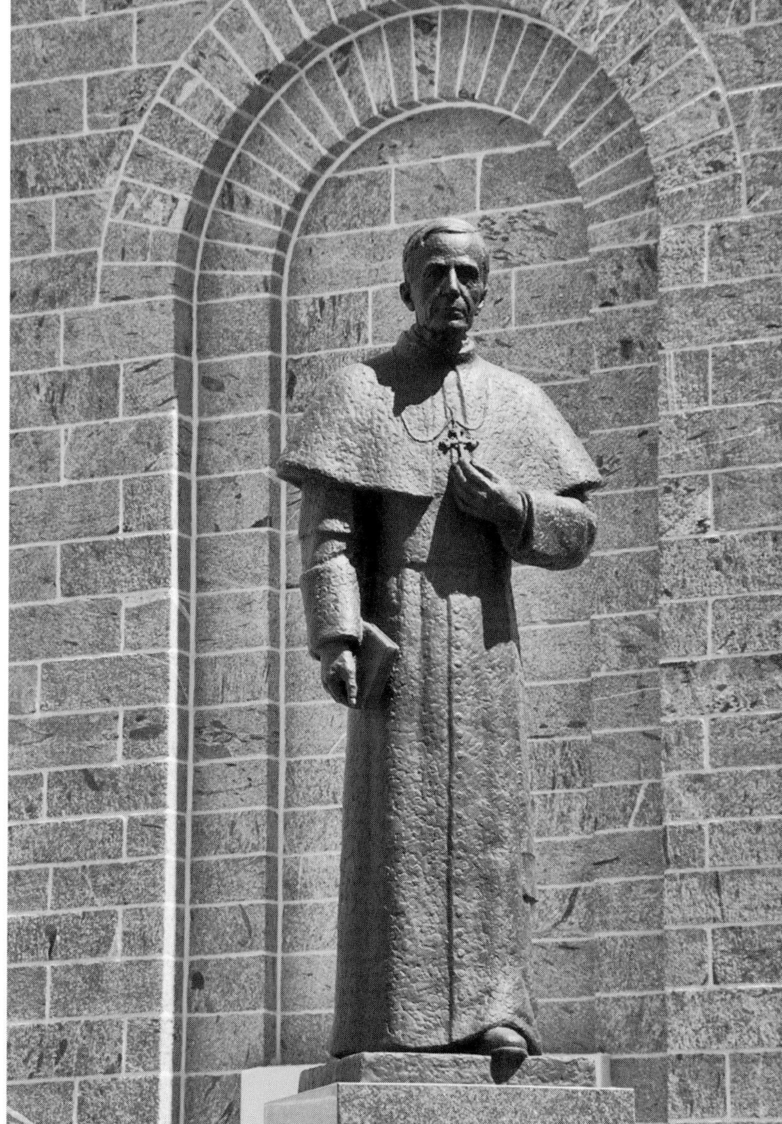

B8

TITLE
Pope John Paul II, 2008

LOCATION
Pope John Paul II Prayer Garden,
N. Charles and Franklin streets

SCULPTOR
Joseph Sheppard (b. 1930)

MEDIUM
Bronze

DONOR
Friends of the Basilica of the Assumption
Historic Trust

The prayer garden at the Basilica of the Assumption was the brainchild of Cardinal William H. Keeler, who was appointed archbishop of Baltimore by Pope John Paul II in 1989 and elevated to cardinal by the same pontiff in 1994. Cardinal Keeler, who had extended an invitation to Pope John Paul II to visit Baltimore, conceived of the garden both as a complement to the basilica nearby and as a way to commemorate the pontiff's 1995 visit.

Opened on October 23, 2008, the garden was designed by the landscape architect Scott Rykiel, a partner at the Baltimore firm of Mahan Rykiel Associates, who is coincidentally both Polish and Catholic. Rykiel imagined the garden as an ecumenical refuge where people of all religions could go. On a granite wall is engraved a quotation on religious freedom and civic tolerance from an address given by the pope at the Cathedral of Mary Our Queen during his Baltimore visit. On the two stone piers that frame this granite wall are metal bands inscribed with symbols of Judaism, Islam, and Christianity, a reference to the pontiff's ecumenical beliefs. A wrought-iron fence crafted by John Gutierrez in his Clipper Mill studio, encloses the space, and pathways throughout are planted with perennials, shrubs, and shade trees. At the garden's center is a statue of the pope by Joseph Sheppard, who won a limited competition against two other sculptors, one Polish and the other based in New York, to earn the commission.

The statue of Pope John Paul II being greeted by two young children is based, with some artistic license, on a photograph taken at Baltimore/Washington International Thurgood Marshall Airport upon the pope's arrival on October 8, 1995. Sheppard had seen this image in a book on the pope's visit that he purchased immediately upon being asked to compete for the garden sculpture. Sheppard, who divides his time between Baltimore and Pietrasanta, Italy, had had an audience with Pope John Paul II in Italy years earlier. In 2008 he completed an oil portrait of the new pontiff, Benedict XVI, which hangs in the North American College in Vatican City today. Sheppard had painted Cardinal William D. Border's portrait and somewhat later painted Cardinal Keeler's. Sheppard's other portraits of Catholic prelates include those of Cardinal Lawrence J. Shehan, archbishop of Baltimore from 1961 to 1974, Cardinal John P. Foley, president of the Pontifical Council for Social Communications in the Vatican from 1984 to 2007, and the new archbishop of Baltimore, Edwin F. O'Brien. Sheppard could be considered the ecumenical sculptor of Baltimore, having now completed a Jewish monument (A15), this Catholic monument, and much earlier a mural of St. John the Baptist for the New Shiloh Baptist Church.

The prayer garden had a somewhat turbulent beginning. The space for the garden was created only after the demolition of the one-hundred-year-old Rochambeau apartment building, owned by the Archdiocese of Baltimore, which the city's preservationists sought to save. The courts, however, sided with the Archdiocese and its plan for the site.

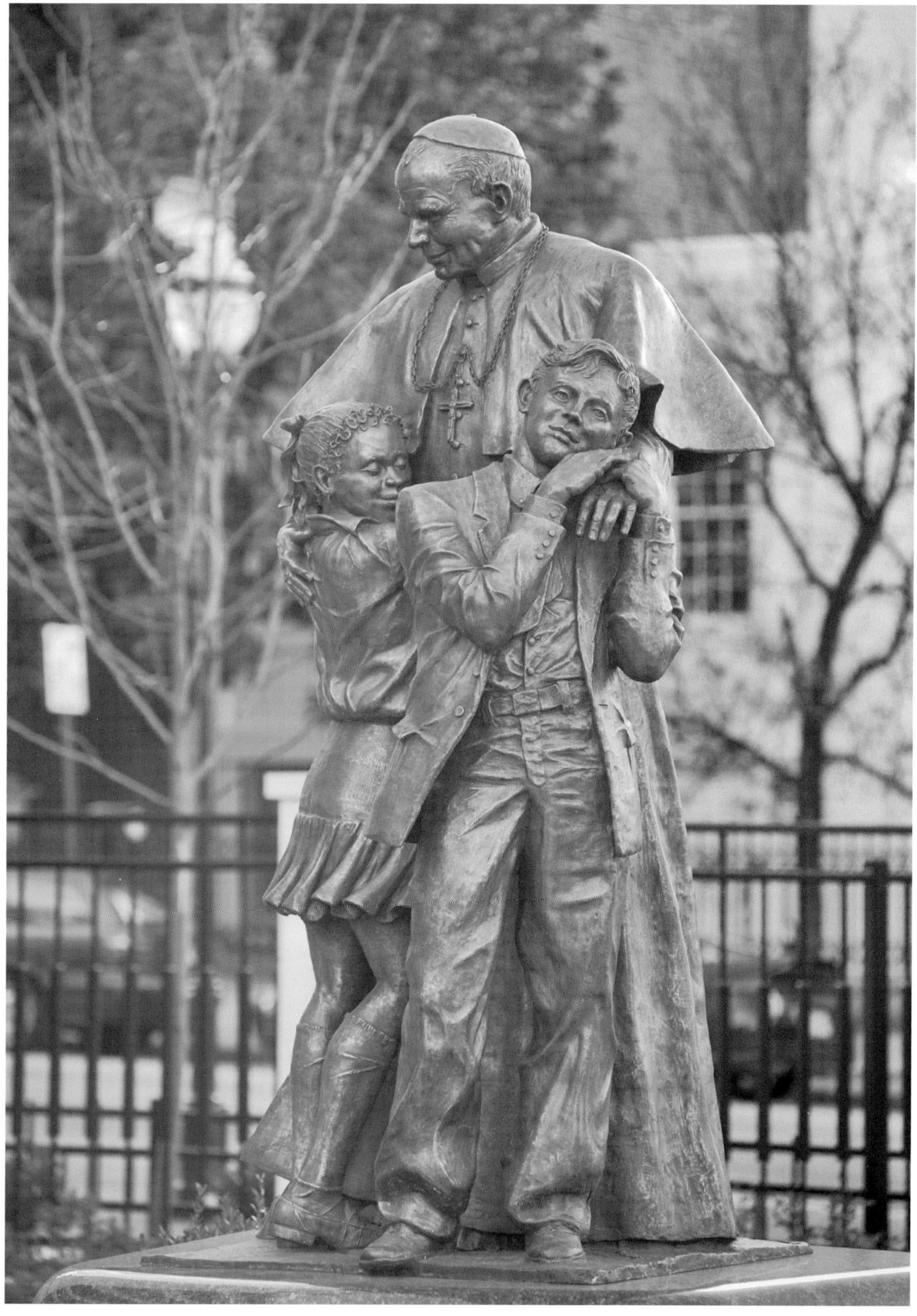

TITLE
Double Gamut, 1991

LOCATION
Franklin Street Garage, 15 W. Franklin Street

SCULPTORS
Linda DePalma (b. 1946) and Paul Daniel (b. 1950)

MEDIA
Painted aluminum, bronze, and copper

DONOR
Baltimore City Percent for Art program

What kind of artwork would be appropriate for the site of a 350-car parking garage in a historic district of downtown Baltimore? This was not a hypothetical question for Ayers Saint Gross, the architectural firm that received an engineering award to build a parking garage immediately adjacent to the Basilica of the Assumption in the Mount Vernon Historic District, which had Percent for Art money associated with it.

Linda DePalma and Paul Daniel, two sculptors who would be collaborating for the first time on a public artwork for Baltimore, wanted the resulting piece to be respectful of the historic neighborhood and at the same time to invoke curiosity and delight. In *Double Gamut,* the playful and witty relief that resulted from their collaboration, they appear to have succeeded. What seems to be a large game board with two player pieces, a red copper ball and a bronze chair, can be seen above the garage entrance off Franklin Street. The fact that this game board and its pieces hang from the side of the building, offering a view perpendicular to the usual view of a game board, is just one of the curiosities here. The chair, which sits in the center of a maze that has itself been placed within a larger, Escher-like grid pattern, is an interpretation of the Baltimore chair, from a style of furniture popular in the nineteenth-century, and thus represents the artists' tribute to the historic nature of the surrounding neighborhood. The image on the seat of the chair recalls the many gargoyles found on nearby historic buildings.

The idea of a game board invokes many metaphors, but the placement of this one, with its two odd game pieces, adds to the challenge of figuring out exactly what the artists had in mind. Certainly the object of their game is not simply finding a parking place. Maybe the title offers a clue; could there be a whole range of games to be played here or a whole range of solutions for one game. One thing is sure: this is Baltimore's best parking garage entrance. A second, almost identical relief—without the three-dimensional player pieces—can be found on the rear facade, facing North Alley.

Linda DePalma received her BA from Marymount College in Tarrytown, New York, in 1968, and she received her MFA from the Mount Royal School of Painting at the Maryland Institute College of Art in 1976. She has received grants from the National Endowment for the Arts, the Maryland State Arts Council, and the Mid-Atlantic Arts Consortium. Her installations, sculpture, and mixed-media pieces have been widely exhibited in New York, Philadelphia, Washington, and Baltimore. DePalma has received commissions for three other outdoor pieces in the Baltimore area. In 1987 she completed *Ground Play* for the Maryland Transit Administration's Old Court Metro Station, and in 1988 *RedwoodArch* was installed at both ends of the 400 block of Redwood Street in Market Center (E4).

Her fountain grates, titled *Flow*, in the newly renovated War Memorial Plaza, was commissioned by the Baltimore City Department of Recreation and Parks and completed in 2005.

Paul Daniel received his BFA from the Kansas City Art Institute in 1973 and his MFA from the Rinehart School of Sculpture at the Maryland Institute College of Art in 1975. He has received numerous awards for his sculpture, including a Maryland State Arts Council Individual Artist Fellowship, a National Endowment for the Arts Fellowship, and a Henry A. Walters Traveling Fellowship. His work has been exhibited throughout the mid-Atlantic region, and he has completed two other permanent public art commissions awarded through the city's Percent for Art program, *Titan* and *Harpie* (N3–N4) at Liberty Elementary School, as well as a commission from the Maryland Transit Administration for *Venter* at the State Center Metro Station and a commission from the Maryland State Arts Council for *Messenger* at the Clifton T. Perkins Hospital Center in Jessup. The majority of these public pieces are kinetic sculptures, for which Daniel is best known. Daniel collaborated with DePalma on public art amenities for Quiet Waters Park in Annapolis, Maryland, creating two unique arbors for the formal garden there.

B10

TITLE
Angel of Truth, 1818; restored 1959

LOCATION
First Unitarian Church, E. Franklin and
N. Charles streets

SCULPTOR
Antonio Capellano (1780–1840)

RESTORATION SCULPTOR
Henry Berge (1908–1998)

ARCHITECT
Maximilian Godefroy (ca. 1765–1840)

MEDIUM
Terra cotta

DONOR
First Unitarian Church

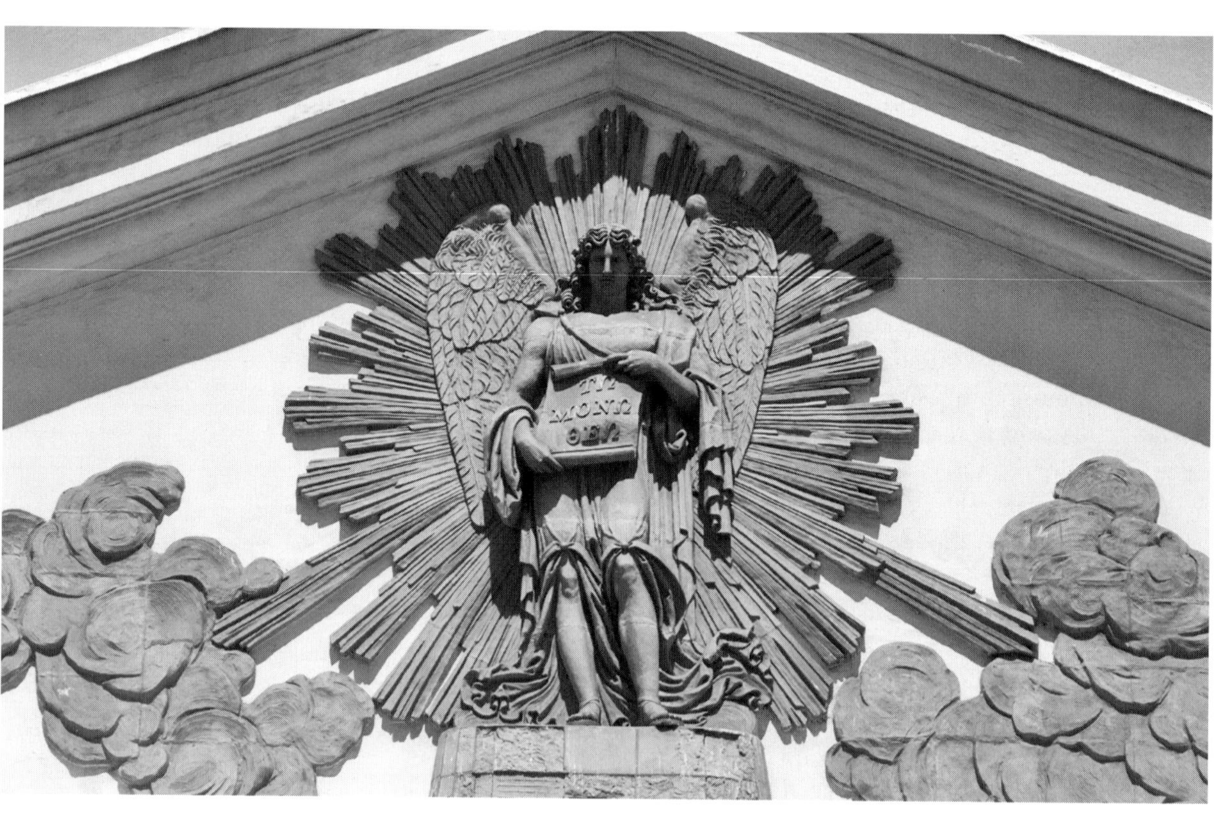

Having come to Baltimore from New York to carve the sculptural elements for Maximilian Godefroy's Battle Monument (D1), Antonio Capellano would begin his collaboration with the architect by executing this statue for the pediment of Godefroy's First Unitarian Church. Godefroy was a French architect who had immigrated to Baltimore in the early 1800s. This church, which is an excellent example of romantic classicism, is considered his masterpiece. Capellano's sculpture was an integral part of Godefroy's design. The angel is depicted in relief standing 7½ feet tall on a pedestal in front of a sunburst of rays. The long robe and fully extended wings contribute to the sense of drama unfolding in the pediment with the appearance of the angel, presenting a scroll written in Greek, "TΩ / MONΩ / θEΩ" (To the One God).

By 1900 Capellano's terra-cotta relief had begun to decay. It was suggested that the original tiles might not have been fired at the proper temperature, that the firing might have been at too high a temperature, or that there might have been too many impurities in the original clay. By 1954 the falling terra-cotta pieces so worried the congregation that they decided to take down what was left of the original pediment design and store it in the church basement until it could be restored.

The commission to restore the sculpture was not awarded until several years later, when Henry Berge agreed to undertake the mammoth job of re-creating Godefroy's pediment relief. The exact duplication of the original was of critical importance to the congregation.

Berge had several challenges to meet immediately. First he had to hire a ceramics expert to advise him on the technical aspects of a medium that was new to him. He chose Walter A. Weldon. Berge then had to find a kiln large enough to cure the sculpture. He approached the Baltimore Gas & Electric Company for help and was put in touch with George Hoffman, who designed a special electric kiln to meet Weldon's curing specifications. The kiln was built in the basement of Berge's studio at 217 W. Lanvale Street.

The third challenge was that the relief had deteriorated so badly that neither of the angel's hands remained. Berge thought there was really only one position for the angel's right hand, as it held the bottom of the scroll, but for the left hand there were several possibilities. Through the newspapers, Berge requested photographs taken by the public over the years that showed the angel's hands. He worried that he might have to use his own imagination for the right hand, only to have someone come forward when the new work was installed and say, "The hands are all wrong and I have the photograph to prove it!" Luckily, a photograph showing the left hand was found in the *News American* archives.

Eighty-one separate pieces were fired to reconstruct the sculpture. The temperature had to be raised so gradually that the firing took most of the summer and fall of 1959. When the angel, with all its embellishments of clouds and sun's rays, was reinstalled on the church pediment in April 1960, six years after the original had been removed, a special church service was held in celebration of the project's success.

Henry Berge was the son of the more famous Baltimore sculptor Edward Berge. The younger Berge, like his father before him, was trained as a sculptor at the Maryland Institute College of Art's Rinehart School of Sculpture, graduating in 1929. Berge created several public artworks for Baltimore, including concrete relief sculptures at two housing projects in the 1940s and 1950s (O7 and R3). Probably his best-known piece is another reproduction, a larger version of his father's well-loved *Sea Urchin*, sited today in the south square of Mount Vernon Place (C16).

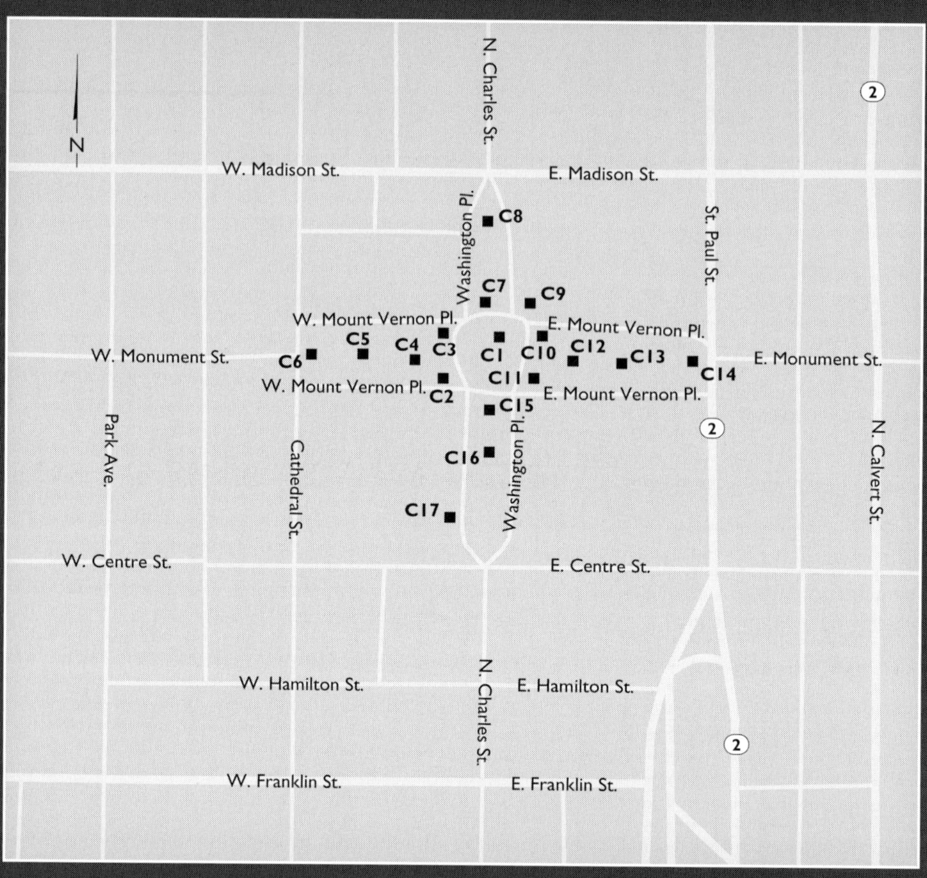

N
W. Madison St.
E. Madison St.
N. Charles St.
Washington Pl.
St. Paul St.
C8
C7
C9
W. Mount Vernon Pl.
E. Mount Vernon Pl.
C5
C4
C3
C1
C10
C12
W. Monument St.
C6
C11
C13
E. Monument St.
C14
W. Mount Vernon Pl.
C2
E. Mount Vernon Pl.
C15
Park Ave.
C16
Cathedral St.
Washington Pl.
C17
N. Calvert St.
W. Centre St.
E. Centre St.
W. Hamilton St.
E. Hamilton St.
N. Charles St.
W. Franklin St.
E. Franklin St.
2
2
2

MOUNT VERNON PLACE

Walking

C1

TITLE
George Washington, 1829

LOCATION
Washington Monument, N. Charles
and Monument streets

SCULPTOR
Enrico Causici (1790–1835)

ARCHITECT
Robert Mills (1781–1855)

MEDIUM
Cockeysville (MD) marble

DONORS
State of Maryland and the citizens of Baltimore

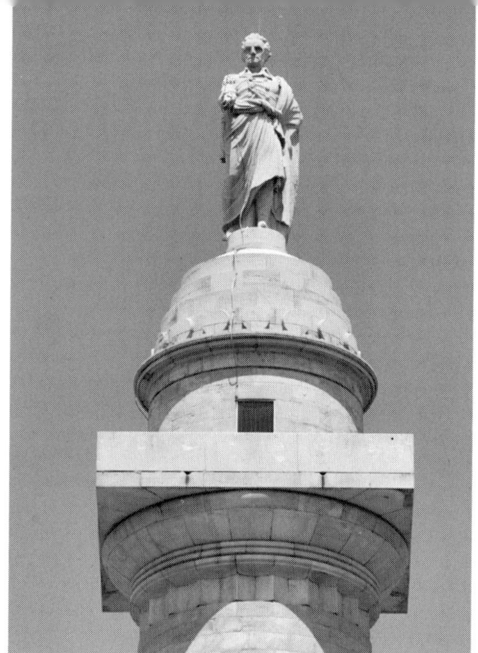

The history of the Washington Monument dates from 1809. In that year, a group of patriotic citizens formed a committee to build a monument to George Washington (1732–99), who was at the time considered almost a god by his fellow countrymen. An architectural competition was held, and four designs were submitted. Maximilian Godefroy, who would later design the Battle Monument and the First Unitarian Church on Franklin Street, submitted a design for a triumphal arch. Joseph Ramee, like Godefroy a recent French émigré, also submitted a design for a triumphal arch. An anonymous design for an obelisk may have been submitted by Benjamin Henry Latrobe, architect of Baltimore's greatest building, the Basilica of the Assumption, and the first Architect of the Capitol. Robert Mills, a 29-year-old native of Charleston, South Carolina, and a student of Latrobe's, won the competition even though his design may have been submitted after the official closing date and his ultraclassical design for an unfluted, colossal Doric column was clearly going to be the most costly to build. Mills went on to design the Washington Monument in Washington, D.C., and the Treasury Building there.

The present site of Baltimore's monument to Washington is not the one originally proposed. The site first proposed was Court Square, where the Battle Monument stands today, at Calvert and Fayette streets. When the Old Court House was removed from the square, the wealthy property owners of the neighborhood petitioned the legislature to be allowed to erect a monument to George Washington on the site. However, when Mills' design was made public, these same property owners became fearful that such a dangerously tall column might fall on their nearby homes and decided that the less lofty Battle Monument should be placed there instead. John Eager Howard came to the rescue, offering land on the southern edge of his estate for Mills' column.

The monument was to be paid for by a $100,000 lottery. The lottery was to sell thirty-five thousand tickets, with prizes ranging from $10 to $50,000. The monument ended up costing more than $200,000 and was paid for by the sale of lottery tickets as well as by a state appropriation and private subscriptions.

On July 4, 1815, the cornerstone was laid before a crowd of more than twenty-five thousand people. A painting of the monument and a painting of George Washington were raised, followed by a thirty-nine-gun salute (the age of the country), strains of "Yankee Doodle," and finally, a one-hundred-gun salute, closing with three volleys from the entire infantry line. That evening there were fireworks at Fort McHenry.

On November 25, 1829, the statue of George Washington, sculpted by the Italian Enrico Causici after Mills' design, was hoisted to the top of the column using an elaborate system of pulleys, a remarkable achievement itself. Causici, who had been working in Washington on the nation's Capitol, was chosen by Mills, who ran his own sculpture competition. Causici spent two years carving the 16-foot-high sculpture of Washington and worrying about how it would be raised. Wrought in three pieces from one block of marble, the statue represents Washington resigning his commission in the Continental army at Annapolis in 1782. He holds a scroll in his extended right hand.

The completed monument is far different from that originally proposed by Mills. There were to be six iron-railed balconies, dividing the shaft of the column into seven sections, six of which were to be covered in inscriptions. The lower section of the column was to have a bas-relief of Cornwallis' surrender. The elevated base was to be pierced by a grand archway, and the figure of Washington atop the monument was to be presented standing with Victory in a quadriga, or chariot, of victory pulled by four horses. None of these decorations were carried out, primarily because of their great expense and the financial difficulties that plagued the project. By 1818 even Mills was recommending that the balconies be omitted, in favor of a simpler design.

The monument and statue are made of marble from Cockeysville, just north of Baltimore, some of which came from the quarry of General Charles C. Ridgely, who had just been elected governor of Maryland. During the years that the monument was being built, there was a marble yard nearby, on the site of the present Peabody Institute. John Eager Howard allowed one house to be built near the site, for the foreman of the stonecutters and the keeper of the monument.

Mills acted as superintendent of the project most of the years that it was under construction, living in Baltimore with his family from 1816 through 1820. He returned to Baltimore from South Carolina in 1827 to resume supervision of the monument and oversee the sculpting and raising of the statue of Washington. Between 1829 and 1840 the room inside the base was finished, the inscriptions were added, and the fencing and pavement around the monument were completed. Although Mills was overseeing these finishing activities, a mistake was made in the inscription. According to the inscription, George Washington became president on March 4, 1789, but in fact he was not inaugurated until April 30. Most of the early presidents were inaugurated on March 4, and it must have been assumed that the same was true for Washington. March 4 of that year was an important date, however, for it was the first day the Congress met in New York under a new constitution.

This monument was the first monument begun to George Washington and the first major monument to him to be completed. There is an important but modest stone monument to Washington near Boonesboro, in Washington County, Maryland, erected by the citizens there in just one day, on July 4, 1827. In 1827 Baltimore's monument to Washington, still incomplete, had been under way for twelve years. Monuments to George Washington did not appear in the country's other major cities until decades later. Even though New York wanted a monument to Washington as early as 1802, Henry Kirk Brown's equestrian monument in Union Square was not completed until 1856. In Washington, work did not begin on Robert Mills' great obelisk until 1848, and it was not completed until 1886. In Philadelphia, Rudolf Siemering's monument to Washington was not installed until 1897.

When John Quincy Adams visited Baltimore in 1827, the column of the Washington Monument awaited Causici's statue and the Battle Monument had recently been completed. At dinner President Adams, who had been shown these two monuments earlier in the day, toasted Baltimore as the "Monumental City," acknowledging that in no other city in the country were there two monuments of similar scale and equal significance. The moniker stuck.

The monument is open five days a week, Wednesday through Sunday, from 10:00 a.m. to 4:00 p.m. Visitors can view an exhibition that includes illustrations of Mills' original design, as well as those submitted by Godefroy, Ramee, and possibly Latrobe, and climb the 228 steps to the top. A $1 donation is suggested.

Note: There is another statue of George Washington in the city. Originally made for the Noah Walker Building on East Baltimore Street by Edward Sheffield Bartholomew in 1857, the marble statue was given to the city when the building was sold and is sited in Druid Hill Park today (M9).

C2–C3

TITLES
War and *Peace,* 1885 copies of 1846 originals

LOCATION
Balustrade west of the Washington Monument

SCULPTOR
Antoine-Louis Barye (1796–1875)

MEDIUM
Bronze

DONOR
William T. Walters

In 1885 William T. Walters presented five bronze sculptures by the French artist Antoine-Louis Barye to the city of Baltimore. Four sit atop the ends of the marble balustrades to the east and west of the Washington Monument. Originally created in stone in 1846 for placement on columns on the facade of the Louvre, these replicas were ordered by Walters through his agent in Paris, the famous Baltimore art collector George Lucas (1824–1909). Over the years Walters collected more than 150 Barye bronzes, most of which are in the Baltimore museum that bears his name; this collection rivals that at the Louvre in both scope and significance. He bought many more bronzes by Barye for the Corcoran Gallery in Washington, on whose board he served.

Antoine-Louis Barye was the first as well as the foremost French *animalier* of the nineteenth century. Born in Paris, he began his career as a goldsmith but entered the École des Beaux-Arts in 1818. He became fascinated watching the wild animals in the Jardin des Plantes, the botanical and zoological garden founded in Paris in 1793, and began making pencil drawings and models. His work is almost exclusively of wild animals, usually revealing their violent side. Many of his bronze sculptures in Paris are in the Luxembourg Gardens, the Tuileries Gardens, or the Louvre. The zenith of his career came between 1837 and 1848, during which time Barye would have made the original *War* and *Peace* and *Force* and *Order* (C10–C11). However, in 1884, when

Walters ordered the bronzes for Baltimore, Barye had died, and Ferdinand Barbedienne, a famous founder in Paris, had purchased most of Barye's plaster casts and models and continued to produce Barye's sculptures. Each of the Baltimore bronzes was cast by Barbedienne, and the foundry medal or an impression of the missing medal can be seen on each of the sculptures.

Each of these sculptures is composed of a seated nude male wrapped in drapery, an animal, and a young nude boy in a way that suggests the allegory. In *Peace* the group comprises a reclining cow; a young boy standing with his back to the male figure and leaning gently against him, looking downward, playing his flute; and a male leaning on a staff, his head tilted downward pensively. The group in *War* includes a reclining horse, alert with head raised and ears forward; a young boy standing, leaning against the male figure and looking outward, sounding his clarion; and the male looking up, about to rise, as he twists his upper torso to reach for his sword. His helmet is tucked behind him, beside the rising horse, and on his head there is a wreath of laurel.

On January 28, 1885, when the four sculptural groups were unveiled in Mount Vernon Place, they were placed in the west square, on the north-south and east-west axes of the fountain built for that square by Robert Garrett, then president of the B&O Railroad, who lived at Nos. 7–9, in a townhouse designed by Stanford White of McKim, Mead & White (and enlarged in 1905

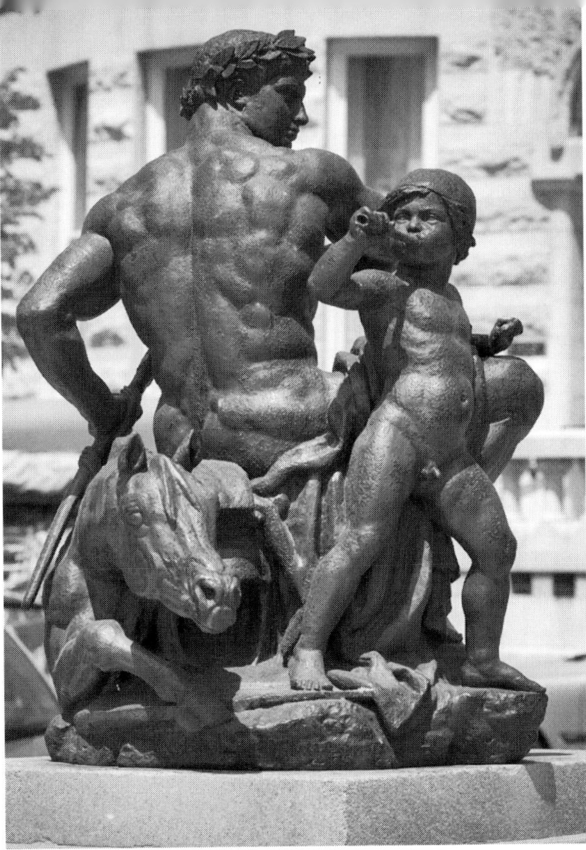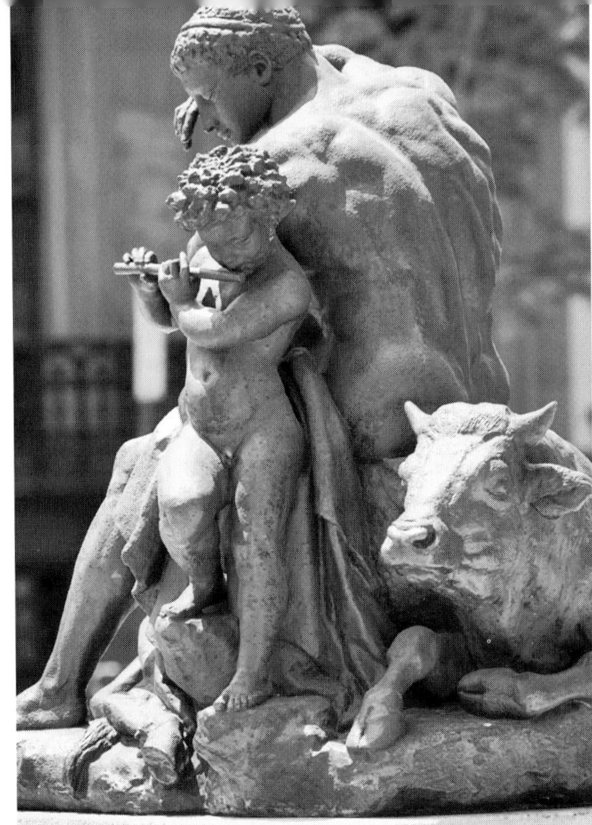

by John Russell Pope). Walters lived nearby, at No. 5, in a house designed by the architects Niernsee and Neilson in the 1850s and purchased by Walters in 1871. The bronzes *War, Peace, Force,* and *Order* were relocated in 1916, when improvements were made to each of the four squares by Thomas Hastings of the New York architectural firm Carrere-Hastings.

Today Walters is probably best remembered as an art collector. He was born in Liverpool, Pennsylvania, in 1820, the son of a banker and merchant. He moved to Baltimore in 1840 and established a very successful liquor business, W. T. Walters and Company. The outbreak of the Civil War put him in such an uncomfortable position, because of his Southern sympathies, that he took his family to Europe, where they settled in Paris. After the war, Walters returned to Baltimore and became more involved in the railroads. Previously, he had held interests in the Northern Central Line, a Maryland and Pennsylvania railroad. The railroad that he consolidated and restructured after the war, the Atlantic Coast Line, traveling between Baltimore and

Wilmington, North Carolina, was later expanded by his son, Henry, who went into business with J. P. Morgan.

While living in Paris, Walters became a serious patron of French nineteenth-century art, buying paintings by Gérôme and Meissonier and sculpture by Barye. With George Lucas, Walters continued to collect not only French nineteenth-century painting and sculpture but Asian art as well. When the collection outgrew his house on the west square, Walters added a gallery off the rear. After Walters died in 1894, his son continued to expand the collection. It was Henry Walters who purchased four pieces of property on the west side of the south square of Washington Place, where the Walters Art Gallery (today the Walters Art Museum) opened in 1909. Upon his death in 1931, Henry Walters gave the gallery and the wide-ranging collection of more than twenty thousand works that he and his father had acquired to the citizens of Baltimore. Today the Walters family home is used for museum offices, and the gallery extension off the back connects the house to the museum. The museum entrance is on Centre Street between Charles and Cathedral streets.

C4

TITLE
Seated Lion, 1885 copy of 1846 original

LOCATION
West square

SCULPTOR
Antoine-Louis Barye (1796–1875)

MEDIUM
Bronze

DONOR
William T. Walters

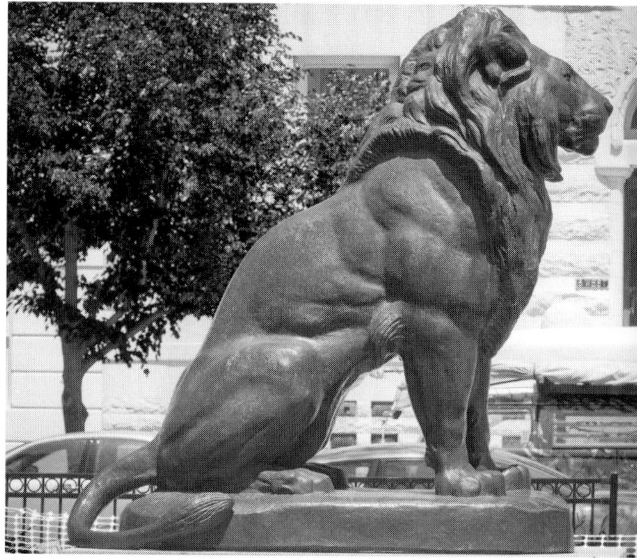

In 1885 William T. Walters presented the city of Baltimore with a fifth bronze by Antoine-Louis Barye—the *Seated Lion.* The other four bronzes were *War, Peace, Force,* and *Order* (C2–C3, C10–C11). The *Seated Lion* is a copy of a sculpture Barye created in 1846 for the Tuileries Gardens in Paris, which Walters certainly knew firsthand. These five Barye sculptures, all ordered through Walters' agent in Paris, George Lucas, were unveiled together on February 1, 1885. Today as in 1885, the statue of the lion sits directly across from No. 5 West Mount Vernon Place, the Walters family home.

Barye's life-size seated lion is majestic in its pose, erect with head raised and ever so slightly turned. The realism of his dense mane and the articulation of his muscular body adds to the sense of monumentality. Barye's *Seated Lion* was so popular that it was made available in four different sizes in his 1847 catalog.

On a shallow ledge on each side of the base is a relief of a lion walking. The traditional association of the lion with royalty is certainly at play here, as the original sculpture was commissioned by the government of King Louis-Philippe, but there may be more specific references to Louis-Philippe here. Louis-Philippe came to power after a revolution that spanned three days in late July. The sign of the zodiac that governs late July is Leo, represented as a walking lion, which is especially relevant for the July Monarchy of Louis-Philippe. The composition may also relate to others of Barye's,

especially his lion for the July Column in Paris, marking the overthrow of another government, that of the Bourbon monarchy in July 1830.

Barye held various posts during his lifetime. He was appointed professor of drawing at the Museum of Natural History, at the Jardin des Plantes, in 1854, a position he held until his death in 1875. He had been named director of casts and models at the Louvre in 1848 but was replaced in 1950 by a follower and his only real competitor as an *animalier,* Emmanuel Frémiet, who was commissioned to create the John Eager Howard equestrian monument in the north square (C8). Barye received many honors during his lifetime, including being made an officer in the Légion d'honneur.

C5

TITLE
Boy and Turtle Fountain, 1916

LOCATION
West square

SCULPTOR
Henri Crenier (1873–1948)

MEDIUM
Bronze

DONOR
Municipal Art Society of Baltimore City

In 1924 the Baltimore Museum of Art opened in a house at 101 West Monument Street, on the southwest corner of Cathedral and Monument streets, where the Peabody Court Hotel stands today. The house had belonged to John Work Garrett, the first president of the B&O Railroad. His daughter, Mary Elizabeth, inherited the house from him and left it in her will to Dr. M. Carey Thomas, for many years the president of Bryn Mawr College. Dr. Thomas lent it to the Baltimore Museum of Art, whose board members later purchased it for use as their headquarters while their new museum building was under construction.

As part of the opening celebration for the museum, an exhibition of garden and fountain sculpture that had been organized in New York in 1923 by the National Sculpture Society was brought to Baltimore by the Rinehart Fund Committee of the Peabody Institute and installed in Mount Vernon Place. This fountain by Henri Crenier was part of that exhibition, and it was sited then where it is today, within the fountain Robert Garrett had had built in the square. The sculpture of a young boy delighted by his discovery of a small turtle almost under his foot seemed so perfectly sited that Grace Turnbull, herself a sculptor and a member of the Municipal Art Society, suggested that it should never leave. Her fellow members of the society agreed. Subscriptions were collected, and the sculpture was given to the city that June.

Henri Crenier was an American sculptor active in art circles in New York City by 1911. His work includes the James Fennimore Cooper Memorial in Scarsdale, New York, a memorial to Christopher Columbus in Mamaroneck, New York, and statuary on the San Francisco City Hall. In the permanent collection of the Metropolitan Museum of Art there is a small bronze sculpture by Crenier of a boy and turtle on a low circular base in a pose identical to that in the Baltimore piece.

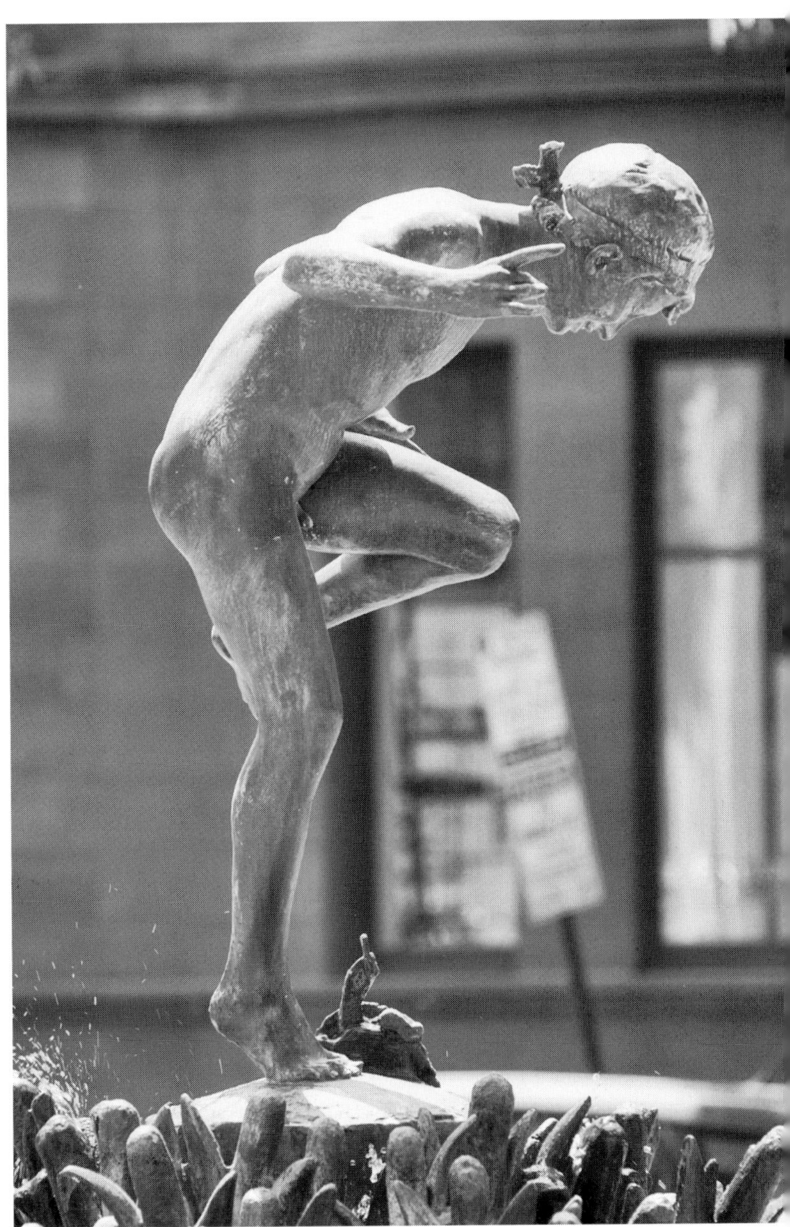

C6

TITLE
Military Courage, 1885 copy of 1879 original

LOCATION
West square

SCULPTOR
Paul Dubois (1829–1905)

MEDIUM
Bronze

DONOR
William T. Walters

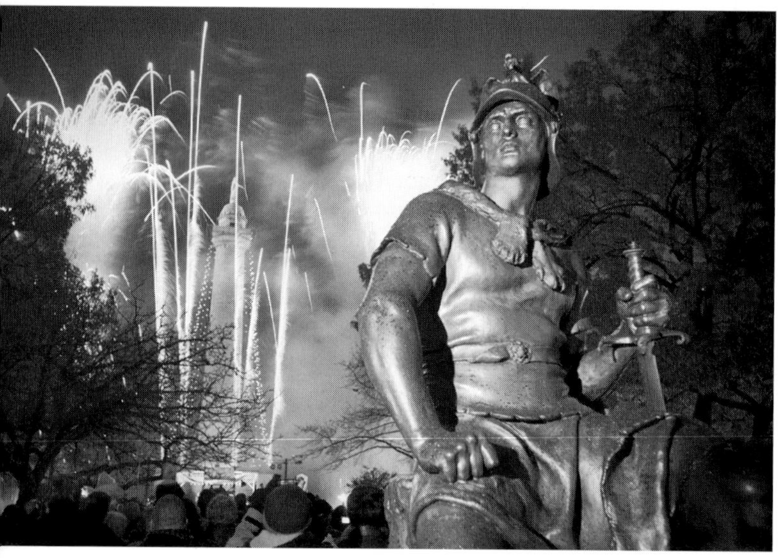

This was the sixth sculpture William T. Walters gave to the city in 1885, the others being the Barye sculptures *War, Peace, Force, Order,* and the *Seated Lion* (C2–C3, C10–C11, C4). It was to complement the *Seated Lion* and was placed on the opposite side of the fountain that Robert Garrett had had built for the square. Thus, by 1885, with four of the Barye bronzes sited around the fountain and the *Seated Lion* and *Military Courage* at either end of the square, the west square had become not only a beautiful city park but also a fitting front garden for the Walters' family home at No. 5 West Mount Vernon Place.

This allegorical figure reminded Walters of Italian Renaissance figures that he loved, most notably the tomb figures by Michelangelo. The similarity of this statue to Michelangelo's statue of Lorenzo on the Medici Tomb, in San Lorenzo in Florence, is easy to see. This figure is also reminiscent of French tomb sculpture and in fact is a copy of one of four terminals Dubois made for the tomb of General Christophe Léon Louis Juchault de Lamoricière, which dates from 1879, in the Cathedral of Nantes. This tomb is considered Dubois' chief work. The majestic helmeted figure sits erect, ever vigilant, his shoulders slightly turned to his left, with his right hand in a fist on his thigh and his left hand holding a sword. There is beautiful detail in the helmet with its winged dragon, the animal skin draped around the figure's neck and shoulder, falling across his leg to his feet, the belt buckle, and the handle of the sword.

Paul Dubois was among the leading Italianate sculptors in France in the latter nineteenth century. Born in Nogent-sur-Seine, he studied at the École des Beaux-Arts and then went to Rome. Dubois' figure of Jeanne d'Arc at Reims Cathedral, from 1889, is also considered among his best work.

C7

TITLE
ROGER B. TANEY MONUMENT,
1887 copy of 1872 original

LOCATION
North square

SCULPTOR
William Henry Rinehart (1825–1874)

MEDIUM
Bronze

DONOR
William T. Walters

Roger Brooke Taney (1777–1864) was appointed chief justice of the Supreme Court in 1836 and held that position for nearly three decades. His most well known opinion is the one he wrote for the Dred Scott decision in 1854. Prior to being appointed to the Court, he served as attorney general of Maryland, U.S. attorney general, and secretary of the treasury under President Andrew Jackson.

This seated portrait of Taney was a gift to the city by William T. Walters. Taney is shown in his court robe with a scroll in his right hand, which is on his right leg, and his left hand resting on a volume labeled "THE CONSTITUTION." Walters commissioned the original statue of Taney for the front lawn of the State House in Annapolis in 1872, and he had this replica made for Mount Vernon Place in 1887. The siting has always been explained by family connections. Immediately to the east of the statue, where the Mount Vernon Place United Methodist Church is today, was the home of one of John Eager Howard's sons, who was married to a daughter of Francis Scott Key. Key was a frequent visitor to the home and actually died there. Taney and Key were brothers-in-law, fellow lawyers, and good friends. Indeed it is through Taney that we have the original handwritten version of Key's "Star-Spangled Banner" (now in the collection of the Maryland Historical Society) and the original details of its writing.

The sculptor, William Henry Rinehart, was an equally famous Marylander. He was born in Union Bridge, Maryland, in what is now Carroll County, the fifth of eight sons. His father was a prosperous farmer. Rinehart showed little interest in farming or in school, so his father sent him to work in the stone quarry on the edge of their farm. Rinehart enjoyed working with stone and was soon making tombstones and mantelpieces. At the age of 21 he left home and settled in Baltimore, where he worked for Baughman and Bevan, the most important marble company in the city. His natural talent was soon recognized, and he was given the firm's more important commissions. During his early years in Baltimore, in the late 1840s, Rinehart began taking evening courses at the Maryland Institute for the Promotion of the Mechanic Arts (today the Maryland Institute College of Art). His earliest appearance as a sculptor was in 1851, when he exhibited a relief that was awarded a gold medal in an exhibition at the Maryland Institute. It was also around this time that he came to the attention of William Walters. Rinehart was sent by his firm to Walters' home to repair a mantle, and legend has it that Walters recognized Rinehart's talent immediately. Whether or not that story is true, what is true is that Walters became Rinehart's chief patron and close friend.

In 1855 Rinehart made his first trip to Italy, living and studying in Florence. After his return to Baltimore, Rinehart received many important commissions. In 1858, with financial assistance from Walters, Rinehart returned to Italy, this time to Rome, where he set up a studio and began creating the sculptures that can be seen today in the Walters Art Museum, the Peabody Institute, Greenmount Cemetery, and Mount Vernon Place. He died in Rome in 1874, shortly after returning from a trip to Maryland, where he had been present at the dedication of the Taney statue in Annapolis.

Rinehart never married. In his will he left sums of money to each of his brothers, and he left the remainder of his estate, about $38,000, to two friends, Walters and Benjamin Newcomer, to use "for the promotion of a more highly cultivated taste for art among the people of Maryland and for assisting young men in the study of sculpture who desire to make it their profession."

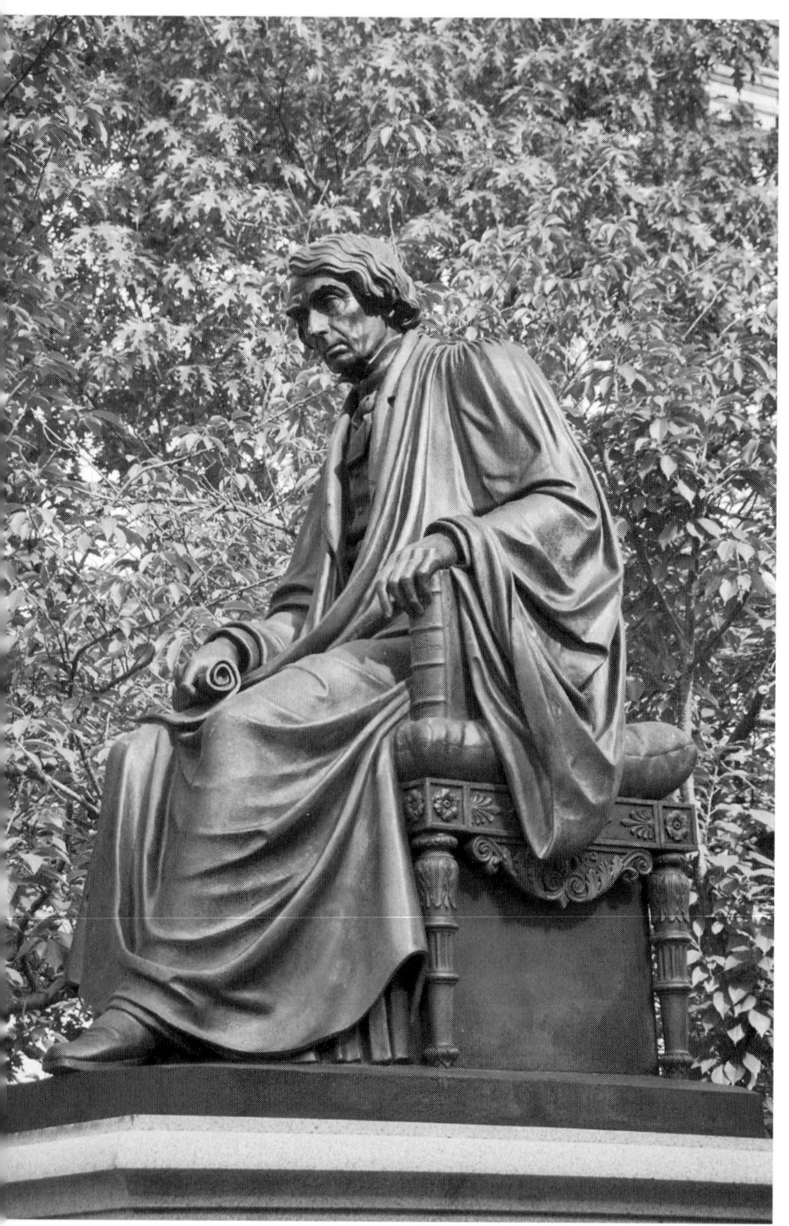

Walters and Newcomer invested the money, and by 1891, when they conveyed the money to the trustees of the Peabody Institute, the sum was approximately $95,000. The Rinehart Fund Committee was established at the Peabody Institute, and Walters was made chair, serving along with Daniel Coit Gilman, the first president of the Johns Hopkins University.

The question of how to use this large sum of money remained unsettled. The committee members decided to begin by funding scholarships for study in Paris or Rome. Each scholarship paid $1,000 annually and was tenable for four years. The first one was awarded in 1895.

Then the idea of establishing a school of sculpture began to evolve. The proposed school of sculpture was to be attached to the Maryland Institute, which had operated successfully in the city since 1826. In 1896 the Rinehart School of Sculpture opened in the Center Market building of the Maryland Institute, and it has operated ever since, graduating 314 students by its hundredth anniversary.

The Rinehart Fund was also used for annual prizes to the most promising students in sculpture, for commissions to young sculptors just returning from abroad, and for purchases and donations to the city of pieces of sculpture. One notable gift to the city by the Rinehart Fund Committee was *On the Trail*, by Edward Berge, in 1916 (K13). More than one-third of all of Baltimore's outdoor sculpture has been created by directors or alumni of the Rinehart School of Sculpture.

Except for this monument and the bust of William Walters on the Charles Street facade of the Walters Art Museum (C17), no other monuments by Rinehart are sited outdoors in Baltimore that are not in cemeteries, which this guide does not cover. To see more outdoor sculpture by Rinehart, visit Greenmount Cemetery. His work is also in the collections of the Walters Art Museum, the Baltimore Museum of Art, the Peabody Institute, the Maryland Institute College of Art, the Metropolitan Museum of Art in New York, the National Gallery in Washington, and the Brooklyn Museum, among others.

C8

TITLE

JOHN EAGER HOWARD MONUMENT, 1903

LOCATION

North square

SCULPTOR

Emmanuel Frémiet (1824–1910)

MEDIUM

Bronze

DONOR

Municipal Art Society of Baltimore City

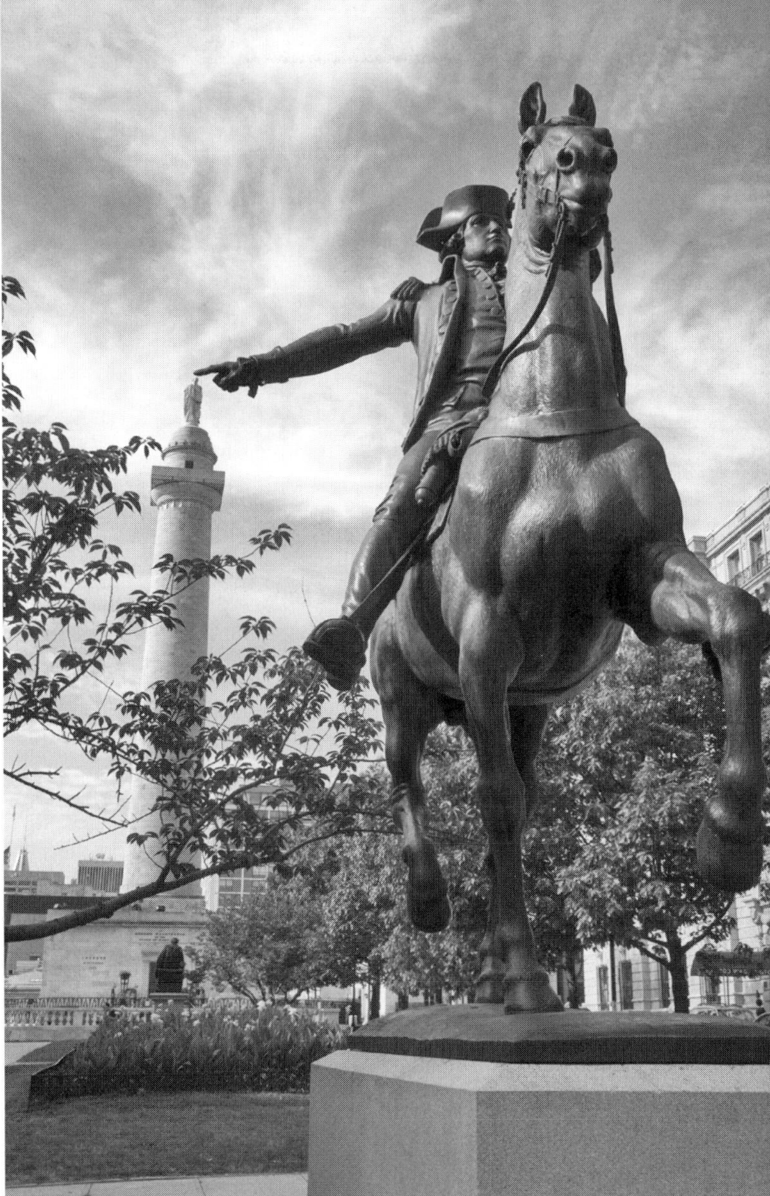

John Eager Howard (1752–1827) was George Washington's chief of staff and Maryland's most distinguished Revolutionary War hero. In the battle of Cowpens in South Carolina in 1781, he led his men into the threatening line of the enemy, exhibiting great military valor, and as a result was credited with bringing about a victory.

The Municipal Art Society of Baltimore City, created in 1899 for "public and educational purposes and especially to provide adequately for sculpture and pictorial decoration for public buildings, streets and open spaces in the city of Baltimore and to help generally beautify the city," set about erecting statues to men who had played an important part in the history of Maryland. Since John Eager Howard had not been chosen to be memorialized in bronze for the National Statuary Hall Collection in the U.S. Capitol—Charles Carroll and John Hanson were chosen instead—which members of the Municipal Art Society thought was a mistake, the first monument the society presented to the city was of Howard at the moment of his greatest wartime victory.

To create an equestrian monument of Howard, the society commissioned one of the foremost French sculptors of the nineteenth century, Emmanuel Frémiet. Next to Barye, who was an early rival, Frémiet was considered the finest French *animalier*. He received his first public commission at the age of 25 and is best known for his 1874 equestrian monument to Jeanne d'Arc in the Place des Pyramides in Paris. There is a replica of Frémiet's *Jeanne d'Arc* in Fairmount Park in Philadelphia. Frémiet spent much time in the Jardin des Plantes in Paris, studying live animals as Barye had before him, and upon Barye's death, Frémiet succeeded him as professor of drawing there. When Frémiet died, his models were sold to the Ferdinand Barbedienne foundry in Paris, just as Barye's had been, and his work continued to be cast until just before World War I.

Frémiet depicted John Eager Howard seated atop a very alert, energetic, muscular horse with left front leg and back right leg raised, suggesting forward movement. Howard, dressed in the uniform of a colonel in the Continental army, looks slightly to his left, with his right arm raised and outstretched, pointing with his forefinger straight out to the right. The sculptor may have been asked to depict Howard at the beginning of his famous charge at the battle of Cowpens, for it is believed that the artist was sent a copy of the congressional medal struck in Howard's honor after that battle. Both sides of the medal are represented in relief on the southern end of the monument's base.

The monument stands on land that was once part of John Eager Howard's estate. Howard had given the city the land for the Washington Monument, and it is appropriate that his statue is sited so near Washington's. The monument to Lafayette (C15), on the opposite side of the Washington Monument from Howard's, is also well sited, for Howard introduced Lafayette to Washington, and the three fought together in the Revolutionary War.

After the war, Howard served in the Continental Congress, as governor of Maryland, and as both a state and later a U.S. senator. He is mentioned in James Ryder Randall's poem "Maryland, My Maryland," written in 1861 and later adopted as Maryland's state song. There is a second monument to John Eager Howard in the city in nearby Howard's Park, at Howard Street and Druid Hill Avenue (E2).

C9

TITLE
Francis Scott Key, 1912

LOCATION
Entrance facade of Mount Vernon Place United Methodist Church, 10 E. Mount Vernon Place

SCULPTOR
Hans Schuler (1874–1951)

MEDIUM
Bronze

DONOR
Daughters of the American Revolution

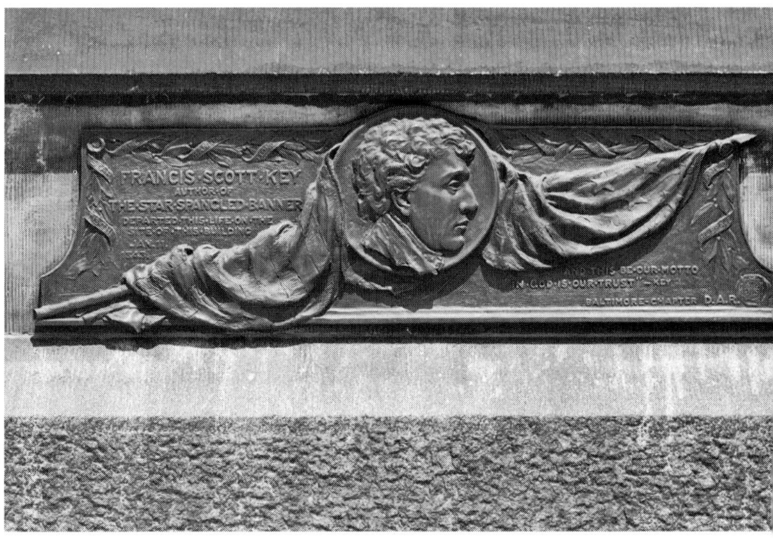

This bronze relief by Hans Schuler was commissioned for the facade of the Mount Vernon United Methodist Church in 1912 by the Daughters of the American Revolution to mark the site where Francis Scott Key (1779–1843) died. Key's daughter Elizabeth Phoebe, who had married John Eager Howard's son Charles, lived in the house that previously had stood on this site, which had been built for the younger Howards by Charles' father, John Eager Howard. Key visited his daughter often, and during a visit on January 11, 1843, he died. Commissioned in 1912 and completed that same year, the marker would have been planned as part of the centennial celebrations of the War of 1812, during which Key wrote the "Star-Spangled Banner."

At the center of the relief is a medallion with a profile portrait of Key. Behind the medallion, a furled flag stretches diagonally across the relief. A branch of myrtle, which extends up the left side of the relief, across the top, and down the right side is bound with a fillet inscribed with words from the "Star-Spangled Banner."

Schuler was a prominent sculptor in Baltimore. From 1925 until his death in 1951 he was president of the Maryland Institute. He was commissioned to create so many of Baltimore's most important monuments, including the Fallsway Fountain (F2) and monuments to Samuel Smith (G2), Johns Hopkins (J13), Martin Luther (K10), Sidney Lanier (J27), and Casimir Pulaski (P3), that he became known as the "Monument Maker of Baltimore." This relief was one of his earliest public pieces in the city.

Schuler, who was born in Alsace-Lorraine when that province was part of Germany, immigrated to the United States when he was 6. He studied at the Maryland Institute and was a member of the first class of the Institute's Rinehart School of Sculpture, along with J. Maxwell Miller and Edward Berge. Receiving a Rinehart Traveling Scholarship to study abroad for four years, he left for Paris, where he entered the Académie Julian and studied with Charles Raoul Verlet from 1900 to 1904. He then returned to Baltimore to set up a studio and begin his long career at the Maryland Institute, where he taught for many years before becoming the president.

C10–C11

TITLES
Force and *Order*, 1885 copies of 1846 originals

LOCATION
Balustrade east of the Washington Monument

SCULPTOR
Antoine-Louis Barye (1796–1875)

MEDIUM
Bronze

DONOR
William T. Walters

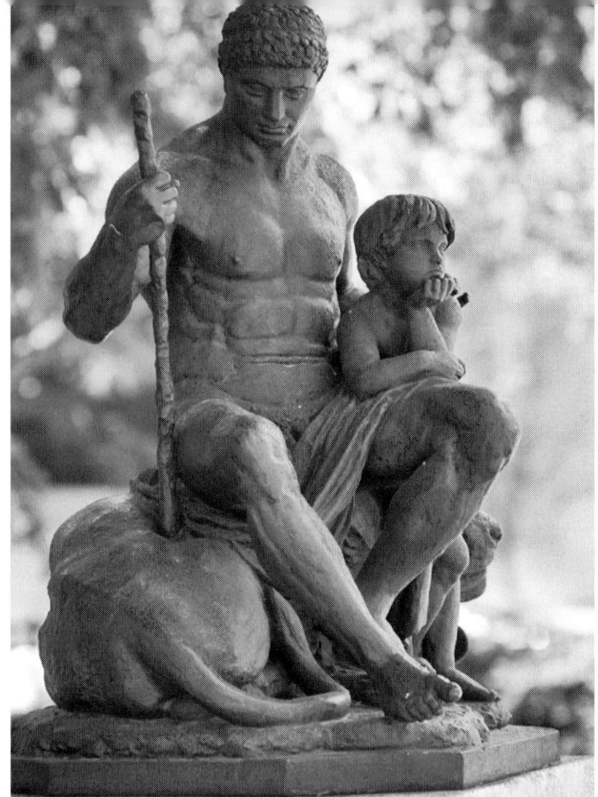

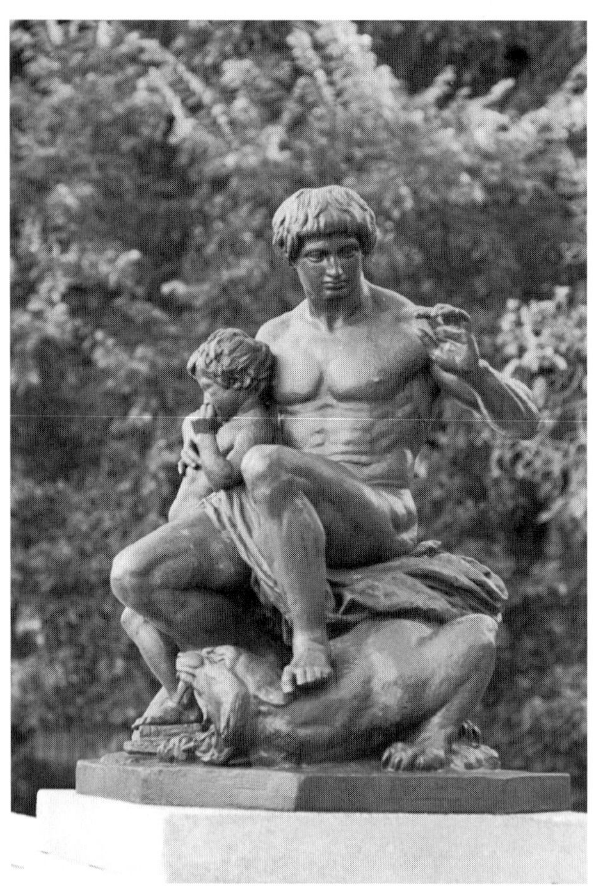

Placed today at the ends of the balustrade east of the Washington Monument, each of these sculptural groups—similar to *War* and *Peace* (C2–C3), their companion pieces on the balustrade west of the monument, is composed of a seated nude male figure with drapery, an animal, and a young nude boy in an arrangement suggesting the allegory. *Force* (*above*), at the north end of the eastern balustrade, is suggested by the gently reclining lion, whose head is raised and alert; the young boy standing, leaning on the left leg of the male figure, his head resting in his hand, and looking outward; and the male, sitting on the lion's back, holding his staff in his right hand and resting his left hand on the young boy's back.

Order (*at left*), at the south end of the balustrade, is suggested by the crouching tiger, who shows his teeth threateningly yet remains held in check by the weight of the male figure's foot, positioned just behind the animal's head; the young boy standing, leaning his back against the male figure, quietly holding a book; and the male, head raised slightly, embracing the young boy with his right arm and raising his left hand to hold a sword, which is missing today but was pointed downward, the tip of its blade resting on the animal.

Force and *Order*, together with *War* and *Peace*, were copies in bronze of the marble statues created originally by Barye for the top of the columns on the facade of the Louvre. They were presented to the city by William T. Walters in 1885.

C12

TITLE
GEORGE PEABODY MONUMENT,
1890 copy of 1869 original

LOCATION
East square

SCULPTOR
William Wetmore Storey (1819–1895)

MEDIUM
Bronze

DONOR
Robert Garrett

This statue of George Peabody (1795–1869) is sited in Mount Vernon Place, across from the entrance to the institute he founded in Baltimore in 1857. This statue, showing Peabody seated in an elegant armchair with his legs crossed, his right hand resting on his right thigh, and his left hand on the left arm of the chair, is a copy of the original commissioned in 1869 for Threadneedle Street in London, where Peabody's philanthropy was more extensive and included the erection of thousands of low-rent housing units for the poor. The sculptor, William Wetmore Storey, shared a studio in Rome during this time with William Rinehart, the famous Baltimore sculptor. The donor of the sculpture for Baltimore was Robert Garrett (1847–96), whose family banking firm, Robert Garrett & Sons, served as Peabody's agent in America. Garrett lived on the west square of Mount Vernon Place and was president of the B&O Railroad from 1884 to 1887.

George Peabody was not from Baltimore, and he did not live in the city for very long. A native of Danvers, Massachusetts, Peabody, like many young men of the time, came to Baltimore in 1815 to make his fortune. Baltimore was then the fastest-growing city in the nation because of its port and the port's location inland. Peabody had met Elisha Riggs during the War of 1812 and afterward joined him in Baltimore to set up a dry goods business, Riggs, Peabody & Company. In 1815 Peabody was 20 years old. By 1829 the company had offices in Philadelphia and New York and was called Peabody, Riggs & Company. However, in the mid-1830s Peabody decided that he wanted to become a financier and that the best place to do that was London. So in 1837, just twelve years after arriving in Baltimore, he left for England, where he would spend the rest of his life.

Peabody did not forget Baltimore or the friends he had made there. Nor did he forget that in 1837 the city did not have a public library, an art museum (the Peale Museum, established by Rembrandt Peale in 1814, had closed by 1830), a university, or a conservatory of music. He addressed all these needs in a letter written in 1857 proposing an institution that would be a haven for the scholar and of use to the public. Peabody gave $1.4 million to establish an institute with four separate departments: a library, a scholarly lecture series, an academy of music, and an art gallery. The first half of the building opened in 1862, and the remainder opened in 1878. Nathaniel Holmes Morison designed the famous library and carried out Peabody's wishes in setting up a library for scholars that the public could use. Morison purchased three hundred thousand volumes, in the United States and abroad, comprising the best works available in every field of the arts and sciences. At the time the collection surpassed even that of the Library of Congress, and today it includes some of the rarest books in the world. When the Johns Hopkins University was founded in 1876, it did not have a library, but the new faculty had access to the Peabody Library.

Peabody's legacy in Baltimore is more than the Peabody Institute. His philanthropy stimulated Enoch Pratt to begin the Pratt Library and Johns Hopkins to establish his university. The interest in collecting art that the gallery of the Peabody Institute initiated certainly must have contributed to what evolved into the collections of the Walters Art Museum and the Baltimore Museum of Art.

William Wetmore Storey was born in Salem, Massachusetts. After attending Harvard College and Harvard Law School and being admitted to the Massachusetts bar, he turned his attention to sculpture. Storey received an important commission from the United States Bar Association for a statue of Chief Justice John

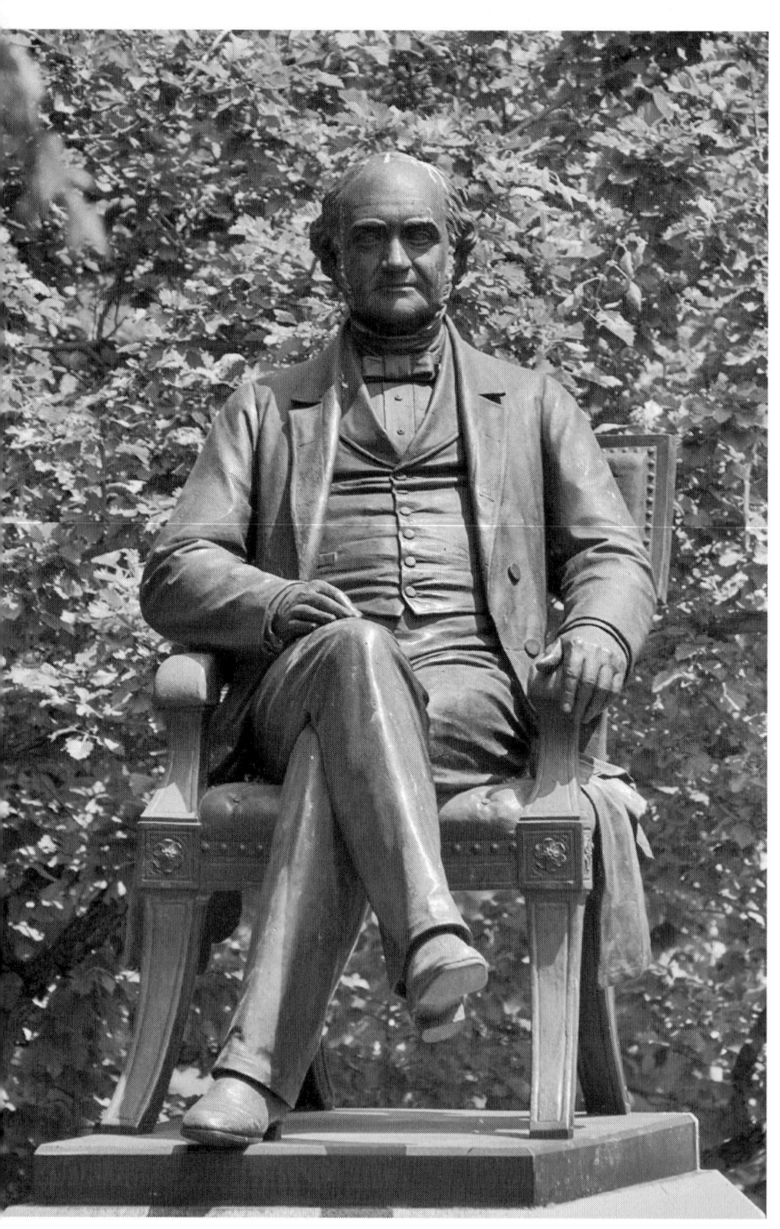

Marshall for the U.S. Capitol. Interestingly, his father, Associate Justice Joseph Storey, had been a longtime colleague of Marshall's on the Supreme Court. Storey's work can be seen today in and around Boston, in the Public Gardens, on the Harvard University campus, and at Bunker Hill, as well as in leading museums around the country. His most famous work, *Cleopatra*, in the Virginia Museum of Fine Arts in Richmond, was mentioned in Nathaniel Hawthorne's book *The Marble Faun* (1860).

While living in Rome as an expatriate, Storey spent much of his creative energy writing poetry, which was widely read during his lifetime. He is buried with his wife in the Protestant Cemetery in Rome, having designed his own grave statue, the *Angel of Grief.*

C13

TITLE
Naïad, 1932

LOCATION
East square

SCULPTOR
Grace Hill Turnbull (1880–1976)

MEDIUM
Bronze

DONOR
Women's Civic League

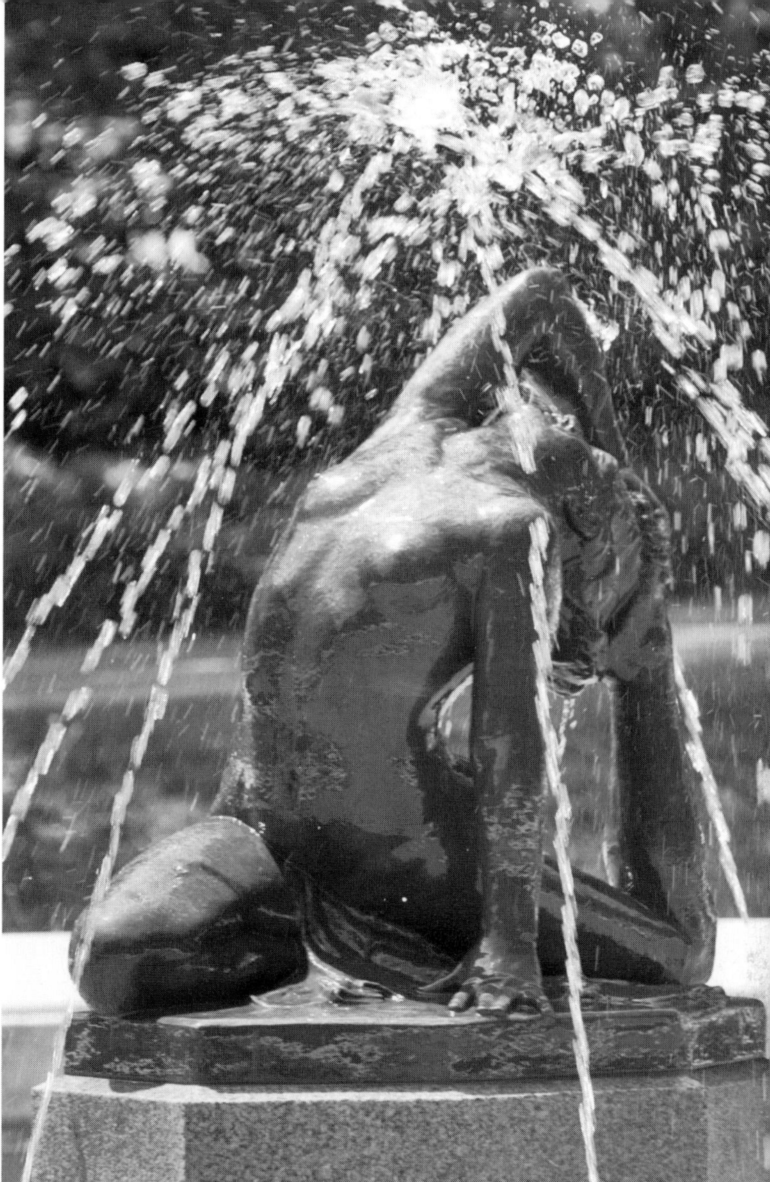

The naïad has long been a favorite subject of artists. In Greek mythology, the naïads were water nymphs that presided over fountains, wells, springs, rivers, streams, and brooks. The naïad was bound to her body of water; if it dried up, she died. The waters associated with a naïad were thought to be endowed with inspirational, medicinal, or prophetic powers, and the naïads were worshipped by the ancient Greeks.

The Women's Civic League thought the naïad could symbolize the reawakening of the city and its downtown and coincidentally replace an ugly pipe in the east square fountain. The gift was made possible through the Coins-in-the-Fountain program. Coins thrown into the fountain in the south square by visitors to three annual spring Flower Marts, which the Women's Civic League sponsored, were used to purchase the gift in 1962. The Women's Civic League, an all-volunteer organization, was formed in 1911 to improve living conditions in the city. The Flower Mart remains their chief fund-raising event.

The figure is shown in quite a dramatic pose. The naïad becomes a closed form, with her right arm reaching for and touching her left foot, which is raised behind her. Her back is completely arched. Nude except for a small bit of drapery falling over her leg, she sits on her folded right leg and holds her head far enough back to touch her raised left foot. When the fountain is on, her body is continually bathed in water, which is directed at her from water jets encircling the sculpture. *Naïad* was the last piece of sculpture to be placed in any of the four squares of Mount Vernon Place.

C14

TITLE

SEVERN TEAKLE WALLIS MONUMENT, 1904

LOCATION

East square

SCULPTOR

Laurent Honoré Marqueste (1848–1920)

MEDIUM

Bronze

DONOR

Municipal Art Society of Baltimore City

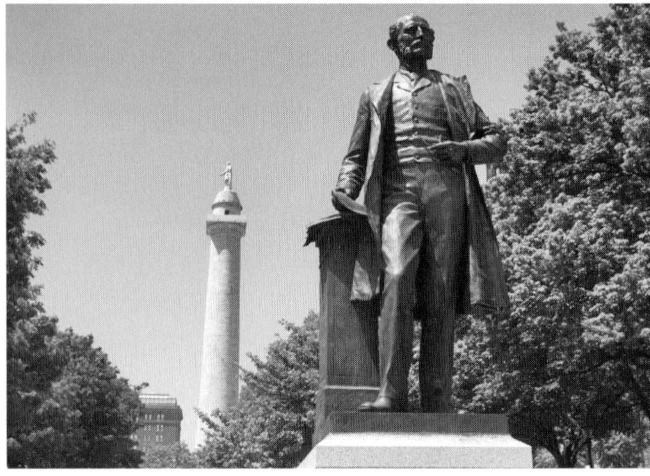

Severn Teakle Wallis (1816–94) was a prominent lawyer in Baltimore during the nineteenth century. He began his brilliant career after being admitted to the bar in 1835, at the age of 19. Later recognized as a wit, a reformer, a poet, a linguist, and an orator, he was Baltimore's leading citizen for almost half a century. His court appearances brought out many colleagues, who would come to hear him argue some obscure point of law as if he had made a lifelong study of it. He could have been elected governor or senator or been appointed a cabinet officer, but he was content to remain a local figure. When the Municipal Art Society of Baltimore City decided to erect statues to men who had played an important part in Maryland history, they chose to commission monuments first to John Eager Howard (C8) and next to Wallis, noting that Wallis had laid the foundation for civil-service reform. In erecting this monument, the society also underscored its belief that "direction is everything, distance nothing," for Wallis died before his reform goals were reached.

Wallis, who remained a bachelor all of his life, devoted much of his energy to the arts. He was a trustee of both the Peabody Institute and the Maryland Institute. He was in fact the juror for an exhibition at the Maryland Institute in 1851 in which William Rinehart first entered a piece of sculpture. Wallis gave Rinehart first place and remained a patron and strong supporter of Rinehart's throughout his career. He was the driving force on the committee that commissioned Rinehart to create a monument to Roger B. Taney, and he spoke at the dedication of that statue in Annapolis in 1872. A replica of the statue was given to the city and stands in the north square (C7).

Laurent Honoré Marqueste was one of the most distinguished French artists of his day. He was born in Toulouse and died in Paris. He won the Prix de Rome in 1871 and made his Salon debut in 1874 in Paris. Thereafter, Marqueste was awarded many first prizes in expositions in France and across Europe. His reputation was well established. Henry Walters suggested him for this commission, and negotiations were carried out in Paris by his fellow Baltimorean, art collector and agent George A. Lucas.

To complete a full standing portrait of Wallis, Marqueste was sent a suit that had belonged to Wallis and a photographic portrait of him. No detail was unimportant. Wallis is shown standing, with his weight on his left leg, his right leg slightly bent at the knee and placed forward to the edge of the base. He is elegantly dressed in his suit and a knee-length coat. His right hand rests on a pedestal, on which his papers are spread. He looks to his left and off to the distance. His moustache, muttonchop whiskers, and slightly bald head are prominent features.

This monument, originally sited in the south square, was moved to its present location in 1920.

C15

TITLE
LAFAYETTE MONUMENT, 1924

LOCATION
South square

SCULPTOR
Andrew O'Connor (1874–1955)

MEDIUM
Bronze

DONOR
City of Baltimore

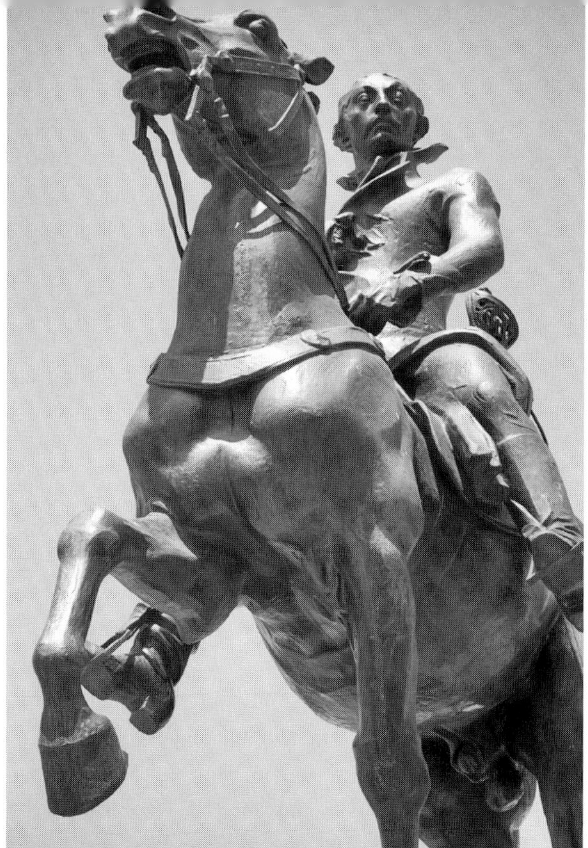

The statue of the Marquis de Lafayette (1757–1834) is one of Baltimore's outstanding war monuments, memorializing, in the name of Lafayette, those soldiers who died in France during World War I. It was also created to honor the young Frenchman for his assistance to America during the Revolutionary War.

This equestrian monument caused great controversy when it was installed. In 1917 the architect Thomas Hastings, from the New York firm of Carrere & Hastings, was hired to relandscape the gardens of Mount Vernon Place. By 1919 Hastings had decided that the new Lafayette statue should be placed just south of the Washington Monument, where it stands today. Such a large pedestal with such a large equestrian statue, it was thought at the time, would block the view of the Washington Monument from the south. Henry Walters, who had just completed the Walters Art Gallery (today the Walters Art Museum), which faced the south square, commented loudly that the placement of the Lafayette statue would be "an artistic crime," and H. L. Mencken wrote that it looked like Washington's spittoon.

The controversy grew. The *Baltimore Sun* chimed in rather frivolously that the goldfish in the pool below would no longer be able to see General Washington. Negative opinions continued to be expressed about the scale of the pedestal, most notably its height. Two leading sculptors in Baltimore at the time, Edward Berge and Ephraim Keyser, even suggested that the base be lowered by four feet. Despite the raging criticism, Mr. Hastings prevailed, and the French nobleman and his mount were placed just south of the Washington Monument and unveiled on September 6, 1924. President Coolidge spoke at the ceremonies, which were attended by some twenty thousand people, including many foreign dignitaries.

Today it is hard to imagine that such a battle took place over this monument, which is such an integral part of the historic site. The placement of Lafayette in close proximity to Washington, the general under whom he served in the Continental army and with whom he became such good friends, seems appropriate. Furthermore, the relationship of the equestrian statues of Howard and Lafayette to the north and south of the Washington Monument, respectively, is also fitting, for Howard introduced Lafayette to Washington, and the three fought together in the Revolutionary War.

The sculptor, Andrew O'Connor, was born in Worcester, Massachusetts. He studied in the studio of John Singer Sargent and worked with his father as a stonecutter and sculptor. By 1906 he had won the second

medal at the Paris Salon, and he won the first medal
in 1928. Then in 1931 he received what many sculptors considered the highest honor in the world: a piece
of his sculpture, a heroic bronze figure of a kneeling
woman, *Mother of Sorrows,* was accepted for permanent display at the Tate Gallery in London. His best-
known works in this country are his statue of Abraham
Lincoln in Springfield, Illinois, and his bronze doors for
St. Bartholomew's Church in New York City. His obituary stated that foreign critics hailed him as the greatest
American sculptor and equated his bronze doors of St.
Bartholomew's to Ghiberti's in Florence and his Lafayette to Verocchio's equestrian statue of Colleoni in Venice. O'Connor lived the last quarter-century of his life
in Paris, London, and Dublin, dying in Dublin. Some
attribute his becoming an expatriate to the bitter controversy surrounding placement of this monument.

C16

TITLE
Sea Urchin, 1959 copy of 1922 original

LOCATION
South square

SCULPTOR
Edward Berge (1876–1924)

MEDIUM
Bronze

DONOR
Frederick R. Huber

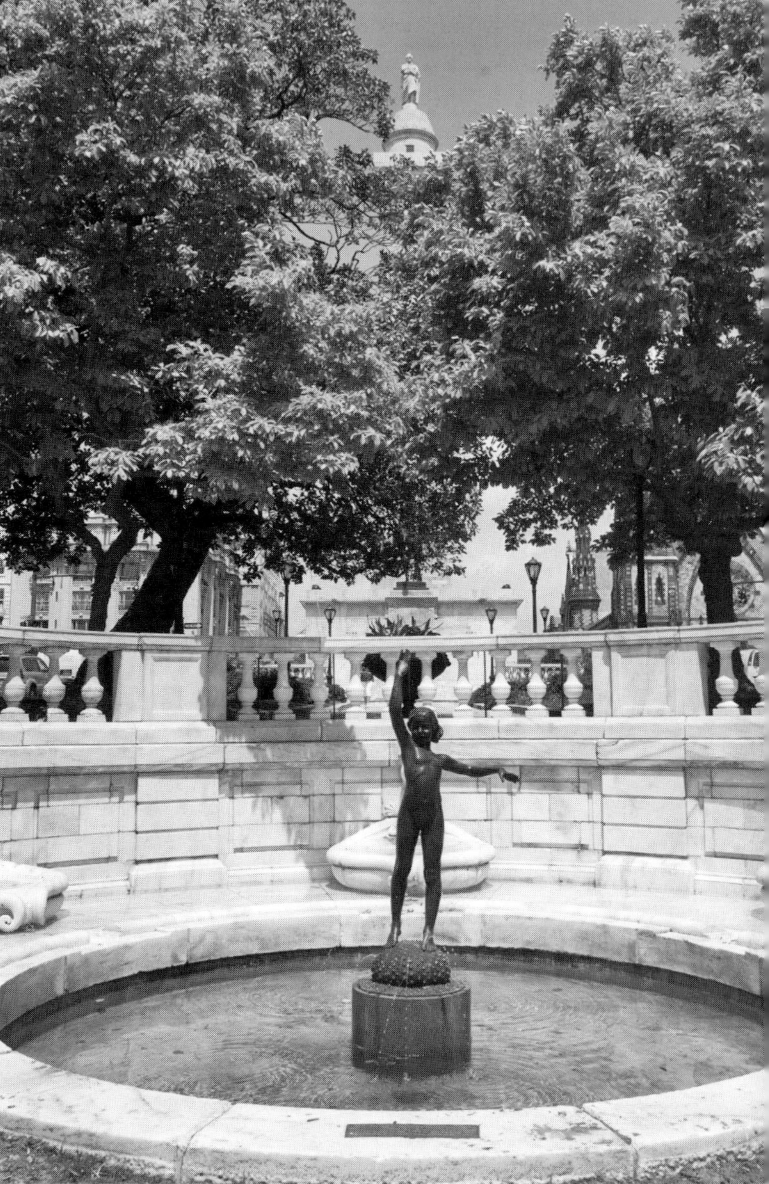

Edward Berge was one of Baltimore's best-loved sculptors. Born in Baltimore, he was one of the seven members of the first class to attend the Maryland Institute's Rinehart School of Sculpture, which opened in 1896. Hans Schuler and J. Maxwell Miller were fellow students. After graduation, Berge, along with Schuler and Miller, went to Paris and enrolled in the Académie Julian, where they studied with Charles Raoul Verlet (1857–1923) for four years. Berge then returned to Baltimore, where he remained until his untimely death. He was a member of the National Arts Club, the National Sculpture Society, and the Charcoal Club, a very active local arts group, and was commissioned to create some of Baltimore's most important monuments.

In Berge's memory, his 3-foot-high sculpture *Sea Urchin* was anonymously given to the city and placed in the fountain in the south square of Mount Vernon Place. It is a statue of a young nude female standing on a sea urchin with her feet apart, her arms raised, and her mouth open as if she were shouting about some delightful discovery, maybe of the sea urchin itself. Berge had designed a remarkable system of copper tubing inside the sea urchin to allow water to spray out of all the holes pierced in its shell.

Berge's *Sea Urchin* was always considered too small for its surroundings, and discussions had been ongoing for almost thirty-four years about its removal and replacement with a larger replica, perhaps by Berge's son, Henry. Frederick R. Huber, the former managing director of the Lyric Theatre and an old friend of Edward Berge's, left $7,500 in his will in 1959 to do just that, and the piece in Mount Vernon today is the replica enlarged by Henry Berge. As the younger Berge said from the beginning, "To the casual eye, it would not be changed except in size."

(For the fate of the original *Sea Urchin*, see J20.)

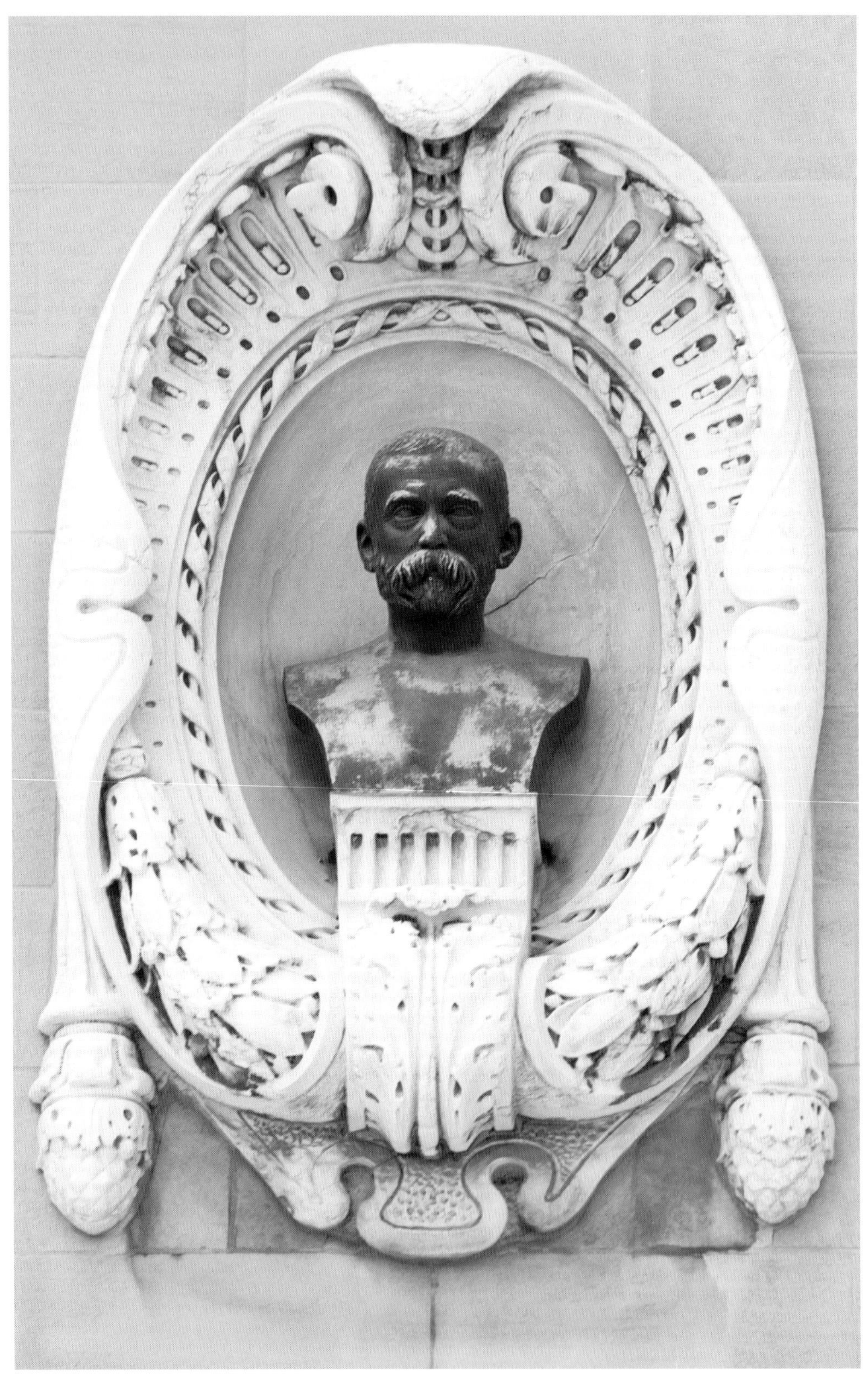

C17

TITLE
William T. Walters, 1907 copy of 1867 original

LOCATION
Walters Art Museum,
niche over the Charles Street entrance

SCULPTOR
William Henry Rinehart (1825–1874)

MEDIUM
Bronze

DONOR
Henry Walters

This large bronze bust of William T. Walters on the facade of the museum that bears his name is an enlargement of an original by William Rinehart, finished in Rome in 1867. When the present Walters Art Museum was under construction, Walters' son, Henry, asked George A. Lucas, his father's agent in Paris and now his own, to arrange for the Barbedienne Foundry to make a twice life-size replica of the bust Rinehart had made of his father in 1867. An entry in Lucas' diary for May 16, 1907, indicates that he wrote to Ferdinand Barbedienne to ask that he begin work immediately on casting the Walters bust. A picture of a marble bust of Walters by Rinehart is published in two catalogs of sculpture by Rinehart, one written by William Rusk and Marvin Ross and one by Anna Ruttledge. In both catalogs it is noted that three bronze copies were made, one of which is said to be the bronze on the facade of the museum.

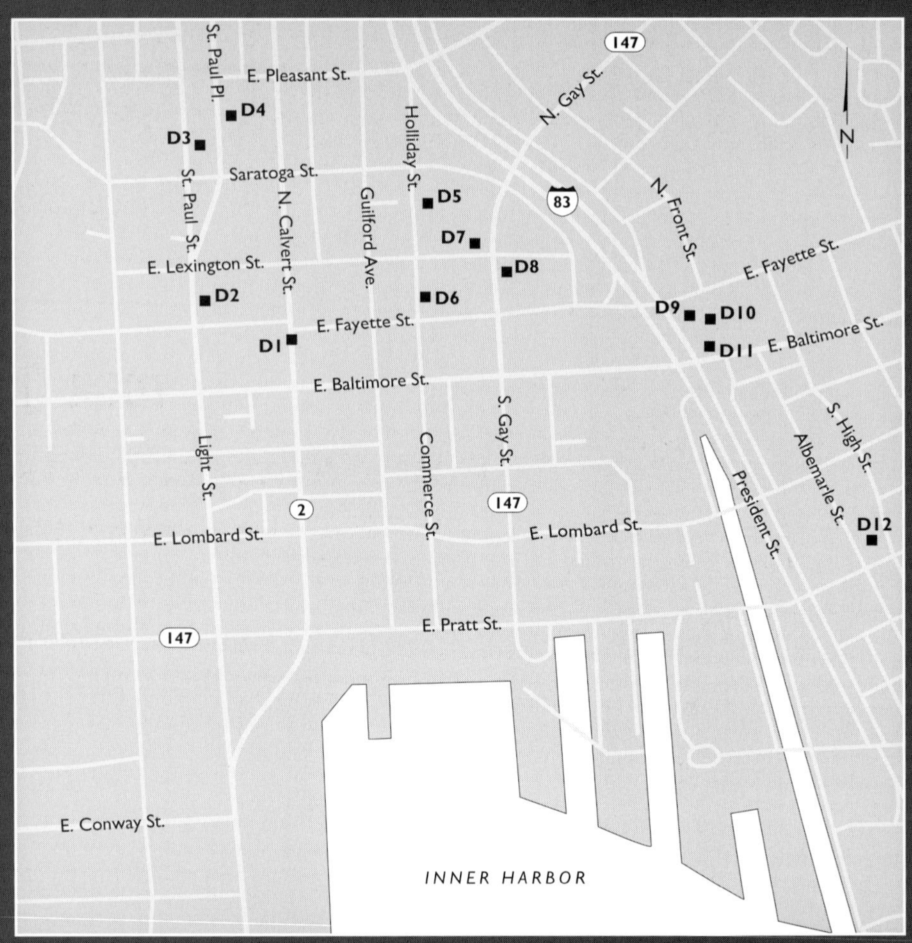

St. Paul Pl.
E. Pleasant St.
N. Gay St.
147
D4
D3
Holliday St.
Saratoga St.
N
83
N. Front St.
St. Paul St.
N. Calvert St.
Guilford Ave.
D5
E. Fayette St.
E. Lexington St.
D7
D8
D2
D6
D9
D10
D1
E. Fayette St.
D11
E. Baltimore St.
E. Baltimore St.
S. High St.
Albemarle St.
Light St.
Commerce St.
S. Gay St.
President St.
2
147
D12
E. Lombard St.
E. Lombard St.
147
E. Pratt St.
E. Conway St.
INNER HARBOR

DOWNTOWN EAST OF CHARLES STREET

Walking

D1

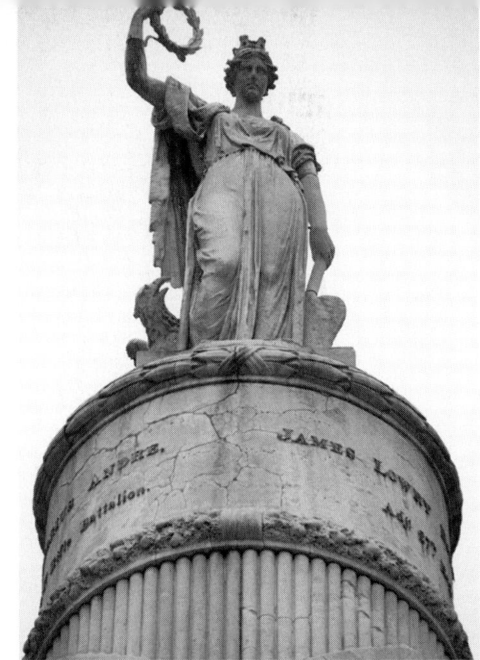

The first and most famous of Baltimore's monuments related to the War of 1812, the Battle Monument was the first true public war memorial in the United States. Dedicated to those slain in the 1814 battle of Baltimore, it bears the names of the thirty-nine men who died fighting at North Point and Fort McHenry.

Maximilian Godefroy, the French émigré who had participated in the defense of the city, was the architect for the monument. He donated the design. Earlier Godefroy had lost to Robert Mills in the competition for the Washington Monument (C1). The sculptor of the four griffins, the two reliefs on the column, and the statue on top of the Battle Monument was Antonio Capellano, whom Godefroy had encouraged to come to Baltimore to work on this project. While in Baltimore, Capellano carved the *Moses* and *Christ* reliefs for the facade of St. Paul's Episcopal Church (B6) and the *Angel of Truth* for the pediment of Godefroy's First Unitarian Church (B10).

The site of the monument is one of Baltimore's most historic squares. In 1768 a courthouse was built on the spot now occupied by the monument. In 1775 George Washington and other Virginia delegates to the Continental Congress were entertained there on their way to Philadelphia, and in July 1776 the Declaration of Independence was read from the courthouse steps. Soon after 1776 a formal square was laid out, and townhouses were built on all four sides. The courthouse was eventually torn down, and a new one was built, not in the footprint of the earlier courthouse but on the west side of the square. The square, unadorned after removal of the old courthouse, was proposed for the Washington Monument. The residents of the square, fearing that the 178-foot-high monument might fall on their nearby homes, refused to allow it; however, they wholeheartedly supported the use of the site for the more reasonably scaled Battle Monument.

On September 12, 1815, the first anniversary of the battle of North Point, the cornerstone was laid. A leather-bound volume listing all the subscribers to the monument, thought to have been placed in the cornerstone, was recently found in the city library. The list included names such as Samuel Chase and Charles Carroll and other well-known Baltimore family names, such as Symington, Merryman, Warfield, Hoffman, and McKim. A total of $40,000 was raised. On that dedication day there was a procession to the square to lay the cornerstone. Among those present were Maj. Gen. Samuel Smith, who commanded all the forces in the defense of Baltimore; Brig. Gen. John Stricker, Smith's commander at the battle of North Point; and Col. George Armistead, his commander at Fort McHenry. A model of the monument was carried to the ceremony in a funeral car drawn by six white horses led by six men in regimentals.

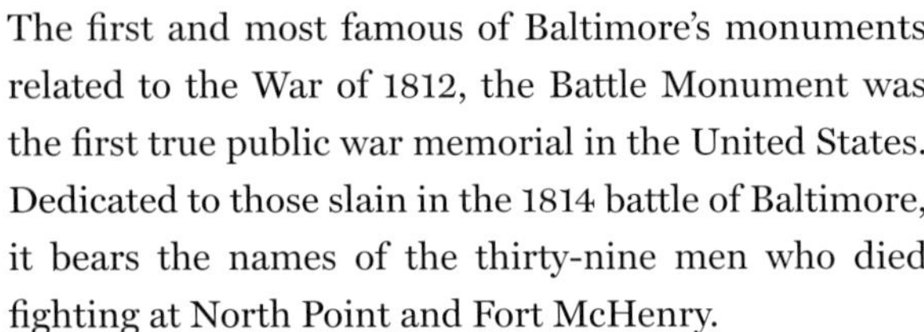

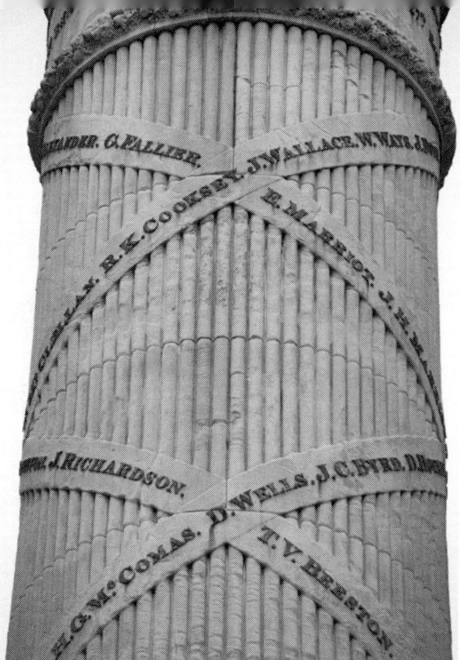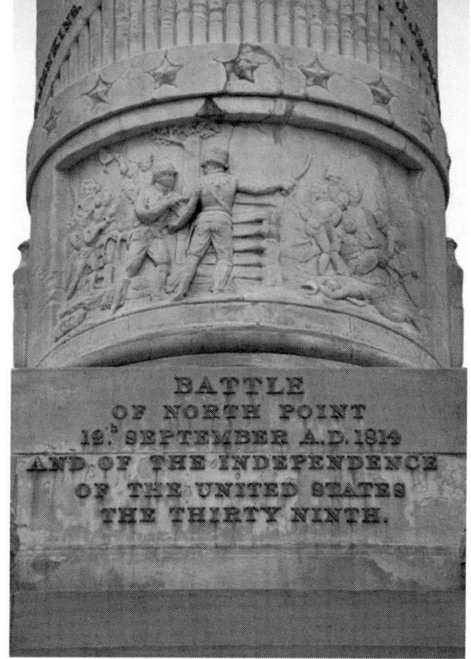

To this day there is no monument like the Battle Monument, and there are few anywhere that are so symbolic in design. The base of the monument was designed to represent an ancient Egyptian tomb. A stone slab or false door was placed on each face of the base to represent an entrance to the tomb. The three steps to reach these doors represent the three years of the war. The eighteen layers of stone that make up the base represent the eighteen states in the Union in 1814. Atop each of the four corners of this tomb is a griffin, a legendary animal with the head and wings of an eagle on a lion's body, symbolizing immortality. These four griffins watch over a column on which there are reliefs depicting the battles of North Point and Fort McHenry. Between the two reliefs, on the east and west sides of the monument, are lachrymal urns symbolizing grief for the dead.

The shaft of the column is carved in the form of a Roman fasces, or a bundle of sticks, the Roman symbol of unity. At the top of the column, between the wreaths of laurel and cypress, are inscribed the names of the three officers killed, and the fillets binding the fasces are inscribed with the names of the thirty-six noncommissioned men killed. Included there are the names of Daniel Wells and Henry G. McComas, the two young riflemen credited with killing the British general Ross in a skirmish just before the battle of North Point began. An unadorned marble obelisk at Monument and Aisquith streets dating from 1873 is dedicated to these two young heroes, whose bodies are locked in a vault under the memorial.

The combined height of the column and pedestal is 39 feet, the number of years since the country's independence. The classical female statue atop the column represents Baltimore and is called *Lady Baltimore*. Looking out toward the harbor, which would have been visible from this site in 1825, she holds a laurel wreath in her raised right hand, and in her left hand is a rudder, a reference to the industry that brought Baltimore its wealth and prosperity. At her feet is an eagle, which looks up at her from behind a bomb like those that exploded over Fort McHenry. In 1827 the monument was adopted as the official symbol of the city.

Capellano's statue has been restored several times over the years. In 1938 the raised hand dropped off in a windstorm and was restored by Hans Schuler, whose monuments adorn the city. In 1975 another well-known Baltimore sculptor, Reuben Kramer, was hired to recreate the left hand and rudder, for which he used stone from Baltimore's ubiquitous marble steps.

(For how the Battle Monument figured in John Quincy Adam's toasting Baltimore as the "Monumental City" in 1827, see C1.)

D2

TITLE
CECILIUS CALVERT MONUMENT, 1908

LOCATION
Clarence M. Mitchell Jr. Courthouse,
100 N. Calvert Street, St. Paul Street entrance

SCULPTOR
Albert Weinert (1863–1947)

MEDIUM
Bronze

DONOR
Society of Colonial Wars in Maryland

Cecilius Calvert (1606–75) was just 26 years old when his father, Sir George Calvert, the first Lord Baltimore, died. Cecilius became the second Lord Baltimore and the first Lord Proprietor of the colony of Maryland. George Calvert had requested and received a grant of 10-20 million acres of land to establish a colony in what became Maryland, but he died as the charter was being issued, so the responsibility of establishing and governing the Maryland colony fell to Cecilius.

It is highly appropriate that this monument is sited at an entrance to the third courthouse to stand on the site, the first dating from 1767. Cecilius Calvert was a champion of three great principles of liberty that became the basis of Maryland law—religious toleration, the separation of church and state, and the right of free men to participate in making the laws they are governed by. Even though Cecilius lived in England all his life, never immigrating to Maryland, he established a sound and prosperous footing there to the depletion of his personal fortune and consistently and innovatively promoted religious toleration for all Christians living in his colony. He sent his brother Leonard to Maryland with a set of instructions to help him govern the colony, titled "Instructions to Colonists by Lord Baltimore," which outlined and underscored the significance of these three liberties. Cecilius Calvert governed Maryland for forty-two years. His son Charles served as governor of Maryland from 1661 to 1675 and as second Lord

Proprietor and third Lord Baltimore from his father's death in 1675 until 1715.

The placement of Calvert's monument on the steps of the courthouse and how he should be depicted generated much discussion and disagreement among members of the Municipal Art Commission. Some city councilmen, lawyers, and courthouse officials thought the entrance to the courthouse was beautiful in its simplicity and should remain unadorned by sculpture, but few agreed. The accuracy of Calvert as a man with long curling hair, clothed in the elegant dress of the day, was suspect, but two answers were given in support of the sculptor's choices. First, all early portraits of Calvert in the Maryland State Archives showed him elegantly dressed with long hair; and second, a handsome man with long curly hair fulfilled their ideal of what Calvert should look like. Case closed.

Francis X. Bushman (1883–1966), an actor originally from Baltimore who at the height of his career was advertised as "The Handsomest Man in the World" claimed to have been the model for Calvert. He also claimed to have been the model for the citizen-soldier in the Union Soldiers and Sailors Monument (J1), Francis Scott Key in the monument at Eutaw Place (I19), and the dying soldier on the Confederate monument on Mount Royal (I12). To supplement his meager earnings as an actor, Bushman worked as a sculptor's model at the Charcoal Club and the Maryland Institute for 50¢ cents an hour. In 1903, in Baltimore again posing at the Maryland Institute, he was asked to help install a sculpture exhibition at the Fifth Regiment Armory. There he met many New York sculptors who, impressed with his physique, invited him to New York to model for them. He posed for Augustus Saint-Gaudens and Daniel Chester French, two of the leading sculptors of the day.

Albert Weinert was born in Leipzig, where he studied art at the Royal Academy. He later studied at the École des Beaux-Arts in Brussels before immigrating to the United States in 1886. He settled in New York and set up a studio in the Bronx. He was a member of the National Sculpture Society and exhibited his work in Chicago, New York, and at the Panama Pacific Exhibition in San Francisco in 1915.

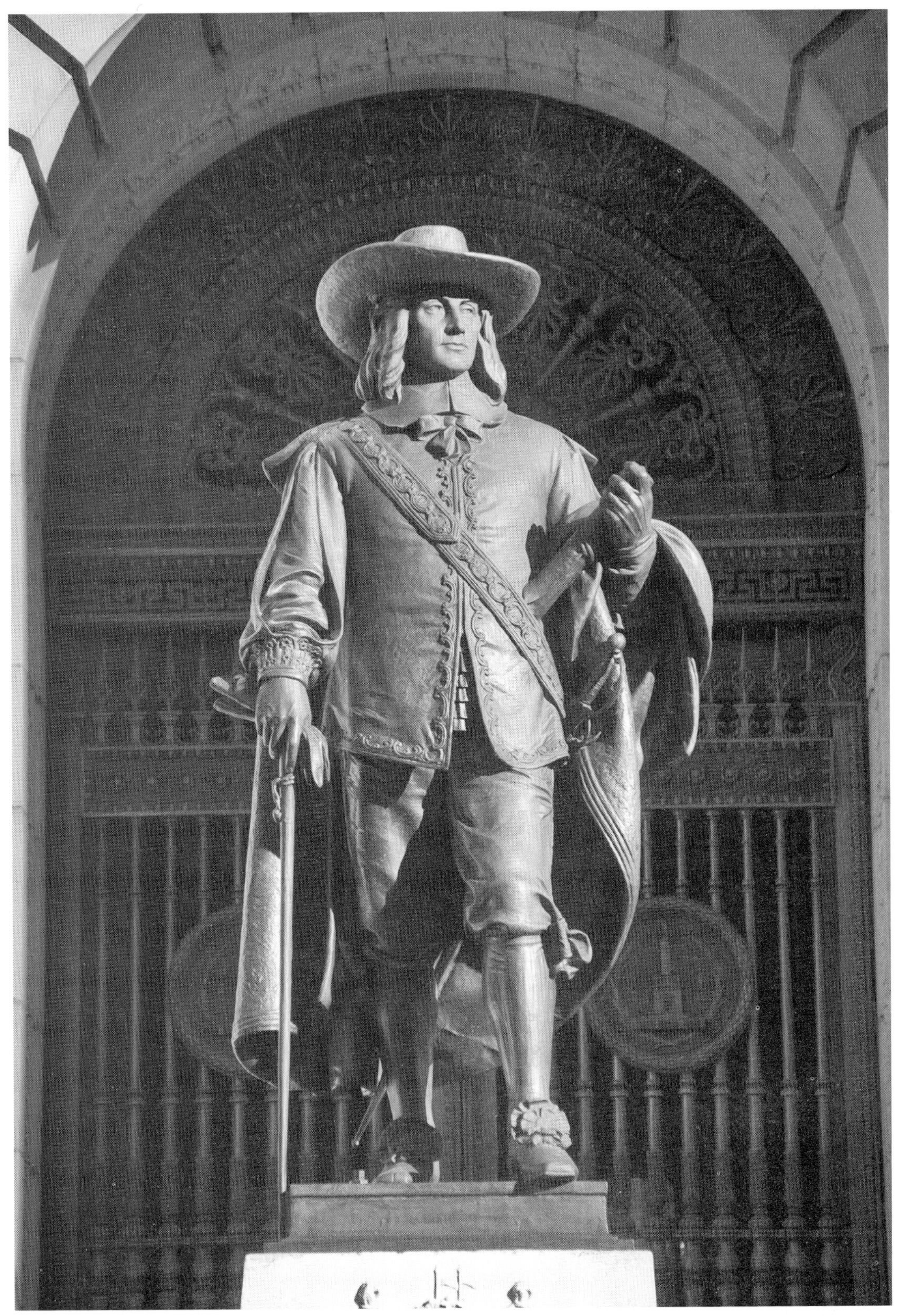

D3

TITLE
JOHN MIFFLIN HOOD MONUMENT, 1911

LOCATION
Preston Gardens, St. Paul Place and Saratoga Street

SCULPTOR
Richard E. Brooks (1865–1919)

MEDIUM
Bronze

DONOR
City of Baltimore

John Mifflin Hood (1843–1906) was the president and general manager of the Western Maryland Railroad from 1874 to 1902. He is remembered chiefly for transforming this debt-ridden, 90-mile-long railroad from being practically bankrupt and a burden to taxpayers into a self-supporting transportation system. When Hood became president, the stock was deemed to be worthless. He completely reorganized what H. L. Mencken referred to as "undoubtedly the worst railroad in the United States," purchased modern steam engines to replace what the Sun called "asthmatic ones," and extended the railroad's tracks 268 miles further into Western Maryland and Pennsylvania. Upon the sale of the railroad to the Fuller Syndicate, Baltimore found that its investment in the railroad, which earlier had been considered a total loss, was now worth more than $8 million. This money was already in the bank when the city needed funds to begin rebuilding after the Great Fire of 1904. Citizens were so relieved to have such funds available that the city council voted to appropriate $10,000 for a statue of Hood and commissioned Richard E. Brooks as sculptor.

The statue of Hood is the closest thing Baltimore has to a monument commemorating the Great Fire of 1904, and it is one of the few statues in the country dedicated to a railroad president. Hood is shown standing in a full-length frock coat. His right hand is on his coat lapel, and in his left hand he holds a sheet of parchment. His weight is on his left leg, and his right leg is forward, extending just beyond the edge of the base. He looks slightly to his left, with a wrinkled brow. His heavy mustache and goatee are prominent features. Just behind his right leg is a train engine wheel framed by oak leaves.

This monument originally was located at the corner of Baltimore and Liberty streets, just one block north of where the Great Fire began. New street patterns for the development of Charles Center and the Civic Center necessitated the relocation of the Hood statue in 1963 to Preston Gardens, where it could be seen from the office window of the then president of the Western Maryland Railroad, who had recommended the new site. The railroad's offices were in the Commercial Credit Building (today the Citifinancial Building), in the 300 block of St. Paul Street, which runs along the western edge of Preston Gardens.

Richard Brooks was born in Braintree, Massachusetts. He established a business making commercial sculpture in Boston. His first opportunity to work from life came with a commission for a portrait bust of Massachusetts Governor William Eustis Russell. The result was so satisfactory that Brooks was encouraged to go to Paris to study, where he subsequently set up a studio. He was awarded a gold medal at the Paris Exposition of 1900 for a statue of Colonel Thomas Case that stands today in Boston's Public Gardens. He also received gold medals in the 1901 Pan-American Exposition and the 1909 Alaska-Yukon-Pacific Exposition, the latter for a statue of William H. Seward, a New York senator and secretary of state under Lincoln, who advocated for the United States to purchase Alaska from Russia, that stands in Volunteer Park in Seattle today. Prior to the Hood commission, the State of Maryland had commissioned Brooks to create two bronze statues, one of John Hanson and one of Charles Carroll of Carrollton, both dated 1903, for Statuary Hall in the Capitol in Washington. He was elected to the National Sculpture Society in 1897 and to the American Academy of Arts and Sciences in 1908.

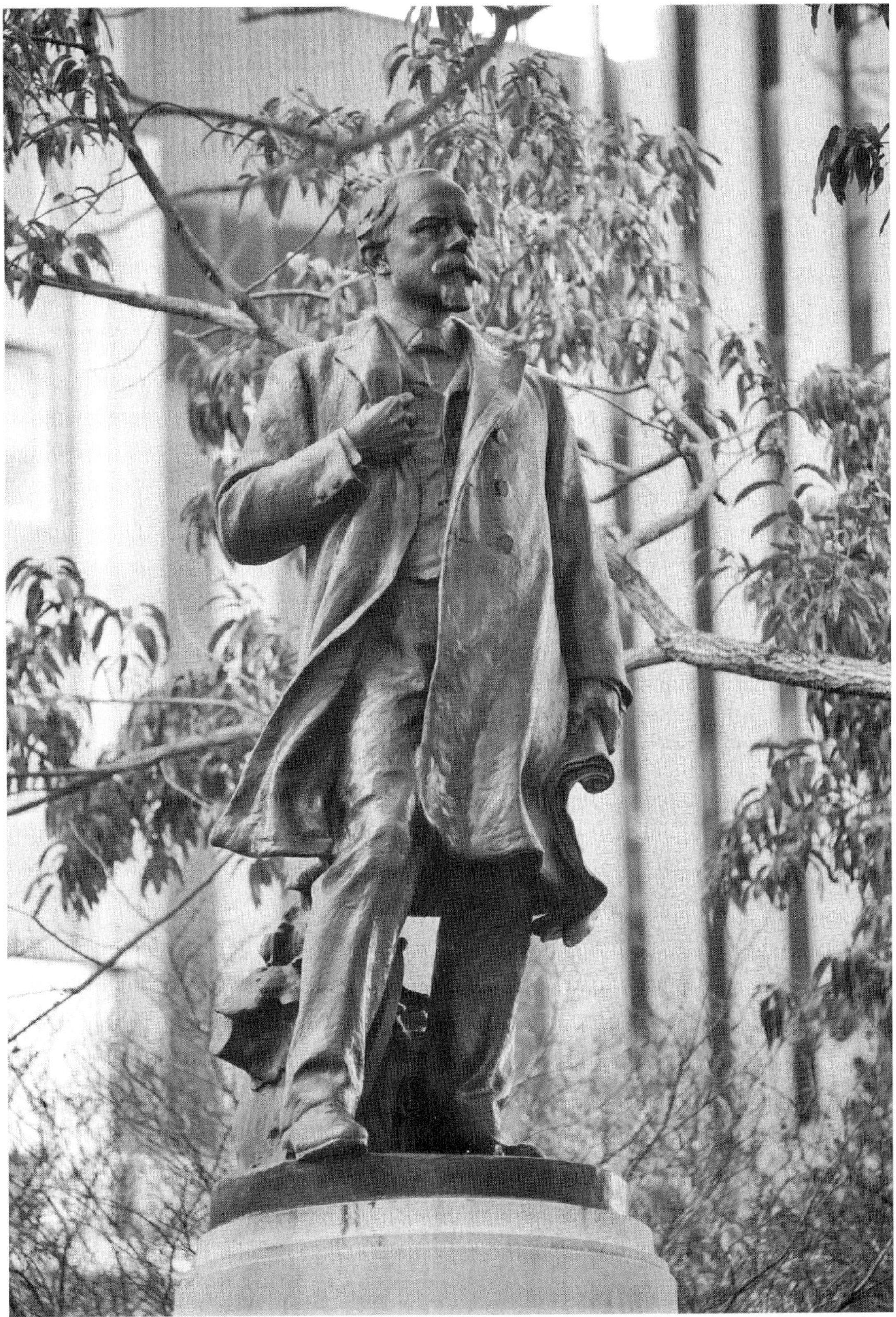

D4

TITLE
Catherine McAuley, Foundress of the Sisters of Mercy, 1831, 2000

LOCATION
Mercy Medical Center, 301 St. Paul Place

SCULPTOR
Sister Marie Henderson (b. 1949)

MEDIUM
Bronze

DONOR
Board of Trustees of Mercy Health Services

Catherine McAuley (1778–1841), founder of the Sisters of Mercy, was born in Dublin, Ireland, into a prosperous Catholic family. Her father died when she was 5, and her mother died fifteen years later. After her mother's death, Catherine first went to live with relatives who did not tolerate her religious practices. In 1803 she was invited to live with William and Catherine Callaghan, serving as Mrs. Callaghan's companion. The Callaghans were childless, and in 1822, after they had both died, McAuley inherited their fortune.

By 1824 McAuley had bought property and begun building a home for religious, educational, and social services for homeless women and poor servant girls. On September 24, 1827, the feast day of Our Lady of Mercy, the first residents moved into what she would eventually call the House of Mercy. Although it was not her original intention, she followed advice to establish a religious congregation of women dedicated to the service of the poor. She founded the Sisters of Mercy on December 12, 1831, after spending fifteen months in formal preparation at the Convent of the Presentation Sisters, in Dublin, where she took vows of chastity, poverty, and obedience.

Mother Catherine lived only ten years after founding the Sisters of Mercy, but by the time she died the community numbered 150. Shortly after her death, small groups of sisters left Ireland for the United States, Argentina, Australia, Newfoundland, and New Zealand, most of them by invitation from a bishop. The group of sisters who came to America was led by Frances Warde, who is credited with founding the Sisters of Mercy in America. They settled in Pittsburgh. On November 11, 1874, six sisters were dispatched from Pittsburgh to Baltimore at the invitation of a group of physicians who asked them to take over a health dispensary at the corner of Saratoga and Calvert streets then called the Baltimore City Hospital. Today that hospital is the full-service Mercy Medical Center.

The sculptor of this statue, Sister Marie Henderson, became a Sister of Mercy herself in 1985, when she was 36 years old. She had received a BA in art from Mercy College in her native Detroit in 1971 and an MA in art education from Eastern Michigan University, in Ypsilanti, in 1984. Before completing her MA, she began a career as a teacher at Mercy High School in Farmington Hills, Michigan, where she taught from 1971 to 2001. It was for the lobby of that high school that she created her first image of Mother Catherine McAuley. It was 1983, and she had just read the book *Mother Catherine McAuley in Her Own Words.* The only known description of McAuley is in that book, written in 1828 by a dear friend and fellow Sister of Mercy, Sister Clare Augustine Moore. That description guided Sister Marie and has guided other artists before her and since.

Sister Clare wrote that Mother Catherine was "upwards of 40 but looked at least ten years younger. . . . Her face was a short oval, but the contour was perfect. Her lips were thin and her mouth rather wide. . . . Her eyes were light blue and remarkably round with the brows and lashes colourless; but they spoke. . . . She was dressed in black British merino which, according to the fashion of the time, fitted tight to her shape. She was remarkably well made; round but not in the least heavy. She had a good carriage. Her hands were remarkably white but very clumsy, very large, with broad square tips to the fingers and short square nails."

Sister Marie focused on the eyes and the hands. She wanted to show Mother Catherine as a person of dignity, compassion, intelligence, and industry. For the hands, Henderson wanted to suggest more than their size; she wanted them to project an openness, a sense of calm, and a willingness to serve. The sculpture Sister

Marie created in 1983 for the high school where she taught has been cast more than one hundred times since, including this statue at Mercy Medical Center. Since creating that first image, Sister Marie has gone on to create portraits of Mother Catherine in oil, watercolor, charcoal, pastel, and ink. All the images represent Mother Catherine at the time she opened the first House of Mercy. The statue in Baltimore was dedicated on November 11, 2000, 126 years to the day after the first six Sisters of Mercy arrived in Baltimore.

Sister Marie continues to create statues of religious figures for Catholic churches, schools, and institutions across the country. Since 2001 she has taught at the School of Architecture of the University of Detroit Mercy.

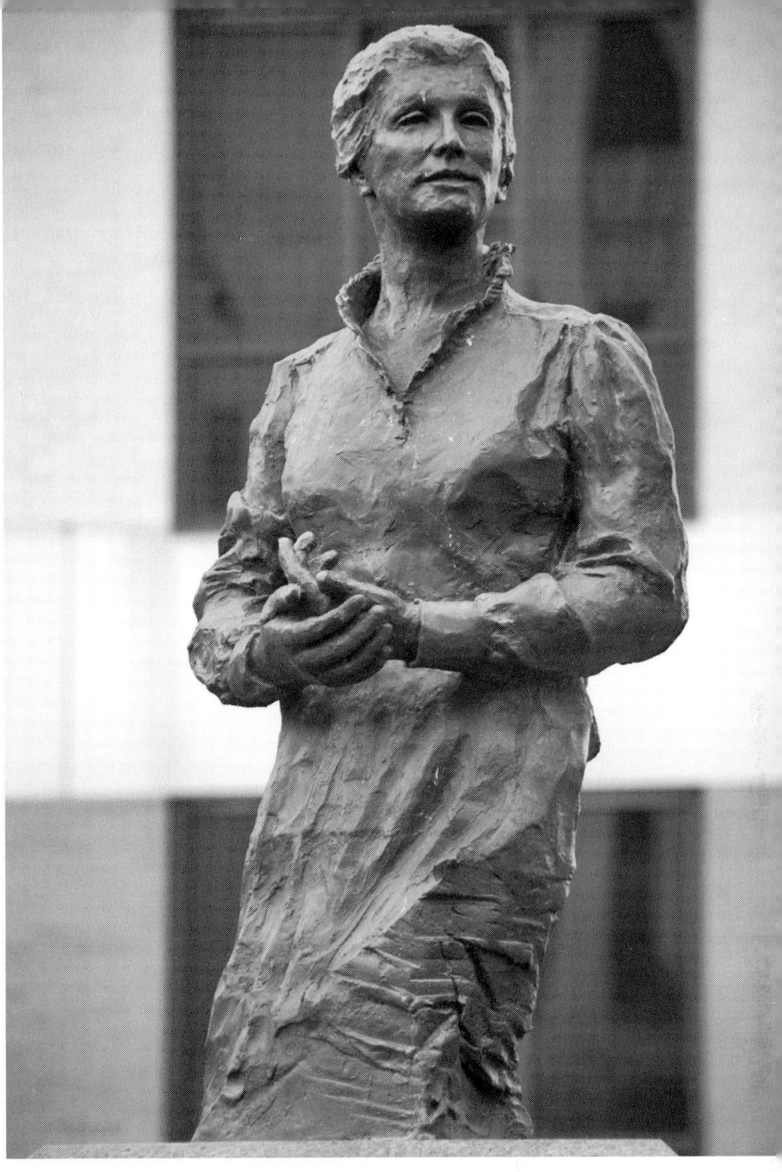

D5

TITLE
Untitled, 1931

LOCATION
Peale Museum, 225 Holliday Street

SCULPTOR
Benjamin Turner Kurtz (1899–1966)

DESIGNER
Robert McGill MacKall (1889–1982)

MEDIUM
Concrete

DONOR
City of Baltimore

The Peale Museum is the oldest building in the country to be erected specifically as a museum. The artist Rembrandt Peale (1778–1860), son of the Revolutionary War painter Charles Willson Peale, built the museum at his own expense to house a collection of art and for exhibitions of fine paintings, natural history specimens, and curiosities. Robert Cary Long Sr. (ca. 1770–1833) was the architect for the museum that opened in 1814.

Peale lived in Baltimore from 1813 to 1822, during which time he developed an apparatus for making gas that could be used to illuminate his museum and the street outside. In addition to pioneering the gaslight, he helped found the Baltimore Gas Light Company, the first of its kind in the country. Peale's museum closed sixteen years later, in 1830, but the building endured. Over the years it served as the city hall, as one of Baltimore's first schools for black students, and as the site of several businesses. In 1929 Mayor William Broening was persuaded to restore the old museum, and in 1931 it reopened as the Municipal Museum of Baltimore. In 1985 the museum became part of the City Life Museums. Unfortunately, the City Life Museums closed in 1997, and all the collections were incorporated into the Maryland Historical Society. From 1997 to 1999, during the last two years of Mayor Kurt Schmoke's administration, the Peale served as a conference center; however, it is closed today. The Baltimore City Historical Society is negotiating to lease the building for use as their headquarters and to establish a history center.

During the 1931 renovation, the pediment decoration for the museum's facade was completed. The relief is the result of a collaborative effort between the sculptor Benjamin Turner Kurtz and the painter and muralist Robert McGill Mackall (1889–1982) to create something that Peale himself might have commissioned. Mackall drew the cartoon for the relief, and Kurtz modeled it out of specially prepared concrete.

These two men were well known and well respected artists in Baltimore. Mackall was trained at the Maryland Institute, to which he returned to become the head of the Department of Fine Arts. He held a similar position at the College of Notre Dame in Baltimore. His paintings are in the collections of the Maryland Historical Society and the Baltimore Museum of Art, where his work was exhibited in 1932. About this time, he was completing murals in the War Memorial Building. Kurtz attended Gilman School and began his art studies at the Rinehart School of Sculpture at the Maryland Institute. For some time he was also a professor at the College of Notre Dame.

The ideas for this pediment were researched and developed by Mackall. He understood that reliefs like this one were planned with no connection to the use of the building and could represent any subject. He chose to include an eagle, a woman reading a book, a column, a retort, and a ship. The eagle is symbolic of patriotism; the reading woman represents learning; the column represents architecture; the retort, a bulblike vessel with a long neck bent downward used for distilling substances by heat, represents chemistry, and the ship is symbolic of the port's activities. The woman is the central figure, with the eagle to her right and the column and retort just behind and under her left arm, respectively. Further to her left is the ship, shown under full sail. This horizontal relief on the third-story elevation was planned so that the perspective worked from street level. The female figure is in classical drapery that reveals her body. She sits on the ledge, as do all the other elements of the relief, with her head turned to her left and her legs stretched out to her right, her right foot hanging just over the ledge. The relief is in the Wedgewood style, white figures against a dark background, a style used in bas-reliefs in the time period of the 1814 building.

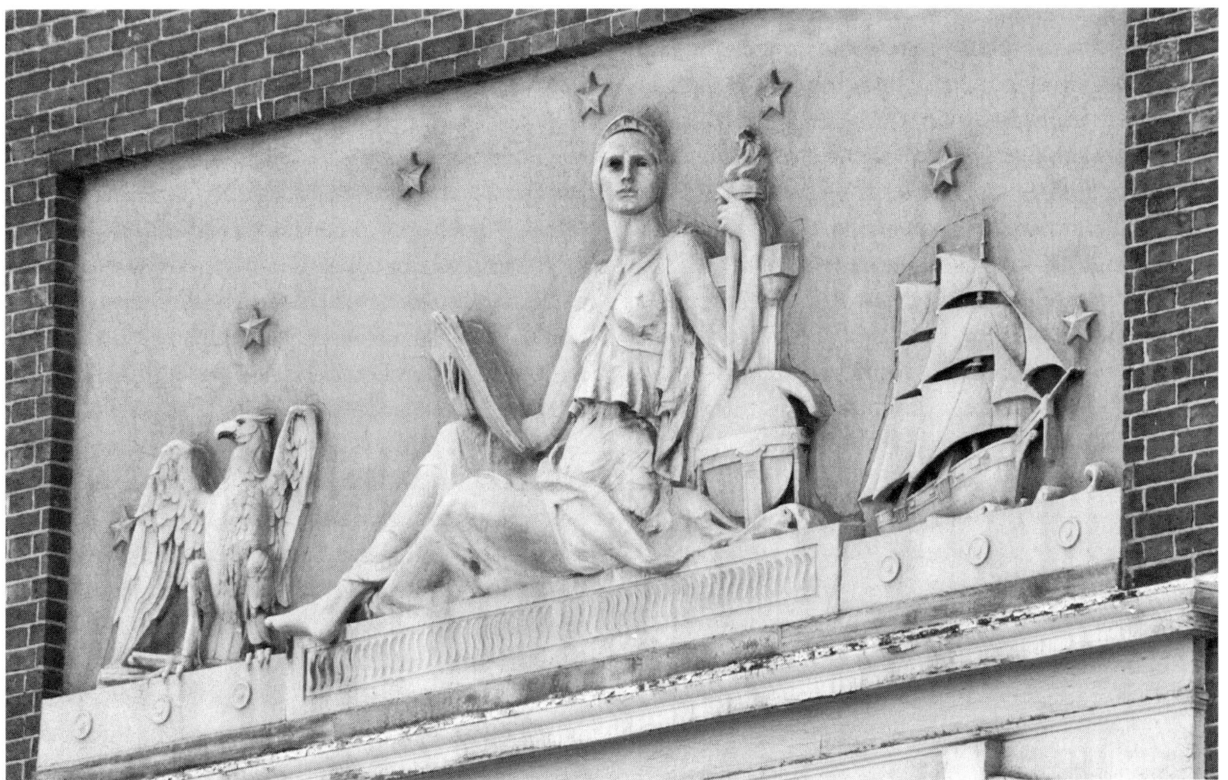

D6

TITLE

NEGRO SOLDIER'S MONUMENT, 1971

LOCATION

War Memorial Plaza, N. Gay and Fayette streets

SCULPTOR

James E. Lewis (1923–2007)

MEDIUM

Bronze

DONOR

Anonymous

The commission for a monument dedicated to Negro soldiers who had fought and died in America's wars was offered anonymously in 1968. A lawyer acting on behalf of a donor who wished to remain anonymous approached the Baltimore sculptor James E. Lewis, as part of a nationwide search, to ask for a sketch and a budget for such a memorial. Lewis was ultimately chosen for the commission. The monument was completed in 1971, but because of difficulties in locating a proper site, it was not installed and dedicated until May 1972.

The anonymous donor had not made clear which city would receive the monument. It was only in response to a request from Lewis that Baltimore was chosen. Once it became certain that the monument would stay in Baltimore, the decision to install it at the north end of Battle Monument Plaza became controversial and its installation was delayed.

The controversy stemmed from the widely held belief that Battle Monument Plaza was hallowed ground and that no other monuments should be allowed there. Battle Monument Plaza was the site of Baltimore's first courthouse, and since 1825 it had been the site of the monument dedicated to the brave men who died in defense of Baltimore in the War of 1812. Both the Park Board and the Art Commission approved locating the monument there; however, the citizens of Baltimore would not accept their decision without a fight, at least in the newspapers and over the radio.

One group of citizens objected to placing the monument at the north end of the plaza because vehicular traffic could only travel north on Calvert Street and therefore people in vehicles could only view the monument through rear-view mirrors or by turning to look back. Others objected to a monument dedicated to one specific group of soldiers rather than to one specific hero who had distinguished himself in battle or to all soldiers who had fought in a particular war, whose names would be listed on the monument. Still others objected to the monument because it was being given anonymously.

The decision to site this monument in Battle Monument Plaza was finally upheld, and it stood there for more than thirty years, its siting remaining problematic. Wisely, in January 2007, after the redesign of War Memorial Plaza and a request from the African American Patriots Consortium to move the monument there, it was relocated to this very prominent location. The consensus seems to be that it is finally in its rightful place.

Lewis had wanted his statue to be a simple one, "of great dignity and poise, which will project an image to give knowledge and pride to the community." The 9-foot-high bronze statue depicts an African American soldier in a modern U.S. Army uniform, holding a wreath instead of a weapon. Hanging from the wreath is a scroll on which the dates of all the wars in which African Americans had participated, from the Ameri-

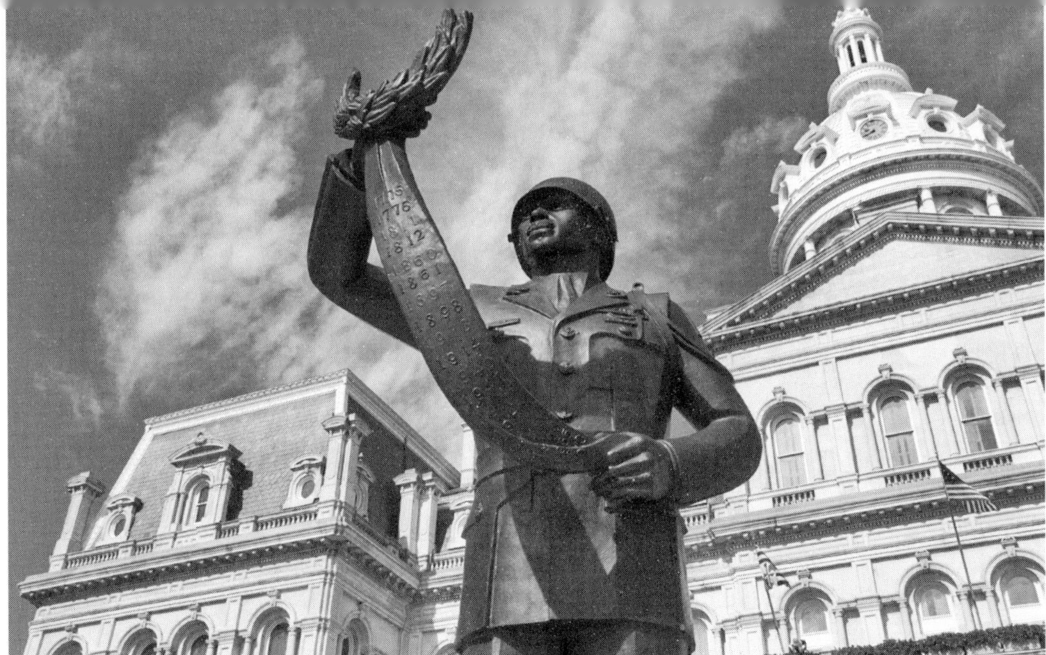

can Revolution to Vietnam, are emblazoned. Assisted by Benjamin A. Quarles, the head of the history department at Morgan State College (today Morgan State University), Lewis listed the years 1775, 1776, 1811, 1812, 1860, 1861, 1897, 1898, 1913, 1914, 1940, 1941, 1949, 1950, 1959, 1960, 1965, and 1970.

James E. Lewis was born in Phoenix, Virginia, and his family moved to Baltimore when he was 2 years old. He graduated from Dunbar High School, where his interest in art developed. He enrolled at the Philadelphia College of Art but interrupted his studies to serve for two years in the Pacific as a Marine. He finished his undergraduate studies at Temple University, staying on to complete his graduate work. He became chair of the art department at Morgan in 1950 and devoted his career to developing that department. Shortly after arriving at Morgan, Lewis was commissioned to create a statue of Frederick Douglass, which he completed in 1956 (K8). In 1970 he stepped down from his post as chair to devote his time to the development of the new campus art gallery, which was dedicated to him in 1990. Located in the Murphy Fine Arts Center, the James E. Lewis Art Museum houses the four thousand works of African American art that Lewis helped to amass for the university.

Nearby, a water feature, *Flow*, animates the western edge of War Memorial Plaza. Linda DePalma was commissioned by the Department of Recreation and Parks to collaborate with Mahan Rykiel Associates, the landscape architectural firm that oversaw the redesign for War Memorial Plaza in 2005, and together they came up with a fountain solution that works almost as well in winter, when the water is off, as it does when the water is on. The grates, cut from aluminum plates and finished with a baked-on black polyester powder coating, are surrounded by granite stone pavers in black and various shades of grey, forming a walkway that is very often chosen as the preferred pathway through the plaza even when the water is shooting twelve feet into the air, which it does all day every day from early spring through late fall. The images incorporated into the three 6-foot-square fountain grates were taken from architectural details on buildings surrounding the plaza, as well as from the plaza itself. Simple flower images carved into stone greet visitors to the War Memorial Building. That same flower image can be found in the center of each fountain grate. The spiral motif anchoring the four corners of each grate was taken directly from a memorial urn in the plaza.

D7

TITLE
FIRE FIGHTER'S MEMORIAL, 1990

LOCATION
Gay and Lexington streets

SCULPTOR
Tylden Streett (b. 1922)

MEDIUM
Bronze

DONOR
Baltimore City Fire Fighter's Monument Committee

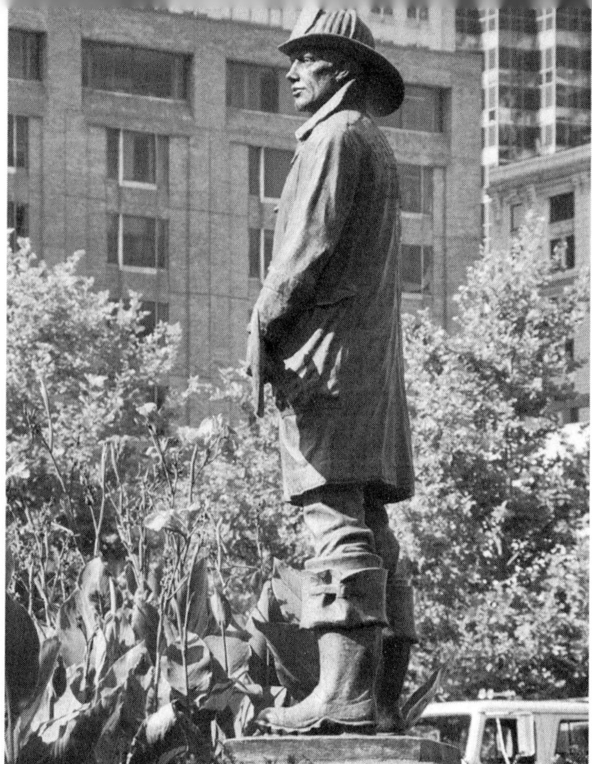

The Baltimore City Fire Fighter's Monument Committee was formed in 1984 to explore the possibility of commissioning an artist to create a monument dedicated to the past, present, and future fire fighters of Baltimore, especially the one hundred fire fighters who had lost their lives in the performance of their duties since a paid fire department was established in Baltimore in 1858. The members of the committee came from within the fire department. Their honorary chairman was then Mayor William Donald Schaefer, and their advisor was Fred Lazarus, president of the Maryland Institute College of Art.

The monument committee's first task was to choose a site for the monument. They chose the corner of the lot where their headquarters building stood; the monument remains there today even though the headquarters has moved. Next the committee decided to hold a competition and invited some thirty artists to participate. Tylden Streett was selected on the basis of the model he submitted. The committee then successfully raised the necessary $107,000 to complete the monument.

Two firemen served as models for Streett's fireman, who is shown standing very straight with his feet apart and firmly planted. He holds his ax horizontally across his body, just below his waist, with both hands. He is dressed in a fireman's hat, large heavy coat buttoned up with collar raised, and high bulky boots folded over at the top. The weight of his gear is clearly depicted and

may serve as a metaphor for the burden of the task that lies ahead. The fireman looks off into the distance, contemplative, his head turned ever so slightly.

Streett was born in Baltimore. He graduated from the Maryland Institute with a BFA in 1954 and received his MFA from the Rinehart School of Sculpture in 1957. From 1957 to 1959 he worked as a studio assistant to Lee Lawrie on the Eastern Shore of Maryland. Then, Raymond Pucinelli, then director of Rinehart, asked Streett to cover for him while he traveled to Italy for two weeks. Streett agreed, and when Pucinelli did not return, Streett was asked to remain as acting director of Rinehart for that 1960-61 academic year. Streett welcomed the arrival of Norman Carlberg, who became director in 1961. Streett remained on the faculty, teaching sculpture, and celebrated his fiftieth year there in 2009. He is still teaching at MICA and at the Schuler School of Fine Arts in Baltimore, where he has taught sculpture since 1990. While a full-time faculty member at the Institute and the Schuler School, Streett has found time to complete several public art commissions in Baltimore and elsewhere.

It is interesting that Streett's daughter, Ferebe Streett, completed a memorial to Baltimore's policemen that is sited nearby.

D8

TITLE
Aquatic Sea Horses, 1927

LOCATION
War Memorial Building, 101 N. Gay Street

SCULPTOR
Edmond R. Amateis (1897–1981)

ARCHITECT
Laurence Hall Fowler (1876–1971)

MEDIUM
Limestone

DONORS
City of Baltimore and State of Maryland

What are these majestic creatures adorning the entrance to the War Memorial Building, and what exactly do they represent? Various answers have been given in guides over the years, but definitive answers can be found in the correspondence between the architect Laurence Hall Fowler and Edmond R. Amateis and several other sculptors. These letters are among Fowler's papers in the Special Collections of the Johns Hopkins University's Milton S. Eisenhower Library, on the Homewood campus.

In 1926 Fowler organized a limited competition to design the sculpture for the flanking pedestals of his new building. Advised by the Baltimore sculptor J. Maxwell Miller, who forwarded Fowler the code for competitions from the National Sculpture Society, Fowler invited Hans Schuler, J. Maxwell Miller, Leo Friedlander, and Edmond R. Amateis to submit models. Lee Lawrie was also invited to participate, but the deadline was too restrictive for him and he declined.

The jury Fowler put in place included the Col. Harry C. Jones, chairman of the War Memorial Commission; Dr. Hugh Young, an architect; E. W. Donn Jr., an architect from Washington, D.C.; and Fowler himself. The sculptor James Fraser was asked but declined. Three models were of "mythological sea horses," which Fowler had stated in a letter to Amateis he thought would be best for the site, and one, submitted by Schuler, was of lions. The jury selected Amateis and awarded him a contract for $14,500 with a deadline of May 30, 1927. In all their correspondence, both Fowler and Amateis referred to these creatures as "sea horses," as did the stone carver working for Amateis, R. A. Baillie of Closter, New Jersey.

Several other letters between architect and sculptor clarify much of the symbolism they decided to include. Fowler sent Amateis copies of the Baltimore and Maryland seals for use in the final sculpture. Held between the front legs of the sea horses are an eagle and an osprey. Amateis explained that he chose the osprey over a hawk because it resembled the eagle more closely and because he had been assured that it was a bird native to Maryland. On the left the osprey, representing the navy, holds the state seal in his talons, and on the right the eagle, representing the army, holds the city seal. In the stylized manner of the artist, differences between the eagle and the osprey are just noticeable by a careful reading of the details on their chests, their extended wings, and their heads. The horses have a very scaly backbone, which makes them look more aquatic, as well as a tail ending in a large fin. These sea horses were to represent the might of America crossing the seas in aid of its allies.

Dating has been another area of disagreement over the years, but the same correspondence pinpoints very closely when the sculptures were completed and installed. A letter from Fowler to Baillie dated October 8,

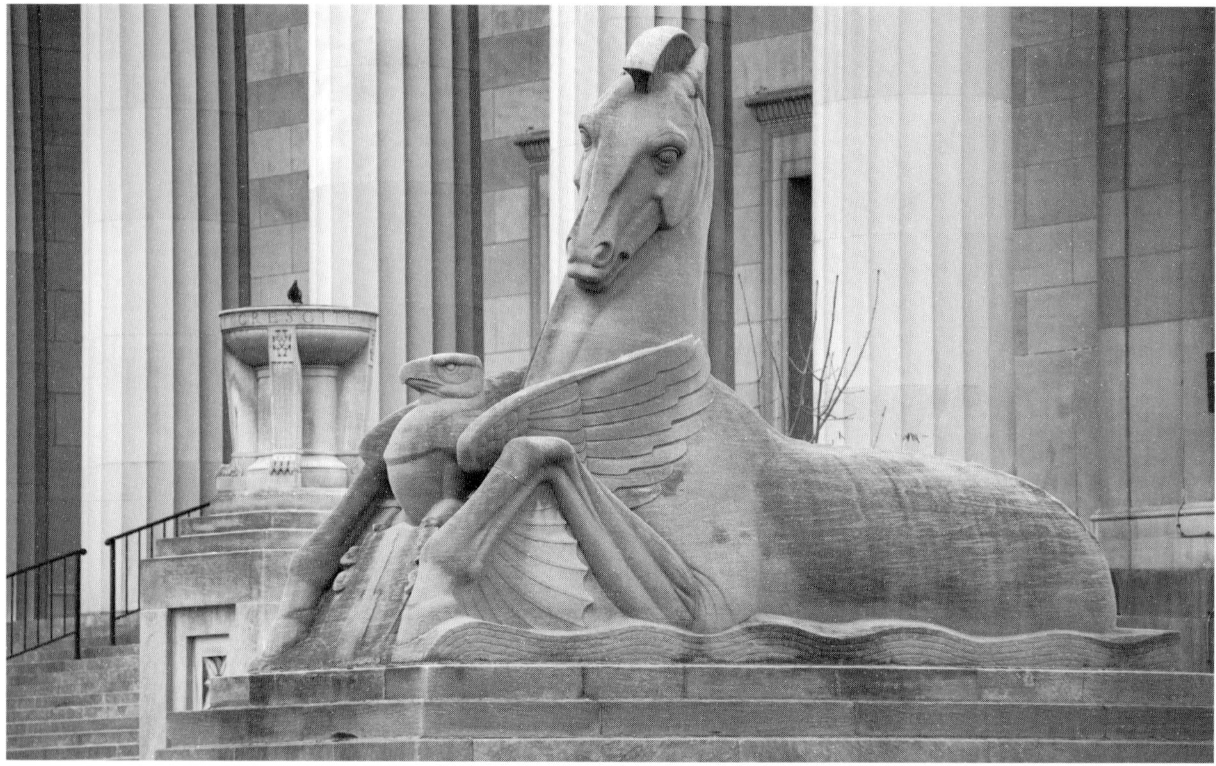

1927, reminds him that the dedication for the War Memorial Square, as Fowler called the plaza in front of the War Memorial Building, also designed by him, was scheduled for November 11, and he wanted the sea horses to be ready by then. Obviously, Amateis had missed the May 30, 1927 deadline stated in his contract, but the sculptures were delivered and installed by Armistice Day, as photographs show.

Edmond Amateis was the son of an Italian architect and sculptor, Louis Amateis, who had immigrated to Washington, D.C., in 1883. The younger Amateis was trained as a sculptor at the Beaux-Arts Institute of Design in New York. In 1921 he won a three-year fellowship to the American Academy in Rome. He completed many commissions in Washington and Philadelphia in the years after his commission for Fowler's War Memorial Building. Before his retirement he was a professor at Columbia University and president of the National Sculpture Society.

D9

TITLE
Amanogawa, 1977

LOCATION:
Shot Tower Park, 801 E. Fayette Street

SCULPTOR
Robert DuBourg (b. 1944)

MEDIA
Black Tennessee marble and stainless steel

DONORS
International Sculpture Symposium of Baltimore and
City of Baltimore

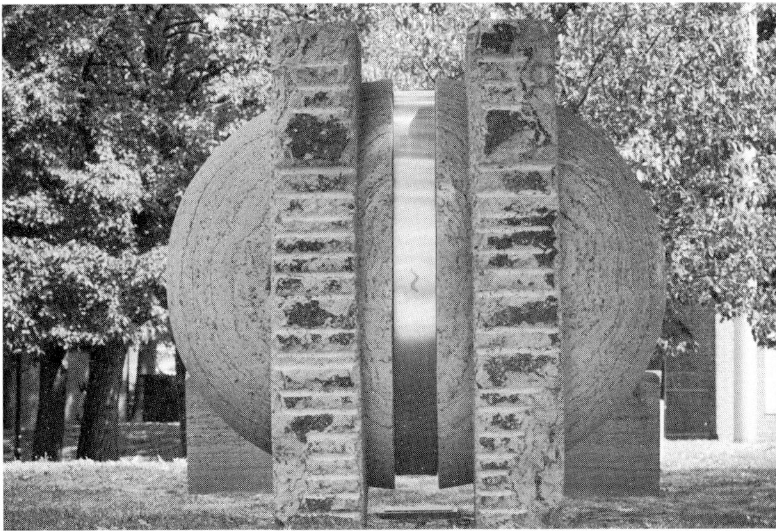

Robert DuBourg not only participated in but also organized Baltimore's first International Sculpture Symposium. He invited three other sculptors to join him in Baltimore—William Bennett, Hiroshi Mikami, and Gerard Höweler. These four sculptors had participated a year earlier in a symposium in West Virginia that DuBourg had organized, and all but Bennett participated in a second symposium organized by DuBourg for Baltimore in 1980. None of the stone sculptures from the 1980 symposium remained on view in the city. DuBourg had hoped that a stone-carving symposium carried out in a very public site would become an annual cultural event in Baltimore, but it did not.

All four pieces of sculpture carved during the 1976 symposium remained in Shot Tower Park until the early nineties, when work on the nearby subway necessitated the relocation of the pieces by Mikami (A12) and Höweler (A14) to Commerce Park.

DuBourg's piece anchors the northwest corner of Shot Tower Park today as it has since the 1976 symposium ended. Carved out of black Tennessee marble, Amanogawa—a Japanese word meaning "river of stars" and used to describe the Milky Way—has five components. The large oval stone and the two rough vertical piers, which appear to suspend it, are actually carved out of one piece of marble. Wrapped around the middle of the smooth, finely polished oval stone is a band of stainless steel. The four smaller pieces, which seem

to mark a pathway to the larger central element, can double as seating.

The site of the Shot Tower was an interesting choice. Erected in 1828, the tower is one of the few such structures remaining in the country. Shot was made by dropping molten lead from a platform at the top, through a sievelike structure, and into a vat of cold water far below. This tower, which was operational until 1892, is designated a National Historic Landmark.

DuBourg is a native Baltimorean who was educated at the University of Maryland in College Park. He has participated in similar symposia in Yugoslavia, Austria, and the elsewhere in the United States. He currently lives and maintains a studio in Harpers Ferry, West Virginia, where he still carves stone.

(For more information on the 1976 sculpture symposium, see A12 and A14.)

D10

TITLE
Baltimore, 1977

LOCATION
Shot Tower Park, 801 E. Fayette Street

SCULPTOR
William Bennett (b. 1949)

MEDIUM
Black Tennessee marble

DONORS
International Sculpture Symposium of Baltimore
and City of Baltimore

Baltimore is one of four pieces created during the 1976 International Sculpture Symposium at the Shot Tower. William Bennett, from Manlius, New York, created this piece after accepting an invitation from Robert DuBourg to join him, Hiroshi Mikami, and Gerard Höweler for a second such symposium, all having participated the previous year in a symposium organized by DuBourg in West Virginia.

Bennett's piece reveals the artist's interest in the contrast between rough and smooth surfaces. The smooth, finely finished front surface differs dramatically from the reverse side, which is as rough as if it had just been unearthed from the ground. The piece is beautifully carved into two vertical sections and four horizontal sections, giving it an overall horizontal emphasis. It is sited at the far eastern edge of Shot Tower Park, near the Pressley Ridge Building.

Bennett studied at Cornell University and did graduate work at the University of Indiana. Like DuBourg, Bennett did not finish his piece that fall. He returned to complete it that following spring.

(For more information on the 1976 sculpture symposium, see A12, A14, and D9.)

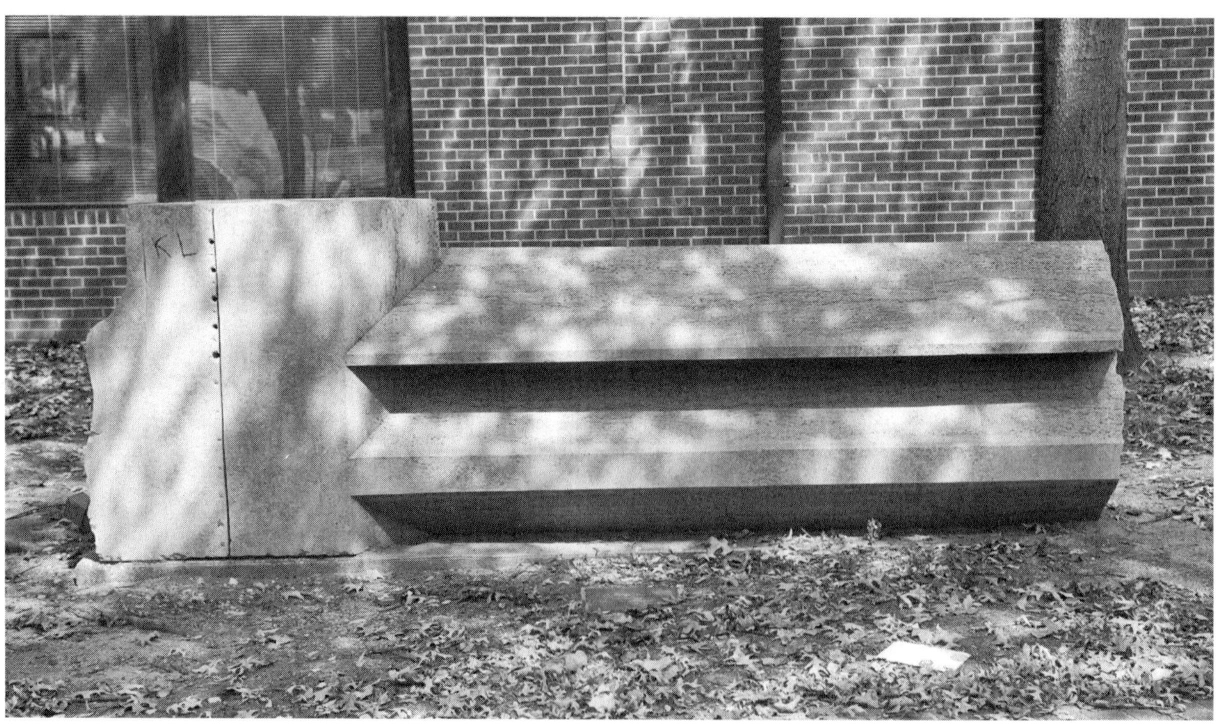

D11

TITLE

BALTIMORE CITY FRATERNAL ORDER OF POLICE
MEMORIAL, 2002–2003

LOCATION:
Shot Tower Park, Fayette and President streets

SCULPTOR
Ferebe Streett (b. 1955)

MEDIUM
Bronze

DONORS
Baltimore City Fraternal Order of Police and the
citizens of Baltimore

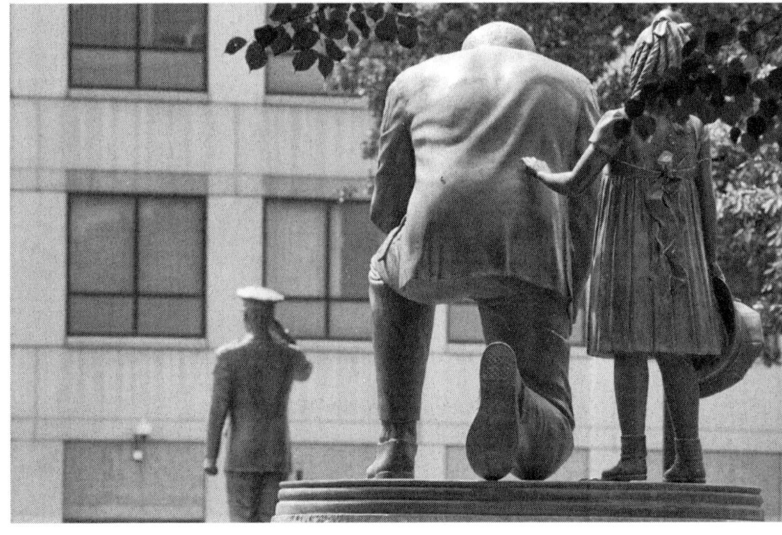

"Their light will shine forever, their deeds never forgotten." This inscription appears on a low wall supporting sixteen polished black granite panels, on which the names of Baltimore's fallen police officers have been inscribed. This wall is the centermost element in the recently completed police memorial. Four life-size figures cast in bronze by Ferebe Streett complete the monument.

Placed closest to President's Street are two of the figures, one male and one female, representing police officers as they might stand at attention at a funeral. The male officer, wearing the dress uniform of a sergeant, salutes; the female officer holds a folded flag. These two figures were completed in 2002. Deeper into the park, on a circular rough-cut granite base, can be seen the figure of a kneeling policeman with his weight on his one bended knee, his head bowed, obviously mourning the loss of a comrade. A young girl stands beside him, looking concerned, with her left hand on his back and his hat in her right hand. A long-stemmed rose lies on the base between them. In these two figures, added to the memorial in 2003, is captured a tender moment of shared personal grief.

Streett is the daughter of Tylden Streett, whose *Fire Fighter's Memorial* (D7) stands close by. She received her BFA from the Maryland Institute College of Art, where her father was on the faculty and where he still teaches today. Although she received her MFA from Towson University, her education as a sculptor probably resulted more from her involvement in many of her father's earlier commissions, most notably *The Immortals*, a relief on the facade of Waverly Elementary School (K2). Streett's selection as the artist to create this police memorial came after she completed a commission awarded in 2000 from the Howard Country Police Department to create bas-relief portraits of three officers who had been killed in the line of duty. In the Baltimore memorial each figure is also an actual portrait. For example, the female officer was a member of the equestrian division, and the young girl was the daughter of a slain police officer. The chief of the Fraternal Order of Police, Gary McIlhinney, made the arrangements for the models. Streett received technical advise from her father on this commission.

This new memorial was added to the site of a memorial dedicated in 1978 by the Police Department to all its members, past and present, who had served their community. The earlier memorial consisted only of an inscribed bronze plaque mounted on a concrete wall with the shield of the department mounted on either side. The inconspicuous nature of the earlier memorial inspired the efforts that led to the creation of this larger, more prominent, and more engaging memorial.

D12

TITLE
Baltimore Passage, 2007

LOCATION
Albemarle Square, Albemarle and Lombard streets

SCULPTOR
David Hess (b. 1964)

MEDIUM
Copper

DONOR
Housing Authority of Baltimore City

How might an artist celebrate three centuries of architectural and urban change in one of the city's most historic neighborhoods? That was certainly a question in the forefront of David Hess' mind after he was chosen to create a monument for Albemarle Square.

Albemarle Square was developed on land that was originally part of Jones Town, one of the three towns (along with Baltimore Town and Fells Point) that combined to form Baltimore in 1797. In the early nineteenth century, the 10 acres on which historic Jones Town had been laid out developed into the "point of entry" neighborhood for immigrants seeking new opportunities. Beginning in the 1820s and 1830s, the Irish, the Italians, and East European Jews settled in this part of the city. Free blacks, originally brought from Africa, settled here too. Mid-twentieth-century urban renewal changed the neighborhood as massive high-rise complexes were built, but recently those complexes have been replaced by new, mixed-income housing modeled on the traditional Baltimore row house. Albemarle Square is one such development.

Hess decided to create something monumental that would celebrate the neighborhood's legacy as a place to make a new start. He wanted to pay tribute to all the immigrants who had come into the port of Baltimore, settling in this old neighborhood, building their churches and synagogues and establishing lasting ethnic communities. Hess chose to incorporate two

forms—one making reference to the ships that brought the immigrants into the port of Baltimore and one acknowledging that the immigrants had come from many distant places around the globe.

One of Hess' challenges was to make something on a large scale for this small plaza. The 14-foot-high abstracted boat form is narrow enough to fit into this median space and consequential enough to hold the globe, which is 9 feet in diameter and constructed out of 2½ inch hollow communication cable, more often found on cell phone towers. The open form of the globe contrasts with the solid, angular form of the boat. The circular form of the globe is repeated on the surface of the plaza, where the sculpture is encircled with Belgium blocks, a material traditionally used for ballast on nineteenth-century ships. The sculpture has been installed on a slight angle to create a more dynamic view from along Lombard, as if the ship were turning.

Much remains today from Jones Town's past, including the Carroll Mansion, home to Charles Carroll of Carrolton, once the wealthiest man in American and the only Catholic signer of the Declaration of Independence; the house where Mary Pickersgill sewed the flag that became the Star-Spangled Banner, today the Flag House Museum; the Shot Tower, a lasting symbol of the area's industrial heritage; the Friends Meeting House; the Lloyd Street Synagogue; and the church of St. Vincent De Paul. *Baltimore Passage* and the new neighborhood of Albemarle Square reflect this history and project it forward.

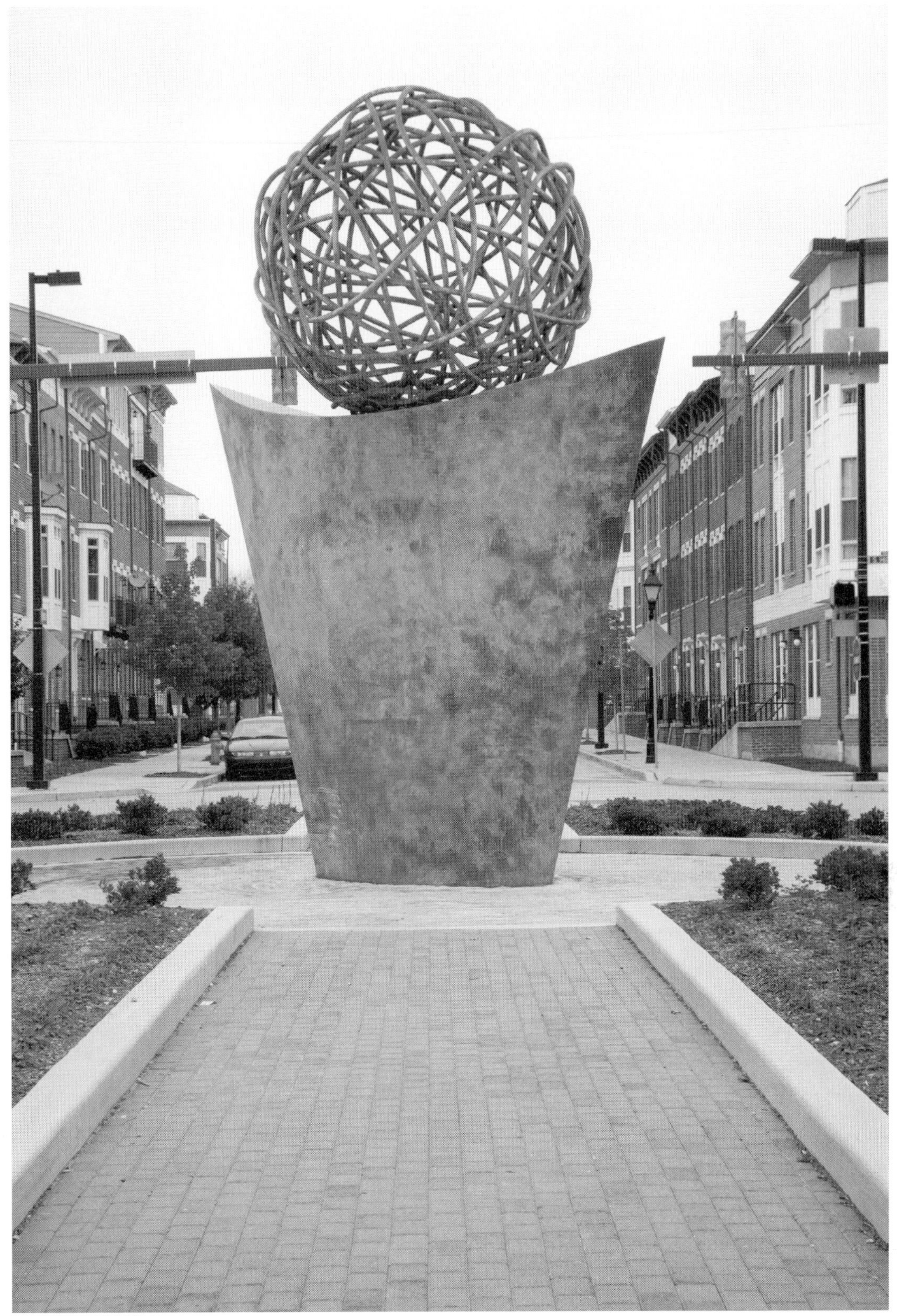

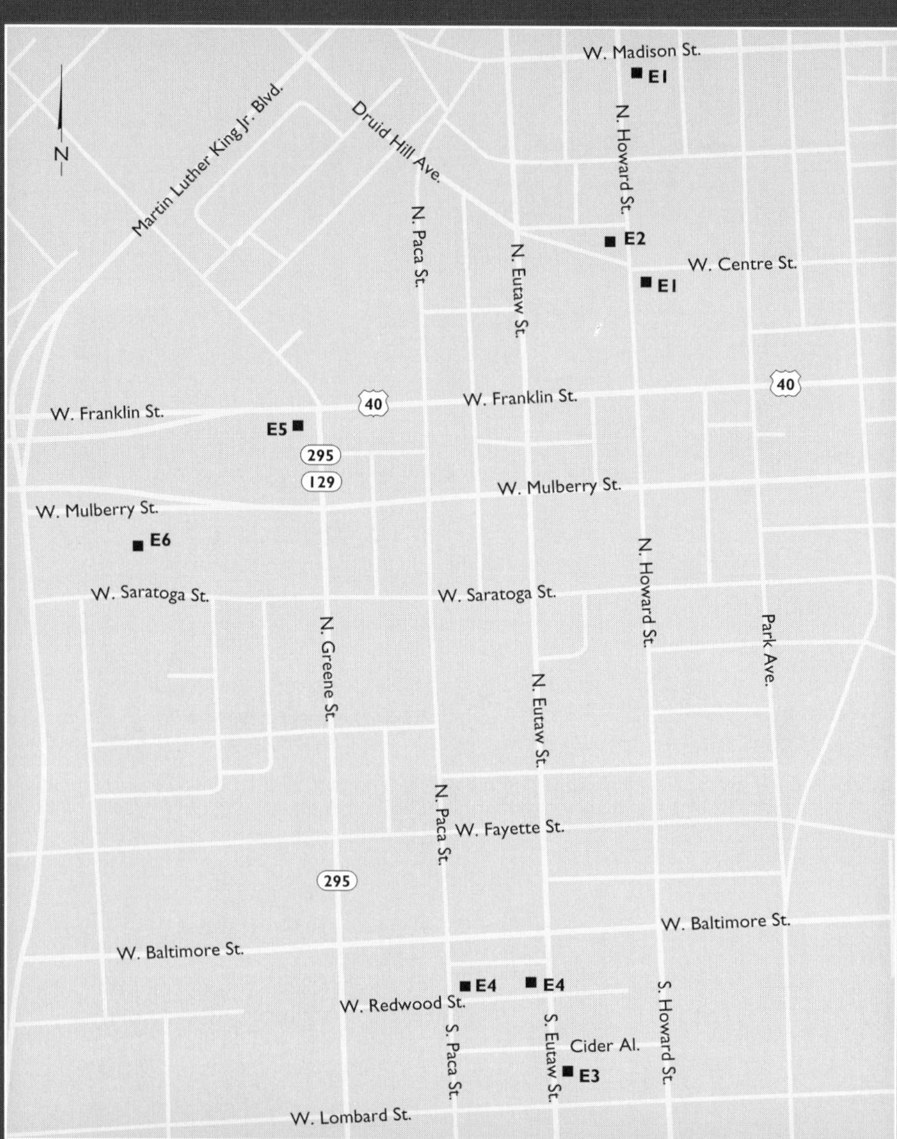

W. Madison St.
E1
N. Howard St.
Martin Luther King Jr. Blvd.
Druid Hill Ave.
N. Paca St.
N. Eutaw St.
E2
W. Centre St.
E1
40
W. Franklin St.
W. Franklin St.
E5
295
129
W. Mulberry St.
W. Mulberry St.
E6
W. Saratoga St.
W. Saratoga St.
N. Greene St.
N. Eutaw St.
N. Howard St.
Park Ave.
N. Paca St.
W. Fayette St.
295
W. Baltimore St.
W. Baltimore St.
E4
E4
W. Redwood St.
S. Paca St.
S. Eutaw St.
Cider Al.
S. Howard St.
E3
W. Lombard St.
N
40

DOWNTOWN WEST OF CHARLES STREET

Walking

E1

TITLE
Thrones for the Eulipions, 2005

LOCATION
N. Howard Street at W. Madison Street and at
W. Centre Street

SCULPTOR
Sam Christian Holmes (b. 1959)

MEDIUM
Steel

DONOR
Maryland Transit Administration
Adopt-a-Shelter Program

In 1997 the Downtown Partnership, the Baltimore Office of Promotion and The Arts, and the Contemporary Museum won a $30,000 grant from the Maryland Transit Administration to redesign bus shelters near the Contemporary's Centre Street home. Sam Holmes received the commission for the shelters.

Holmes began his involvement in this public art project by riding the bus and spending time at the two shelters in order to discover the community for whom he would be making the piece. He wanted to make a work of art that would be connected to the "moment" a traveler or a pedestrian was at the bus stop, and he wanted to elevate the "moment." It was while he was riding the bus that he got the idea of somehow making the seats in the bus shelter thrones.

Holmes chose the design elements for the thrones from his heritage. From the pantheon of African saints he remembered Ochoosi, a traveler's guardian who is similar in appearance to an American Indian and whose symbol is an arrow. He rediscovered Ochoosi on a trip to Brazil, where he found arrows in every taxicab and over every doorway. For the screenlike structure behind the thrones, which looks like a curvilinear drawing in space, Holmes chose symbols of the African diaspora. The grand circles and swirls represent the universe, and the cross represents a crossroad, where direction can change but where there can be a moment of rest and contemplation. This screen rests on the vertical backs of a line of individual seats, above each of which, at just the right height, is a crown.

Part of the title of this piece was taken from the jazz saxophonist Rahsaan Roland Kirk's "Theme for the Eulipions," from his 1975 album *The Return of the 5,000-Pound Man*. Eulipions were the musicians, artists, and poets who performed on the subways and the sidewalks. Kirk said that the "art" of these performers was their duty-free gift for the traveler. Holmes offers these transformed bus shelters as his "duty-free" gift to the travelers along Howard Street.

Sam Holmes earned his BFA in 1984 and his MFA in 1994, both from the Maryland Institute College of Art, where he taught in the general fine arts and graphic design departments from 1996 to 1999. He then went to Howard University in Washington, D.C., where he was a professor and head of the digital art program from 1999 to 2005. From Howard, Holmes went to teach at Morgan State University. In 2008 he returned to the Maryland Institute, where he is a visiting artist and lecturer.

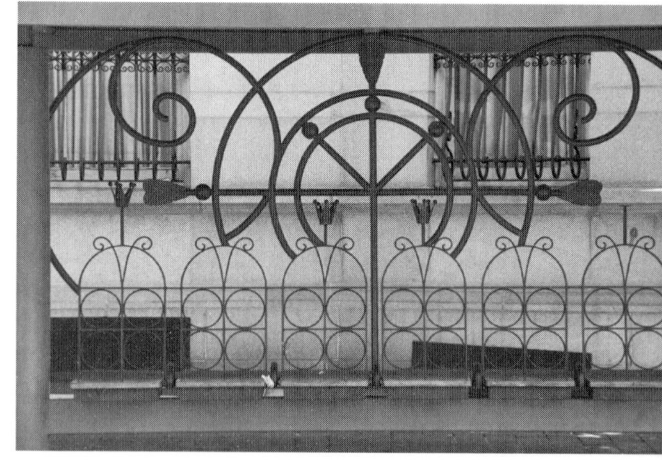

E2

TITLE
John Eager Howard, 1985

LOCATION
Howard's Park, N. Howard Street and
Druid Hill Avenue

SCULPTOR
David L. Gerlach (b. 1950)

MEDIUM
Red brass

DONORS
Market Center Development Corporation and the
Municipal Art Society of Baltimore City

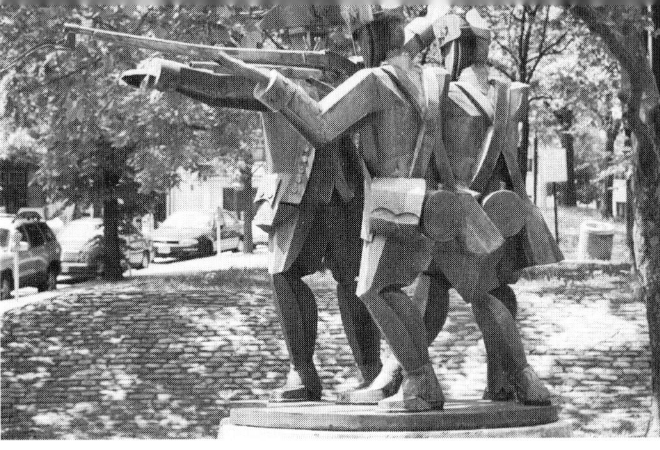

This public artwork was the first of several to be commissioned as part of the revitalization of the west side of downtown Baltimore, generally known as Market Center and bounded by Liberty Street to the east, Pratt Street to the south, Preston Street to the north, and Martin Luther King Jr. Boulevard to the west. The urban-renewal initiative was to develop the area into a vibrant mixed-use neighborhood around the famous Lexington Market that would support the continuing growth of the University of Maryland at Baltimore and the University of Maryland Medical System, the largest institutional neighbors. The two other outdoor sculptures commissioned by the Market Center Development Corporation for this area are by Linda DePalma (E4) and Jeff Schiff (appendix 3).

The green space in which this sculpture is sited is actually part of John Eager Howard's original estate, which spread from the Jones Falls on the east to Eutaw Street on the west and from Biddle Street on the north to Centre Street on the south.

The sculptural group consists of three stylized figures fabricated out of red brass. The choice of red brass was predicated on its ease of handling, its durability, and the limited budget, which prohibited the use of bronze. It is the only piece made out of red brass in the city. John Eager Howard is shown standing to the right of his men, with his right arm forward and his left arm back. His forward hand once held a sword, as he is shown leading his men into battle in 1781 at Cowpens, where he ordered a bayonet charge. The two other figures hold bayonets as they step forward with arms raised, taking aim at the enemy. The infantrymen are depicted in their Revolutionary War uniforms with helmets protecting their heads and canteens and shot bags crossed over their backs. The placement of John Eager Howard on the ground with his troops is largely symbolic of Howard's feelings for his men and their feelings for him. He would have been on horseback, as he is shown in an equestrian monument by Emmanuel Frémiet in nearby Mount Vernon Place (C8).

John Eager Howard (1752–1827) was one of Maryland's great Revolutionary War heroes. He lead his men into battle with great valor at Cowpens, in South Carolina, for which he was awarded a congressional medal, and later at Eutaw Springs, where he received wounds that ended his career. Nearby Eutaw Street was named for that battle. One of George Washington's most trusted generals, Nathanael Greene, said of Howard: "Col. Howard is as good an officer as the world afforded, and deserves a statue of gold, no less than the Roman or Grecian heroes." The phrase about Howard's deserving a monument appears on the plaque that is mounted on the circular concrete base. (For more information on John Eager Howard, see C1 and C8.)

David Gerlach was born in Washington, D.C., and educated at the Corcoran College of Art and Design in Washington, the Cooper Union in New York City, Montgomery College in Montgomery County, Maryland, and the Rinehart School of Sculpture at the Maryland Institute College of Art, from which he received his MFA in 1982. He lives and maintains a studio in Baltimore.

E3

TITLE
Fire Chariot, 1973

LOCATION
John F. Steadman Fire House, S. Eutaw and
W. Lombard streets

SCULPTOR
Roger Majorowicz (b. 1931)

MEDIUM
Bronze

DONOR
Baltimore City Percent for Art program

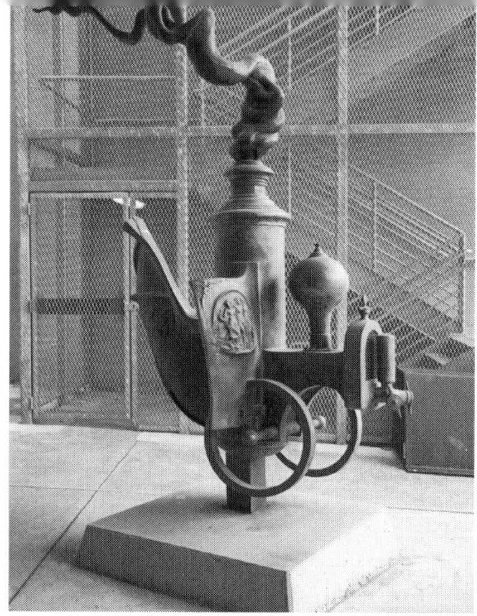

Completed in 1973, Roger Majorowicz's *Fire Chariot* stands at the Eutaw Street entrance to the firehouse that wraps around the historic Bromo-Seltzer Tower, at the corner of South Eutaw and West Lombard streets. As the title implies, the piece makes reference to fire trucks of old. With smoke billowing out the top and wheels lifting off the ground as if racing over uneven terrain with necessary haste and implied speed, this fire vehicle looks as if it might actually be leaving the fire station.

This 12-foot-high, 1-ton sculpture was cast in twenty-three separate pieces that were then welded together. To learn about historical fire equipment, the sculptor visited fire museums in Maryland and Philadelphia. As a result of his painstaking research, all the elements included in the design of this piece represent details found on seven different historical fire wagons on display in these museums. The vertical steam boiler with black smoke billowing out the top and the pressure globe with an American eagle were adapted from a horse-drawn American-LaFrance steam truck that dates to 1918. The front hose connector is from a 1917 Ahrens-Fox truck, and the radiator cap with its honeycomb grill was taken from a 1924 steam-driven Seagrave truck.

The beautiful relief on this fire chariot's wing, showing two women carrying another woman from a fire, is a tribute to one found on the 1819 Jeffers & Nuttall, a parade hose carriage the artist found in the

Heaver Museum in Lutherville, Maryland. The Christie tractor, the Silsby, and the Clapp & Jones truck also provided inspiration for the artist. The flowing wing at the rear is meant to underscore the sense of motion and suggest the excitement of a fire truck rushing down the street with the firemen's coats flapping in the wind. Between the steam boiler and the wing there is a saddle seat where children can sit.

Originally the fire chariot was bright gold, the edge of the wing was bright red, and the smoke was black. Today, unfortunately, the chariot has been painted instead of giving the bronze a new patina, and the eagle is missing, removed by vandals years ago.

Majorowicz was born in South Dakota, where he learned blacksmithing on his father's ranch. He graduated from the Minneapolis College of Art in 1958 with a BFA in sculpture. That same year, he received a Fulbright Fellowship to study in Florence, where he remained until 1961. After teaching at the University of Illinois in Urbana for four years, Majorowicz moved to Baltimore, where he taught sculpture at the Maryland Institute College of Art from 1965 to 1983, the first ten years as head of the sculpture department. In 1983 he moved to Maine, where he lives and maintains a studio. His work has been featured in museums and galleries in New York, Chicago, Los Angeles, and Washington, D.C., as well as in Milan and Rome. He has completed over forty public commissions around the country, many of them for the Percent for Art program in Maine. Four of them were through Baltimore City's Percent for Art program (O3, O6, and Q4).

E4

TITLE
RedwoodArch, 1988

LOCATION
W. Redwood Street between S. Eutaw and
S. Paca streets

SCULPTOR
Linda DePalma (b. 1946)

MEDIUM
Painted steel

DONORS
Market Center Development Corporation and
City of Baltimore

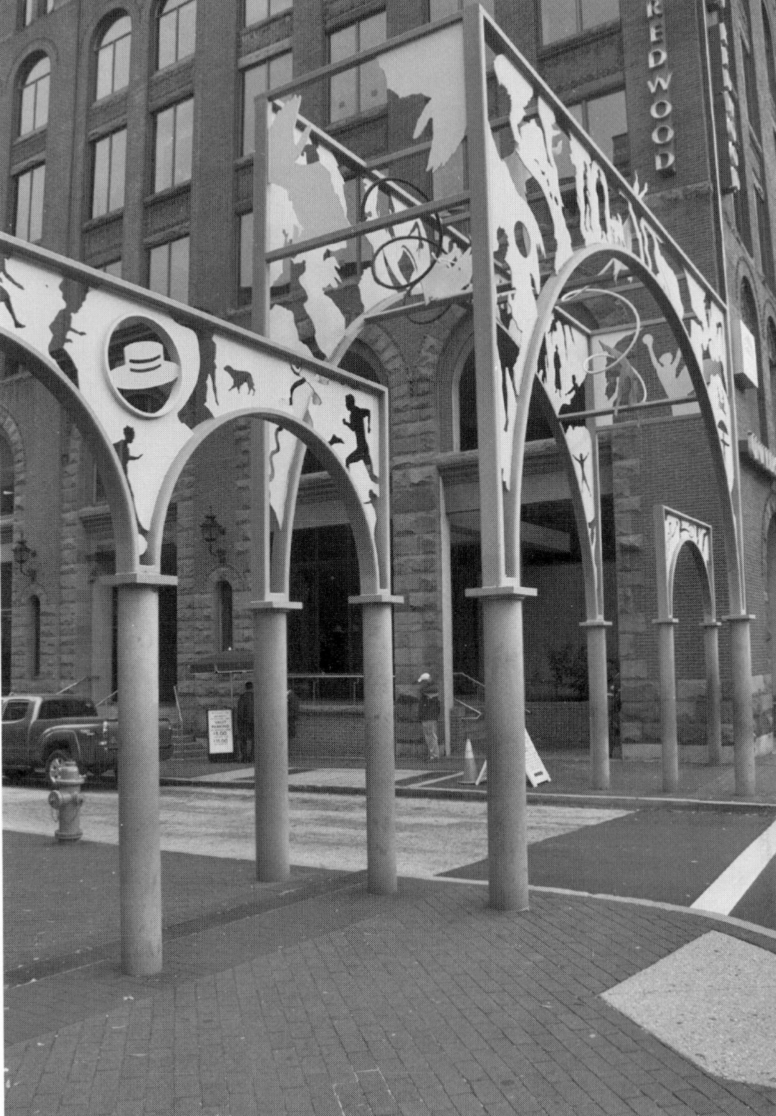

A dense, complex mass of images drawn from the garment industry—hats, scissors, ribbons, and threads and men and women in coats, suits, and dresses—are combined with very expressive figures of runners, fighters, divers, dancers, and dogs, not to mention Fred Astaire and Ginger Rogers dancing together one last time. What could this mean? Why were these silhouette images cut out of brightly painted steel and inserted into the framework of five arches of an expansive gateway across Redwood Street? The answer lies in the artist's examination of and reflection on the rich history of this site. After commissioning David Gerlach to create a piece of sculpture for Howard's Park (E2), the Market Center Development Corporation teamed up with Maryland Art Place, a not-for-profit center for contemporary art in Baltimore, to develop a more comprehensive public art program that would contribute significantly to their development of this west-side downtown urban-renewal area. Maryland Art Place helped with site selection and with designing an artist-selection process. Linda DePalma was chosen to create a new public artwork for Redwood Street, and Jeff Schiff was selected to create one for Liberty Plaza that would visually connect the east and west sides of Liberty Street.

Redwood Street, which was known as Lovely Lane and then German Street before it was renamed Redwood Street to honor the first Baltimore soldier killed in Europe, Lt. George Buchanan Redwood, was of particular importance. The 400 block of Redwood was the last remaining fully intact block of the Loft District, as the whole garment-manufacturing area had been called. This periodically interrupted street running from South Street to Martin Luther King Jr. Boulevard had been the site of large loft buildings that housed garment, hat, and other sewing manufacturers and wholesalers.

DePalma set about celebrating the industries formerly housed along this street as well as the new ones related to the medical fields. For the intersection of Redwood and South Paca streets, DePalma designed the largest and most celebratory element—the gateway—with a main arch spanning the roadway that stands 24

feet high and a series of smaller pedestrian arches defin-
ing the walkways. At the east end of the block where
Redwood intersects with South Eutaw Street, DePalma
placed two single columns to punctuate the streetscape.
The figures on the tops of these two columns were
clearly cut from the main gateway at the opposite end
of the street. Easily recognizable on the south side of
the street is Leonardo's ideal man. The young woman
leaping through a cutout of a man in a large overcoat
on the opposite side of the street is a direct reference
to *Ground Play,* DePalma's concurrent public artwork
made for the Maryland Transit Administration's Old
Court Metro Station.

This public artwork can be interpreted as reflecting the transitional nature of the neighborhood for
which it was created. Some figures relate to the history
of the site, and some relate to its current use, but almost
every figure is active, energized, as the area is today.
Optimistic, engaging and challenging, the piece offers
many narratives of the past, the present, and the future.
DePalma suggested that the gateway could be seen as a
metaphor for the garment district, with the viewer as a
tailor. The silhouettes are the patterns that can be constructed or stitched together, but instead of ending up
with a piece of clothing, the viewer creates one of these
narratives, uncovering the stories so beautifully embedded in the piece.

E5

TITLE
Chorale, 1981

LOCATION
Social Security Administration, Metro West Center, N. Greene and W. Franklin streets

SCULPTOR
Isaac Witkin (1936–2006)

MEDIUM
Painted steel

DONOR
Art in Architecture Program, U.S. General Services Administration

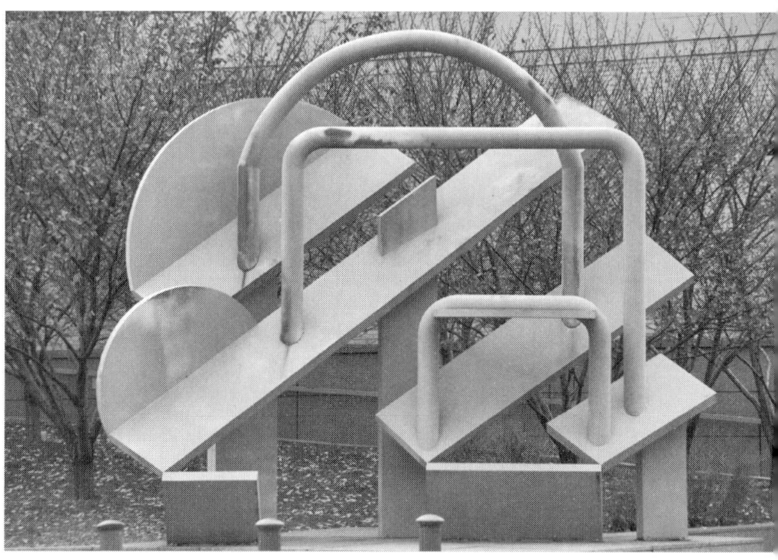

The General Services Administration planned to have three artworks for the new federal complex on North Greene Street. Isaac Witkin and Ronald Bladen were selected to create outdoor pieces for the site, and Loren Madsen was chosen to develop an interior piece for the atrium lobby.

Witkin's 17-foot-high abstract sculpture of painted steel is a complex arrangement of bold forms, angular and rounded, open and closed, rising and expanding in space. The resulting sculpture is well balanced, a study in contrasts. The granite base anchors the piece to the corner site, where it stands as a kind of gateway for people driving south or west out of the city.

Witkin often used musical titles for his sculptures, which may have been autobiographical. His mother was a concert pianist, and one of his daughters is a pianist and composer. He said that he titled this piece Chorale "because it contains rising and falling cyclic rhythms and counterpoints." The two-part color scheme was selected to harmonize with the building, echoing its blue and salmon brick hues. Today, the original colors are difficult to imagine; the paint has faded and taken on a chalky appearance that masks the effect of the delicate spraying of magenta over a blue-grey.

Witkin was born in Johannesburg, South Africa. When he was 21, he emigrated to London, where he enrolled at St. Martin's School of Art and studied with the English sculptor Anthony Caro. After completing his formal education, he worked for two and a half years as an assistant to another English sculptor, Henry Moore. In 1965 Witkin came to the states to replace Caro on the faculty of Bennington College in Vermont. In the 1980s he moved to New Jersey.

The first exhibition to include his work—New Generation, featuring the group of avant-garde British sculptors emerging in the sixties—opened at Whitechapel Art Gallery in London in 1964. In 1966 Witkin's work was included in the landmark exhibition Primary Structures, at the Jewish Museum in New York, the first major exhibition devoted to Minimalism. Shortly thereafter, Witkin's work won first place at the Quatrième Biennale in Paris. It was an auspicious beginning for a young sculptor.

Throughout the 1970s, Witkin continued to exhibit his welded steel sculptures in New York, across the country, and in Europe. He was a sculptor with an international reputation and an international life, connecting three continents. Today his work can be seen at Grounds for Sculpture in Hamilton, New Jersey, and in the permanent collections of the Tate Museum in London, the Hirshhorn Museum and Sculpture Garden in Washington, and Storm King in New York.

(For more on the federal government's Art in Architecture Program, see A2.)

TITLE
Host of the Ellipse, 1981

LOCATION
Social Security Administration, Metro West Center, Mulberry Street between Martin Luther King Jr. Boulevard and Greene Street

SCULPTOR
Ronald Bladen (1918–1988)

MEDIUM
Cor-Ten steel

DONOR
Art in Architecture Program, U.S. General Services Administration

Ronald Bladen, considered by many to be a founding father of Minimalism, is widely recognized for his monumental geometric sculptures. For this sculpture, commissioned by the General Services Administration for its new Social Security building, Bladen used two vast triangular forms placed at an angle to each other to create a powerful presence. One element reaches 35 feet into the air. What he was after, he said, was "to create a drama out of a minimal experience."

Bladen was born in Vancouver, British Columbia, and studied at the California School of Fine Arts in San Francisco from 1939 to 1943. In 1955 he moved to New York. A painter for almost twenty years, by the mid-sixties he had begun making sculpture. For the 1966 exhibition at the Jewish Museum in New York, Primary Structures, Bladen made *Three Elements*, a piece composed of three identical, 10-foot-high rectangular slabs installed side by side, all leaning at an angle of 65°. One year later, he was one of three artists, along with Barnett Newman and Tony Smith, invited to participate in the groundbreaking 1967 exhibition Scale as Content at the Corcoran Gallery of Art in Washington, D.C. Included in that exhibition was Bladen's monumental, 23-foot-high black sculpture entitled *X*.

These early seminal works earned Bladen much critical acclaim. During the next two decades he exhibited regularly and taught intermittently at the Parsons School of Design and the School of Visual Arts in New York City and the Skowhegan School of Painting and Sculpture in Skowhegan, Maine. Since his death, one-man exhibitions of his work have been mounted at the San Francisco Museum of Modern Art, the Weatherspoon Art Gallery at the University of North Carolina in Greensboro, and the P.S. 1 Contemporary Art Center in New York.

Years after this piece was installed, the outdoor playground with its high protective fence was constructed for a new day care center that was incorporated into the building. Unfortunately this play area was constructed too close to the artwork and encroaches into the space

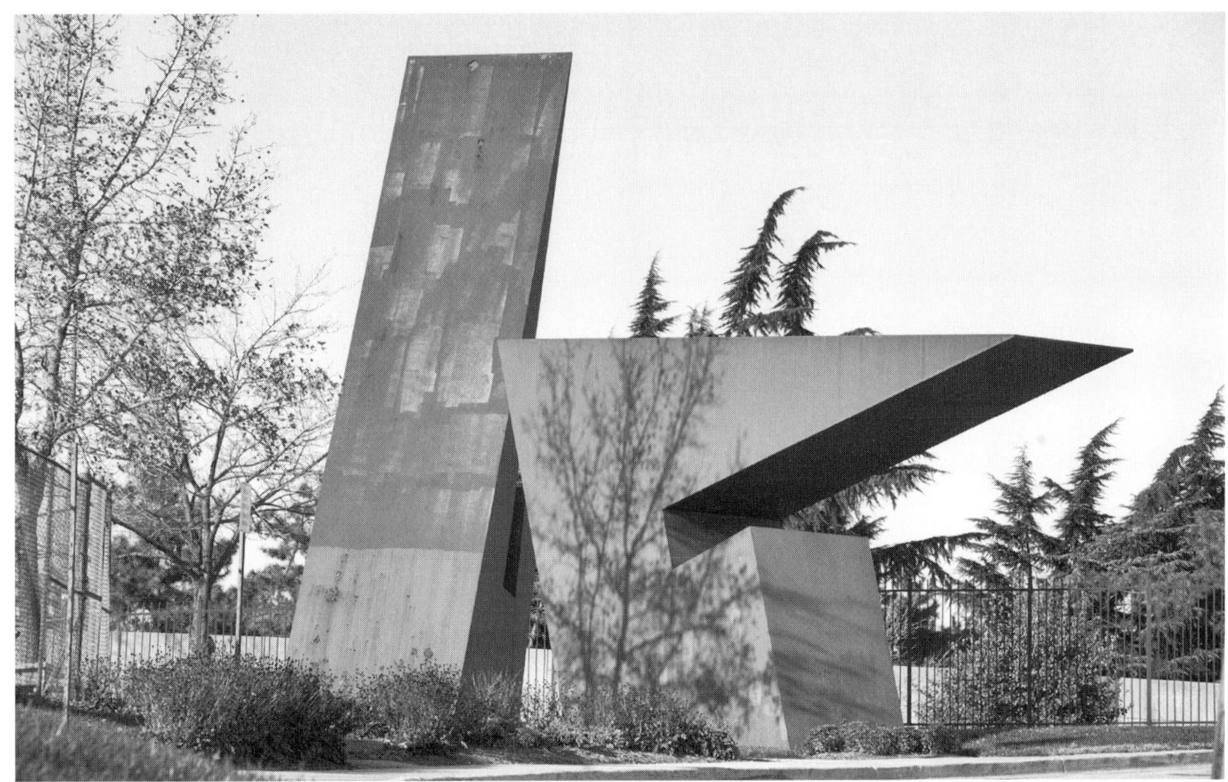

carved out by the sculpture, compromising the original intent for viewing and experiencing the artwork.

In addition to this piece by Bladen and the piece by Isaac Witkin (E5), a third piece of art was commissioned for the Metro West Center: an interior stone relief for the atrium lobby created by Loren Madsen. Like Witkin and Bladen, Madsen completed his commission in 1981. In the late 1970s, the Social Security Administration built a computer center on Security Boulevard in Woodlawn, just outside Baltimore, for which Richard Fleischner was commissioned through this same public art program to create a site-specific piece for the grounds. Completed in 1980, Fleischner's *Baltimore Project* consists of ten abstract elements sited throughout an expansive wooded grove adjacent to the building.

(For more information about the federal government's Art in Architecture Program, see A2.)

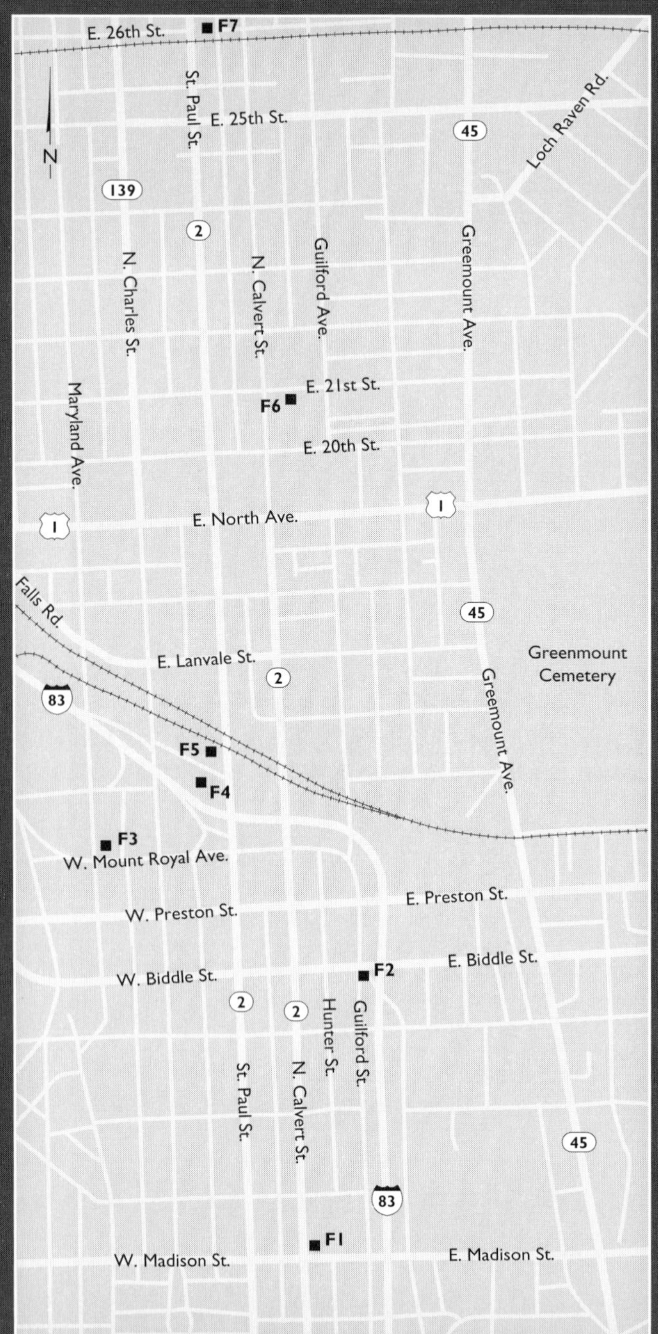
E. 26th St.
F7
St. Paul St.
E. 25th St.
45
Loch Raven Rd.
N
139
2
N. Charles St.
N. Calvert St.
Guilford Ave.
Greemount Ave.
Maryland Ave.
E. 21st St.
F6
E. 20th St.
E. North Ave.
1
1
Falls Rd.
E. Lanvale St.
2
83
Greemount Ave.
Greenmount Cemetery
F5
F4
F3
W. Mount Royal Ave.
E. Preston St.
W. Preston St.
E. Biddle St.
W. Biddle St.
F2
2
2
Hunter St.
Guilford St.
N. Calvert St.
St. Paul St.
45
83
F1
W. Madison St.
E. Madison St.

MOUNT VERNON PLACE TO 26TH STREET

Driving

F1

TITLE
Arbor, 2005

LOCATION
Mount Vernon Children's Park, E. Madison
and N. Calvert streets

SCULPTOR
David Hess (b. 1964)

MEDIUM
Stainless steel

DONORS
Maureen and Louis Van Dyck

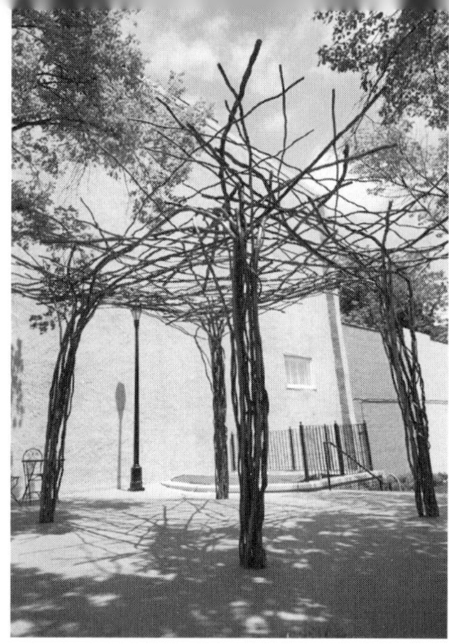

The artist David Hess was commissioned to create a unique element—a structure that was part pergola, part folly—for a park designed for the children of the Mount Vernon–Belvedere neighborhood. Using the Midtown Community Benefits District office as their fiduciary agent, community volunteers raised money for the construction of this park. Joan Flora, a landscape architect, was hired to help design the play area and its equipment, and the firm of Whitney Bailey provided the engineering.

Arbor is a freestanding structure made of stainless steel pipe of varying dimensions that Hess twisted in his studio and then assembled and welded together on site. The four vertical elements at the corners of this pergola-like structure are constructed of several twisted steel pipes woven together to resemble several small tree trunks, and these 14-foot-high elements support an open flat roof of similarly interwoven twisted steel pipes that resemble more tree trunks and branches. Hess had used the same material for his bird's nest at the American Visionary Art Museum (AVAM), completed the previous year (G4). In both pieces the reference to nature is clear, and the illusion is achieved by extraordinary craftsmanship. Each stainless steel element was twisted and patinated to a silver grey color to mimic the appearance of cedar tree trunks and branches, which might have been dragged from the woods for use in these construction projects. The real leafy twigs that fall from nearby trees onto the roof of this piece heighten the illusion that it was a naturally occurring structure offering a sense of protection and some shade and that the playground was constructed around it.

Hess was born in Baltimore. After earning a degree in visual arts at Dartmouth College, he returned to Baltimore and set up a studio in Monkton. He is probably best known in Baltimore for *Working Point,* his piece at the Baltimore Museum of Industry (G15), and *Nest* at AVAM. Before his commission for the latter, Hess had been commissioned to design and fabricate the central staircase, garden gates, handrails, benches, restaurant and bar fixtures, and other architectural details throughout the museum. In 1996 Hess received the Craftsman of the Year for Ornamental Ironwork award from the Building Congress and Exchange for his work there.

Hess is also known for designing and fabricating unique pieces of furniture; his outdoor benches can be seen in Tide Point, at the former Procter and Gamble factory, and throughout the Weinberg Cancer Center at Johns Hopkins Hospital. He often incorporates found objects into his sculpture and his furniture that make them site-specific. Hess used gears, wheels, chains, marine rigging, and boiler parts from Baltimore industries in his piece at the Museum of Industry, and he incorporated cast-iron elements from the Proctor and Gamble factory into the benches at Tide Point. His 2005 entry into the Kinetic Sculpture Race won the grand prize.

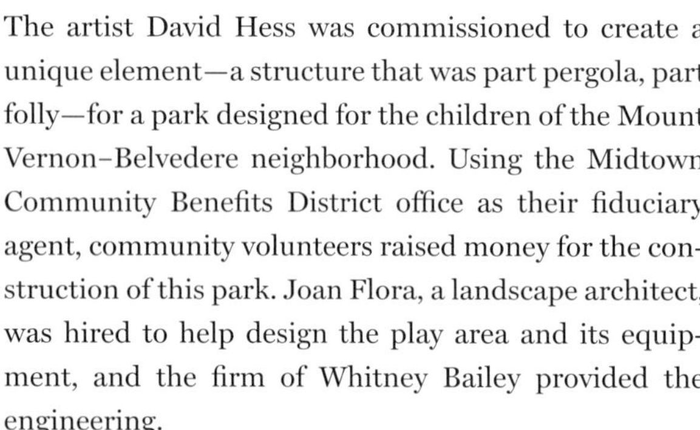

F2

TITLE
Fallsway Fountain, 1915

LOCATION
Guilford Avenue, E. Biddle Street, and The Fallsway

SCULPTOR
Hans Schuler (1874–1951)

ARCHITECT
Theodore Wells Pietsch (d. 1930)

MEDIUM
Marble

DONOR
City of Baltimore

This fountain, with its beautiful bare-breasted female figure wearing a laurel wreath, seated atop the 25-foot-high plinth, gracefully holding a large urn in one hand and a shield of the City of Baltimore in her other, was erected in 1915 to celebrate the completion of The Fallsway. The new road leading into the center of the business district had been built over the Jones Falls, eliminating eighteen street bridges and three railroad spans. Begun in August 1911 and not completed until December 1914, the project reclaimed 600,000 square feet of land, allowing for this new 75-foot driveway from Mount Royal Avenue to Baltimore Street. All this information, as well as the name of the mayor and the names of all the engineers and other city officials and planners involved on the project, is inscribed on the sides of the plinth, between the elegant corner Corinthian columns.

Prior to the building of The Fallsway, the Jones Falls had run through the middle of downtown and into the harbor. This stream, which had carried boats as far north as Saratoga Street, flooded frequently, causing much damage over the years, so much damage, in fact, that the city had spent $2 million a generation earlier to confine it within a stone retaining wall, which was still breached on occasion. At other times it was an offense to eyes and nostrils. The city's chief engineer at the time, Calvin V. Hendrick, set about building a real sewer system for the city. As part of that system, he devised a way to force the Jones Falls stream into a huge concrete pipe. Other pipes were laid to carry storm water, and still others were laid to carry ordinary sewage. Over all these pipes was laid a concrete bed covered with paving for the broad driveway into the city.

Considered one of the most remarkable feats of engineering of the time, the resulting new boulevard provided a way for farmers from Pennsylvania to more easily bring their goods to market in downtown Baltimore or into the port for shipping abroad. In 1915 most of the goods brought into the city were still transported by horse-drawn wagons. Thus, for all those horses traveling to the terminus of The Fallsway, it made perfect sense to incorporate a semicircular water basin into this monument. There are even drinking places for cats and dogs. But long before it was relocated in 1967 from The Fallsway and Eager Street to allow for the extension of the Jones Falls Expressway, it ceased to function as a fountain. Since its relocation to this rather meaningless spot, the fountain, once one of Baltimore's grandest monuments, has been all but forgotten, as has the fact that this monument was an important early work of Hans Schuler. Theodore Wells Pietsch was the architect.

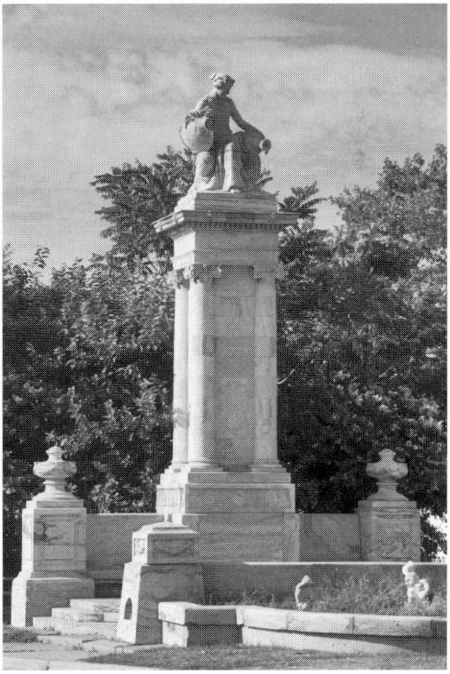

F3

By 1930 this monument had become known as "the statue of the missing letters." An inscription carved into the monument's original base, long ago destroyed, contained a badly misquoted line of poetry from *The Raven*, one of Edgar Allan Poe's most famous poems. When the monument was presented to the city in 1921, the line read: "Dreamng dreams no mortals ever dared to dream before." The omission of the *i* from *Dreaming* did not cause a problem, but, oh, what a ruckus the addition of the *s* to *mortal* created among Poe enthusiasts, especially one Edmond Fontaine, a tree surgeon and poet.

After many letters to the editor over the years, Fontaine decided to take matters into his own hands. In his final letter to the *Evening Sun,* dated May 28, 1930, Fontaine served notice that if the letter *s* was not removed by June 1, he would go and chisel off the "offending letter . . . for the good of my soul." For some reason he did not wait until June 1; on the evening of May 29, in less than two minutes, he removed the *s*, for which he was immediately arrested for defacing public property. After spending one night in jail because he could not raise the $100 collateral required, the Park Board showed leniency and let him off with a warning. It was determined that Fontaine had not carried out an act of vandalism but rather had acted out of reverence for the memory of the poet. The national press the inci-

dent generated did not hurt his case either. There was rejoicing all around.

The curious history of the Poe monument does not end here. It all started when the members of the Women's Literary Club of Baltimore decided at their April 12, 1907, meeting to erect a memorial to Edgar Allan Poe (1809–49). A week later, members of the group incorporated as The Edgar Allan Poe Memorial Association of Baltimore. By 1911 they had enough money to approach Sir Moses J. Ezekiel about creating a statue of Poe, and he accepted with enthusiasm. A first statue, finished in 1913, was being shipped from Rome, where Ezekiel maintained a studio, to Berlin for bronze casting when it was destroyed in a customs-house fire at the border. A second statue, completed in 1915, was destroyed in an earthquake in Rome. Undaunted, Ezekiel completed a third statue in March 1916, but shipment was delayed due to perceived risks in shipping the statue across the Atlantic during World War I. Ezekiel died on March 27, 1917, and it was not until 1921 that the statue arrived in Baltimore. It was installed and dedicated on October 20, 1921, on the southern edge of Wyman Park.

In 1983 the Poe monument was moved from its original site in Wyman Park to the University of Baltimore's new plaza in front of its law school. This new location is appropriate for two reasons. First, since the early 1970s, UB has provided a home to the Poe Society and has been the repository of the society's archives, which date back to 1923. Second, Poe once considered law as a profession, registering in the District Court of Philadelphia to study law in the office of his friend Henry B. Hirst. For those who know that Poe lived in Baltimore from 1829 to 1836, during which time he had his first success as a poet, the fact that his monument is no longer hidden under trees and shrubs in a forgotten part of a city park is reason enough for the relocation.

Sir Moses Jacob Ezekiel was one of the most prolific American sculptors during the period between the Civil War and World War I. Maintaining a studio in Rome for more than forty years, he was acclaimed on both sides of the Atlantic and was knighted by three European monarchs. But he is largely forgotten today except in Virginia and in academic circles. Born in

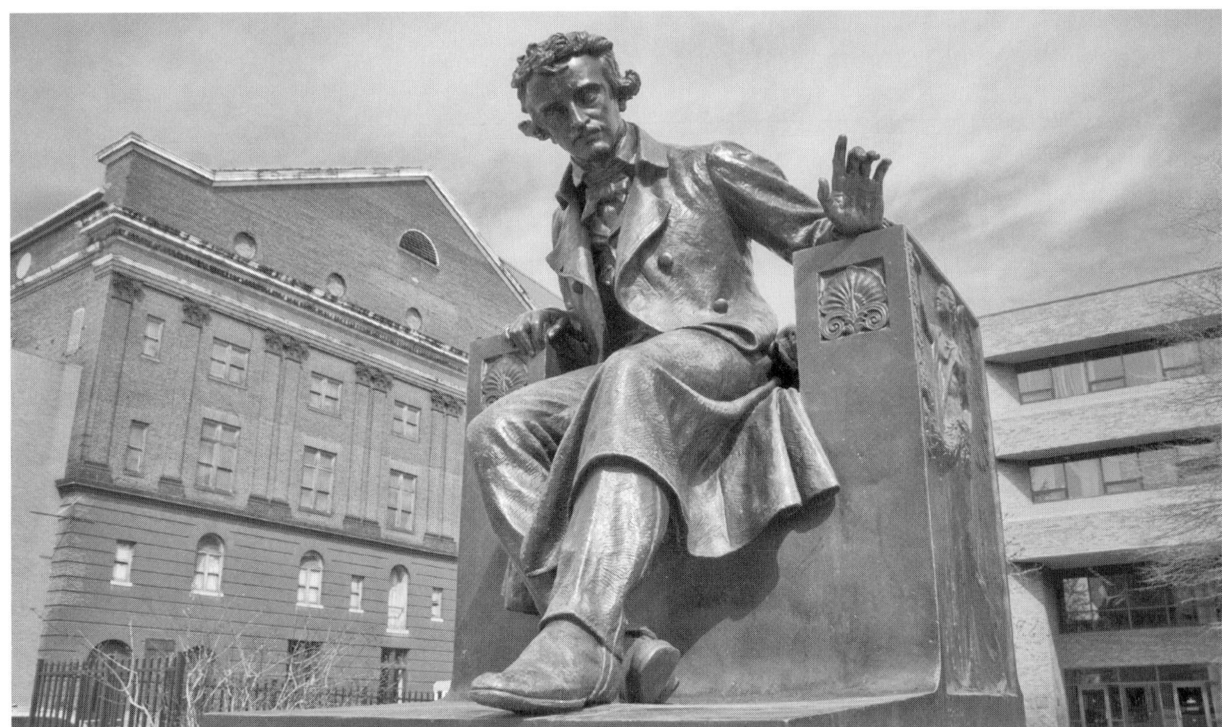

Richmond, Virginia, he was the first Jewish cadet at the Virginia Military Institute, from which he graduated in 1866 after a hiatus to serve in the Confederate army. Soon thereafter, he spent a year studying anatomy at the Virginia Medical College and decided to become a sculptor. He received his artistic training in Europe, first in Germany and later in Rome, where he was to remain for the rest of his life. After completing his first large commission from America for the 1876 Centennial Exhibition in Philadelphia, a statue titled *Religious Liberty,* which is sited today in Fairmount Park, his studio in Rome became a busy place. He quickly established himself as a portrait sculptor and created many busts and full-length figures.

The portrait of Poe, which came very late in his career, is considered his finest. Poe is shown dressed formally, in a full-length coat that spills over the back of his chair, leaning forward as if listening to the Muses, who might be represented in the two beautiful relief panels on the outer surfaces of this chair. On Poe's right side, a winged female figure, shown in profile, is depicted in a long flowing gown playing a lyre with thistles at her feet. She could represent Terpsichore, the Muse responsible for judging a work's artistic component. On his left side, another winged female, similarly draped and in profile, is shown raising a festoon of laurel. She is harder to identify. Just under Poe's right elbow, balancing on one corner of his chair, is a book, a certain reference to his life as a poet, a short-story writer, literary critic, and editor. Ezekiel most certainly had seen portraits of Poe, for his depiction of him as a handsome, shy-looking man, slightly built and 5 feet eight 8 inches tall, with curly hair and mustache, is accurate. Just one year after completing the Poe monument, Sir Moses died. He was buried in Arlington National Cemetery beside his Confederate Memorial.

F4

TITLE
Male/Female, 2004

LOCATION
Pennsylvania Station, 1515 N. Charles Street

SCULPTOR
Jonathan Borofsky (b. 1942)

MEDIUM
Aluminum

DONORS
Municipal Art Society of Baltimore City and
the Penn Station Fund

In celebration of their centennial, the members of the Municipal Art Society of Baltimore City decided to commission a large-scale, site-specific work of art from a world-class artist for Baltimore City. They hired the Public Art Fund, a nonprofit arts organization in New York City, which had been presenting artists' projects, new commissions, and exhibitions in public spaces for more than thirty years, to advise them on the artist-selection process, and they got permission from the city to locate their gift in the newly reconfigured circular plaza in front of Penn Station.

Jonathan Borofsky, a sculptor currently based in Ogunquit, Maine, was on the Public Art Fund's short list, and he was eventually selected by the nine-member board that constitutes the Municipal Art Society today—a far cry from the 500-member organization it was when it was founded in 1899.

At the time this commission was awarded, Borofsky was well known for his monumental figurative pieces sited across the United States, Europe, and Asia.

He has made multiple copies of many of his images, including *Hammering Man, Molecule Man, Walking Man, Singing Man,* and *Man with a Briefcase.* He has made twenty-four versions of his now world-famous mechanized *Hammering Man,* which can be found in Seattle, Dallas, Frankfurt, Germany, Basel, Switzerland, and Seoul, Korea, to name just a few cities. Borofsky says that he would like to make as many versions of *Hammering Man* as possible, because they represent the worker in all of us and can thus connect working people around the world with one another.

Borofsky was born in Boston. He did his undergraduate work at Carnegie Mellon and his graduate work at the Yale School of Art and Architecture. For the past decade he has focused almost exclusively on outdoor sculpture, all of it on this superhuman scale. An early *Hammering Man* is 70 feet high, and the *Molecule Man* in Berlin measures 100 feet. One reason he gives for working on such a large scale is drawn from his childhood: he loved listening to his father tell stories of

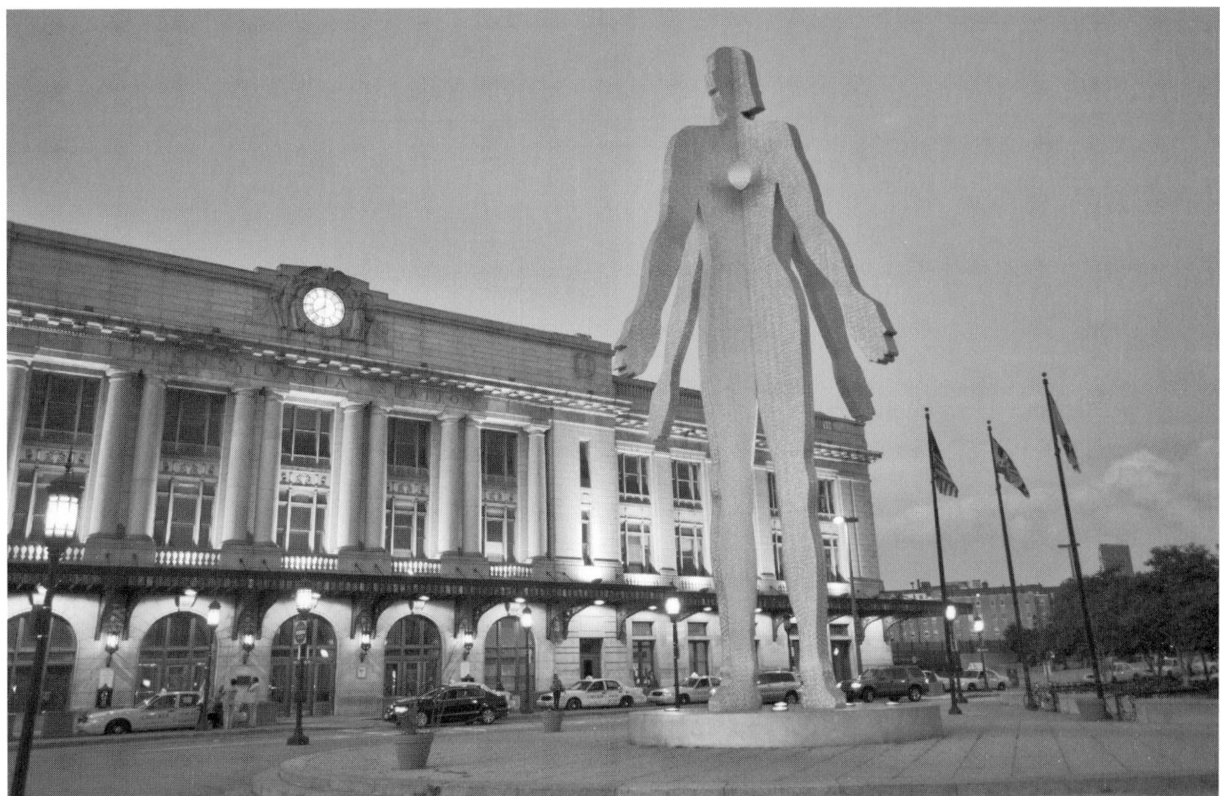

a friendly giant who lived in the sky and did good things for people. Borofsky also says that each of his works is a kind of self-portrait. He thinks that an artist reveals something of him- or herself in every work. He considers his own work a kind of record, an ongoing portrait of his life and maybe by extension, an exploration into what constitutes humanity.

There is no doubt that this sculpture is Borofsky's. The colossal scale alone might announce that, but so also do the schematized human figures, which have no identifying features to make the implied narrative more explicit. That narrative is left entirely to the viewer. *Male/Female* is another work that Borofsky has grown fond of and has made multiple times. A 24-foot version was made for Kagoshima, Japan, and a 30-foot one was made for Bielefeld, Germany. The Baltimore piece stands 52 feet tall and is made of 14 tons of burnished hollow-core aluminum. Borrowing an idea from his 140-foot-high *Heartfelt Man,* in Tokyo, Borofsky has inserted a pulsating light-emitting diode, or LED,

at the intersection of the male and female silhouettes that changes from cobalt blue to fuchsia every sixty seconds to represent the heart and denote spiritual energy. Borofsky says the figures represent two energies that come together to create a greater force.

Another theme in the work is balance, a theme Borofsky has dealt with most recently in *Walking to the Sky,* sited during September and October 2004 in Rockefeller Center in New York City by the Public Art Fund and now permanently sited on the campus of his alma mater, Carnegie Mellon.

Baltimoreans remain conflicted as to whether the artist followed the Municipal Art Society's instructions that the work be welcoming, identifiable, unique, colorful, and reasonable.

F5

TITLE
Untitled, 1978

LOCATION
Pennsylvania Station, 1515 N. Charles Street

SCULPTOR
William Leizman (b. 1926)

MEDIUM
Mayari-R steel

DONORS
Municipal Art Society of Baltimore City and
the citizens of Baltimore

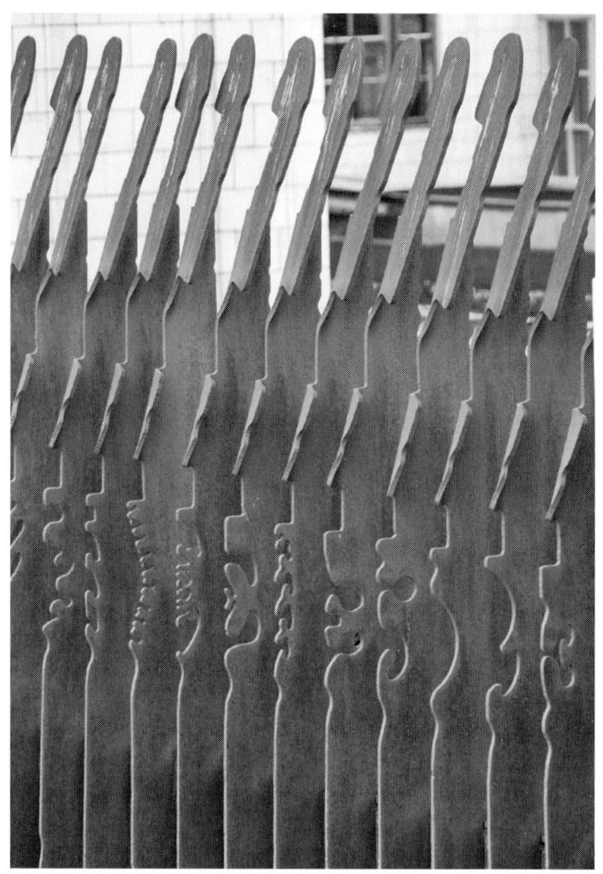

The tall windscreen designed for Penn Station comprises sixty slabs of steel, each 10 feet high, about 12 inches wide, and ½ inch thick. The designs cut into the metal edges of each slab are unique and give a rhythmic flow across the wide-open space leading from the train station toward St. Paul Street, framing the northern perimeter of a small parking lot beside the station and acting as a barrier fence for the railroad tracks below. The slabs stand at a slight angle to the low wall to which they are attached and are silhouetted against the sky.

For his sculpture, William Leizman always used Mayari-R steel, which for years was made at the nearby Bethlehem Steel Company. Like Cor-Ten, Mayari-R steel is a weathering steel that cures beautifully, forming a rich brown velvety surface that can still be detected here.

Leizman went to the steel plant and supervised workmen as they flame-cut his designs into the steel slabs. After they were cut, each 300-pound slab was then bent using a 250-pound press. The pieces were then shipped to the site, and Leizman bolted them into place himself. The project took two years to complete. Originally sited on the west side of the train station, where it could be seen from N. Charles Street and where it welcomed travelers into a side door, the piece was relocated to the east side of the station during renovations in 2004. Today the piece languishes in this much less visible site and is further compromised by multiple parking signs that have been insensitively installed across the whole expanse of the artwork.

William Leizman was born in Baltimore, where he lived and worked until moving to Florida in 1996. He studied art at the University of Maryland, the Maryland Institute College of Art, and at Carnegie Mellon. He worked with Hans Hofmann in Provincetown, Massachusetts, for two years and spent three years in Paris as a student of Fernand Léger's. Throughout his life he was an avid collector of tools, and these old tools inspired his art. In his studio on Caroline Street, tools hung from the ceiling and across the surface of every wall, lining many shelves as well. He owned more than five hundred hammers. Leizman created five outdoor sculptures in Baltimore, four through Baltimore City's Percent for Art program (N9, Q3, and Q5).

F6

TITLE
Caterpillar, 1976

LOCATION
Dallas F. Nicholas Sr. Elementary School,
201 E. 21st Street

SCULPTOR
Norman Carlberg (b. 1928)

MEDIUM
Cor-Ten steel

DONOR
Baltimore City Percent for Art program

Norman Carlberg has always been interested in the formal elements in sculpture. The results of his continuing investigation of these elements reveal a certain classicism in the directness and simplicity of his work. He is an internationally acclaimed sculptor who came to Baltimore in 1961 to serve as director of the Rinehart School of Sculpture at the Maryland Institute College of Art, retiring in 1996. During those thirty-five years Carlberg continued making art, completing two Percent for Art commissions in Baltimore, of which this is the earlier one.

Caterpillar is constructed out of a single module that is repeated over and over and grows in varying directions to form four caterpillars that seem to have been captured in various poses as they crawled across the plaza in front of the new elementary school. Carlberg identifies his style of sculpture as "modular constructivism." He was introduced to this style at the Yale School of Art and Architecture, where he studied with Josef Albers, and since that time all his sculptures have been designed using identical modules. The identical modules in this charming and playful piece are curvilinear, geometric, and hard edged.

Carlberg was born in Roseau, Minnesota, and studied art at the Minneapolis School of Art and the University of Illinois before earning his MFA from the Yale School of Art and Architecture. After teaching at the Universidad Católica in Santiago, Chile, Carlberg came to the Maryland Institute, where he ushered in the modernist spirit after a long tradition of figurative sculpture. His work has been widely exhibited, beginning with a group exhibition in 1959 at the Museum of Modern Art titled Recent Sculpture USA and a Whitney Annual in 1962. His work is included in the permanent collections of the Whitney Museum of American Art and the Guggenheim in New York, the Hirshhorn Museum in Washington, and the Baltimore Museum of Art, among others.

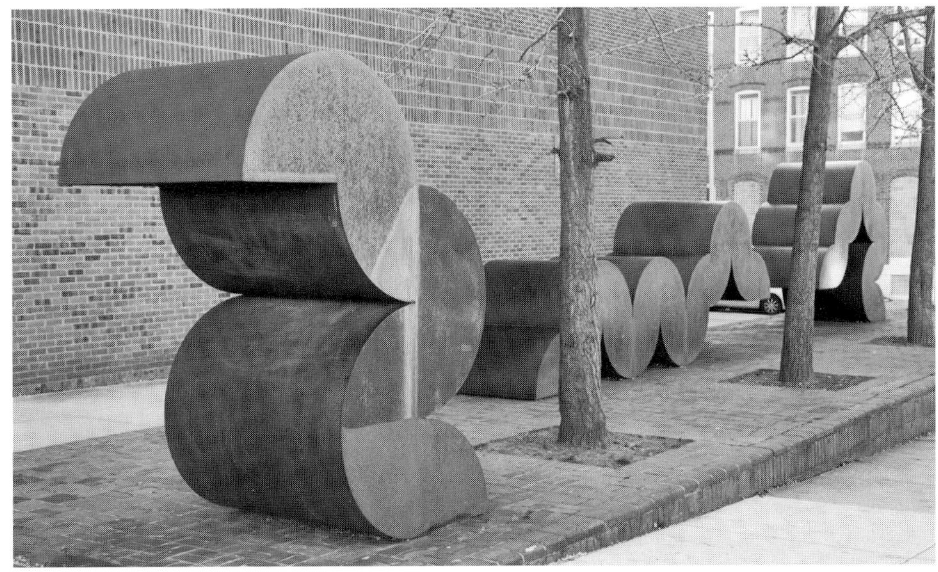

F7

TITLE
Samurai Rocker, 1979

LOCATION
Margaret Brent Elementary School,
100 E. 26th Street

SCULPTOR
Richard D. Gottlieb (b. 1951)

MEDIUM
Cor-Ten steel

DONOR
Baltimore City Percent for Art program

Serendipity played a major role in the awarding of this commission. The young sculptor Richard Gottlieb had a 6-foot model of a piece of sculpture he wanted to build. At the time he was living in Great Neck, New York, but he had a connection in Baltimore that led to his being asked to submit his model for consideration for a Percent for Art commission for a new elementary school. The Civic Design Commission (today the Public Art Commission) ultimately approved the commission.

Gottlieb, who had graduated from the Atlanta College of Art in 1975, titled the piece *Samurai Rocker,* although he thinks that titles sometimes do a disservice to objects, limiting how they can be viewed. Gottlieb did say that the curving lines of the piece reminded him of the actor Toshiro Mifune in repose while playing a samurai in a film by Akira Kurosawa, even if the samurai in this piece may have posed atop a rocking horse. The piece has a simplicity and grace that have endured over thirty years. The arching line of the uppermost element in the piece mimics the arching line of the entrance of the building, although that was not planned.

Behind the school, just outside the kindergarten room, is another piece of sculpture commissioned at the same time. Frayda Shalowitz's *Seal,* cast in bronze, was designed to lie on the ground, with its head turned backward and its front flippers apart, elevating its upper body slightly. The schoolchildren obviously enjoy climbing on the piece.

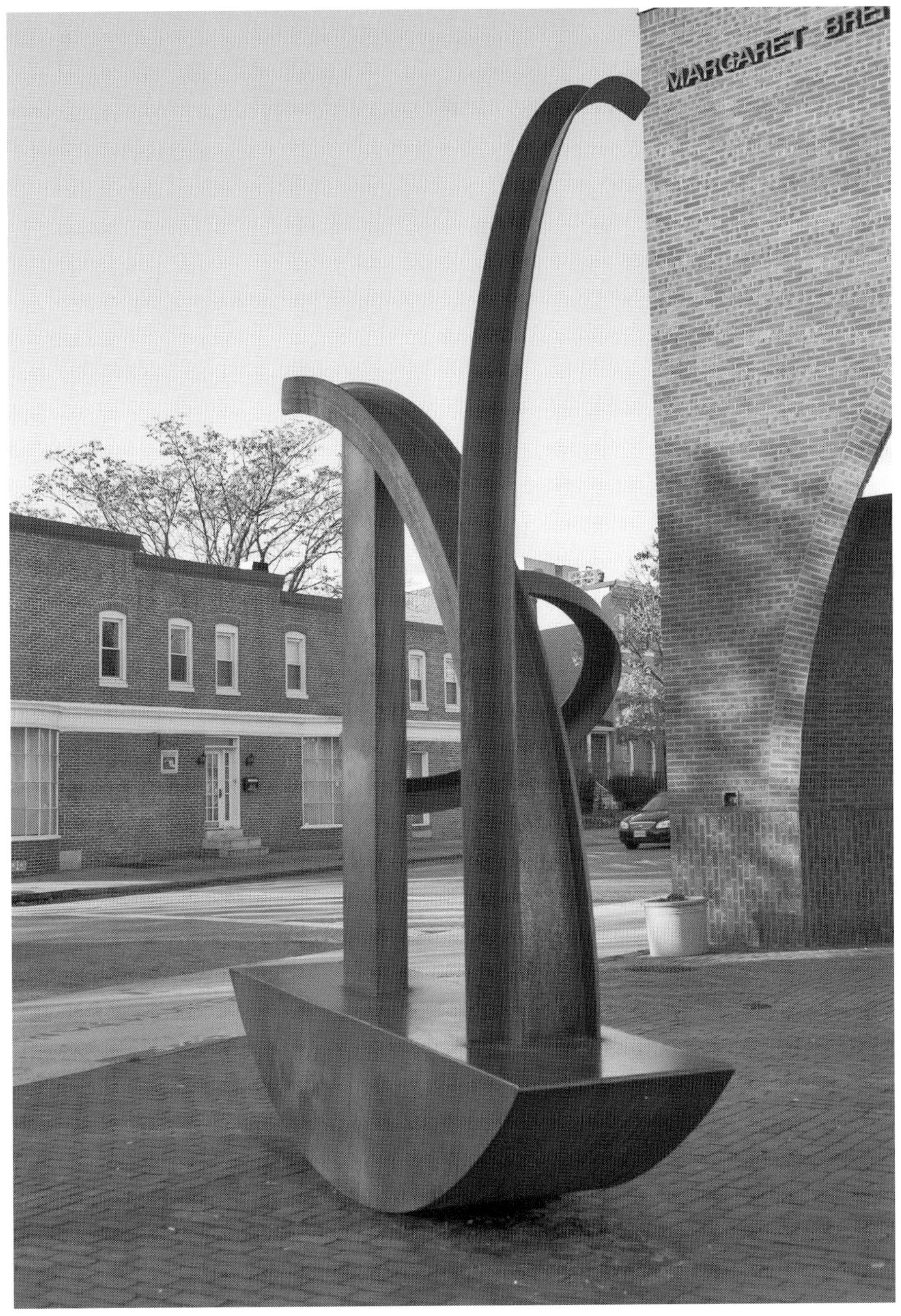# MARGARET BRE

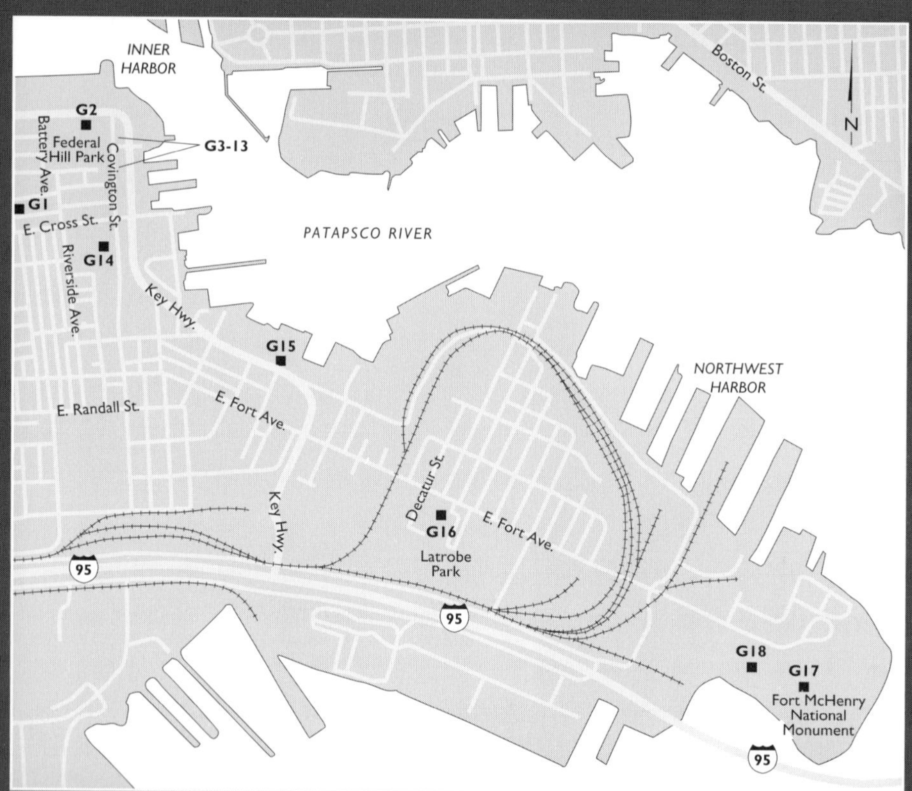

INNER HARBOR
Battery Ave.
Federal Hill Park
Covington St.
E. Cross St.
Riverside Ave.
Key Hwy.
E. Randall St.
E. Fort Ave.
Key Hwy.
PATAPSCO RIVER
Boston St.
N
NORTHWEST HARBOR
Decatur St.
E. Fort Ave.
Latrobe Park
Fort McHenry National Monument
G2
G3-13
G1
G14
G15
G16
G18
G17
95
95
95

FEDERAL HILL, INNER HARBOR SOUTH, AND FORT MCHENRY

Driving

G1

TITLE
Untitled Crab, 1972

LOCATION
Federal Hill Elementary School,
1040 Williams Street

SCULPTOR
Edmund Whiting (1918–1975)

MEDIUM
Copper

DONOR
Baltimore City Percent for Art program

Edmund Whiting, a sculptor from Pennsylvania, was commissioned by the Baltimore architect Charles M. Nes (1907–89), of Nes, Campbell & Partners, to create this fountain for his newly designed elementary school. One of the earliest Percent for Art commissions, the fountain was completed when the new school opened.

The free-form fountain is made of copper sheet. The rather architectonic, abstract shapes clearly suggest the idea of a crab lumbering across the school plaza, with his eyes on the viewer and his legs spread wide. There are small openings, with covers, over the entire surface. Water is supposed to drizzle out of these holes and fall as droplets into the pool beneath before being recycled. Much of the charm of the piece is missing when the water is off, and it is only turned on intermittently. The vertical streaks down the copper on all of the surfaces of the fountain suggest how the piece might originally have looked and sounded.

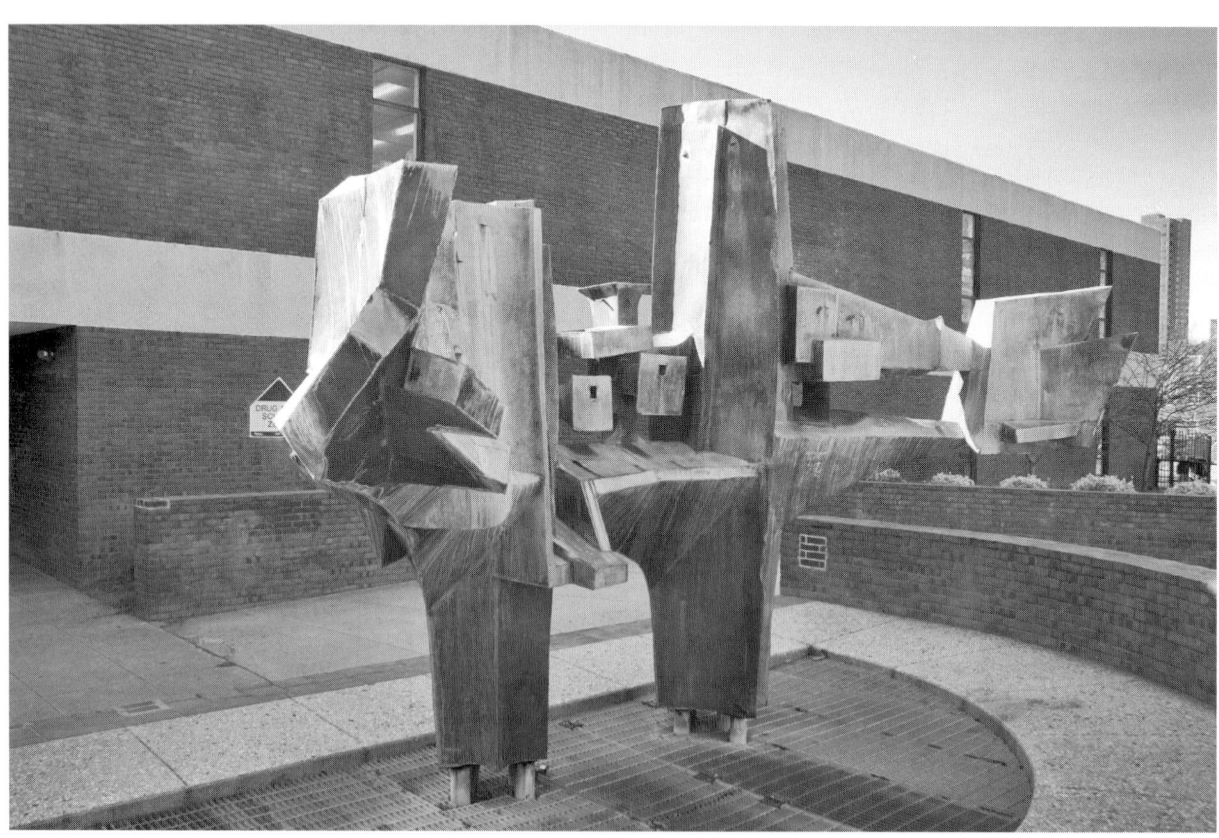

G2

TITLE
MAJOR GENERAL SAMUEL SMITH MONUMENT,
1917

LOCATION
Federal Hill Park, Warren Avenue and Key Highway

SCULPTOR
Hans Schuler (1874–1951)

MEDIUM
Bronze

DONOR
National Star-Spangled Banner Centennial
Commission

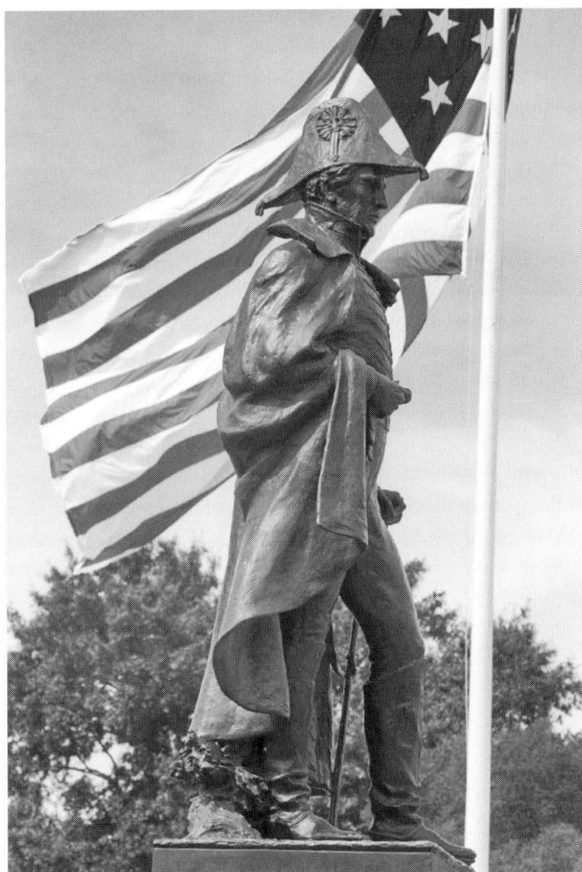

Major General Samuel Smith (1752–1839) was the commander of the Maryland forces that fought in the battle of Baltimore at North Point and at Fort McHenry on September 12–14, 1814, in which the British were repulsed and defeated, saving Baltimore from ever being occupied by foreign forces. Before the War of 1812, Smith had been a hero of the Revolutionary War. The battles he fought in are listed on the monument. After an exemplary military career, Smith continued his life of public service by serving forty years in Congress and becoming president of the U.S. Senate, secretary of the navy, and, when he was 80 years old, mayor of Baltimore. Little wonder that there is a monument dedicated to him.

There were many parades and celebrations in Baltimore to mark the centennial of the War of 1812, and several sculptural monuments, including this one, were commissioned as part of those celebrations. Hans Schuler received this commission and two others. One, from the National Society of the U.S. Daughters of 1812, designed for a niche on the facade of City Hall, was of a bronze, screaming eagle of war standing on a flagpole around which an American flag was wrapped, held by a fillet on which words from the "Star-Spangled Banner" are visible. A companion piece, an eagle of peace, for the opposite side of the facade was never completed, and recently the screaming eagle was moved indoors to the upstairs rotunda in City Hall. The Daughters of the American Revolution commissioned Schuler to produce a small relief with a portrait of Francis Scott Key for the facade of the Mount Vernon United Methodist Church (C9). A fourth sculpture commissioned for the occasion, by J. Maxwell Miller, is in Patterson Park, paid for by money collected by schoolchildren (P1).

General Smith is shown standing in his military uniform from the War of 1812. Thrown over his shoulders is a full-length cape. In his right hand he holds his gloves at about waist level, and the weight of his left hand rests on a sword whose tip is planted behind his left leg. Even though this is a relatively early Schuler monument, the figure has been beautifully designed; with his full weight on his right leg and his left leg forward, the figure conveys a sense of movement and the energy of an officer in full command.

Originally sited on the southeastern edge of Wyman Park, near where the Union Soldiers and Sailors Monument stands today, this sculpture of Smith was moved in 1953 to a park named for him at the corner of Light and Pratt streets and then to its present location in 1970. The Federal Hill Park site was to be temporary, with plans for the monument to be re-sited somewhere along the water's edge.

Luckily for the city and for this old soldier, Major General Smith has remained in his perch, high above the harbor and near a much earlier monument honoring Col. George Armistead, with whom he fought in the War of 1812. Armistead was the commander at Fort McHenry when the British fleet attacked on September 13, 1814, during the battle of Baltimore. The architectural firm of G. Metzger designed this monument in 1882. The outline of Armistead's career is inscribed on the shaft of the column, whose cornice is surmounted by a ball banded with stars. This monument was sited in Eutaw Place until residents complained about the scale of the piece and it was moved to Federal Hill. A second monument, a heroic bronze portrait statue of Armistead by Edward Berge, is sited at Fort McHenry, seen later on this tour (G17). This later Armistead monument was the fifth piece of sculpture commissioned in 1914 to commemorate the centennial of the defense of Baltimore, and the Francis Scott Key monument, also at Fort McHenry (G18), was the sixth.

G3

TITLE
Whirligig, 1995

LOCATION
American Visionary Art Museum, 800 Key Highway

SCULPTOR
Vollis Simpson (b. 1919)

MEDIUM
Found metal objects

DONOR
Ryda H. Levi in memory of her husband,
Robert H. Levi

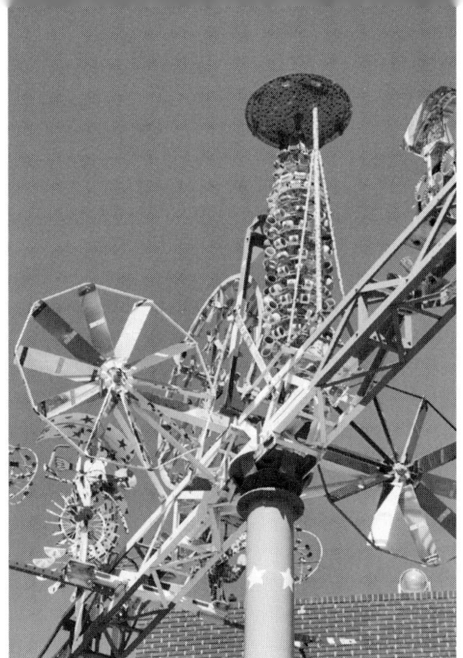

Vollis Simpson's monumental, multicolored, wind-powered sculpture, which stands 55 feet tall and spins in the harbor breezes, was commissioned for the American Visionary Art Museum (AVAM) by its founding director, Rebecca Hoffberger. Its installation coincided with the opening of the new museum in November 1995. Simpson created the whirligig as a salute to Federal Hill, which overlooks the museum, and to life, liberty, and the pursuit of happiness.

AVAM is the national museum for "outsider" art, or art made by self-taught artists. Fittingly, the first commission went to Simpson, a retired mechanic, farmer and visionary artist from Lucama, North Carolina, about fifty miles east of Raleigh. Simpson made his living repairing trucks and farm machinery and designing and building equipment to move buildings. He accumulated tons of miscellaneous machine parts over the years, and since his retirement in 1985 he has been welding them together just for the fun of it to see how they would move in the wind. His work can also be seen at the North Carolina Museum of Art in Raleigh and near the Courtland Avenue Bridge in Atlanta, for which he was commissioned to create four sculptures for display during the 1996 Olympics. But the best place to see his whirligigs is on his farm in Lucama, where as many as two dozen, some more than 40 feet high, are installed in the fields and pastures.

Simpson is a master recycler. For his piece at AVAM, like all his earlier pieces, he has welded or bolted together highway signs and reflectors, bicycle wheels, model airplanes and airplane propellers, oil filters, tin cans, pinwheels large and small, milkshake canisters, air filter cups, old saucepans and other kitchen appliances, and scrap metal cutouts of animals (there's a Cheshire cat up there) and implements like wheel barrels that Simpson has fashioned himself. All these objects are arranged along a large crossbeam mounted atop a tall pivot pole that once stood at an Exxon gas station. As the crossbeam turns in the wind, so does almost everything attached to it. And it is all perfectly balanced! He is more than a master recycler; he is a brilliant engineer. Simpson's explanation for what he has been doing since he retired is simple: "I just had a lot of material out there. Had to do something with it."

The daytime experience of the whirligig is very different from the nighttime experience. The red, white, and blue with splashes of yellow give way, as the sun sets and the car headlights are turned on, to the reflectors attached to elements all over the piece. The wind also changes the experience. Planted 13 feet into the ground, the whirligig has withstood 80-mile-an-hour winds. Overcast days with light winds are the best for viewing this piece.

G4

TITLE
AVAM Nest, 2004

LOCATION
American Visionary Art Museum, 800 Key Highway

SCULPTOR
David Hess (b. 1964)

MEDIUM
Stainless steel

DONOR
American Visionary Art Museum

This may be the only balcony in Baltimore that is made out of 6,000 linear feet of hollow stainless steel pipe. It may also be the only balcony that doubles, visually at least, as a bird's nest.

When AVAM acquired the old whiskey warehouse next door, it gutted it and with Cho, Benn Holback + Associates created an addition named the Jim Rouse Visionary Center, after the Baltimore visionary urban planner and real estate developer James Rouse (1914-96) whose crowning achievement in the 1960s was the planned community of Columbia, Maryland, which was followed by the creation of festival markets like Quincy Market in Boston and Harborplace in Baltimore and the Enterprise Foundation to make affordable housing available across the country. This addition, which houses new gallery space, an education center, offices, and conference rooms, more than doubled the museum's footprint at the base of Federal Hill.

The space in between these two buildings was developed into an entrance plaza with a bird theme. David Hess created the *AVAM Nest* as a work of art that not only fit into the larger plaza environment with Dr. Evermor's 40-foot-high *Phoenix* (G5) and Andrew Logan's *Cosmic Galaxy Egg* (G6) nearby but also functions as a balcony for the new three-story building.

The sculpture is made out of three hundred 20-foot lengths of stainless steel pipe of differing diameters that have been braided together, some mechanically, to give a natural effect, on a gigantic scale, of a nest of twigs woven together by birds. The patina was chosen to add to the realistic effect. The nest was designed to fit over the concrete floor and the metal framework for the balcony and wrap around the outer railing.

Hess has been involved in projects at AVAM since it opened in 1995. He was first asked to design the interior, curving staircase for the main building, which he fabricated out of twisted steel pickets bound by a bronze railing. Other projects included the AVAM gates outside and the chandeliers on all three floors in the addition.

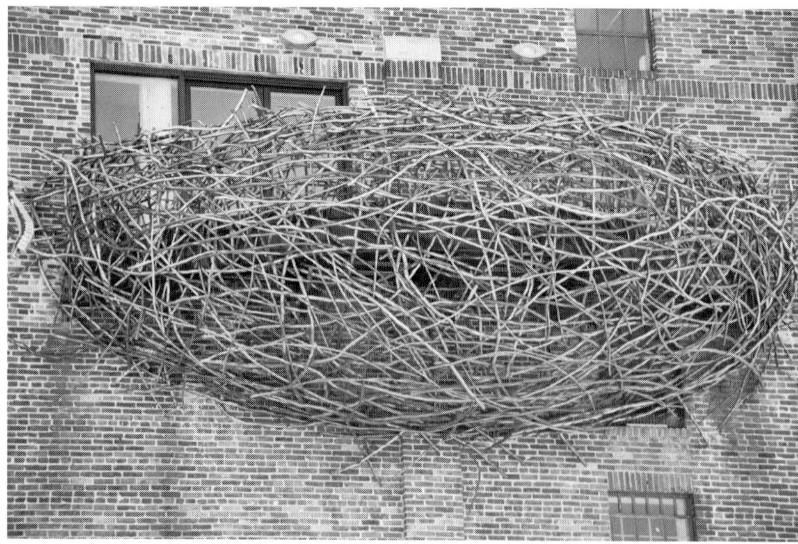

G5

TITLE
Phoenix, 1997

LOCATION
American Visionary Art Museum, 800 Key Highway

SCULPTOR
Dr. Evermor (b. 1938)

MEDIUM
Found metal objects

DONOR
American Visionary Art Museum

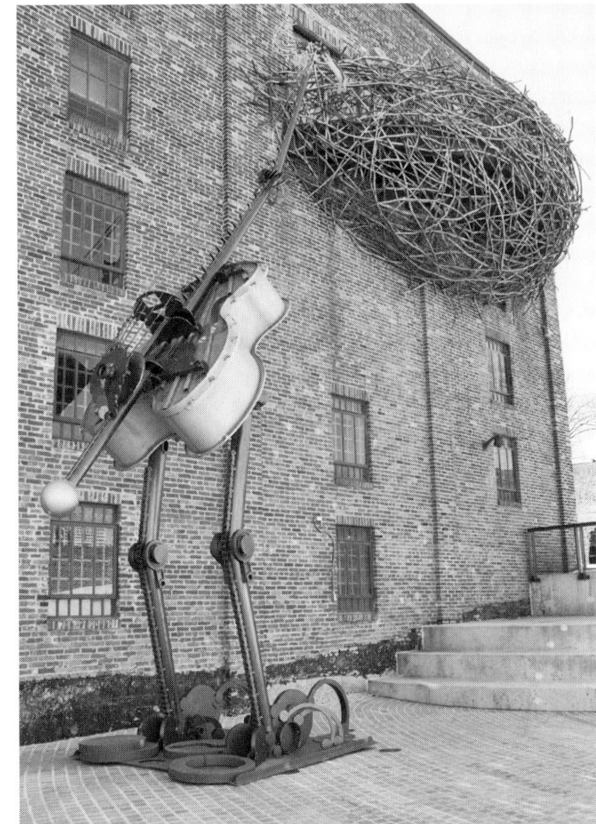

This 40-foot-high bird stands right up against the Jim Rouse Visionary Center on two long spindly-looking legs. Facing the *AVAM Nest,* three stories up, the bird extends its head and very long neck up to the nest as if it were trying to peer in.

This is a "miniature" sculpture by the visionary artist known as Dr. Evermor, from Baraboo, Wisconsin. After spending more than three decades as an industrial wrecker, working at manufacturing sites like breweries, mills, and factories that had become commercially outmoded, Tom Every began questioning his role in the destruction of all these sites. In 1983 he gave his wrecking business to a son, renamed himself Dr. Evermor, and began building the now legendary 300-ton *Forevertron.* Constructed out of industrial artifacts, including an x-ray machine, old carburetors, a fast-food sign, scrap generators, and old thrusters, the *Forevertron* measures 50 feet high, 120 feet wide, and 60 feet deep.

The *Forevertron* can be seen at the Evermor Sculpture Park, in New Freedom, Wisconsin, just south of Baraboo, where hundreds of his creations can be seen. One of the big attractions there is a multi-member *Bird Band,* from which *Phoenix* was plucked in 2005. Dr. Evermor claims that it is the only bird band in the world. Many of the birds were crafted out of brass bedposts, old tools and other hardware, gear chains, survey markers, and gasoline nozzles. This bird was made out of a Hubbard tank, an automobile-sized metal vessel once used by doctors to provide hydrotherapy to polio patients. The shape of the tank reminded Dr. Evermor of a guitar, to which he then added some conveyor-belt parts, cables, and other found objects. Some of the birds actually make music, such as the ones whose frames incorporate chimes or cymbals. This piece, like many other *Bird Band* members, looks like a giant string instrument, with strings extending from the back of its head to its midsection. Industrial wreckage never looked so good.

G6

TITLE
Cosmic Galaxy Egg, 2004

LOCATION
American Visionary Art Museum, 800 Key Highway

SCULPTOR
Andrew Logan (b. 1945)

MEDIUM
Bronze, shell, colored glass, and fiberglass

DONOR
American Visionary Art Museum

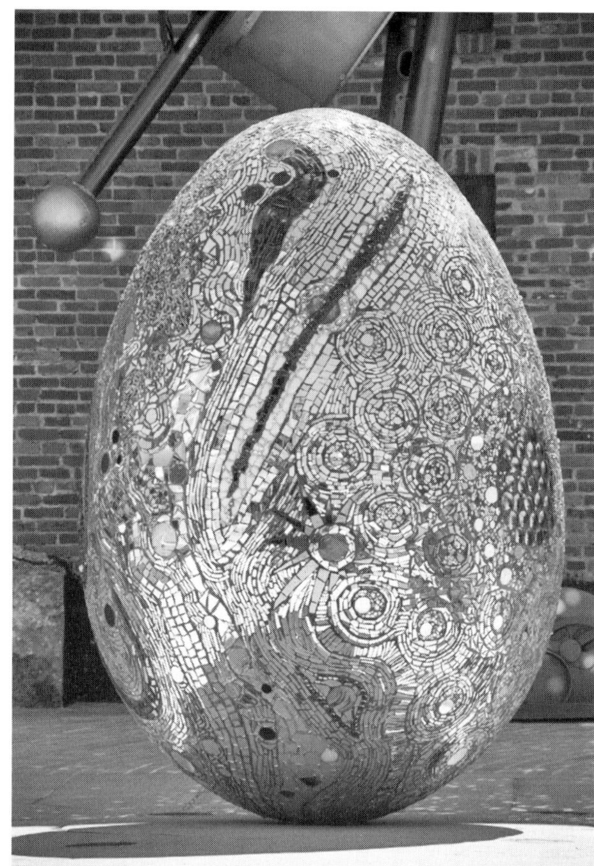

This sculpture is a smaller version of Andrew Logan's 15-foot-high *Cosmic Egg,* which was fabricated in 1983 and can be seen today in the Andrew Logan Museum of Sculpture in Welshpool, Wales, the only museum in Europe dedicated to the work of a living artist. The Baltimore version of Logan's fantastic, glittering, mirrored egg, while standing only 8 feet high, nonetheless displays the exuberant excess for which Logan's work is known.

The designs on the surface of this egg were inspired by pictures of deep space posted on the Web site of the Hubble Space Telescope. These images, converted by the Space Telescope Science Institute at the Johns Hopkins University in Baltimore from Hubble data into images that people can view on line, are of amazingly colorful planets, stars, nebulae, galaxies, and more.

The British sculptor Andrew Logan has worked in the fields of decoration, sculpture, stage, drama, opera, parades, and festivals. He won fame in 1972 as the founder of the alternative Miss World competition, in which men and women compete on equal terms. Logan had been a friend of Divine's for many years when he invited Divine to participate in one of the early alternative Miss World competitions. Today Logan's statue of Divine is part of AVAM's permanent collection. Divine was the drag persona of Harris Glenn Milkstead (1945–88), an actor and singer who stared in several John Waters films, including *Pink Flamingos, Female Trouble,* and *Polyester.*

A third piece of sculpture by Logan in the museum's permanent collection is *Black Icarus,* a less than traditional representation of the ill-fated Greek legend about a boy who flies too close to the sun. Visible from Key Highway at night, *Black Icarus* is raised and lowered mechanically through the hollow of the main stairwell of the museum. Logan covered Icarus' wings in colored glass and mirror mosaic, and he used a similar approach for the surface of the *Cosmic Galaxy Egg.*

G7

TITLE
Fountain Heads, 1988–2003

LOCATION
American Visionary Art Museum, 800 Key Highway

SCULPTOR
Ted Ludwiczak (b. 1927)

MEDIUM
Stone

DONORS
Gift of the artist and American Visionary
Art Museum

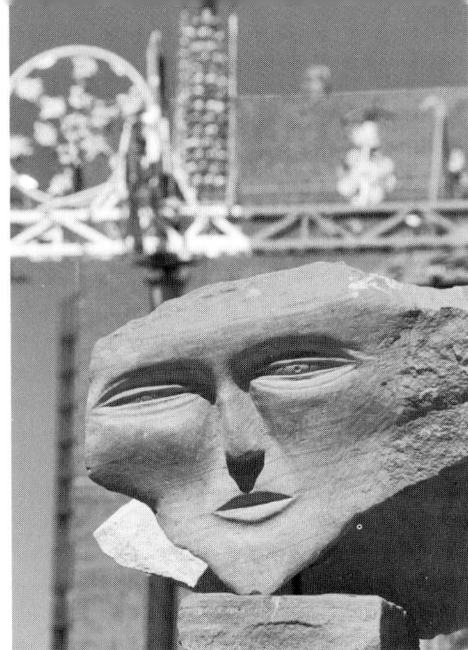

Theodore "Ted" Ludwiczak immigrated to New York City from his native Poland in 1956. In New York, he learned to grind contact lenses and ran his own business until his retirement in 1986. After his wife died in 1988, he moved to Haverstraw-on-the-Hudson to be near his daughter. It was there that he began carving stone heads.

He built a retaining wall on his property along the Hudson River, but when he completed it, he thought it looked bare. Looking around, he noticed on the beach a large rock in which he saw a face. He thought he could see eyes and maybe even a mouth. So using an old, bent lawn mower blade he went to work, following the shape of the stone, and carved a face in the rock. He added it to his retaining wall. The one stone head looked lonely, so he made another. He has continued adding heads ever since. Today the retaining wall is literally covered with stone faces, carved mostly out of the red sandstone found on the riverbank.

Ludwiczak's house and property also are covered by his carved stone heads. Ranging in height from 6 inches to more than 4 feet, they are carved from red sandstone, which he used for the earliest heads, as well as from granite from an abandoned quarry nearby, white limestone, marble from Vermont, and even stone curbing he saved after the city replaced the old curbing on his street. All the stone he uses is found, and all his tools are rudimentary, either found or made by him. In addition to his lawn mower blade, he has used a railroad spike and a simple hammer.

Ludwiczak does not part with his heads easily. He would really like to keep them all. He says he needs an extended period of time with each before he can part with it and feels guilty each time he lets one go. He considers them part of his family, and families don't like to be split up.

So how did AVAM get so many faces for the creation of this water feature? In October 2003, twenty-seven of Ludwiczak's carved stone heads were included in the annual exhibition at AVAM, titled Golden Blessings of Old Age / Out of the Mouths of Babes. When the exhibition ended in September 2004, seventeen heads were returned to him; he had donated five, and the museum purchased five. The ten stone heads, each about 2 feet high, were installed on a wall over which water cascades. The resulting fountain was a partnership between AVAM and the TKF Foundation, a private grant-making foundation that funds the creation of public sanctuaries and green spaces to connect people to the natural world. The bench installed near this fountain is an integral part of the sacred space that TKF has helped to create. The fountain was begun in the fall of 2007 and was completed in the spring of 2008.

TITLE
Meditation/Wedding Chapel, 1996
LOCATION
American Visionary Art Museum, 800 Key Highway
SCULPTOR
Ben Wilson (b. 1963)
MEDIUM
Wood
DONOR
American Visionary Art Museum

For Ben Wilson, one of Britain's most outstanding outsider artists, spontaneity is the key to his process of making art and spontaneity is only possible in an atmosphere of freedom. Wilson has felt this way since his days as a young art student, when he rejected the constraints of the classroom and chose instead to work on the college grounds to make his first major work of art, a massive human figure and chair out of wood he had collected. Today his work is found in many countries around the world, but in unexpected woodland settings, rarely in galleries or museums.

Understandably, then, Wilson finds it hard to work on commission. He feels that his process would be compromised by giving a completion date or even providing a description of what the finished work might look like. When he begins work on a new project, Wilson has no idea when he will finish or what form the piece will take. Wilson believes that the process of making the piece is the experiment and that if you already know what it is going to be, then there's no reason to do it.

So it was quite remarkable that Wilson agreed to come to Baltimore to make one of his vast wooden constructions, which it was hoped would be completed in time for the November 24 opening of the new visionary art museum. It is probably less remarkable that the piece was not finished on schedule.

The inaugural exhibition was The Tree of Life, featuring four hundred works created from wood and tree products that celebrated man's connection with nature. It was the curator of the exhibition, the folklorist Roger Manly, who approached Wilson about making a piece for the museum that could also be included in the exhibition. Wilson approached building this complex environment as he always had—with no idea of the end result. He did not set out to build a meditation/wedding chapel; that is how the museum has defined the structure. The giant wildflowers, aromatics, and climbing vines that encircle the structure were added later. Working with complete freedom—with the "power of no idea," as Wilson puts it—he spent long hours on site during very cold weather (from October to January, three and a half months total). The wood he used he had gathered from the city stump dump, behind the zoo; from Sandy Point State Park, where driftwood was available; and from a Cromwell Valley property in northern Baltimore County, where he found many fallen branches. The wood was a mix of red oak, yellow oak, poplar, cedar, polonia, and locust. With the many smooth wooden pieces he either carved or used as found, he built a structure that spreads horizontally along the back garden wall. The tall entrance leads past one small side chamber, which has seating, to a stairway that rises gradually and culminates in a slightly larger end chamber with seating and three windowlike openings. Wilson crafted a covering for this chamber that is arched and constructed out of short, smooth pieces of wood arranged in a series of

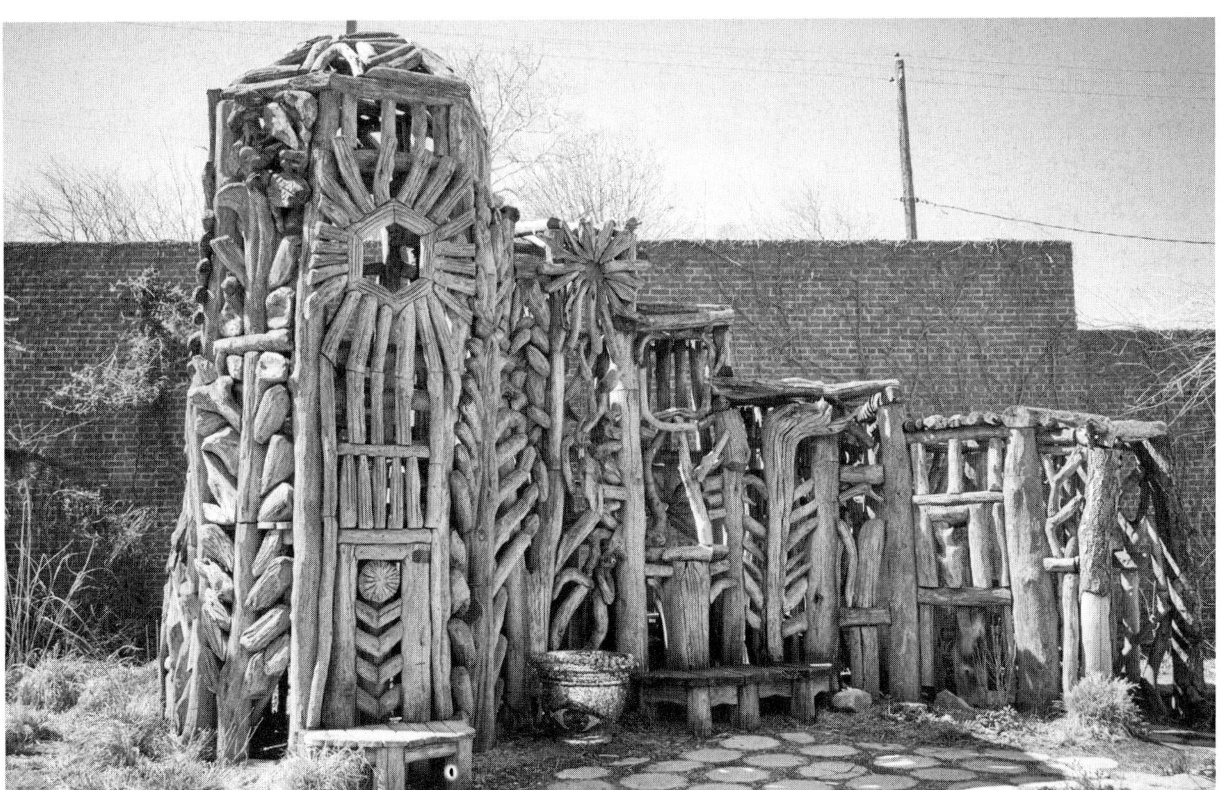

triangular openings that reveal the sky beyond. From the ground entrance to the highest point of the structure, which is reached in the end chamber, the structure increases gradually in height, and each level is covered with wooden pieces arranged to give a sense of protection and enclosure but also to reveal the sky. Included in the walls of the structure are arrangements of wooden pieces that look like a flower or a face, and the steps are scored with designs. The experience of being in the structure is one of being transported to a magical place that offers a sense of calm as well as a sense of mystery. Looking out from the structure, one sees, among other things, Vollis Simpson's *Whirligig*, which was going up at the same time.

Today Ben Wilson lives and works in Muswell Hill, in North London. He has been called a lay naturalist because of his longstanding approach to art in woodland settings and his concern for those environments. Wilson has a mischievous streak, expressed by his covering over billboards with bold white murals of figures and trees. These illegal paintings were his protest against billboards that disturb nature and against advertisers' categorizing people. But after one too many entanglements with the law over his spontaneous mural

paintings, Wilson began a new body of work—miniature paintings made on discarded chewing gum in situ. This activity is not illegal and does not require prior permission, so he can work spontaneously, as he has always preferred. All along the High Streets of Barnet, where he grew up, and Muswell Hill, where he now lives, Wilson has been painting tiny masterpieces, of faces, animals, flowers, suns, abstract designs, and often of something specifically requested of him. The chewing-gum paintings began as an act of protest against all the rubbish and waste that has become part of urban society. Now the paintings seem to be a way to connect people, including himself, more closely to their surroundings and give them a sense of place.

Wilson's work has been included in a few recent exhibitions. In 2000 his work was included in the exhibition Art Without Precedent: Nine Artists from the Musgrave Kinley Outsider Art Collection, which is on indefinite loan to the Irish Museum of Modern Art. In 2001 his work was part of the exhibition Obsessive Visions: Art Outside the Mainstream, at England & Company, a London gallery, and in 2008 his work was selected for the major exhibition of British outsider art at the Musée La Halle Saint Pierre in Paris.

G9

TITLE
Critters, 1982–2006

LOCATION
American Visionary Art Museum, 800 Key Highway

SCULPTOR
Clyde Jones (b. 1938)

MEDIUM
Painted wood

DONOR
Gift of the artist

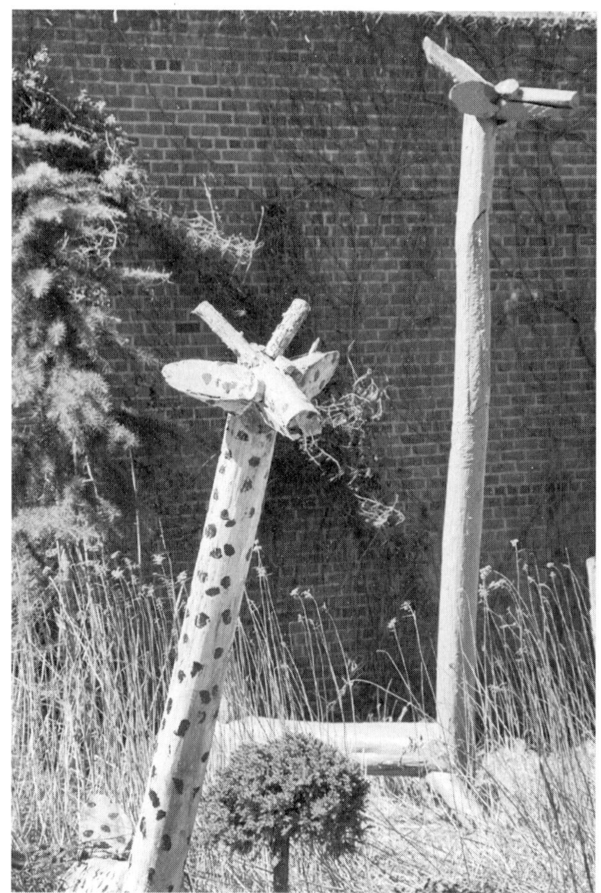

Clyde Jones is known for his critters and his paintings. He lives in Bynum, North Carolina, just south of Chapel Hill, where hundreds of these critters can be seen—in and around Carrboro and Chapel Hill and at his home.

Jones was a laborer and logger at a nearby mill until 1979, when he severely injured himself with a chainsaw. In 1982, during a long convalescence, he began making critters and painting. He uses log remnants and large root stumps from hickory and ash trees that grow along the Haw River, which flows nearby. Jones makes these animals, often referred to as Haw River critters, out of four or five pieces of found hickory and ash wood, which he cuts quickly with his chain saw and nails together, with or without paint. There are signs around Bynum that read "Haw River Critter Crossing."

Eight of these critters were exhibited at AVAM in its exhibition Home and Beast, which ran from October 2006 to September 2007. Afterwards Jones made a gift of two of his critters—these two giraffes—to the museum's permanent collection. Seeing a resemblance between the two requires imagination. One is painted yellow with spots, the other Carolina blue. Both have long necks, short bodies, stubby legs, and two horns between their short, broad ears. And they exude a whimsical charm and innocence that is completely disarming.

It is said of Jones that he is in his element with a pile of wood at his feet and a chain saw in his hands.

With a mill house on his property, that is how he is most often found. His work has been shown at the Sawtooth School for Visual Art and at the Southeastern Center for Contemporary Art, both in Winston Salem, North Carolina; in the New Orleans Museum of Art; and at the North Carolina Museum of Art in Raleigh.

G10

TITLE

Universal Tree of Life, 2005–2007

LOCATION

American Visionary Art Museum, 800 Key Highway

SCULPTOR

Bob Benson (b. 1930)

MEDIA

Double-sided mirrors, stained glass, steel, and concrete

DONOR

Gift of the artist

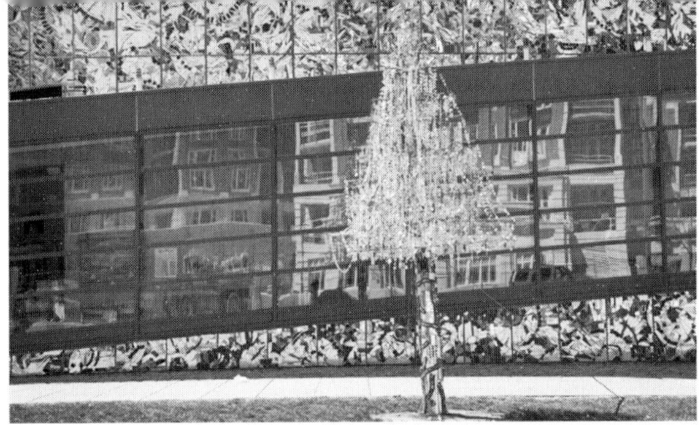

What does a man do after he retires from a long and successful career in arts administration, public radio, and music criticism? If that man is Bob Benson, who was the director of community development at the Maryland State Arts Council for two decades, host of a classical music program at WJHU-FM for ten years after working at WFDS-FM, WBAL-FM, and WBJC-FM, and a writer of music criticism for several publications, he makes art with mirrors.

Since a 2004 trip to the Lower Eastern Shore, where he saw a simple string of double-sided mirrors attached to a filament swinging in the breeze, reflecting the sun, Benson has been making what he calls "mirror art." This piece, located outside at AVAM, is one of three major mirror-art projects Benson has done for AVAM. The two others are inside the museum, and both are associated with *Black Icarus* by Andrew Logan (see G6), which is mechanically raised and lowered in the main hallway of the museum. *Oceanus* symbolically represents the ocean Icarus fell into after flying too close to the sun, and Benson's newest addition, *The Sun,* 5 feet in diameter, is made from thousands of pieces of red-, gold-, and silver-colored mirror; it hangs just below the mechanism that raises and lowers *Icarus.* Benson also created a 17-foot-wide *Mirror Tapestry* for the bar in Mr. Rain's Fun House, the restaurant that opened in AVAM in 2010.

The *Universal Tree of Life* was not the first tree Benson made for AVAM. In 2005 Benson was invited to decorate a live oak tree just outside the museum's entrance on Key Highway. His decorations included strands of quarter-inch double-sided mirrors of various lengths attached to 50-pound filament, which he calls "flashies," as well as objects made out of brilliantly colored double-sided mirrors and stained glass, called "mirror creations." The latter might be discs of varying sizes with images of butterflies, crabs, and unnamed creatures. The tree died the following year. Benson decorated a second tree, which was planted near the site of the first tree. The second tree died from termite infestation, which may also have been the cause of the demise of the first tree. It was decided that the third tree should be made entirely of metal and mirrors to avoid further termite problems!

The *Universal Tree of Life* is a collaboration between Benson and his neighbor, the sculptor Rick Ames, who also collaborated with Benson on *Oceanus.* In 2005 Benson decided he wanted a Christmas tree for his front yard, so he engaged Ames to weld a metal frame and branches for a tree that he would then decorate with his double-sided mirrors. The upper part of this tree—the top 8 feet—stood in Benson's front yard for almost three years. In the fall of 2007 it was decided to move the tree to AVAM, but this relocation necessitated certain modifications. A 7-foot trunk and three lower branches were added to the original tree, as were many new "flashies" and "mirror creations," especially new colored ones. Today the tree stands 21 feet tall, and the new trunk is wrapped in mirrors with a meandering vine decoration. In the wind, the sound of the tree, with all its limbs laden with dangling mirrors, is as engaging as the view.

G11

TITLE
Bicycle Man, date unknown

LOCATION
American Visionary Art Museum, 800 Key Highway

SCULPTOR
Vollis Simpson (b. 1919)

MEDIUM
Found metal objects

DONOR
Gift of the artist

Vollis Simpson just called it *Bicycle Man.* It had been included in the museum's 1996 exhibition titled Wind in My Hair, and afterwards it was permanently installed in its present lofty site over Key Highway. The wedge-shaped part of the building below the sculpture will be covered in mosaics during the next phase of the youth apprenticeships, in which young people have covered other areas of the museum's facade in mosaics. The figure in *Bicycle Man,* which is constructed out of found objects and scrap metal in much the same way as his *Whirligig* (G3), can be seen magically balancing himself on a machine modeled after a unicycle. He rests only on days when there is no breeze. In profile, the handlebars, a basket, the large front wheel, and the small back wheel can be clearly seen.

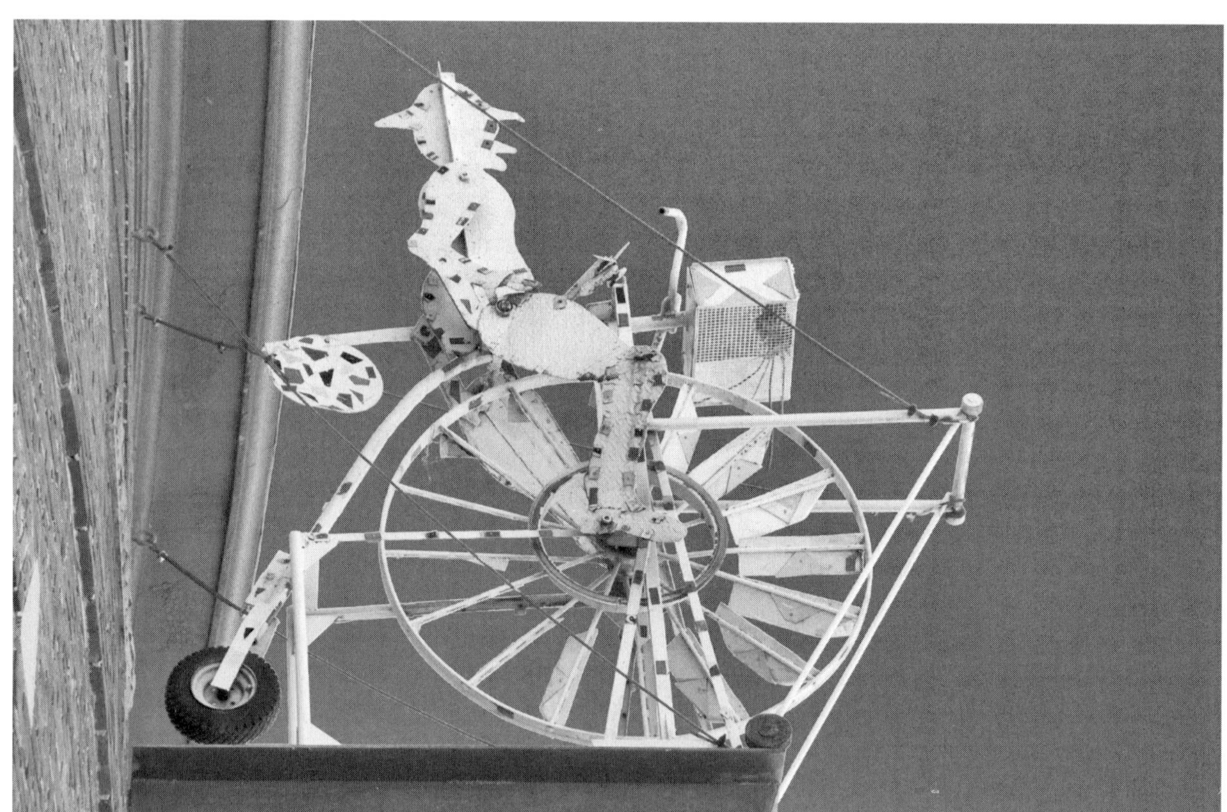

G12

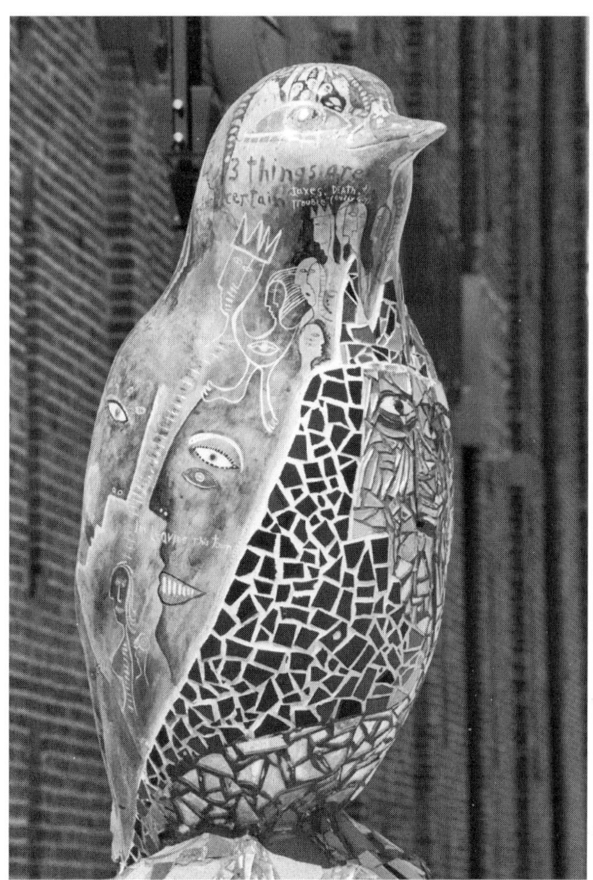

If you think you have seen this bird before, you may have. Originally titled *Outsider Bluebird II*—the first *Outsider Bluebird* was vandalized—this second bluebird stood for three months, from August to October 2003, at the intersection of Rhode Island Avenue and 34th Street in Mt. Rainier, Maryland. It was part of a public art project in Prince George's County called Birds I View, in which seventy-four 5-foot-high fiberglass forms modeled on the eastern bluebird, the county's official bird, were designed by regional artists. This public art program, like the crabs in Baltimore and the cows in Chicago, culminated in a reception and live auction of the birds to benefit arts in education in Prince George's County. Dick Brown bid on his own bird and gave it to the American Visionary Art Museum. AVAM's *Bluebird of Happiness,* renamed by the founding director, Rebecca Hoffberger, is perched on a wall that runs along Key Highway just south of the new Jim Rouse Visionary Center. It is the first artwork in the museum's permanent collection that visitors see when they arrive from Interstate 95.

Dick Brown has a PhD in counseling psychology and has an active practice in Baltimore. He was trained as a wood sculptor in Texas and studied bronze casting at Prince George's Community College, but it is as a self-taught painter and mosaicist that he has been most active recently. This sculpture is his first effort at combining mosaics and painting. He has used a variety of recycled materials: mirrors, stained glass, broken china, pieces of glazed pottery and tiles. Most of the painted surface areas are covered in abstracted heads shown in profile. He thinks that his professional focus on real people's heads and what is inside them explains why he is fascinated artistically with painted heads. The inscriptions written on the bluebird refer to blues songs, which Brown says he often listens to as he is making art. "3 things are certain taxes, death and trouble (Buddy Guy)" is a line from Buddy Guy's song "Trouble Man." Quotations from two other favorite blues songs also appear on the bird: "I'm Leaving this town" and "Morals matter."

G13

TITLE
Golden Hand of God, 2004

SCULPTOR
Adam Kurtzman (b. 1957)

LOCATION
American Visionary Art Museum, 800 Key Highway

MEDIA
Fiberglass and metal leaf

DONOR
Patrick Hughes

When the renovation was being planned that would expand the American Visionary Art Museum by creating the Jim Rouse Visionary Center out of the an old whiskey warehouse, there were plans to have a movie screen held up by a couple of "hands of God" on the Collington Street side of the building, which faces Federal Hill. In the tradition of Little Italy's *cinema paradiso,* people would be invited to use the east side of Federal Hill as a natural amphitheater from which to watch AVAM's movie presentations.

AVAM founding director, Rebecca Hoffberger, invited a Los Angeles–based sculptor to tackle this problem. Adam Kurtzman decided that one hand would be best and set about making a hand large enough to have a real presence on that side of the building. First he created a 15-foot-high hand out of papier-mâché. He then covered it in a half-inch layer of fiberglass, eventually removing the papier-mâché. The hand is hollow and relatively lightweight. The gold leaf has tarnished to a handsome patina, golden but not the blinding gold it was when first installed. Visually the hand appears to hold the 35-foot-wide movie screen between thumb and forefinger.

Kurtzman maintains a studio in Los Angeles' historic Brewery Building, where he works in papier-mâché, bronze, and glass. This was the first time he had worked on such a large scale, and he says that he looks at the world a little differently now. His work has been exhibited in New York, Los Angeles, San Francisco, and San Diego. He is represented by Blackman+Cruz in Los Angeles and by galleries in San Francisco and Chicago.

AVAM shows family films during the summer on eight consecutive Thursday nights at 9:00 p.m., when it is good and dark. Flicks from The Hill Summer usually begins in July and runs through August.

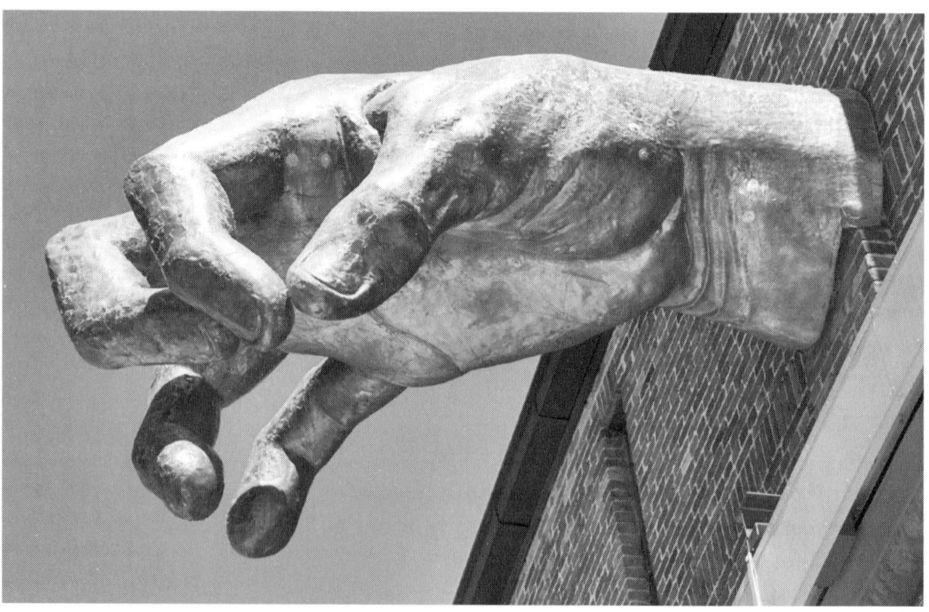

G14

TITLE
Untitled, 1978

LOCATION
Digital Harbor High School, 1100 Covington Street

SCULPTOR
David von Schlegell (1920–1992)

MEDIUM
Painted aluminum

DONOR
Baltimore City Percent for Art program

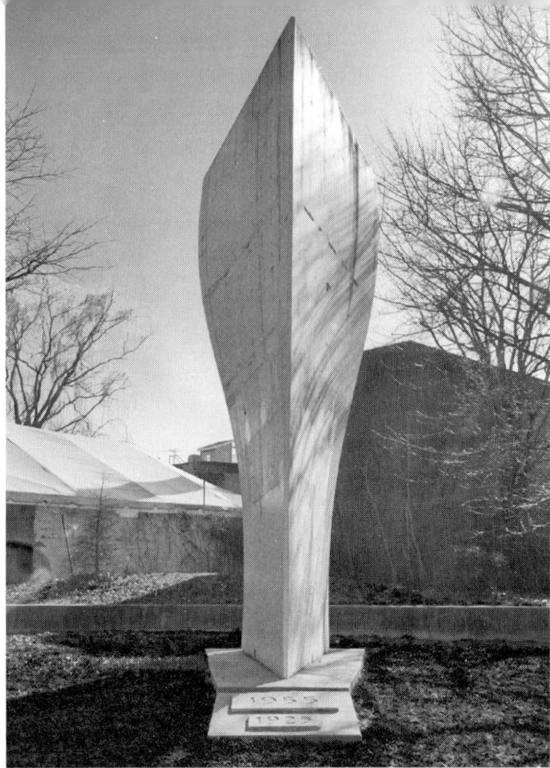

Originally sited on a plaza in front of Southern High School (renovated and renamed Digital Harbor High School in 2002), which once offered a panoramic view of Baltimore's harbor, this 26-foot-high abstract sculpture by David von Schlegell made a direct reference to the prow of a ship. The scale and simplicity of its form and the boldness of the artist's choice of color—white— were striking when one stood in that plaza beside the sleek, tall, broad sides of the sculpture or looked up at it from Collington Street or from Key Highway. Unfortunately, during the school's renovation, von Schlegell's sculpture was moved to the back of the facility. Today it can be reached more directly from East Cross Street.

Von Schlegell's Baltimore piece is thought to be his first painted public sculpture. Earlier pieces were on the same heroic scale and clearly referenced ships, but none had been painted. The question of why von Schlegell chose to continue his use of nautical references in Baltimore, especially for a site that overlooked the harbor, is easily answered, but there may be more interesting and personal reasons for the form and color of this piece. Von Schlegell loved Herman Melville. He owned a boat named *Whitejacket,* the title of one of Melville's novels. Von Schlegell had read *Moby Dick* and often referred to the "whiteness of the whale," a powerful symbol that may have influenced his choice of color for this piece.

Born in St. Louis, von Schlegell studied painting at the Art Students League in New York before turning to sculpture in the 1960s. In 1966 his work was included in Primary Structures at the Jewish Museum, an exhibition that helped establish minimalism; works by Isaac Witkin (E5) and Ronald Bladen (E6) were also included. In 1971 he was appointed director of graduate studies in sculpture at Yale University, where he taught until his retirement in 1990. His work is in the permanent collections of major museums and sculpture parks across the country, including the Whitney Museum of Art in New York, the Hirshhorn Museum in Washington, D.C., the DeCordova Museum and Sculpture Garden in Lincoln, Massachusetts, the Storm King Art Center in Mountainville, New York, and the Laumeier Sculpture Park in St. Louis. During the 1970s and 1980s he completed more than thirty public commissions for cities across the country, from New Haven to Miami to Sacramento. The commission that immediately preceded the Baltimore commission is his most celebrated piece, *Voyage of Ulysses,* a fountain sculpture at the James A. Byrne Federal Courthouse in Philadelphia. The Philadelphia and Baltimore pieces are clearly related in their scale, their minimalism, and their reference to ships. The architect of Southern High School, Hoult Verkerke, of the firm SCV, chose von Schlegell for the Baltimore commission.

G15

TITLE
Working Point, 1997

LOCATION
Baltimore Museum of Industry, 1415 Key Highway

SCULPTOR
David Hess (b. 1964)

MEDIA
Steel, stainless steel, and cast-iron found and
fabricated parts and concrete

DONOR
Municipal Art Society of Baltimore City

This sculpture by David Hess may represent the most
imaginative use of 90 tons of industrial equipment.
Commissioned in 1990 by the first director of the Baltimore Museum of Industry, Dennis Zembala, Hess
made a model of a sculpture that would document the
rapidly disappearing industrial heritage of Baltimore,
which had been the mission of the museum since it
was founded in 1977. Then he spent seven years driving around Baltimore, to old industrial sites and behind
abandoned industrial buildings, collecting the heavier
industrial materials, which he identified on the basis
of shape.

Hess wanted the piece to resemble a large toy,
maybe even a dangerous toy. He wanted it to appear as if
the huge old crane from Dundalk, already on site, could
pick up and move his sculpture, and he chose its specific location accordingly. Hess also wanted this toy—or,
alternatively, a giant creature that had just crawled up
from the harbor and stretched out on land, or maybe
even just a pile of industrial junk—to appear to be stuck
on a turntable. The turntable idea led Hess to design
the circular angled landscape around the piece. The tilt-
ing turntable creates a wonderful sense of anticipation,
suggesting that the toy, or creature, or junk pile, might
topple over, and then what would that look like? The
setting had become a kind of anti-plaza, which seemed
perfect for the industrial museum.

The easiest industrial parts to identify are those
that have been arranged on the turntable. They are a
ship propeller, a ship anchor chain, and an anchor
shank, the piece that takes the chain and digs into the
mud at the bottom to secure the ship. For the large central sculpture Hess used eighteen large found industrial elements, some of which are easier to identify
than others. The pole that reaches far into the air is
an old cast-iron street lamppost. The large sphere just
below it is a hollow boat mooring, 6 feet in diameter,
which was originally attached to a ship's anchor chain
and floated on the water's surface. The cone is a hop-
per from Rhone Planck, a chemical company in Curtis Bay, that was used for mixing chemicals. There are
two giant flywheels from a paper company and a roller
mill from Lee High Cement Company that was used for
crushing rock. There is even a boiler from the National
Bohemian Brewery Company, which operated long ago
in Baltimore. The piece at the easternmost end, which
looks like either the claw of the toy or the mouth of the
creature, is a big alligator sheer from Cambridge Iron
and Metal, which would have been used to cut into
bite-size pieces all the nonferrous metal that scrappers
brought in as junk.

The title of the piece may have more than one
meaning. As stated on a plaque nearby, the working
point is that point on a construction drawing that is
used as a reference for all the other measurements and
calculations. Surely, Hess needed to calculate all the
loads accurately off just such a point to construct this
magically balanced sculpture. And the title probably
also makes reference to Locust Point, an industrial part
of town where working points were always needed. The
title may also be shorthand for a series of questions: Are
you working? Why? What's the point?

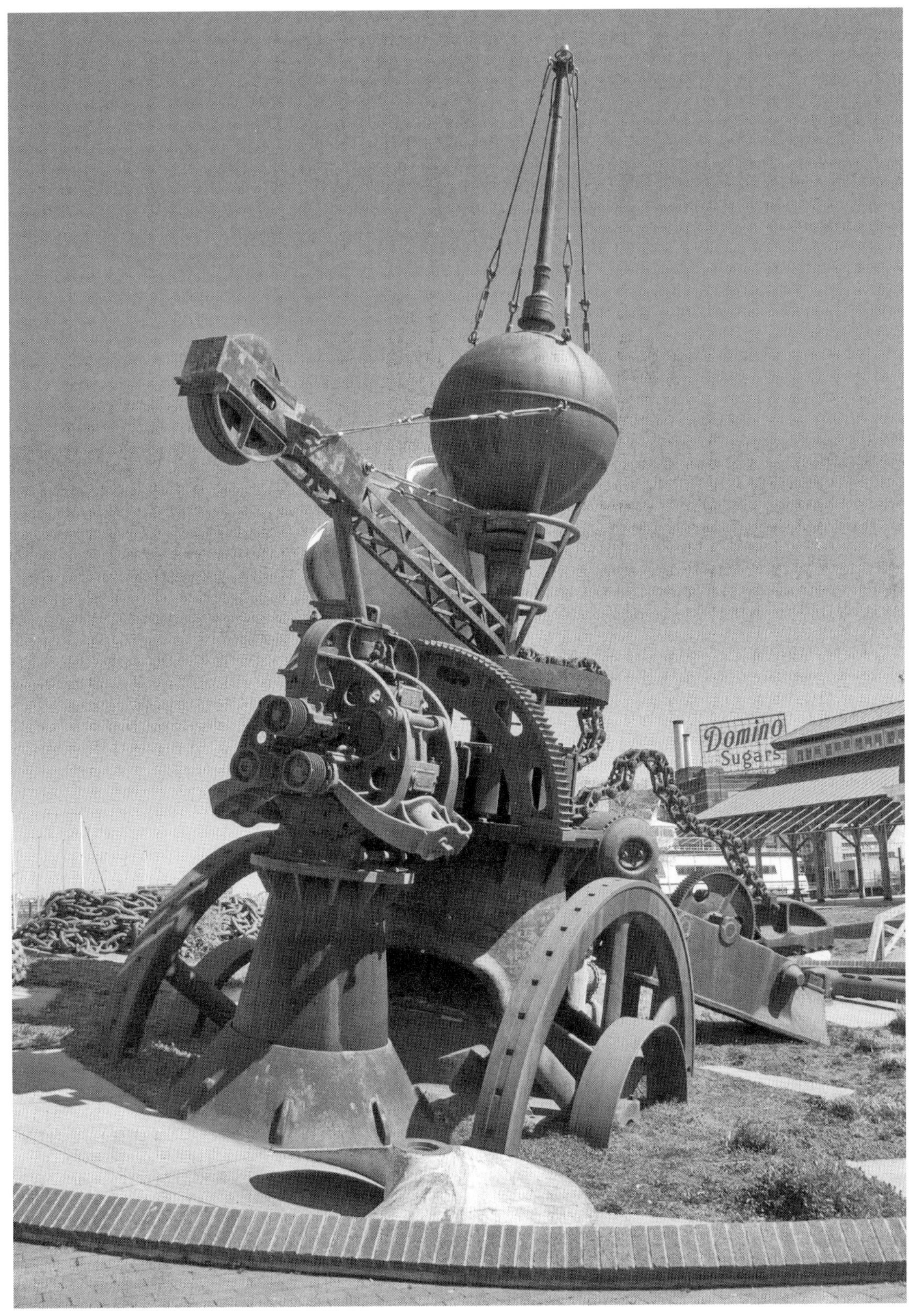
Domino
Sugars

G16

TITLE
Untitled, 1988

LOCATION
Francis Scott Key Elementary School,
1425 E. Fort Avenue

SCULPTOR
John D. McCarty (b. 1940)

MEDIUM
Painted steel

DONOR
Baltimore City Percent for Art program

Anthony M. Mileto, the architect who had recently been awarded a contract to build the new Francis Scott Key Elementary School, saw an exhibition of new, large abstract steel sculpture by John McCarty in the spring of 1985 at the C. Grimaldis Gallery in Baltimore. Mileto admired the work and invited McCarty to propose an outdoor sculpture for the new school. McCarty presented a maquette for the piece and won the commission, signing a contract later in 1985.

After several delays the new school was completed and the piece could be installed in the open plaza area in front of the school. The 20-foot-high piece was fabricated by the artist out of new steel, not constructed out of found objects, as might be first surmised. The two vertical pipes of differing diameters stand at an angle to each other, meeting high above to form a triangular interior space, easily suggesting the legs of a figure. A short horizontal tube that is closed at each end is held atop the two vertical elements. Three other elements, both square and tubular, are mounted at different angles off the horizontal tube, furthering the idea of some kind of robotic figure. McCarty painted the huge vertical sculpture bright red when it was first installed so that it would be lively and stand out against the school.

McCarty was thinking about many things when he was working on this piece, including Francis Scott Key, bombs bursting in air, and canons shooting from the fort, but none of these ideas completely informed the final sculpture, and while they are interesting to think about, all were incidental. It is interesting, in this context, to recall a statement made by McCarty. He said that he was "interested in how a work can act as a trigger, evoking the vague recollection of a place, a site, a structure or an event."

Born in Washington, D.C., McCarty graduated from the University of Virginia in Charlottesville and received his MFA from the Pratt Institute in New York City. He is an associate professor in sculpture at the University of Maryland in College Park, where he has taught since 1990, and lives close by in Delaplane, Virginia. His sculpture has been exhibited in Virginia, Washington, New York, and Baltimore, and he has completed several public art projects in the United States as well as in Berlin and Ghana.

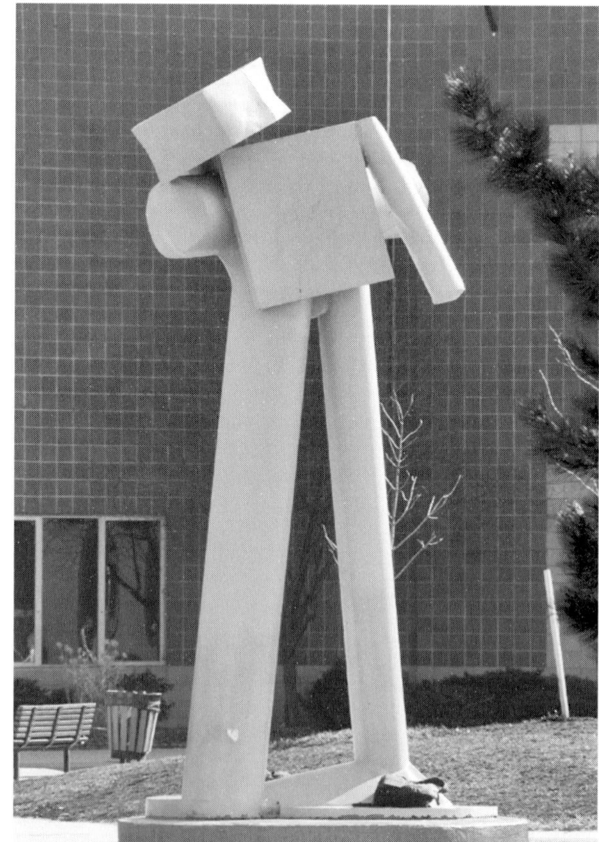

G17

TITLE
COL. GEORGE ARMISTEAD MONUMENT, 1914

LOCATION
Fort McHenry, E. Fort Avenue

SCULPTOR
Edward Berge (1876–1924)

MEDIUM
Bronze

DONORS
City of Baltimore and the Society of the War of 1812

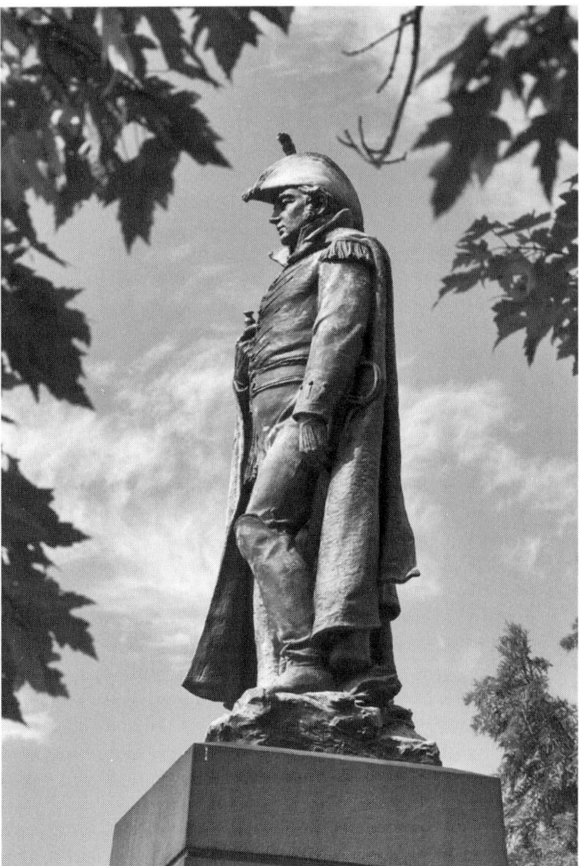

The earliest monument in Baltimore to Colonel George Armistead (1779–1818) stands on Federal Hill near the statue of Major General Samuel Smith (G2). This monument to Armistead was commissioned by the City of Baltimore, with some monetary support from the Society of the War of 1812, to mark the centennial of the battle of Baltimore, at North Point and at Fort McHenry, and Armistead's role as commander of the fort during the British attack on September 13–14, 1814. Armistead and his one thousand men withstood twenty-five hours of bombardment, until several of the British vessels tried to pass the fort and were fired upon. The British suffered heavy losses and were driven back. Francis Scott Key happened to be on board one of the British vessels that evening when the British attacked. From that vantage point, he wrote the poem that became America's national anthem.

The 8-foot-high portrait statue of Armistead stands on a 14-foot granite base just north of one of the points of the star-shaped fort nearby and east of the visitors' center. Armistead is depicted looking out over the Patapsco River toward where the British ships would have appeared. As if it were the eve of battle, Armistead holds a looking glass in his right hand against his chest, and in his left hand he holds a sword pointing downward just visible behind his left leg. Dressed for a cool September night, Armistead wears his uniform and a cape, which appears to be falling off his left shoulder, as if to suggest his forward movement. His stance, with his weight clearly resting on his left foot, reinforces that active quality. His uniform is complete with a helmet with a plumb. Robert M. Graf, a Maryland Institute model, served as Berge's model, as he did for the Latrobe Monument (O11).

G18

TITLE

FRANCIS SCOTT KEY MONUMENT, 1922

LOCATION

Fort McHenry, E. Fort Avenue

SCULPTOR

Charles Henry Niehaus (1855–1935)

DATE

1922

MEDIUM

Bronze

DONOR

U.S. Government

In 1914, on the centennial of the defense of Fort McHenry and the writing of the "Star-Spangled Banner," Congress appropriated $75,000 to commission a monument dedicated to Francis Scott Key (1780–1843), the author of the poem that would be set to music and become the national anthem, and to the soldiers and sailors who fought in the 1814 battle of Baltimore, at North Point and at Fort McHenry. In 1814 Key was the district attorney of Washington, D.C., and was seeking the release of Dr. William Beane whom the British had arrested and were holding on board a vessel in the British fleet located near the present-day Francis Scott Key Bridge, about two miles from the fort. Key successfully negotiated Beane's release, but both men were detained aboard the ship for fear they might have overheard the British planning the imminent attack on Fort McHenry. Key penned his poem while watching and listening to the bombardment of the fort throughout the evening of September 13, 1814, and until dawn the next day, from a porthole on that British ship.

In 1916 the U.S. Fine Arts Commission held a national competition to which thirty-four sculptors submitted entries. Charles Henry Niehaus, then of Grantwood, New Jersey, was selected. The monument was not installed and dedicated until Flag Day, June 14, 1922. The delay was blamed in part on the fact that a number of marble pieces, supplied by local masons, were rejected by federal inspectors. President Warren G.

Harding gave the address at the dedication ceremony, with several thousand people in attendance, the first remarks by a U.S. president to be broadcast coast to coast on live radio. Harding extolled Key's patriotism and paid tribute to him as a "modest genius" who was raised "in one flaming hour to a place among immortals." Harding continued, "Key reached the sublime heights and wrote the poetic revelation of an American soul aflame."

The colossal, 24-foot-high nude figure atop the huge, 15-foot-high circular base is Orpheus, the Greek god of music and poetry, who is depicted playing a five-string lyre. It is believed to have been the largest bronze ever cast by that time. The naturalism so readily apparent in the gently twisting body of Orpheus reflects the neoclassical taste of the times and the classical training of the sculptor, who had studied at the Royal Academy in Munich and later in Rome. The frieze on the drum of the marble base makes the dedication of the monument clear. A soldier on one side and a sailor on the other hold a portrait shield of Key, who is depicted in profile. The frieze, in low relief, continues full circle with a procession of classical Muses paying tribute to both the army and the navy. The lively, clearly celebratory procession is filled with classically inspired men, women, and young boys, nude or partially clothed in diaphanous drapery, most playing musical instruments as they follow one another around in a circle, sometimes so crowded that the figures are shown overlapping, a remarkable feat in low relief.

After his training in Europe, Niehaus returned to the United States by the 1890s, from which time he was in constant demand as a sculptor. He created monuments all over the country. Two monuments by him in nearby Washington are the Samuel Hahnemann Memorial and the Commodore John Paul Jones Memorial. Niehaus was the first runner-up for the Ulysses S. Grant Memorial there. He also created eight of the one hundred figures in Statuary Hall, including statesmen from Ohio, Kentucky, Kansas, Michigan, and Indiana.

This monument originally stood in the middle of the road leading into Fort McHenry. It was moved in 1962 to its present location, in the process losing its wide exedra with benches and cannon and balls. The choice of the figure of Orpheus to memorialize Key has long been debated. Key's relatives complained to Congress that the statue in no way typified the spirit of patriotism that led Key to write his poem. A great many admirers of Key's agreed that it was an inappropriate solution. Hans Schuler certainly agreed; he had competed with a heroic figure of Key himself, while Niehaus said he had been unable to come up with such a figure and thus had turned to allegory.

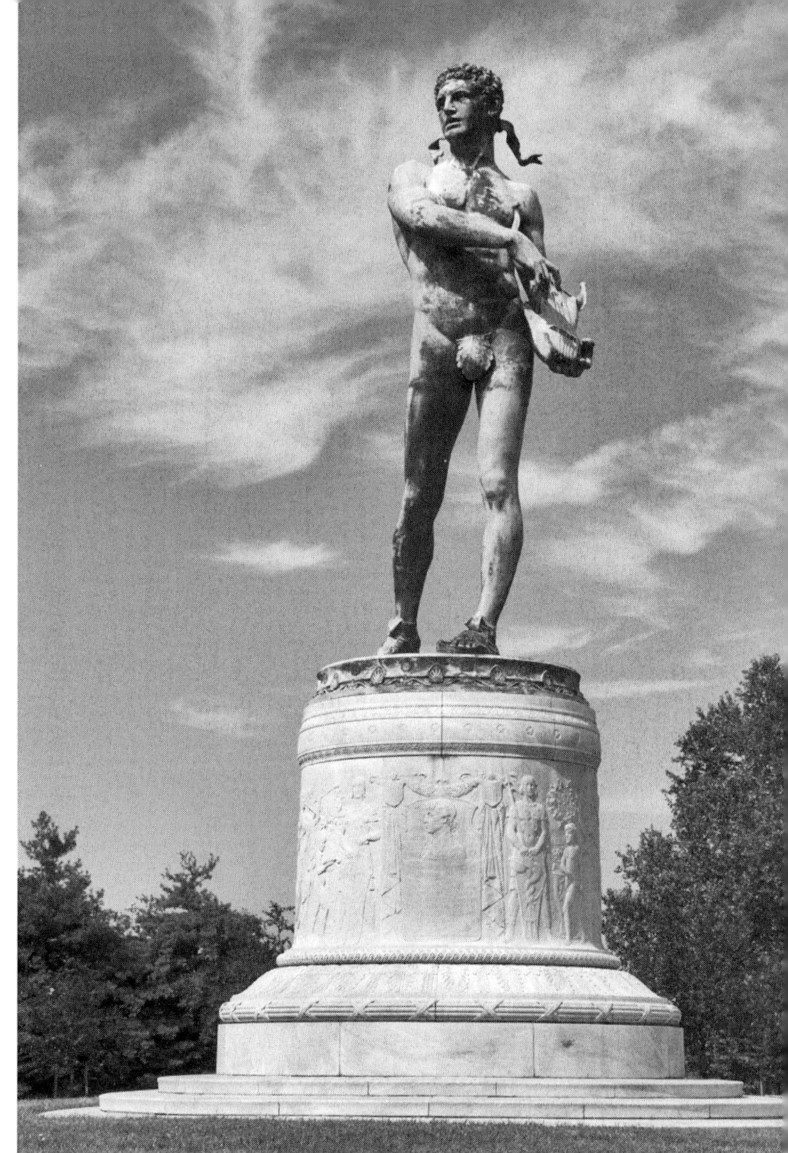

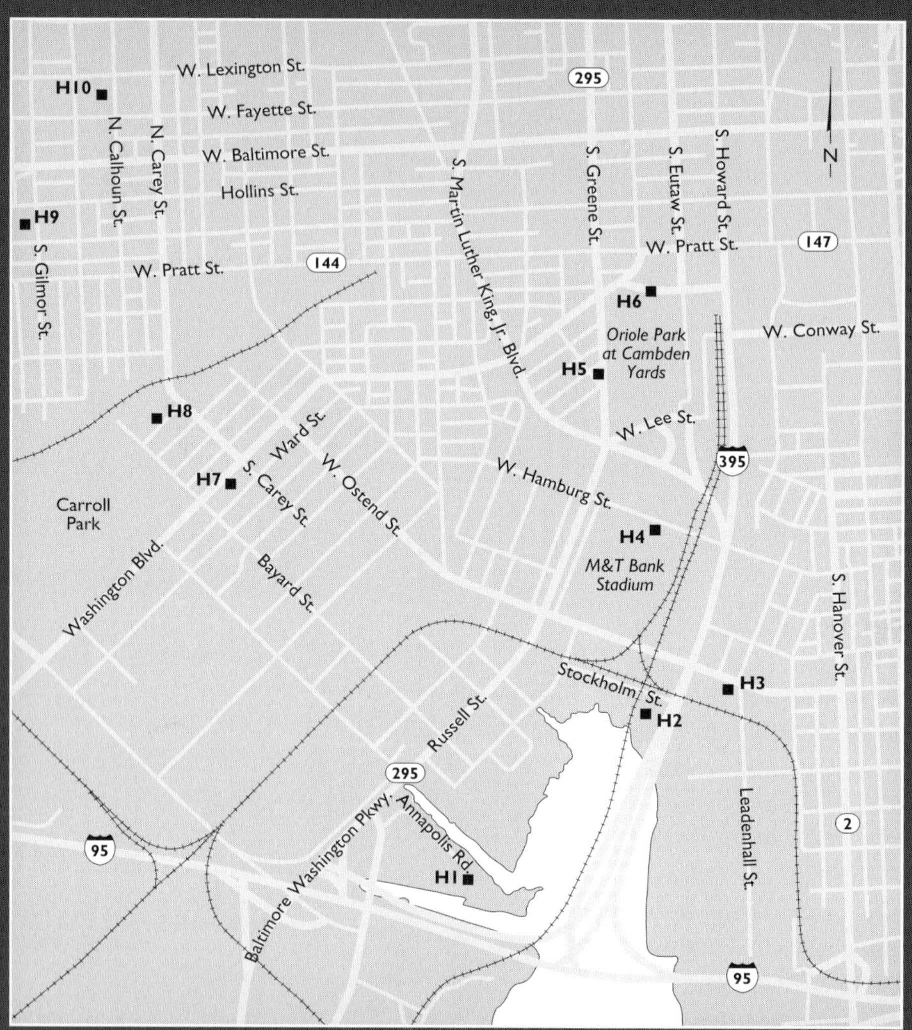

H1	*Energy,* p. 150	**H6**	*Babe's Dream,* p. 159
H2	*Dogs and Cats,* p. 153	**H7**	*Untitled,* p. 160
H3	*Subvator,* p. 153	**H8**	*Untitled,* p. 161
H4	*The Golden Arm,* p. 155	**H9**	*Children's Round Square,* p. 162
H5	*Atlantic Blue Roller Column,* p. 157	**H10**	*Steel Henge,* p. 163

SOUTH BALTIMORE

Driving

H1

TITLE
Energy, 1970

LOCATION
Wheelabrator Baltimore, 1801 Annapolis Road

SCULPTOR
Francesco Somaini (1926–2005)

MEDIUM
Bronze

DONORS
Baltimore Gas & Electric Company and the citizens of Baltimore

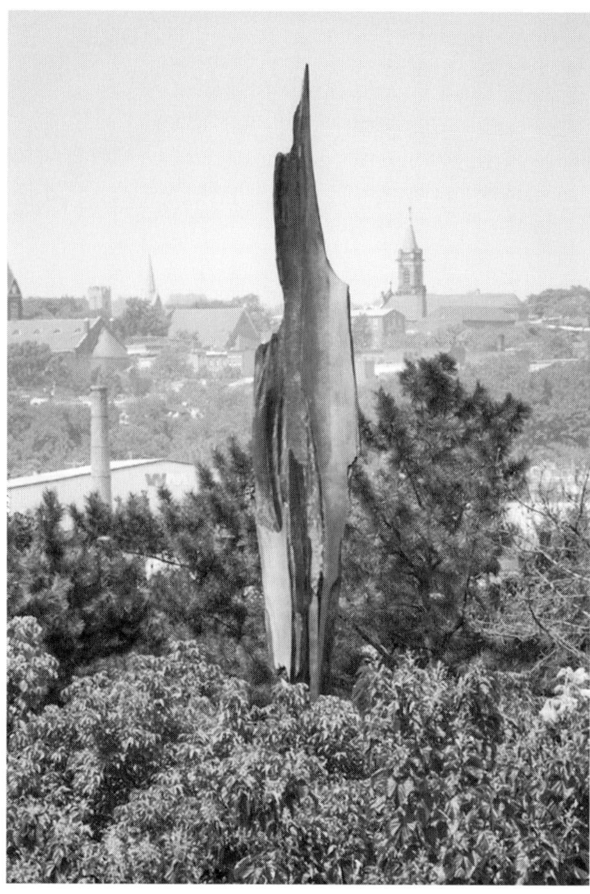

The first corporate gift of sculpture to the city, this piece was commissioned by the Baltimore Gas & Electric Company (today Constellation Energy) for its new building going up on Center Plaza. It quickly became seen as the centerpiece of Charles Center, the city's most important redevelopment project of the decade. With the dedication of Somaini's sculpture in June 1970, that phase of the city's redevelopment came to a successful close.

J. Jefferson Miller, chairman of the board of Charles Center–Inner Harbor Management, the development arm of the city at the time, was familiar with Somaini's work. When he saw a photograph of a sculpture similar to *Energy*, he thought of the new BG&E Building on Center Plaza. Informal discussions led to a $60,000 commission for Somaini to create a piece for Baltimore. BG&E's gift of sculpture to the city was followed by USF&G's purchase of a Henry Moore sculpture for the plaza of its new building and the C&P Telephone Company's (today Verizon Maryland) commissioning Michio Ihara to create a piece of sculpture for its new building on the southwest corner of Light and Pratt streets.

The 33-foot-high bronze resembles a giant piece of driftwood or a towering flame. It was referred to once as a huge stalagmite. Half of the twisting shaft of bronze is highly polished and golden; the other half, in contrast, is a darker, rough-hewn metal. This contrast is very typical of Somaini's work. The artist said that the sculpture is a monument to human energy, adding, "You cannot forget that which remains to be done, the unfinished part."

So perfect for its setting in close proximity to BG&E's new headquarters, *Energy* was written about widely and celebrated with great fanfare. Then in 1985, due to the weight of the sculpture, which could no longer be supported by the structural beams of the parking garage beneath it, the piece was moved to the entrance to Baltimore's new Refuse Energy Systems Company Operation (RESCO) plant, today called Wheelabrator Baltimore, which burns municipal solid waste, basically household trash, to heat boilers that produce steam, which turns a turbine to produce electricity. Opened in 1984, the plant has processed more than 9 million tons of waste and can provide electricity for as many as forty thousand homes. The plaque installed nearby stated that the sculpture was a gift to the recycling plant from BG&E and the citizens of Baltimore.

Energy looked very handsome in its new setting, where it was visible to everyone traveling into and out of the city along Russell Street. Unfortunately, due to the need for new traffic patterns around the plant, the work had to be moved again, this time to an isolated site behind the plant. Today none of the three early corporate gifts of sculpture is located downtown. Henry Moore's *Reclining Connected Forms* was sold at Sotheby's to a collector in Paris, and Ihara's untitled piece was removed in 2008, when a new owner renovated the building and redesigned the entrance.

Francesco Somaini was born in northern Italy, near Lake Como, but lived in Milan. In the 1950s he was considered one of the most prominent young sculptors in Italy. His sculpture was uncompromisingly abstract. In 1959 he won the Best Foreign Sculpture prize in the São Paulo Biennale in Brazil. His works may be seen in museums and public places across Europe and the United States, and they are in many private collections, including those of Governor Nelson A. Rockefeller, the architect Philip Johnson, and William Paley, the former head of CBS radio and television.

Note: Wheelabrator Baltimore is a working waste-to-energy plant that operates twenty-four hours a day, seven days a week. It is also on private property. Visitors who wish to see Somaini's *Energy* should call in advance to make arrangements to view the sculpture.

H2

TITLE
Dogs and Cats, 1986

LOCATION
Municipal Animal Shelter, 201 Stockholm Street

SCULPTOR
Harvey Peterson (b. 1949)

MEDIUM
Neon

DONOR
Baltimore City Percent for Art program

Dogs and Cats is one of the few neon artworks in the city and the only one to be commissioned through the city's Percent for Art program. Harvey Peterson was not known for working in neon, but he wanted something visible from a distance, given that the shelter was in a somewhat isolated location. Installing the piece on the roof made it visible from several arteries leading into and out of the city from the south.

The flat rooftop on this one-story building offered a good site for neon. Fabricated by Claude Neon Signs of Baltimore and maintained by them for many years, the seven blue dogs and four red cats chase one another around in a circle against a black rectangular background. Just barely visible in the daytime, the piece is much more prominent at night, when the lights are on.

Born in Seattle, Washington, Peterson attended the Maryland Institute College of Art, from which he received his BFA in 1973 and his MFA in 1982. He then spent more than two decades teaching art at Gilman School in Baltimore, where he was head of the art department, before moving to Belfast, Maine, in 1997, where he creates folk-inspired figurative sculpture. *Dogs and Cats* was his second Percent for Art commission. The first, in 1979, was for the interior of the Lilly M. Jackson School.

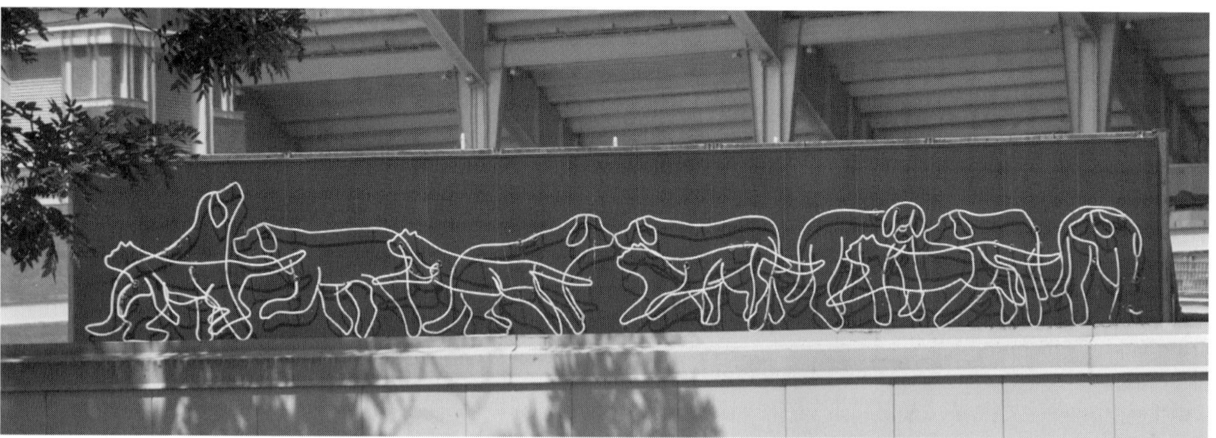

H3

TITLE
Subvator, 1989

LOCATION
Spring Garden Business Park, 175 W. Ostend Street

SCULPTOR
Rodney Carroll (b. 1949)

MEDIA
Aluminum, steel, concrete, gravel, and found objects

DONOR
Samuel Himmelrich Jr.

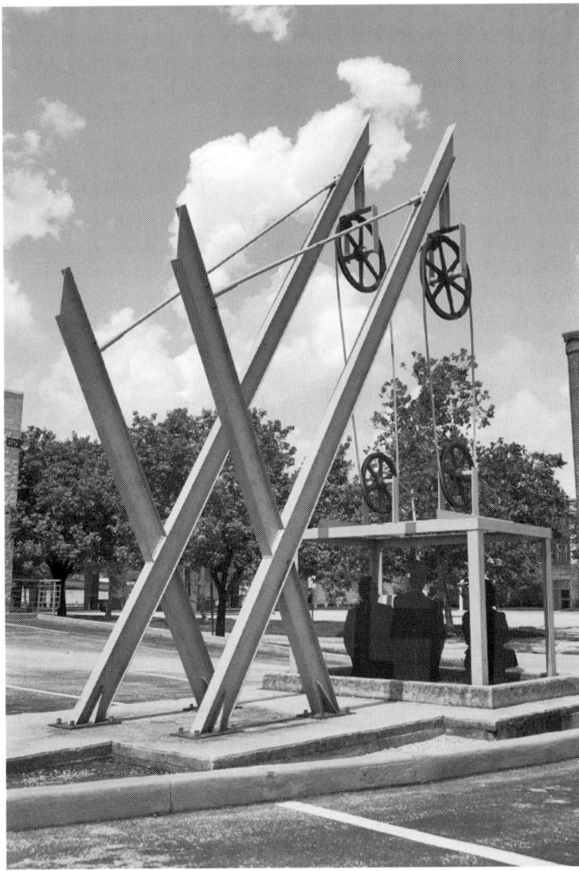

How did an elevator from a historic building find its way into a new work of public art? The story begins in 1988, when Samuel Himmelrich Jr. was developing the Ross Murphy Finkelstein Building, a one-hundred-year-old manufacturing facility at 190 W. Ostend Street, into a commercial office complex.

The following year, diagonally across the street, at 175 W. Ostend Street, Himmelrich began construction of the Spring Garden Business Park. Spring Garden's one-story buildings, whose early tenants included the American Federal Employees Union and industrial "to the trade" stores, wrapped around a central parking lot.

Wanting a piece of sculpture for the center of this business park, Himmelrich approached Rodney Carroll about the project. At the time, Carroll's studio was in a nearby building. Himmelrich was removing an old elevator from the Finkelstein Building, and he wanted Carroll to incorporate it into his sculpture for the business park across the street.

Using found materials was a new challenge for Carroll, but working with the concept of transportation interested him. The finished piece incorporates only the pulleys and the wind-up drum, or cable spool, from the old elevator, along with the idea of transporting people. Here, however, the idea is to bring people only from below, at which the title of the piece hints.

In the elevator car, looking toward the street are silhouettes of three figures. Facing the street, the figures appear to be just rising from below; their bodies are visible to just below the waist. They represent, from left to right, Himmelrich's wife; his father, Sam Sr.; and Tom Rapponatti, the executive director of the American Federation of State, County and Municipal Employees (AFSCME), whose office was housed on site at the time. These cutouts were recognizable to people in the neighborhood, as demonstrated by the large number of flowers left at the base of the sculpture just after Mr. Rapponatti died.

High above this transport cage are two sets of cables and pulleys. Four I-beams have been arranged in the shape of two *X*'s to appear as part of the transportation system. At the rear of the sculpture is the wind-up drum from the old elevator. The figures and pulleys are painted black, the I-beams are painted grey, and the aluminum cables are silver. The wind-up drum is very

dark, almost black, and although it is physically uncon-
nected to the cables and pulleys, it is visually integrated
into the idea of lowering the figures and bringing them
to the surface again

Rodney Carroll was born in Norfolk, Virginia, and
attended Old Dominion University, receiving a BFA in
1974. He received his MFA from the Rinehart School of
Sculpture at the Maryland Institute in 1983 and has
maintained a studio in Baltimore ever since. His first
public art commission, *Tank Dancing*, for Kitakyushu,
Japan, was completed in 1985. An unusual beginning
no doubt, but Norfolk and Kitakyushu are sister cities,
and Carroll had been involved in a cultural-exchange
program between universities in the two cities. Since
that time, he has completed public art projects in Res-
ton, Arlington, Fairfax, Alexandria, McLean, and Newport News, Virginia; in Washington, D.C.; in Greenville
and Columbia, South Carolina; in the City of Ormond
Beach, Florida; in Bellingham, Washington; in Cary,
North Carolina; and across Maryland. His sculpture
is held in many private collections. He has completed
three other outdoor pieces for Baltimore (I2, I8, and
K11).

H4

The Baltimore Colts quarterback for seventeen years, Johnny Unitas (1933–2002), who wore number 19 on his jersey, is shown standing in the pocket, ready to make what most assuredly would be another touchdown pass to his favorite target, Raymond Berry. There were other great receivers, including Lenny Moore, Alan Ameche, and L. G. "Long Gone" Dupre, all of whom played with Unitas in the 1958 NFL championship game, still considered the greatest game of football ever played, when Unitas led his Colts in a win over the New York Giants at Yankee Stadium. Unitas and his teammates Berry, Moore, Art Donovan, Gino Marchetti, and Jim Parker, all of whom played in that game, all entered the Hall of Fame at the end of their careers. The poster from that celebrated game has an image of Unitas standing back, ready to throw the ball, just as he is in this statue. And certainly it was his heroics in the fading minutes of that overtime game that made his a household name.

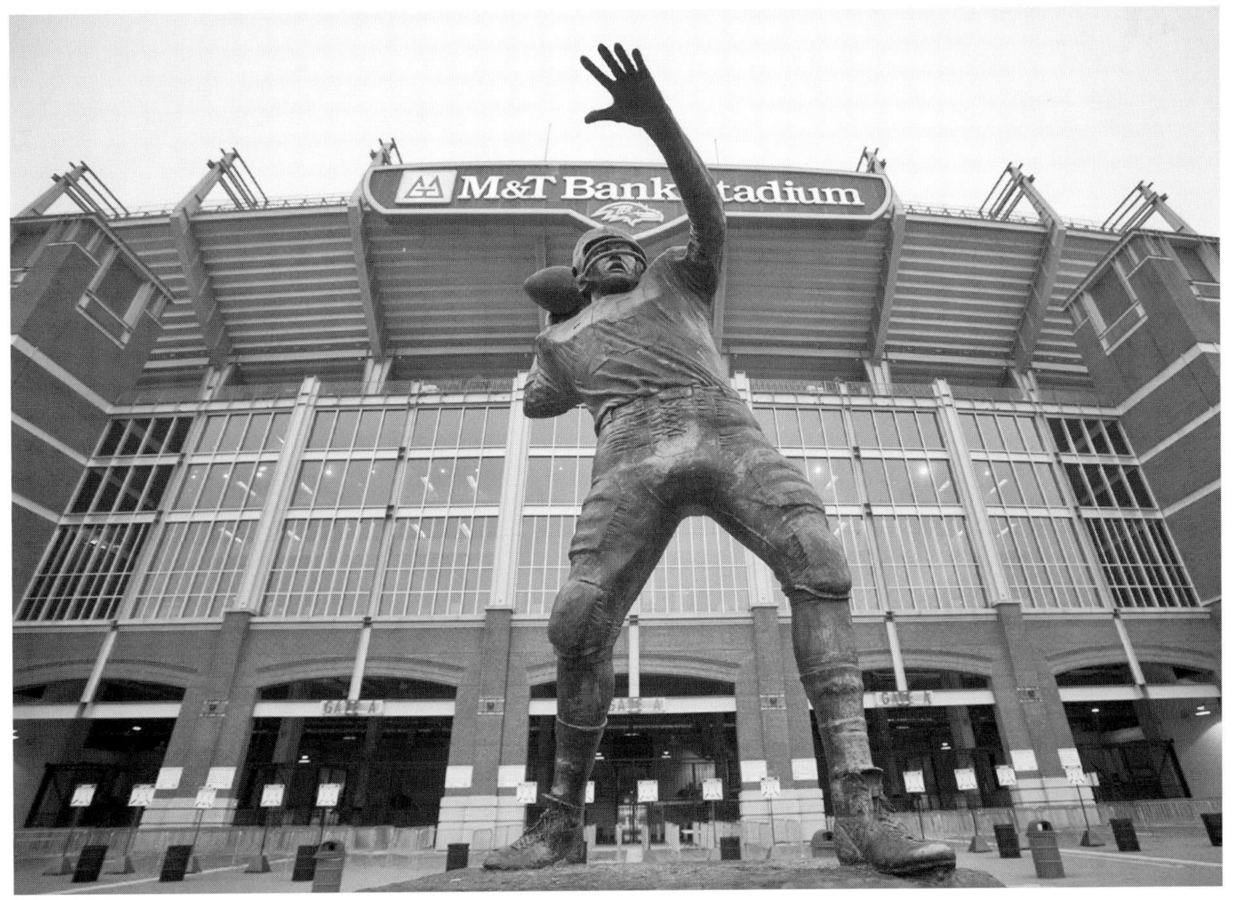

Johnny Unitas and the 1958 championship Colts were credited with the exploding popularity of football, which ushered in the TV era of sports coverage. Unitas became the team's legendary hero. He retired in 1973, after more than 40,000 yards passed and 290 touchdown passes, both records at the time. Considered by many the greatest quarterback who ever played the game, Unitas is an enduring symbol of football that is linked to Baltimore.

Frederick Kail, a 1959 graduate of the Maryland Institute and the owner of a design company for forty years, knew Johnny Unitas and had already received commissions for a bust and a statue of Unitas. In 1973 he had sculpted a bust for a group of Colts fans who wanted to honor Unitas, and the bust was given a place of honor in Unitas' living room. The statue had been for the University of Louisville, Unitas' alma mater, to whom Unitas had recommended Kail. With these two projects under his belt, Kail himself decided that Baltimore's new football stadium should have a statue of Johnny Unitas out front, and in 1999 he approached the Ravens and the Maryland Stadium Authority about the idea. With their approval and with approval from Unitas, Kail set about raising the money he would need to create such a statue. Three years later, but unfortunately for the artist a month after Unitas died, *The Golden Arm* was unveiled outside the Ravens' M&T Bank Stadium and dedicated not only to Unitas but to all the great Baltimore Colts.

When Kail began working on a small clay model for what would become the 14-foot-high monument, he called Unitas and asked him to come to his studio. Kail wanted to be sure Unitas would be pleased with the statue. Unitas told Kail just to depict him in the typical pose of a quarterback, and as Unitas looked at the model, he started pushing the clay around himself, moving the arm higher and the foot further under the figure's shoulder. The humble Unitas did not seem to realize that there was something very specific and characteristic about *his* stance, which was so clearly captured in that 1958 poster.

Even though Unitas had agreed to this statue, in part because his friend Kail would be creating it, he never felt completely comfortable with the idea. He had said to Kail that he did not want to be the only athlete represented by a statue at the stadium, and Kail promised Unitas that he would propose a "Walkway of Legends," a series of statues of Hall of Fame football and baseball players to be placed along the 250-yard stretch between the Ravens' stadium and Oriole Park. Unitas really liked the idea of celebrating the sports history of Baltimore, but that idea has not yet come to fruition.

A detail about the model that tickled Unitas was that Kail had captured the way Unitas tied his shoes—with a kind of double knot. Today, fans form long lines to touch the toe of Unitas' left foot for good luck before entering the stadium. A high polish has developed at the tip of the boot, where that double knot is easily noticed.

H5

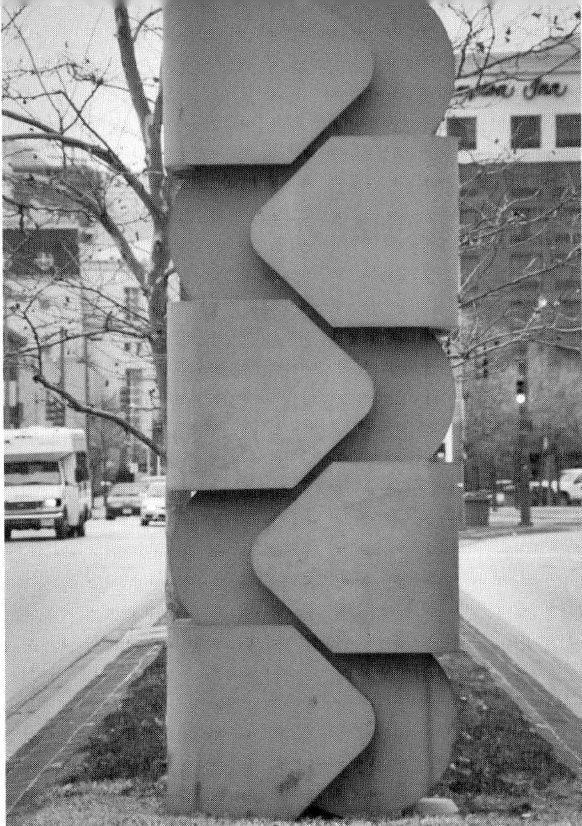

Dominick Cea created this abstract painted steel sculpture in 1977 as part of a sculpture symposium sponsored by the city and administered by the Department of Housing and Community Development. The four artists invited to participate were Greg Moring, James Adajian, Jim Sanborn, and Cea. They were commissioned to create gateway pieces for four major entrances into the city. Offered fifteen sites from which to choose, Cea selected Russell Street, one of the major points of entry into the city from the south, where it intersected Washington Boulevard. (It was moved further south in the median in 1992 as part of the highway construction project around the new baseball stadium.) Moring chose the grounds of the old City Hospitals (today Johns Hopkins Bayview Medical Center) along Eastern Avenue; Adajian chose East Cold Spring Lane near Falls Road; and Sanborn chose a site in Cherry Hill Park between Reedbird and Potee streets, another major entry into the city from the south. Only one other piece from this symposium remains in the city today—Jim Sanborn's *Patapsco River Project* (R4).

Cea was born in New York City and joined the navy before finishing college. After his service, he took a job at the National Bureau of Weights and Standards and settled in Gaithersburg, Maryland. At that time he began working toward his college degree. He earned enough credits to be accepted at the Maryland Institute College of Art, from which he graduated, fulfilling a lifelong dream. He then attended the Rinehart School of Sculpture at the Maryland Institute, graduating in 1978. It was while he was at the Rinehart School that he was chosen to participate in this sculpture symposium.

At the time of his selection, which was facilitated by J. Arthur Benson, then head of the sculpture department at MICA, Cea had just finished making a model in which he had worked out the ideas for a simple sculpture made of interlocking pieces that he felt could be appreciated at 30 miles an hour. He decided to use that model for this commission. The city made it as easy as possible for the artists to create large-scale, site-specific artworks that they otherwise might not have been able to undertake early in their careers. The city gave these four artists a downtown site in the 600 block of St. Paul Street (where Waterloo Place is today) to work in, a $2,000 honorarium, all the materials they needed, six assistants, and the heavy equipment needed to handle steel, the material all of them were using. Twenty-five Baltimore industries, suppliers and fabricators donated, among other things, steel, treated wood, grinding wheels, welding equipment and CO_2.

Cea's use of a repeating geometric unit, with one side curved and the other angular, stacked one inside the other, reflects the strong influence of his mentor, Norman Carlberg, then director at Rinehart, whose own pieces are constructed using a single modular unit (see F6). Cea stacked five units and alternated the orientation of the units, so that viewed from any angle the curvilinear units appear to be set in between the angular units. He hoped that by repeating and manipulating one simple shape he could produce something that had a new synergy. Because he wanted form to retain primacy, he chose a color that would not erase that form: Atlantic blue, which also gave him an idea for a title for the piece. When taken apart, the individual units look like rollers, which provided the rest of the title.

Today, Cea lives in California and works as a contract engineer in the power industry, training for which he received in the navy.

H6

TITLE
Babe's Dream, 1995

LOCATION
Oriole Park at Camden Yards, 333 W. Camden Street

SCULPTOR
Susan Luery

MEDIUM
Bronze

DONORS
Baltimore Orioles, Maryland Stadium Authority, Maryland Baseball Ltd. Partnership, and several citizens and corporations

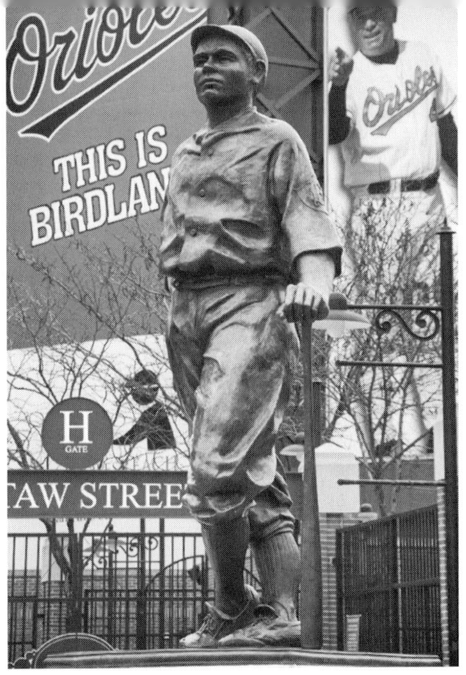

In 1993 Susan Luery was approached by the Babe Ruth Museum about designing a statue of Babe Ruth (1895–1948). The city supported the idea and promised to make a site available.

Luery began working on a maquette early in 1994. She had decided to depict the young, 18-year-old George Herman Ruth at the very beginning of his baseball career, just as he set out on his improbable journey to becoming an American icon. She wanted to depict the youthful, six-feet-one-inch, two-hundred-pound athlete who began playing baseball with the Baltimore Orioles, a minor-league franchise in the International League. This statue is of the youthful Ruth looking off into the distance as if imagining his destiny.

Luery used old family photographs and early team pictures from the museum to capture the face of the young Ruth. Then she engaged Michael Carter as her model for Ruth's youthful physique. She had met Carter, an aspiring opera singer who had never modeled before, in an Italian class. Since he was the same height and weight as the 18-year-old Ruth and thus could fit into the International League uniform she had gotten from the Babe Ruth Museum, she persuaded him to serve as her model.

In order to show the range of the youthful Ruth's talent, Luery decided to depict him with his left hand on a Louisville Slugger and holding a glove in his right hand to reflect his pitching ability as well as his versa-tility in the field. It was the glove that caused a ruckus, for it is a right-handed fielder's glove and Babe was a lefty. The Babe Ruth Museum sent the glove to Luery to use as a model, but something was lost in the communications. The mistake was not discovered in time to make any changes. One story has it that when Ruth was playing ball at St. Mary's Industrial School for Boys in Baltimore he might not have had the option of using a left-handed glove and might actually have used a right-handed glove: he would catch the ball, lose the glove, and fire away to get a runner out. But that was probably not the case by the time he was 18 and a left-handed rookie pitcher for the International League Orioles, which is how Luery chose to depict Ruth in her statue.

The sculpture was planned to celebrate the centenary of Ruth's birth, and it was unveiled on February 5, 1995. The siting at Oriole Park was confusing at the time of the dedication, because it was not widely known that the Sports Legends Museum would be located at Camden Yards, just across the plaza from the statue, in the old Camden Station, as it is today.

Luery was born in Baltimore and studied at the Maryland Institute. Before graduating, she left for Italy to continue her studies. Returning to Baltimore, she set up a studio and created work that can be seen at Oregon Ridge and in the courtyard in front of the Towson County Seat. Today Luery lives in Hingham, Massachusetts.

H7

TITLE
Untitled, 1976

LOCATION
Charles Carroll Barrister Elementary School,
1327 Washington Boulevard

SCULPTOR
Fernanda Zopf (b. 1922)

MEDIUM
Granite

DONOR
Baltimore City Percent for Art program

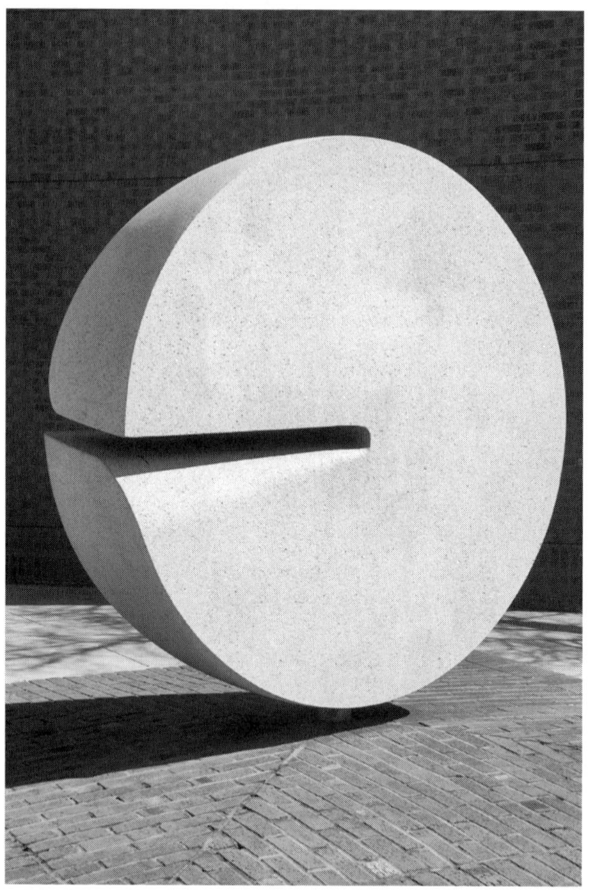

This untitled piece of sculpture, sited at the entrance to an elementary school, came to be known affectionately as "Pac-Man" by the students, after the Japanese arcade game was introduced in the United States in 1981 and quickly became a social phenomenon. Based on the geometry of a circle, the sculpture was carved out of Salisbury pink granite with a narrow section missing, resembling the Pac-Man character that gobbled up every dot in its maze in the video game.

Fernanda Zopf was born in Teramo, Italy, and received her BS degree from the University of Naples. She studied painting in Italy, Germany, and Canada before arriving in Baltimore in 1954. She earned her BFA from the Maryland Institute College of Art and then received a fellowship to the Rinehart School of Sculpture, where she worked with Norman Carlberg, the director at the time. After receiving her MFA in sculpture in 1965, she became an instructor at the Maryland Institute and began exhibiting her work around Maryland. Public art commissions soon followed.

This was Zopf's third commission through the city's Percent for Art program. She was continuing her experiments with geometric shapes, especially the circle, and decided to use that form for this project. She made many different models based on the circle, in various sizes, and the architect for this school, Anthony Iannello, chose the model and scale he preferred. The sculpture was carved at a quarry in Georgia and then shipped to Baltimore, where it was installed in the middle of a wide, low brick base.

In recent years Zopf has returned to painting. Most recently her work has been shown at the Gallerie Françoise et Ses Freres, in Lutherville, Maryland, in 2003 and at the College of Notre Dame, in Baltimore, and the Washington County Museum of Fine Arts, in Hagerstown, Maryland, in 2004 (see L15 and M4).

H8

TITLE
Untitled, 1967

LOCATION
Diggs-Johnson Middle School, 1300 Herkimer Street

SCULPTOR
Peter van Rossum

MEDIUM
Aluminum

DONOR
Baltimore City Percent for Art program

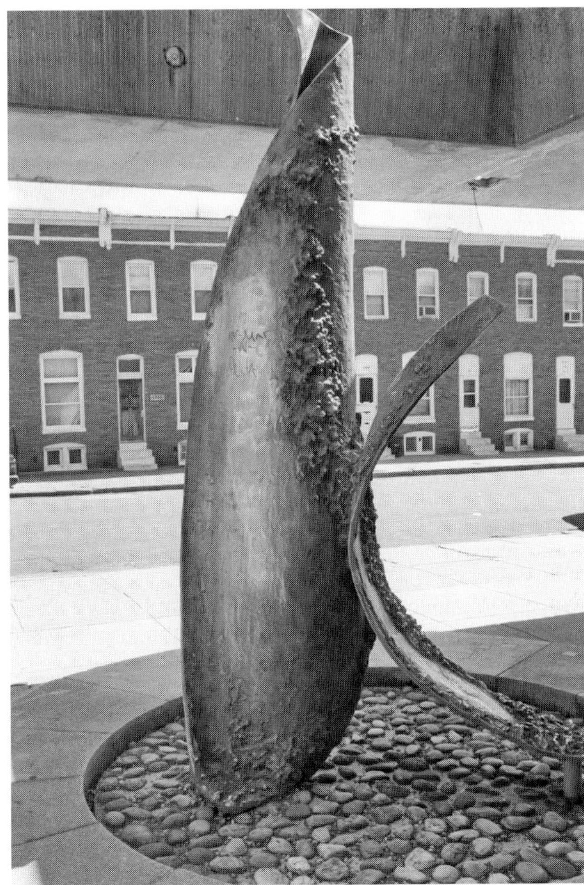

This was one of the first three pieces of outdoor sculptures to be commissioned through the Percent for Art program in Baltimore, and it is the first of five commissions that Peter van Rossum received through this program.

This untitled piece is made of cast aluminum. The vertical element stands 8 feet high and folds in on itself. The interior smooth surface contrasts to the rough, textured outer surface. A more delicate curving arc is tangential to the strong central vertical form. Sun spills down onto the sculpture through a square opening in the overhang at the entrance of the building in front of which the sculpture is placed. In contrast to the square opening is the low, broad circular brick base with granite caps. The center of the circular base is filled with 3-inch stone aggregate.

Van Rossum's four other commissions were architectural in nature. For the Light Street branch of the Enoch Pratt Library, he designed a pattern of brick rustication for the facade, as he did for the facade of the James McHenry Elementary School. For Westside Elementary he designed a pattern of black, white, and grey aggregate for a series of facade panels. A fourth project, at Rosemont Elementary School, again aggregate facade panels, was cemented over and destroyed. All five pieces were completed between 1967 and 1971.

H9

TITLE
Children's Round Square, 1969

LOCATION
Steuart Hill Elementary School, 30 S. Gilmore Street

SCULPTOR
Alfredo Halegua (b. 1930)

MEDIUM
Concrete

DONOR
Baltimore City Percent for Art program

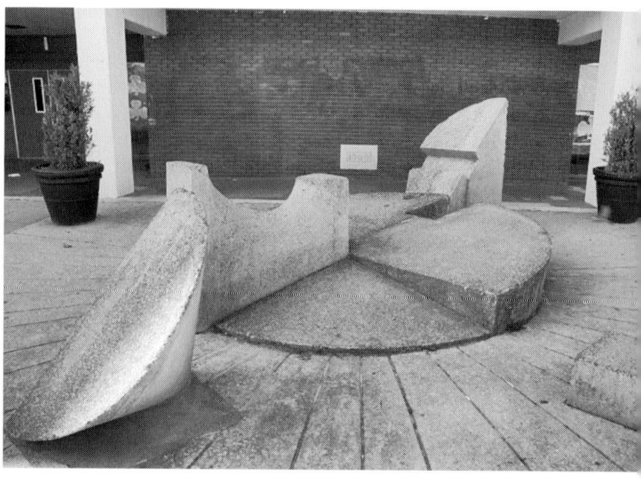

Alfredo Halegua's challenge was to create a work of art for a very shallow space in front of this new elementary school. The resulting artwork, made out of reinforced concrete, doubles as a seating and play area for the children as they wait for school to open in the morning or for someone to pick them up in the afternoon. The sculpture might also be a three-dimensional puzzle to be deciphered by the waiting students. If all the pieces in different shapes and sizes, apparently randomly placed, could be fit back together, what form would they take? A circle or a square is suggested, but in reality neither is possible. The question remains to be pondered year after year by new students. Halegua designed the sculpture to be an integral part of the larger entrance plaza area for the school, and he used incised lines radiating out from the piece across the plaza to suggest just that.

Alfredo Halegua was born in Montevideo, Uruguay. He moved to Baltimore in 1959 and settled in Washington, D.C., in 1961. Halegua has earned a national reputation for his large, abstract steel sculptures, which have been exhibited across the country for the past forty years and included in many important public and private collections, including those of the Baltimore Museum of Art, the National Gallery of Art in Washington, the Mint Museum in Charlotte, North Carolina, and the Ringling Museum in Sarasota, Florida. He has created public artworks for many cities all across the country, including Washington, Charlotte, Miami, Jacksonville, and Oklahoma City.

The very understated sculpture that Halegua designed for the entrance to this school is quite atypical of his signature work. He usually prefers to work in metal and on a more monumental scale. The very next year the architects for this school offered Halegua a much larger commission, for the city's new senior center (I1). In 1970 Halegua also completed a large abstract aluminum sculpture for a courtyard at Walbrook High School that had to be brought in by helicopter (Q1).

H10

TITLE
Steel Henge, 1977

LOCATION
Vivien T. Thomas Medical Arts Academy School,
100 N. Calhoun Street

SCULPTOR
Alton Parker Balder (b. 1924)

MEDIUM
Painted steel

DONOR
Baltimore City Percent for Art program

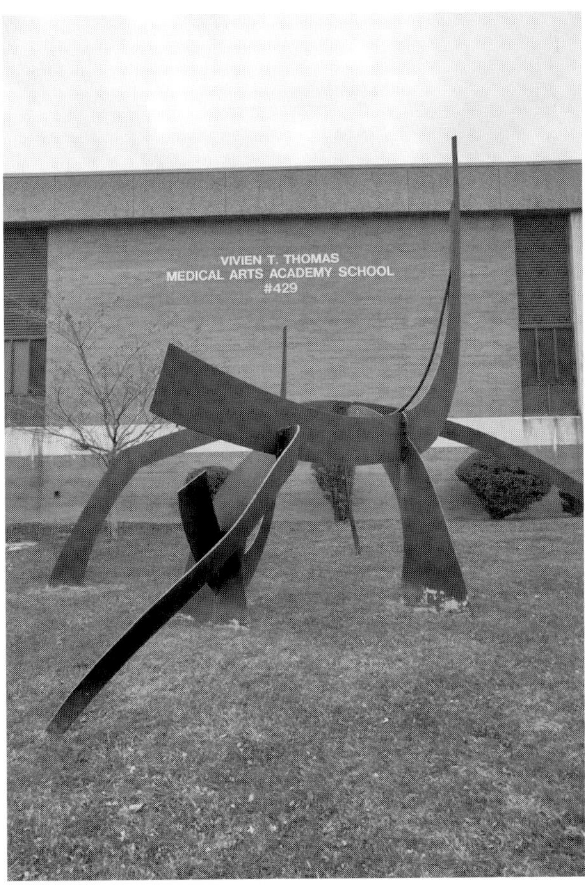

In 1977, when this school opened as the Francis M. Wood Senior High School, A. P. Balder was commissioned to create a work of art for the front lawn. He did so by cutting and bending five arching steel forms, each wider at one end and narrowing toward the other, and interweaving them.

Variation has also been woven into the piece. The curvature of each arc is different. Three arcs bend downward and into the ground; the other two are more open and sweep upward. Some of the arcs are bolted together; others connect by slipping through a cut in the wider end of another. The resulting composition is like that of a drawing, made with broad sweeping motions through space. The arrangement of these intersecting, curvilinear forms is very pleasing.

Although the piece was painted vermillion when it was first installed, it is blue today, after years of being yellow. The history of these colors can be read on the piece.

Balder attended City College High School in Baltimore and graduated from the Johns Hopkins University. During World War II he was an interceptor-plane pilot in the European Theater. Returning to Baltimore, he studied part time at the Maryland Institute College of Art. The artists he worked with there were featured in a book he wrote in 1955 titled *Six Maryland Artists.*

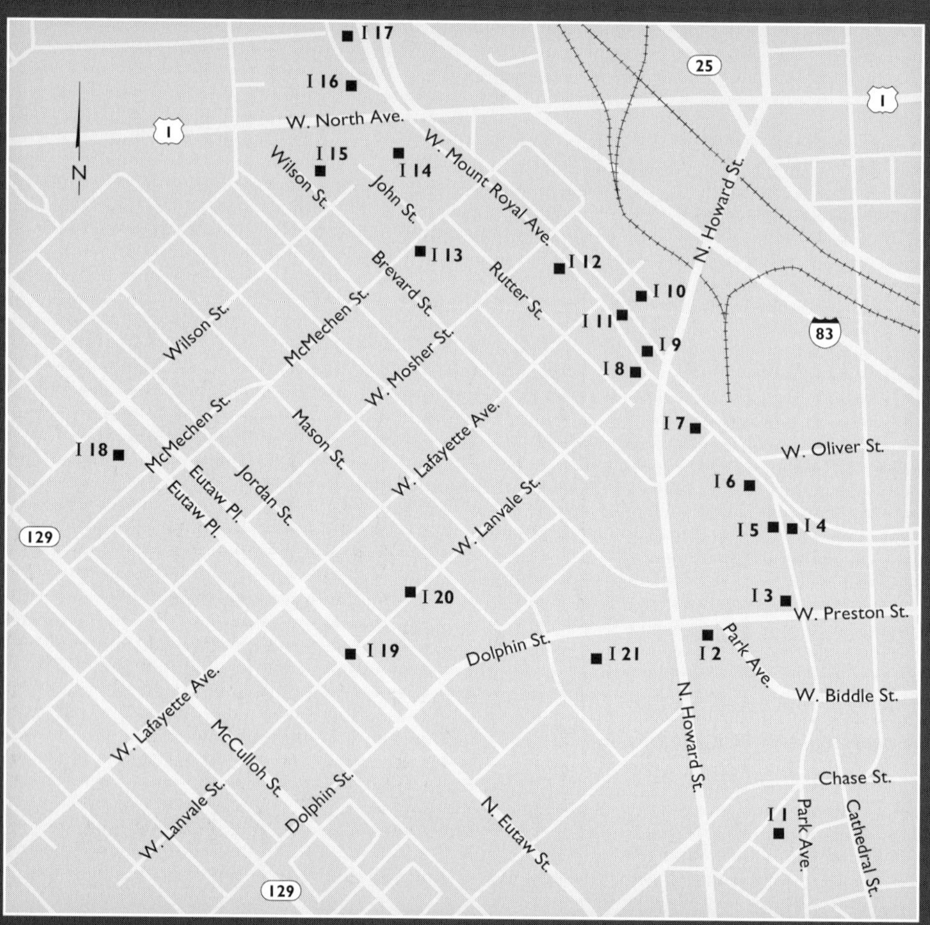

I 17
I 16
25
1
W. North Ave.
1
N
Wilson St.
I 15
I 14
W. Mount Royal Ave.
John St.
N. Howard St.
Brevard St.
I 13
Rutter St.
I 12
I 10
Wilson St.
McMechen St.
I 11
I 9
W. Mosher St.
I 8
83
McMechen St.
W. Lafayette Ave.
I 7
W. Oliver St.
I 18
Mason St.
W. Lanvale St.
I 6
McMechen St.
Eutaw Pl.
Jordan St.
I 5 I 4
Eutaw Pl.
129
I 3
W. Preston St.
I 20
Park Ave.
Dolphin St.
I 19
I 21
I 2
W. Biddle St.
W. Lafayette Ave.
N. Howard St.
McCulloh St.
Chase St.
W. Lanvale St.
Dolphin St.
N. Eutaw St.
I 1
Park Ave.
Cathedral St.
129

MOUNT ROYAL AVENUE AND BOLTON HILL

Walking

TITLE
Colossus I, 1972

LOCATION
Waxter Center for Senior Citizens, 861 Park Avenue

SCULPTOR
Alfredo Halegua (b. 1930)

MEDIUM
Cor-Ten steel

DONOR
Baltimore City Percent for Art program

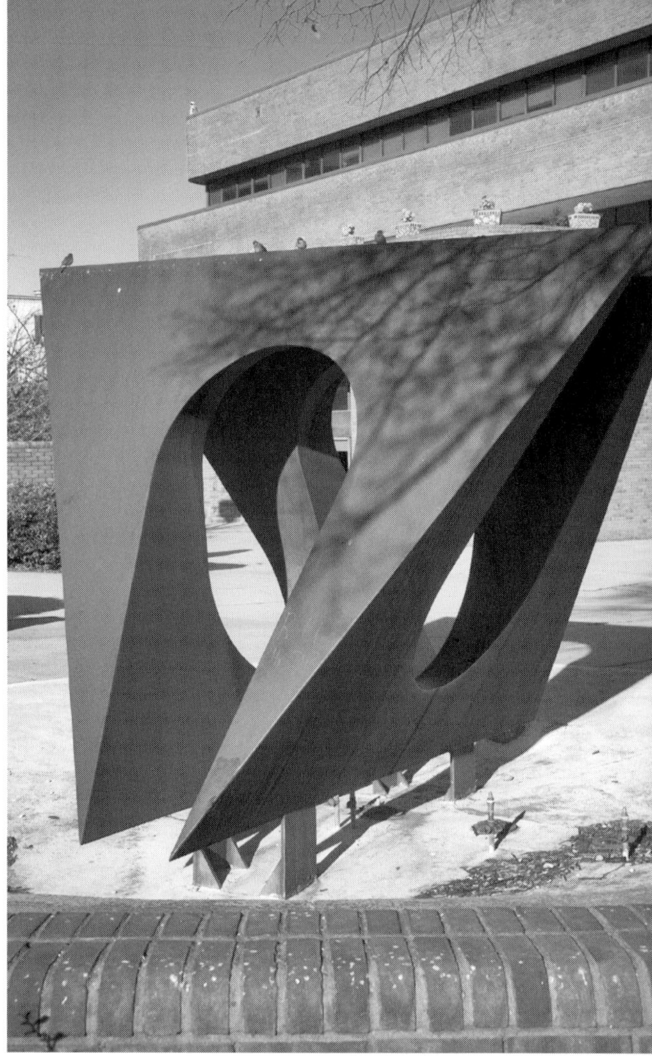

Alfredo Halegua was commissioned by the architectural firm of Tartar and Kelly to create a piece of sculpture for the city's new center for senior citizens. Tartar and Kelly had worked with Halegua at Steuart Hill Elementary School (H9) the year before and were pleased to be able to offer him another larger commission.

Halegua had no limitations imposed on him here. He could choose the specific location and decide what kind of sculpture would be appropriate. From the beginning, Halegua wanted to include water, thinking that the sound of falling water would be soothing and therapeutic.

Originally standing in a circular pool of water, the sculpture comprises four modules of weathering steel welded together. Each module is defined by three straight edges and one curving line, which cuts out an interior space in its surface. If inverted and turned 90°, the sculpture would look the same. The water jets were designed to push a curtain of water up through the middle of the sculpture, and then the water would come cascading back down over the piece and into the pool below. It was very beautiful when the water was running. A low, semicircular brick wall was built around the street side of the piece, with benches installed along the curving wall.

In 1977 Halegua made a second *Colossus,* out of the same material but in slightly different proportions, for the Ringling Museum of Art in Sarasota, Florida, where it became the first work to be installed in the new sculpture garden. The Florida sculpture does not include a fountain.

12

TITLE
Firebird, 2005

LOCATION
Symphony Center

SCULPTOR
Rodney Carroll (b. 1949)

MEDIA
Bronze, stainless steel, and copper

DONORS
David S. Brown Enterprises and the Maryland
Transit Administration

In 2000 a national competition was held to select an artist to create a work of art for the plaza at the southeast corner of Howard Street and Park Avenue, between Symphony Hall and a light-rail stop and outside an office and apartment complex called Symphony Center. Rodney Carroll was selected to receive this commission in the heart of the city's cultural district.

Because of the site's direct relationship to Symphony Hall, Carroll wanted to have a piece of music in mind as he approached the design of his sculpture. He chose as his inspiration *The Firebird*, by Igor Stravinsky (1882–1971), a 1910 work commissioned by Sergey Diaghilev, director of the Ballets Russes in Paris, and based on a Russian folk tale featuring a handsome prince, a lovely princess, and the magical intervention of the firebird. The music, which brought the young Stravinsky overnight success, was remarkable for its brilliant orchestration and harmony, flamboyant romanticism, evocative power, and an orchestral palette that included forceful passages as well as lighter ones.

Carroll strove not only to make his sculpture a visual interpretation of the music of Stravinsky and related to the curvilinear lines of Symphony Hall but also to make it a gateway piece, welcoming pedestrians coming from any direction to walk through the piece, not around it. Each of the sculpture's four sides presents a different profile. Echoes of Stravinsky's music can be seen in the pairing of the weighty silver buttressing elements, one on either side of the central bronze towering element, with the five lighter, more graceful steel pipes that bend ever so slightly as they lean against the central tower between the arms of the buttresses and extend 50 feet into the air, making illusions to the five bars on which music is written. The copper element wrapping around the tower and between the two wings that ground the piece so completely may make reference to organ pipes. Even the coloration in the piece, resulting from the incorporation of bronze, copper, and steel, is a reminder of orchestral color, especially noted in Stravinsky's upbeat soaring flight of fantasy for the Ballets Russes.

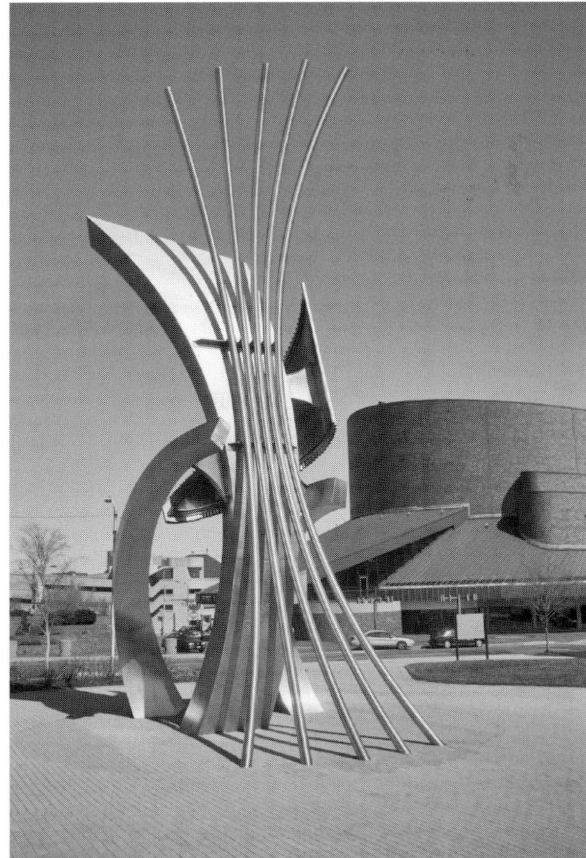

13

TITLE
Pearlstone Park, 1985

LOCATION
Cathedral and Preston streets

SCULPTOR
Scott Burton (1939–1989)

MEDIA
Sandblasted concrete and brick

DONORS
Mayor William Donald Schafer, the citizens of Baltimore, and the Pearlstone Charitable Income Trust

Pearlstone Park is unique in the city because a sculptor was given artistic autonomy over the entire site and its design. Scott Burton had committed himself to making public art throughout his career, always referring to himself as a "public sculptor" and repeatedly stating that he wanted "to get some social meaning back into art." His approach is readily apparent in this park situated in the heart of the city's cultural district.

The one acre that Burton was asked to design is directly across the street from Symphony Hall and up a hill from the Mount Royal Station, which houses the Rinehart School of Sculpture of the Maryland Institute. Two north-south city streets serve as the eastern and western perimeters of this green space and an east-west city street marks its southern boundary. Thinking of the park as a total environment, Burton designed settees and light standards, planned for a semicircular esplanade where the seating and lights would be arranged, determined the placement of the pathways that crisscross the entire space, and planned for the planting of forty large leafy trees to provide shade for the seating area.

Burton chose concrete and brick, materials that blended well with the existing city sidewalks that boarded the park and related to the brick used on Symphony Hall and in its plaza as well as to the red tile roof of the Mount Royal Station building just to its north. The six lampposts are made of cast concrete, and their bases are of brick. The sixteen settees, which allow seating on four sides and on their tops, are also of cast concrete. The benches and light standards are placed on a concrete swath that cuts through the middle of the curving brick esplanade and touches the linear concrete pathways tangentially.

With his thoughtful design of every element and his "furniture sculptures," Burton managed to create a handsome and useful urban park out of a piece of left-over land whose development had languished for years. A proposal from the Pearlstone family for a park on this site dedicated to the memory of the late Jack Pearlstone had been well received by then Mayor William Donald Schaefer, and with the personal and financial involvement of the family the project was completed in 1985. The next year, a one-person exhibition of Scott Burton's work opened at the Baltimore Museum of Art.

Two years before Pearlstone Park was completed, Burton created a terraced outdoor garden with chairs cut from boulders for the grounds of the National Oceanic and Atmospheric Administration (NOAA) campus in Seattle. The same year that Pearlstone Park was completed, Burton's collaboration with the architect I. M. Pei and two other artists, Kenneth Noland and Richard Fleischner, on the Wiesner Building at the Massachusetts Institute of Technology was completed. Burton designed the public seating, the stairwell, and the balustrades for the atrium of that building. Burton

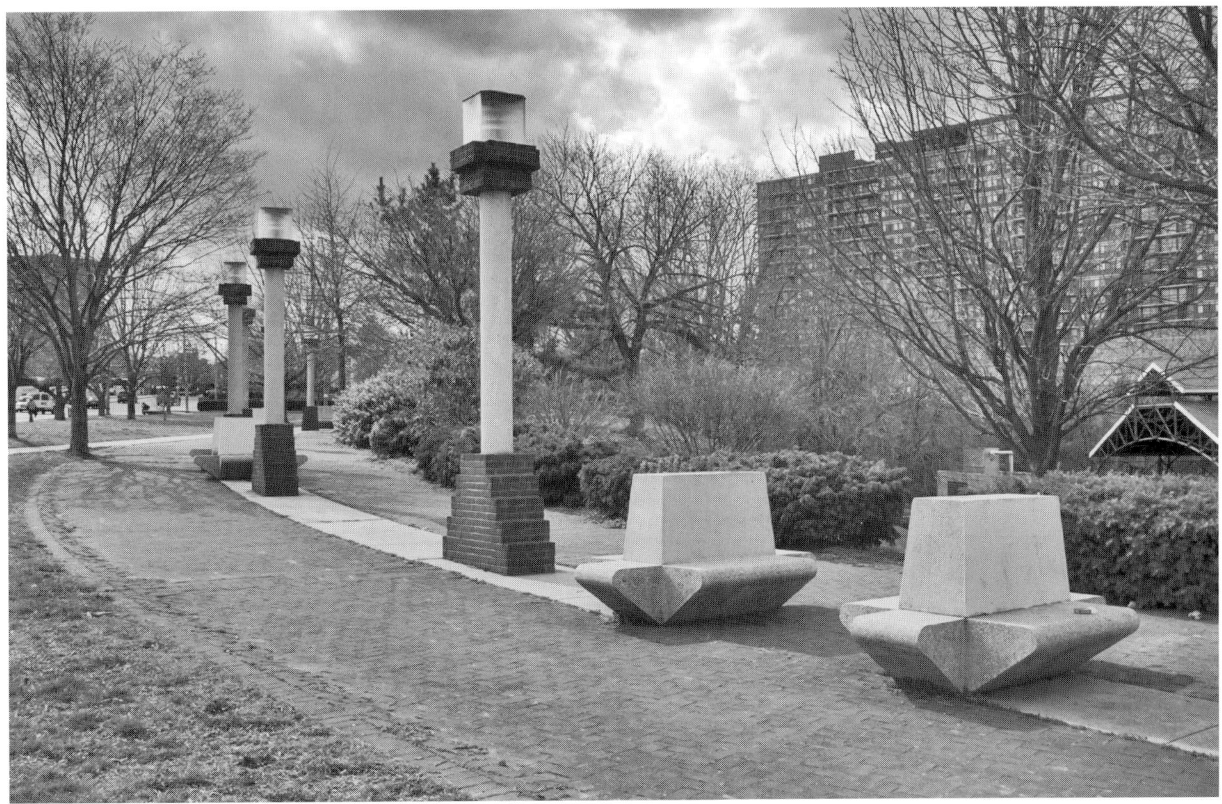

also collaborated with his close friend, the Minneapolis-based artist Siah Armajani, the architect Cesar Pelli, and the landscape architect Paul Friedberg on the plaza for the World Financial Center in Battery Park City in New York City.

Burton, who was born in Greensboro, Alabama, and educated at Columbia and New York universities in the 1960s, worked as a critic and an editor for *Art News* and *Art in America* before becoming a full-time artist. But by the 1980s Burton had devoted himself to the design and production of functional objects, mainly seating and tables, for public spaces, including corporate offices and parks. Blurring the lines between sculpture and furniture, and merging form and social function, he created environments in cities across the country following his belief that art should "place itself not in front of but around, behind, underneath its audience." This approach is realized in Pearlstone Park, which, like Burton's other environmental artworks, requires the spectator's presence to complete them.

TITLE
Goddess of Liberty, 1901

LOCATION
Maryland Line Monument, E. Mount Royal Avenue
and Cathedral Street

SCULPTOR:
A. L. Van den Bergen (Berghen) (1850–1921)

ARCHITECT
Hodges and Leach

MEDIUM
Bronze

DONOR
Maryland Society of the Sons of the American
Revolution

"TO ALL THE PATRIOTS OF MARYLAND WHO DURING THE
REVOLUTIONARY WAR AIDED ON LAND OR AT SEA IN
GAINING THE INDEPENDENCE OF THIS STATE AND OF
THESE UNITED STATES AND TO THE MARYLAND LINE
"THE BAYONETS OF THE CONTINENTAL ARMY"

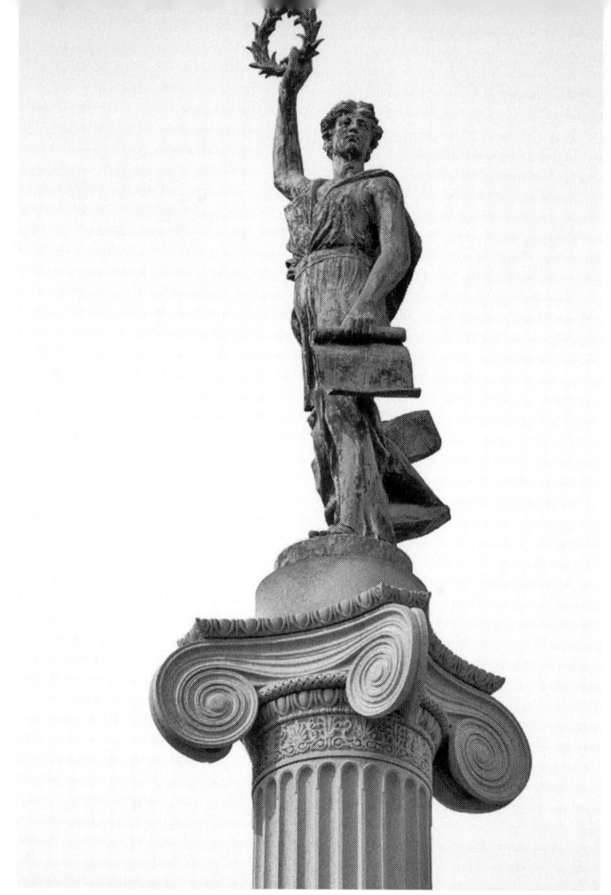

This is Maryland's Revolutionary War monument, most often called the Maryland Line Monument. "Maryland Line" refers to the infantry regiments of the Continental army from Maryland who fought under George Washington, earning the proud reputation of being among the best in the army.

The monument committee of the Maryland chapter of the Sons of the American Revolution solicited contributions from residents all across Maryland, and except for one donation of $104 from the Ancient and Honorable Artillery Company of Massachusetts, the monument was paid for by Marylanders. The local architectural firm of Hodges and Leach was hired to prepare the design for the monument, and A. L. Van den Bergen was commissioned to create the heroic statue of the Goddess of Liberty that stands 11 feet tall atop the very beautiful Ionic column. Van den Bergen was associated with the Art Institute of Chicago at the time of this commission. William Boyd (1882–1947) was hired to carve the granite column. A three-step granite platform with a granite pedestal supporting the column completes the monument, which measures 60 feet from the ground to

the top of the victor's laurel wreath that the Goddess of Liberty holds aloft in her right hand. In her left hand is a scroll representing the Declaration of Independence.

On October 19, 1901, on Peggy Stewart Day, the monument was unveiled and dedicated on what was then a much larger Mount Royal Plaza. Peggy Stewart Day commemorates Maryland's own Tea Party. In 1774 a vessel owned by Anthony Stewart and named for his daughter sailed into the Annapolis harbor loaded with two thousand pounds of tea, for which Stewart had decided to pay the importation taxes required by the British. His fellow citizens became angry and demanded that he burn his ship or be hanged. On October 19, 1774, Stewart ran his ship aground and put the torch to it himself. This episode demonstrated the determination Marylanders felt to challenge England for the taxes that were being imposed on them. The Boston Tea Party had occurred ten months earlier, on December 16, 1773, and "the shot heard round the world" was fired six months later, on April 19, 1775, starting the American Revolutionary War.

Four bronze tablets are mounted on the pedestal, one on each face. One tablet has the coat of arms of the Society of the Sons of the American Revolution, the Maryland coat of arms used during the Revolution, the U.S. coat of arms, and the original, thirteen-star flag. On two tablets are listed the various engagements in which the Maryland Line fought and their dates. On the fourth tablet is a list of notable bodies of the time and specific actions they took.

In Prospect Park, in Brooklyn, New York, there is a monument of marble, granite, and bronze dedicated to the Maryland 400 that was designed by Stanford White in 1895. This monument commemorates the contributions and sacrifice of the Maryland Line in 1776 at the battle of Long Island, in which 256 Marylanders were killed and another 100 wounded or captured. These gallant Marylanders from the Fifth Regiment led a rearguard action to check the British advance on New York by way of Brooklyn and protect the retreat of Washington's outnumbered army.

The action of these Marylanders saved Washington's army from assured destruction and also made

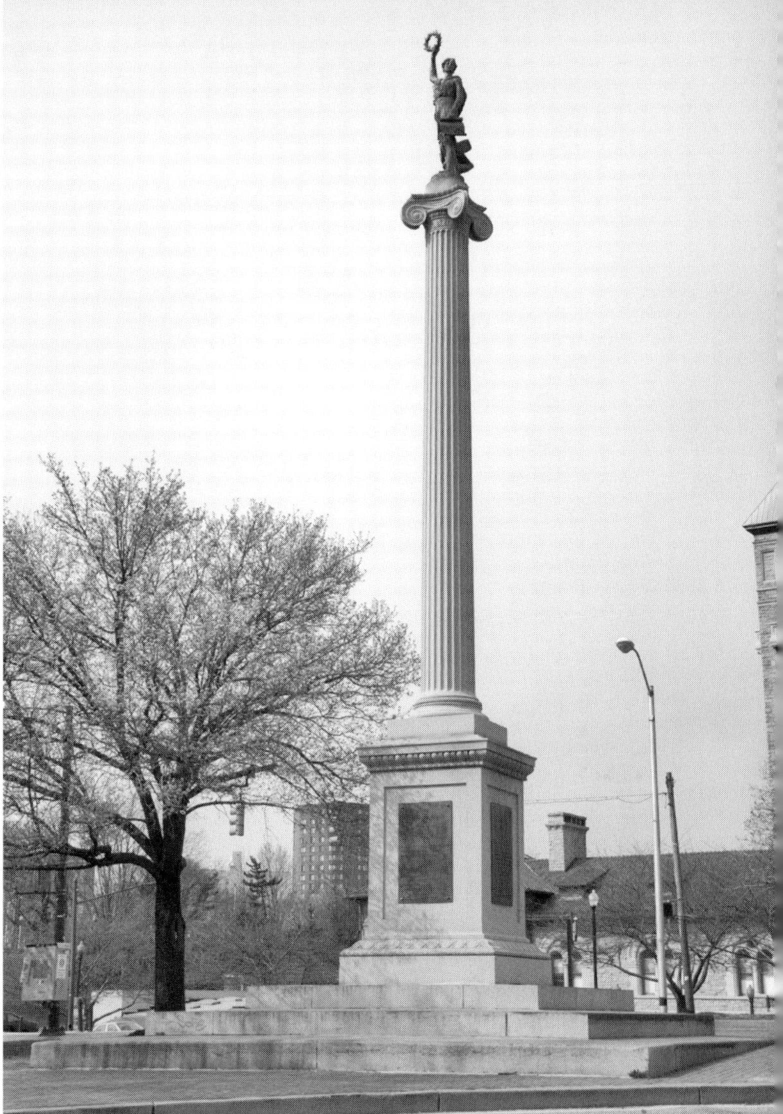

history, for the Maryland Line was the first in the American army to use bayonets. A bayonet is simply a blade that is attached to the barrel of a rifle for use in close combat. The Marylanders became famed for their forceful use of this weapon, which earned them the moniker inscribed on this monument, "The Bayonets of the Continental Army." Unlike other militia, who did not care for military action away from their home communities, Marylanders were often present among Washington's troops wherever they were fighting. George Washington is thought to have referred to the Maryland units as "his old line," which led to one of the state's nicknames, "Old Line State." Washington may have first used this tribute during the battle for Long Island.

I5

TITLE
Untitled, 1996

LOCATION
Maryland Institute College of Art, Mount Royal
Station entrance, 1400 Cathedral Street

SCULPTOR
René A. Townsend (1952–1998)

MEDIUM
Cast concrete and ceramic tile

DONORS
On loan from Linda Day Clark and Carl Clark

Fifteen sculptors from across the country who were alumni of the Rinehart School of Sculpture at the Maryland Institute College of Art were invited to create new works of art for an Artscape exhibition planned by the city for the summer of 1996 to mark the centennial of the founding of that graduate program. Titled Celebrating Rinehart, the exhibition was curated by this author. The exhibiting artists were Robert Alholm (class of 1982), Rodney Carroll ('83), Paul Daniel ('75), Laure Drogoul ('82), John Ferguson ('71), Chris Gavin ('88), Paul Glasgow ('81), Paul Gregg ('95), Drake Hawthorne ('96), Gregory Henry ('87), Eunice Kambara ('94), Allyn Massey ('89), Steve Reber ('85), Christy Rupp ('77), and René Townsend ('87). The pieces by Carroll, Henry, Massey, Rupp, and Townsend have remained on site. The piece shown here was made for that 1996 exhibition.

After completing her MFA at Rinehart, the first African American woman to do so, Townsend returned to Chicago to join the faculty of the School of the Art Institute of Chicago, where she had earned her BFA. She participated in numerous community art projects, including the Gallery 37 Project, sponsored by the Chicago Department of Cultural Affairs, and received several commissions through the Chicago Percent for Art program, including projects for the Thurgood Marshall Branch Library and the Forest Glen Elementary School. Her work can be found in West Chatham Park and at the Chicago Transit Authority's Bronzeville Green Line Station.

Many of Townsend's public artworks combined a life-casting technique with mosaics. For the DuSable Museum of African American History, in Chicago, she created a life-size sculpture representing the four children who survived the 1839 mutiny by African captives on the *Amistad.* With a group of children as her models, she used her life-casting technique. Covering her young models with Vaseline to protect their skin during the model-making process, she applied a thick layer of plaster of Paris and allowed it to harden into a negative mold. She then created a papier-mâché sculpture from all the body casts, and the museum had them cast in bronze and reconfigured for display in 2003.

Townsend employed her life-casting technique for this piece. She asked an old friend, the Baltimore artist Linda Day Clark, to be her model for the female form, and then she asked other friends in Baltimore for pieces of old ceramics, which she supplemented from thrift shop purchases. With the mold of the figure and with all the collected ceramics broken into fragments, Townsend worked on site, outside the Rinehart studios, which are located in the Mount Royal Station, at the foot of this driveway.

A female figure appears embedded in an upright rectangular block whose surface has been decorated front and back with the ceramic tile fragments. The head and nude upper body, made from the life casting, is "dressed" in drapery that hangs from the figure's waist down to the ground, in folds created by manipulating the concrete and setting the ceramic pieces in the layers. Surrounding and accentuating the head, which is tilted slightly upward, are rows of white shells. The figure's face, neck, chest, and arms are decorated with small brown rectangular stones that have been set in bands around the figure's arms and in strands that run up and down the torso. Townsend seems to have created this piece as a tangible document of her years in Baltimore and as a reminder of the lasting friendships she made.

Note: This piece was to be given to Morgan State University and was to be moved there at the close of the exhibition in 1996. In November 2010 the piece was still in front of the Mount Royal Station building; if it is no longer there, it can probably be seen somewhere on the Morgan State University campus.

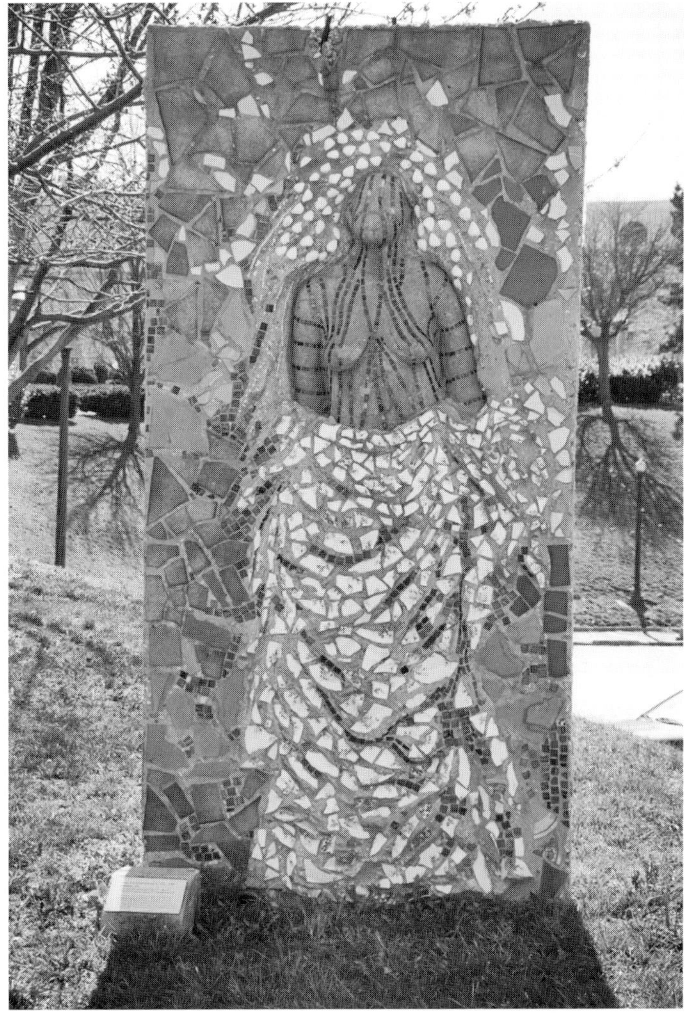

TITLE
Maya Queen Empowered, ca. 1989
LOCATION
Maryland Institute College of Art, Mount Royal
Station, 1400 Cathedral Street
SCULPTOR
Lila Katzen (1925–1998)
MEDIA
Stainless steel and bronze
DONOR
On loan from the artist's estate

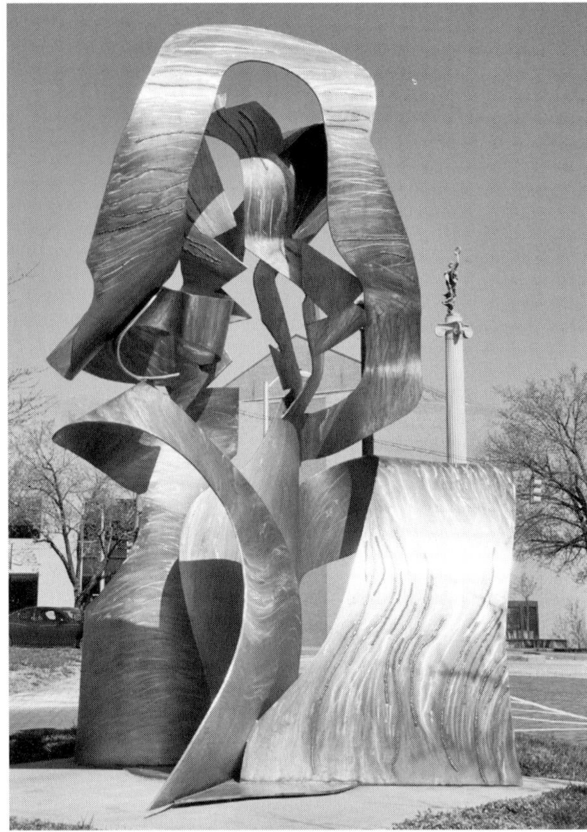

Lila Katzen began her career as a painter. Born in Brooklyn, she trained initially at the Art Students League and then at New York's Cooper Union, where she earned her BFA. In 1948 she moved to Baltimore. As early as 1955, as an accomplished painter, she was given her first one-person exhibition at the Baltimore Museum of Art. In 1962 Katzen accepted a position at the Maryland Institute College of Art, where she remained on the faculty until 1980. During that time her interests turned to sculpture, and she began experimenting with nontraditional materials. She achieved international acclaims for her *Liquid Tunnel,* a light and fluorescent liquid sculpture shown at the 1970 São Paulo Biennale in Brazil. In 1988 she was the American representative to World Expo 88 in Brisbane, Australia, where she exhibited a 20-foot-high sculpture of Cor-Ten steel.

For much of her sculpture made in the 1970s, 1980s, and 1990s she used stainless steel and Cor-Ten, the weathering steel that she would allow to develop its natural patina of rust, as can be seen in *Fanned Arena,* at the Johns Hopkins University's Olin Hall (J18). After a visit to several Mayan sites on a 1981 trip to the Yucatán Peninsula, Katzen became fascinated with Mayan society and culture, and certain Mayan references began to appear in her work. As the title of this piece suggests, Katzen imagined a Mayan ceremonial robe made of ribbonlike fabric layered around an imaginary figure, curving and twisting as if blowing in the wind. The bronze and stainless steel weldments, or linear welts, serve a decorative role here and help suggest a richly textured fabric. The weldments were new for Katzen and very different from the smooth planes in her earlier work. Although she never wavered in her commitment to abstraction, some of her works from this period reflecting a Mayan influence also seem to suggest the figure.

Katzen had a prolific career, exhibiting extensively in both solo and group shows. Her work is held in the collections of the DeCordova Museum in Lincoln, Massachusetts, the National Gallery of Art in Washington, the J. Paul Getty Museum in Los Angeles, and the Wadsworth Atheneum in Hartford, Connecticut, as well as in the outdoor sculpture collection at Wichita State University, in Kansas, where Katzen was a visiting professor in 1995.

This piece was originally exhibited at the 1989 International Art Expo, held at the Chicago Navy Pier, and then was on display at the Time-Life Building in Chicago before coming to the Maryland Institute in 2002.

I7

TITLE
Time Flies, 1996

LOCATION
MICA Store, 1200 W. Mount Royal Avenue

SCULPTOR
Christy Rupp (b. 1949)

MEDIUM
Man-made stone, steel, and clock

DONOR
On loan from the artist

This piece was one of the fifteen artworks commissioned for the 1996 Artscape exhibition, Celebrating Rinehart, and one of five pieces to remain on site. It was also one of four pieces funded in part by the Municipal Art Society of Baltimore City to inaugurate a new Revolving Sculpture Project, whose aim was to place long-term temporary sculptures around the Maryland Institute campus. (For more information on that exhibition, see I5.)

The snail that appears to be slowly climbing up the wall of the college store, weighted down by the clock mounted in its shell, was a charming and humorous addition to the exhibition celebrating the centennial of the Rinehart School of Sculpture. One of Rupp's most successful early works, *Social Progress,* sponsored by the Public Art Fund in 1986 and installed on the corner of 23rd Street and 5th Avenue in New York, featured a 3½-foot-high snail pulling a 17-foot-long ear of corn behind it with a 20-foot rope. As a metaphor for struggle and a weighty slowness, the piece was as witty as it was serious, just as her Baltimore piece is.

In 1997 Rupp completed a New York City Percent for Art commission for which she made clock housings for six hall clocks in Early Childhood Center #2 in the Bronx. Cutouts of a turtle, racing rabbits, a sloth, a jaguar, a comet, and a fossil, in bronze, aluminum, and brass, were paired on three floors to reflect the slow and fast passage of time.

All of Rupp's work forces the viewer to think about the environment. With wit and a lot of environmental information, Rupp has dealt in her other public artworks with water issues, bacterial pathogens, urban ecology, and genetically engineered foods. A 1973 graduate of Colgate University, Rupp, who was born in Buffalo, New York, then earned a master of arts in teaching from the Rhode Island School of Design in 1974 and an MFA from the Rinehart School in 1977. In 1981 and again in 1985 she was awarded an Individual Artist Fellowship by the National Endowment for the Arts. Over the years Rupp has taught at Bard College in Annandale-on-Hudson, New York, at Brooklyn College, and at Lehman College in the Bronx. For a 2008 exhibition titled Extinct Birds Previously Consumed by Humans, at the Frederieke Taylor Gallery in New York, Rupp recreated some endangered species of birds, constructing them from bones collected from fast-food outlets.

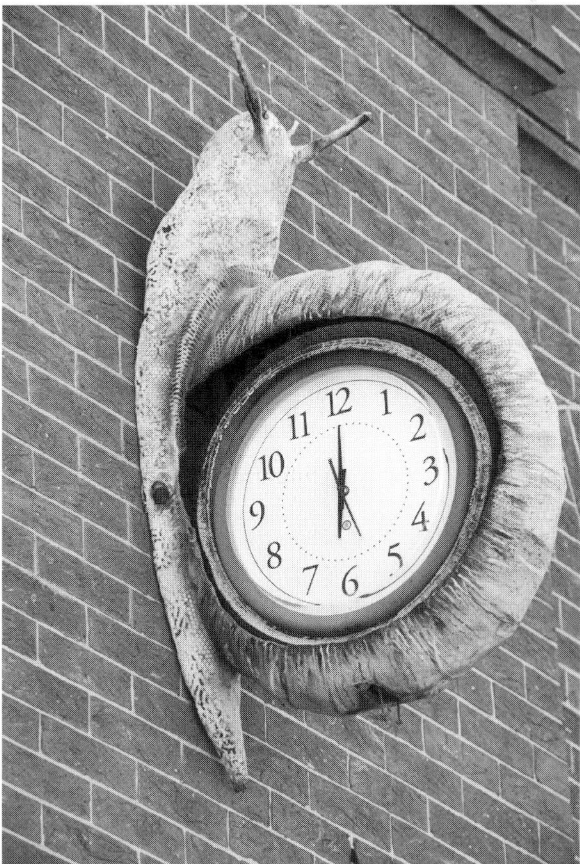

TITLE
Tenchi-Nage, 1996

LOCATION
Maryland Institute College of Art, Main Building,
1300 W. Mount Royal Avenue

SCULPTOR
Rodney Carroll (b. 1949)

MEDIUM
Steel

DONOR
On loan from the artist

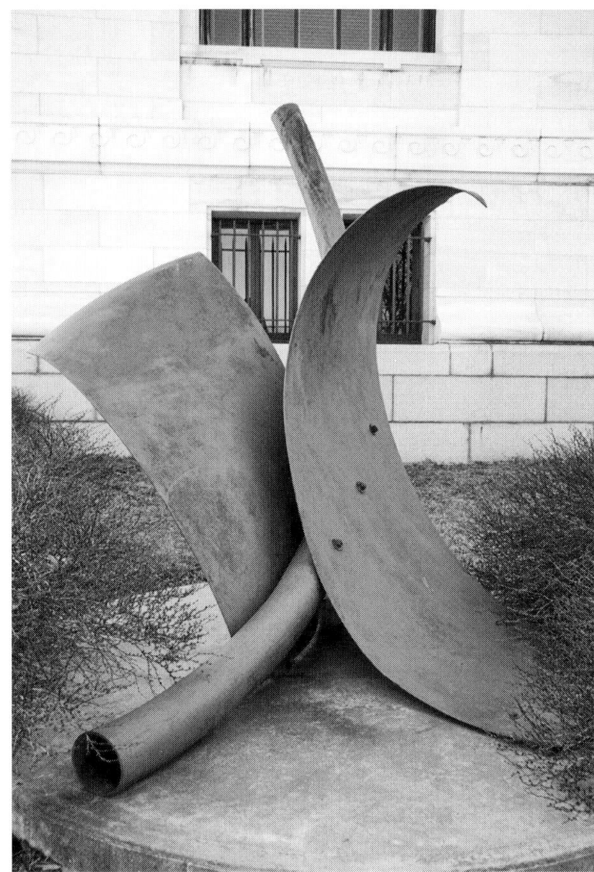

Further up Mount Royal Avenue from Christy Rupp's *Time Flies* (17) is this sculpture by Rodney Carroll, one of the pieces of sculpture commissioned for the 1996 Artscape exhibition, Celebrating Rinehart, that has remained on site. Carroll's choice of this site determined the scale of his piece. Most of Carroll's sculptures at the time had a verticality that would not have worked here. Concurrent with this exhibition commission, Carroll was working on a Percent for Art commission for a sculpture that would stand 20 feet high in front of the Montebello Elementary School (K11).

Carroll began a new series of sculptures that would deal with the dynamic relationship between two people or two elements. For inspiration he turned to Aikido, a Japanese martial art that focuses, not on punching or kicking an opponent, but rather on using one's own energy to gain control of an opponent in order to throw that opponent away from oneself, never to permanently harm him or her. Tenchi-Nage is one such throw. Literally translated as "Heaven and Earth Throw," it was so named because, during the throw, one hand travels upward toward the heavens while the other hand travels downward toward the earth. Here the arcing element on the left represents the figure that is lifting and throwing his opponent, who is represented by the element on the right. The energy exerted between the two elements, or opponents, is represented by the central curving tubular form, which extends 9 feet into the air.

The three elements are bolted together and mounted on a circular concrete base. When the piece was first installed, the uncoated steel had a silver color, which today has weathered to a rich reddish-brown.

The building behind Tenchi-Nage is the main building of the Maryland Institute. After the Great Fire of Baltimore in 1904 destroyed the Institute's 1852 Market Place Building, plans to rebuild in a new location began in earnest. A building site adjacent to Corpus Christi Church was donated by the Jenkins family, and a competition was held, which was won by Pell and Corbett Architects. The new building was completed and occupied in 1907 as the permanent home for the oldest fully accredited degree-granting college of art in the country, which has operated in the city since 1826.

19

TITLE
The Pulse of Time Starts and Stops, 1996

LOCATION
Median at W. Mount Royal Avenue
and W. Lanvale Street

SCULPTOR
Gregory Henry (b. 1961)

MEDIUM
Painted steel

DONOR
On loan from the artist

Whether he is making a drawing, a print, a painting, or a piece of sculpture, Gregory Henry uses simple, everyday objects from his childhood, spent on a chicken farm in Guyana. Roosters and chickens figure prominently, as do bulls and cows as well as utilitarian vessels—pots and pans, kettles and water buckets. For his contribution to the 1996 Artscape exhibition, celebrating the Rinehart School of Sculpture, Henry chose two of his iconic forms, the rooster and a vessel.

Henry's choice of the rooster for this exhibition celebrating one hundred years is particularly fitting, for roosters are the guardians of time, protectors of the night and announcers of the morning. The inclusion of the rooster may offer a hint at the title, suggesting that the sculpture deals with the passage of time and the simpler things in life, which are sometimes overlooked and underappreciated. The silhouette of the vessel may also serve as a metaphor for the passage of time. When the sculpture is approached from the front, the vessel that doubles as the base appears broad and rectangular; from the side the curving shape is so thin it almost vanishes, reminding the viewer of a slice of time, a snapshot of life.

It is also appropriate that Henry made a piece of sculpture so clearly tied to his Guyanese culture, which he had turned away from after emigrating to Brooklyn, New York, with his family, but to which he returned while in graduate school at Rinehart. He has since added to his icons and fables from Guyanese culture to include African and other South American cultures.

Henry, who was born in Esequibo, Guyana, earned his BFA from Ohio University in Athens, Ohio, in 1985 and then attended the Rinehart School of Sculpture at the Maryland Institute, where he earned his MFA in 1987. Today he is an associate professor of art at the Christopher Newport University in Newport News, Virginia. His work has been exhibited widely in Virginia, North Carolina, New York, Maryland, and Kentucky and is included in the permanent collections of the Corcoran Gallery in Washington; the Harriet Tubman Museum in Atlanta; the museum of Hampton University in Virginia, where he was on the faculty; the Kansas African American Museum in Wichita; and the museum of Ohio University. He has completed two public art commissions recently, a Monument to Service, for the Newport News Police Headquarters in 2008, and the design for a floor medallion in the new Terminal B at the Ronald Reagan Washington International Airport. He has also illustrated a children's book—*Chickens! Chickens!*—for which he won the 1995 Parents' Choice Silver Honors.

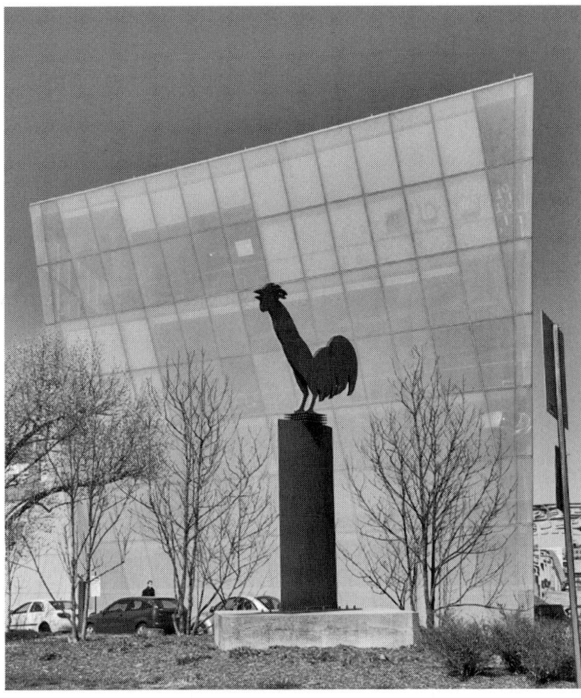

TITLE
Untitled, 1996

LOCATION
Maryland Institute College of Art, Fox Building,
1301 W. Mount Royal Avenue

SCULPTOR
Allyn Massey (b. 1949)

MEDIUM
Steel

DONOR
On loan from the artist

In 1980 the former Cannon Shoe Company warehouse was renovated and opened by the Maryland Institute as the Fox Building, providing more faculty offices, classrooms, studio space, and the Meyerhoff Gallery. In 1992 the Institute continued its expansion along West Mount Royal Avenue by purchasing the Maryland AAA headquarters building and renovating it for classrooms, gallery space, and a new home for the Decker Library. When Allyn Massey was invited to make a site-specific work of art for the 1996 Artscape exhibition, celebrating the centennial of the Rinehart School of Sculpture, of which she is an alumna, she decided to make a piece of sculpture that would clearly mark these two buildings as belonging to the Maryland Institute.

Massey's proposal drawing for this piece showed an open sphere on the northwest corner of the roof of the Fox Building with a 102-foot beam that extended downward, meeting the ground at the southeast corner of the former AAA building, connecting the two buildings visually. Massey hoped that with further investigation she would figure out a way to light the beam.

Many roadblocks prevented the full realization of that remarkable proposal. Funding was key to being able to light the beam. But money might have been raised if the city had allowed that beam to cross what turned out to be a city street running between the two buildings. Even today it looks like an alley, which could have been closed at least temporarily. Having to raise

the beam twenty feet off the ground where it met the former AAA building removed too much of the poetry of the piece for Massey to proceed with the necessary engineering and lighting studies. Remarkably, the sphere was installed on the roof of the Fox Building, where it remains.

Massey had been incorporating round forms into her work for a long time. The sphere is all encompassing and nonthreatening. This commission was an opportunity to work with the form on a much large scale than she had done before. This sphere is 14 feet in diameter and sits on a 6-foot-high platform that is hidden from view because the roof is 6 feet below the top of the parapet. Massey fabricated the entire piece by hand. What is so remarkable about this fact is that four months before she received this commission, her Clipper Mill studio, along with the studios of twenty-three other artists, had burned to the ground. She did not have a screwdriver. She did not even have a vice. She had lost everything— all her artwork stored there, her drawings, her journals, her slides of earlier work, and her tools. With a little insurance settlement money, she bought a welder; she borrowed everything else she needed, including a wooden worktable, and set to work cutting and bending 1-inch solid steel rods.

The sphere is made up of four major pieces—like an orange cut in half, with each half then cut in half. The quarters were then locked together along what serves as the two equators of this sphere using bulldog clips, which she fabricated—flat steel plate cut in short, 3-inch strips and bent into U-shaped pieces, which Massey then drilled holes into and bolted around two rods from each section to secure the piece together. These bolts are visible to the eye. Set on axis, the transparent sphere can be seen to have other bracing elements. The openness of the piece was necessitated by weight restrictions for placement on the roof and for wind resistance.

The timing of this commission led Massey to remember the myth of Sisyphus. Her desire to incorporate a reference to this myth in a new artwork was what led to the original design, incorporating the slanting beam with the sphere, and what made it so difficult to give up. Sisyphus was the founder and king of Corinth, but more importantly for Massey, he had been condemned by the gods to ceaselessly roll a boulder up to the top of a mountain, from which the boulder would fall back by its own weight, and Sisyphus would have to begin again. The myth represented the idea of starting over and how difficult that is—something Massey was having to do, beginning with this project, coming as it did on the heels of the devastating fire.

Massey is a professor in the Department of Art and Art History at Goucher College in Towson, Maryland. She received her BFA from the Corcoran School of Art in Washington in 1986 and her MFA from the Rinehart School in 1989. Upon graduation from Rinehart, Massey was awarded the Henry A. Walters Traveling Fellowship and the Amalie Rothschild Award for Sculpture. She received Individual Artist Fellowships from the Maryland State Arts Council in 1992, 1995, and again in 1998. Her sculpture has been exhibited extensively in Baltimore and throughout Maryland, as well as in Washington and Virginia.

Just below Massey's piece is a very large Buddha that was built in 1994 by a student from Japan, Noriko Ikaga. Close to 7 feet high and made out of adobe, cement, and sand, unfired and unglazed, the Buddha was Ikaga's senior thesis project. The idea of leaving the Buddha in its natural state, allowing it to weather naturally, is a reflection of the Buddhist teaching of impermanence. Admirers have been unable to allow the natural deterioration to occur and have been restoring the piece. Originally Ikaga incised a brick pattern in the clay surface with white mortar lines to resemble the brick buildings of Baltimore and reflect her new environment.

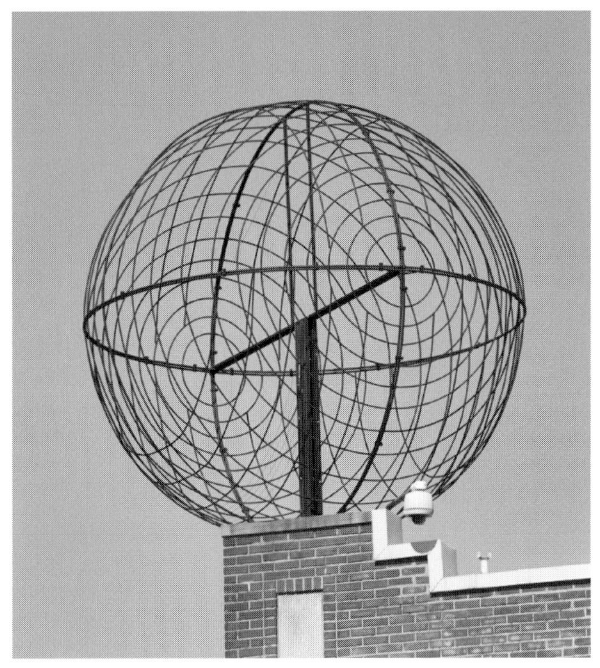

I11

TITLE
Untitled, 1976

LOCATION
Median at W. Mount Royal and Lafayette avenues

SCULPTOR
John Parker (b. 1948)

MEDIUM
Painted steel

DONOR
Gift of the artist

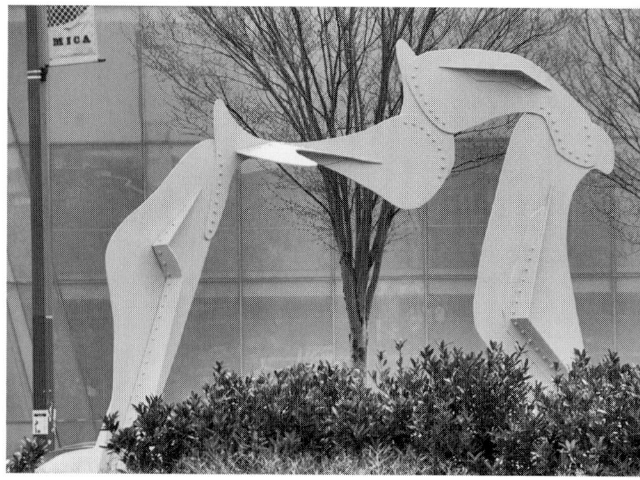

This untitled piece of sculpture was first exhibited by John Parker in his thesis exhibition, a requirement of all students graduating from the Rinehart School of Sculpture at the Maryland Institute. Parker, a 1977 graduate, was interested in making a gateway piece. Thinking about the atrium space of the library on the second floor of the Mount Royal Station building, which also houses the Rinehart studios, and the experience of walking through that space led him closer to a design for a work of art that people could walk through.

There were other influences at work here. A collector of insects since high school, Parker continues to add a half-dozen species a year to his collection. References to the shapes and gestures of insects can be seen in the individual shapes he used to build his arch. He cut the shapes from steel plate and then fitted them together, bolting or welding the overlapping patterns. The bolts are both functional and decorative.

A secondary fascination of Parker's, which may have contributed to the design of this piece, is his love of dinosaurs. One way of looking at the archway is to see it as a gigantic, larger-than-life insect spread out across the median, maybe some form of praying mantis. The bright yellow color adds to its playfulness and accentuates its curvilinear silhouette.

Today Parker owns The Painted Garden in Glenside, Pennsylvania, where he sells his own, unique hand-crafted iron garden structures. He has continued to make and exhibit his sculpture, primarily with the Midwest Sculpture Initiative, which organizes several exhibitions of outdoor sculpture annually throughout the Midwest.

TITLE
CONFEDERATE SOLDIERS AND SAILORS
MONUMENT, 1902

LOCATION
W. Mount Royal Avenue near Mosher Street

SCULPTOR
F. Wellington Ruckstuhl (1853–1942)

MEDIUM
Bronze

DONOR
Maryland Daughters of the Confederacy

How difficult must it have been to live in Baltimore during the Civil War? William T. Walters, keenly aware of the difficulty his Southern sympathies would cause him in Baltimore, moved with his family to Paris for the duration. John Work Garrett had to overcome his Southern sympathies to acknowledge his aversion to the idea of Southern secession, for he had spent his professional life knitting the country together as president of the B&O Railroad. Johns Hopkins, a B&O Railroad board member, joined Garrett in encouraging the other board members to keep the railroad in the service of the Union.

An examination of Baltimore's public monuments associated with the Civil War provides another measure of the challenges of living in this border state during the war. Baltimore may be the only city in the country that has monuments to both Union and Confederate soldiers and sailors. The Maryland Daughters of the Confederacy raised the money for their monument privately and commissioned a Southern sympathizer from New York, F. Wellington Ruckstuhl. Here Glory supports a fallen soldier, his standard lowered but her wreath of History held high. Glory's huge wings reach dramatically upward toward the sky. The inscription on the base of the monument is "GLORIA VICTIS," meaning "Glory to the Vanquished," making the outcome of the war as clear in this monument as it is in the Union

monument in Wyman Park, on the corner of N. Charles and 29th streets (J1).

Two other public monuments in the city, both privately commissioned, are dedicated to the Southern efforts in the war: the Lee and Jackson Monument, across from the Baltimore Museum of Art on the edge of Wyman Park (J2), and the Confederate Women's Monument, at the corner of N. Charles Street and University Parkway (J25). What an investigation of all four Civil War monuments makes clear is that while the state government kept Baltimore officially on the side of the Union, there were many in the city who were clearly, if unofficially, sympathetic to the Southern cause.

When this monument was dedicated on May 2, 1903, less than forty years after the War Between the States, the thousands who attended the unveiling had very vivid memories of the war. Many in attendance were local veterans. Others were people who had been personally touched by the war and were there to remember their sweethearts, husbands, brothers, fathers, and grandfathers. The veterans gathered at the Washington Monument to organize for a parade to Mount Royal for the unveiling. Some were on horseback, and some were marching, led the whole way by Andrew C. Trippe, major general of the United Confederate Veterans of Maryland and an officer who had been wounded and captured during the war. With the bands playing "Dixie," they marched up Charles Street waving swords and hats, carrying their regimental banners and, of course, their Confederate flags. It was a very emotional scene at the memorial. Women wept, and so did men. They were remembering their lost comrades and loved ones and their broken hopes of the past.

In New York only a few weeks later, on May 30, 1903, Augustus Saint-Gaudens' Sherman Monument— the gilded statue of Sherman on horseback being led by a female figure on foot, Victory, who carries a palm branch of peace—was dedicated. The monument stands on the corner of 5th Avenue and 59th Street. Also in New York there was a military parade in which some of Sherman's own men marched and during which the bands played "Marching through Georgia." The dedication in New York was as celebratory as

the one in Maryland was sad. The contemporaneous
dedications of these two monuments clearly illustrate
that the coals of civil strife die slowly, and as much a
part of history as the Civil War is today, in the early
years of the twentieth century it was still being fought.

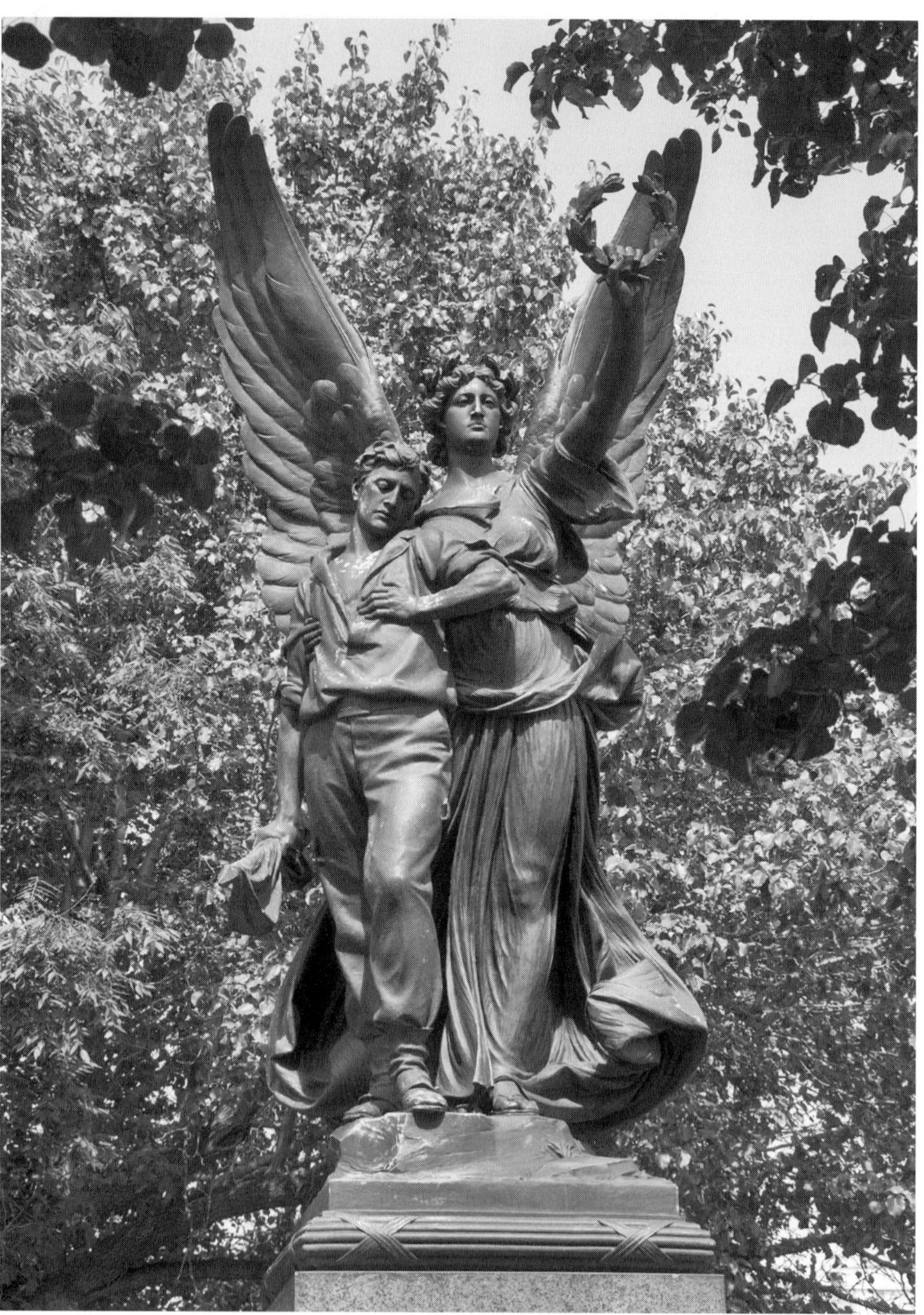

I13

TITLE
Nut and Bolt, 1982

LOCATION
Mount Royal Elementary / Middle School,
121 McMechen Street

SCULPTOR
J. Arthur Benson (b. 1933)

MEDIUM
Painted steel

DONOR
Baltimore City Percent for Art program

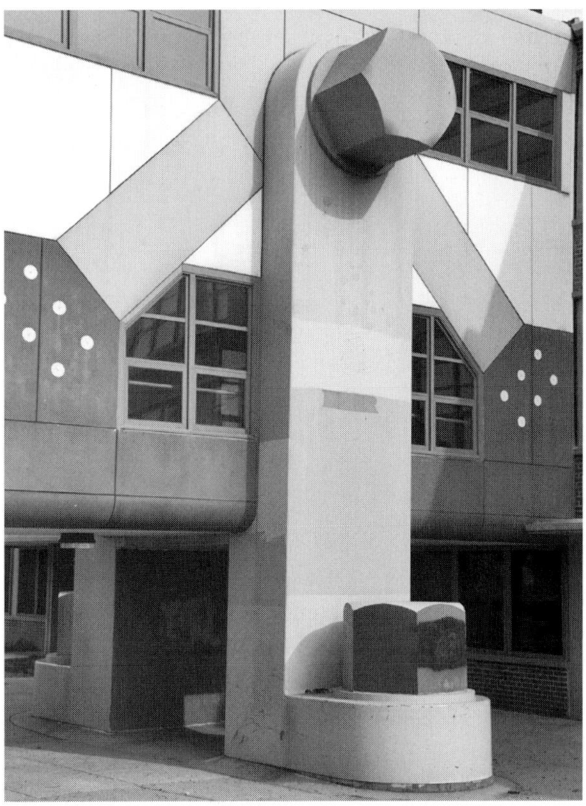

Art Benson lives in Baltimore, where he was on the faculty at the Maryland Institute College of Art for three decades, from 1972 to 2002, serving as the head of the undergraduate sculpture department. He received this commission in 1981 from James Pettit, the project architect for Ayers Saint (today Ayers Saint Gross), who designed the new addition to the existing school.

The artwork was to be developed as part of an elevated, two-story pedestrian bridge connecting the new building to the older one. The walkway is clad in metal panels that were painted yellow, white, and red and arranged to emphasize the mechanical nature of the bridge. The sculpture appears to be an integral part of the bridge, functioning as a visual anchor but also serving to hide structural columns that turned out to be needed to support the bridge above the plaza area. The two large L-brackets, origially painted bright royal blue, one designed for each side of this elevated passageway, appear to have been fixed in place by four nuts and bolts, two for each bracket, one at the top to attach it to the passageway and one at the bottom to affix it to the plaza. The nuts were painted a deep green, and the bolts were painted the yellow of the bridge panels. The mild plate steel used in the fabrication of this piece is $^{3}/_{16}$ inch thick and was originally painted with epoxy and an Emron coating.

Because this addition was being built to a school in the historic district of Bolton Hill, the Preservation Commission was involved in approving the architect's and the artist's proposals. The commission raised serious questions about the appropriateness of the pedestrian bridge, with its accompanying artwork, and decided that the proposed addition was not "historically correct." The neighborhood was very much involved on both sides of what became a bit of a controversy. After a long delay and an agreement to take some of the sheen off of the original colors, the project was allowed to proceed. The architect and artist collaborated to produce a work of art that would be fun and colorful and visually related to a tinker toy. After all, this was a school for young children, and *Nut and Bolt* would be installed near where these students played every day.

TITLE
Babette, 1982

LOCATION
Maryland Institute College of Art, the Commons,
120 McMechen Street

SCULPTOR
Paul Daniel (b. 1950)

MEDIUM
Steel and stainless steel

DONOR
On loan from the artist

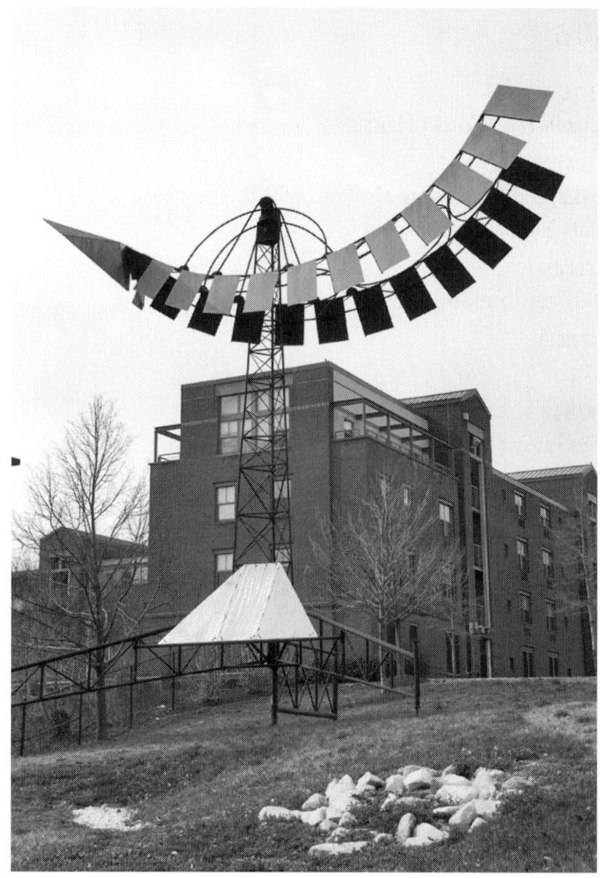

Paul Daniel began building the base of this sculpture with no clear idea of the rest of the piece, only knowing that he wanted to build something large scale that was kinetic. The piece he ended up making is an assemblage of leftover materials from Daniel's earlier sculpture projects—*Titan* and *Harpie,* commissioned through the city's Percent for Art program for Liberty Elementary School (N3–N4), and *Aeolian,* a temporary wind-driven piece that floated on the reservoir in Druid Hill Park for more than a year.

The base of this piece would have to be stable enough to hold, at its height, the weight of a moving element. Steel pipes in varying sizes were used to construct the three arms of the base, which were then arranged like a tripod. The trussed tower, which projects 25 feet into the air, functions as support for a 23-foot-long steel construction with a swooping crescent profile, from which steel panels hang. These panels, whose outer surface is painted yellow and whose inner surface is black, increase in size toward the open end. At the closed end, where these two horizontal pipes converge, Daniel added multifaceted panels, which give a flourishing finish to this top structure. This top structure can rock front to back and can rotate 360° in the wind before returning to its original position. The pitch of the vertical truss refers to Italian towers, with which Daniel was fascinated at the time.

The title *Babette* came from a 1959 French film, *Les Quatre Cents Coups,* or *400 Blows,* directed by François Truffaut, which Daniel saw in 1982. Babette was one of the characters, and the name appealed to him. In 1994 the piece was moved from outside Daniel's Clipper Mill studio to the grounds behind the Commons, an apartment complex for Maryland Institute students that opened in 1992.

I15

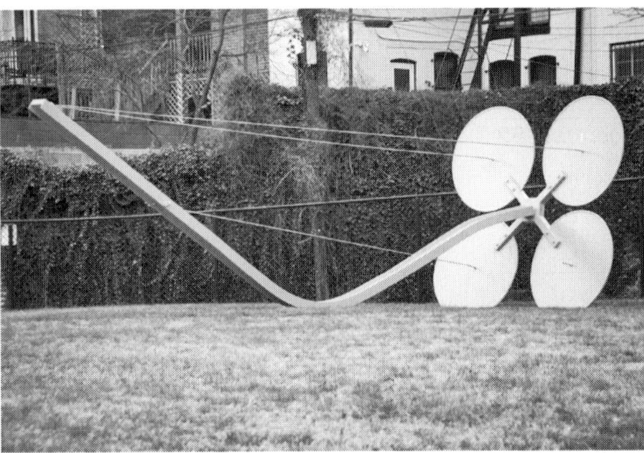

A found object at a wreckage site became the impetus for this sculpture by Jeffrey Johnson. The idea for what to do with the found object came from a drawing of an aerial view of Idaho farmland.

In 1973 Johnson was a graduate student in the Rinehart School of Sculpture at the Maryland Institute. Deutsches Haus, up the hill and across the street to the south from his studio in the Mount Royal Station, was being torn down, and he was fascinated. Originally built to house the Bryn Mawr School, the building had been sold to house ten Baltimore German singing societies. Today it is the site of the Meyerhoff Symphony Hall. As Johnson watched the work progress, a very large steel beam caught his eye. The beam had been bent by the wrecking ball being used on site, and he found its new shape very sensuous. One night he talked his friends into helping him recover that beam from the work site and take it to his studio.

Now that he had his beam, Johnson began thinking about making a new piece of sculpture. He remembered a drawing he had made quickly during a plane trip that took him over Idaho. He was intrigued by the green cloverleaf patterns in the fields that had resulted from the use of a particular type of watering machine for irrigation. Designed as a way of conserving water, the machine watered four fields at a time from one central pipe. Off the central pipe were four smaller pipes, each leading to a sprinkler that traveled in a circle. The resulting pattern, which he recorded in his sketchbook, now provided the inspiration for another element of his new sculpture. He fabricated four steel discs, which he bolted into an 8-foot-square cloverleaf pattern. Tension cables stretch from the center of each disc of the cloverleaf to the opposite end of the steel beam, an expanse of approximately 27 feet. The cloverleaf stands at a 20° angle, held in place by the tension cables.

That year Anne Arundel Community College invited the Rinehart sculptors to exhibit work on their campus for six months. Johnson sent this piece. Its success led him to begin a series of tension sculptures using steel plates, beams, and cables. He continued the series in Houston, where he went to teach at the University of St. Thomas in 1974, immediately after graduating from the Rinehart School.

Three years later, in 1977, Johnson decided to return to California, where he had been born and raised. He eventually joined the faculty at Los Medonas Community College, outside San Francisco, where he served as art department chair, teaching sculpture and ceramics, for seventeen years. He retired in 2006 and lives on five acres outside Sacramento, where he works in his sculpture and ceramics studios and raises sheep.

The title of the piece is a reference to another influence in Johnson's work. His uncle owned a yacht club in California, where he learned to sail at age 9. Johnson says that all his sculpture is horizontal, and he thinks that his passion for sailing is embedded in all his work. It is not too hard to imagine a boat under sail when looking at this piece of sculpture.

TITLE
LT. COL. WILLIAM H. WATSON MONUMENT, 1902

LOCATION
Mount Royal Terrace at North Avenue

SCULPTOR
Edward Berge (1876–1924)

ARCHITECT
Hodges and Leach

MEDIUM
Bronze

DONOR
Maryland Association of Veterans of the
Mexican War

Come! 'tis the red dawn of the day,
Maryland!
Come with thy panoplied array,
Maryland!
With Ringgold's spirit for the fray,
With Watson's blood at Monterey,
With fearless Lowe and dashing May,
Maryland! My Maryland!

The fourth stanza of the nine-stanza poem written by James Ryder Randall in 1861, which became the state song of Maryland, remembers this gallant hero of the Mexican War. William H. Watson was a prominent lawyer in Baltimore with a wife and three children when the war with Mexico broke out in 1846. He had served on the city council and was then serving in the House of Delegates. He did not have to answer President Polk's call to service, but he did. It may have been his West Point education that led to his decision to volunteer. He was made a lieutenant colonel and given command of an infantry battalion that became known as "Baltimore's Own."

After a grueling sea voyage, the battalion was sent immediately into the battle for Monterey. Watson led attacks on the Mexican army, which was entrenched on a well-fortified hill from which the Mexican riflemen could pick their targets. Watson was shot dead on one of those raids. His body was brought home and buried in Greenmount Cemetery with great pomp and circumstance on February 8, 1847. It was not until 1890 that thought was given to the creation of a monument to honor Watson and his comrades who had died in battles at Monterey, Buena Vista, Sonoma, and Mexico City.

The Maryland Association of Veterans of the Mexican War got a grant for $3,000 from the state legislature and commissioned Edward Berge to design the monument. An appropriation from the city council and some private donations supplemented the state funds. A bronze heroic portrait of Watson in uniform with his sword drawn stands atop a 22-foot-high pedestal of Maryland granite. The shaft of the tall pedestal is decorated with four Corinthian pilasters and a handsome entablature with a very sculptural cornice. Watson is depicted with his very recognizable muttonchop whiskers. Four plaques on the shaft list the names of those killed in battle in the years 1846–48, the names of those on the monument committee, the names of the surviving members of the association, and the names of the deceased members, respectively.

When the monument was unveiled on February 22, 1903, the anniversary of the battle of Monterey, it stood in the middle of Mount Royal Avenue at Lanvale Street. When there, the monument included four stands of cannonballs and two Mexican mortars. In 1930, when plans for an extension of Howard Street included an underpass at that intersection, the monument, whose weight was a concern, was moved to just inside what was then the entrance to Druid Hill Park. What is left of the original gates of Druid Hill Park can be seen nearby. Regrettably, the four stands of cannonballs were lost in the move. Not until May 2004 were four new stands of cast-iron ornamental cannonballs restored to the foot of the monument. These antique cannonballs were given to the city by the staff at Fort McHenry and are smaller than ones that might have been fired by the Mexican mortars on site. G. Krug & Sons installed the cannonballs, and the cost was underwritten by two longtime residents of Mount Royal Terrace.

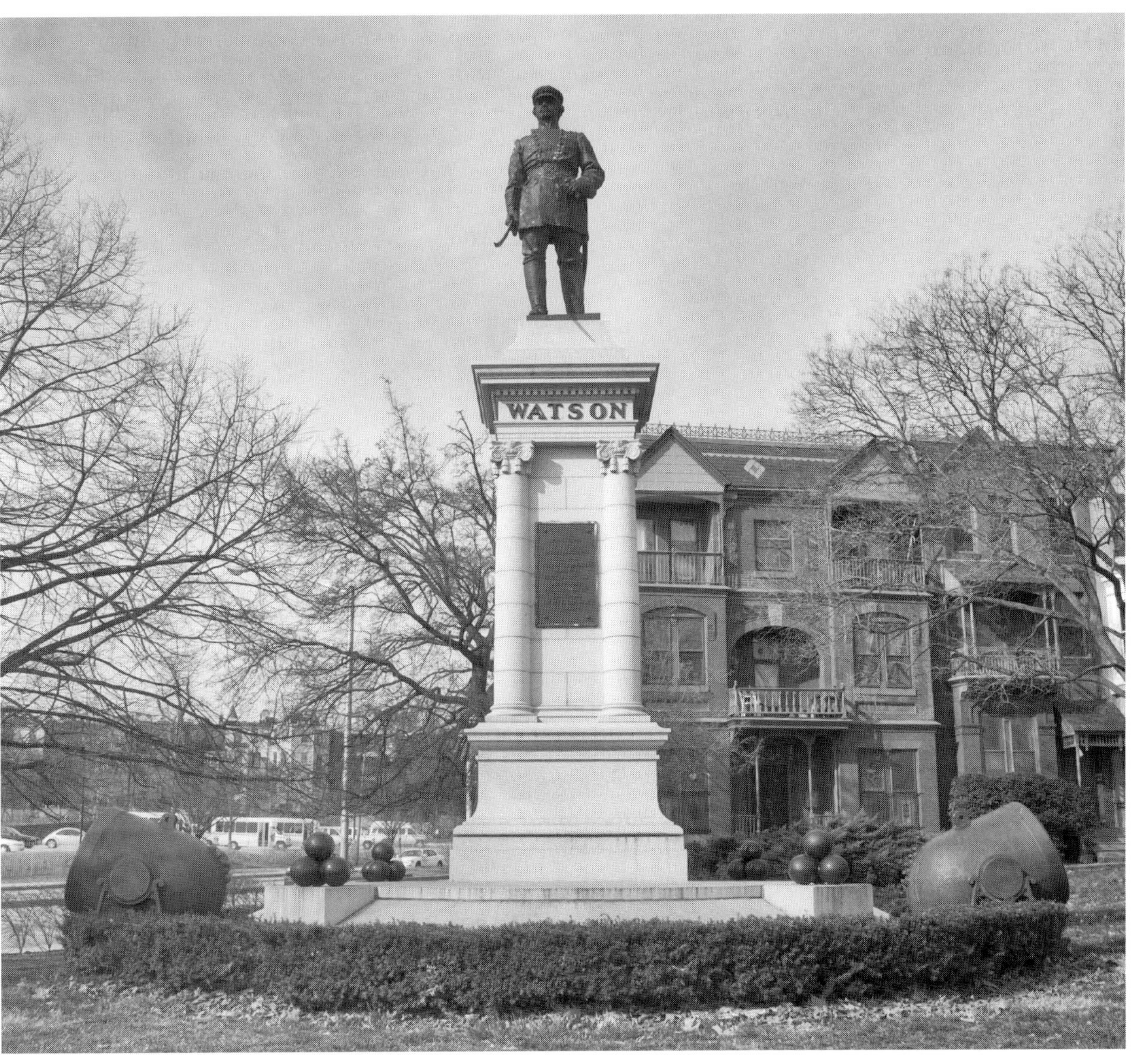

117

TITLE
Lady Baltimore, 1880

LOCATION
Mount Royal Terrace at Lennox Street

SCULPTOR
Herman D. A. Henning (1841–1893)

MEDIUM
Limestone

DONOR
City of Baltimore

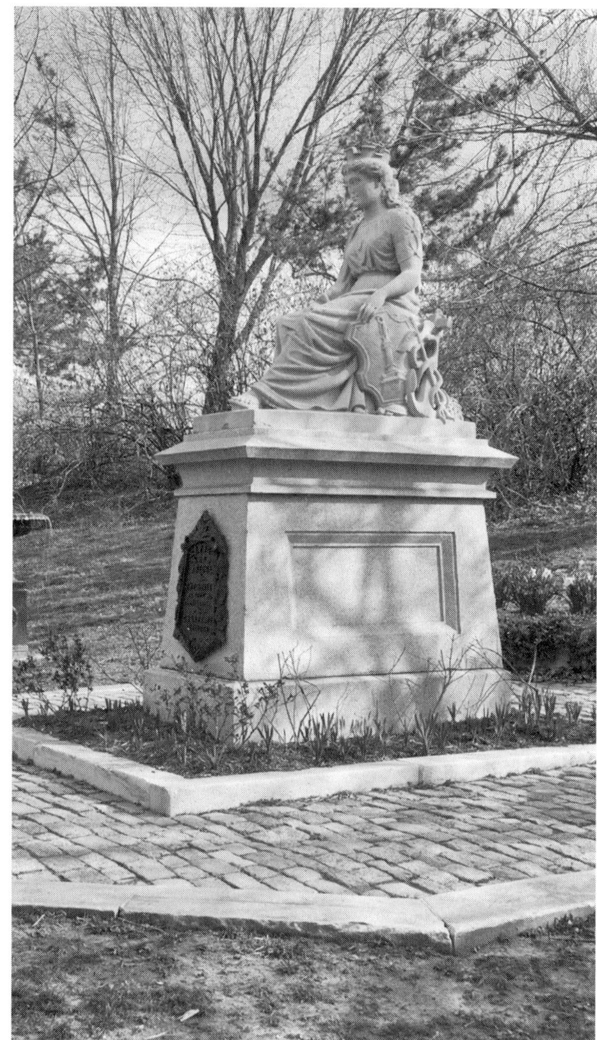

This seated figure was christened *Lady Baltimore* not because she was thought to be the wife of George Calvert, the first Lord Baltimore, but because of her attributes. All the symbols of the history, commerce, and industry of Baltimore placed around her feet led to the interpretation of the figure as an allegorical representation of Baltimore. She wears a crown and an elegant full-length gown. Her left hand rests on a shield bearing the outline of the Battle Monument, which was on the city seal, and her right hand reaches down to touch a hammer, an anvil, gears, and other nautical equipment. Near the shield are an anchor, a caduceus, and a rope and pulleys.

There are three other statues identical to this one, and all four were originally made for the St. Paul Street Bridge, over the Jones Falls. That bridge had been built in 1880 after the designs of the engineer C. H. Latrobe. Herman D. A. Henning, a German-born sculptor who was an instructor at the Maryland Institute at the time, carved the four figures out of limestone, and they were placed on granite bases at the approaches to the bridge. A photograph in a 1910 *Guide to Baltimore* shows their placement.

In 1957 the city of Baltimore began construction of the Jones Falls Expressway, which necessitated the rebuilding of several bridges, including the St. Paul Street Bridge. The four ladies were temporarily moved to storage. Then, on June 21, 1974, one of the four statues was sent to Baltimore, Ireland, which is considered the ancestral home of the Calverts, Maryland's founding family, as a gift from one Baltimore to another. At about the same time the other three statues were moved to Cylburn Park and sited in the garden there.

Then, in 1979, one of those ladies from Clyburn appeared as the centerpiece of this narrow but charming two-block green strip along Mount Royal Terrace. This strip, with its 8-foot-high berm and heavy tree planting, was created to protect the nearby neighborhood from the noise and view of traffic traveling on the new Jones Falls Expressway, just behind it.

I18

TITLE
Untitled, 1967

LOCATION
Eutaw-Marshburn Elementary School,
1624 Eutaw Place

SCULPTOR
Thomas F. Hoffmaster (b. 1923)

MEDIUM
Bronze

DONOR
Baltimore City Percent for Art program

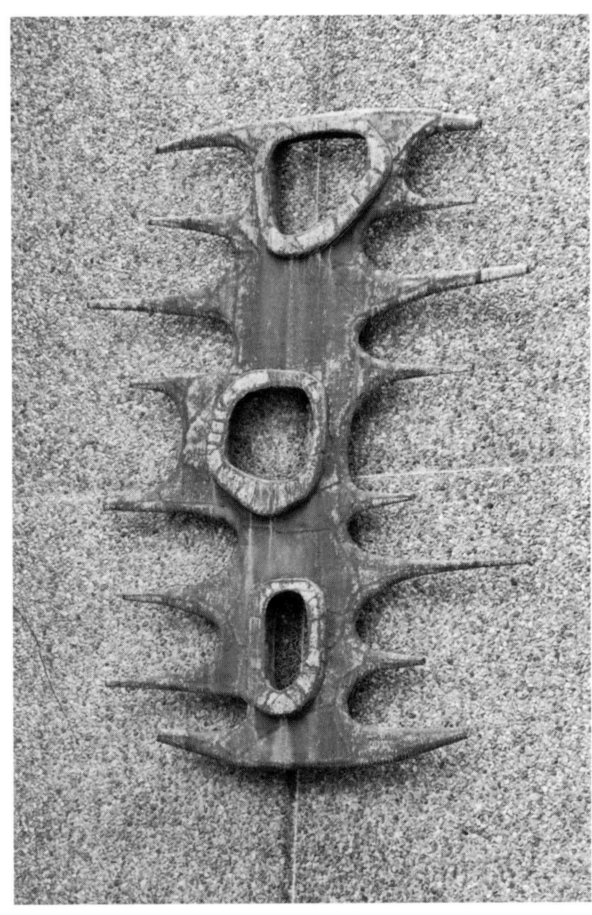

This abstract bronze wall relief, installed over the entrance to the Eutaw-Marshburn Elementary School when it first opened, is one of the earliest artworks completed under the city's Percent for Art ordinance, passed in 1964 by the city council. (For more information about the early history of Baltimore's Percent for Art program, see A5.) The first year that artworks commissioned through this program appeared was 1967, when three sculptures were sited outdoors.

A Baltimorean by birth, Thomas Hoffmaster began taking art classes at the Maryland Institute when he was just 13. He attended the Johns Hopkins University, where he earned a degree in biology, and went on to a career as a medical artist and photographer. He continued making sculpture and received a second commission through the Percent for Art program.

This untitled bronze is abstract, having three vertically stacked amorphous-shaped openings and eight projections of random lengths extending from each side. His second commission was awarded in 1971 for the interior of the Waverly branch of the Enoch Pratt Library. Hoffmaster's approach for that commission was very different: he created a frieze of metal figures representing well-known writers such as Edgar Allan Poe, Frederick Douglass, and H. L. Mencken and literary characters such as Tom Sawyer, Paul Bunyan, Don Quixote, and Long John Silver.

TITLE

FRANCIS SCOTT KEY MONUMENT, 1911

LOCATION

Eutaw Place at Lanvale Street

SCULPTOR

Marius Jean Antonin Mercié (1845–1916)

MEDIUM

Granite, bronze, and marble

DONOR

Charles L. Marburg

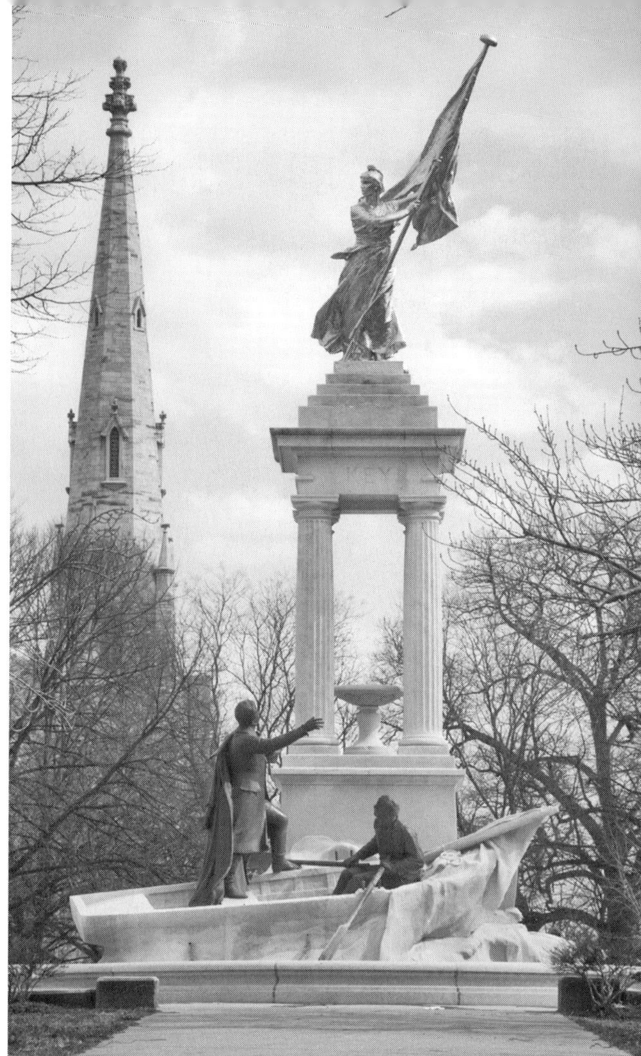

In 1907, just weeks before his death, Charles L. Marburg gave $25,000 to his brother, Theodore, to commission a monument to his favorite poet, Francis Scott Key (1779–1843). Charles and Theodore Marburg were members of a very prominent mercantile family in Baltimore. Theodore was the best-known family member, celebrated as an author, art collector, founding member of the Municipal Art Society of Baltimore, and a former ambassador to Belgium. Charles was head of Marburg Brothers, a tobacco manufacturing company that was later sold to the American Tobacco Company. Their father, William A. Marburg, had started the business as a cigar importer during the 1860s. Sometimes this monument is referred to as the monument that tobacco built.

The monument is by the French sculptor Marius Jean Antonin Mercié and was unveiled in 1911. It was originally designed as a fountain. Within a circular, granite-walled basin that held water, there is a boat on the crest of a wave. In the boat are two bronze figures, a seated barefoot sailor with his hands on the oars and a figure standing opposite the sailor, a long cloak hanging from his shoulder as if dislodged by his raised right hand. That standing figure is Francis Scott Key, shown presenting his poem to Columbia, the gilt bronze female figure standing atop the architectural structure that rises from a boulder in the center of the basin. Four Doric columns carry an architrave and cornice, above

which rise three steps, atop which Columbia stands holding the national flag high and to her left.

On opposite sides of the base of the square temple-like structure are two gilt bronze reliefs. One depicts the bombardment of Fort McHenry, and the other depicts the guns and ramparts of the fort. The monument clearly refers not only to Francis Scott Key's writing of the "Star-Spangled Banner" but also to the circumstances under which he wrote it. Key had boarded a British ship in the harbor the day before the attack on Fort McHenry. A lawyer, he was acting on behalf of a client who had been detained on board that ship. The British decided that it was too risky to allow Key and his client to return to land, because they might have overheard them planning the attack. Thus Key's experience of the bombing of Fort McHenry was as a detainee on a British ship out in the harbor. The sculptural tableau

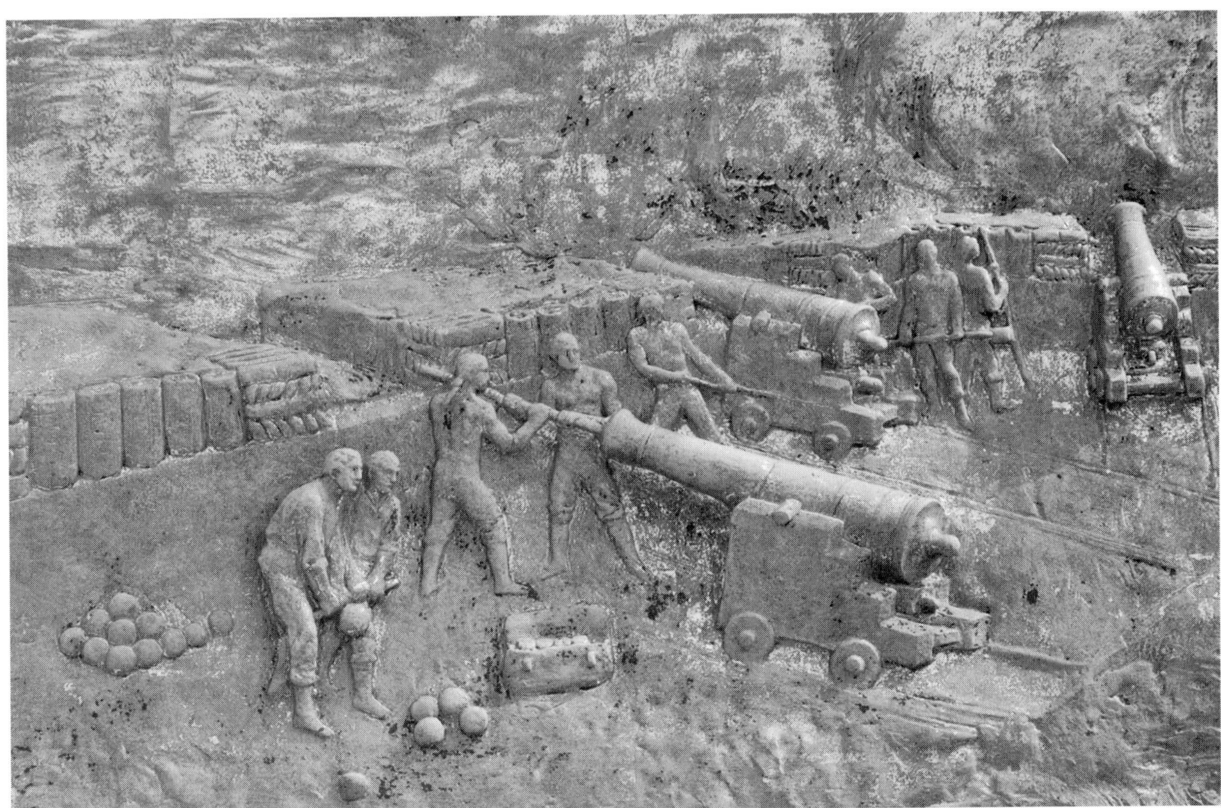

of the memorial depicts Key presenting his poem to the country after his return to shore following the bombardment of the fort.

Mercié, a native of Toulouse, was one of France's leading sculptors in the nineteenth century. He attended the École des Beaux-Arts in Paris, where he was a student of François Jouffroy and Jean Alexandre Joseph Falguière and was awarded the Prix de Rome in 1868. An early success was his *Gloria Victis* in the courtyard of the Hôtel de Ville in Paris in 1874. Mercié taught at the Academie Julian in Paris and was elected a member of the Académie française in 1891 and an officer of the Légion d'honneur in 1913. Also in 1913, he became president of the Société des artistes français. His many statues are sited around Paris, and there are three important ones in the United States. In addition to the Key Monument, he was commissioned in 1890 to create an equestrian monument to Robert E. Lee for Richmond, Virginia, and he collaborated in 1891 with his mentor Falguière on the Lafayette Monument in Lafayette Park in Washington, D.C. Mercié had many students who also created monuments in America. One was F. Wellington Ruckstuhl, who was commissioned to create the Confederate Soldiers and Sailors Monument on Mount Royal, his own *Gloria Victis* (I12).

The placement of the Key Monument was cause for some controversy. Even though in 1911 Eutaw Place was considered to be the city's most distinguished avenue—it is thought to have been the first great urban boulevard with a park down its center to be created in America, and it became the prototype for all subsequent American landscaped parkways—Key's family and many citizens felt that a monument to Key should have been designed for Mount Vernon Place, the historic heart of the city and a more prominent site for a monument. Key's family also was not pleased with Baltimore's second monument to Francis Scott Key, raised at Fort McHenry by the federal government in 1922 to mark the hundredth anniversary of the writing of the "Star-Spangled Banner" (G18).

TITLE
Calvert Street Bridge Lions, 1879

LOCATION
Lanvale Park, Lanvale and Mason streets

SCULPTOR
Herman D. A. Henning (1841–1893)

MEDIUM
Limestone

DONOR
City of Baltimore

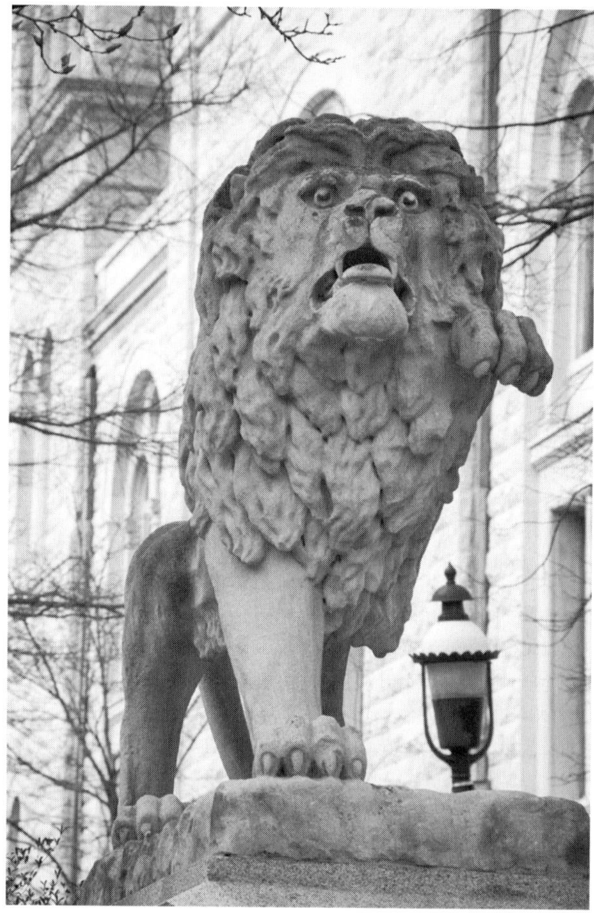

These three lions have a history similar to that of the four statues of Lady Baltimore (I17). Originally these three lions and one other, which was subsequently damaged, were placed at the north and south approaches to the Calvert Street Bridge, just as the four statues of Lady Baltimore were placed on the St. Paul Street Bridge. Herman D. A. Henning, the sculptor of the *Lady Baltimore* statues, is thought to have carved these lions about the same time.

Legend has it that in 1883, while the lions were still on the Calvert Street Bridge, an Irish nationalist named Larry Finnegan took a sledgehammer and knocked off their tails to demonstrate his anger at the British. Supposedly the lions looked British. The lions were given new tails soon thereafter, a repair that is noticeable today.

When the Calvert Street Bridge was taken down in 1957 for construction of the Jones Falls Expressway, the lions, like the statues of Lady Baltimore, were sent to Druid Hill Park for storage. While in storage, they were vandalized again, some say by Finnegan's ghost. Originally each held a shield in his raised right paw. A newspaper photograph from February 1957 of one of these statues being lifted from its base on the Calvert Street Bridge reveals that each lion held a shield with the image of the Battle Monument, the seal of the City of Baltimore.

Early plans to re-site the lions at the entrance to the Baltimore Zoo did not come to fruition, but the three remaining lions did find a new home in 1976 in this small Bolton Hill park created in the midst of a group of new townhouses at Lanvale and Mason streets. LDR International, an urban design and planning firm based in Columbia, Maryland, designed the park.

TITLE
To the Glory of Maryland, 1923

LOCATION
Fifth Regiment Armory, 29th Division and
Dolphin streets

SCULPTOR
Hans Schuler (1874–1951)

MEDIUM
Bronze

DONOR
Gift to the State of Maryland by the Women's Board
of the Armory

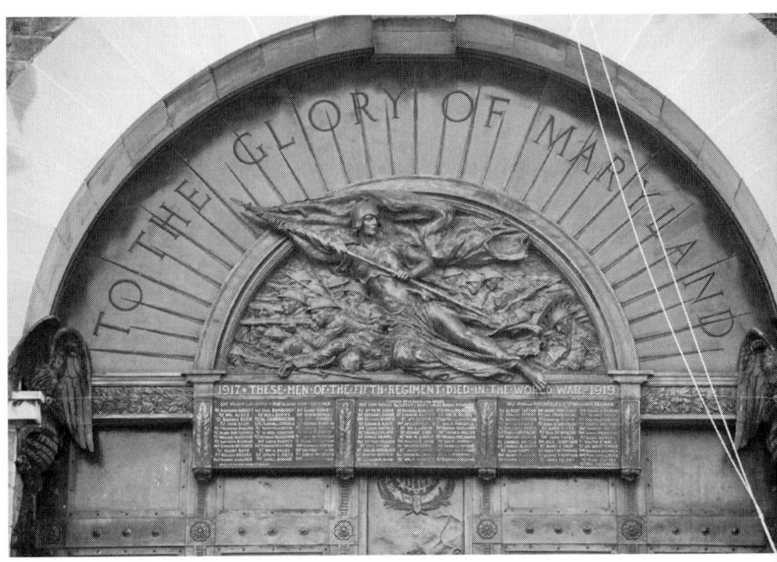

On Armistice Day, November 11, 1925, a bronze relief sculpture by Hans Schuler was dedicated "To the Glory of Maryland." Designed to fit in the lunette over the main entrance to the armory, it commemorated the participation of Maryland's Fifth Regiment in World War I.

This huge relief tablet features portraits of some of the men who served in the Twenty-ninth Division of the Fifth Regiment and were killed at the front. Hans Schuler spent a year designing and modeling the memorial from photographs of former soldiers and officers. The group portrait depicts the regiment at zero hour, charging over a trench and into battle. One soldier lies dead across the parapet. Another is shown reloading his rifle. A third can be seen holding onto his gas mask, which has come off, as he sinks to the ground. All around these men others push forward. Soaring above the men is Victory, wearing a diaphanous gown and a helmet, carrying a standard diagonally across her body as she turns to look back over her shoulder. Written over her are the words "TO THE GLORY OF MARYLAND." Across the lower half of the relief is the inscription "1917 THESE MEN OF THE FIFTH REGIMENT DIED IN THE WORLD WAR 1919," and below the inscription, in three panels, are listed the names of the 116 men from this regiment who made the ultimate sacrifice.

In addition to Schuler's relief, there are two large American eagles surmounting bronze tablets that bear the names of the 2,070 men who enlisted in the regiment and saw service during World War I. These tablets were the gift of the officers of the regiment. The bronze casting was done at the J. Arthur Limerick Company, a foundry in Baltimore.

The Fifth Regiment Armory was designed by the architectural firm of Wyatt & Nolting and built between 1901 and 1903 on land that had originally belonged to George Grundy, whose estate was know as Bolton. The building has quite a history of its own, from renting out space to businesses after the Great Fire of 1904 to hosting the 1912 Democratic National Convention, which finally nominated Woodrow Wilson, who four years later activated the military, including units of the Fifth Regiment, to fight in World War I. Many other national politicians spoke here as well, including Alfred E. Smith, Franklin Delano Roosevelt, Dwight D. Eisenhower, and John F. Kennedy.

Today the building is on the National Register of Historic Places.

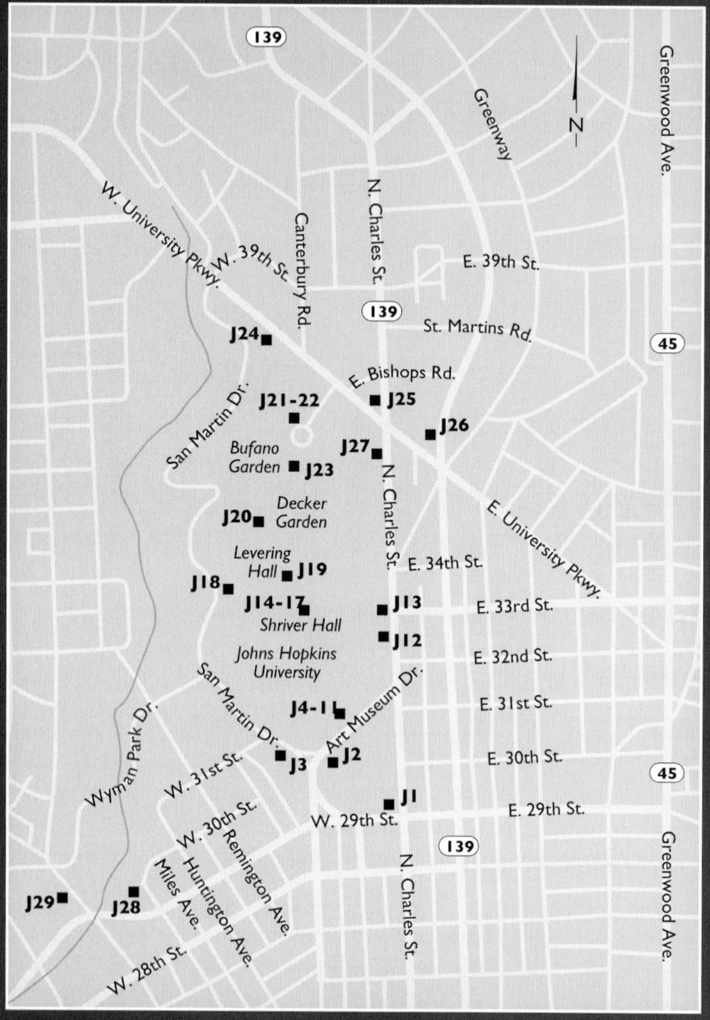

139
Greenway
Greenwood Ave.
N
W. University Pkwy.
W. 39th St.
Canterbury Rd.
N. Charles St.
E. 39th St.
139
St. Martins Rd.
45
J24
E. Bishops Rd.
San Martin Dr.
J21-22
J25
J26
Bufano Garden
J27
J23
N. Charles St.
Decker Garden
J20
Levering Hall
J19
E. 34th St.
J18
J14-17
J13
E. 33rd St.
Shriver Hall
J12
E. 32nd St.
Johns Hopkins University
E. University Pkwy.
San Martin Dr.
J4-11
Art Museum Dr.
E. 31st St.
J3
J2
E. 30th St.
45
Wyman Park Dr.
W. 31st St.
J1
W. 30th St.
W. 29th St.
E. 29th St.
Remington Ave.
139
N. Charles St.
Greenwood Ave.
J29
J28
Huntington Ave.
Miles Ave.
W. 28th St.

JOHNS HOPKINS UNIVERSITY
HOMEWOOD CAMPUS AND ENVIRONS

Walking and Driving

J1

UNION SOLDIERS AND SAILORS MONUMENT, 1909

LOCATION
Wyman Park, N. Charles and 29th streets

SCULPTOR
Adolph Alexander Weinman (1870–1952)

MEDIUM
Bronze

DONOR
State of Maryland

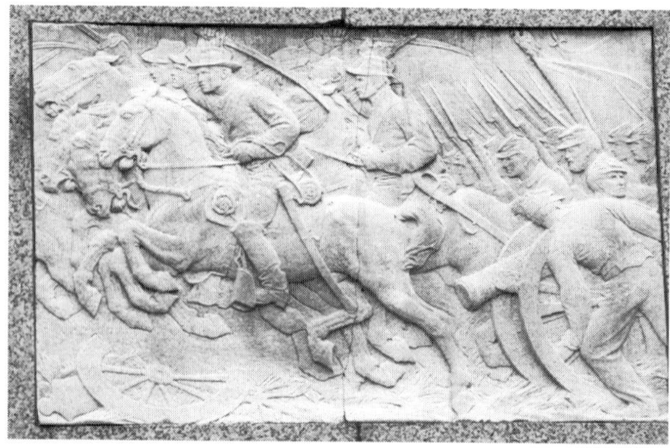

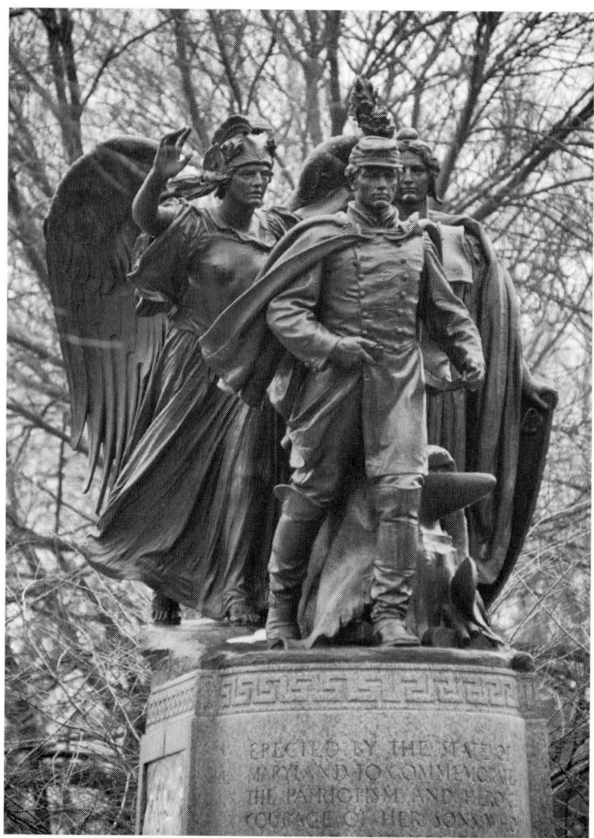

The largest of the four Civil War–related monuments in the city, this monument created by Adolph Alexander Weinman honors the soldiers and sailors who fought to preserve the Union. It was erected in 1909 as the state's official Civil War monument.

Weinman was born in Germany and immigrated to the United States at the age of 10. He attended the Cooper Union in New York City and then studied under Augustus Saint-Gaudens, Charles Henry Niehaus, and Daniel Chester French. He opened his own studio in 1904. Weinman designed the dime and the half dollar in 1916 and is credited with much architectural decorative-relief sculpture. This monument to the Union soldiers and sailors is among his earliest monumental public sculptures, and it earned him well-deserved acclaim. His other work in Baltimore was done later, for the new Baltimore Museum of Art: the architect John Russell Pope hired him to design the lions symbolically guarding the museum and the relief for the pediment (J7–J8). Weinman served on the U.S. Fine Arts Commission and was president of the National Sculpture Society.

The influence of Weinman's mentors, especially of Saint-Gaudens, is abundantly clear in the sculptural group that completes this monument. The central figure of the group is a farmer turning from his plow and anvil, shown behind him and to his left, to buckle on the belt of his uniform and go off to war. This handsome young man is attended by two female figures, Victory on his right and Bellona (the goddess of war) on his left.

The keen sense of drama and energy is created in part by the forward motion implied in all three figures. Each leans forward with weight on one foot. Their clothing responds to their apparent forward motion. The citizen-soldier's cape is blown back away from his body, revealing his uniform underneath. Victory's drapery flutters, as do her sleeves, and her huge wings are fully extended behind her. Bellona's drapery is treated similarly, and both gesture forward and upward with their arms, urging the young man onward.

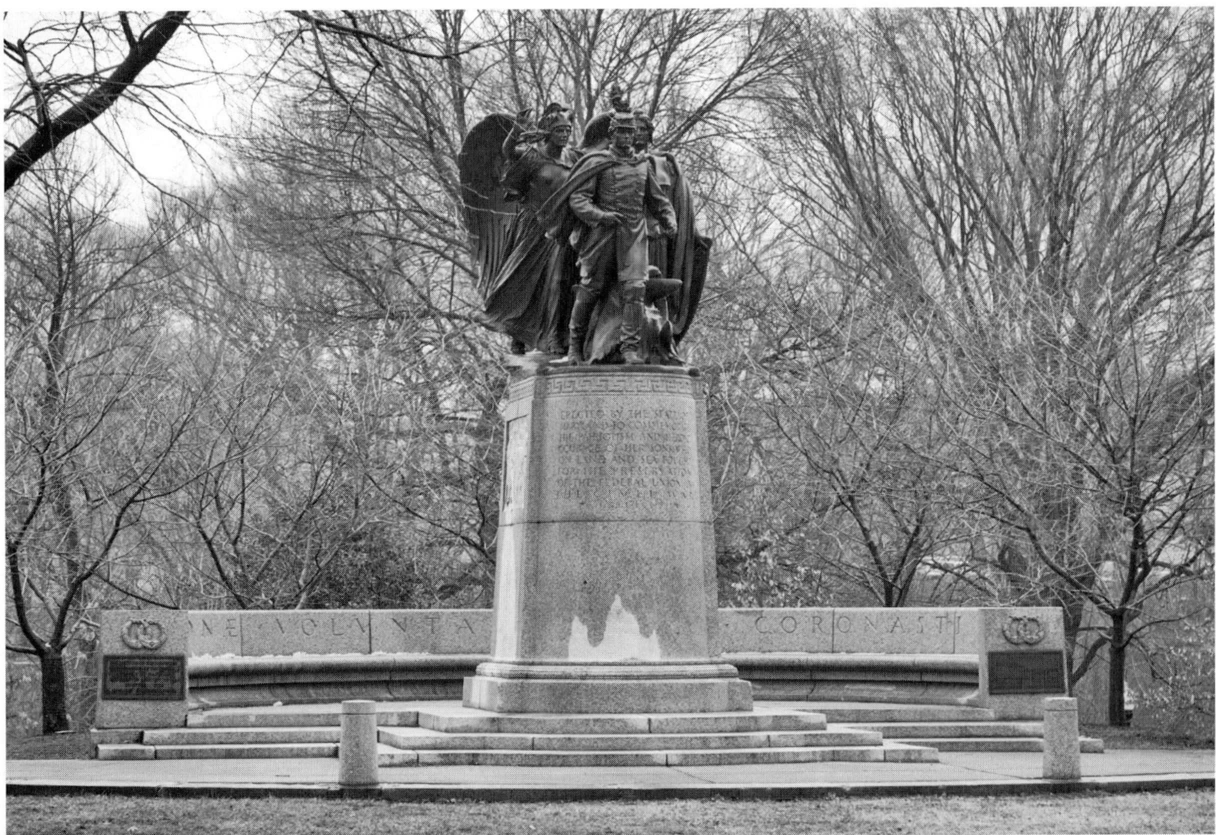

The 12-foot-high granite base on which the beautifully amassed figural group stands has two relief panels. One, on the north side, depicts a charge by the cavalry and the infantry, and the opposite relief depicts a naval attack. At the rear of the base are military symbols, including a sword, an eagle, a shield, and an anchor. The inscription on the front reads, "ERECTED BY THE STATE OF / MARYLAND TO COMMEMORATE / THE PATRIOTISM AND HEROIC / COURAGE OF HER SONS WHO / ON LAND AND SEA FOUGHT / FOR THE PRESERVATION / OF THE FEDERAL UNION IN / THE CIVIL WAR / 1861–1865." A beautiful exedra, or curving bench, set on a platform three steps high with cannon posts around the edge completes this monument. The Latin inscription on the exedra, "SCVTO BONAE VOLVNTATIS TVAE CORONASTI NOS," which means "With favor wilt thou compass us as with a shield," is taken from the Maryland state seal.

The inclusion of Victory and Bellona with the very handsome and energetic young citizen-soldier shown leaving to serve his country erases any doubt about who won this war. Compare this monument to the smaller, more poignant Confederate Soldiers and Sailors Monument, showing another handsome young man, dying in the arms of Glory (I12). The Confederate monument, on W. Mount Royal Avenue, was paid for by the Maryland Daughters of the Confederacy and created by a Southern sympathizer from New York. The inscription on the base of that monument is "GLORIA VICTIS," or "Glory to the Vanquished," making the outcome of the war as clear in that monument as it is in this one.

Originally this monument stood at the intersection of Lake Drive and Mount Royal Avenue, at the edge of Druid Hill Park. The costly relocation to Wyman Park in 1959 was necessitated by the construction of the Jones Falls Expressway and the associated entrance and exit ramps at that location. The Luther Monument (K10) and the Fallsway Fountain (F2) also had to be relocated for development of the expressway.

J2

TITLE
LEE AND JACKSON MONUMENT, 1948

LOCATION
Wyman Park, Art Museum Drive

SCULPTOR
Laura Gardin Fraser (1889–1966)

ARCHITECT
John Russell Pope (1873–1937)

MEDIUM
Bronze

DONOR
J. Henry Ferguson

Robert E. Lee and Thomas J. "Stonewall" Jackson were childhood heroes of J. Henry Ferguson (1849–1928), a bachelor banker who organized the Colonial Trust Company and served as its president until his death. He left $100,000 in his will for the creation of a public monument to the two men, whom he wanted held up as good examples for the youth of Maryland. Ferguson had stipulated that the money for the monument could come to the city only after the death of his sister, Mrs. Ella F. Ward. When she died in 1934, the money and very specific instructions were given to the Municipal Art Society of Baltimore City, the organization chosen by Ferguson to organize a design competition and oversee the creation of the monument.

Ferguson's will spelled out exactly what should be represented, what the inscriptions should be, and who should serve as members of the jury for a limited competition. These individuals were also charged with selecting the site for the monument, which had to be within ten miles of City Hall.

Six sculptors were invited to take part in the competition, held in 1935: Lee Lawrie, Paul Manship, and Edward McCartan, all of New York; F. William Sievers, of Richmond, Virginia; Hans Schuler, then director of the Maryland Institute in Baltimore; and Laura Gardin Fraser, of Westport, Connecticut. Fraser won. She was one of the very few women who distinguished themselves in the field of sculpture in the first half of the

century. When she won this competition, she was best known as a designer of medals. She was the first woman to receive the Saltus Medal, the highest award for medal designers in the United States. Fraser designed and created more that one hundred medals. Among her most important designs were for the congressional medals honoring George C. Marshall, Charles Lindbergh, Benjamin Franklin, George Washington, and Admiral Richard E. Byrd. Fraser was also known as an *animalier*. She had always had a passion for horses and had created many polo trophies, all portraits of famous horses. She was married to another well-known sculptor, James Earl Fraser, who had been her teacher. She was elected to the National Sculpture Society in 1912, the National Academy of Design in 1931, and the National Institute of Arts and Letters in 1931.

Fraser spent twelve years creating this monument, much to the frustration of the Municipal Art Society and the citizens of Baltimore. It had been announced that the project was expected to take two years. The sculptor commissioned John Russell Pope, the architect of the Baltimore Museum of Art, located across the street from the site, to design the granite base. By 1939 a very impressive base with all the required inscriptions had been completed at a cost of $50,000. Two of the inscriptions are quotations from one of these men about the other. The quotation from Lee, "STRAIGHT AS THE NEEDLE TO THE POLE JACKSON ADVANCED TO THE EXECUTION OF MY PURPOSE," appears on the side of the base closest to Jackson, and the quotation from Jackson, "SO GREAT IS MY CONFIDENCE IN GENERAL LEE THAT I AM WILLING TO FOLLOW HIM BLINDFOLDED," is inscribed on the side closest to Lee.

The double equestrian monument was not completed until 1948. The delays were due in part to problems in purchasing Italian clay, which was in short supply in the United States during the 1940s. There were also severe restrictions on the use of metal for anything other than national defense. It was clear, too, that the sculptor was working very slowly and carefully on this very important monument. In the bronze, just behind the back hoof of Lee's horse, Fraser left a tribute to the Gorham Company, which had been responsible for casting the piece: she thanked them for holding to the original contract, "to their own intrinsic loss."

The double equestrian monument represents the parting of Lee and Jackson on May 1, 1863, the eve of the battle of Chancellorsville, one of the most important battles of the Civil War. Lee is shown seated on his famous horse, Traveller, wearing a long overcoat and his well-recognized wide-brimmed hat. To Lee's right, Jackson, seated atop Little Sorrel and dressed in his Confederate uniform, has just signaled to his horse to leave. Little Sorrel holds his head high, and his front left leg is raised to step and turn away. With this sculpture, Fraser depicted four portraits—Lee and Jackson, Traveller and Little Sorrel—and captured the exact moment of the generals' parting, which took place in a clearing much like the one offered by this site at the edge of Wyman Park. The drama of the moment depicted is heightened by the knowledge that Jackson received a mortal wound in the battle that followed.

May 1, 1948, was a glorious day in Baltimore. Three thousand people, including the sculptor and the grandchildren of the two generals, as well as the governor of Maryland, the mayor of Baltimore, and other notable citizens, were in attendance. The marching band from the Virginia Military Institute, where Jackson was teaching at the outbreak of the Civil War, performed. Members of the old Fifth Regiment, the "Dandy Fifth," led the parade.

A letter written to *Time* magazine on April 10, 1948, made note of the installation of this double equestrian monument and stated that it was thought to be the only double equestrian monument in the United States or Europe. Shortly thereafter, on June 14, 1948, a letter and photograph appeared in *Time* documenting the 1936 double equestrian monument *Lee and a Soldier,* by A. Phimister Proctor, in Dallas, Texas, abruptly ending Baltimore's short-lived primacy in this area.

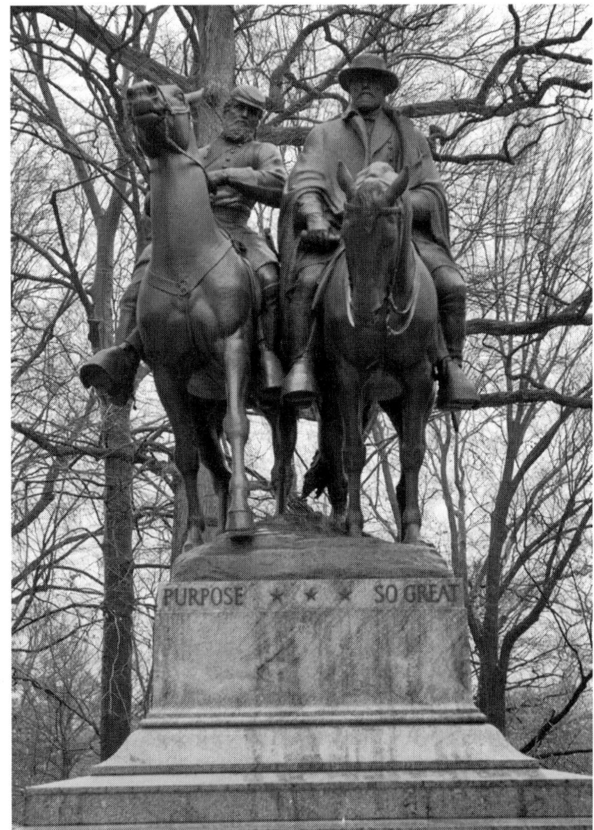

TITLE
CHAPIN A. HARRIS MONUMENT, 1922

LOCATION
Wyman Park, Wyman Park Drive between San Martin and Art Museum drives, opposite the south entrance to the Johns Hopkins University

SCULPTOR
Edward Berge (1876–1924)

MEDIUM
Bronze

DONOR
Maryland State Dental Association

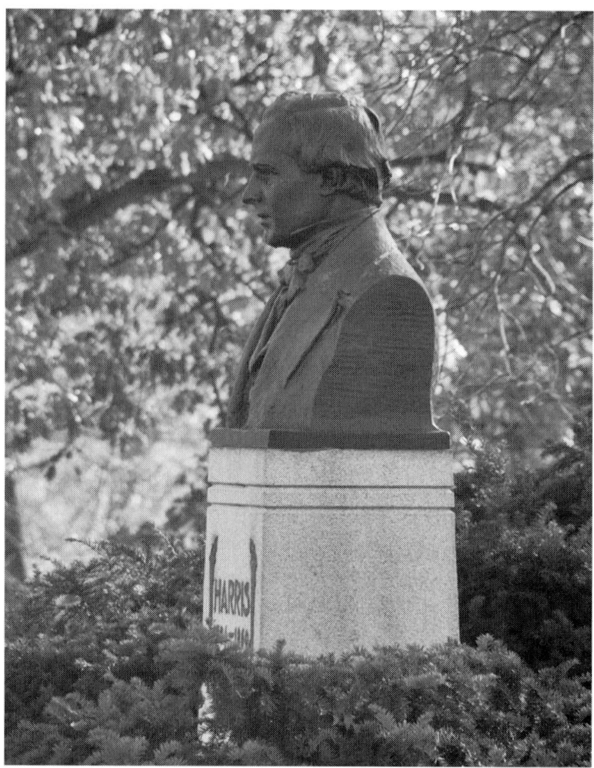

Chapin A. Harris (1806–60), widely heralded as the father of modern dentistry, was born in New York City and moved to Baltimore in 1835. In 1839, in association with Horace H. Hayden, he founded the Baltimore College of Dental Surgery, the first college of its kind in the world. The college was granted a charter by the Maryland General Assembly in 1840 and has since become the University of Maryland School of Dentistry. Harris was a physician and surgeon as well as a dentist. He wrote a number of books on dentistry, compiled a dictionary of dental science, and established the first dental periodical, the *American Journal of Dental Science,* for which he served as editor. He died in Baltimore and was buried in Mt. Olivet Cemetery.

In 1911 a committee was appointed by the Maryland State Dental Association to collect funds for a memorial to this pioneer in dentistry. Contributors included colleges, dental associations, and individuals across the United States and in England, France, Sweden, and Norway.

This small monument stood at the corner of North and Linden avenues before it was relocated in 1939 to this site, just off Art Museum Drive, west of the Baltimore Museum of Art, on a slice of land that is actually part of Wyman Park. It had originally been planned for the corner of Cathedral and Preston streets, but even before the design was complete the Municipal Art Commission and the Park Board changed the site.

For this bronze portrait bust Edward Berge took a very traditional approach. Harris' head, neck, shoulders, and chest are depicted frontally. His attire is formal—a coat with wide lapels, a vest, a shirt with a high collar, and a scarf tied at his neck into a bow. He is depicted as a handsome man with a gentle countenance.

The choice of this site for the Harris monument was questioned by a correspondent for the *Evening Sun* and elicited a humorous response from one of the editorial writers. The correspondent asked why Harris would be placed in such "a high-toned, artistic and literary atmosphere as Wyman Park," so near the Baltimore Museum of Art, the Johns Hopkins University, and across the park from the monument to Edgar Allan Poe, still in its original site at the time (F3). The editorial writer responded by suggesting that "Harris' contribution to human happiness and welfare is probably equal to that of any poet, artist, or writer, living or dead." Harris' contribution was, in effect, to remove the practice of dentistry from the hands of barbers, blacksmiths, and charlatans and place it in the hands of competent practitioners.

J4–J5

TITLES
Discus Thrower, 1902 copy of 480–455 BC original, and *Seated Mercury*, mid-19th-century copy of 323–146 BC original

LOCATION
Baltimore Museum of Art, Art Museum Drive

SCULPTORS
Unknown, after Myron of Eleutherai and an unknown Italian, respectively

MEDIUM
Bronze

DONOR
Gift of the City of Baltimore, Department of Recreation and Parks

The Baltimore Museum of Art *Discus Thrower* is a copy, cast in Naples in 1902, after the long-lost original *Diskobolos*, by the Greek sculptor Myron of Eleutherai (fl. 480–455 BC), known through Roman copies. The *Seated Mercury*, shown here as a classical youth, resting, wearing only his winged sandals, is thought to have been made in Naples in the nineteenth century after a Hellenistic statue known today only through its Roman copies. One of those copies, originally discovered at Herculaneum in 1758, is in the Museo Nazionale in Naples. These sculptures were at one time sited on the grounds of the now vanished Alexandroffsky, the urban villa built in West Baltimore in 1853 by Thomas Winans (1820–78), the oldest son of Ross Winans, an engineer and railroad pioneer. The younger Winans, an engineer and inventor, was sent off to Russia with his brother William by their father to help supervise the construction of the railroad linking St. Petersburg and Moscow. The brothers' involvement in the development of Russia's first railroad made them both millionaires.

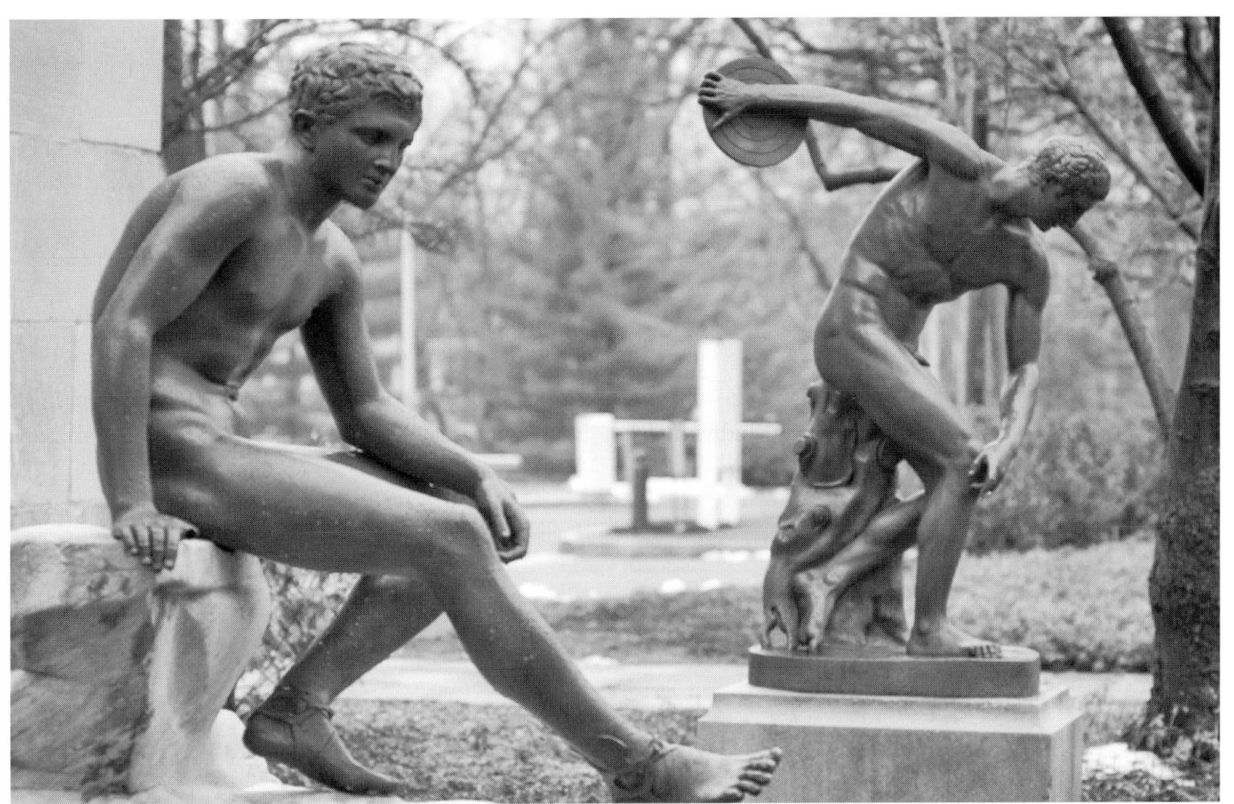

Thomas Winans returned to Baltimore in 1851 with his Russian-French bride, and in 1853 he built Alexandroffsky for her. Throughout the grounds, in the formal gardens, around the tennis courts, and along the winding drive up to the villa there were bronze and marble statues collected by Thomas Winans, and his family after him, on travels throughout Europe—nudes and scantily clad figures, heroic figures and classical deities. The *Discus Thrower* and the *Seated Mercury*, sitting near each other today in the museum's west garden, were both installed along the drive.

Winans' neighbors along Fremont and Hollins streets complained vociferously about the nude statues on his estate, in full public view, which they thought were indecent and a corrupting influence on their children. In addition to the two statues seen here, there was a heroic nude Pan hoisting an infant to his shoulders. In response to these complaints, Winans surrounded his property with a 12-foot-high fence, which of course caused a bigger problem. In his will, Winans stated that under no circumstance should the fence come down.

Thomas Winans' daughter, Celeste Hutton, inherited Alexandroffsky and lived there with her family until she died in 1925. At that time the property was offered for sale, first to the city for $400,000, an amount considered too high, and then to a Baltimore–New York syndicate, which bought it for $260,000. The Winans family moved many family treasures out to Crimea, which had been Thomas Winans' country estate, and then sold at auction the remaining collections of Oriental rugs, Arctic bearskins, Chinese tapestries, and Turkish wall hangings. The syndicate then sold off parcels for commercial development. By 1928 Alexandroffsky had been razed.

Luckily for the city, Winans' summer home on his Crimea estate had a better fate. The city was able to purchase the lower half of the estate in 1942 with a bequest from J. Wilson Leakin solely for buying parkland. In 1948 the city purchased the rest of the estate. Once the city owned all the property, the Department of Recreation and Parks, acting as agent, distributed throughout the city the sculpture found there. The *Discus Thrower* and the *Seated Mercury* were given to the museum in 1948, and two other bronzes, *Athena Parthenos* and *Apollo Belvedere* (L8–L9), went to the Evergreen Museum and Library. Two lions went to the Baltimore Zoo (M13).

J6

TITLE
Guardian Lions, mid-19th-century copies of
1792 originals

LOCATION
Baltimore Museum of Art, Art Museum Drive

SCULPTOR
Unknown after Antonio Canova (1757–1821)

MEDIUM
Marble

DONOR
Gift of the estate of Margaret Anna Abell

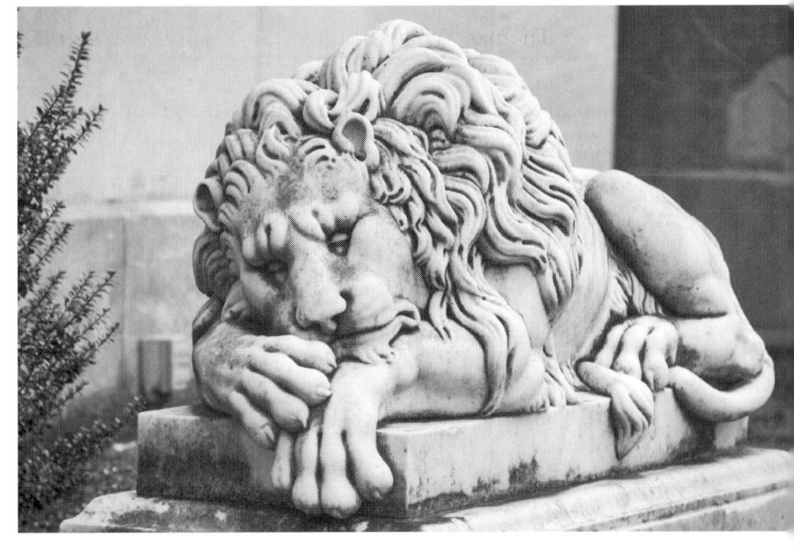

These two charming lions would probably not be in the west garden of the Baltimore Museum of Art if Anna Schley Abell (1870–1948), widow of A. S. Abell II (1866–1914), had not lost her court battle against the Greenmount Cemetery to have them installed beside her husband's tomb, a large marble monument not far from the tomb of his grandfather, A. S. Abell, founder of the *Baltimore Sun* newspapers.

Before coming to the museum in 1977, these recumbent lions, lying with their heads turned slightly to the side, guarded three Abell properties in the city: the entrance to an estate in Guilford; a city residence on St. Paul Street; and a house on Roland Avenue near Northern Parkway. Margaret Anna Abell, the donor, was one of seven children born to A. S. Abell II and Anna Schley Abell.

The lions are thought to be nineteenth-century copies after ones carved by the leading European sculptor of his time, the Italian Antonio Canova, for the tomb of the Venetian pope Clement XIII in St. Peter's in Rome, completed in 1792. The two great guardian lions were placed at the base of this papal tomb monument, on either side of the door leading to the tomb chamber. Copies were made in marble, terra cotta, and bronze in all sizes to meet the demands of contemporary tourists.

TITLES
To the Fine Arts and *Lions,* 1929

LOCATION
Baltimore Museum of Art, Art Museum Drive

SCULPTOR
Adolph Alexander Weinman (1870–1952)

CARVER
Charles E. Klutch (1871–1952)

ARCHITECT
John Russell Pope (1873–1937)

MEDIUM
Limestone

DONOR
Baltimore Museum of Art

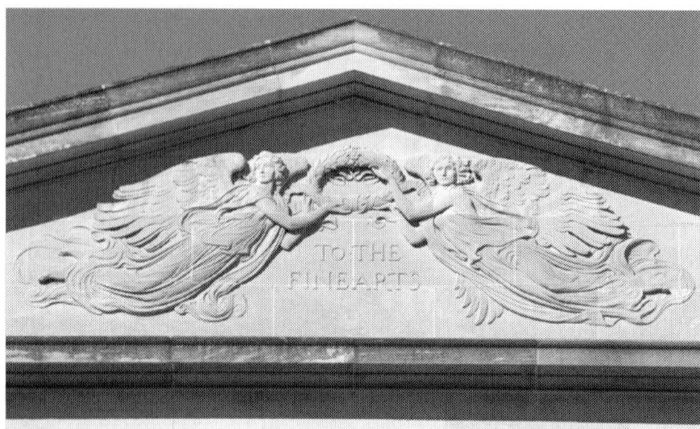

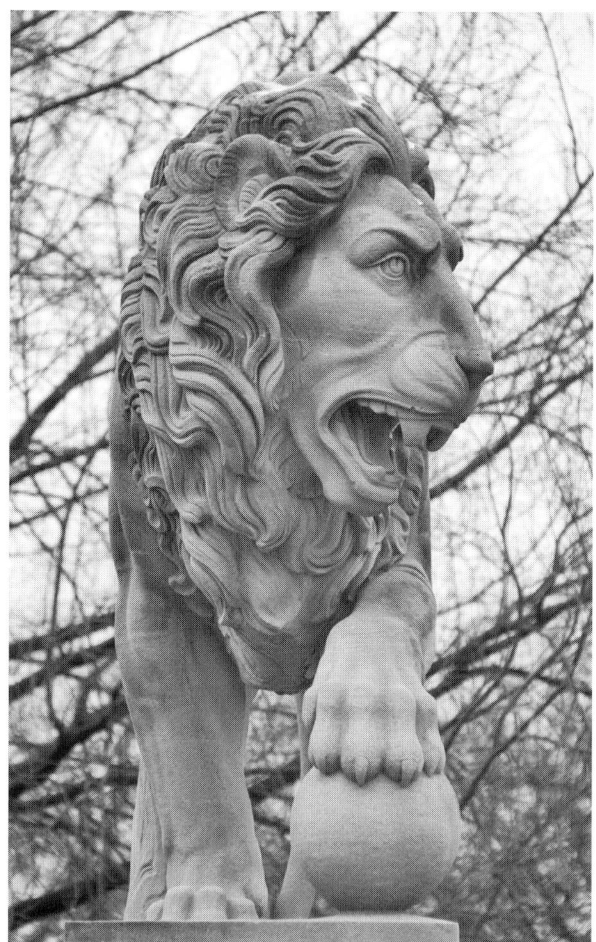

In 1924 there was a bond issue on the ballot asking the citizens to approve $1 million to build a permanent municipal museum. It passed, and the architect John Russell Pope was engaged to design the new building on six acres of land in Wyman Park, donated by the Johns Hopkins University. The cornerstone was laid on October 20, 1927, and the building was opened eighteen months later, on April 18, 1929.

Adolph Alexander Weinman was selected by Pope to design the relief for the museum's pediment and the two lions that were to stand at the front of the property, symbolically guarding the museum. The pediment was to be filled with two angels holding between them a wreath made of acanthus leaves, and the words "To the Fine Arts" were to be inscribed below the wreath. The angels, clothed in diaphanous, flowing gowns, appear to hover high over the entrance to the museum.

The two stone lions, which stand on massive stone bases to the far left and far right of the building facade, are mirror images of each other. Their threatening demeanor is somewhat tempered by their pose. Their eyes are wide open, their nostrils are flared, and their open mouths reveal sharp teeth, but their heads are slightly turned and their left paws rest quietly on a sphere. Weinman may have chosen as a model for these lions ones that stood at one time outside the Villa Medici in Rome but now stand outside the Loggia dei Lanzi in Florence. Weinman probably modeled the lion in clay, and then an enlargement was made in plaster. The plaster model, in the museum's collection, is dated 1929. Charles E. Klutch, a well-known stone carver in Baltimore, is credited with carving both the pediment and the lions.

J9

TITLE
Violins Violence Silence, 1981–1982

LOCATION
Baltimore Museum of Art, Art Museum Drive

SCULPTOR
Bruce Nauman (b. 1941)

MEDIUM
Neon tubing and clear glass tubing

DONORS
Gift of Leo Castelli Gallery, New York, and Sperone Westwater Fischer Gallery, New York

Bruce Nauman, born in Fort Wayne, Indiana, received his BFA from the University of Wisconsin–Madison in 1964 and his MFA from the University of California–Davis in 1966. Since the early 1970s he has been considered one of the most innovative and provocative contemporary artists. Throughout his career, his work has taken countless forms, as diverse as sculpture, video, film, printmaking, performance, and installation. Yet he has always been fascinated by neon and by experimenting with light. He was chosen to be the U.S. representative at the 2009 Venice Biennale.

Nauman made two versions of a neon work in which the words "Violins," "Violence," and "Silence" are superimposed, flashing brightly in a sequence that moves forward and then backward. One was triangular and was designed for an interior installation; the other, designed for an exterior installation, was to run horizontally along the top of a building and around one

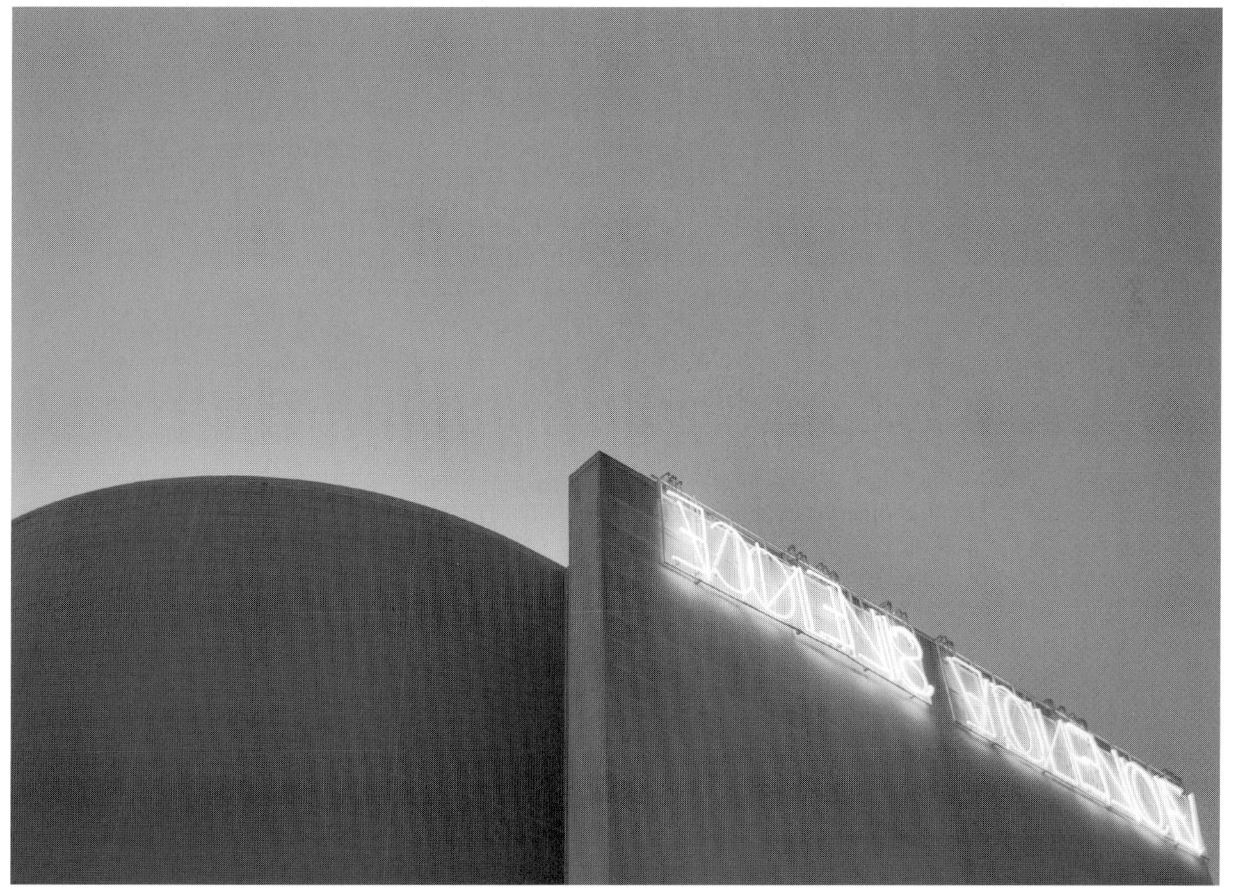

corner. The colors and flashing sequences for the two pieces were similar. Nauman had originally designed the exterior piece for the music department at the California State University–Long Beach, which in the end did not follow through with the commission.

In 1982 the Baltimore Museum of Art mounted an exhibition of Nauman's neons and included both versions of *Violins Violence Silence.* The exterior piece was fabricated and mounted on the south and east faces of the museum's new wing. The letters for the Long Beach building were necessarily enlarged twofold, to 4 feet high, to fit the museum's larger scale. When the exhibition ended, the two galleries representing Nauman, which together had underwritten the production of the exterior piece for the exhibition, placed the piece on indefinite loan to the museum and then offered it as a gift in 1983.

The pattern of words repeats, forward, then backward, superimposed on one another, in bright colors of orange and green, turquoise and peach, white and hot pink, yellow and fuchsia, blue and red, coral and sky blue. The pattern includes seconds when all the words are visible, as well as seconds when they are all off.

Presenting these three flashing words, Nauman invites the viewer to consider the shift in meaning that occurs when a letter here or there is changed—when, for example, "SILENCE" becomes "VIOLENCE" or "VIOLINS" becomes "VIOLENCE." He leaves his audience considering the relationship between the words as they get so tangled up as to become almost impenetrable. Which word is more powerful—*silence* or *violence, violins* or *violence*? Over his career, Nauman has made many provocative neon signs that confound and challenge the viewer to consider the human predicament: SILENCE IS GOLDEN/TALK OR DIE; WHITE ANGER, RED DANGER, YELLOW PERIL, BLACK DEATH/EAT; NONE SING/NEON SIGN; RAW WAR (also in the BMA collection), and RUN FROM FEAR/FUN FROM REAR. He has also always enjoyed subverting the commercial purpose of neon in advertising.

Violins Violence Silence was not especially well received in its early days on the museum. Some neighbors threatened to go to the zoning board, saying that neon had no place on the museum.

J10

JANET AND ALAN WURTZBURGER SCULPTURE GARDEN, opened 1980

LOCATION
Baltimore Museum of Art, Art Museum Drive

LANDSCAPE ARCHITECT
George E. Patton

DONORS
Janet and Alan Wurtzburger

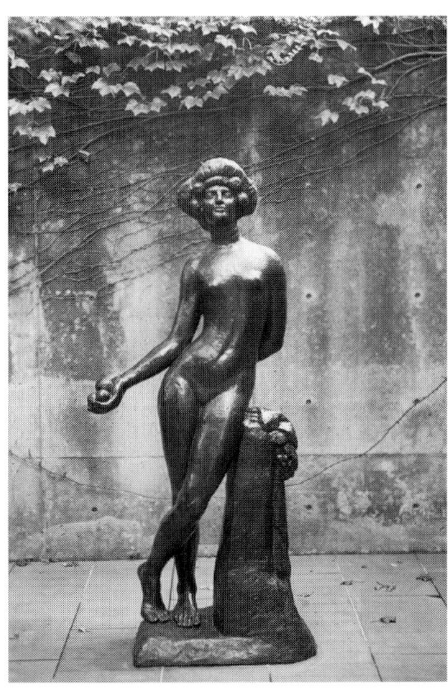

Janet and Alan Wurtzburger were art collectors and rank among the most important benefactors of the Baltimore Museum of Art. Alan Wurtzburger was a real estate investor who, together with his wife, collected more than 136 objects of African art, which the couple donated to the museum in 1955. They then began collections of Pacific Island and ancient American art with the express intention of donating these collections to the museum. Their resulting gift of 423 African, Oceanic, and pre-Columbian objects made the BMA one of the first museums in the country able to form such a collection, and in 1958 the Wurtzburger Gallery of the Primitive Arts opened at the museum. This was followed in 1982 by the Alan and Janet Wurtzburger Gallery for the Arts of Africa, the Americas, and Oceania.

The Wurtzburgers' passion for sculpture began in the 1940s, when they were collecting African art, and eventually grew to include contemporary art. Between 1955 and 1973 they purchased examples of modern sculpture that they then installed at Timberlane, their estate in Stevenson, Maryland. From the beginning, they intended their sculpture collection to go to the BMA, and they included in their bequest their wish that the sculpture be displayed in an outdoor garden. The Wurtzburgers both died prematurely, he in 1963 and she in 1973. In 1980 their wishes were brought to fruition with the opening of the Janet and Alan Wurtzburger Sculpture Garden.

The Wurtzburgers' gift of modern sculpture included thirty-five works of art, nineteen of which were installed in the sculpture garden; these works ranged from Emile-Antoine Bourdelle's *Fruit* (1911) to Max Bill's *Endless Ribbon* (1953) and Henry Moore's *Three Piece Reclining Figure No. 1* (1961–62). Other pieces in the garden, all in the figural tradition, include Alexander Calder's *Four Dishes* (1967), Raymond Duchamp-Villon's *The Horse* (1919), Jacob Epstein's *The Visitation* (original 1926, cast 1955), Pablo Gargallo's *The Prophet (St. John the Baptist)* (1933), Gaston Lachaise's *Standing Woman* (original model 1912–18, cast ca. 1945 or later), Henri Laurens' *Large Bather* (1947), Jacques Lipchitz's *Mother and Child II* (1941–45), Giacomo Manzu's *Young Girl on a Chair* (1955), Gerhard Marcks' *Prometheus Bound II* (plaster original 1944, cast 1948), Marino Marini's *The Miracle* (1954), Mario Negri's *Seen from a Wall in the Memory* (1960) and *Large Monumental Allegory* (ca. 1960), Isamu Noguchi's *Untitled* (1958), Germaine Richier's *Tauromachy* (1953), Auguste Rodin's *Balzac* (original 1892–93, cast 1957), Fritz Wotruba's *Man Walking* (1952), and Ossip Zadkine's *May 1940: The Destroyed City* (1957).

The sculptures in the garden may rotate from time to time, as when the Balzac was included in the temporary exhibition Rodin: Expression and Influence in the Cone Wing in 2007–8 or for conservation. Pieces of sculpture given to the museum by the Wurtzburgers that are not installed in the garden are on display inside the museum.

J11

TITLE
RYDA H. AND ROBERT H. LEVI SCULPTURE GARDEN, opened 1988

LOCATION
Baltimore Museum of Art, Art Museum Drive

LANDSCAPE ARCHITECT
Joseph Hibbard, Sasaki Associates, Inc., Boston

DONORS
Ryda H. and Robert H. Levi

The Levi Sculpture Garden highlights works from the second half of the twentieth century. Together with the Wurtzburger Sculpture Garden (J10), it offers a one-hundred-year survey of sculpture from the figural to the abstract.

This sculpture garden was established with a gift of fourteen pieces of sculpture from Ryda H. and Robert H. Levi and funded in part by a city bond and a matching grant from the State of Maryland. The Johns Hopkins University provided the land, as it had done years before when the museum built its new home on Art Museum Drive.

Since 1960, when the Levis began collecting sculpture, many of these pieces had been displayed on the grounds of their Baltimore County estate on Greenspring Avenue. In addition to the pieces that they gifted to the museum, the Levis funded the museum's acquisition of six pieces specifically for the sculpture garden: Ellsworth Kelly's *Untitled* (1986), Scott Burton's *Rock Chair* (1986–87), Barry Flanagan's *Large Boxing Hare on Anvil* (1984), Michael Heizer's *Eight-Part Circle* (1976–87), Joel Shapiro's *Untitled* (1985), and Tony Smith's *Spitball* (1961).

The Levis' collection of sculpture also includes Alexander Calder's *100 Yard Dash* (1969), José Ruiz de Rivera's motorized and slowly turning *Construction 140* (1971), Mark di Suvero's *Sister Lu* (1978–79), Anthony Caro's *Sheila's Song* (1982), Isamu Noguchi's *Noh Musicians* (1958–74), Louise Nevelson's *Seventh Decade Forest* (1971–76), Joan Miró's *Head (Tete)* (1974), Masayuki Nagare's *Time and Happiness* (1973), and George W. Rickey's *Space Churn with Spheres, Variation III* (1972).

Robert H. Levi (1915–95) was chairman and president of the Hecht chain of department stores in the Baltimore-Washington area. In 1958 he oversaw the merger of the chain with the May Department Stores Company. He remained as a vice president of the May Company until his retirement in 1967. He then joined the Mercantile-Safe Deposit & Trust Company, retiring in 1985. He was born in Baltimore and graduated from the Johns Hopkins University in 1936. He remained devoted to the university, serving over a thirty-year period as a trustee for both the university and the hospital. Ryda H. Levi (d. 2008) was internationally known for her ongoing support of art and education.

In 1975, the same year that they made the bequest for Rickey's *Space Churn with Spheres*, which today is part of the sculpture garden, the Levis gave the museum *Four Lines Up*, created by Rickey in 1965, which is sited outdoors in the center of the Schaefer Court, formerly know as the Antioch Court. Made of stainless steel, it stands 10 feet tall, and its four blades swing in parallel planes.

Like the sculpture in the Wurtzburger Garden, the sculpture in the Levi Garden may rotate from time to time.

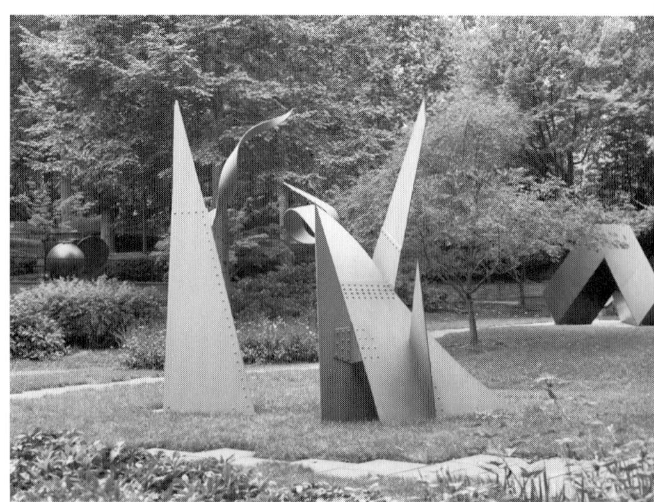

J12

TITLE
Spirit of Music, 2002

LOCATION
Mattin Center, Johns Hopkins University

SCULPTOR
Jud Hartmann (b. 1948)

MEDIUM
Bronze

DONORS
Family and friends of Rex Chao

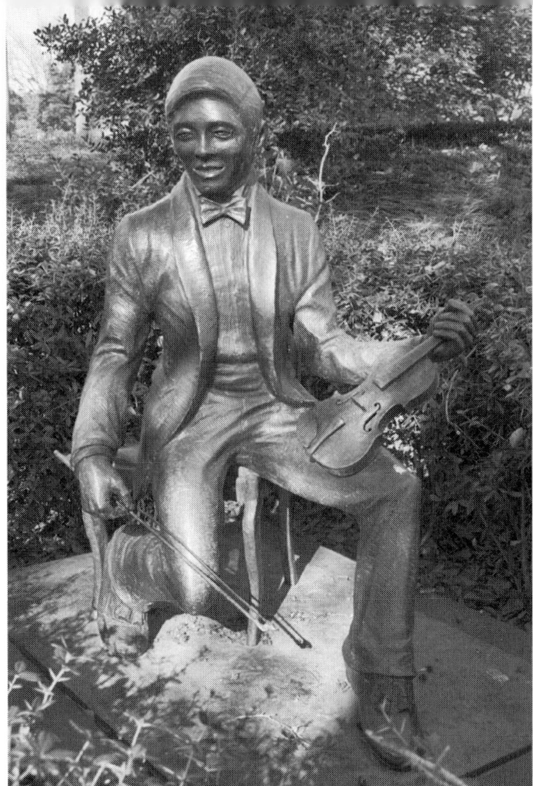

Rex Chao (1976–96) was a 19-year-old sophomore and political science major at Johns Hopkins University when he was shot and killed on the campus by an estranged friend and classmate in 1996. Many students in the class of 1998, wanting to ensure that Chao's memory would live on after they graduated, began searching for a way to pay a lasting tribute to him. Because Chao was a talented violinist who played in the Peabody and Hopkins symphony orchestras, they decided to commission a bronze sculpture of a seated figure in his likeness, playing a violin. His girlfriend, Suzanne Hubbard, and her friend Amy Clair Brusch volunteered to head the Rex Chao Memorial Committee, organized to raise the funds that would enable them to commission the memorial. They chose the Maine sculptor Jud Hartmann, who had completed the Lacrosse monument in front of the nearby Lacrosse Museum and National Hall of Fame (J24).

Raising funds initially seemed to be a daunting task, but the committee got a boost when U.S. congresswoman Susan Molinari, for whom Chao had interned on Capitol Hill, pledged her remaining campaign chest to the project.

Originally proposed for the interior of the Mattin Center, the university's new performing arts facility, but sited today outdoors between the center and the Baltimore Museum of Art's sculpture gardens, the almost life-size cast bronze statue depicts a young man on the edge of his chair, his body twisting in space just enough to suggest movement, with his violin in his left hand and the bow in his right, smiling as if he might have just finished playing a piece. Hubbard visited Hartmann in his Blue Hill, Maine, gallery while he was working on the piece and left with him a tape of Chao playing a Mendelssohn violin concerto. Hubbard hoped the recording would inspire Hartmann to create an image that would remind people of Chao's life and talents, not of the tragedy that ended his life.

Hartmann worked from a number of photographs of young Chao and met with his parents several times. However, the statue is less a portrait of Chao and more a reflection of a young man's love of and talent for music.

Hartmann has had no formal art training. He is completely self-taught. He began sculpting in wood after college and then worked for a while in stone. Since 1983 he has worked solely in bronze and primarily on a project depicting the Woodland Tribes of the Northeast. By 2000 he had created more than fifty sculptures of these Iroquois and Algonquin Indians. His work can be found in private and corporate collections nationally and internationally. Hartmann lives in Brooklin, Maine, with his wife and family and maintains a studio there.

J13

TITLE
JOHNS HOPKINS MONUMENT, 1935

LOCATION
N. Charles and 33rd streets

SCULPTOR
Hans Schuler (1874–1951)

ARCHITECT
William Gordon Beecher (1877–1963)

MEDIUM
Bronze

DONOR
Municipal Art Society of Baltimore City

Sometime before World War I the Municipal Art Society decided to erect and give to the city a memorial to Johns Hopkins (1795–1873) in recognition of his generosity in founding both the university and the hospital that today bear his name. These early plans were interrupted by the war but were revived in the early 1930s. Hans Schuler was chosen as the sculptor, and he was to work in association with the architect William Gordon Beecher.

The site chosen for the monument was an oval at the intersection of N. Charles and 34th streets, directly opposite the entrance to the university's Homewood campus. Included in these early plans were two fountains, one on the north side of the monument and one on the south.

Schuler proposed that there be a heroic bronze bust of Johns Hopkins on top of a tall marble pylon, with two allegorical figures seated at its base, on the east-west axis of the monument. The female figure on the east side, with bare breasts, a laurel wreath in her hair, holding a bowl from which a snake twists around and up her arm, would represent healing and the hos-

pital; the male figure opposite her, with a bare chest, beautiful flowing drapery over his crossed legs, and a scroll spread across his lap, would represent learning and the university. The inclusion of flowing water was to be symbolic of the enduring benefits of this gift to the city and the world.

The portrait is a very good likeness of the Quaker merchant and banker who spent his summers at his Clifton Park mansion, set on five hundred acres, from which he could see Federal Hill, where flags were raised to signal which ships were entering the harbor. From Clifton's tower Hopkins could learn when ships headed to unload at his warehouses were arriving. He became involved in real estate, including building modern warehouses and office buildings along the harbor, which improved the port area for the city and brought him high returns. He also became a finance capitalist, lending money to young men to whom banks would not lend, which brought him as much satisfaction as did making money for himself. He was a Unionist and an abolitionist, and together with his good friend John Work Garrett, Hopkins worked to overcome the South-

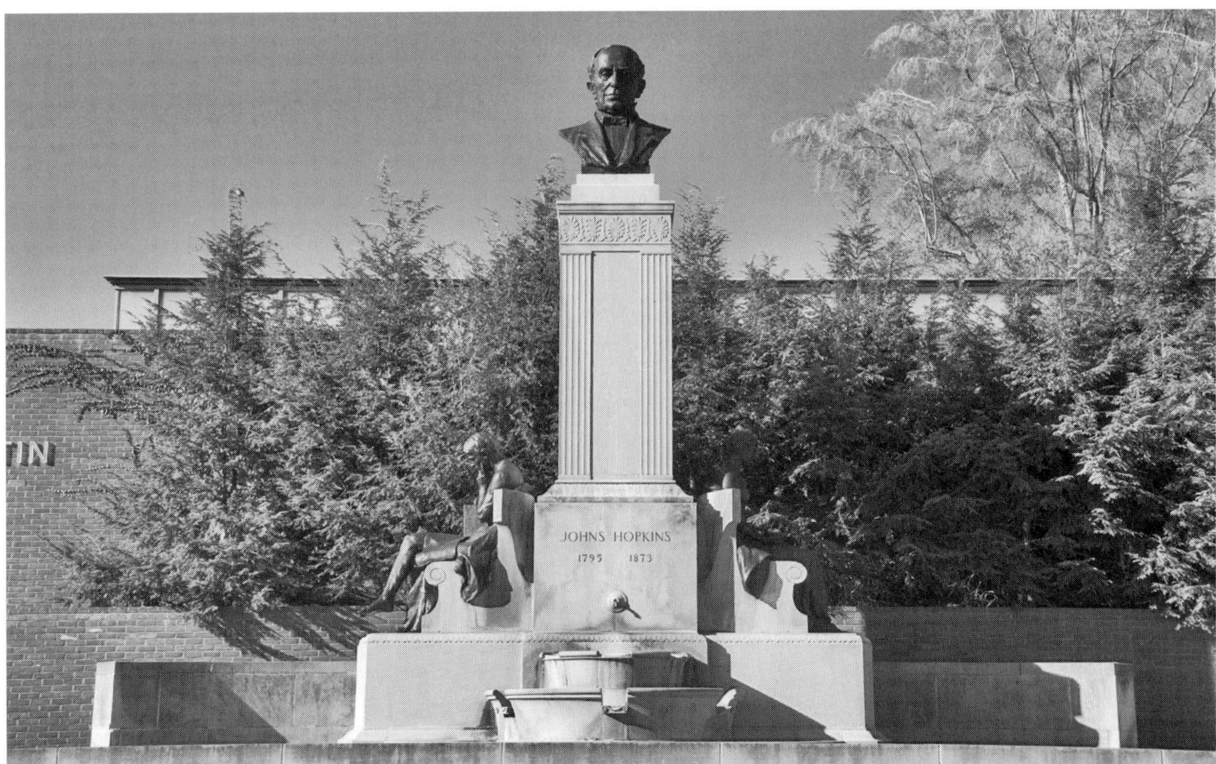

ern sympathies of his fellow members of the board of the B&O Railroad to keep the railroad in the service of the Union. It is widely held that it was John Work Garrett who invited Johns Hopkins to dine with George Peabody shortly after the Peabody Institute was dedicated in 1867 and shortly before Hopkins made his will later that same year. Hopkins was greatly influenced by Peabody and his philanthropy, and it is thought that this dinner set Hopkins on his course of establishing a university and a hospital. When he died on Christmas Eve six years later, those two institutions had been incorporated into his will. His bequest to the university, the largest ever made to an American institution of learning, was B&O Railroad stock and his Clifton mansion; his other real estate holdings made up his bequest to the hospital.

It is hard to imagine that the Johns Hopkins Monument was ever a traffic hazard, but many area residents believed that it blocked the view of both motorists and pedestrians traveling north and south on N. Charles Street, and they worried that accidents might result. In June 1952 their fears were confirmed when two fire trucks rushing to a fire on the campus, one traveling south and one traveling north, collided as they turned into the campus because the monument blocked their view of each other. Two city firemen were killed, and six others were injured.

Shortly thereafter letters to the editor and articles in the local newspaper documented the rising concern over the monument's placement in the middle of a roadway and the suggestions being offered for its relocation. Many thought the monument should be moved onto the Homewood campus, on the lawn inside the circular drive often referred to today as "the Beach." Others suggested the "spacious lawn" in front of the Hopkins hospital on Broadway. Composite pictures appeared in the newspapers showing the monument on the lawn in front of Gilman Hall and at the top of 33rd Street, where it stands today. It took the city and the university three years after the accident to work out an agreement for placing the monument on a small plot of land belonging to the university, land that the university transferred to the city.

J14–J15

TITLES
William Henry Welch and *Daniel Coit Gilman,* 1956

LOCATION
Shriver Hall, Wyman Quadrangle,
Johns Hopkins University

SCULPTOR
Sidney Waugh (1904–1963)

MEDIUM
Bronze

DONOR
Alfred Jenkins Shriver

Alfred Jenkins Shriver (1867–1939), a bachelor and prominent Baltimore attorney, left the bulk of his estate to his alma mater, the Johns Hopkins University, to be used to build a lecture hall. To receive this money, the university had to agree to the very detailed instructions in Shriver's will concerning the artwork required for the building. There were to be murals inside and sculpture outside. On the interior walls there were to be portraits of the early faculty of philosophy and the original faculty of the medical school; the original boards of trustees of the university and the hospital; the members of the class of 1891, in which Shriver had ranked first, graduating Phi Beta Kappa; Baltimore clipper ships; the ten leading Baltimore philanthropists; and the mural that would cause the greatest stir, one of the ten most beautiful women of Baltimore in Shriver's era in his estimation.

Outside there were to be portrait statues of Daniel Coit Gilman (1831–1908), the first president of the university, who served in that capacity from 1875 to 1901 and was the man chiefly responsible for establishing Johns Hopkins as the first great American research university in the German tradition, who was also active in founding the Johns Hopkins Hospital (1889) and the Johns Hopkins Medical School (1893), and William Henry Welch (1850–1934), the first professor of pathology, the first dean of the medical school, and the first dean of the school of hygiene and public health. There was also to be a portrait bust of Isaiah Bowman (1875–1950), the fifth president of the university. If the Johns Hopkins University board had not accepted these conditions, a similar offer would have been made to Loyola College and then to Goucher College. The board of the Johns Hopkins University accepted these terms but not Shriver's stated preference that the lecture hall be sited on the "oval fronting the Carroll Mansion."

Architectural surveys for the new lecture hall were done by Laurence Hall Fowler in 1944, but the building was not started until after the end of the war, and Shriver Hall was not completed until 1954. The murals were in place by 1956, and the sculpture followed. Sidney Waugh was commissioned to do the statues of Gilman and Welch. At the time, Waugh was the director of the Rinehart School of Sculpture at the Maryland

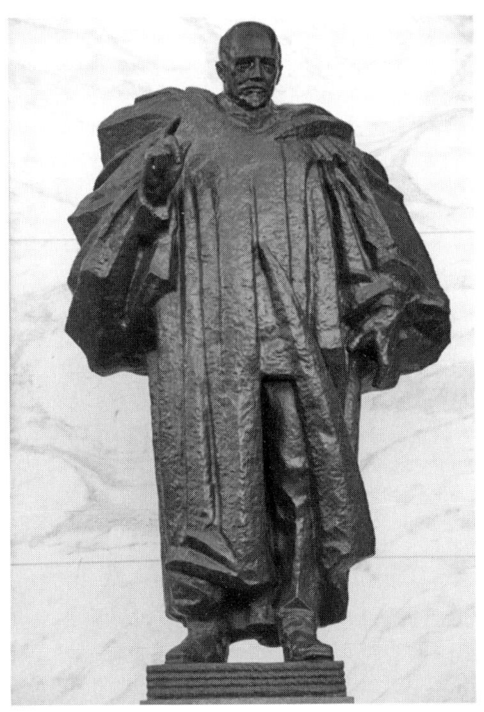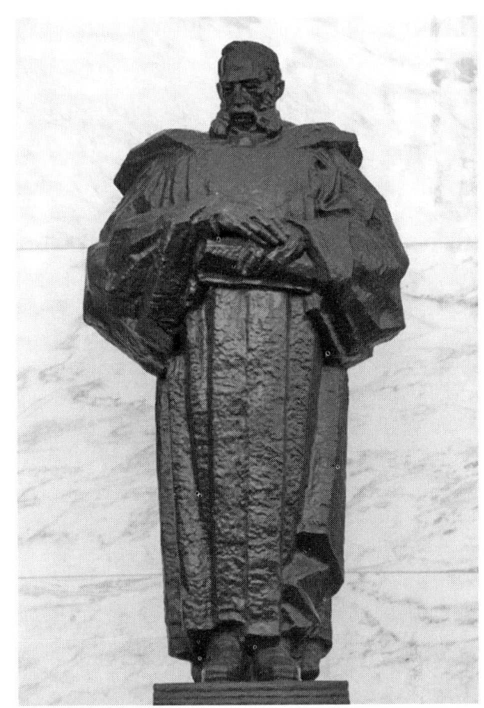

Institute College of Art, a position he held from 1942 to 1957. He had been educated at Amherst and the School of Architecture at MIT and then turned to sculpture, studying at the École des Beaux-Arts in Paris, at the American Academy in Rome, and at the Rinehart School of Sculpture. From 1933 until his death he was the chief associate designer for the Steuben Glass Company. He created many public portrait sculptures in Washington, D.C., most notably at the National Archives Building, and in Philadelphia, in addition to his statues of Gilman and Welch.

To plan these portrait statues, Waugh asked the university to provide him with written materials and photographs of the two men when he visited the university just after January 25, 1954. He had signed a contract for the two statues on November 5, 1953. In an undated document titled "The basic material which I will require," Waugh asked for brief biographical sketches of the men, including their academic specialties and their other interests; all available photographs of the two men, every likeness that could be found, official, unofficial, even snapshots, which he said would be very useful in creating a good likeness; brief physical descriptions of the two men, including any typical gestures and movements; and photographs of persons—any persons—in academic robes, posed and otherwise, in processions and in groups, "off-angle shots," which might be useful in developing the composition. Waugh stressed that in this kind of work it was impossible to have too much material at hand. "The sculptor may find something of real interest in a photograph which might seem trivial to others," he said. The resulting portraits of the two men in their academic robes are good likenesses and capture the differences in their personalities. Gilman is shown standing quietly, pensive, contemplating the sheaf of papers he holds in his very large hands, his mustache and flowing side whiskers clearly in evidence. Welch is shown in a more active pose, robe billowing, with his right hand and forefinger elevated, as if making a point while delivering a speech. Both statues are 9 feet tall on granite bases of equal height and appear larger than life, as both men were in reality.

J16

TITLE
Isaiah Bowman, 1955

LOCATION
Shriver Hall, Wyman Quadrangle,
Johns Hopkins University

SCULPTOR
Laura Gardin Fraser (1889–1966)

MEDIUM
Bronze

DONOR
Alfred Jenkins Shriver

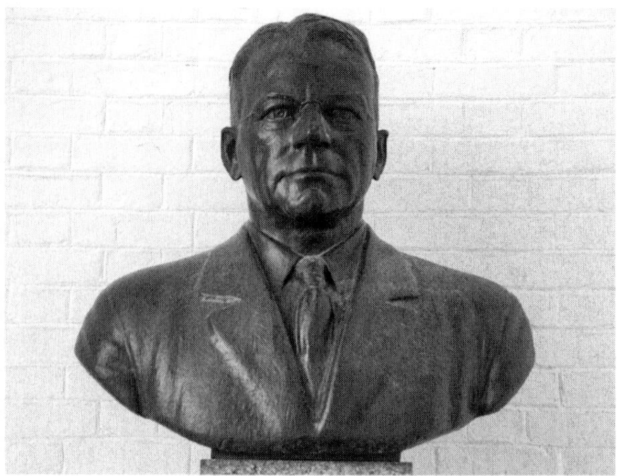

Isaiah Bowman (1878–1950) was the fifth president of Johns Hopkins University, serving in that capacity from 1935 until his retirement in 1948. Alfred Jenkins Shriver, who left money to Johns Hopkins University for a new lecture hall, specified that certain murals and statues had to be created for the building. A portrait bust of Bowman was to be placed near the entrance of the new hall, together with heroic portraits of Daniel Coit Gilman and William H. Welch, giving a clear indication not only that Shriver knew Bowman but that he approved of the choice of Bowman as president. (For a more complete discussion of Shriver's gift and its requirements, see J14–J15.)

Bowman was born in Waterloo, Ontario, and earned a BS degree from Harvard in 1905. In 1909 he received his PhD from Yale, where he taught geography from 1905 to 1915. Among other endeavors, he led the first Yale expedition to South American in 1907 and served as a geographer-geologist on the Yale expedition to Peru in 1911. In 1913 he led the American Geological Society expedition to the central Andes. By the time he was appointed president of Hopkins, he had distinguished himself as a geographer, educator, and author. He published several books, including one on his expedition to Peru and one on his trip to the Andes. He served as the chief territorial adviser to President Wilson at the Versailles Conference, and later, during his tenure at Hopkins, he served the Department of State as a territorial adviser during World War II. He served on numerous commissions and boards, including those of the Association of American Geographers, the Council of Foreign Relations, and the National Academy of Sciences.

Laura Gardin Fraser created this portrait bust of Bowman, which is traditional except that she chose to depict him in glasses, a subtle and unusual, but noticeable, touch.

J17

TITLE
Give Peace a Chance, 1972

LOCATION
Shriver Hall, Wyman Quadrangle,
Johns Hopkins University

SCULPTOR
Theodore C. Scuris (b. 1940)

MEDIUM
Aluminum

DONOR
Johns Hopkins University class of 1970

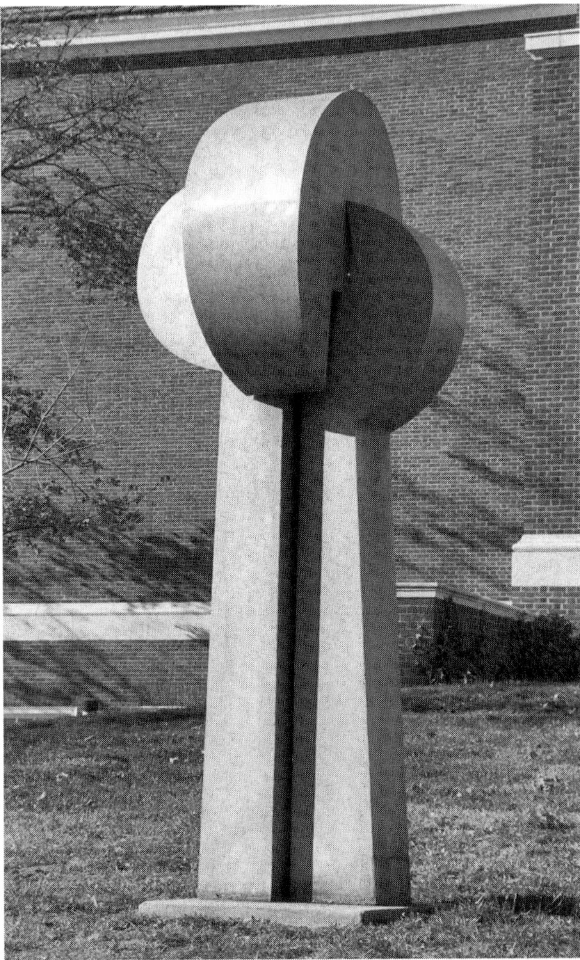

Originally sited at the north end of Wyman Quadrangle opposite Shriver Hall, this sculpture, commissioned as a gift to the university by the class of 1970, was moved to the eastern side of Shriver Hall during a relandscaping of the campus. The sculptor was Ted Scuris, who that year received both an MA from the Writing Seminars at Hopkins and an MFA from the Rinehart School of Sculpture at the Maryland Institute College of Art. He would go on to teach sculpture at Goddard College in Plainfield, Vermont.

Even though Scuris insisted that the piece was purely abstract, students over the years have compared the sculpture to an elephant, a wrench, and even a question mark. The students in the class of 1970 wanted to leave their alma mater with a piece of art that was not grounded in the past but could be a modern symbol for the future.

Made of burnished aluminum, the 8-foot-high piece was constructed by welding three separate pieces together. The title may have more to do with contemporary events in Southeast Asia than anything else. Some saw in it a clenched fist that represented the student activism on campuses across the country at the time. The United States had invaded Cambodia that April, and in early May the Ohio National Guard, reacting to demonstrations on the campus of Kent State University, had shot thirteen students, killing four. Scuris said only that he would like to dedicate it to the memory of Elliott Coleman, a poet and teacher who had started the Writing Seminars program at Hopkins, whom Scuris admired and respected.

TITLE
Fanned Arena, 1979

LOCATION
Olin Hall, San Martin Drive,
Johns Hopkins University

SCULPTOR
Lila Katzen (1925–1998)

MEDIUM
Cor-Ten and stainless steel

DONOR
On loan from the Baltimore Museum of Art

Lila Katzen made *Fanned Arena* in an edition of two. This is the first piece she made. It was on view first at the Phillips Collection, in Washington, D.C., but then became part of the collection of Donald L. Thal, of Bergenfield, New Jersey, who in 1981 put it on long-term loan to the Baltimore Museum of Art. The BMA in turn lent it to Johns Hopkins University, where with full cooperation and supervision of the artist, it was sited in front of the university's new building for earth and planetary sciences, which opened in 1981. The building was named in honor of John M. Olin, chairman of the Olin Mathieson Chemical Company, whose foundation provided the money for the building. Olin, who was an inventor, industrialist, conservationist, and philanthropist, served on the university's board of trustees from 1953 to 1974.

This work is composed of four large semicircular, or fan-shaped, pieces of steel—three of Cor-Ten and one of brushed stainless steel. The abstract forms sit right on the ground. The artist explained that the Cor-Ten steel represents the earth and the stainless steel represents the extension of life on earth. This explanation supports its placement before the entrance to Olin Hall. Several of the boulders originally planned for that location made their way there in spite of the installation of *Fanned Arena*—possibly a small protest of the change of plans.

The second *Fanned Arena,* made in 1980, is in the collection of the Grand Rapids Museum of Art, in Grand Rapids, Michigan, where it is sited on the museum's front lawn.

Note: This piece is to be returned to the executor of the estate of the donor at some time in the near future.

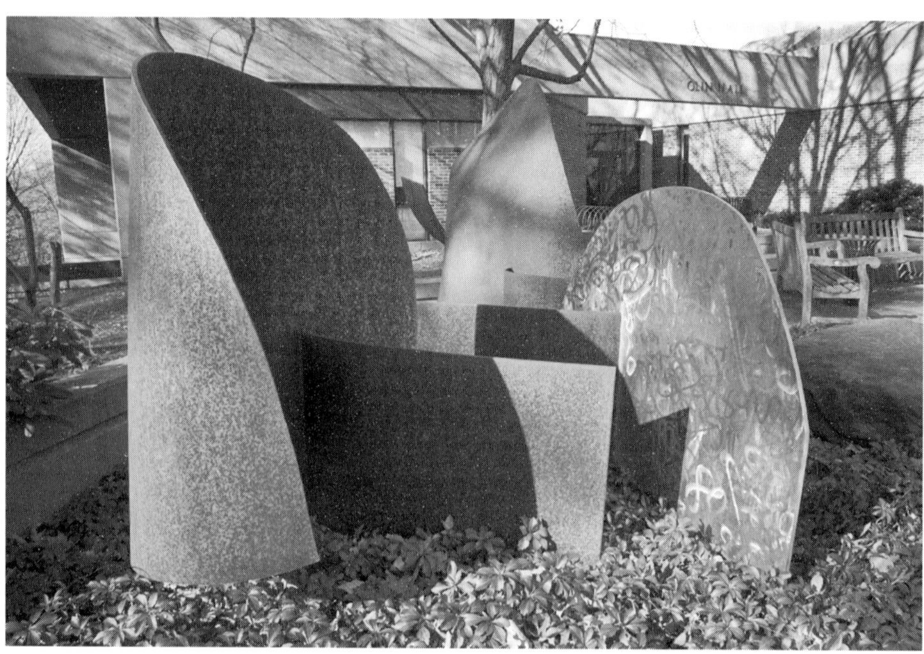

J19

Willow, 2002–2005

LOCATION
Levering Hall, Johns Hopkins University

SCULPTOR
Martin Kline (b. 1961)

MEDIUM
Bronze, unique

DONOR
Stephen Mazoh

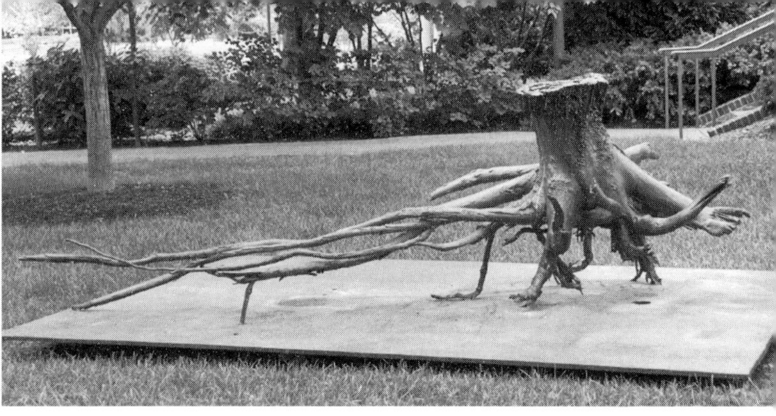

A huge tree that stood on Martin Kline's property in upstate New York fell onto his driveway during the remnants of a tropical storm that had worked its way north. Most of the tree was cut up for removal, but the tree stump, with its long, entangled root system, was so intriguing that Kline kept it in the yard with the vague notion of possibly using it in an artwork sometime in the future.

Several years passed, and Kline moved from making drawings to making drawings with encaustic. He then began making oil paintings with encaustic, applying more and more layers of hot wax until the paintings took on a sculptural quality. This process of hot-wax painting on canvas led him to think about casting canvas and frame as a whole. It did not involve a great leap to start casting small branches with interesting shapes. *Willow* was another step forward because of its scale.

Casting this found object—the tree stump and its roots—was no simple task. It actually took three years from start to finish. Kline worked with a foundry to develop the process. The stump and branches would be cast directly, but they would have to be cut into smaller pieces and made lighter. Kline had made an earlier piece using the stump by simply layering beeswax on the top cut surface of the stump. This top part of the stump, with its layers of wax, was cut off and cast separately. Welding it back onto the stump after the stump had been cast gave *Willow* a smooth, lustrous surface.

Additional bronze welding material was used to camouflage the weld.

Before the stump itself could be cast, it had to be hollowed out by a slow, tedious process of burning out the entire cavity, and the roots were cut into shorter pieces. A ceramic shell had to be built to hold the hollow stump and the short root pieces during the casting process. Many other decisions had to be made about the patina and about how to present the piece. Kline chose a rusty steel mounting plate from the foundry as the base; he didn't want the piece to blend too completely into nature.

Kline was born in Norwalk, Ohio, and earned his BFA from Ohio University in Athens in 1983. His drawings and paintings have been included in many group exhibitions in galleries and museums across the country and in solo exhibitions at the ACP Gallerie in Zurich; the Allez les Filles Gallery in Columbus, Ohio; and the Marlborough Gallery and Jason McCoy, Inc., in New York City. In the spring of 2005 he was awarded a grant to live and work in Miyonojo City, on the Japanese island of Kyushu. In 2007 his drawings, paintings, and sculpture were exhibited in a solo exhibition at the Haggerty Museum of Art in Milwaukee, Wisconsin. His work is held in numerous public and private collections, including those of the Metropolitan Museum of Art, the Whitney Museum of American Art, and the Brooklyn Museum, all in New York City; the Cleveland Museum of Art; the High Museum in Atlanta; and the Baltimore Museum of Art.

Willow was given to the Johns Hopkins University in memory of Stephen Mazoh's brother-in-law Ron Fish, a Baltimore lawyer who had died a few years earlier. Mazoh was a 1962 graduate of the Johns Hopkins Krieger School of Arts and Sciences.

J20

TITLE
Sea Urchin, 1922

LOCATION
Decker Garden, Johns Hopkins University

SCULPTOR
Edward Berge (1876–1924)

MEDIUM
Bronze

DONOR
Paul M. Higinbothom

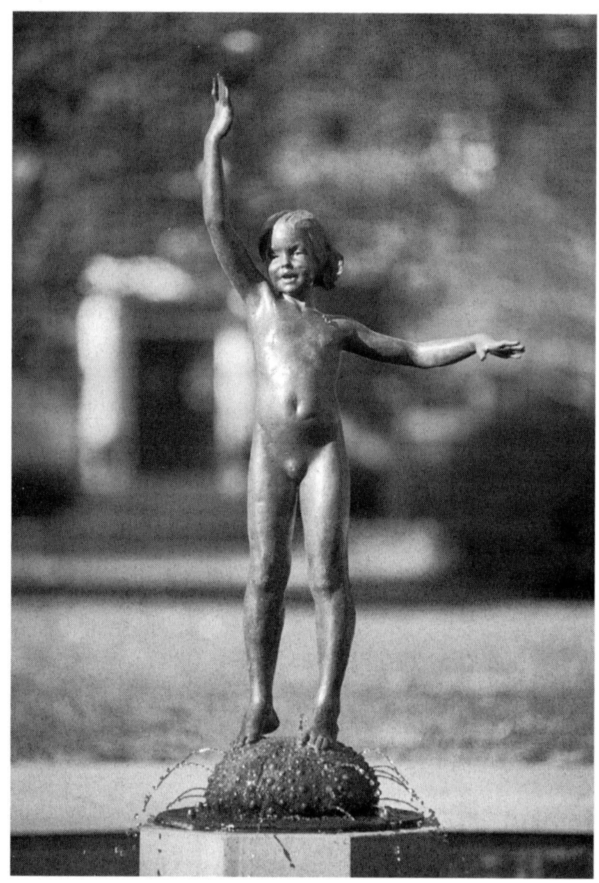

For such a small statue, this piece has a very long history, sometimes controversial but always interesting.

In 1924, very unexpectedly and prematurely, the sculptor Edward Berge died. The following year, a memorial exhibition of his work was mounted at the Baltimore Museum of Art, then located in Mount Vernon Place. Two sculptures titled *Sea Urchin* were among the sixty-five artworks on exhibit. The exhibition document stated that many of the works were for sale by the Berge estate. An anonymous donor said to have purchased *Sea Urchin* from the Berge estate in 1925, possibly one of the two exhibited in that memorial exhibition, presented to the city the 3-foot-high bronze figure of a small female child standing gleefully on a sea urchin, and it was placed in the fountain in the south square of Mount Vernon Place in memory of Edward Berge.

Over the next thirty-four years, before this original *Sea Urchin* was relocated to the lily pond in Decker Garden on the Johns Hopkins University campus, just east of the president's house, it endured countless indignities. It was twisted from its pedestal and kidnapped more than once, and it was vandalized many times. It has had its arms ripped off, it has been covered in red paint, and it has suffered a number of minor abrasions over the years. Continually, often after one of these incidents, there were calls for the piece to be relocated, primarily because it was "woefully out of scale with the monumental surroundings," as someone wrote to the Sun newspapers.

Then, in 1959, Frederick R. Huber, formerly the managing director of the Lyric Theatre and a close friend of Edward Berge's, died, leaving to the city $7,500 to replace the 3-foot-high *Sea Urchin* with a new, larger version, to be made by the sculptor's son, Henry (C16). Through his will Mr. Huber also made arrangements for the disposition of the original, which he wanted given to Paul M. Higinbothom, his lawyer and the executor of his will. Mr. Higinbothom felt that a piece of sculpture that had been in the public domain for more than three decades should remain so, and he and two friends, Dr. Richard T. Shackelford and Dr. Edwin B. Jarrett, drove around the city looking for a fitting site, settling in the end on this one, on the Hopkins campus, where in warm weather water sprays out of the tiny horns that protrude in circles around the sea urchin's shell and goldfish can be seen swimming under the water lilies.

J21–J22

TITLES
Discus Thrower and *Runner,* 1964

LOCATION
Newton H. White, Jr., Athletic Center,
Johns Hopkins University

SCULPTOR
Joe Brown (1909–1985)

MEDIUM
Bronze

DONOR
Mrs. Newton H. White Jr.

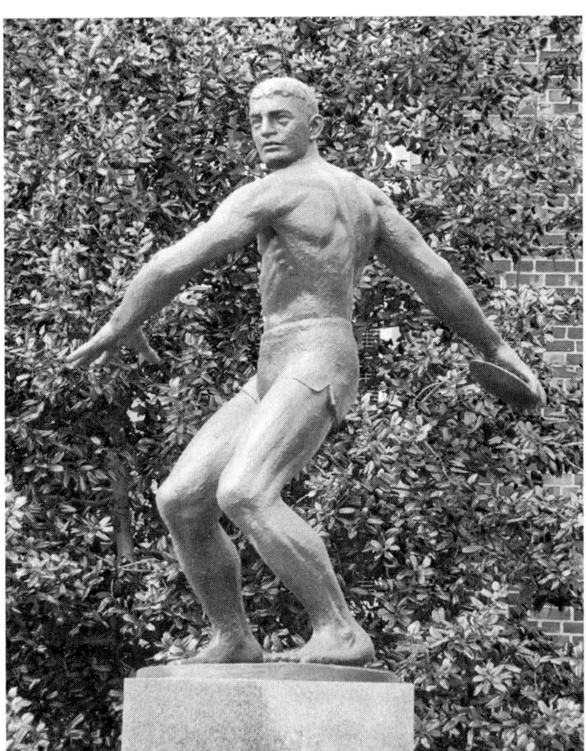

The Johns Hopkins University commissioned two sculptures from Joe Brown, an athlete, educator, and artist, for the new athletic center that opened in May 1965. Brown chose to depict a discus thrower in a contemporary pose for throwing the discus and a runner, who could symbolize all athletes in a running sport. They make interesting companions, reflecting different types of athletes—one solid, stocky and tough, the other tall, thin, and probably known for his endurance.

For his models Brown used athletes on the track team at Princeton University, where he was on the faculty. He had been hired as Princeton's boxing coach in 1937. His is an interesting story, one that began in a tough neighborhood of South Philadelphia. He entered Temple University in 1927 on a football scholarship and earned a bachelor's degree in physical education in 1931. In his second year at Temple he became captain of the boxing team, and in his junior year, to earn money, he turned from amateur boxing to professional boxing. A national contender as a light heavyweight, he fought nine professional bouts before deciding not to pursue boxing as a career but to return to amateur status for his senior year at Temple.

Brown began sculpting by chance. Again to earn extra money, he posed for the sculptor Walter Hancock at the Pennsylvania Academy of Fine Arts. Challenged to try his hand at sculpting, he made a small figure. The next year, he had three pieces accepted in the academy's

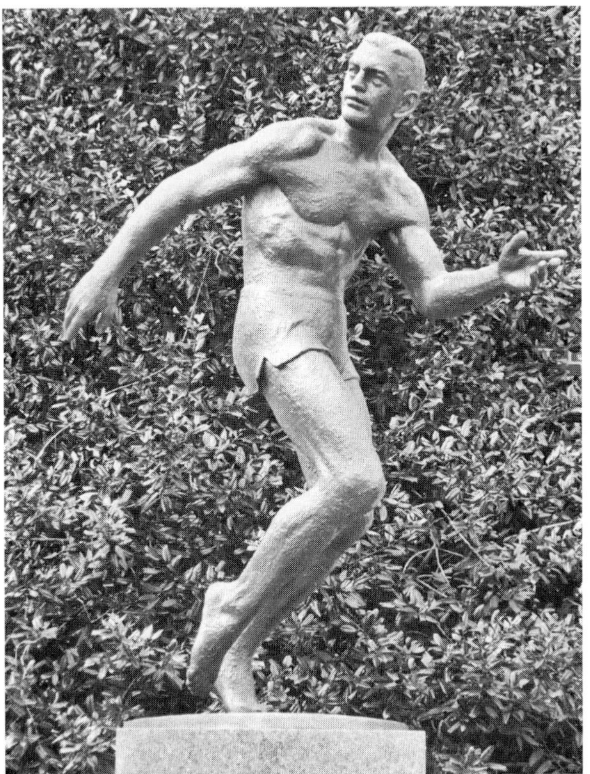

annual exhibition. He then took a seven-year apprenticeship with R. Tait McKenzie, Brown's mentor and friend. But his goal remained education, and he sought and won the job at Princeton, where he coached boxing and began teaching sculpture, eventually becoming a full professor in the School of Architecture.

Brown's association with McKenzie has bearing on another piece of sculpture in Baltimore, McKenzie's *The Boy Scout,* at the Morris and John D. Schapiro Scout Service Center (J29). In 1937 McKenzie created the life-size sculpture of a Boy Scout that was to be used across the country as a symbol of scouting at local and regional headquarters. After McKenzie died in 1938, Brown was designated as the person to approve all copies of *The Boy Scout* before they were shipped. Brown probably oversaw the casting and approval of Baltimore's *Boy Scout,* which was cast in 1969.

Seventeen pieces of Brown's sculpture can be seen in nearby Westminster, Maryland, at McDaniel College (founded as Western Maryland College). Many of these works of art had been exhibited in art galleries, in major corporate headquarters, and in solo exhibitions at Expo 67 in Montreal and at the XIX Olympiad in Mexico City. In 1996 the Joe Brown Foundation sent this gift to the college from Brown's estate and many were put on public display in buildings across the campus. It turns out that Brown had received an honorary degree from the college in 1978. Dr. H. Samuel Chase, a professor of exercise science and physical education there, had sponsored Brown for the honor. Chase, who had been at Johns Hopkins in 1964, had met Brown when he was working on the two sculptures at the athletic center, and the two had become friends. During research for the proposal for Brown to get the honorary degree, it was discovered that Brown had boxed at the college while a student at Temple, when Western Maryland College was a nationally ranked boxing power. Brown had won his match there.

Four of Brown's heroic bronze statues of sports figures were originally sited around Veteran's Stadium in Philadelphia. Now there is a new stadium, and the sculptures can be seen in other parts of the city.

The athletic center at Johns Hopkins was named in honor of Captain Newton H. White Jr., whose widow donated the money for it. White was the commander of the aircraft carrier USS *Enterprise* before World War II. He became interested in Johns Hopkins after reading Hopkins professor Ira Remsen's textbook on chemistry. Earlier in 1954 White and his wife had established scholarships, named after him, to support students who for financial reasons would not have been able to attend the university.

J23

TITLE
BUFANO SCULPTURE GARDEN, opened 1983

LOCATION
Dunning Park, Johns Hopkins University

SCULPTOR
Beniamino Bufano (1898–1970)

MEDIUM
Cast granite

DONORS
Erskine Bufano and the Bufano Society of the Arts

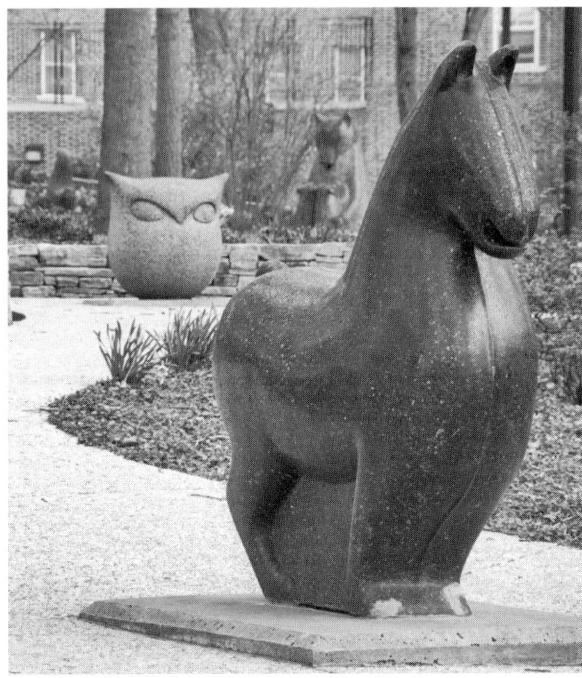

Beniamino Benvenuto Bufano was born in San Fele, Italy, and came to New York City with his family when he was 3 years old. He grew up in the city, and attended the Art Students League from 1913 to 1915, when he moved to San Francisco to work on sculpture for the 1915 Panama-Pacific International Exposition. He settled there, teaching at the University of California–Berkeley and at the California College of Arts and Crafts in Oakland and making sculpture that can be seen throughout the San Francisco Bay area today. His statue of the Chinese leader Sun Yat-sen in San Francisco's Chinatown is one of his best-known works. His large-scale stone animals and religious figures, several of St. Francis, especially the St. Francis at the Mondavi Winery, with its mosaic skirt, are widely admired and loved.

After Bufano's death, his son, Erskine, wanted to introduce Bufano's work to people on the East Coast to gain greater visibility for his father's work and expand his reputation across the country. He decided that a university might offer the best environment for doing this, and so together with members of the Bufano Society of the Arts he approached the Johns Hopkins University about a gift of ten animal sculptures. Certain site conditions had to be met, but by 1983 the university had agreed to accept the gift. Dunning Park, just east of the athletic center, was selected as the site. The animals include *Penguins Praying, Mother Bear and her Cubs, Bactrian Camel, Dromedary Camel, Snail, Ram, Elephant, Cat, Horse,* and another *Penguin.* These cast granite figures, with their simple shapes and smooth, rounded, highly polished surfaces, capture the gentle personalities of the animals they represent. That is their charm. In 2003 several of the sculptures were restored after having been vandalized several years earlier, and the park was relandscaped.

J24

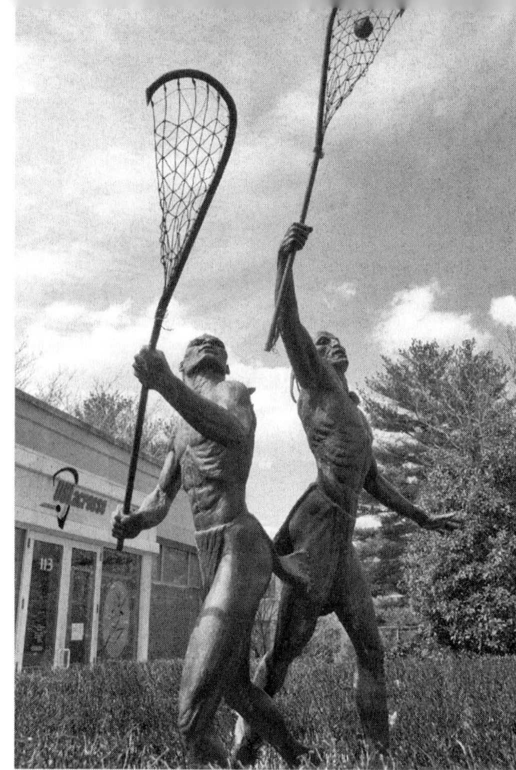

This bronze sculpture was commissioned to honor the Iroquois Indians, from whom the modern game of lacrosse descends, and to commemorate the 125th anniversary of modern organized lacrosse in North America.

Hartmann had become fascinated in college with the Northeast Indian tribes, and in 1983 he began what has become his life's work: creating a series of bronzes representing the Woodland Tribes of the Northeast, the Iroquois and the Algonquins. By the time he received this commission, Hartmann had completed twenty-eight sculptures in the series, ranging in size from 20 to 36 inches, each cast in an edition of four to ten. Today the series numbers more than fifty. His respect for the Native American Indians and his love of the game of lacrosse, which he played at Hobart College in Geneva, New York, a Division III powerhouse at the time, were a perfect blend for approaching this project.

An early idea for the sculpture to be sited in front of the new building that would house the museum and national hall of fame was to depict two mid-fielders facing off for the ball. But the donor, Emil "Buzzy" Budnitz, who had played for Johns Hopkins and after college for the Mt. Washington Club in Baltimore and was inducted into the Lacrosse Hall of Fame in 1976, wanted to represent the very beginnings of the sport, saying that the game could still change and that face-offs might be done differently in the future. The Lacrosse Hall of Fame invited three sculptors to submit proposals. To confirm the historical authenticity of the artists' interpretations of how the early game was played, the Hall of Fame invited several members of the Iroquois community, one of whom was Oren R. Lyons Jr., a Native American who had grown up in the Onondaga nation in upstate New York, had been an All American goalkeeper at Syracuse University, and was now a member of the International Lacrosse Hall of Fame, to review the three proposals.

The two Iroquois Indians are shown in graceful action as they both reach for the ball, which can be seen in the net of the higher stick. Depicted only in loincloths and soft shoes, their strong, muscular bodies are on display, underscoring how physically demanding the game is. Hartmann has also captured the power of their concentration, which seems equal to their physical prowess. The two opponents are attached at the calves of their right legs, and the one who has caught the ball appears to be in midair. Hartmann has succeeded in conveying the physical and mental challenges of the game of lacrosse and in honoring the creators of the game he loves.

Probably as a result of this commission, Hartmann received the commission to create the memorial to Rex Choa, the Hopkins student who was killed on campus in 1996 (J12).

J25

TITLE

CONFEDERATE WOMEN'S MONUMENT, 1915–1917

LOCATION

N. Charles Street and University Parkway

SCULPTOR

J. Maxwell Miller (1877–1933)

MEDIUM

Bronze

DONORS

Daughters of the Confederacy, United Confederate Veterans, and the State of Maryland

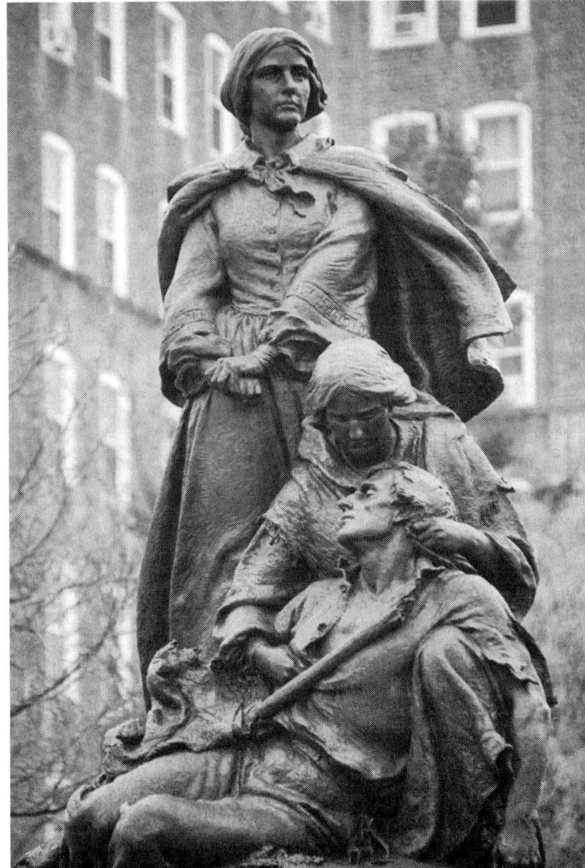

The Daughters of the Confederacy and the United Confederate Veterans worked for years to raise enough money to erect a monument to Maryland's Confederate women. Finally, in 1914, the state legislature gave them the funds they still lacked.

J. Maxwell Miller was awarded the commission to create a monument to honor the sacrifices and contributions of Confederate women. At the time, Miller was teaching at the Maryland Institute, where he would become director of the Rinehart School of Sculpture in 1923, a post he held until his death. This was not his first public commission in the city. He had been commissioned jointly with Edward Berge to create a monument to Ferdinand C. Latrobe, seven times mayor of Baltimore (O11), and he was commissioned to create a monument to celebrate the centenary of the writing of the "Star-Spangled Banner," which is in Patterson Park today (P1). But this monument to the Confederate women would be the most challenging.

Miller designed a composition with three bronze figures to be placed atop the monument. The three figures represent a fallen soldier being attended by a crouching woman behind whom stands a younger woman, hands clutched together, cape blowing in the wind, as she stares to her left and into the distance. The young man's left arm is draped over the woman's bended knee, he leans his head and upper body back against her chest, and his legs are tucked under him. The body of

the soldier cuts diagonally across the front of the woman nursing him. This diagonal line is repeated in the placement of the standard gripped by the soldier. The strong diagonal created by his body focuses the viewer's concentration on the dying soldier, heightening the emotional content of the monument and underscoring what the mothers, wives, sisters, and aunts of Confederate soldiers had endured during the Civil War. The dedication on the front of the monument reads, "TO THE / CONFEDERATE WOMEN / OF MARYLAND / 1861–1865 / TO THE BRAVE AT HOME." The inscription on the back of the monument continues the tribute: "IN DIFFICULTY AND DANGER / REGARDLESS OF SELF / THEY FED THE HUNGRY / CLOTHED THE NEEDY / NURSED THE WOUNDED / AND / COMFORTED THE DYING."

David J. Carver, a graduate student at the Johns Hopkins University at the time, was Miller's model for the dying Confederate soldier. The very well known portrait painter Thomas C. Corner recommended Carver to the young sculptor when he was looking for a model in 1917. Carver would tell of gazing in awe at himself when the monument was unveiled in November 1918. He ranked his involvement in the creation of this monument among the most profound and exciting experiences of his life. He received his PhD from the School of Arts and Sciences at Johns Hopkins in 1919 and went on to become a teacher, businessman, and art collector.

Miller was born in Baltimore and studied at the Maryland Institute. He was a member of the first class of the Rinehart School of Sculpture at the Institute, along with Edward Berge and Hans Schuler. After graduating from the Rinehart School, the three men traveled together to Paris, where they studied for four years at the Académie Julian under Charles Raoul Verlet. All three would have notable careers in Baltimore.

J26

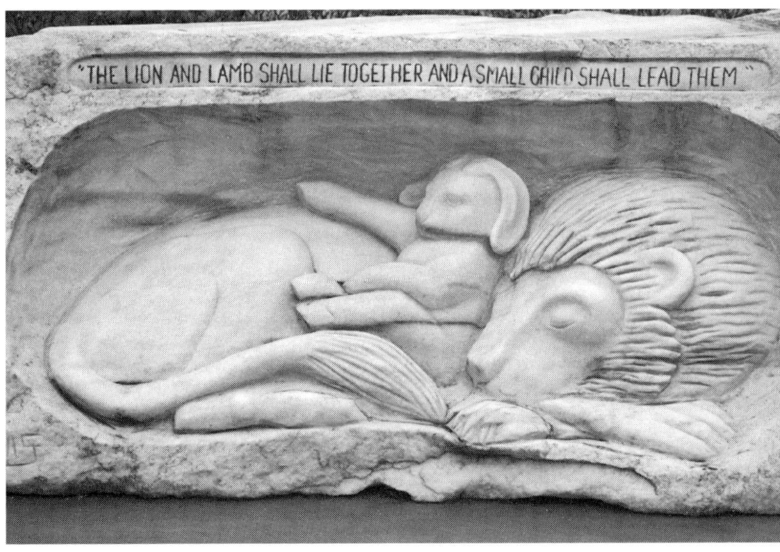

TITLE

CHILDREN'S PEACE MEMORIAL, 2005

LOCATION

Episcopal Cathedral of the Incarnation, N. Charles Street and University Parkway

SCULPTOR

William Sunderland (b. 1930)

MEDIUM

Marble

DONOR

Gift of the artist

Near the main entrance to the Episcopal cathedral, on the right, is a relief sculpture of a lion and a lamb lying peaceably together carved out of a piece of Georgia white marble. This sculpture is only one part of a meditative space that includes a winding footpath across a wooden footbridge and handcrafted tiles bearing the names of Baltimore children who died because of neglect, abuse, or violence.

This meditative space was a partnership between the cathedral's Children's Peace Center and the TKF Foundation, a private grant-making foundation based in Annapolis that helps fund the creation of public sanctuaries like this one. Benches such as the one installed near this sculpture are an integral part of the sacred spaces that TKF helps to create. The sculptor, William Sunderland, is a Baltimore native who lives in Atlanta. Sunderland's brother is a member of the congregation at the cathedral. Floura Teeter Landscape Architects, Inc., designed the garden.

Nearer to N. Charles Street and clearly visible from University Parkway is the Victory Cross, which dates from 1920. The Cathedral League, an organization of women from every parish in the Episcopal diocese of Maryland, decided to place a large, impressive cross in memory of victory in World War I on the cathedral grounds. Every woman member would share in this work. The cross was not to be understood as a memorial to fallen soldiers but as a witness to victory.

The project was unanimously adopted at a league meeting on February 5, 1919. It was noted in the minutes to that meeting that a drawing of the Peace Cross at the Washington Cathedral was shown as an example of what was being proposed. At the league's April 22 meeting it was reported that the cross had been ordered from the Hilgartner Marble Company and that it would stand 21 feet tall on a base 10 feet square. At this same meeting it was decided that the names of all Maryland men of the church who had died in the war would be engraved on a copper plate to be placed inside the cornerstone of the base of the cross; instead, the plate was mounted on the rear of the base, where it can be seen today. The cross was dedicated on January 27, 1921.

The design of the Victory Cross at the Episcopal Cathedral is obviously related to that of the Peace Cross at the Washington Cathedral, dedicated in 1898 to mark the end of the Spanish-American War. It seems clear that the Cathedral League sent the drawing of the Washington Peace Cross to the Hilgartner Stone Company and that the carvers there used the drawing as their guide.

J27

TITLE

SIDNEY LANIER MONUMENT, 1941

LOCATION

N. Charles Street near University Parkway, on the
Johns Hopkins University campus

SCULPTOR

Hans Schuler (1874–1951)

MEDIUM

Bronze

DONOR

Municipal Art Society of Baltimore City

Sidney Lanier (1842–81) was a poet, tutor, soldier, lecturer, clerk, scholar, linguist, novelist, and musician, all before the age of 39, when he died while living in his adopted city of Baltimore. At the time of his death, he was considered one of the country's great poets, ranking just after Poe, Whitman, and Emerson.

Lanier was born in Macon, Georgia. At the age of 14 he entered Oglethorpe University in Midway, Georgia. After graduating in 1860 at the top of his class, he was appointed a tutor there, but after Georgia voted to secede from the Union, Lanier resigned and volunteered as a private in the Confederate army. In 1864 he became a signal officer on a blockade-runner, and in November of that year he was captured off the coast of North Carolina. Imprisoned at Camp Point Lookout, in southern Maryland, Lanier suffered terribly from the bitter cold, contracting consumption, a disease that would plague him the rest of his life. Released in a prisoner exchange in February 1865, he walked all the way to Macon, which took him two months. He was dangerously ill when he got to Macon, but after two months he had recovered enough to join his brother Clifford in Montgomery, Alabama, where he took a job as a hotel clerk and bookkeeper. A year later, in 1867, he became the head of a country academy in Prattsville, Alabama, he married Mary Day, and his novel *Tiger Lilies*, begun while he was a prisoner of war, was published.

Lanier's longest continuous employment was the four years he spent in his father's law office, 1868–72, while looking for a position on the faculty of a southern university. In 1873, on one of his many trips to New York seeking publication of his poems, he stopped in Baltimore and auditioned for the orchestra at the recently opened Peabody Institute. He was hired as the first flutist. Mary and their four sons would join him in Baltimore. This steady employment and his salary of sixty dollars a month allowed him to turn his attention to his writing and to his poetry. In 1876 he was invited to pen the words for the cantata to be sung at the Philadelphia Centennial Exposition. His verse was judged so uplifting and so reflective of the reunified nation that he was asked to write the centennial poem, published in *Lippincott's Magazine*, for which he was paid handsomely. Lanier's success with the centennial cantata and poem led Daniel Coit Gilman to invite him to become a lecturer in English literature at Hopkins, fulfilling his lifelong ambition of university teaching and scholarship. In 1877 his first volume of poems was published, and he began a period of financial independence that ushered in the most productive period of his literary career.

While in Baltimore, Lanier wrote most of his best-known poems—"The Marshes of Glenn," "The Symphony," "Psalm of the West," "Ballad of Trees and the Master," and "Ode to the Johns Hopkins University." These few short years, from 1873 to 1881, were the happiest of his life. He worked incessantly on the public lectures that he gave at Hopkins and Peabody and above all on his poetry, for which many felt he had forsaken his first love, music. But by 1881 he had entered the last stages of his consumption and had moved temporarily with his family to Ashville, North Carolina, for the healing air of the mountains. It was there that he died, just after completing "Sunrise," considered one of his greatest poems.

A line from this last poem—"I am lit by the sun"—appears on his grave marker in the Turnbull family plot, and it is referred to in the relief behind the seated figure of Lanier in the monument commissioned by the Municipal Art Society of Baltimore City to mark the centenary of his birth. Just to the left of the two female

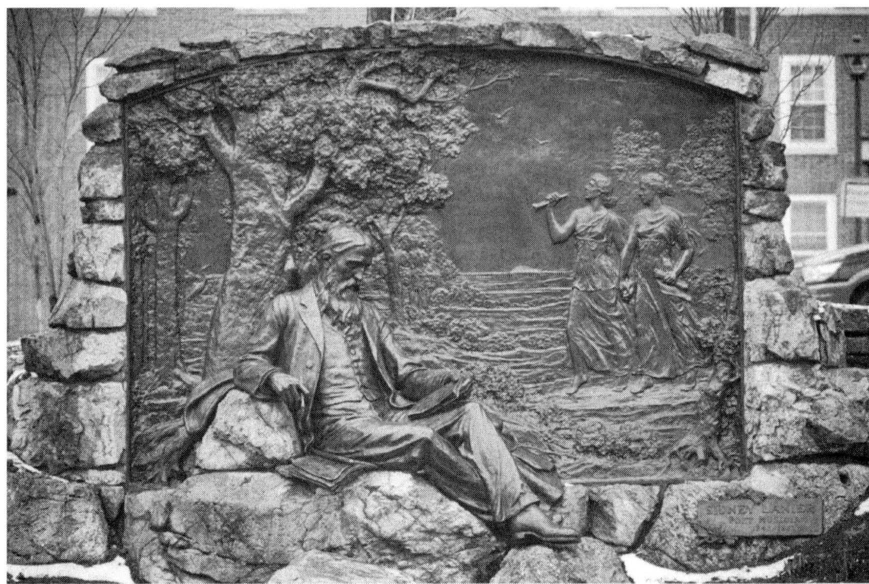

figures representing the muses of poetry and music can be seen the sun and the sun's rays on the horizon.

On February 3, 1942, on what would have been Lanier's one hundredth birthday, Johns Hopkins president Isaiah Bowman accepted the gift of Hans Schuler's unique monument from R. E. Lee Taylor, president of the Municipal Art Society. Gilman had described Lanier as "striking in appearance, his looks, manner and speech distinctive." Those words and his personally rewarding life in Baltimore as an acclaimed flutist and poet are reflected in this unusual portrait. Lanier is depicted with the long beard seen in all representations of him, even though it makes him appear older than his years. He is shown seated on a cluster of natural boulders placed in front of a huge bas-relief. He is formally dressed, and his tall, elegant frame is much in evidence. Schuler chose to present Lanier deep in thought, working on a poem, evidenced by his gaze focused on the book in his lap and the pencil in his right hand. His flute is nearby, a clear reflection that poetry and music both contributed to the happiness he experienced in Baltimore, most notably his appointment to the faculty of Johns Hopkins. The tinge of sadness inherent in the monument serves to mark the shortness of his life and raises the question how much more he might have achieved.

The Johns Hopkins University opened the Lanier Room on the third floor of Gilman Hall that same February day to further mark the centennial of his birth. In this room, which looked like the working library of a poet, was Lanier's great swell-front walnut desk, Mrs. Lanier's own small desk, Lanier's dictionary on an old-fashioned stand, his glass-front bookcase filled with books reflecting his interests, his art—an oil painting and engravings—and several of his favorite chairs. The more than two thousand letters written by Lanier and contributed from descendants of his friends were to be made available to the students. Original manuscripts of some of his great poems—"Corn," "Sunrise," and "Ballad of Trees and the Master"—were also on display in this room. There was a small trunk in which Mrs. Lanier kept her letters from her husband, as well as the chair she sat in to reread those letters. In one letter, written just after his selection as first flutist in the Peabody orchestra, Lanier told his wife that "we might dwell in the beautiful city, among the great libraries, and midst of the music, the religion, the art we love, and I could write my books, and be the man I wish to be. I do thank God, even for this dream."

The Municipal Art Society's decision to give the university a monument to Sidney Lanier seems even more prescient today, for the Peabody Institute became a division of the Johns Hopkins University in 1977.

J28

TITLE
Untitled, 1978

LOCATION
Greenmount School, 501 W. 30th Street

SCULPTOR
Judith Chodak Goldberg (b. 1942)

MEDIUM
Ceramic tiles

DONOR
Baltimore City Percent for Art program

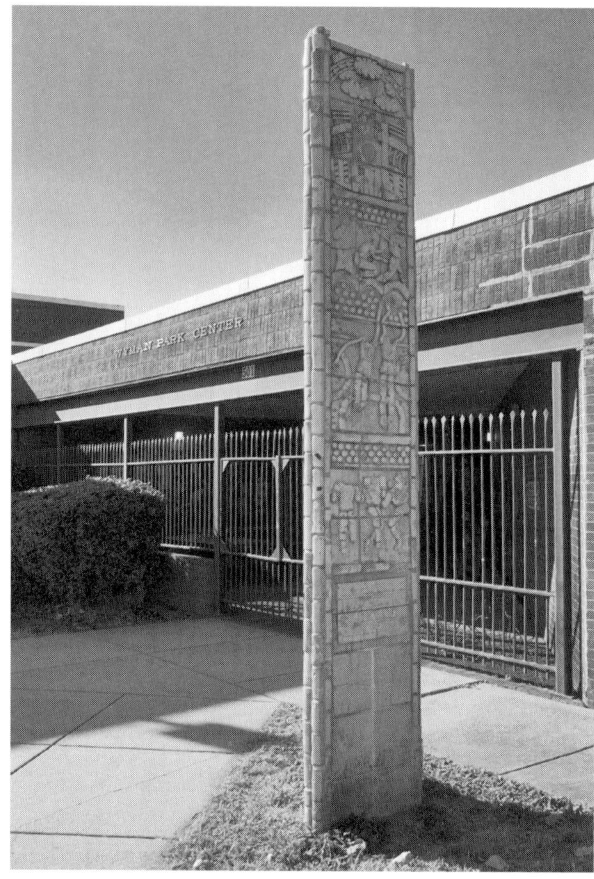

Today the Greenmount School owns this building, but when it was built in 1977 it was the Wyman Park Multi-Purpose Center, housing a recreation center and a mayor's station.

The neighborhood residents made it clear to the architect that they wanted an artist from the neighborhood to create any artwork that might be commissioned for the new building through the Percent for Art program. The architect held a small competition among five artists living around Wyman Park. Artists were asked to submit a drawing of their proposed artwork. Judith Chodak Goldberg, who had received her BFA from the Maryland Institute College of Art in Ceramics in 1966 and her MFA in art education from the same institution in 1975, was selected.

Goldberg created a triangular obelisk made of white ceramic tiles over a concrete core. On each face there is a vertical series of scenes in high relief that tell the story of the community at work and at play. On one face, above the inscription "OUR COMMUNITY IS PEOPLE ON THE MOVE . . . WORKING," are depictions of a fire truck en route to a fire, an ambulance and its driver, a bus, and two police cars with sirens blaring. Above these scenes is the Washington Monument, making clear that the community is Baltimore. On a second face, above the inscription "OUR COMMUNITY IS PEOPLE . . . RELAXING AND PLAYING," are scenes showing three figures playing football and two figures playing basketball; above these,

a batter and catcher are engaged in a game of baseball; and the uppermost scene is of a stadium. On the third face, above the inscription "OUR COMMUNITY IS MADE OF MANY DIFFERENT PEOPLE," are figures representing priests, doctors, teachers, and construction workers.

The third face is particularly hard to read today, as are many areas on the two other faces. Unfortunately, the same week the obelisk was installed, it was badly vandalized. And even though there were discussions about asking Goldberg to restore the obelisk, she was never asked, and it never happened.

J29

TITLE
The Boy Scout, 1969 casting of 1937 original

LOCATION
Morris and John D. Schapiro Scout Service Center,
701 Wyman Park Drive at Sisson Street

SCULPTOR
R. Tait McKenzie (1867–1938)

MEDIUM
Bronze

DONORS
Morris and John D. Schapiro

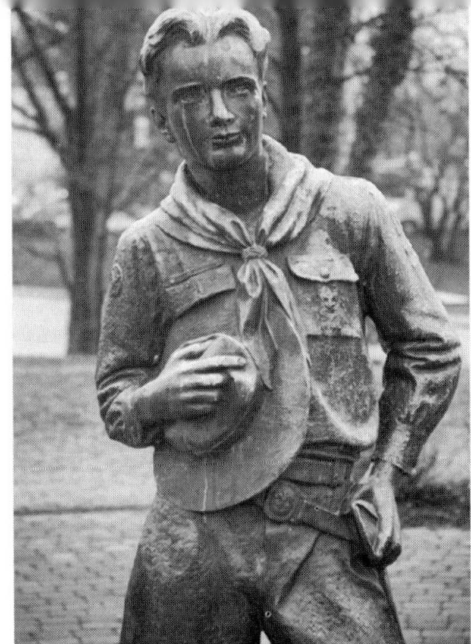

R. Tait McKenzie was a personal friend of the founder of the Boy Scouts, Sir Robert Baden-Powell, and was active in organizing the first Philadelphia chapter of the Boy Scouts in 1908. He was asked to create the statue known as *The Boy Scout,* and in 1911 he presented a model for the piece as an 18-inch bronze figure. Ten copies were made of that original figure.

In 1937 McKenzie made the first life-size bronze statue. He used four different young boys as models. The resulting figure is of a serious but kindly American youth dressed in his Scout uniform, shorts and a long-sleeved shirt with "BOY SCOUTS OF AMERICA" above the pocket. His head is uncovered to suggest reverence, proper obedience to authority, and a well-ordered discipline. The youth's hat is in his right hand, held against his chest, and his left hand rests on the head of his hatchet, which hangs from his belt. The placement of the young man's hand on his hatchet serves as a symbol of truthfulness. He stands directly on the ground, out in front of the scouting center, about 6 feet tall, with his weight on his right foot. His boots are untied, and his socks are pulled up to his knees.

McKenzie made the statue available to any community that wished to buy one. Almost every one did. These statues can be found at scouting headquarters all over the country. Baltimore's was ordered for the opening of the Schapiro Scout Service Center in 1969. Each of the life-size statues was cast by the Modern Art Foundry in Long Island City, New York, and after McKenzie's death each casting had to be approved by Joe Brown, the sculptor of *Discus Thrower* and *Runner* at the Johns Hopkins University athletic center (J21–J22), before shipping.

McKenzie began his professional life as a medical doctor. Born in Ontario, Canada, he worked his way through college and medical school at McGill University. He was the Canadian intercollegiate champion in the high jump, a good hurdler, a first-rate boxer, and a member of the varsity football team, and he excelled in swimming and fencing. It is not surprising that his chosen field of medicine was orthopedic surgery. He was on the faculty at McGill Medical School in the Department of Anatomy and as medical director of physical training from 1894 to 1904. He left McGill to head the new Department of Physical Education at the University of Pennsylvania and to serve on the medical faculty there. In 1931 he asked to be relieved of his duties in order to devote more time to his sculpture.

Initially McKenzie was drawn to sculpture as a way to demonstrate points in his anatomy lectures when he could not find other examples. His early work in exhibitions around Philadelphia was not well received by critics. He studied European masters and traveled to Europe to continue his studies. He then worked closely with two scholars studying Greek sculpture. His work improved, and he won recognition as a sculptor. His other sculptures are of runners, discus throwers, skaters, sprinters, punters, and pole-vaulters. He became known as the "Sculptor of Athletes."

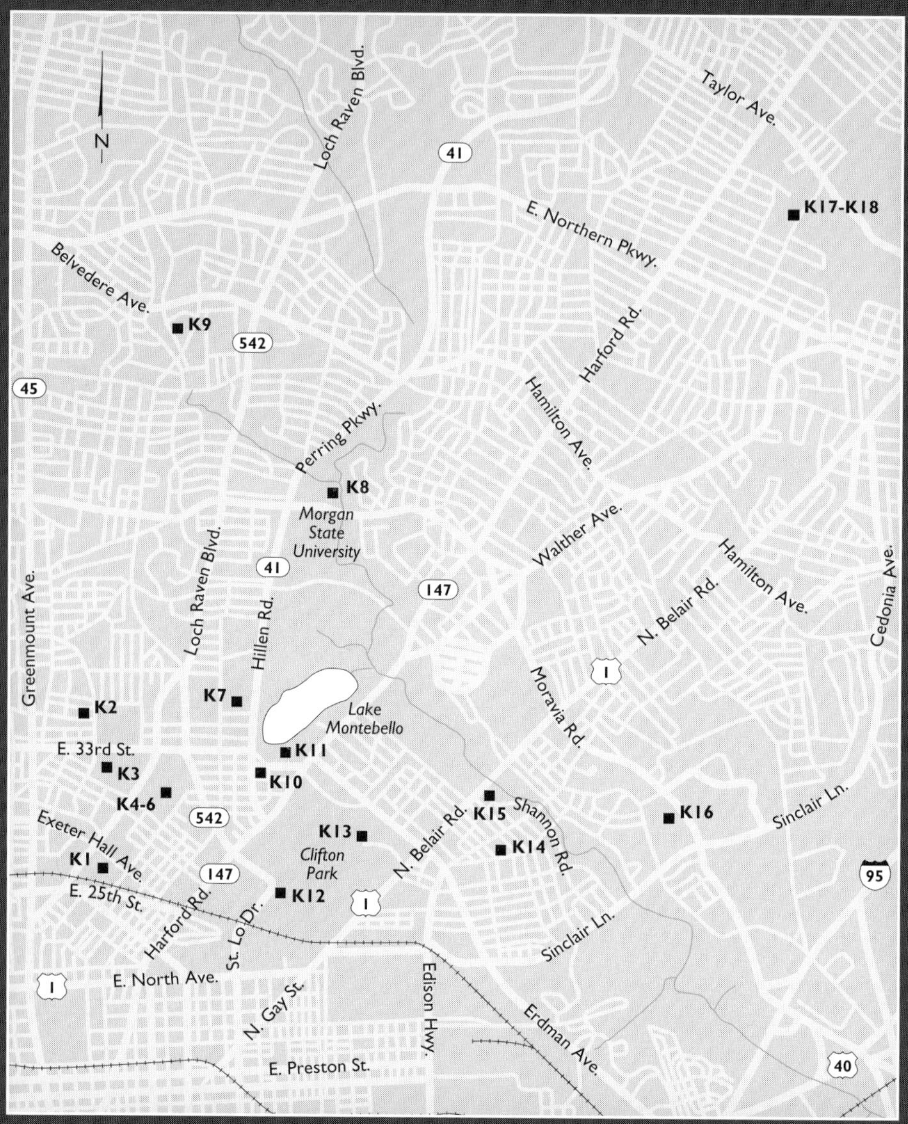

N
Loch Raven Blvd.
Taylor Ave.
41
E. Northern Pkwy.
K17-K18
Belvedere Ave.
K9
542
Harford Rd.
45
Hamilton Ave.
Perring Pkwy.
K8
Morgan State University
Walther Ave.
Hamilton Ave.
147
N. Belair Rd.
Cedonia Ave.
Loch Raven Blvd.
Hillen Rd.
41
1
K2
K7
Lake Montebello
Moravia Rd.
Greenmount Ave.
E. 33rd St.
K11
K3
K10
Sinclair Ln.
K4-6
542
K15
Shannon Rd.
K16
K13
K14
Exeter Hall Ave.
Clifton Park
N. Belair Rd.
K1
147
95
E. 25th St.
Harford Rd.
K12
1
E. North Ave.
St. Lo Dr.
Sinclair Ln.
1
N. Gay St.
Edison Hwy.
Erdman Ave.
E. Preston St.
40

WAVERLY, CLIFTON PARK, AND ENVIRONS

Driving

K1

TITLE
Untitled, 1969

LOCATION
Cold Stream Park Elementary School,
1400 Exeter Hall Avenue

SCULPTOR
Earl F. Hofmann (1928–1992)

MEDIA
Aluminum and ceramic tiles

DONOR
Baltimore City Percent for Art program

Across three wide sections of brick wall and just below the narrow, ribbed cap of the school building, Earl F. Hofmann installed his expansive aluminum relief. Composed of sixteen aluminum cutouts, most of them ornamented with high-glazed red, orange, yellow, and blue ceramic tiles, the relief is bright and colorful with sweeping, energetic forms.

One main, double-door entrance and three single-door entrances are spread across the front of the building. Hofmann chose to accentuate those entrances with a broad band of colorful ceramic tiles above each one. For the main entrance, he used bright orange tiles, through which patterns of black tiles can be seen, and for the smaller entrances, he employed a more static pattern of bright red and black tiles. Hofmann related the tiled entrances to the larger relief through the use of the same high-glazed ceramic tiles.

Architect George Vaeth invited Hofmann to create artwork for his new school. They were friends, and Vaeth wanted to work with Hofmann on the project. Together they came up wit the scheme that can be seen today.

Hofmann was somewhat of an unlikely choice for this commission, because he was primarily known as a painter. He graduated from the Maryland Institute in 1953, where he had studied with Jacques Maroger, a recent émigré from France who was credited with the rediscovery of the oil painting medium used by Jan van Eyck and other Renaissance painters. Along with Joseph Sheppard, John Bannon, Frank Redelius, Thomas Rowe, and Evan Keehn, Hofmann was a member of the Six Realists, a group of painters in Baltimore who exhibited together in the 1960s. Their most celebrated exhibition was a Salon des Refusés, organized in 1961 in response to their being excluded from the Maryland Annual Exhibition at the Baltimore Museum of Art. In 1970, Hofmann became artist-in-residence at St. Mary's College of Maryland, where went on to teach for many years.

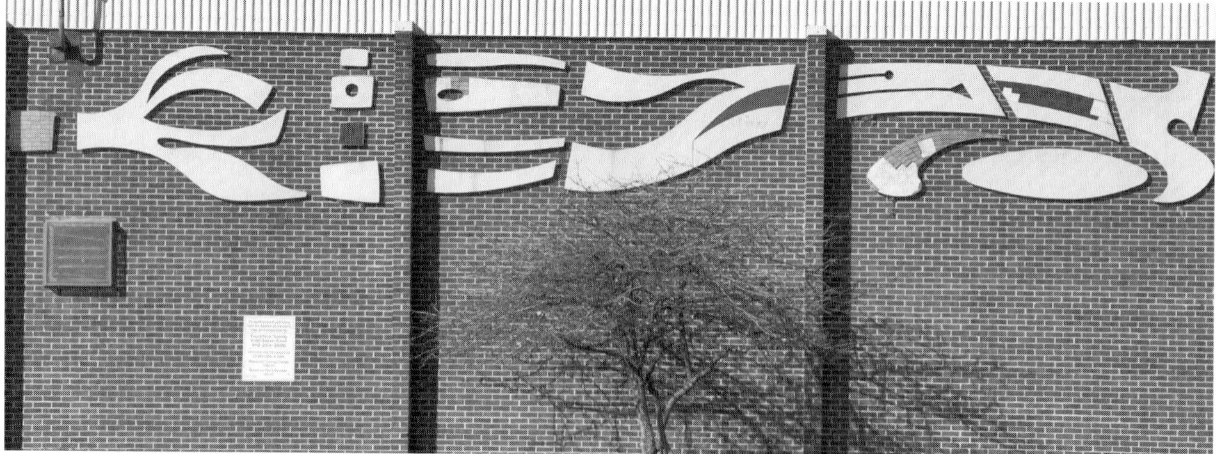

K2

TITLE
The Immortals, 1980–1982

LOCATION
Waverly Elementary School, 3400 Ellerslie Avenue

SCULPTOR
Tylden Streett (b. 1922)

MEDIUM
Glass-reinforced polyester resin

DONOR
Baltimore City Percent for Art program

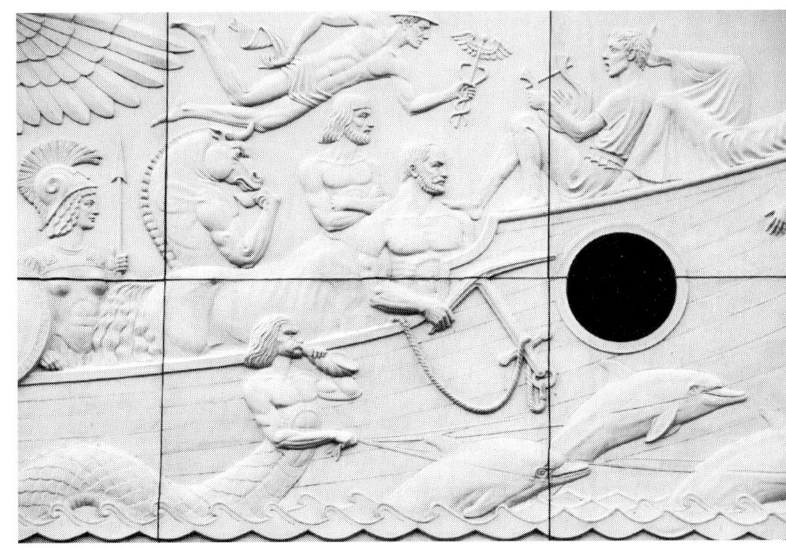

The round window over the entrance door to this new school would have to be incorporated into any artwork designed for the facade. The window suggested a boat with a porthole, and that is where Tylden Streett began the project. The twelve mythological figures came later.

Streett designed the huge relief as an eight-panel composition. He worked first in clay, assisted by his daughter, Ferebe, and Mike Lasell, then a student at the Maryland Institute. Plastic molds of the clay panels were made by a specialty automobile company. These eight plastic molds were then taken to another automobile factory, where the glass-reinforced polyester resin panels were made. The process was not unlike that used to make a Corvette. No coating was needed, but Streett did add some coloration to the resin in the area cut to suggest waves and water.

The life-size mythological figures are, from left to right: Artemis, the goddess of the hunt and the wilderness, with wings; Eros, the god of love, with arrows; Helios, the god of the sun, with his attribute of a shinning aureole of the sun behind him; Silenus, a satyr and companion of Dionysus, on his ass; Icarus, who flew too close to the sun with wings fashioned out of wax by his father, Daedalus, for their escape from Crete and died; Pallas Athena, the goddess of war and of wisdom and justice, with her war helmet; Hermes, the messenger of the gods, with his winged hat; the Minotaur, half man and half bull; Chiron, the centaur who is half man, half horse; Heracles, a son of Zeus who completed the twelve labors he needed to complete to become immortal, holding the anchor; Orpheus, the greatest of all musicians, holding his lyre; Triton, the messenger of the deep, in the water, represented as being half man, half fish; one of the nine Muses, possibly Clio, with her trumpet and three dolphins. The profile of Heracles is that of the artist.

For the recreation center next door, Streett carved into the brick facade a winged horse rising up on his hind legs.

K3

TITLE

LIZETTE WOODWORTH REESE MONUMENT, 1939

LOCATION

Johns Hopkins at Eastern, 1101 E. 33rd Street

SCULPTOR

Grace Hill Turnbull (1880–1976)

MEDIUM

Marble

DONOR

Gift of the artist

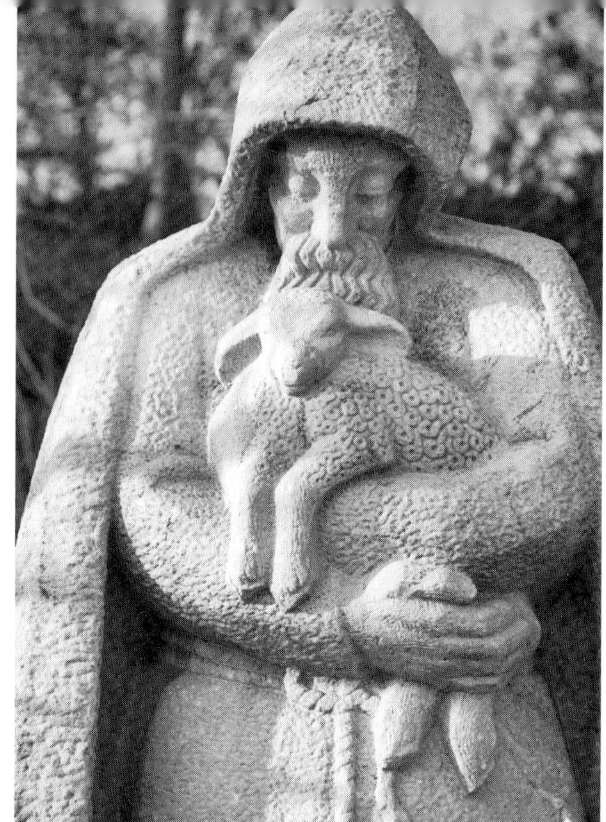

Lizette Woodworth Reese (1856–1935) was once regarded by American and European critics alike as a poet on par with Robert Frost, Elinor Wylie, and Edna St. Vincent Millay. H. L. Mencken considered her sonnet "Tears" one of the three greatest sonnets in the English language. Mencken, who was a pallbearer at her funeral, praised Reese as "the most notable woman Maryland has produced." Tributes to her were published in the leading newspapers across the country, where often her sonnet "Tears" was reprinted. Today most of her books of poetry are out of print, even though lines from "Tears" can still be found in reference books like Bartlett's.

Reese began writing poems at the age of 14. She was a Phi Beta Kappa graduate of Goucher College in Baltimore. In 1934 she was named the year's National Honor Poet. She was a good friend of Grace Turnbull's parents, who encouraged her and published a work of hers when she was only 17. Turnbull knew and admired Reese and donated this monument to Eastern High School, where Reese had been a student. The monument was moved to the Lake Clifton High School, where students from Eastern were moved after their school closed in 1985. At the urging of the Eastern High School alumnae, the monument was moved back to the grounds of the former Eastern High School in June 2009.

Turnbull makes reference in the monument to Reese's poem "The Good Shepherd," seven four-line stanzas of which are incised into the pink Georgia marble. Sheep and lambs and shepherds and their dogs were recurring themes in Reese's poetry. She loved to see the shepherd of Clifton Park tending his flock. Here a shepherd, holding a lamb, stands in the center of a semicircular row of sheep—seven sheep on his right and six sheep and his dog on his left. The shepherd is dressed in a short tunic tied at the waist with a rope. He wears sandals with straps reaching up to his knees. A hooded cape covers his bowed head and shoulders.

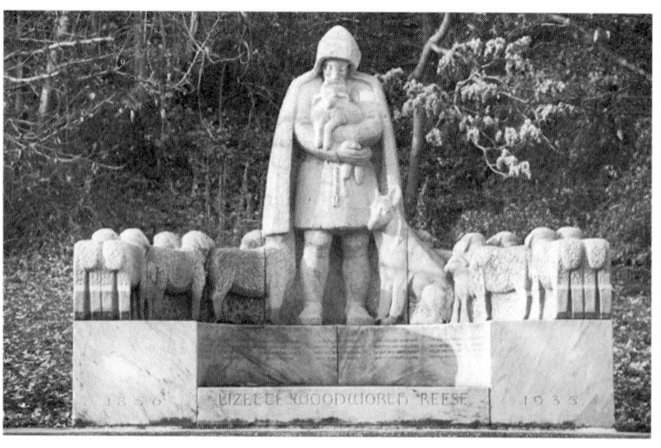

"

K4

TITLE
The Guide, 1980

LOCATION
Baltimore City College High School,
33rd Street and The Alameda

SCULPTOR
Ayokunle Odeleye (b. 1951)

MEDIUM
Galvanized steel

DONOR
Baltimore City Percent for Art program

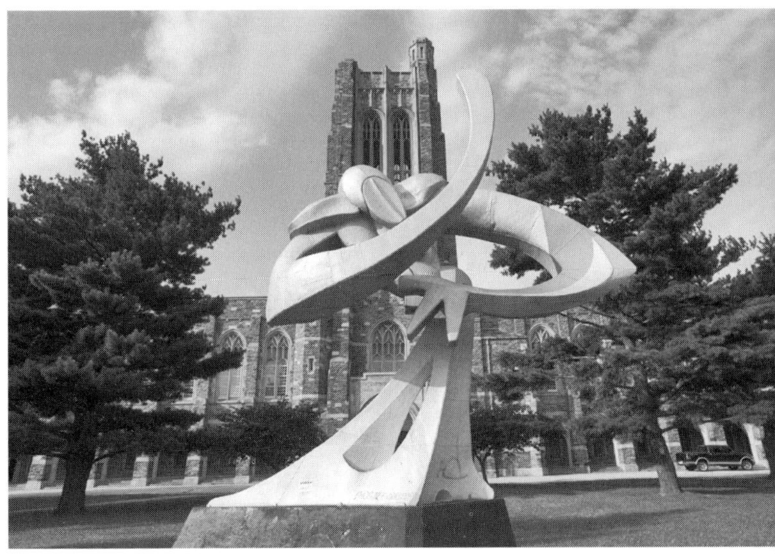

Baltimore City College High School is the third oldest high school in the country, established in 1839 as an all-male school. Originally located on the site now known as St. Paul Place, it moved into a new English Gothic Revival–style building on Howard Street, opposite Centre Street, in 1875. That building was replaced by one designed by Baldwin & Pennington in 1895. The 1895 building was the original site of the World War I Memorial relief by J. Maxwell Miller (K5).

In 1928 Baltimore City College High School moved to its current 38-acre campus and into a new Gothic stone castle. The school is often referred to as the "Castle on the Hill" or just "City"; it is also known as the "Home of the Knights." So in 1978, when the school underwent a major renovation, works of art were commissioned from thirteen artists. Ayokunle Odeleye was selected to create a large-scale, site-specific piece for the front campus. Since little was done to the exterior of the building during this renovation, Odeleye's sculpture was to be the visual symbol of the major changes that had taken place at the school.

With *The Guide*, Odeleye gave the students their knight. Although the piece is very abstracted and gestural, the large figure of a knight can be deciphered. On his oval head there appears to be a helmet, and armor appears to protect his shoulders, from which long arms extend endlessly as they wrap around the figure. The torso is pinched in at the waist, and legs are only suggested by two broad linear elements that sweep to the left. That this figure is a knight is evident when it is viewed from the back as well. Standing almost 20 feet high, the knight's silver silhouette perched on the hill in front of his castle can be seen from a great distance.

Odeleye is a full professor of art at Kennesaw State University, outside Atlanta, Georgia, where he has been on the faculty since 1989. He received his BFA and his MFA from Howard University in 1973 and 1975, respectively, and has been teaching ever since. He has completed many public art projects in cities across the country, including Richmond, Virginia; Savannah, Georgia; Wilmington, North Carolina; Pensacola, Florida; Dallas; Spring Valley, New York; and Atlanta. Among the several in Atlanta are pieces for the Olympic Stadium in 1995-96 and for the Hartsfield International Airport in 2002. *The Guide* was one of his earliest pieces.

K5

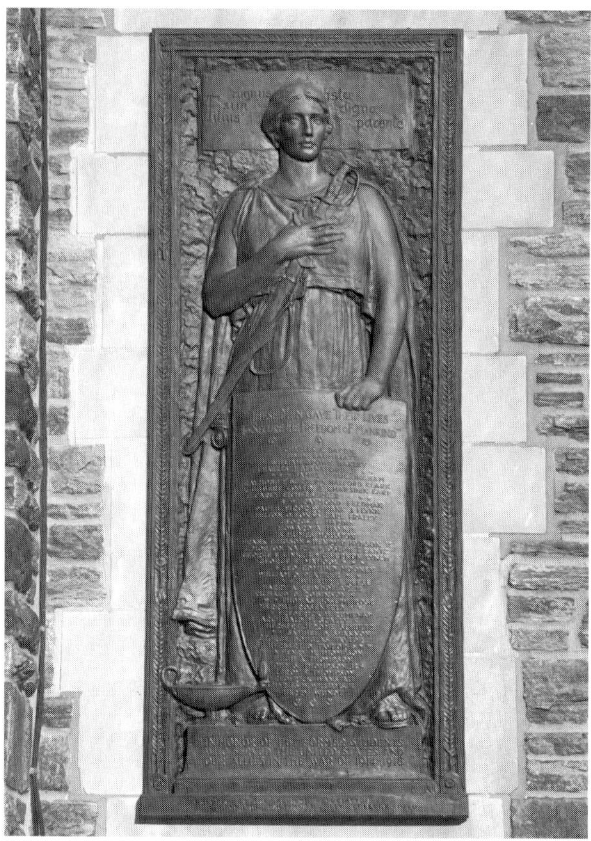

Against a background of oak leaves, the figure of Alma Mater stands behind a shield on which are inscribed the names of those graduates of City College who fought and died in World War I. The inscription across the top of the shield reads, "THESE MEN GAVE THEIR LIVES TO SECURE THE FREEDOM OF MANKIND." The relief also honors all those young men from City College who fought in the war, as the inscription on the base on which Alma Mater stands indicates: "IN HONOR OF 1167 FORMER STUDENTS WHO SERVED THE UNITED STATES AND OUR ALLIES IN THE WAR OF 1914–18."

The classical figure that Miller created to symbolize Alma Mater holds a sword and laurel in her right hand against her bosom. She quietly stares off into the distance. Her long gown, exposing her bare shoulders and arms, hangs to the ground, her sandaled feet just visible under the generous folds of drapery. The lamp symbolizing wisdom and teaching that usually accompanies images of Alma Mater is in the lower left corner of the relief.

Alma mater in Latin means "nourishing mother." It was taken from *alma mater studiorium,* meaning "nourishing mother of studies," which is the motto of the University of Bologna, one of the oldest universities in Europe. Miller's unusual choice of Alma Mater for this war memorial adds poignancy to the subject, a poignancy heightened by the figure's youthful beauty and mournful expression. Behind her head is an unrolled scroll with another Latin inscription, "DIGNUS ISTA SIM DIGNA FILUS PARENTE," "MAY I BE A SON WORTHY OF SUCH A MOTHER."

Originally placed on the facade of City College when the school was located on Howard Street, the relief was reinstalled on this new school building, just to the left of the main entrance, in 1928. Nearby are portraits of Riggin Buckler and George Corner Fenhagen, the two principal architects of the school. They were carved in stone and placed at each end of the archway over the main entrance to the school. Buckler is the one smoking a cigarette, and Fenhagen smokes a pipe.

K6

TITLE
Citisphere, 1979

LOCATION
Baltimore City College High School,
33rd Street and The Alameda

SCULPTOR
Robert G. Fergerson (b. 1949)

MEDIUM
Stainless steel

DONOR
Baltimore City Percent for Art program

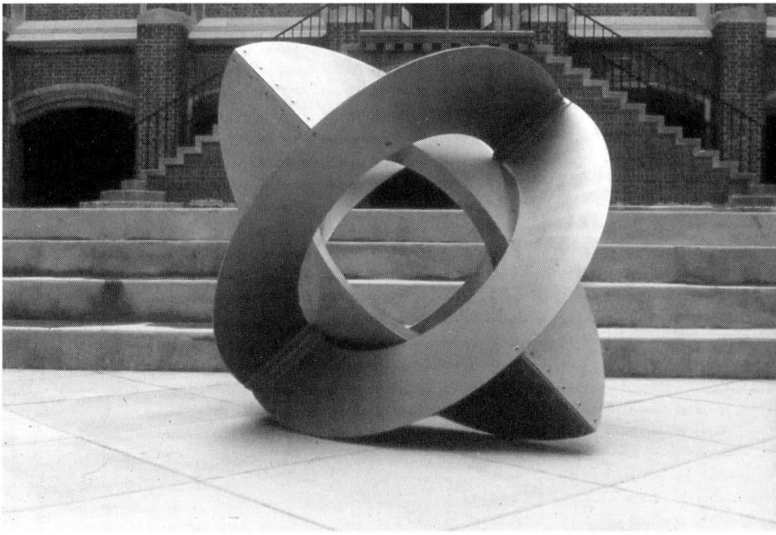

Citisphere has often been described as origami in steel. Robert Fergerson began with the idea of using repeated modular elements in shapes mirroring those of the Gothic windows on the school's facade. Four circles are formed by eight semicircular rings cut out of ½ inch stainless steel. Two circles intersect at right angles to each other. The other two circles are folded at a 60° angle and tucked inside the two intersecting circles. This arrangement creates a multifaceted spherical structure of curves and spaces measuring 8 feet in diameter; it sits directly on the plaza outside the school cafeteria. When the sun shines brightly onto the piece, an additional element of light and dark patterns appears, as half of the stainless steel rings strongly reflect the sunlight and the other rings are in shadow.

The choice of stainless steel as a medium resulted from directives from the architect, Leon Bridges: the piece had to be maintenance free and vandal proof; it could not be painted; and it could not be made of Cor-Ten steel, which would rust and stain the plaza. (No doubt Odeleye's choice of galvanized steel for *The Guide*, out in front of the school [K4], was determined by these same directives.) To fabricate the piece, Fergerson turned to Dixie Manufacturing. Following Fergerson's full-scale drawings—blueprints really—Dixie cut and bent the pieces. Fergerson did the final grinding, cleaning, and surface finishing and then assembled the piece on site.

Fergerson was born in Syracuse, New York, and earned a BFA from Syracuse University. After spending the year 1971–72 at St. Martin's School of Art in London, he attended the Rinehart School of Sculpture at the Maryland Institute College of Art, graduating in 1974. After graduation he accepted a job teaching three-dimensional art at the Maret School in Washington, D.C., where he still teaches today. His work has evolved over the years; today he is primarily involved in woodworking and the design and fabrication of furniture.

Note: This outdoor sculpture is sited on a terrace within the school for which there is limited access. When school is in session, the sculpture may be viewed between 10:00 a.m. and 5:00 p.m.; visitors must first check in at the school's main office. During the summer months, visitors are advised to call ahead to confirm the hours of operation.

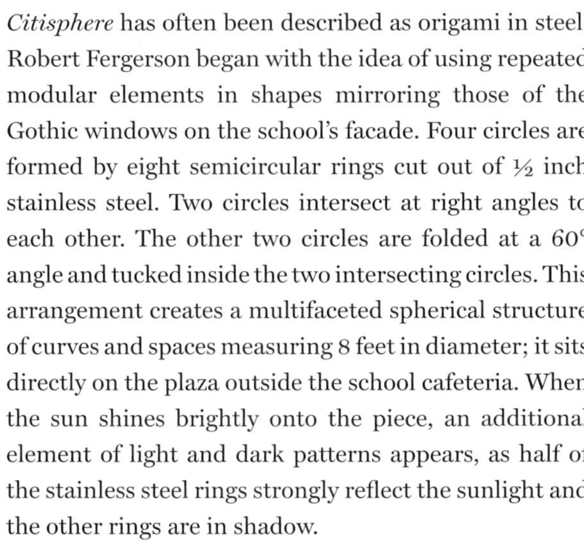

K7

TITLE
Inertia Study, 2002

LOCATION
Mergenthaler High School,
35th Street and Hillen Road

SCULPTOR
David Hess (b. 1964)

MEDIUM
Stainless steel

DONOR
Baltimore City Percent for Art program

When this high school opened in 1953 as a vocational and technical school, it was named for Ottmar Mergenthaler (1854–99), a German-born American inventor who arrived in Baltimore in 1872 and took a job in a machine shop. In 1886 he designed and built his first linotype machine. Regarded as the greatest advance in printing since the development of moveable type four hundred years earlier, Mergenthaler's machine allowed the two operations of setting and casting type in leaden lines to be performed simply by touching the keys of a board similar to the keyboard of a typewriter. The machine was first used by the *New York Tribune* in 1886. Prior to that time, no newspaper had been more than eight pages long. This linotype machine was in use until the 1970s, when phototypesetting and then computerized typesetting arrived. Today an operational linotype is on display in the print shop at the Baltimore Museum of Industry.

Mergenthaler contracted tuberculosis and died at the age of 44. One other building in Baltimore bears his name: Mergenthaler Hall, built in 1940–41 on the Homewood campus of Johns Hopkins University, paid for by a gift from his widow and son.

In 2002 a major renovation was completed at MERVO, as the Mergenthaler High School is most often called. This renovation was subject to the Percent for Art ordinance, and David Hess received a commission to create a work for the school. Hess' longstanding interest in discarded industrial machinery has lead him to incorporate these found objects into his art. Nowhere can that approach be better documented than in his 1997 piece for the Museum of Industry, *Working Point* (G15). Hess has been inspired in other ways by the industrial detritus of Baltimore, whose shapes and textures have also found their way into his art.

Inertia Study is composed of five stainless steel cylinders, each 10 feet in diameter and 4 feet wide with a 4-foot opening in the center. Their size and weight and the obvious precision with which they were made gives them an industrial quality. Where did they come from? Were they ever part of some larger industrial machinery that got refurbished for their introduction here? Their installation with what appears to be a certain randomness adds to their mystery.

Three of the huge cylinders stand on a wide ledge that cantilevers over the front entrance of the school.

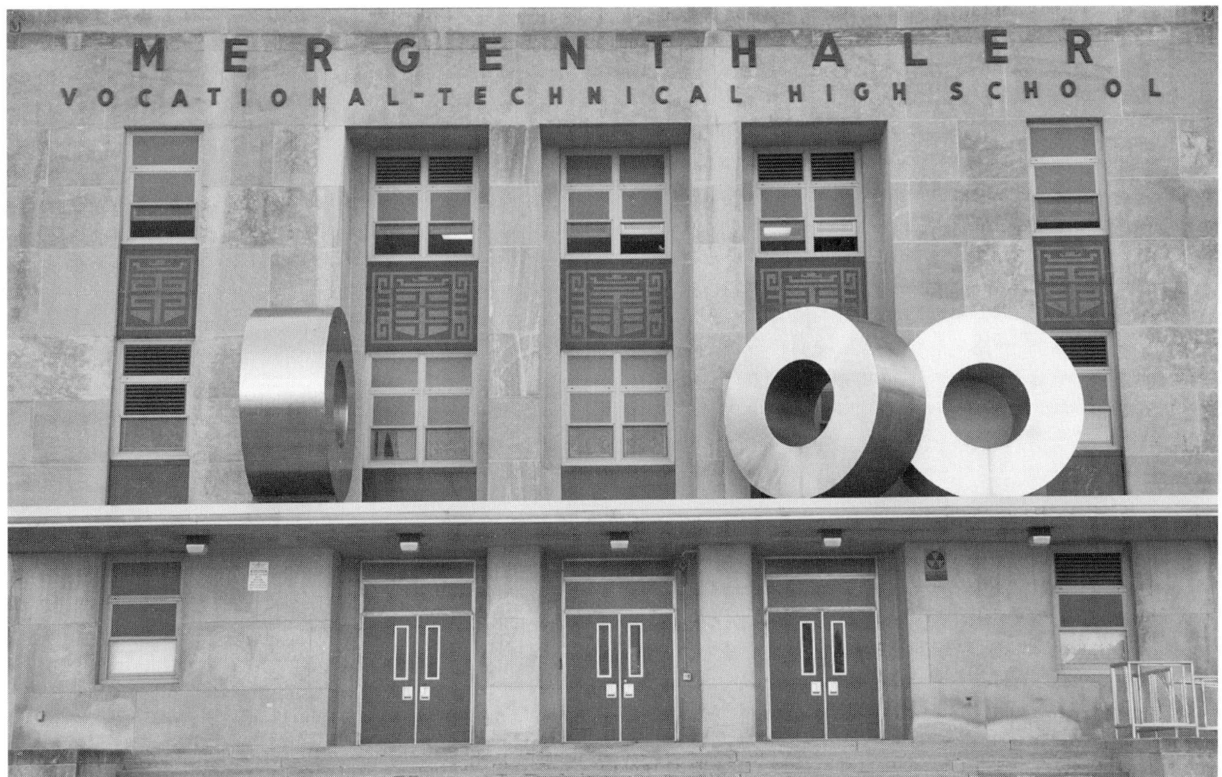

Two other cylinders appear to have rolled off that ledge, one coming to rest on the grass to the left side of the entrance and one out in front on the grass in the center of the school's entrance drive. Might the other three cylinders roll off too? How might that happen? Will the two cylinders be put back up on the ledge eventually? Hess has created an active, even precarious environment, but one that is humorous too. One clue from the title is that these pieces might stay where they are.

In addition to being playful and mysterious, Hess' piece is also rich in historical references to MERVO and to Baltimore. There are layers of meaning in the form itself, which could certainly remind Baltimoreans of the 4-foot-wide coils of rolled steel totaling 20,000 pounds that could be seen at Sparrows Point. The size and shape of these cylinders are also reminiscent of the huge reams of paper used at printing companies around town. And the five cylinders are perfect reminders of the donuts that were produced in the school's baking program long ago.

K8

TITLE
Frederick Douglass, 1956

LOCATION
Morgan State University, 1700 E. Cold Spring Lane

SCULPTOR
James E. Lewis (1923–2007)

MEDIUM
Bronze

DONOR
Maryland Educational Association

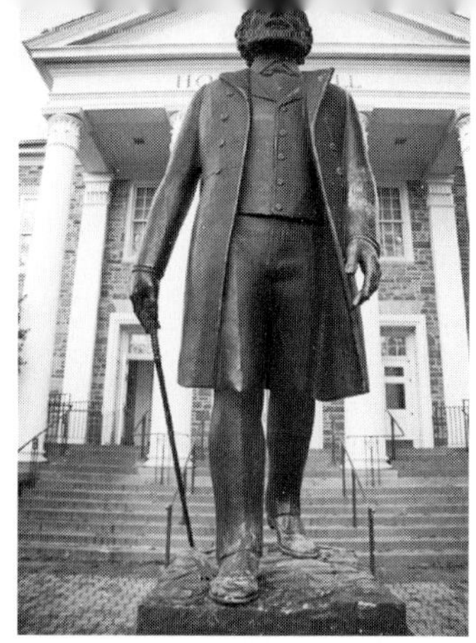

James E. Lewis was an associate professor and head of the art department at Morgan State University when he was commissioned to create a statue of Frederick Douglass, the man who began life as a slave on Maryland's Eastern Shore and died an author, orator, diplomat, and statesman.

Thirteen years before the statue was unveiled, the idea for it was presented to the Maryland Educational Association, then the state teachers' organization exclusively for Negroes. After the idea was approved, the association began raising money: pennies and dimes from students in the city's schools were supplemented by contributions from parent-teacher associations, service clubs, and other interested individuals. When $10,000 had been raised, Lewis was invited to present a maquette, on the basis of which he was awarded the commission.

Given Douglass' life story, it is fitting that the Maryland Educational Association commissioned this statue. In 1825, when Frederick Augustus Washington Bailey (only later Frederick Douglass) was 8 years old, he was sent to Baltimore from his Talbot County plantation to work for Hugh Auld, a relative of his master's. There, in the Auld household, Douglass learned to read and write. Mrs. Auld was so impressed with the young boy's obvious intelligence that she defied the law of the day and gave him reading lessons. Eventually Mr. Auld discovered the lessons and stopped them, but Douglass had had the world opened before him. Years later he managed to escape from the South and travel to New Bedford, Massachusetts, where he began working against slavery.

To prepare for this commission, Lewis traveled to the Douglass home in Anacostia, a neighborhood in southeastern Washington, D.C., where he studied life and death masks and photographs of the famed abolitionist and sat for hours reading his letters, all so that he could imbue the statue with Douglass' true spirit. Lewis wanted to capture the seriousness of purpose that characterized Douglass' life. After two years of work, Lewis depicted Douglass later in his life, standing straight and tall, reflecting on the successes of the abolitionist movement but aware of the remaining challenges facing black men and women everywhere. Douglass is presented here elegantly dressed, in a frock coat worn over a suit, his long hair and full beard neatly trimmed. He holds his head high, his brow furrowed with determination, his eyes firmly focused on the distance, as he strides forward, using the cane said to have been given to him by Abraham Lincoln, whom he advised on many occasions.

The statue stands in front of Holmes Hall, the university's most widely recognized architectural landmark. The inscription on the front of the granite base reads, "FREDERICK DOUGLASS / 1817–1895 / HUMANITARIAN / STATESMAN." A plaque mounted on the back of the base tells the early history of the statue: "ERECTED / BY THE / MARYLAND EDUCATIONAL / ASSOCIATION / THROUGH CONTRIBUTIONS OF / CHILDREN IN COLORED SCHOOLS / AND CITIZENS OF MARYLAND / IN THE YEAR 1956." A quote from Douglass follows: "I AM AN AMERICAN / AND AS AN AMERICAN / I SPEAK TO AMERICA."

K9

Untitled, 1985

LOCATION
Fire Station #43, 1100 Walters Avenue

SCULPTOR
George Greenamyer (b. 1939)

MEDIUM
Forged, fabricated painted steel

DONOR
Baltimore City Percent for Art program

For more than thirty years, George Greenamyer has been making site-specific sculptures for train stations, fire stations, airports, metro stations, parking facilities, zoos, and parks and for libraries, science buildings, and athletic centers at colleges and universities across the country, most often through Percent for Art programs like the one in Baltimore.

Like all of Greenamyer's sculptures, this untitled piece is constructed of mild steel that is machined, hot-forged and welded and then painted in high-gloss epoxy colors. In all his sculptures he pursues a direct narrative, telling a visual story in a very straightforward manner. Often the story relates to the history of the site or the region or to the work done by people at the site, as in this case. These stories are usually celebratory, told with whimsy and humor. Here the stage for firefighting is designed to make reference to the fire trucks of old, with large and small wheels connected and framed by a long horizontal bar that intersects with a vertical beam, all painted black. Fourteen diminutive firemen, all dressed alike in red hats and coats, blue pants, and high black boots, carry a long ladder across the horizontal bar toward the burning house that sits atop the beam. The firemen march in step, as if they were in a parade rather than rushing to a fire. And luckily the house seems completely resistant to the red flames pouring out of windows on each side.

Greenamyer was born in Cleveland, Ohio. He received his BFA from the Philadelphia College of Art (now the University of the Arts) and his MFA from the University of Kansas in Lawrence. Since 1968 he has taught at the Massachusetts College of Art and Design in Boston. Retired since 2005, he still teaches one welding class there.

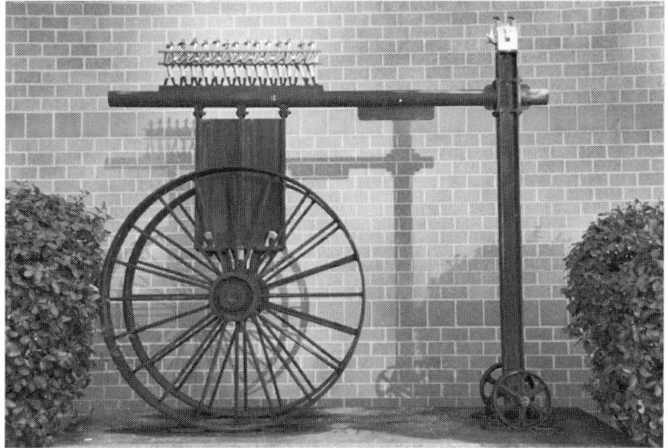

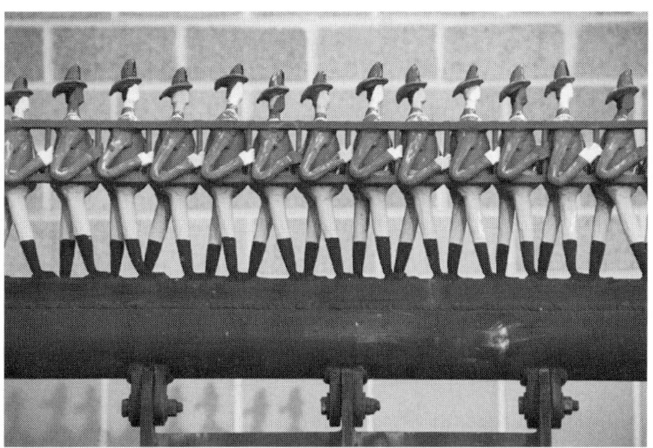

K10

TITLE

LUTHER MONUMENT, 1936

LOCATION

31st Street at Hillen Road

SCULPTOR

Hans Schuler (1874–1951)

MEDIUM

Bronze

DONOR

Arthur Wallenhorst

By 1936 there were other monuments in the United States dedicated to Martin Luther (1483–1546), the Christian theologian and Augustinian monk whose teachings inspired the Protestant Reformation, but they had all been cast from originals in Germany. This monument is thought to be the first "American" Luther.

Arthur Wallenhorst (1850–1933), a very successful Gay Street jeweler, watchmaker, and expert in gems and a familiar figure in the local German colony in Baltimore for years, left $50,000 in his will to commission a monument to Luther. Wallenhorst had had a deep respect for Luther throughout his life and had always dreamed of creating a monument to him.

In the first paragraph of his will, Wallenhorst named the trustees who were to oversee the creation of the monument. They chose the sculptor—Hans Schuler—and the Municipal Art Commission chose the site—just inside the Mount Royal entrance to Druid Hill Park. The monument was relocated to its present site overlooking Lake Montebello in 1959, a move necessitated by the development of the Jones Falls Expressway.

Hans Schuler said that after receiving this commission he studied contemporary portraits of Luther, particularly those by Lucas Cranach, who painted Luther from life, and read biographies written by Luther's contemporaries. Schuler was quoted as saying,

"I conceived of Luther coming as a herald and I have portrayed him as moving with a Bible in his hand." Luther had been the first person to translate and publish the Bible in the commonly spoken dialect of the German people, which Schuler no doubt had learned from biographies of Luther.

The 18-foot-high statue stands on a 12-foot-high granite base designed by William W. Emmart, the municipal architect. With right arm raised, the bronze figure of Luther dressed in his traditional full-length robe presents a dramatic silhouette against the sky. Gazing into the distance, Luther stands with his left foot forward, extended just over the edge of the base, suggesting forward movement.

The monument was unveiled on October 31, Reformation Day, so designated because on that day in 1517 Luther nailed to the church door at Wittenberg his Ninety-five Theses, accusing the Roman Catholic Church of heresy, an act considered by many to be the starting point of the great religious revolt of the sixteenth century. More than eight thousand people attended the ceremony. Three thousand children from Lutheran Sunday schools in Baltimore paraded from the Fifth Regiment Armory to the monument, led by the Police Band. One of the featured speakers was the German ambassador to the United States, Dr. Hans Luther, who was a descendant of Luther's and whose daughter was to unveil the statue. The ambassador's words on that late October day in 1936 are interesting: "May our Lutheran inheritance coming to us out of the depth of history prove to be a foundation of genuine mutual understanding between the great people of the United States and of Martin Luther's fatherland, and be a constructive force in the maintenance of peace throughout the world." Hitler, of course, had other ideas, and the ambassador was called home.

Wallenhorst's only stipulation concerning the monument was that it bear the inscription, "Given by a Baltimore Jeweler," which appears on the rear of the base. Appearing on the front of the base is the first line of Luther's *Hymn of Faith*, "A mighty fortress is our God." Luther's hymns sparked the development of congregational singing in Christianity.

K11

TITLE
Winged Youth, 1999

LOCATION
Montebello Elementary School, 2040 E. 32nd Street

SCULPTOR
Rodney Carroll (b. 1949)

MEDIA
Bronze, aluminum, and Cor-Ten steel

DONOR
Baltimore City Percent for Art program

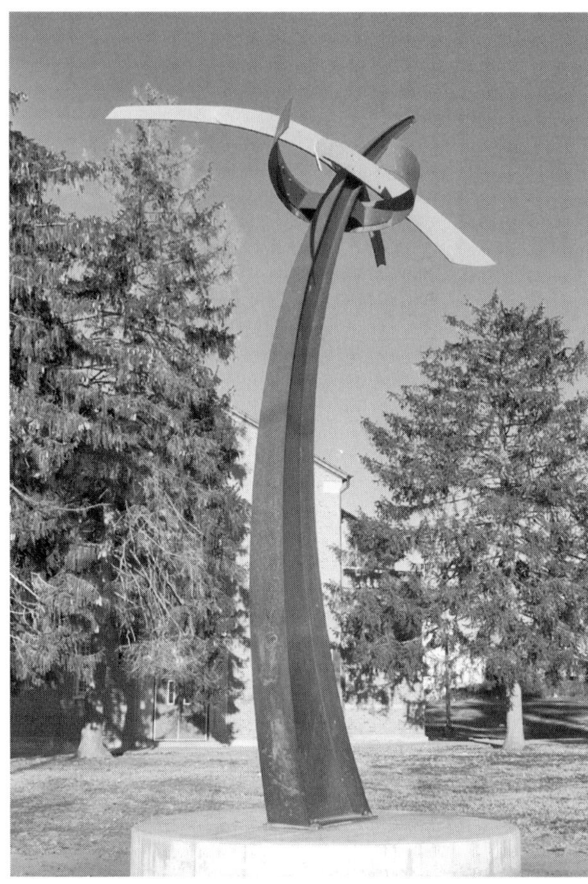

Rodney Carroll made three important decisions immediately upon receiving the commission to create a work of art for Montebello Elementary School, decisions that determined not just his choice of materials but the design itself.

Carroll decided, first, that the sculpture should not block the view of the beautiful classical arcade on the facade of the school building; second, that it should be in harmony with the three tall cedar trees that have stood for decades in front of the school; and third, that it should be for and about the students.

Carroll has always said that each element in his sculpture has a specific meaning and is related to every other element. Here Carroll designed a bold, sweeping arc extending 26 feet into the air that narrows as it bends to reach its terminus. This arc represents the youthful, energetic student, and the narrow design of the arc and its placement on the left side of the facade help avoid any disruption to the view of the arcade on the first floor of the building. Carroll's use of Cor-Ten for the arc was his way of acknowledging the cedar trees on the site and attempting to have the sculpture blend in with them. The two aluminum elements that span the Cor-Ten arc perpendicularly on either side represent the "wings" of the student, who will be inspired by all the experiences at school and soar to great heights as a result. The third element, made out of bronze, which curves around the main arc and supports the silver "wings," represents the spirit of the student.

Winged Youth was designed as a tribute to every young student at the school who searches for self-knowledge and is inspired to soar to greater heights than ever imagined.

K12

TITLE
Untitled, 1969

LOCATION
Lake Clifton Campus (formerly Lake Clifton High School), 2801 St. Lo Drive

SCULPTOR
Harry Bertoia (1915–1978)

MEDIUM
Bronze

DONOR
Baltimore City Percent for Art program

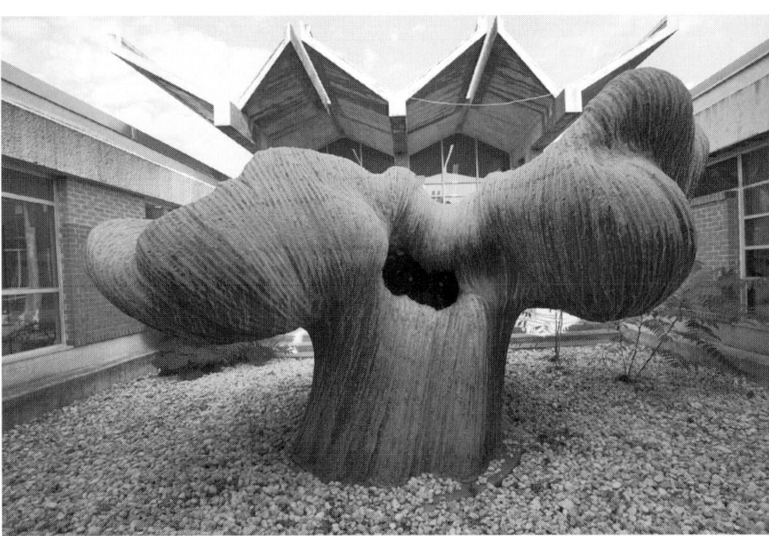

The first public art commission awarded to Harry Bertoia was for Eero Saarinen's General Motors Technical Center in Detroit in 1953, and his last public commission, for the Federal Reserve Bank in Richmond, Virginia, was completed in 1978. During his twenty-five year career in the field of public art, Bertoia became well known across the country for his monumental sculptures designed for plazas, ceilings, and walls for schools, colleges, and universities, for banks and other corporations, for museums, art centers, libraries, and parks. More than 160 sculptures can be attributed to him.

Bertoia's commission for the new Lake Clifton High School came at a time when he was interested in liberating sculpture from its base. This amorphous and dynamic bronze sculpture, which completely fills the school's central courtyard, sits on an almost unnoticeable base on the concrete floor. It appears as if one huge wave has just rolled into the space. Most of his sculptures are strong, organic shapes with textured surfaces. The idea of water pouring into this interior space may have come from the fact that the school was built directly on the bed of the former Lake Clifton, drained in 1964.

Bertoia always claimed that his sculpture evolved as the jewelry he was designing kept getting larger and larger. Besides jewelry, he also designed furniture, most notably the Diamond chair, known as the Bertoia chair, which he designed for Knoll Associates in 1952.

Born in Italy, Bertoia came to the United States when he was 15 years old. He studied at the Detroit Society of Arts and Crafts and then at the Cranbrook Academy of Art in Bloomfield, Michigan, where he established a metalworking department and taught from 1937 to 1943.

Note: This outdoor sculpture is sited in a courtyard within the school for which there is limited access. When school is in session, the sculpture may be viewed between 10:00 a.m. and 5:00 p.m.; visitors must first check in at the school's main office. During the summer months, visitors are advised to call ahead to confirm the hours of operation.

K13

TITLE
On the Trail, 1902

LOCATION
Clifton Park, Indian Drive

SCULPTOR
Edward Berge (1876–1924)

MEDIUM
Bronze

DONOR
Gift of the Peabody Institute William H. Rinehart Fund

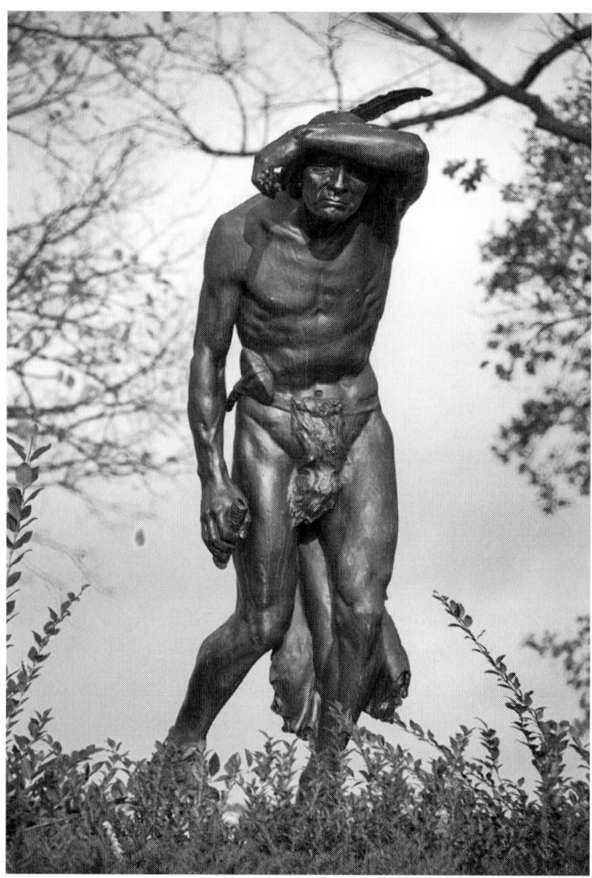

Clifton, the summer estate of Johns Hopkins, the founder of the university and hospital that today bear his name, was purchased by the city in 1895 and turned into a public park. *On the Trail* was the first piece of sculpture to be installed there, in 1916.

The trustees of the Rinehart Fund at the Peabody Institute gave this sculpture by Edward Berge to the city. Prior to the founding of the Rinehart School of Sculpture at the Maryland Institute in 1896, the money left by William Rinehart for the support of young men pursuing careers as sculptors was used to underwrite study abroad for young sculptors and to purchase sculpture from those artists when they returned to Baltimore—sculpture that would then be given to the city. This was such a gift.

Every detail of this larger than life-size Indian suggests that he has been hunting for a long time. Wearing only a breechcloth and ankle-high moccasins, the weary-looking Indian stands on a rough boulder looking out over the park grounds and beyond. With stooped shoulders and slightly bent knees, holding three arrows in his left hand, he shades his eyes with his left arm, which rests across his forehead. A stone ax is tucked into the strap that holds his breechcloth, and his bow, missing today, appeared to dangle slightly behind him from his right hand. He wears an empty arrow pouch on his back, suggesting that the end of the hunt is near. Berge's Indian represents a very careful study in anatomy. It was originally exhibited at the Louisiana Purchase Exposition in St. Louis in 1904.

Berge's son Henry was called on from time to time to repair this sculpture. In 1945 the younger Berge was asked to recast the bow and the three arrows, which had been broken when the statue was knocked off its base. Henry Berge commented at the time that he thought *On the Trail* was a good piece of sculpture but not one made for endurance in a public space.

K14

TITLE
Knowledge + Love = Brotherhood, 1993

LOCATION
Brehms Lane Elementary School, 3536 Brehms Lane

SCULPTOR
Lisa Kaslow (b. 1953)

MEDIUM
Painted steel

DONOR
Baltimore City Percent for Art program

To the right of the school entrance and balancing on top of a stack of three large and colorful books—one red, one orange, and one yellow—is a bright pink heart-shaped element. A bright blue circle sits right on top of the heart. Around this circle is a ring of colorful cutout figures—dancing, leaping, running, and all holding hands. Written on the base plate are the words "KNOWLEDGE + LOVE = BROTHERHOOD." These concepts are clearly represented in the compositional elements of the piece and are understood by the students.

Lisa Kaslow is a graduate of Yale College and the Rinehart School of Sculpture at the Maryland Institute College of Art. She has been working in the public arena for more than thirty years, making freestanding and relief sculpture for schools, colleges, and universities, for community centers and transit facilities and parks in Maryland, where she lived for many years, in New Jersey, where she lives now, and in many other states across the country. In nearby Beltsville, Maryland, seventeen larger than life-size sports figures made by her, in the collection of Balcor Property Management, are placed around the Ammendale Technology Park. She completed three other Percent for Art commissions for Baltimore City (N6, P6, and Q8).

For the lobby of this school, Kaslow was commissioned to create two ceramic-tile panels titled *In Our Universe*. Together they measure 54 inches high by 78 inches wide.

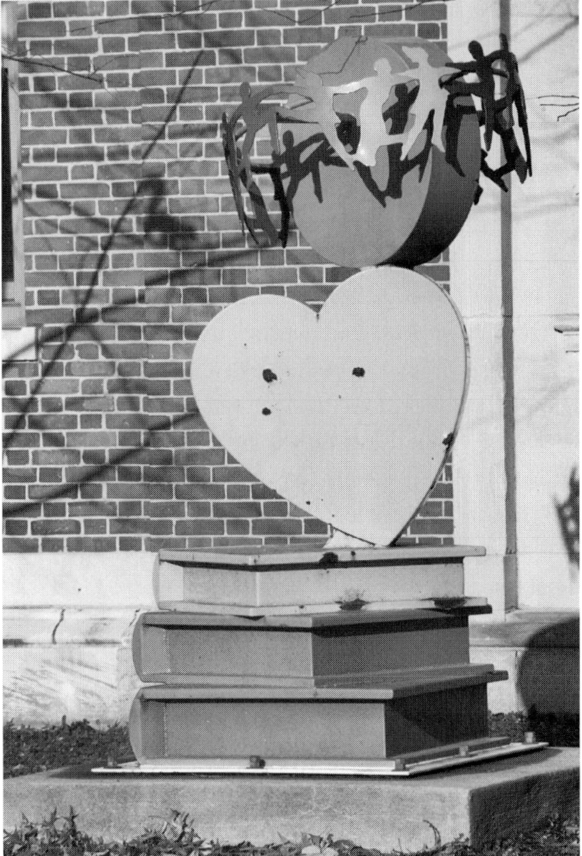

K15

TITLE
SERVICEMEN'S MEMORIAL, 1921

LOCATION
Herring Run Park, Belair Road and Shannon Drive

SCULPTOR
Edward Berge (1876–1924)

MEDIUM
Bronze

DONORS
The people of Belair Road and vicinity

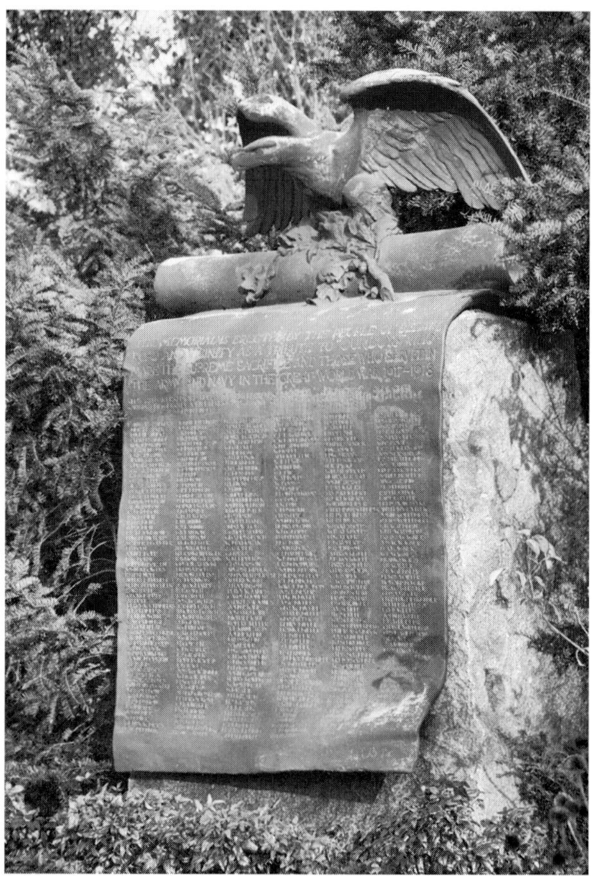

Edward Berge was asked to design a memorial with a field for many names, at a modest cost, and without using a tablet scheme. This modest monument of unusual plan was the result.

Berge sculpted an eagle perched atop an unfurled scroll that hangs down one side of a large granite boulder. The eagle's wings are completely outstretched, and in its claws it holds an oak branch of carefully detailed leaves and acorns. Inscribed on the scroll are the names of 358 young men from families who lived in the Belair Road area—from Kingsville to Erdman Avenue, from Harford Avenue to Old Philadelphia Road—who served in the U.S. Army, Navy, or Marine Corps. The names of those who died in service to their country are starred.

This monument has been relocated more than most in the city. Dedicated in 1921 at Glenmore Avenue and Belair Road, it was moved a few years later to Herring Run Park, near Parkside Drive. It was moved to its third and present site in 1933 and rededicated on July 4 that year.

K16

TITLE
Boanerges, 1978

LOCATION
Northeast Middle School, 5001 Moravia Road

SCULPTOR
Mary Ann Mears (b. 1946)

MEDIUM
Cor-Ten steel

DONOR
Baltimore City Percent for Art program

Mary Ann Mears was selected by the architect William McMillan to create a piece of sculpture for the new school he had designed. The original idea was to site a piece in front of the school, but after giving the project more thought and visiting the new building, Mears decided that she wanted to make a sculpture that students would see throughout the day, not just when they were arriving and leaving school. In other words, she chose to make a piece for the students, not for the neighborhood, a piece for the outside that could be experienced from the inside. She decided on the raised patio off the back of the building, which can be seen from the library, above it, and from the cafeteria, which opens just off of it.

Scale was another important factor. Mears wanted the piece to *feel* really big, not just *look* really big. By designing a piece that would more than fill this exterior space, which can be seen only in sections from both the first and second floors inside the school, she hoped to offer the students a close-up, personal experience with sculpture.

Out of Cor-Ten steel, Mears designed a sculpture in five sections, each three-sided closed form welded to the next. Three sections sweep across the patio, and two reach dramatically upward, one almost as high as the roof. The wedge-shaped curvilinear piece touches down in two places as it wraps around as a starched three-dimensional ribbon might.

Searching for a title for her sculpture, Mears decided on *Boanerges,* referring to any declamatory or vociferous orator or preacher. In the Bible, Jesus gave James and his brother John the title *Boanerges,* meaning "sons of thunder" and "speaking loudly." Mears liked the sound of the title and hoped that her sculpture would be seen not only as calligraphic but also as oratory.

Note: This outdoor sculpture is sited on a terrace within the school for which there is limited access. When school is in session, the sculpture may be viewed between 10:00 a.m. and 5:00 p.m.; visitors must first check in at the school's main office. During the summer months, visitors are advised to call ahead to confirm the hours of operation.

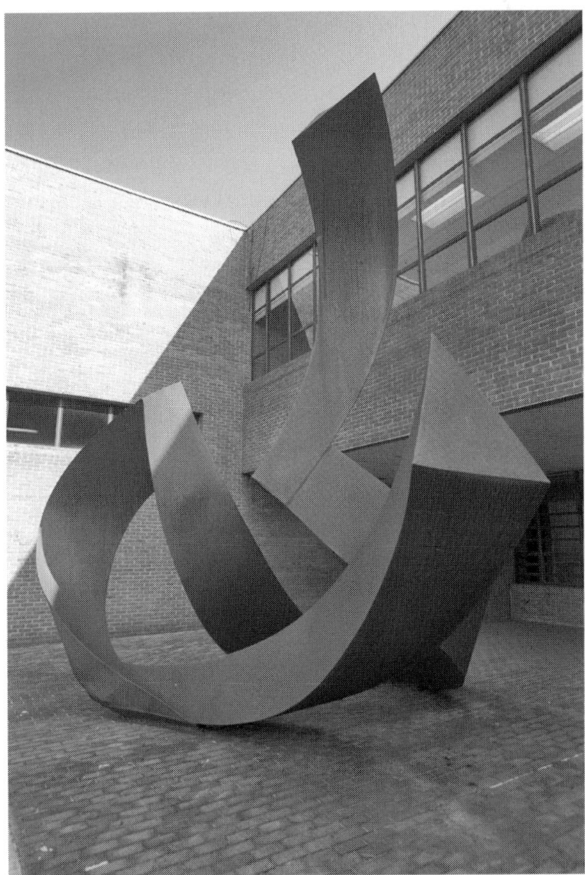

K17–K18

TITLES
Form in Space and *Winged Victory*, 1969

LOCATION
Woodholme Elementary School, 7300 Moyer Avenue

SCULPTOR
Harry Hilson

MEDIUM
Fiberglass resin and steel

DONOR
Baltimore City Percent for Art program

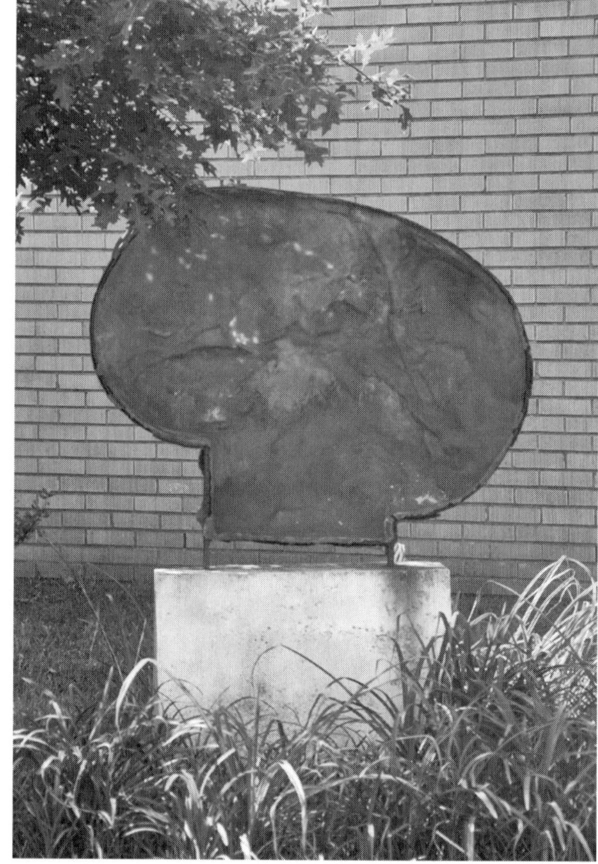

Sited in a courtyard enclosed by this one-story elementary school are two pieces of sculpture by Harry Hilson. Selected by the school's architect, J. Prentiss Browne, Hilson made three sculptures out of fiberglass resin that he molded into various sizes and shapes and colors and then mounted within steel frames.

Only two of the pieces remain. The larger of the two pieces is composed of four winglike elements set at right angles to one another. Each wing has a different surface texture, and the colors range from green to blue to rusty brown. When the piece is viewed with the sunlight behind it, the colors appear richer, and the "wings" become almost transparent. Mounted on a low circular base, the wings clearly look as if they could spin around in the wind.

The round, concave shape of the smaller piece has reminded students of a seashell. Rust in color, it exhibits the same quality of transparency in direct sunlight. The view into this textured, colorful piece when it is filled with light suggests deep space, a galaxy far away. The contrast between the way these sculptures appear when they are infused with sunlight and the way appear without the sun pouring through them is intriguing.

Note: These outdoor sculptures are sited in a courtyard within the school for which there is limited access. When school is in session, they may be viewed between 10:00 a.m. and 5:00 p.m.; visitors must first check in at the school's main office. During the summer months, visitors are advised to call ahead to confirm the hours of operation.

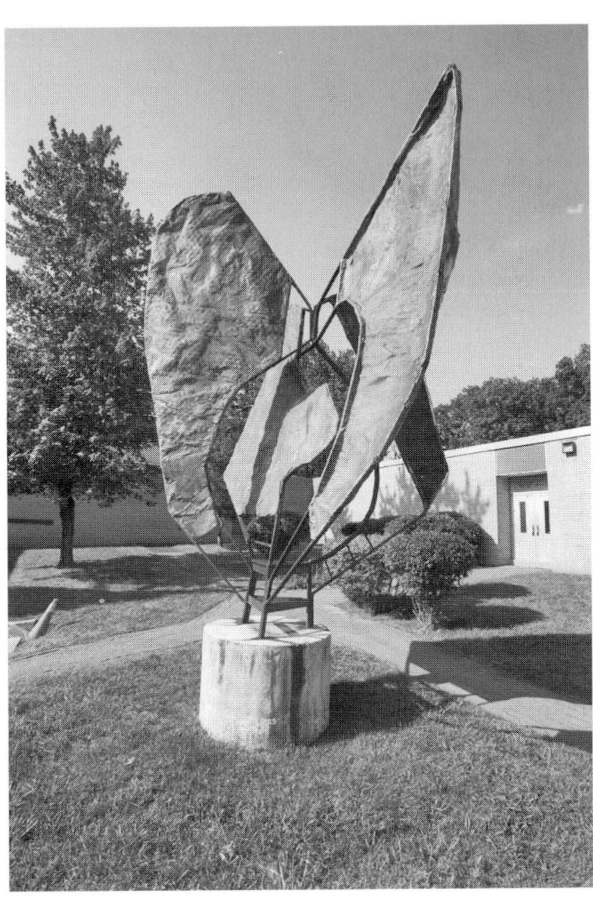

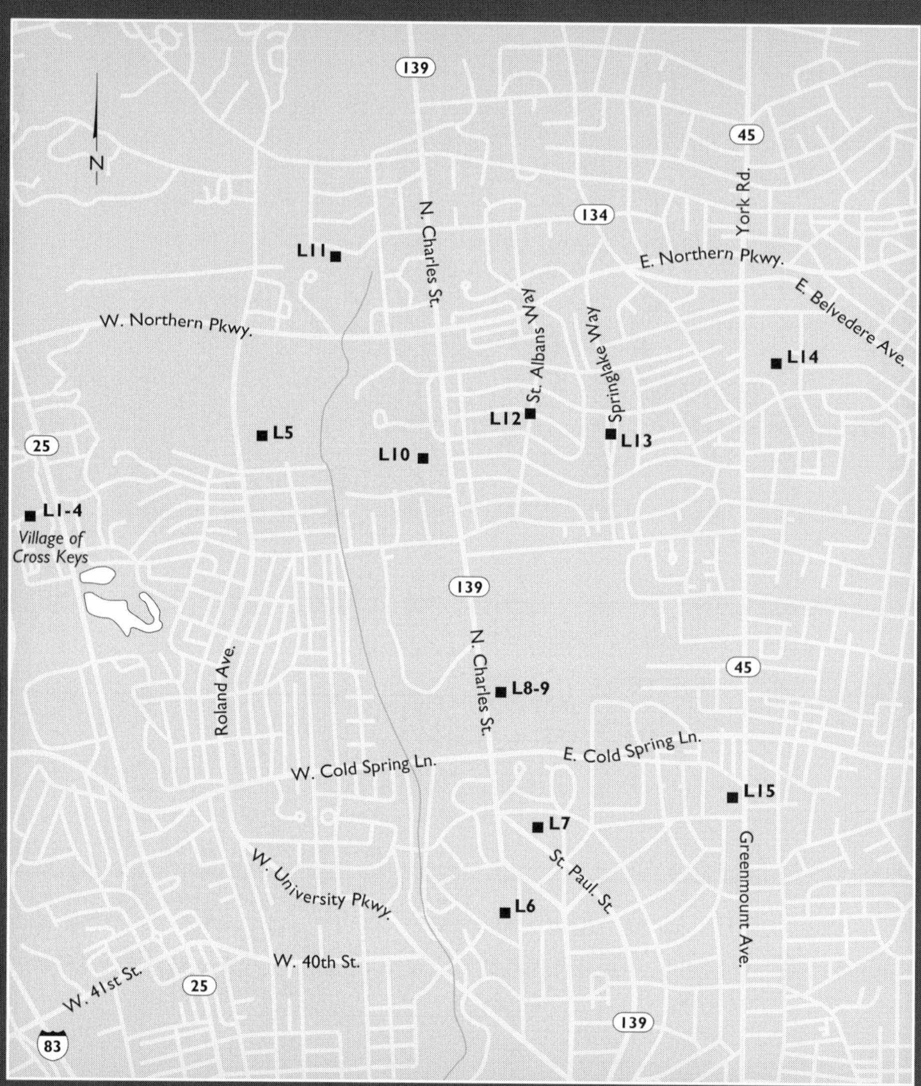

139
45
134
York Rd.
E. Northern Pkwy.
E. Belvedere Ave.
N
N. Charles St.
W. Northern Pkwy.
St. Albans Way
Springlake Way
L11
L14
25
L5
L12
L13
L10
L1-4
Village of
Cross Keys
139
Roland Ave.
N. Charles St.
45
L8-9
E. Cold Spring Ln.
W. Cold Spring Ln.
L15
L7
St. Paul St.
Greenmount Ave.
W. University Pkwy.
L6
W. 41st St.
W. 40th St.
25
83
139

NORTH BALTIMORE

Driving

L1

TITLE
No. 10, 1974

LOCATION
Village of Cross Keys, 5100 Falls Road

SCULPTOR
John Ferguson (b. 1939)

MEDIUM
Cor-Ten steel

DONOR
The Rouse Company

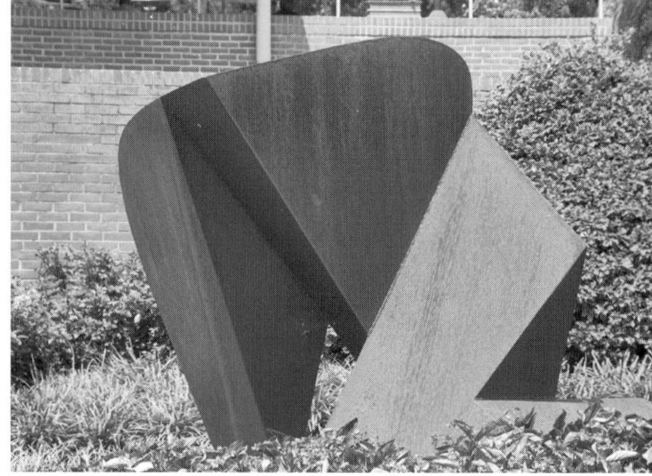

The Village of Cross Keys was an early experiment in community development by the Rouse Company, once one of the largest publicly held real estate development and management firms in the United States, whose founder was James W. Rouse. The Cross Keys development, on land purchased from the Baltimore Country Club west of Falls Road between Cold Spring Lane and Northern Parkway, was a planned-use development that included townhouses, apartments, and a shopping center.

The Rouse Company had a program called Art in the Marketplace, designed for purchasing or commissioning contemporary art for its developments. This piece by John Ferguson was purchased by the Rouse Company and placed in the interior courtyard of the centrally located commercial area. Some years later, it was moved to its present location across from the entrance gatehouse.

Made of Cor-Ten steel, this abstract piece rests directly on the ground. The piece is vertical, rising higher in the center. It is composed of three wedge-shaped sections that have been cut and welded together. Each section is composed of straight edges and curving ones, and the piece unfolds across the ground like a hand of cards.

John Ferguson received an MFA from the Rinehart School of Sculpture at the Maryland Institute College of Art in 1971. He has had many solo exhibitions at the Henri and Kornblatt galleries in Washington, D.C., and in 1990 he had a solo exhibition at the Phillips Collection. His work is in the collections of the Hirshhorn Museum in Washington and Goucher College in Baltimore. He received a Percent for Art commission in Baltimore at the Maree Garnett Farring Elementary School (R5) and has two pieces of sculpture sited on the lawns of private apartment complexes along Park Heights Avenue—*Veronica* at the Green Acres Apartments, in the 6700 block, and *Sidney* at the Park Place Apartments, in the 7200 block. The 2007–8 Baltimore Sculpture Project, sponsored by the Baltimore Office of Promotion and The Arts, included a sculpture by Ferguson that was temporarily sited on Pratt Street between Howard and Hanover streets. Ferguson currently teaches an introductory sculpture class at the Harford Community College.

L2

TITLE
On Point, 1976

LOCATION
Village of Cross Keys, 5100 Falls Road

SCULPTOR
John Ferguson (b. 1939)

MEDIUM
Cor-Ten steel

DONOR
The Rouse Company

On Point was the third piece of sculpture by John Ferguson that the Rouse Company purchased for the commercial center in the Village of Cross Keys. Using a similar approach to that used in all his other sculptures, Ferguson composed this abstract piece by welding together three elements, each having both straight and curved edges.

The piece extends upward and out, making a gentle reference to a dancer or a bird. As in most of his pieces, Ferguson used Cor-Ten steel. Originally and for years, its surface resembled that of *No. 10,* at the entrance to Cross Keys (L1). However, recently the piece was painted yellow.

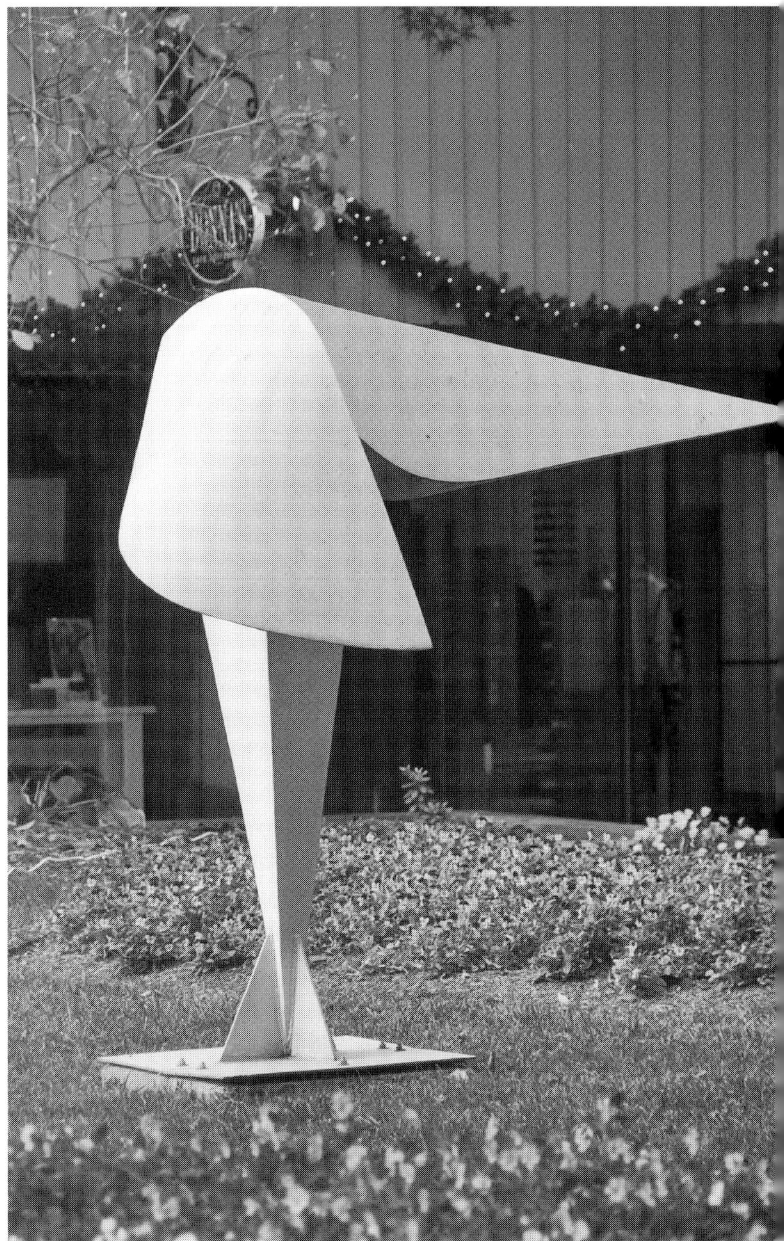

L3

TITLE
Implement XXV / River Arc, 1995

LOCATION
Village of Cross Keys, 5100 Falls Road

SCULPTOR
John Van Alstine (b. 1952)

MEDIA
Stone and bronze

DONOR
The Rouse Company

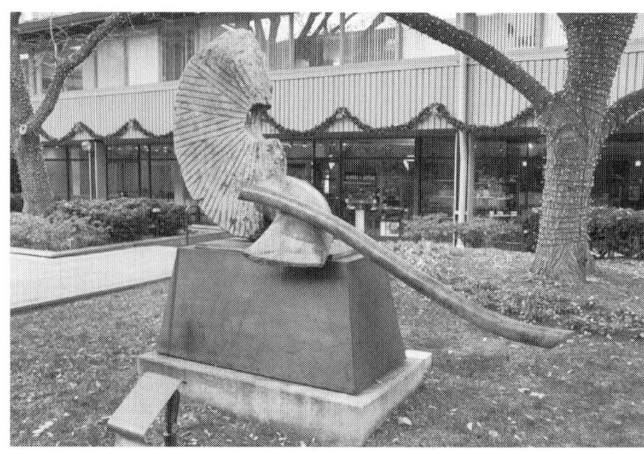

For John Van Alstine stone is everything. Van Alstine's early sculptures were composed only of stone, which he carved. Since 1975 his approach has been one of assemblage, in which he juxtaposes stone and steel, perfectly balanced. As his art continued to develop, he added found objects and bronze castings of stones and other found objects to his assemblages. Most of his work has been on a monumental scale, and most often rough cut stone—granite or slate or limestone—is visually connected to an arc or circle created out of metal—bronze, steel or iron, either forged or cast.

This sculpture by Van Alstine was purchased by the Rouse Company and installed in the courtyard of the commercial center in the Village of Cross Keys in 1997. It offers a slightly different experience from that of his monumental work. Here the scale is more intimate, and the stone is the arc, held in place by two beautifully patinated bronze arms, one very long and graceful, extending out into space. The stone, once used in a gristmill, had been dredged from the bottom of a river near Van Alstine's studio in Wells, New York. Van Alstine did nothing to the stone, so that it retains its natural weight and texture and thus its integrity. The radiating marks were cut into the stone long ago for grinding grain, and the opposite dark surface resulted from being buried in the river floor. The stone adds a hint of historicity to this contemporary piece, transporting the viewer back in time, if only for a moment. The bronze arms look as if they might have come from some antique farm implement, which also contributes to the sense of a distant time and place.

Implement XXV / River Arc was given in memory of James Rouse (1914–96), the founder of the Rouse Company, which developed Cross Keys. The company headquarters was located in Cross Keys for many years; it was where Rouse designed the new city of Columbia, Maryland, where he held meetings, and where he could always be found. Because he loved Cross Keys, it seemed a fitting place for a sculptural tribute to him. On a plaque placed in front of the sculpture is inscribed the following statement by President Bill Clinton: "Jim Rouse proved we could reclaim and recreate our urban frontiers. His life was defined by faith in the American spirit, and he showed us that we could build communities worthy of the character and optimism of our people."

Van Alstine received a BFA in sculpture, ceramics, and glass from Kent State University in 1974 and an MFA from Cornell University in 1976. His work has been exhibited in museums and galleries across the country. One of his earliest exhibitions was Directions '79, at the Hirshhorn Museum in Washington, D.C., and one of his most recent was Olympic Circles, at the C. Grimaldis Gallery in Baltimore in the summer of 2008. One of his first public art commissions was for Billings, Montana, and three of his most recent projects were for the Indianapolis Airport, the State University of Indiana in Terra Haute, and the 2008 Olympics in Beijing (*Rings of Unity—Circles of Inclusion*).

L4

TITLE
No. 9, 1968

LOCATION
Village of Cross Keys, 5100 Falls Road

SCULPTOR
John Ferguson (b. 1939)

MEDIUM
Painted steel

DONOR
The Rouse Company

For many years the Baltimore Museum of Art held an exhibition of works by regional artists called the Maryland Annual. In 1968 John Ferguson received the Rouse Company Purchase Prize for this red abstract sculpture, which was installed in the company's newly opened Village of Cross Keys, just outside the inn, at the western edge of the courtyard of the commercial area. Two other sculptures by Ferguson were purchased for Cross Keys in 1974 and 1976 (L1 and L2).

Three discrete elements make up this piece. Ferguson believed that using three elements together allowed him to achieve a certain balance in his sculpture. And in all his sculpture, he enjoyed welding straight and curvilinear surfaces together to create each element.

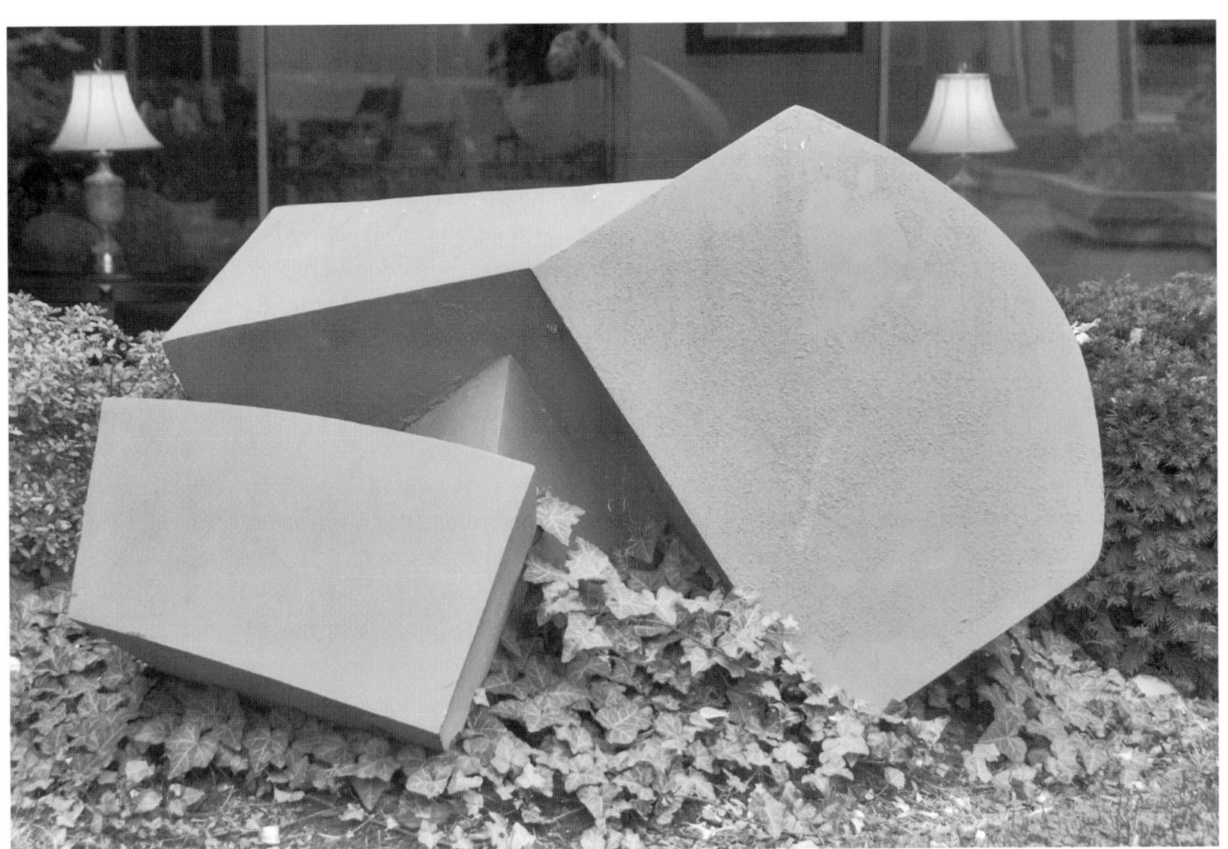

L5

TITLE
Fish Fence, 1997–2003

LOCATION
Roland Park Elementary and Middle School,
5207 Roland Avenue

SCULPTOR
Greg Moring (b. 1949)

MEDIUM
Painted steel

DONOR
Roland Park Elementary and Middle School
Parent-Teacher Association

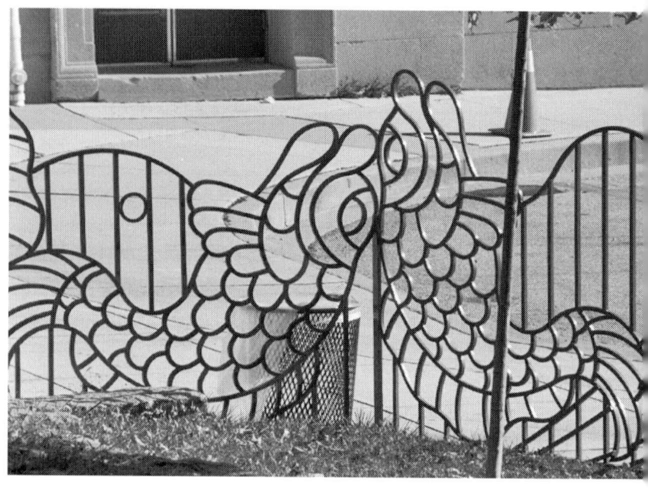

Since "image is everything," in the mid-1990s the parents of students at this public school set about improving the appearance of the school grounds along Roland Avenue. In this huge undertaking they were enormously successful.

A committee of the school's parent-teacher association (PTA) was set up to determine and implement a range of improvements to the front of the school campus. They began by designing a garden for the northern edge of the school property and made a list of plants that would be needed. Soon these plants had been donated. To control the erosion across much of the school property, the grounds committee decided to terrace it, gathering old cobblestones not being used by the city to support the terraces. And then, with a grant from the Neighborhood Improvement Program and through fund-raising projects such as the school's May Mart, the PTA raised enough money to commission a sculptor to create a fence for the grounds—not a solid, unfriendly fence but an open structure to outline the entrances and animate the pathways.

Three artists were asked for proposals and Greg Moring was chosen to continue working with the school administrators and parents. In addition to the design selected—with fish, waves, and bubbles—he offered a design with leaves and flowers and one using the letters of the alphabet.

The project was carried out in phases. The first phase was to construct the gate and fence for the garden. The second phase was to fabricate and install the linear expanse of the fence along Roland Avenue. During a third phase, the fence along the walks up to the front door of the school was completed and installed. The last section of the fence to be installed extended from the parking lot to the front door; this was the most playful section, with fish tumbling down the stairs on top of one another. Each phase required more fund raising, and the entire project took eight years. Moring took a faculty position at Youngstown State University not long after the project got under way but after it had been completely designed. Chris Gavin, a fellow sculptor, fabricated much of the fence following Moring's designs.

The design follows function but manages to be inventive as well as playful. Fish appear at the ends of each linear expanse of fence and as the featured element of each gate. Most often the tails of the fish are pointed up into the air, but for the double gate leading from the parking lot the two fish face each other with their heads held high. Bubbles and waves fill the spaces between the fish. The trim on the school building now matches the blue-green color of the fence. The garden and the fence together have contributed to an enduring impression of success and well-being at this school and have become a landmark for the neighborhood.

L6

TITLE
Pegasus, 2008

LOCATION
Calvert School, 105 Tuscany Road

SCULPTOR
William F. Duffy (b. 1953)

MEDIUM
Bronze

DONORS
The family, friends, and classmates of Molly Harris and the Marion I. & Henry J. Knott Foundation

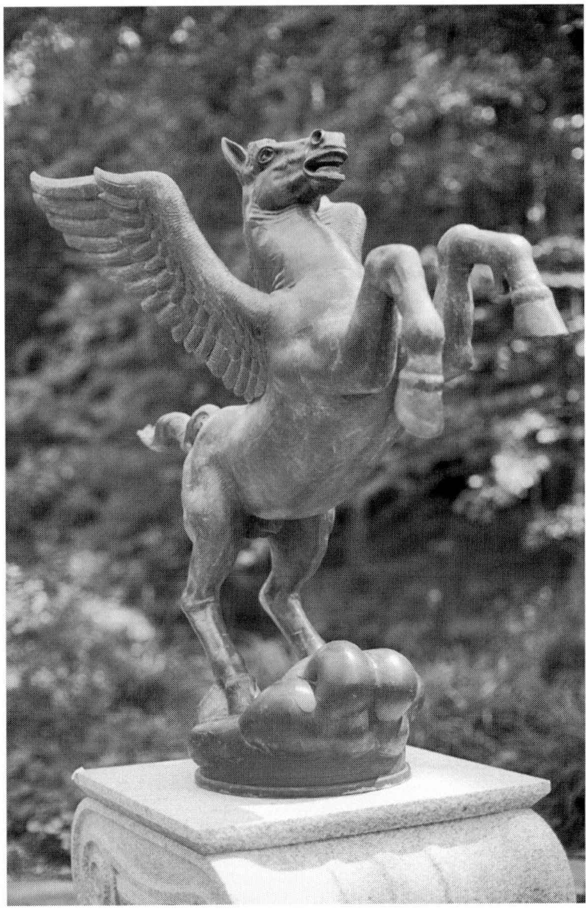

Down the hill behind Frank J. Carey Hall, along a stream that meanders through the campus, is a garden filled with herbaceous perennials and ornamental grasses designed by Wolfgang Oehme, a principal at the Washington, D.C., firm of Oemhe, van Sweden. At the center of this beautiful garden is a bronze statue of the winged horse Pegasus rising on his hind legs as if flying through the clouds toward the heavens, where, according to the Greek myth, he became a constellation. Pegasus was the son of Poseidon and Medusa, from whose head he sprang. (See O3 for more details.)

Edward and Laura Harris commissioned this garden with its statue of Pegasus in memory of their daughter Molly, a student at Calvert in the 8th age class who died very suddenly and unexpectedly in the spring of 2007. The Harrises visited William Duffy's studio to discuss the possibility of his creating a statue in remembrance of their daughter, and they saw his small model for Pegasus. Since Molly loved both Greek mythology, which is taught at Calvert in the 8th age class, and horses, Pegasus seemed an appropriate subject for a statue for the campus. Duffy has depicted Pegasus in flight, with a suggestion of clouds around his back feet. With his large wings raised skyward, his tail elevated and extending outward, his nostrils flared, and his mouth open, Pegasus appears as a muscular and energetic horse in flight.

Initially Duffy wanted Pegasus to sit directly on the slate pavers laid on the ground in the garden, but eventually he decided that the sculpture should be elevated, but not too high above the young members of the student body. The idea of using a truncated Ionic column for the base fit his parameters. An adjunct professor of 3-D computer modeling in the art department at Towson University, he used the computer-aided design (CAD) system he teaches to design the base. He then used the CAD-CAM (computer-aided manufacturing) software to direct a CNC (computer numerical control) milling machine to cut the granite.

Duffy received his BFA, with a concentration in figurative sculpture and drawing, from the School of the Museum of Fine Arts in Boston in 1975 and his MFA from the University of Maryland–College Park in 1983. In 1980 he earned a technical diploma from the Johnson Atelier Technical Institute of Sculpture in Princeton, New Jersey. Born in Cambridge, Massachusetts, he has lived in Baltimore since completing his graduate degree at Maryland. Duffy has continued working in the public arena, creating sculpture for Gaithersburg and Rockville, Maryland; for Columbus and Youngstown, Ohio; and for Harrisburg and Philadelphia, Pennsylvania. His most recent Percent for Art piece in Baltimore was made for Ashburton Elementary School in 1999 (N7). Another of Duffy's pieces, *Synergy,* can be seen in the lobby of the Benton Municipal Building, on East Fayette Street. Duffy most often works in bronze, creating intricately designed figural groups as likely as not for the centerpiece of a fountain.

Note: Visitors to the campus of this private school are asked to check in with the receptionist in the Lower School building, at the Tuscany Road address. You will be directed to the path that leads directly to the Mary W. "Molly" Harris '13 Memorial Garden.

L7

TITLE
Simon Bolivar, 1948

LOCATION
Bedford Square, St. Paul and N. Charles streets

SCULPTOR
Felix G. W. de Welden (1907–2003)

MEDIUM
Bronze

DONOR
Government of Venezuela

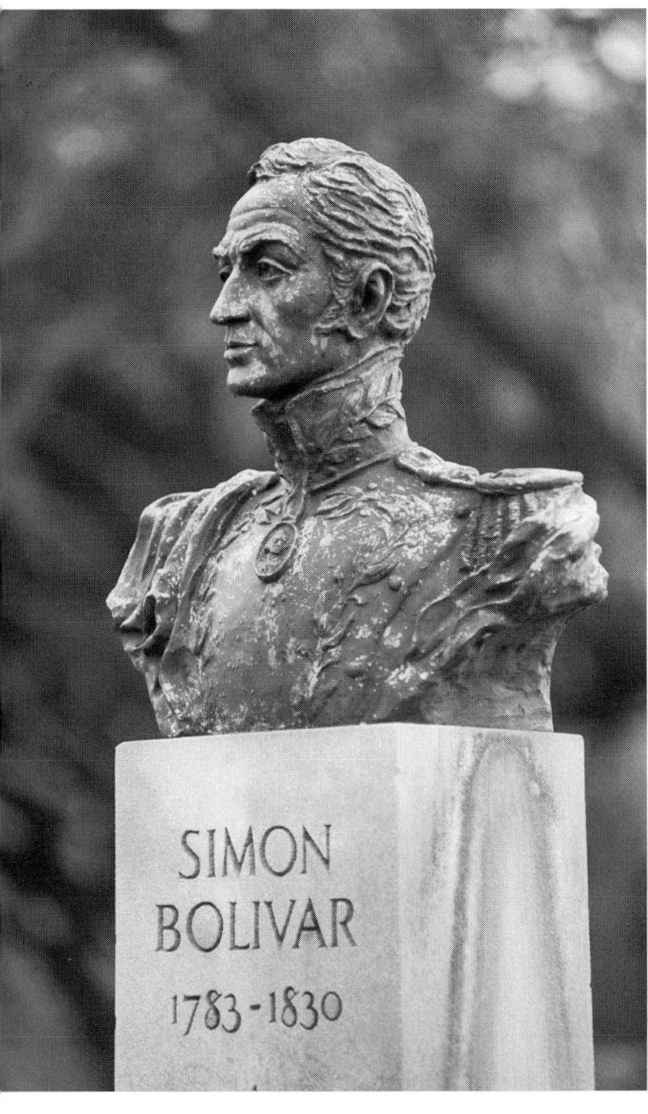

Felix G. W. de Welden, the sculptor of the famous Iwo Jima Memorial, in which five Marines are depicted raising the American flag on top of Iwo Jima's Mt. Suribachi, the first Japanese territory captured in World War II, created more than twelve hundred public memorials, many of which were small portrait busts of important men, like this one of Simon Bolivar.

The original of this portrait of Bolivar was cast in 1948. Today eight casts of this bust exist. Three were gifts to the cities of New Orleans, Bolivar, Missouri, and Bolivar, West Virginia. In 1960, when this gift was arranged for Baltimore, four busts remained and the Venezuelan ambassador was looking for appropriate places to erect them. The sculptures were being given to American cities as a means of generating better understanding between the countries as well as better economic relations and trade. Since Bolivar is known as the George Washington of South America and is held in as high esteem in Latin America as Washington is in the United States, he was the perfect subject of a state gift of sculpture to cities in the United States.

De Welden's portrait bust of Bolivar is a very traditional one, depicting the head, shoulders, and chest. Bolivar is presented frontally, with very handsome features, and dressed in a uniform. A high collar is beautifully decorated with branches of leaves and berries, the same decoration that can be seen on his chest. Around his neck is a chain holding a medallion with a portrait of George Washington, with whom he had a personal friendship. On the base, below his name and life span, is a bronze medallion showing the country of Venezuela and bearing the following inscription:

19 DE AVRIL DE 1610   20 DE FEBRERODE 1869

INDEPENDENCIA   FEDERACION

REPUBLICA DE VENEZUELA

Simon Bolivar (1783–1830) was born in Caracas, Venezuela, the son of a wealthy Spanish nobleman who owned large tracts of land and many slaves. After his widowed mother died, the 15-year-old Bolivar was sent to Spain to complete his education. At age 19 he married a woman of Spanish nobility and returned to Venezuela. A year later, she died, and Bolivar, brokenhearted, returned to Europe, traveling extensively in Italy and France. In 1805 in the city of Rome, Bolivar decided to devote the rest of his life to freeing Venezuela. He returned to Caracas in 1806 and soon thereafter became the leader of the movement for independence from Spain, which was spreading across Latin America. He was instrumental in winning independence for Bolivia, Columbia, Ecuador, Peru, and Venezuela, as inscribed on the front of the limestone base. The hero of more than two hundred bloody battles, Bolivar's most notable achievement was to lead a tattered and ill-equipped army across the high Andes. He defeated the Spanish forces and was received in Bogota as the Liberator of Nueva Granada (now Ecuador). He died at age 47, in poverty. Today his body is enshrined in the national pantheon in Caracas.

De Weldon was born in Vienna, Austria. He was educated at the University of Vienna's Academy of Creative Arts and Sciences and School of Architecture, from which he received his MA, MS, and PhD, all by the age of 22. He left Vienna and lived in London from 1933 to 1937, then immigrated to the United States in 1938, becoming a citizen in 1945. Among his public memorials, thirty are in and around Washington, D.C. The Iwo Jima Memorial, his interpretation of the Pulitzer Prize–winning photograph taken by Joe Rosenthal on February 23, 1945, has become a national memorial to Marine Corps heroes of all wars. De Weldon completed several equestrian monuments, including one of Simon Bolivar that was dedicated in Washington, D.C., in 1959.

This portrait bust was dedicated in Baltimore in 1960. It was April 19, Independence Day in Venezuela. The site, which seems to have been chosen based on availability, was decided on after successful negotiations between the Department of Recreation and Parks and the Guilford Neighborhood Association.

L8–L9

TITLES
Athena Parthenos, 1902 copy of 438 BC original,
and *Apollo Belvedere,* 1902 copy of 320 BC original

LOCATION
Evergreen Museum and Library,
4500 N. Charles Street

SCULPTORS
Unknown, after Leochares and Phidias, respectively

MEDIUM
Bronze

DONOR
City of Baltimore, Department of Recreation
and Parks

These two early twentieth-century copies of statues
from classical antiquity that are known to us today only
from Roman copies are sited in the back gardens of the
Evergreen Museum and Library. This estate belonged
to T. Harrison Garrett and then to his son, John Work
Garrett. Johns Work Garrett left the property to the
Johns Hopkins University in 1942, with life tenancy for
his wife, Alice Warder Garrett. Mrs. Garrett established
a foundation to care for her collections and to help
ensure that her husband's wishes be honored. In 1990
the house was opened as a museum and library, and it
has been administrated jointly by the university and the
foundation ever since.

The early provenance of these statues is not known,
but their appearance in Baltimore was as part of the collection of the Thomas Winans family. Winans became
famous and wealthy for building the first railroads in
Russia. He and his family after him purchased examples of classical sculpture in their travels across Europe
for their in-town estate, Alexandroffsky. The sculptures
were eventually moved to the Winanses' summer estate,
Crimea, in 1925, and after the Crimea property was sold
to the city in 1948, several of the sculptures were given
to the Baltimore Museum of Art, the Baltimore Zoo,
and Evergreen. (For more biographical information on
Thomas Winans and a more detailed discussion of the
provenance of these artworks, see J4–J5.)

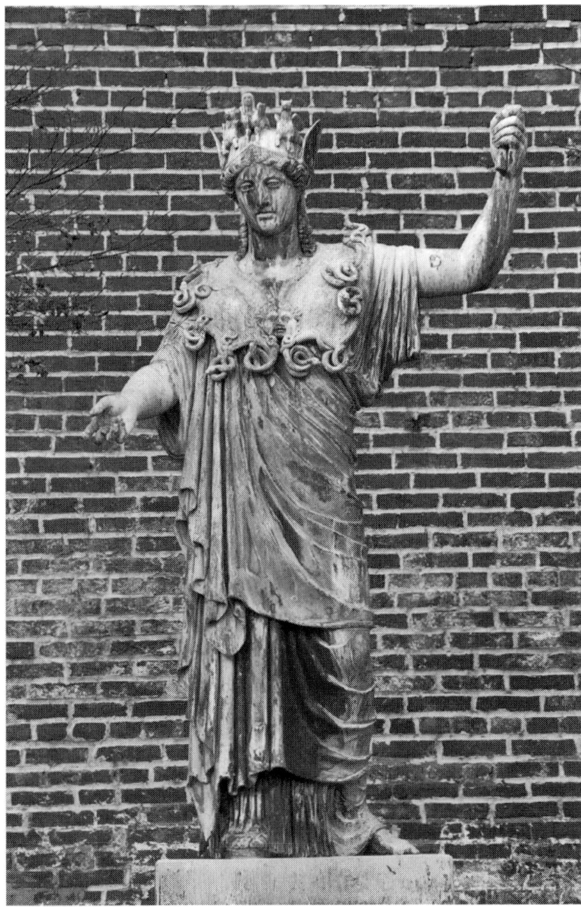

Athena is one of the twelve gods of Olympus. The
goddess of wisdom, she is always dressed as a warrior,
carrying a spear (which is missing here) and wearing
a helmet, shield (also missing), and breastplate. This
sculpture, like the one of Apollo, is a copy of a masterpiece of classical antiquity known today only through
Roman and Hellenistic copies of the sculptor Phidias'
fifth-century original, made for the Parthenon. Phidias'
Athena, completed in 438 BC, stood erect, wearing a
tunic, a shield, and a helmet, holding a Nike (a goddess of victory) in her extended right hand and a spear
in her left. Except for the missing Nike and spear, this
describes the Evergreen statue exactly, including the
extended arm with upturned hand, which would have
held the figure of Nike. The breastplate has a border of
snakes, and a head is imprinted in the center. Athena's
helmet, with figures of a sphinx and two winged horses

on the top, has long been her symbol. Her sandals are just visible below her tunic. If the shield that was beside her in Phidias' original were present here, it would have the head of Medusa on it, for Athena helped Perseus kill Medusa, and he presented her with the Gorgon's head.

This bronze statue of Apollo, the Greek god of the sun and of music and poetry, is a copy of a much-celebrated marble statue that was discovered in 1489 near Rome. That marble statue is itself a copy of a masterpiece of Greek art made about 320 BC by the Greek sculptor Leochares, who was employed by Alexander the Great. The marble copy came into the possession of Giuliano Della Rovere, who, when he became Pope Julius II in 1503, transferred the statue to the Vatican, to the small sculpture court, the Cortile del Belvedere, from which it derives its name. Today that famous marble copy, known as the *Apollo Belvedere,* is housed in the Museo Pio-Clementine. Contemporary engravings by Marcantonio Raimondi of the newly discovered statue of Apollo helped spread awareness of it and fueled the Renaissance passions for classical antiquity and mythology. Soon copies were in great demand.

Apollo is shown having just killed the serpent Python, who was terrorizing the Delphi coast. The arrow has just left his bow, which is missing here, but a fragment can be seen in his left hand. The pose of Apollo's nude body was much admired in the Renaissance. The drapery, clasped at his right shoulder, hangs down behind him and wraps over his left forearm. Besides the drapery, he wears only beautifully detailed open-toed sandals, the straps of which wrap around his feet to above his ankles, and his quiver, whose strap diagonally crosses his chest from his right shoulder to under his left arm. His head band, drawn through his very curly hair, denotes him as a god.

On the base of each sculpture can be seen the founder's mark, indicating that both were cast in 1902 by Sabatino de Angelis & Fils, a foundry that had been operating in Naples since 1840.

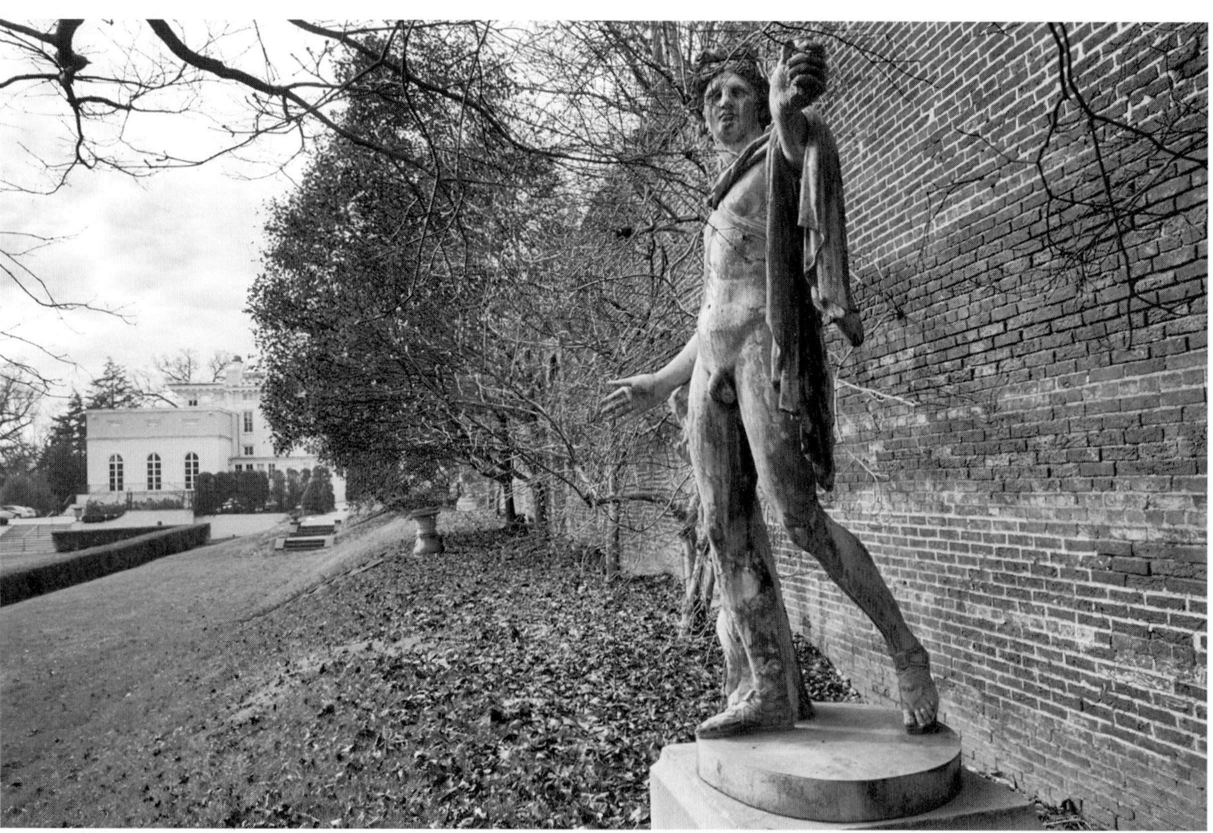

L10

TITLE
Friends, 1999

LOCATION
Friends School of Baltimore, 5114 N. Charles Street

SCULPTOR
Bart Walter (b. 1958)

MEDIUM
Bronze

DONOR
Friends School of Baltimore

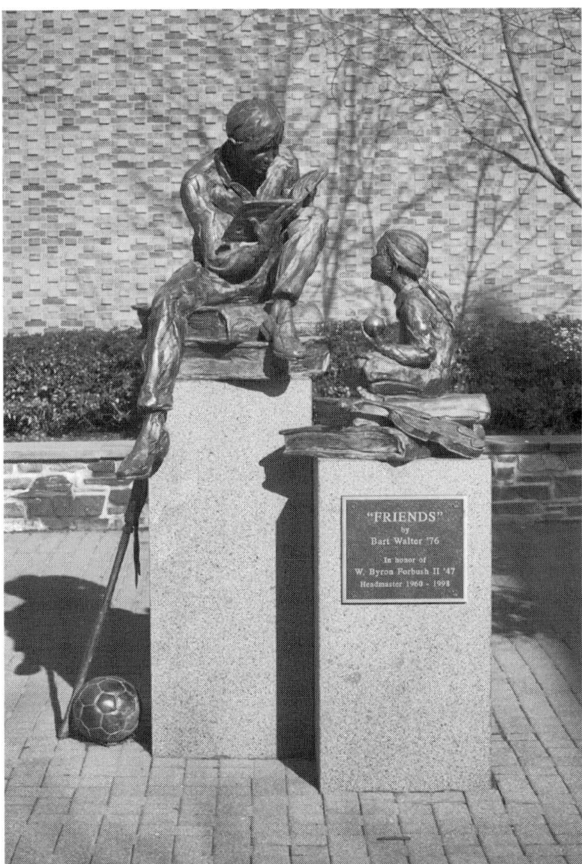

Located in the quad between the high-school auditorium and the math and science building is a sculpture commissioned by the school to honor its recently retired headmaster, W. Bryon Forbush, who led the Quaker school for almost forty years. Bart Walter, a 1976 alumnus of the school, was selected to create a work of art capturing the student experience at the school during Forbush's tenure in some iconic way.

Friends School of Baltimore was founded in 1784 on the Quaker ideals of truth, equality, simplicity, community and peaceful resolution of conflict and is the oldest school, public or private, in Baltimore. The school offers a pre-K through twelfth-grade coeducational college-preparatory program with a commitment to educating the whole person, morally, intellectually, and physically. Regular meeting for worship offers students a way to practice the values that permeate every aspect of a Quaker school life: simplicity, reflection, meditative concern, and hope.

In this sculpture, Walter has tried to capture some of the breadth of the educational experience at Friends School. Two students sit on oversize books. The older boy is seated on thicker books atop a taller base than those on which the younger girl is seated. He appears to be reading out of the book that he holds open against his elevated knee. The young girl, sitting cross-legged with rounded shoulders, looks up and leans in as if listening. Her violin rests half on the base and half on one of the books under her. On the ground beside the boy and leaning against his base are a lacrosse stick and a soccer ball. The girl may be holding the lacrosse ball. The signature style Walter developed for adding slabs of clay to the surfaces of his sculpture is in evidence here, on the two figures.

Walter was born and raised in Baltimore. After attending Friends, he earned a BA at Hiram College in Ohio. Today he lives in Westminster, Maryland, where he maintains a studio. Before receiving this commission from Friends School, he was commissioned to create a sculpture for the new entrance at the Baltimore Zoo, today the Maryland Zoo in Baltimore, titled *Otter Rocks* (M12). The zoo subsequently purchased several more of Walter's sculptures, which are sited around the zoo.

Note: Visitors who wish to view this sculpture are asked to check in with the receptionist in the Business and Development Office, which is clearly signed on the entrance drive from Charles Street.

L11

TITLE

silence, 2002

LOCATION:

Bryn Mawr School, 109 W. Melrose Avenue

SCULPTOR

Brece V. Honeycutt (b. 1960)

DATE

2002

MEDIA

Forged steel, slate, and brass

DONOR

Gift of the artist

"This sculpture is about facts that are forgotten, history that gets erased." So stated Brece Honeycutt at the dedication of her sculpture celebrating the philanthropy of Mary Elizabeth Garrett (1854–1915), a founder of Bryn Mawr School, a private college-preparatory school for girls, and of the Women's Medical School Fund, an endowment that would ensure not only that the Johns Hopkins Medical School would open in 1893 but that it would be open to women as well as men.

Honeycutt originally made *silence* for the 2002 sculpture exhibition at Evergreen Museum and Library, for which ten artists were invited to create temporary, site-specific works that responded to the landscape or to the history of the property that had belonged to the Garrett family before it was given to Johns Hopkins University in 1942 and opened as a museum in 1997. She was intrigued by a brief mention of Mary Elizabeth Garrett included in the exhibition materials. Honeycutt had a longstanding interest in women's history and women's work and had made several pieces of sculpture about women, including a piece about Clara Barton, the founder of the Red Cross, and a piece about the early suffragettes.

Mary Elizabeth Garrett was the youngest child and only daughter of John Work Garrett, president of the B&O Railroad. Her brother T. Harrison Garrett and his family lived at Evergreen, while Mary Elizabeth lived with her father on Mt. Vernon Square. She displayed

enviable business acumen and had been her father's confidante and traveling companion for years. Upon his death in 1884, she inherited the family home and a fraction of his estate, making her one of the wealthiest women in the country.

Since women did not follow in their fathers' footsteps in those days, she devoted her attention and her huge fortune to women's rights and women's education. Her philanthropic gift to Bryn Mawr preceded her gift to the Johns Hopkins Hospital. Miss Garrett, together with her friends Bessie King, Julia Rogers, Martha Carey Thomas and Mary "Mamie" Machall Gwinn, formed the Women's Fund Committee in 1890 to help raise the rest of the money needed to open the Johns Hopkins Medical School. The committee raised $111,300 from men and women across the country. The gift was made with one stipulation: women must be admitted on the same basis as men. The contribution was accepted, but by December 1892 less than $200,000 of the $500,000 needed to open the medical school had been raised. Thus the trustees were relieved to receive Mary Elizabeth Garrett's letter of December 22, 1892, offering to donate the remainder, but this gift came with its own stipulations: that the men and women to be admitted must have college degrees—this medical school would be a graduate school—and all the students must be proficient in French and German as well as physics, chemistry, and biology. She believed the trustees wanted these requirements, which had been set forth by the founding faculty in 1884. Despite the trustees' growing fears that few students would meet these conditions, they eventually agreed to these terms, and the medical school opened within a year, another of the terms of the gift, in 1893. Miss Garrett's total gift to the hospital was $354,764.

In a sunny corner of the middle-school courtyard stand seven tall desks made of steel and slate, each with a book of metal pages held in place by two brass rings. On each page of each book are etched excerpts from Miss Garrett's letters and ledgers, which together tell the story of her philanthropy. Many pages are filled with the names of the men and women who donated to the Women's Medical School Fund and the amounts they donated. Other pages are etched with excerpts from

Miss Garrett's letter to President Gilman and the trustees outlining the terms of her gift to the new hospital. On another page is a list of equipment she required for Bryn Mawr's new gymnasium, a facility almost unheard of for women: locker rooms, showers, baths, a swimming pool measuring 50 by 20 feet, a running track, and a basketball court.

Miss Garrett insisted that the women attending the school be given silent study time. The title of the piece comes in part from that requirement. Honeycutt etched one letter of the title on the front cover of each book, and on the last page of each she etched the full title. Also etched on one page is a definition of *silence:* "absence of mention." By that definition, the title could certainly apply to the life of Miss Garrett and her philanthropy on behalf of the education and advancement of women.

Honeycutt received a BA in art history from Skidmore College, in Saratoga Springs, New York, and an MFA in sculpture from Columbia University. In 2007 she received an artist fellowship from the D.C. Commission on the Arts and Humanities in Washington and exhibited her work at Wave Hill in the Bronx. In 2008 Honeycutt was a resident artist at Pocket Utopia in Brooklyn, New York, and exhibited here work there.

Note: Visitors to the campus of Bryn Mawr School are asked to check in with the receptionist in the Howell Center, which is clearly signed and easily reached from the main entrance driveway off Melrose Avenue.

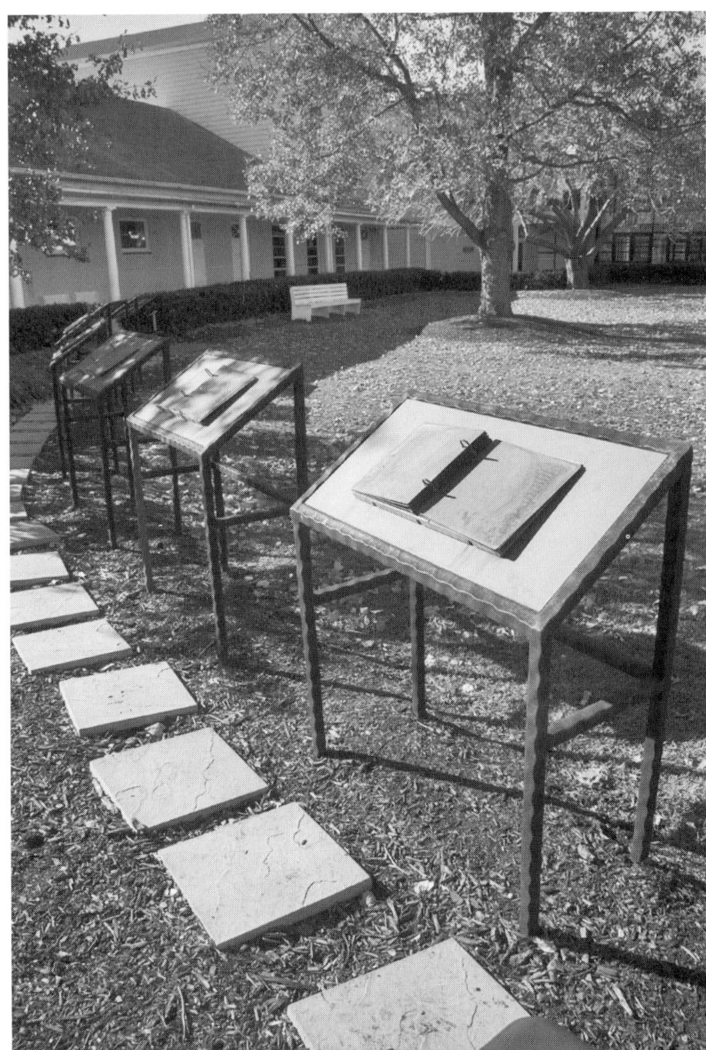

L12

TITLE
Boy with Fish, date unknown

LOCATION
Median, St. Albans Way

SCULPTOR
Unknown

MEDIUM
Bronze

DONOR
Homewood Garden Club

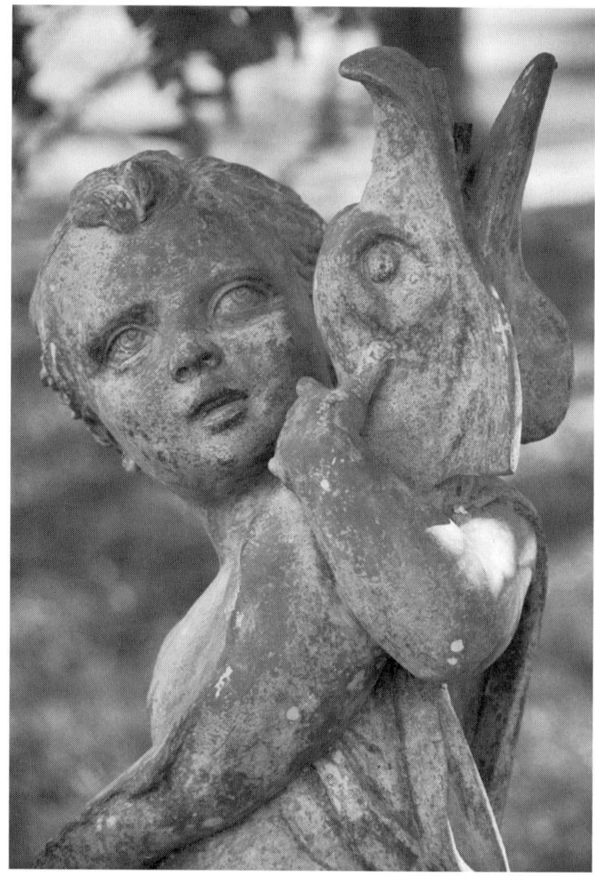

The plaque reads "Homeland Garden Club 1976," suggesting that the garden club gave this sculpture to the Homeland neighborhood in 1976, but very little else is known about the small bronze sculpture of a young boy holding a fish. There are no markings on the sculpture, and no records can be found in the files of the Homeland Garden Club, the Homeland Association, or the Department of Recreation and Parks to indicate how the city came to own this piece, what its earlier provenance might have been, who the sculptor was, or why it was placed in the median of St. Albans Way, which meanders through this residential neighborhood.

The sculpture must have originally been designed as a fountain, for the fish's mouth contains a spout for water. The young boy stands with his weight clearly on his left foot, leaning back against what appears to be a stump. The boy is nude except for a wisp of drapery around his waist and groin. Holding the fish high against his chest and left shoulder, he turns his head to look at the fish. The boy's left arm is wrapped around the fish's body, and his right hand holds the fish's tail.

L13

TITLE
Wildflower, 1923

LOCATION
5200 block of Springlake Way

SCULPTOR
Edward Berge (1876–1924)

MEDIUM
Bronze

DONOR
The Roland Park Company

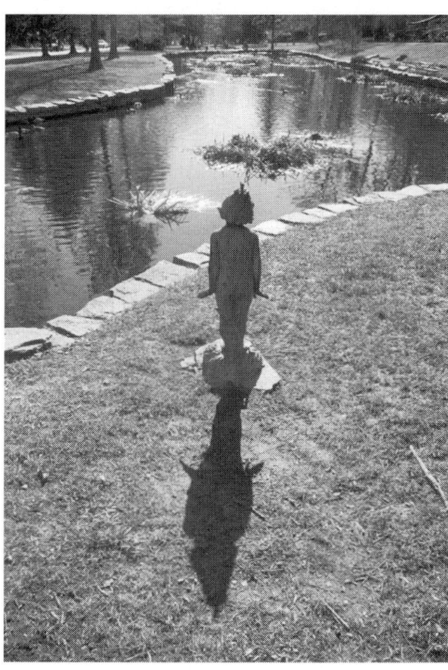

This was the most popular small bronze that Edward Berge made. Three examples of this piece are listed in the brochure printed for the memorial exhibition held at the Baltimore Museum of Art in February and March of 1925, a year after Berge's untimely death. Of the three pieces listed in the brochure, one was a life-size bronze dated 1909, the earliest known piece of this subject; one was a medium-size bronze from 1916, and the third was a small bronze from 1923. Exact dimensions were not given, nor were there even short descriptions of the pieces.

Here, along Springlake Way, near the water's edge, the very small spritelike female figure, which may be another casting of the small bronze in the Baltimore Museum of Art exhibition, is shown wearing only a flower as a hat. The flower may be a morning glory or the blossom from a pumpkin plant. The young girl leans slightly forward from her waist, with her feet together and her arms held close to her sides. Her hands are held out from her body, her fingers pressed tightly together. There is a hint of a grin in the expression on her face. At the back of this sculpture, tall grasses rise behind and against the young girl's legs as she stands on a mound of flowers.

An almost identical version of Berge's *Wildflower* was given to the Keswick Multi-Care Center, on 41st Street across from The Rotunda. The small statue at Keswick must originally have been part of a fountain, for instead of tall grasses behind the young girl it has cattails, designed to hide the waterspouts that are visible upon closer inspection. Much later in life Berge's young model for this piece was a resident at Keswick, a private nonprofit multicare center for seniors, which may have been the reason for the gift in 1961 from the Stoney Run Garden Club. The piece at Keswick is not accessible to the public, as it is sited in a private garden used by the residents.

The sculpture on Springlake Way originally stood on land that formed a small island in the lake. The Roland Park Company, which developed Roland Park, Homeland, and Guilford, first began selling homes and property in Homeland on October 10, 1924, and had mounted an exhibition of sculpture around the lakes and in the caretaker's house to draw people to the new neighborhood. *Wildflower* was purchased from this exhibition by the Roland Park Company and given a permanent home by the lake. It quickly became the symbol of Homeland and was used on its letterhead.

A sculpture that has become known over the years as *The Homeland Wolf,* also by Berge, was included in the same 1924 exhibition. A life-size plaster cast of the *Wolf* dating from 1919 was included in Berge's memorial exhibition at the Baltimore Museum of Art. The piece remained in Homeland for years after the exhibition and then seemed to vanish. In fact, it had been on loan and was removed by Mrs. Berge and sold at auction at Weschler's in Washington, D.C.

L14

TITLE
The Of Course Culture Horse, 1980

LOCATION
Govans Elementary School, 5801 York Road

SCULPTOR
Stan Edmister (1938–2007)

MEDIA
Painted steel

DONOR
Baltimore City Percent for Art program

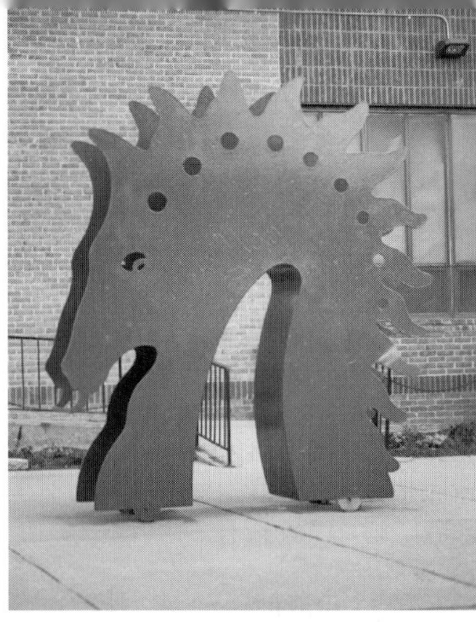

This playful sculpture was designed for the entrance plaza of the new Govans Elementary School. As stated in the artist's contract, it was to consist of double silhouettes of a horse, a rider, and a hand cut out of metal and painted. The wording in the contract was wonderfully misleading, for only a fraction of what was expected appeared on the plaza.

The artist designed double silhouettes of a horse, a rider, and a hand. The largest double silhouette, standing more than 6 feet tall, was a somewhat stylized head and neck to suggest the frisky horse on the plaza. The two identical horse heads are connected by a steel bar, which suggests a bridle, and by a solid sheet of steel framing a central opening in the neck, contributing a sense of volume and three-dimensionality. Stan Edmister cut ten round openings in each silhouette, one for the eye and the others as decoration for the mane, suggested by triangular edges that radiate out from the horse's head and neck, giving a sense of movement and action. Each silhouette appears as a shadow of the other, which further animates the space.

Unfortunately, the double silhouette of the horse is the only element that remains today. The missing silhouettes suggesting the rider and the hand were equally animated and engaging. Cowboy chaps were used to suggest the rider, and cutouts of a thumb and forefinger represented the hand. The chaps were smaller than the horse, the hand was smaller than the rider, and the three elements were spread out across the plaza. Represented by a thumb and forefinger, the hand seems to point to the horse and rider, as if anyone needed encouragement to come and play. Each element was attached directly to the concrete plaza with L-brackets and bolts. The brackets of the two smaller elements may have loosened and failed.

Originally Edmister painted all of the cutouts blue, with touches of red at the edges. Today the horse head is painted the same green as the front doors of the school.

Stan Edmister was born in Tulsa, Oklahoma, and raised on a farm in Lee's Summit, Missouri. He earned a BFA at the Kansas Art Institute before moving to Baltimore to study at the Maryland Institute, where he earned an MFA in 1969. He first became known in Baltimore for his nontraditional playground sculptures. An early one was constructed at Calvert and 26th streets in 1979, and others followed in East Baltimore, Cherry Hill, Hampden, and Park Heights. His most recent playground—a double-helix-molecule sculpture and climbing toy—was built adjacent to Bryn Mawr School's new science building. His first commission through the city's Percent for Art program was for the David E. Weglein School, on Central Avenue, in 1976; it was removed from view when the property was sold to the Culinary Institute. During the late 1980s and early 1990s, Edmister was involved in what he called "The Gateway of Color" project, to design the color schemes for sixteen bridges that crossed the Jones Falls Expressway, funded in part by the National Endowment for the Arts and the Municipal Art Society of Baltimore City.

L15

TITLE
Untitled, 1971

LOCATION
Guilford Elementary School, 4520 York Avenue

SCULPTOR
Fernanda Zopf (b. 1922)

MEDIUM
Polyester resin

DONOR
Baltimore City Percent for Art program

In 1971 Fernanda Zopf received the first of her three Percent for Art commissions for the city public schools. A new addition was being designed for Guilford Elementary School, and Zopf was to create a sculpture for the courtyard.

Zopf had been experimenting with geometric shapes, especially the circle. She decided to take two circles, pinch them in the middle, cut each one, and join them together so that the resulting object would have one continuous surface. Made of polyester resin and painted black, the piece was sited in a raised bed at the edge of the courtyard. Today the courtyard forms part of the main entrance to the school, and Zopf's sculpture stands along this entrance corridor. It has been painted a light blue.

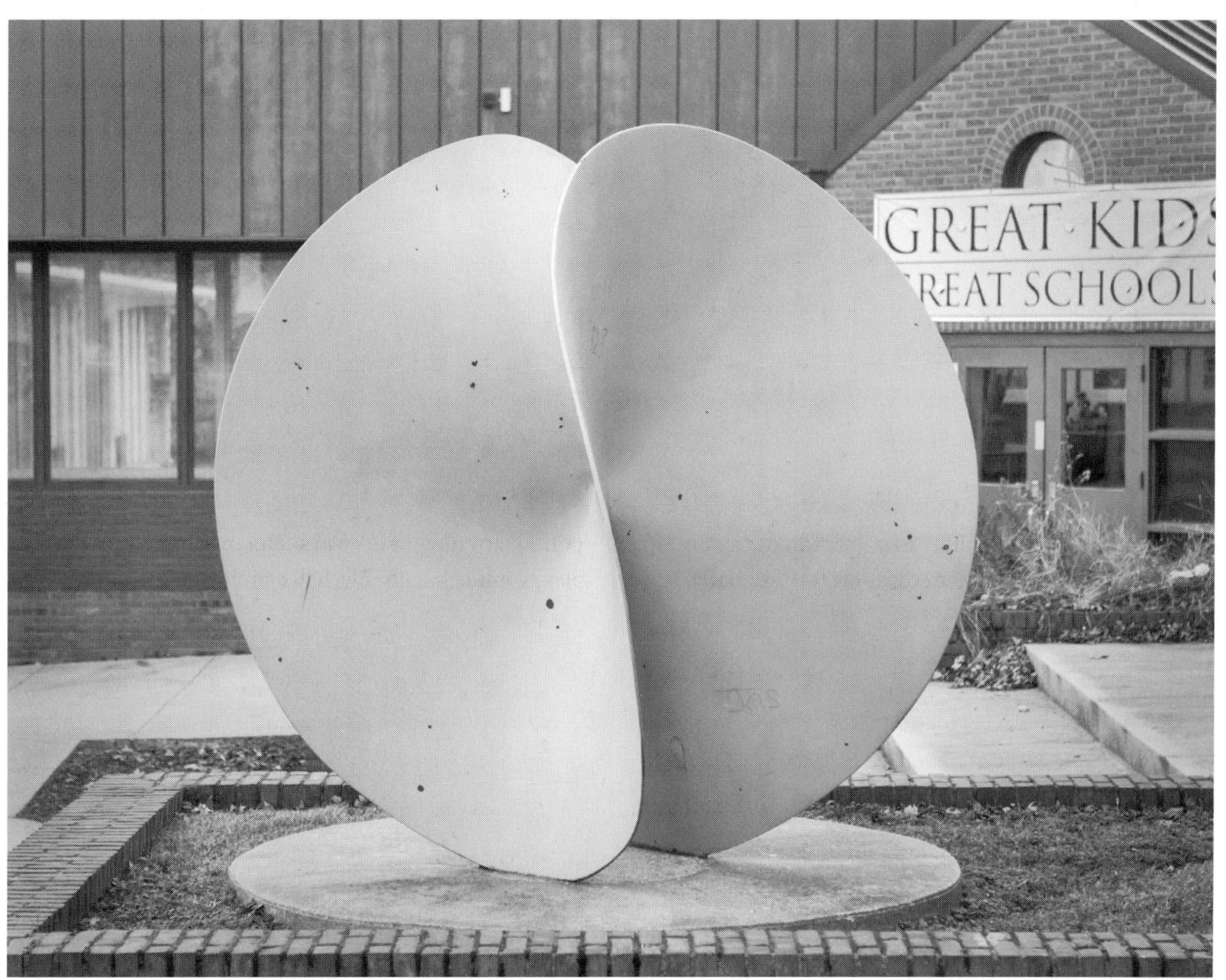

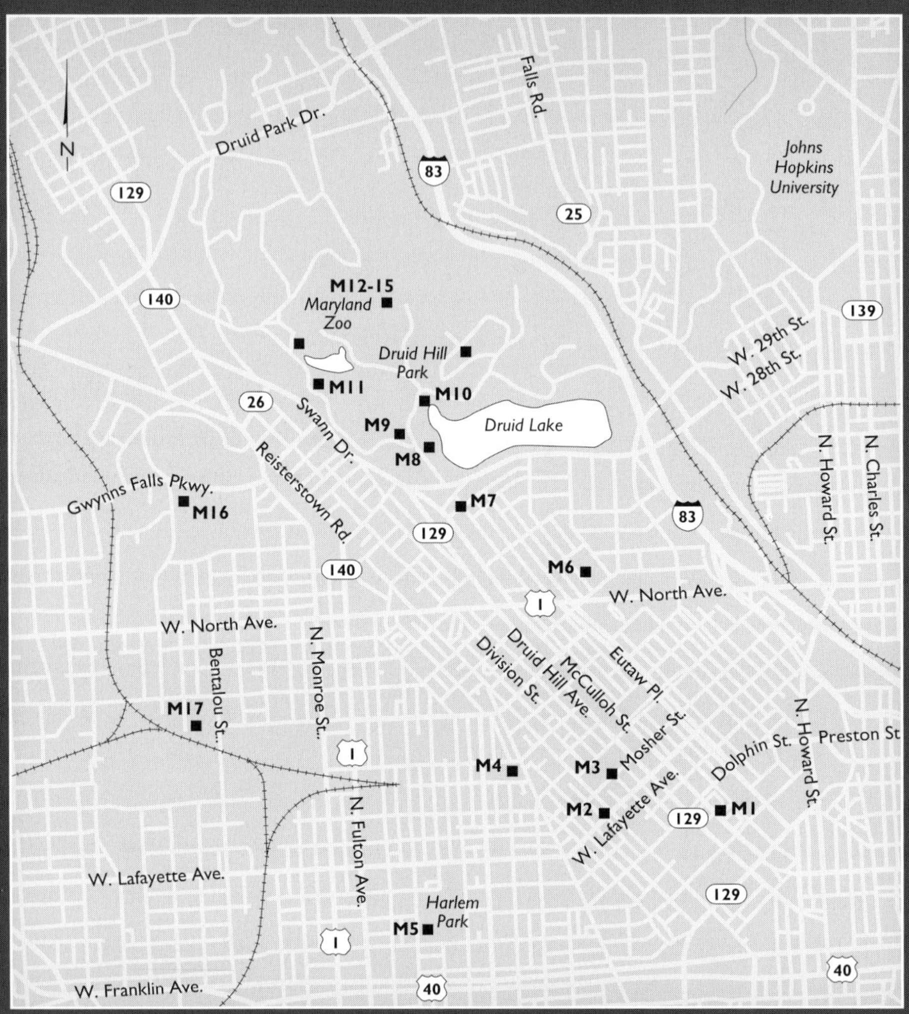

Falls Rd.
Druid Park Dr.
N
129
83
25
Johns Hopkins University
140
M12-15
Maryland Zoo
139
Druid Hill Park
M11
M10
26
W. 29th St.
W. 28th St.
M9
Druid Lake
M8
Swann Dr.
Reisterstown Rd.
Gwynns Falls Pkwy.
M16
N. Howard St.
N. Charles St.
M7
129
140
83
M6
W. North Ave.
1
W. North Ave.
Druid Hill Ave.
McCulloh St.
Eutaw Pl.
Division St.
Mosher St.
Bentalou St.
N. Monroe St.
M17
Dolphin St.
N. Howard St.
Preston St
1
M4
M3
M2
M1
129
N. Fulton Ave.
W. Lafayette Ave.
129
W. Lafayette Ave.
Harlem Park
1
M5
40
W. Franklin Ave.
40
40

DRUID HILL PARK AND ENVIRONS

Driving

M1

TITLES
Recreation and *Education,* 1940

LOCATION
McCulloh Homes, McCulloh Street between
W. Preston and Dolphin streets

SCULPTOR
Henry Berge (1908–1998)

MEDIUM
Concrete

DONOR
Housing Authority of Baltimore City

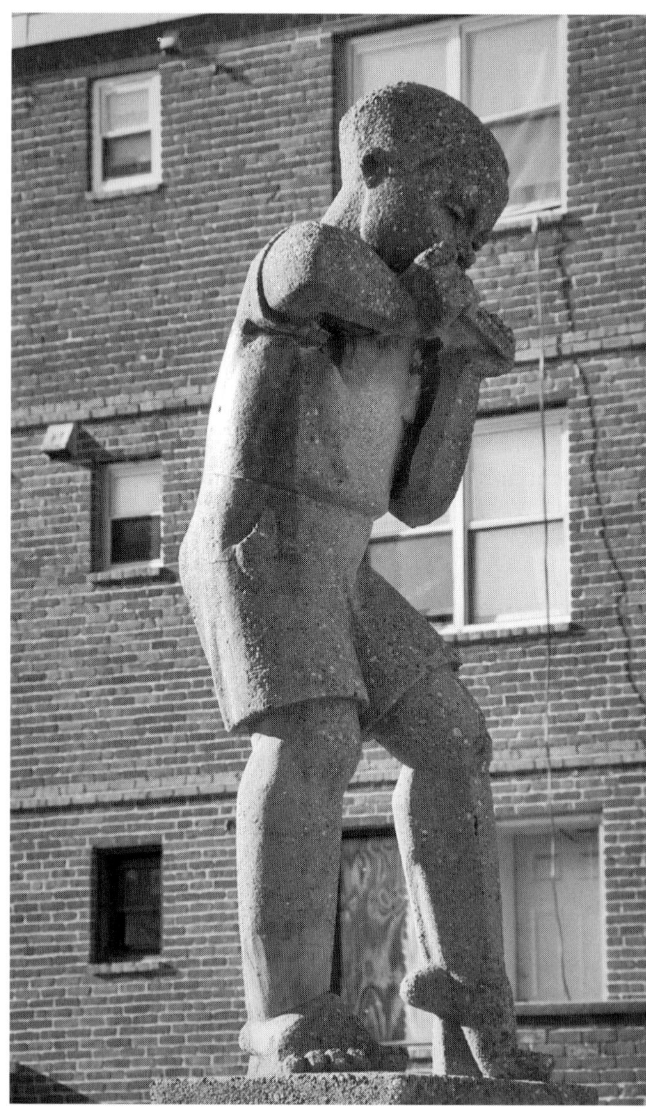

Over a period of approximately fifteen years the architect Edward C. Minor, the chief of design for Baltimore's Housing Authority, commissioned Henry Berge to develop artwork for three housing projects—McCulloh Homes and Lafayette Courts, today called Pleasant Garden View, in 1940 and Cherry Hill Homes in 1954 (see O7 and R3).

The first commission Minor awarded was for the McCulloh Homes, the first units of which were rented in 1941. Minor asked Berge specifically to create free-standing figures of a girl and a boy for placement at the entrance to the housing project. Berge developed the concept of recreation and education and cast the pieces in aggregate in his backyard. He received $1,400 for his work.

The young boy who represents recreation, shown here, stands on a brick base capped in concrete, holds a harmonica in both hands as he presses it to his mouth. He is leaning slightly forward with his left foot raised, as if he keeping time to the music. He is dressed in a shirt and shorts and appears to be barefooted. The young girl representing education stands about 15 feet away, on a similar concrete-capped brick base, holding in her arms an open book, which she appears to be reading. She wears a short dress and is also barefooted.

M2

TITLE
Billie Holiday, 1983–2009

LOCATION
Billie Holiday Plaza, Pennsylvania and Lafayette avenues

SCULPTOR
James Earl Reid (b. 1942)

MEDIUM
Bronze

DONOR
Baltimore City Department of Housing and Community Development

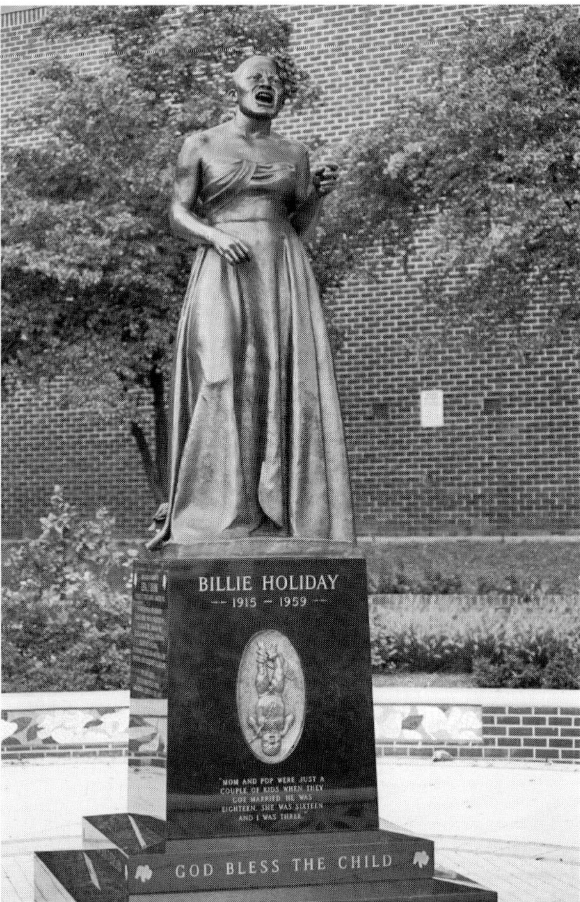

Billie Holiday (1915–59), the legendary jazz singer, grew up on the streets of Baltimore, and for that she is claimed as one of its own. She might actually have been born here if her young teenage mother, Sadie, had not tried to hide her pregnancy by going to Philadelphia to give birth.

Born Eleanora Harris, Holiday grew up on South Durham Street, an alley street in Fells Point. Her father, Clarence Holiday, was a jazz guitarist in Fletcher Henderson's band, but he was not much in evidence. Eleanora got a job running errands for Alice Dean's brothel, drawn there to listen to the jazz and blues music that played in the parlor. When she was 14, she moved with her mother to New York, where she began singing in obscure Harlem nightclubs. She took her professional name from the screen star Billie Dove, and the jazz performer Lester Young, with whom she sang, gave her the nickname "Lady Day." She toured with Count Basie and Artie Shaw before going solo. She was the first black woman to sing with an all-white orchestra, which was quite an accomplishment in her day. Life never became easier for her, and in the 1940s she became addicted to alcohol and drugs, which led to her death at just 44. Among her major hits were the songs "Lover Man," "Billie's Blues," "This Year's Kisses," "God Bless the Child," and "Strange Fruit."

Billie Holiday returned to Baltimore on occasion, performing at the Royal Theatre, one of Baltimore's premier jazz clubs in the 1930s and 1940s, which stood diagonally across the intersection from the newly created pocket park where this statue was installed. In 1983 James Earl Reid completed the 8½-foot bronze statue of Holiday singing, dressed in a strapless evening gown, with her trademark gardenias in her hair, which is braided and pulled back in a knot. However, the statue of Holiday was not placed on the 6-foot-high base that Reid had designed for it, and he did not participate in its unveiling.

After almost twenty-five years of trying to resolve this situation, Reid was finally allowed to create the bronze relief panels that had been planned for the base but were deemed "too controversial" in the 1980s. In 2007 the city council approved funding for a much larger base to support the new relief panels, which contain more of the history and social context of Holiday's life and work. One relief depicts an African

American infant attached to an umbilical cord, in reference to the Holiday standard "God Bless the Child," and a second relief makes a clear reference to Holiday's signature song, "Strange Fruit," illustrated by a lynching, the "strange fruit" of bodies hanging from trees. Added onto the bronze base, just behind the figure and just above the artist's signature, is a crow, a symbol of the Jim Crow laws, eating a gardenia. The retooled statue of Billie Holiday, with its new base, was reinstalled and rededicated in the newly redesigned park on July 17, 2009.

James Earl Reid was born in Princeton, North Carolina, and earned his BFA from the Maryland Institute College of Art in 1966, where he studied with Joseph Sheppard. After receiving his MFA in sculpture from the University of Maryland–College Park, he taught there for eleven years, followed by teaching appointments at Spellman College, Atlanta University, Morgan State University, Goucher College, and the Baltimore School for the Arts. In 1979, the same year that Reid received the commission for the statue of Billie Holiday, the Community for Creative Non-Violence, in Washington, D.C., asked him to make a public sculpture depicting a homeless nativity scene. Reid presented a homeless mother, father, and child living over a heating grate. A controversy arose when the Community for Creative Non-Violence and Reid both filed for copyright to the piece. The landmark case reached the Supreme Court, which ruled in 1989 in support of artists' rights to retain creative and intellectual property.

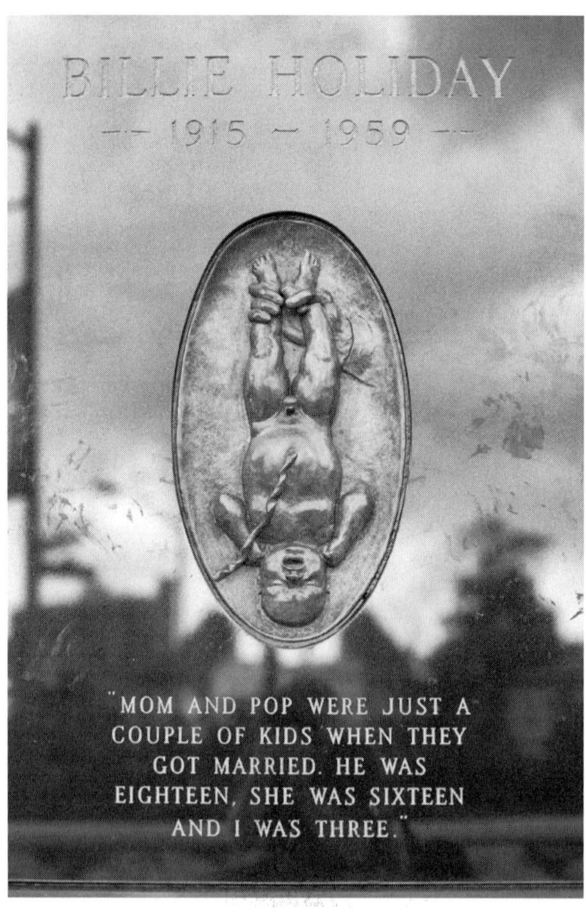

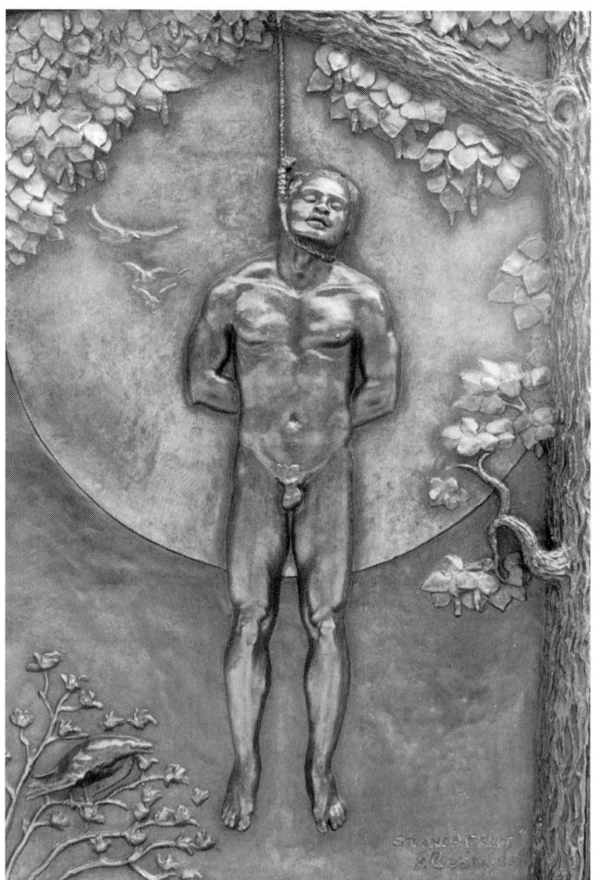

M3

TITLE
OM, 1979

LOCATION
Total Health Care, Division and Mosher streets

SCULPTOR
Oliver Patrick Scott (b. 1940)

MEDIUM
Mayari-R steel

DONOR
Baltimore City Percent for Art program

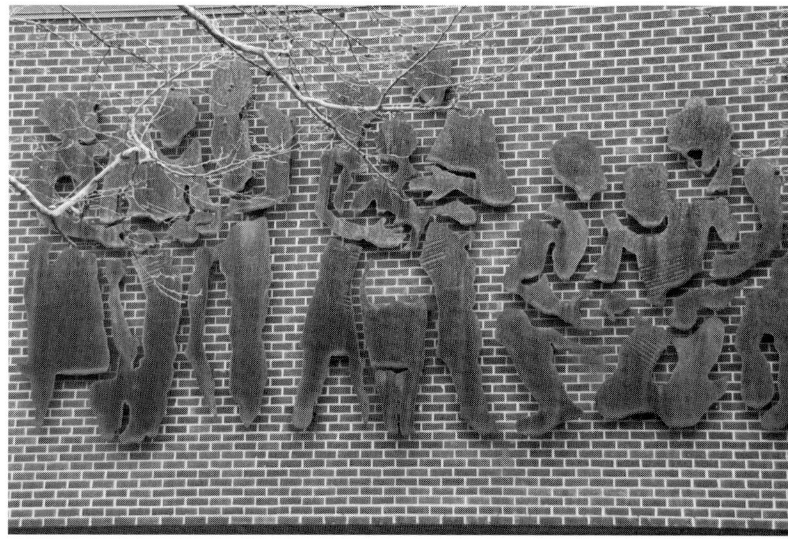

OM is a vibratory and healing mantra and an interesting title for a relief about healing and caregiving. In 1978 the architectural firm of Sulton, Campbell was awarded the commission to build a new community health center. The firm's Washington office handled the project and commissioned Oliver Patrick Scott to create an artwork for the building.

The original contract was for one wall relief of ¼ inch weathering steel measuring 11 by 30 feet. The single relief referred to in this contract can be found today on two walls of the center, the entrance wall and the long wall that faces Mosher Street. At some point after the design was approved, it was decided by all involved to break the relief into two parts, allowing for some decoration on the entrance facade.

The group that includes a mother and father holding an infant was chosen for the entrance wall, and the three remaining figural groups were installed on the wall facing Mosher. Horizontal in composition, the three figural groups here, like the grouping on the entrance facade, are composed of three figures. All of the groups are abstracted cutouts, each figure made of two, three, or four separate parts, yet in each group it is clear that two figures are caring for the figure between them.

The relief was cut out of Mayari-R steel, a weathering steel manufactured locally at Bethlehem Steel. The broad, flat surfaces of each piece of steel have been allowed to weather and develop the characteristic smooth, rich, almost velvety surface. Several of the pieces have been scored with short, close parallel lines, primarily in the midsections of the figures. These lines were created using black epoxy paint. Scott signed the piece with the same epoxy paint.

Born in Fort Smith, Arkansas, Oliver Patrick Scott grew up in Baltimore, where he lives today. He received his BS degree from Morgan State University, in Baltimore, in 1960 and his MA in painting from the University of Maryland–College Park. He joined the Morgan faculty in 1964 as director of the Fine Arts Center and taught there for twenty-two years. In 1972 he became chairman of the art department. Primarily a painter, he turned brush drawings into life-size cartoons, which were cut out of steel by the Seaboard Company in Baltimore.

TITLE
Untitled, 1975

LOCATION
William H. Pinderhughes Elementary School,
1200 N. Fremont Avenue

SCULPTOR
Fernanda Zopf (b. 1922)

MEDIUM
Concrete

DONOR
Baltimore City Percent for Art program

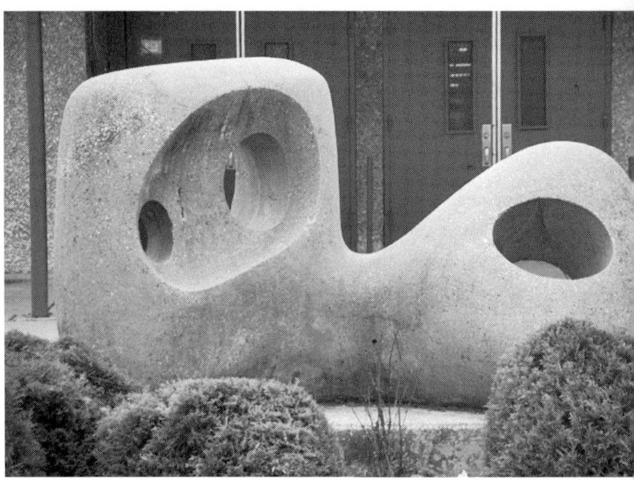

In 1975 Fernanda Zopf received her second commission through the city's Percent for Art program. The first was completed in 1971 for Guilford Elementary School (L15), and a third commission was completed in 1976 for yet another elementary school, Charles Carroll Barrister Elementary (H7).

The architect designing this new school asked Zopf to create a piece of sculpture to be sited near the entrance. At the time, she was continuing her experiments with geometric shapes, especially the circle, and she wanted to use that form here. The architect asked her to make her form more organic and to create something that the children could play on. He went further to suggest that she might consider doing something resembling Henry Moore's work.

The sculpture Zopf made for this school was in direct response to the architect's request and was limited by the $5,000 allowance for the artwork, which did not even cover the cost of the concrete. The abstract, horizontal, rounded form that makes reference to a reclining figure has three openings. It is mounted on a low concrete base so that students can play on it.

M5

TITLE
JAMES L. RIDGELY MONUMENT, 1885

LOCATION
Harlem Park, Edmondson Avenue between
N. Gilmor and N. Calhoun streets

SCULPTOR
Unknown

MEDIUM
Bronze

DONOR
Fraternal Order of Odd Fellows

In 1885 a monument to James L. Ridgely (1807–81) was erected in Harlem Park. Ridgely was a distinguished member of the Order of Odd Fellows in Baltimore and is remembered in this monument as a patriot, a legislator for his city and state, a patron of education, and a representative American citizen.

The 27-foot-high granite base culminates in an 8-foot bronze portrait statue of Ridgely dressed in a buttoned knee-length formal coat. His right arm rests on a cluster of three low columns, and the scroll that he holds in his right hand opens downward, revealing the words "ODD / FELLOWSHIP / ESTO / PERPETUO." Ridgely's left hand rests on his waist, and his elbow is held outward. He stands with his weight resting solidly on his left foot, and his right foot is slightly forward, extending just over the edge of the base.

William Rusk, in his *Art in Baltimore Monuments and Memorials*, states that the statue was made by "an authoress who resides in Kentucky" and attributes this information to Nelson's *History of Baltimore*, and under Ridgely's forward right foot can be seen the inscription "DOGLE SC" Rusk also states that the base was built by the Muldoon Monument Company, which has operated nationally out of Louisville, Kentucky, since 1855, designing, fabricating, and erecting monuments, supplying granite for the pedestals for other monuments, and even operating as a foundry as recently as 1987. That fact lends weight to the idea that a sculptor

from Kentucky named Dogle, unknown today, created the figure.

The monument was placed in the center of a brick and concrete plaza measuring 58 feet in diameter in the nearly 10-acre Harlem Park, created on land the city had acquired several years earlier, in 1868. Harlem Park became known throughout the city for its great variety of trees and its endless beds of exotic flora. Goldfish ponds were created sometime after 1890 around the edges of the park.

The Fraternal Order of Odd Fellows was founded on the North American continent in 1819, in Baltimore, by Thomas Wildey, to whom another Baltimore monument was dedicated in 1865 (O10). In seventeenth-century England it was odd for men and women to organize specifically to give aid to those in need, but the many who did were called Odd Fellows. Their best-known symbol is three linked ovals, containing the letters *F, L,* and *T,* representing their principles of "Friendship, Love and Truth." This symbol can be found on both monuments.

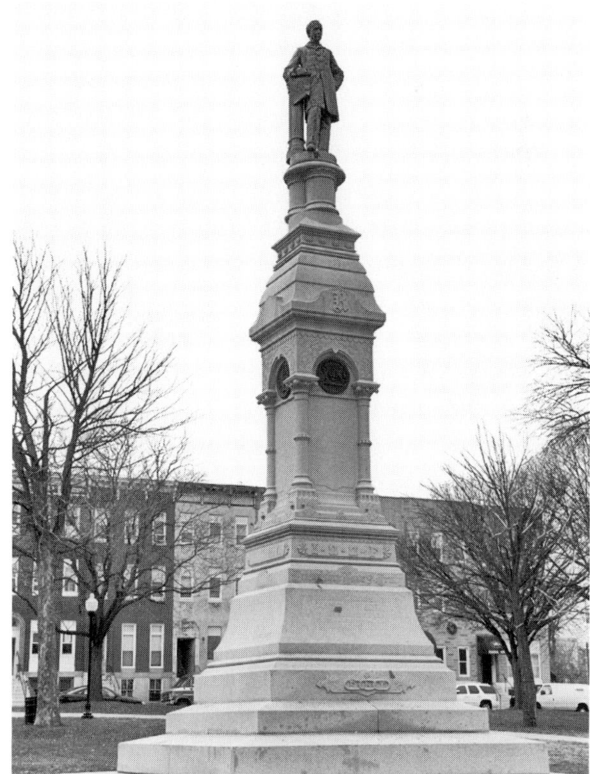

M6

The Learning Tree, 1982

LOCATION
John Eager Howard Elementary School,
2011 Linden Avenue

SCULPTOR
Patrick F. McGuire

MEDIUM
Painted plate steel

DONOR
Baltimore City Percent for Art program

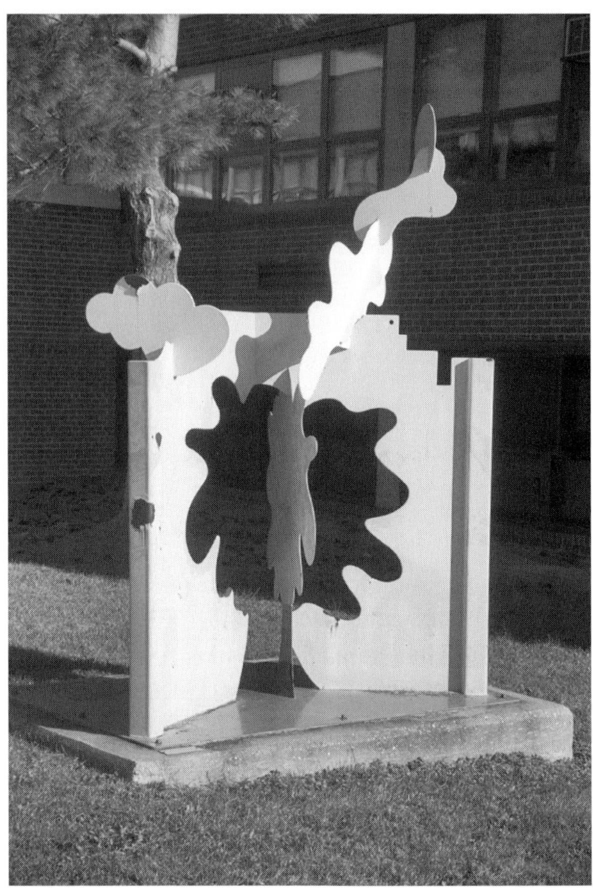

Patrick McGuire received this Percent for Art commission from Benjamin Brotman, the architect for the addition to the John Eager Howard Elementary School. The sculpture was installed in front of one entrance to the school, on a lawn designed as a play area for the children.

In a simply constructed vignette, McGuire uses a tree and the sky with three clouds and the sun to suggest a connection between the elementary students and the universe beyond their school environment. The simple forms can be easily understood. The brown tree trunk, with its stylized canopy of foliage painted green, was cut out of a large sheet of ¼ inch steel and turned at an angle to the sheet. The remainder of the sheet of steel, painted blue, represents the sky. The three puffy white clouds and a bright yellow sun, also cut out of steel, are stacked on top of the steel sheet, all at angles to one another. The tree is bolted to a steel plate that is bolted onto a concrete foundation.

McGuire received his BFA from the Minneapolis College of Art and Design and his MFA from the Rinehart School of Sculpture at the Maryland Institute in 1965.

TITLE
Untitled, 1890

LOCATION
Department of Recreation and Parks headquarters,
2600 Madison Avenue

SCULPTOR
John Monroe

MEDIUM
Granite

DONOR
William H. Parker Sr.

Just inside the Madison Avenue entrance to Druid Hill Park, on the lawn of the headquarters for the Department of Recreation and Parks, is a stone relief that originally was set over the Fayette Street entrance to the Old Post Office. The exact subject of this relief panel, with its putti and corn and grapes, remains somewhat elusive.

There is more than one mystery associated with this relief. John Monroe was an English sculptor who, the plaque states, had just completed work on the Albert Memorial in London's Hyde Park when he was brought to Baltimore to carve more than twenty relief panels for the new post office that was going up in Baltimore between 1880 and 1890. What happened to all those stone panels when the Old Post Office was razed in 1930?

The plan was to save all the relief panels and create some kind of memorial in Druid Hill Park. However, only two panels are known to have survived—this one and one that can be found on the front lawn of a property in Roland Park that formerly belonged to William H. Parker Sr., who had worked on the Old Post Office at the time of its construction and had helped set the relief panels. This was no small task, since this one is 4 feet high, 8 feet wide, and 2 feet deep and weighs 8 tons. When parts of the building were offered for sale to employees or given to local cemeteries, such as Louden and the Hebrew Cemetery, Parker, who by then was the

contractor and builder of the Emerson Hotel nearby, bought two relief panels; he presented this one to the Board of Park Commissioners and kept one for his own front yard.

Mr. Parker presented his gift to the parks board in 1932, and the timing of his gift led to the misunderstanding of its subject matter. Beer returned to Baltimore about this time, and the legend that the subject of the panel was repeal grew as viewers focused only on what they thought was a still for making liquor in the background. The presence of corn and grapes further supported this idea.

Today it seems clear that the real subject of the panel is actually the arts and sciences. This interpretation is supported by the identification of the retort, not a still, on the left side of the panel and an understanding that the retort had long been used as a symbol of chemistry. Here the retort sits on a tripod, under which there would be a flame, and nearby is a condenser, into which a liquid would flow. Another symbol of the sciences might be the telescope that the larger, more central nude boy holds in his right hand. On the right side of the panel, where two of the four young nude males are seated, one holds paintbrushes and a palette, and the other rests both hands on the head of a bust as if sculpting. A lyre, representing music, lies on the ground between them.

John Monroe is credited with some of the carvings on Brown Memorial Park Avenue Presbyterian Church in Baltimore and on the Mount Vernon Place United Methodist Church. His involvement on the Albert Memorial, commissioned by Queen Victoria to commemorate her beloved late consort, must have been as an assistant to one of the eight sculptors known to have been involved. The Albert Memorial is a huge architectural structure with eight figural groups in addition to the figure of Albert and a continuous frieze around the memorial. Monroe most certainly would have brought fresh ideas from the great sculptural program of the Albert Memorial, which includes allegorical representations of the continents Europe, Asia, Africa, and America; the industrial arts (agriculture, engineering, manufactures, and commerce); the greater sciences (geometry, physiology, astronomy, rhetoric, chemistry [carrying a retort], medicine, geology, and philosophy); and the virtues and angels. The frieze is composed of relief portraits of famous poets, musicians, painters, architects, and sculptors.

The subject of the companion panel in Roland Park seems to be two of the industrial arts—engineering and agriculture. The composition is the same as in this panel, with two larger nude male youths sitting on a low capital in the center and two other nude youths in the lower corners. The main figure on the right wears a bib apron and rests his right arm on an anvil, with a furnace in low relief behind him and gears and a spindle at his feet. The figure in the lower right corner holds a ball, possibly of twine, as if he is wrapping it, and a spinning wheel is in low relief behind him. The main figure on the left sits before a crude plow and holds some other implement, which is hard to decipher as much of it is missing. The figure in the lower left corner has a lap full of corn, a symbol of agricultural bounty. The subject matter here supports the idea that the subject of the panel at the Department of Recreation and Parks headquarters is the arts and sciences and indicates that Monroe might have been following, at least in part, the program of ideas from his most recent job in London.

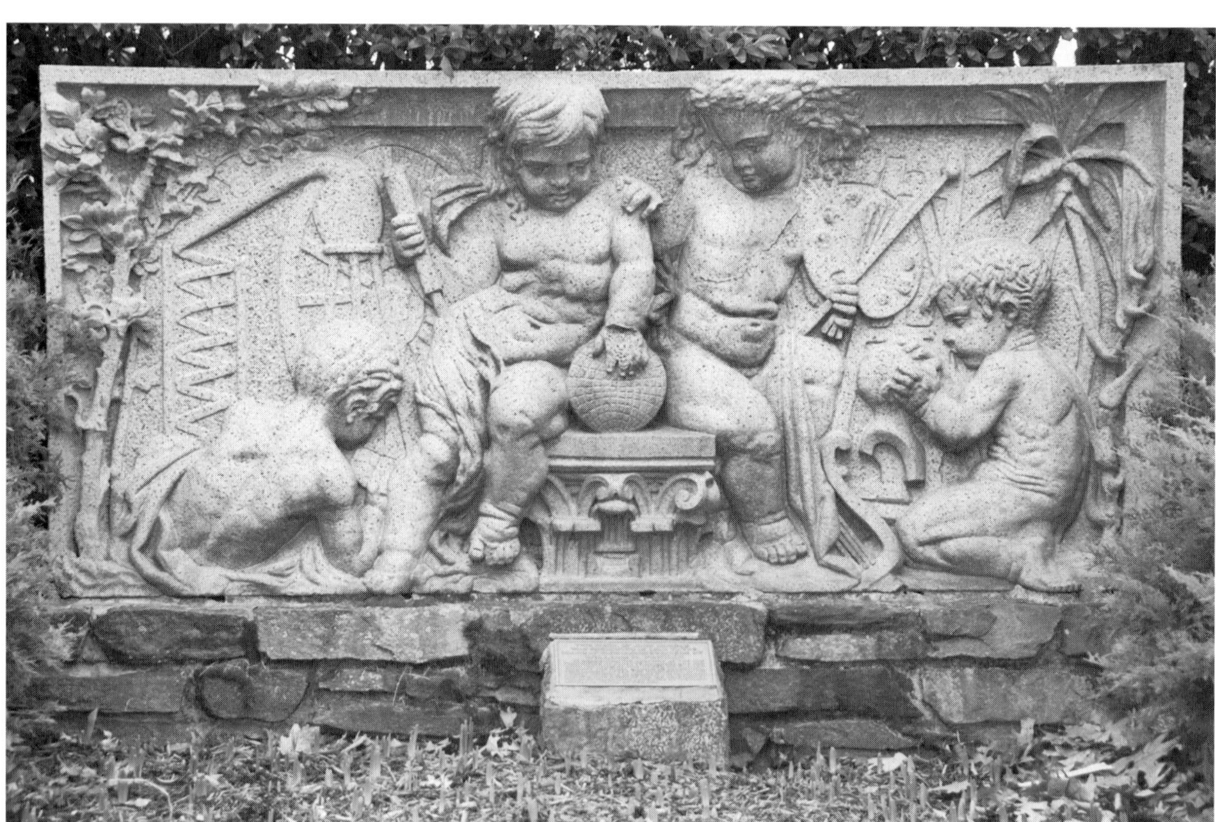

M8

TITLE:

WILLIAM WALLACE MONUMENT, 1893 copy of 1869 original

LOCATION:

Druid Hill Park

SCULPTOR:

D. W. Stevenson (1842–1904)

MEDIUM:

Bronze

DONOR:

William Wallace Spence

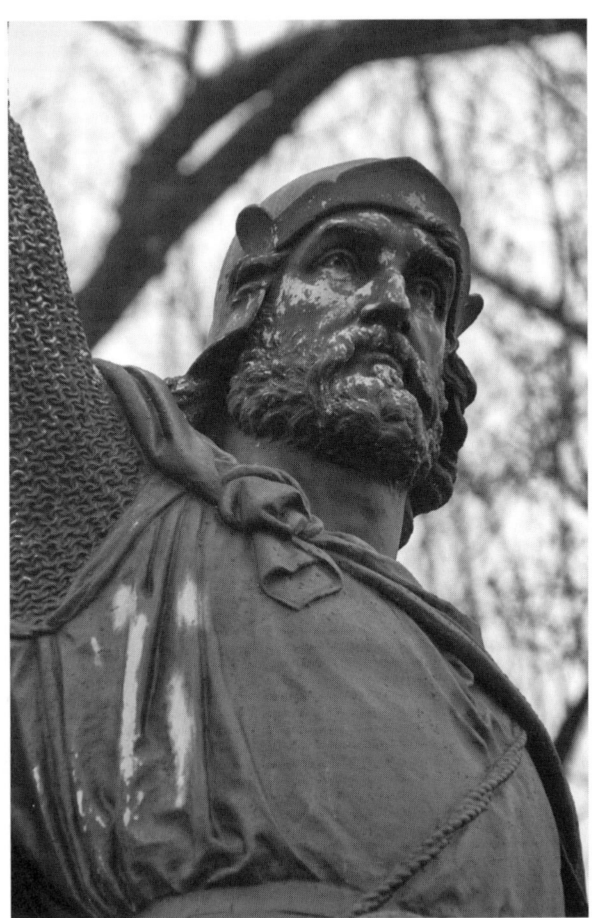

Why is a champion of Scottish liberty represented by a statue in Druid Hill Park, one might wonder, upon viewing the armored warrior holding aloft a huge sword at the western end of the park reservoir.

The statue is of William Wallace (ca. 1272–1305), one of Scotland's greatest national heroes and the undisputed leader of the Scottish resistance during the early years of struggle to free Scotland from English rule at the end of the thirteenth century. One of his early victories over the English came in 1297 in the battle of Stirling Bridge, when the Scots regained control of Stirling Castle. Never before had a Scottish army triumphed so completely over an English aggressor. Five thousand British lost their lives that day, and for the moment Scotland was almost free of occupying forces. Wallace was knighted and made Commander of the Army of the Kingdom of Scotland. In his few remaining years Wallace continued his strong committment to the struggle for Scottish independence. But in 1305 he was captured, taken to London, condemned, hanged, and quartered, and the quarters were sent to Newcastle, Berwick, Stirling, and Perth. He became a martyr and the very symbol of Scotland's struggle for freedom. His death revived the national rebellion that would finally lead to Scottish independence.

William Wallace Spence, a Baltimore businessman born in Edinburgh, so greatly admired his ancestor that he ordered a copy of a famous statue of Wallace for placement in Druid Hill Park. Spence lived at Bolton, a mansion built about 1800 that stood where the Fifth Regiment Armory stands today. Bolton Street led directly from his estate to the site of the monument in Druid Hill Park.

The original bronze statue of Wallace, by the Scottish sculptor D. W. Stevenson, stands atop the Wallace Monument, a tower built on Abbey Craig, near Sterling Castle, in 1861. Wallace is shown standing in his helmet and full body armor, his shield by his side and his long sword drawn and raised. Wallace was said to have struck this pose as he watched from Abbey Craig as the army of Edward I gathered for the battle at Stirling Bridge. In Druid Hill Park, the drama of the stance is heightened by the scale of the figure and the base on which it stands. It is some 30 feet from the ground to the tip of the sword, the figure standing almost 16 feet tall on a 14-foot-high rough-hewn granite base. It was unveiled on November 30, St. Andrew's Day, celebrating the patron saint of Scotland.

Stevenson was born at Ratho, just west of Edinburgh. He was trained at the Trustee's School in Edinburgh before traveling to Rome, where he continued his studies. He worked with the sculptor Sir John Steell on the Prince Albert Memorial in Edinburgh's Charlotte Square and was a member of the Royal Academy of Scotland.

Three years after this monument was installed in Druid Hill Park, Spence gave another monument to Baltimore: *Christus Consolator* (The Divine Healer), which stands today in what was originally the main lobby of the Johns Hopkins Hospital on Broadway Avenue. This statue of Christ is a copy of one by the Danish sculptor Bertel Thorvaldsen. A Presbyterian and a friend of Johns Hopkins', Spence answered the request of Daniel Coit Gilman, the president of the university and the hospital, for a religious work of art, which people seemed to think was needed for the hospital. Hopkins, a Quaker, had made it clear in his will that the hospital should have no religious affiliation.

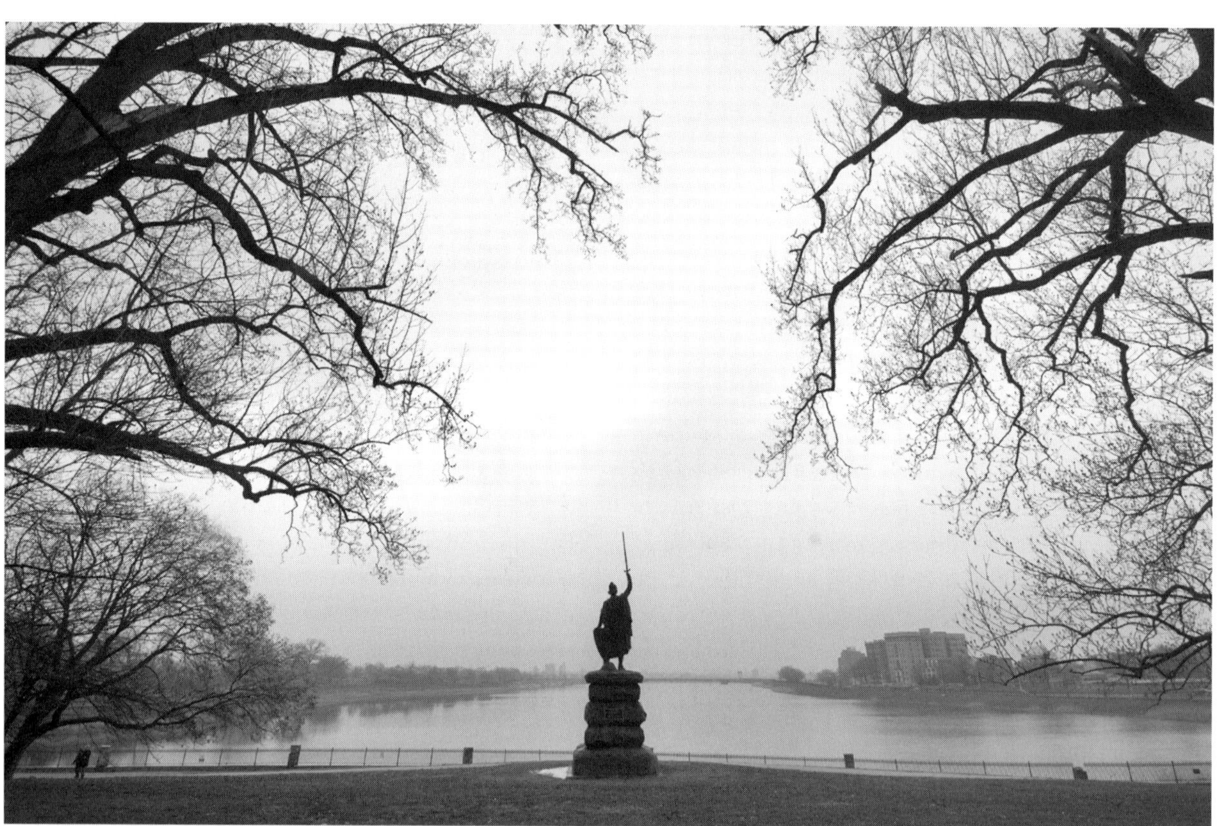

M9

TITLE
George Washington, 1857

LOCATION
Druid Hill Park

SCULPTOR
Edward Sheffield Bartholomew (1822–1858)

MEDIUM
Marble

DONORS
Noah Walker family and Enoch Pratt

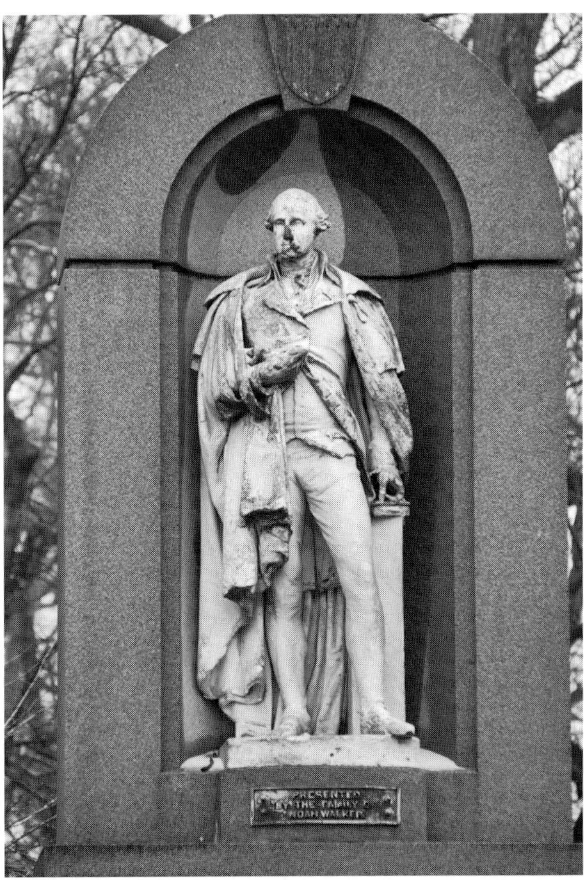

Like the nearby statues of Christopher Columbus and William Wallace, most statues of great men depict them standing alone on top of an impressive base. So why did this gift of a statue of George Washington necessitate a gift by Enoch Pratt of a niche for Washington to stand in? The answer can be found in the statue's provenance.

Originally this statue of Washington was prominently displayed in a third-floor niche on the facade of the building that housed Noah Walker's clothing and dry goods emporium on E. Baltimore Street. Between 1850 and 1870 Noah Walker's clothier shop was one of the biggest and best-known businesses in the city. It was where families of taste and fashion shopped. The building became known as the "Washington Building." The statue was even visible at night, framed by a circle of gas-lighted stars. Washington is depicted wearing the uniform of the commander in chief of the Continental army, holding a scroll in his right hand and resting his left hand on a book lying on a stand. He wears a military cloak over his shoulders.

A friend of Enoch Pratt's, Walker was urged by Pratt, as were Pratt's other wealthy friends, to visit the studio of Edward Sheffield Bartholomew in Rome when they were on the grand tour, which Walker did. It was in Rome that Walker ordered a statue of Washington from Bartholomew for the niche on the facade of his store. For $6,000 Walker got a statue without a back! It didn't need one. Years later, long after Walker's death in 1874, when the family sold the building, they decided to give the statue to the city. But it needed a niche. Pratt immediately paid to have a granite niche designed and constructed by George Mann & Son. This was one more effort by Pratt to support Bartholomew; it had been Pratt's financial backing that made it possible for Bartholomew to study and work in Rome. Bartholomew made Pratt's tomb in Greenmount Cemetery, ordered years before Pratt's death. Bartholomew's other works in Baltimore include *Shepherd Boy* at the Peabody Institute, a bust of Pratt on the second floor of the main library that bears his name, and the tomb monument for John Eager Howard's family in Greenmount Cemetery. Bartholomew also created a statue of Charles Carroll of Carrollton for the chapel at Doughoregan Manor, Carroll's country home in Howard County.

M10

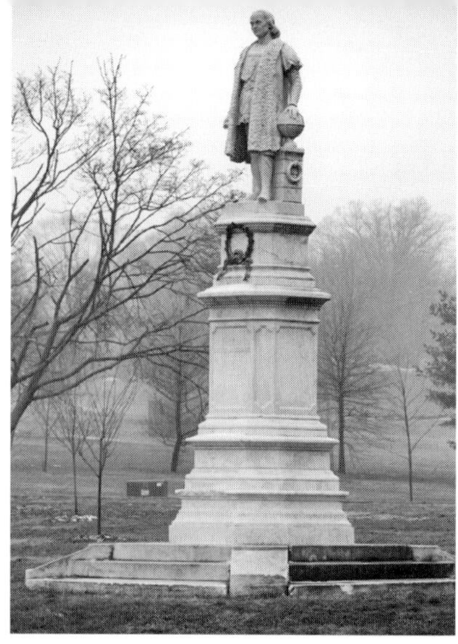

TITLE:
COLUMBUS MONUMENT, 1892

LOCATION:
Druid Hill Park

SCULPTOR:
Achille Canessa (1856–1905)

MEDIUM:
Marble

DONOR:
Italian United Society of Baltimore

In 1892, cities across the country rushed to commemorate the four-hundredth anniversary of Christopher Columbus' discovery of America by raising monuments dedicated to him, and Baltimore was no exception. The Italian United Society of Baltimore chose to present the city with a statue of Columbus by the Genoese sculptor Achille Canessa. On October 12, 1892, Mayor Ferdinand Latrobe accepted the gift from the Italians on behalf of the city, and Cardinal Gibbons gave the benediction.

Achille Canessa created monuments for cities across Italy as well as for cities as distant as Santa Cruz de Tenerif, Spain, and São Paulo, Brazil. Much of his sculpture was made for funeral monuments like the grand pantheon of the Sabino de Arriaga family and the monument to the Ereñozaga brothers in the medieval cemetery of Plentzia, Spain. Monuments to Columbus made after the one he made for Baltimore can be found in San Juan, Puerto Rico, and Lima, Peru.

This is the second of Baltimore's three monuments celebrating Columbus' discovery of the New World. The earlier monument, which is the oldest monument in the country dedicated to Columbus, is an obelisk in Herring Run Park that dates from 1792. Like Baltimore's newest monument to Columbus, in the Inner Harbor (A10, where more details about the 1792 obelisk can also be found), the monument in Druid Hill Park is a life-size marble statue that depicts Columbus as a young man with shoulder-length hair, dressed in his traditional sleeveless coat, or tabard, with one hand resting on a globe and the other holding a partially unfurled scroll. Here the globe sits on the edge of a low stone wall from which a mooring ring hangs. This arrangement differs slightly from that of the Inner Harbor statue, as does the base, which in the Inner Harbor has six relief panels, depicting Columbus' ships, his birthplace, his landing, and his meeting the Indians in the New World.

Every year on October 12 Italians gather to place a wreath at the base of the monument and to celebrate the achievement of their fellow countryman. Years ago, an annual parade of military detachments, veteran organizations, and other groups preceded the ceremony.

A 37½ inch bronze statue in the Mariners' Museum in Newport News, Virginia, is a copy of the Columbus Monument in Druid Hill Park. This small bronze was originally displayed in the Baltimore neighborhood of Forest Park, in the backyard of Giovanni Schiaffino, who had immigrated to Baltimore as early as 1879 from Genoa and who was by the early 1890s the Italian consul in Baltimore. Schiaffino is thought to have commissioned a Columbus statue from Canessa on behalf of the Italian community and arranged for shipping the statue to Baltimore. It seems that Schiaffino asked Canessa to copy an existing Columbus monument in Genoa, and for this commission Canessa gave Schiaffino the small bronze. When the Schiaffino family home was sold in 1935, the bronze sculpture was purchased by the K. Hettleman & Sons scrap yard in Baltimore from Giovanni Schiaffino's grandson. The Mariners' Museum acquired the bronze from the scrap yard in 1939.

M11

TITLE:
Wagner, 1900

LOCATION:
Druid Hill Park, Mansion Lawn

SCULPTOR:
R. P. Golde

MEDIUM:
Bronze

DONOR:
United Singers of Baltimore

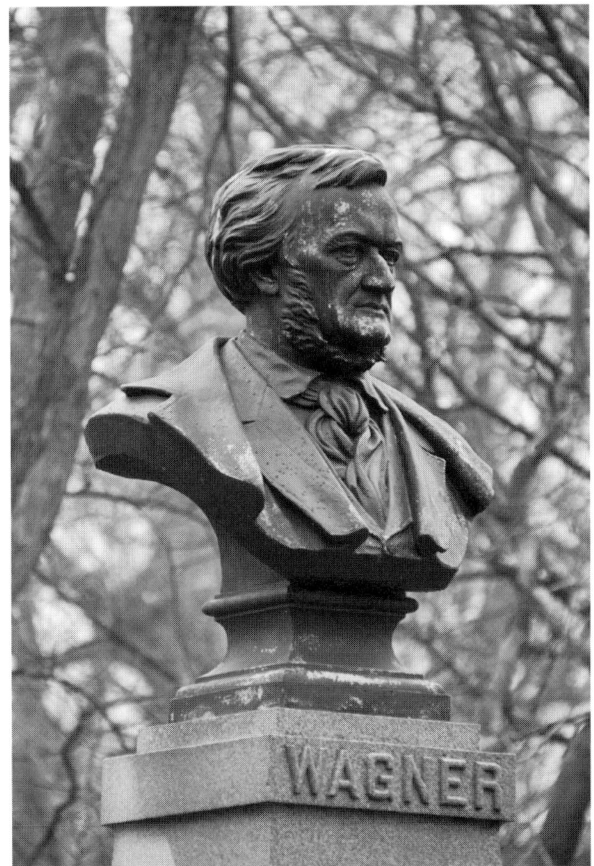

This bronze bust of Richard Wagner (1813–83), the German composer and conductor known primarily for his operas, was awarded to the United Singers of Baltimore as the first prize at the 19th National Saengerfest, a German singing festival and competition, which took place in Brooklyn, New York, in 1900. The United Singers in turn presented the bust to the city the following year. The inscription on the red granite base gives the details of the festival and the results of that year's competition. The song the Baltimore group sang to win first place was "Scheiden," meaning "parting," written by D. Melamet.

Golde was a German-born sculptor who came to the United States in 1884 and was living in New York City when he received the commission for this bust. Wagner is depicted with his characteristic long sideburns, dressed formally in a shirt with a scarf tied around his neck, over which he wears a vest. Two outer garments, a jacket and possibly a cape, are suggested. He looks out slightly to his left. A model for this portrait bust may have been a nineteenth-century portrait of Wagner similar to the one painted by Franz von Lenbach, which depicts Wagner in similar attire with the same facial features.

The Saengerfest, which drew five thousand singers to Brooklyn from June 25 to July 4 in 1900, continues today as a triennial event, not the annual event it was up until World War I. The most recent festival was held in Washington, D.C., in 2009.

There is a related sculpture, a bronze bust of Conradin Kreutzer, another famous German composer, in Patterson Park (P2). That bust was presented to the United Singers of Baltimore when they won first place in the 24th National Saengerfest, held in Brooklyn fifteen years later. It too was given to the city, to be installed in another city park. Golde was the sculptor, and the history of that year's festival is inscribed on the base.

M12

TITLE
Otter Rocks, 1993

LOCATION
Maryland Zoo in Baltimore, 3100 Auchentoroly
Terrace, Schaefer Plaza

SCULPTOR
Bart Walter (b. 1958)

MEDIUM
Bronze and concrete

DONOR
Maryland Zoological Society

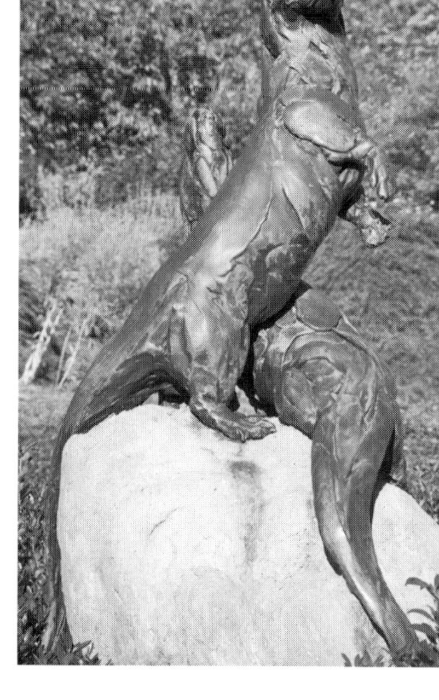

The Maryland Zoo in Baltimore (formerly the Baltimore Zoo) is the third oldest in the country, opening in 1876. Today its 167-acre campus is home to more than fifteen hundred animals. This sculpture by Bart Walter was installed as part of the new entrance plaza, named for the former mayor of Baltimore and governor of Maryland, William Donald Schaefer.

Although the circular pool of water into which visitors threw coins no longer exists, the three river otters still attract their share of attention as they appear to play on several large concrete rocks. Walter has captured a playful moment in their day: two of the river otters become intertwined as they scramble up one of the taller rocks to look off into the distance, and the third otter looks in the direction of what was the pool, where now shrubs are planted. *Otter Rocks* is the result of Walter's combining two previously independent sculptures, *Entwined* (the pair of river otters) and *Fluid Motion* (the single otter below).

Walter developed a signature surface for his sculpture, and it is in evidence here. After developing the concept, he builds an armature of metal pipe, rebar, aluminum wire, and foam, over which he applies an initial layer of clay to establish the form and mass of the figure. Assistants may participate in this process. Then Walter adds layer upon layer of his signature slabs of clay to develop the final surface. A mold is then made, and the piece is cast in bronze at a foundry. The environment is then created, and each bronze figure is pinned into its base.

The Maryland Zoological Society subsequently decided to commission other sculptures from Walter for installation around the zoo. His life-size *Mountain Silverback Gorilla* is in the Chimpanzee Forest, and his *Polar Bear* is in the Polar Bear Watch. Soon to be installed are seven more sculptures: *Ostrich Trio, Two Hunting Lionesses, Grooming Cheetah, Reclining Cheetah, Coiled Snake, Singing Toad,* and *Humble Toad.* These commissions were proposed in the strategic plan created in 2003 under then director Roger Birkel and the zoo's master-plan team.

Although Walter also creates works that involve the human figure, such as his piece for Friends School (L10), he is best known for his animal sculpture, which has been widely exhibited and commissioned. In 2005 he completed his largest sculpture to date, for the town of Westminster, outside Denver, Colorado, titled *Wapiti Circle,* of five monumental elk that he studied and sketched in the Gallatin Mountains of Montana. Most often Walter studies the animals he sculpts on site, as he did for *Wild Imaginings,* a sculpture at the Monmouth County Library in Shrewsbury, New Jersey. For the library he sculpted a lion as a guardian and companion of a young boy, as imagined from children's literature. He traveled to Kenya to study and sketch the lions there.

M13

TITLE
Lions, ca. 1857

LOCATION
Maryland Zoo in Baltimore, 3100 Auchentoroly
Terrace, Schaefer Plaza

SCULPTOR
Unknown

MEDIUM
Cast iron

DONOR
City of Baltimore

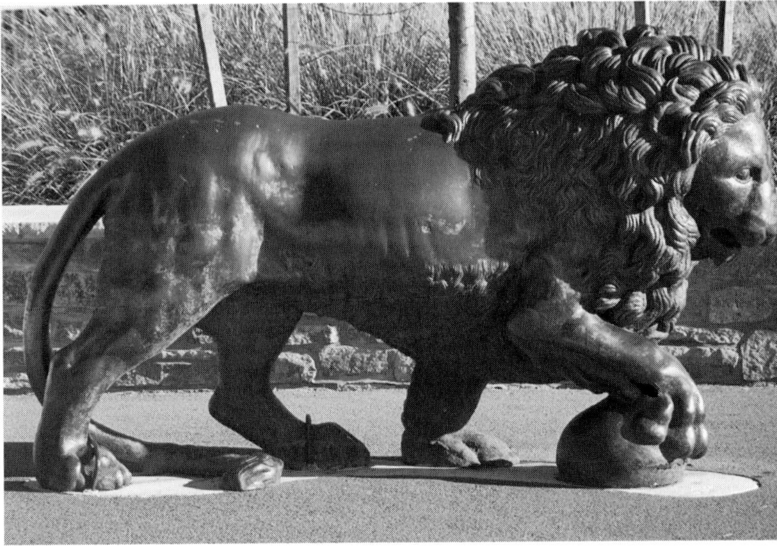

Two lions were cast in Russia at the request of Thomas Winans and shipped to Baltimore to be installed at the entrance to his new country house on the estate he named Crimea. The country house was built between 1856 and 1857, after his in-town mansion, Alexandroff-sky, was completed in 1853, providing a possible date for the lions. Winans had recently returned from Russia, where he and his brother had been involved in building Russia's first railroad, between St. Petersburg and Moscow. (See J4–J5 for a biography of Thomas Winans and a discussion of his art collection.)

Almost a century later, the city purchased the Winans estate, in two parcels, the first in 1942 and the second in 1948. The second parcel included the country house and several pieces of sculpture, which were then distributed around the city by the Department of Recreation and Parks acting as agent. Sculpture went to the Baltimore Museum of Art (J4–J5), the Evergreen Museum and Library (L8–L9), and the Baltimore Zoo (today the Maryland Zoo in Baltimore). Luckily for the city, the purchase of the land for development as a park allowed for the house to stand. Today it is home to the offices of the Parks and People Foundation.

It is likely that the lions, only one of which is shown here, arrived at the zoo in 1948, when two pieces arrived at the Baltimore Museum of Art and two pieces arrived at Evergreen. Today the two life-size, fierce-looking lions, standing 40 inches tall, greet visitors deep inside the entrance plaza, where they are surrounded by a rubberized surface so that children can climb on their backs.

"

M14

TITLE
Boy with Goose, 1851 copy of a 2nd-century
BC original

LOCATION
Maryland Zoo in Baltimore, 3100 Auchentoroly
Terrace, Children's Zoo

SCULPTOR
Unknown, after Boethus

MEDIUM
Bronze

DONOR
George Bartlett, Esq.

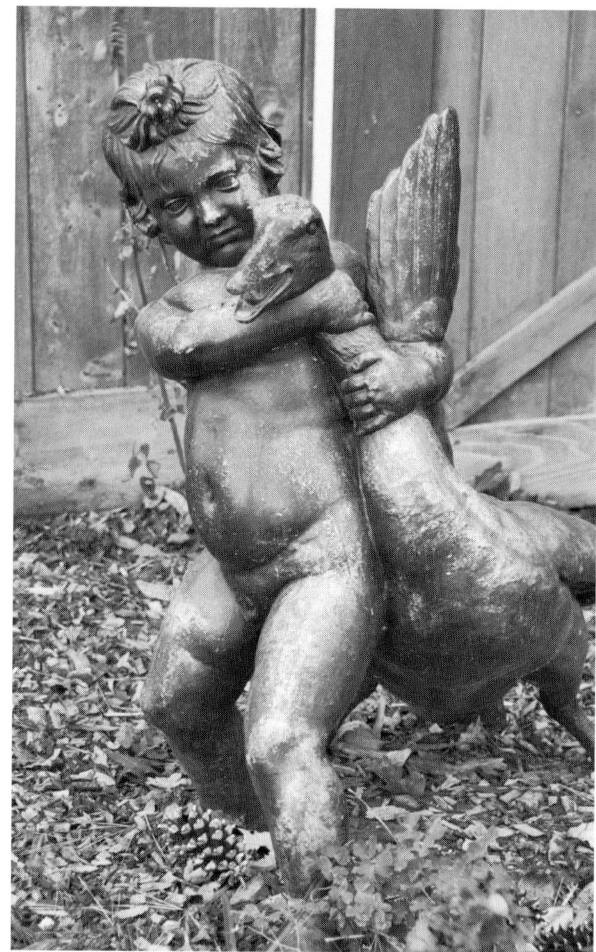

Boethus was a Greek sculptor from Chalcedon who is
thought to have been active during the second century
BC. He was noted for his representations of children,
and his original bronze sculpture of a young boy with a
goose was described in the writings of Pliny the Elder.
It is also known today through Roman copies. It was
a favorite subject, and many marble and bronze copies
were made. A marble copy is in the Louvre.

Boethus depicts the chubby boy, nude with curly
hair, struggling with a goose that is almost as big as he
is. In a very active pose, his feet wide apart but flat on
the ground, the boy wraps both his arms tightly around
the big bird's neck, either hugging or strangling it. That
he may at least inadvertently be strangling the goose is
suggested by the bird's open mouth as he appears to be
gasping for air.

Geese were often found around Greek houses. They
were considered model companions for housewives and
for children, occupying a position similar to that of the
domestic cat in modern households.

The inscription at the rear of the base of the sculpture, "A. BUJAC / PARIS / 1851," probably refers to the
foundry. Inscribed around the edge of the base is the
name of the donor but no date. It may have been given
to the zoo in 1966. The piece was sited in Druid Hill
Park until it was moved into the zoo, where it can be
seen in the Children's Zoo, near the entrance to the
Meeting Barn.

M15

TITLE
John Daniel II Gorilla, 1927

LOCATION
Maryland Zoo in Baltimore, 3100 Auchentoroly
Terrace, African Journey

SCULPTOR
Valerie Harrisse Walter (1892–1984)

MEDIUM
Bronze

DONOR
Gift of the artist

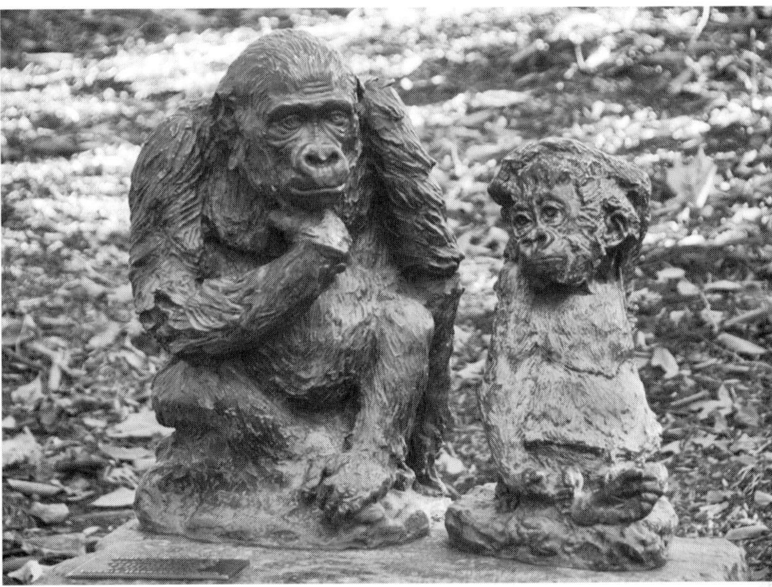

Valerie Harrisse Walter presented this small sculpture of two gorillas to Arthur Watson, the first director of the Baltimore Zoo (today the Maryland Zoo in Baltimore) sometime after his tenure began in 1948, and he kept it on his desk. When Roger Birkel arrived as the new director in 1995, he decided that it should be sited outdoors. It has recently been re-sited along the walk through the Chimpanzee Forest.

Born in Baltimore, Walter studied at the Art Students League in New York City and then returned to Baltimore to attend the Rinehart School of Sculpture at the Maryland Institute, graduating in 1917. Her sculpture was exhibited at the Corcoran Gallery in Washington, D.C., the Detroit Institute of Art, the Pennsylvania Academy of Art in Philadelphia, the Seattle Museum of Art, and the Whitney in New York City. Walter was fascinated with gorillas and sculpted them from life. These small gorillas were among the many she sculpted throughout her career.

The gorilla on the left is a portrait of John Daniel II when he was about three years old and weighed about 80 pounds. He is shown sitting on his crossed legs with his right hand under his chin. His left arm rests on the ground behind him. The smaller gorilla sits on his right foot and wraps his left arm over and around his head. His left foot is out in front of his body, and his right hand is cupped in his lap. The sculpture is listed in the catalog of an exhibition of the Society of Washington Artists held at the Corcoran Gallery of Art in 1934. The catalog entry states that John Daniel II was from French West Africa and was modeled from life.

M16

TITLE

Untitled, 1995–1997

LOCATION

William S. Baer School, 2001 N. Warwick Avenue

SCULPTOR

Peter Otfinoski (b. 1951)

MEDIA

Metal, wood, and found objects

DONOR

Baltimore Marine Center

Driving along Gwynns Falls Parkway, it is hard to miss the unusual sculptures that dot the landscape of the William S. Baer School, at the corner of Warwick Avenue. Upon closer inspection, it becomes clear that the sculptures, the likes of which have never been seen at any other public school in Baltimore, are of musicians holding their instruments and athletes with their sports equipment. Where did they come from, and how did they end up here?

Peter Otfinoski, an outsider artist from Loxahatchee, Florida, made the more than twenty sculptures found here. An outsider artist is someone working outside the fine-art system of schools, galleries, and museums, who produces works of extreme individuality, and inventiveness that owe nothing to tradition or fashion—like work found at the American Visionary Art Museum on Key Highway. The figures on the grounds here are primarily musicians and athletes. Among the figures are what appear to be a musical quartet and a group of jazz musicians, as well as a football player, a basketball player, and a golfer, made of hammered metal over very similarly constructed wooden forms that are individualized with paint and found objects. Soldering wire is used for the eyebrows, and metal tubes for the eyes. Almost everything about these whimsical figures—their heads, their bodies, their legs and feet—is flattened, abstracted, and rectangular, and yet each is unique and in character.

In 1997 these sculptures were installed along the Promenade of the Baltimore Marine Center. The sculptures had been commissioned by My Daddy's Gallery, in Owings Mills, from which they were purchased by the developers of the marine center. In 2004, after the marine center was expanded to include new homes, the sculptures were donated to the William S. Baer School, a city public school that provides education and therapeutic services to students aged 3–21 with multiple disabilities and health impairments and to students aged 3–5 without disabilities in a reverse-inclusion model program. The sculptures have been integrated throughout the school building, near the swimming pool, outside the kitchen, in the butterfly garden, and around an interior courtyard, as well as outside on the school grounds.

Several of the sculptures were vandalized while at the marine center and have been restored by Jack McWilliams. Most often it was an instrument or a piece of sports equipment that was missing. McWilliams also reinstalled each sculpture in a garden setting designed and planted at the school by his colleagues at Maxalea, the company he owns.

Otfinoski was born on a small farm in Middletown, Connecticut. Trained as a social worker and self-taught as an artist, he learned how to weld metal by watching his uncles repair farm equipment. He began exhibiting his work in art fairs and festivals across the country.

In 1990, when he bought three acres of land in rural Loxahatchee, he began building his sculpture park, the Love Happiness Institute. Most of the stainless steel figures there were assembled from discarded restaurant kitchen equipment. That same year, he received a fellowship from the Pollock-Krasner Foundation, which awards grants to artists of recognizable artistic merit and demonstrable financial need who have worked professionally over a significant period of time. Seven of his sculptures have been purchased and installed in Leu Gardens, in Orlando, Florida, the first of many artworks by Florida artists that will be installed throughout the 50 acres of gardens.

M17

TITLE
Linear Growth Structure, 1968

LOCATION
Easterwood Recreation Center, 1530 Bentalou Street

SCULPTOR
E. Clifton Boudman (b. 1941)

MEDIUM
Painted steel

DONOR
Baltimore City Percent for Art program

What could Norman Carlberg, then director of the Rinehart School of Sculpture at the Maryland Institute, do when he was offered $3,000 to make three sculptures for three new recreation centers? Give these commissions to three of his graduate students? Exactly. Carlberg subcontracted these projects to three Rinehart students. The only piece that remains today is *Linear Growth Structure,* on the front lawn of the Easterwood Recreation Center.

The painted steel sculpture is very simple in concept. Eight steel pipes, each 3½ inches in diameter, rise up from a circular concrete footing. Each pipe loops on itself at its midpoint and then continues upward toward the sky at a slight outward angle. At the time of the commission there were no trees in front of the recre-ation center, and Boudman's idea was to give the center a tree—that is, his conceptual version of a tree.

The staff and the children at the recreation center have always appreciated the sculpture. Since there was never a plaque giving a title for the piece, the young children who played there nicknamed it the "What Knot," and all the sports teams from that recreation center are called the Easterwood What Knots.

Clifton Boudman was born in Bloomsburg, Pennsylvania, and received his BFA from Virginia Commonwealth University in Richmond, Virginia. After receiving his MFA from the Rinehart School in 1966, he moved to northern Maine, where he joined the faculty at the University of Maine at Presque Isle. He is a senior fine-arts professor there today.

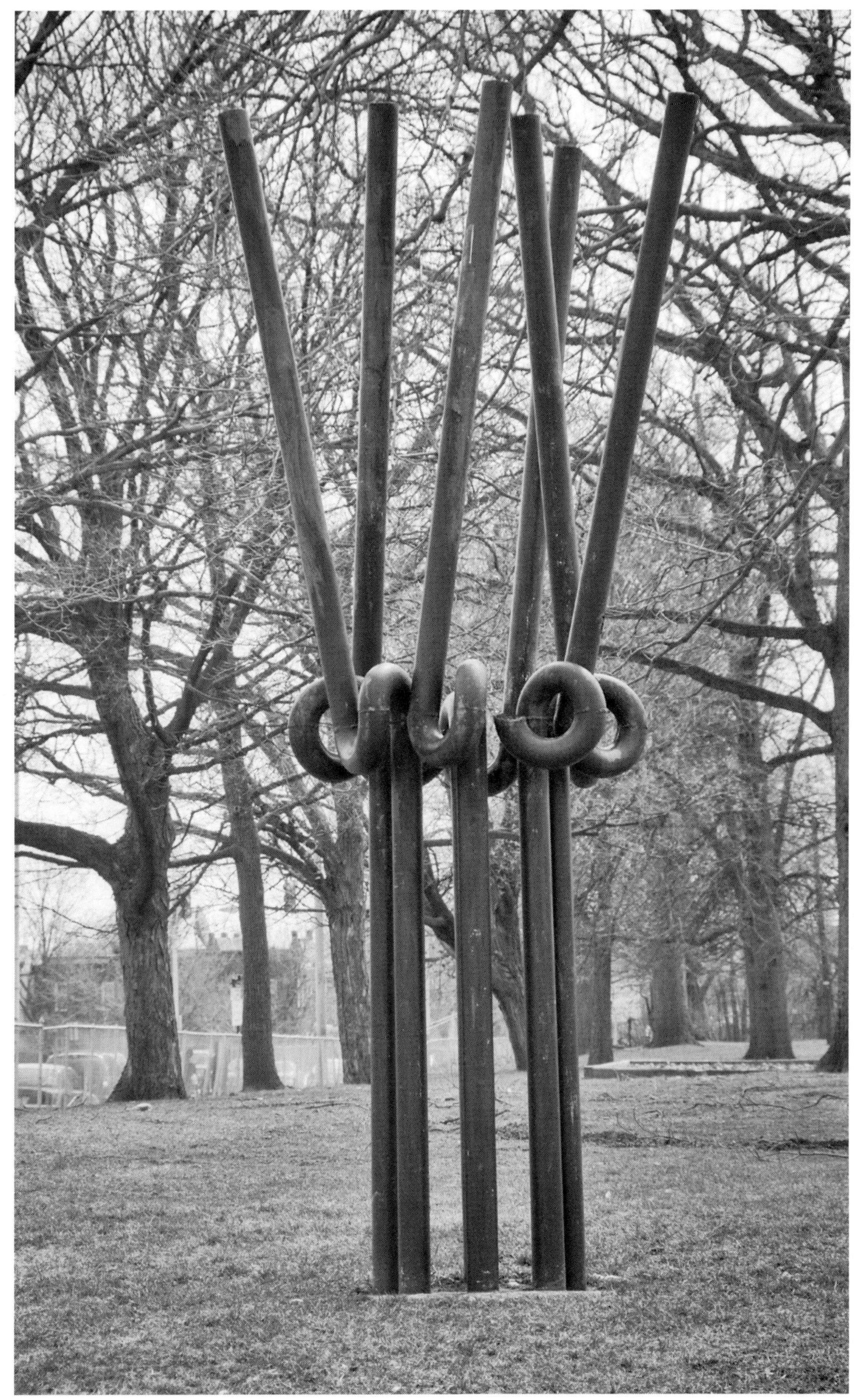

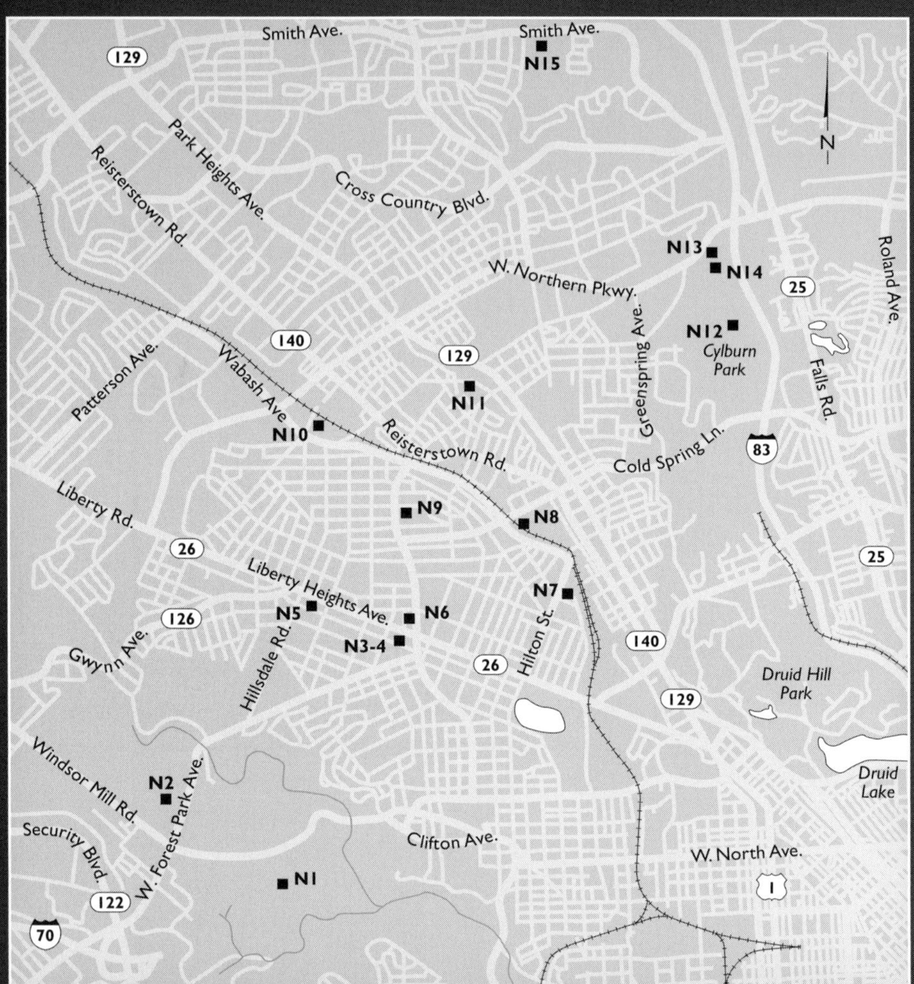

Smith Ave.
Smith Ave.
N15
129
Park Heights Ave.
Reisterstown Rd.
Cross Country Blvd.
N
N13
N14
W. Northern Pkwy.
25
Roland Ave.
140
N12
Cylburn Park
Greenspring Ave.
Falls Rd.
Patterson Ave.
Wabash Ave.
129
N11
83
N10
Reisterstown Rd.
Cold Spring Ln.
25
Liberty Rd.
N9
N8
26
Liberty Heights Ave.
N7
N5
N6
Hilton St.
126
N3-4
140
Gwynn Ave.
26
129
Hillsdale Rd.
Druid Hill Park
Windsor Mill Rd.
N2
W. Forest Park Ave.
Clifton Ave.
Druid Lake
Security Blvd.
N1
W. North Ave.
122
1
70

NORTHWEST BALTIMORE

Driving

N1

TITLE
Bird in a Tree, 1989

LOCATION
Carrie Murray Nature Center, 1901 Ridgetop Road

SCULPTOR
William F. Duffy (b. 1953)

MEDIUM
Painted steel

DONOR
Baltimore City Percent for Art program

William Duffy was commissioned by the architect William F. Kirwin to create two pieces of sculpture for the grounds around the Carrie Murray Nature Center.

Established in the late 1980s through a generous donation from the former Orioles player and Baseball Hall of Famer Eddie Murray, the nature center is named for his mother. Visitors are welcomed to the center year-round to learn about thousands of animals and insects native to Baltimore. It is a place where permanently injured birds of prey are rehabilitated and where an insect zoo with indigenous and exotic species is housed.

Bird in a Tree was installed beside the drive leading into the nature center's campus. It is made of forged steel. Within a square frame supported above a concrete base by two 2-foot steel posts are two birds perched on curving branches covered in leaves. It is not a realistic scene: the stylized birds, painted pink and blue, do not represent a particular species, and even though the leaves are pale green, they too are stylized. A second piece of sculpture commissioned from Duffy for the site, *Boy Releasing a Bird,* is no longer on view.

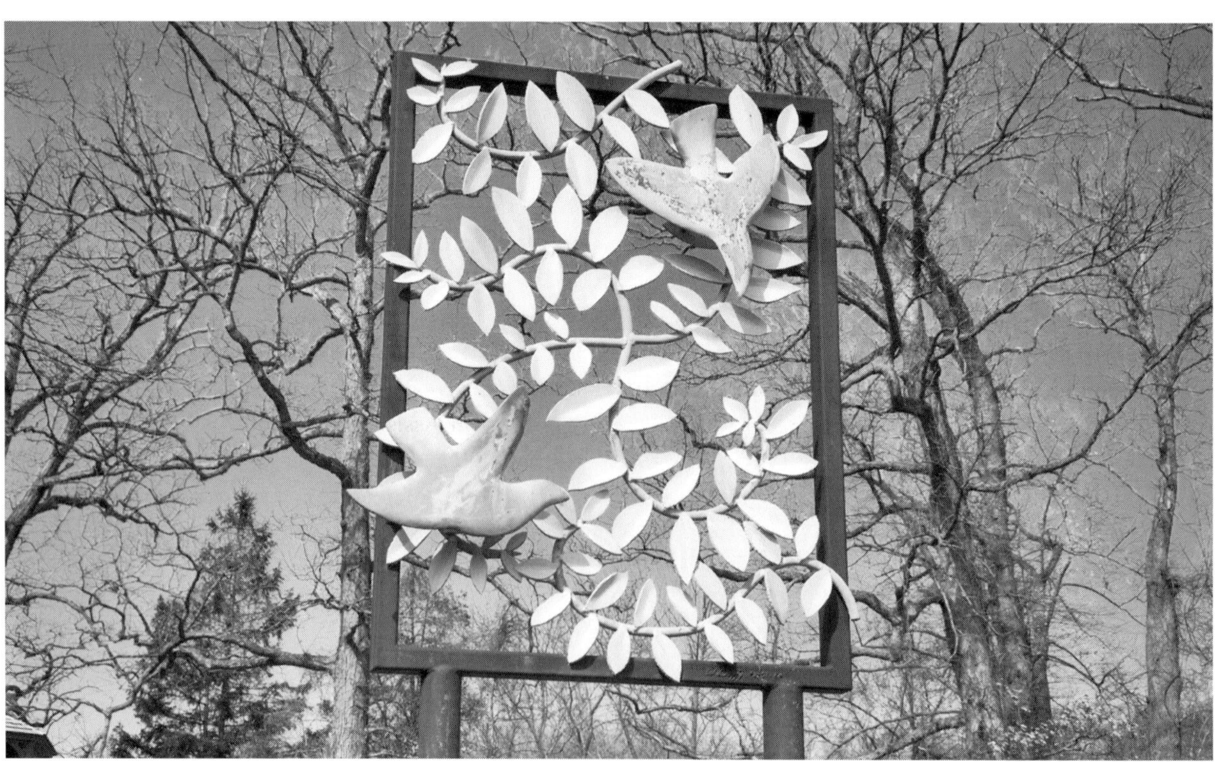

TITLE
St. Francis of Assisi, 1937

LOCATION
James Lawrence Kernan Hospital,
2200 Kernan Drive

SCULPTOR
Henry Berge (1908–1998)

MEDIUM
Concrete

DONOR
Arundell Club

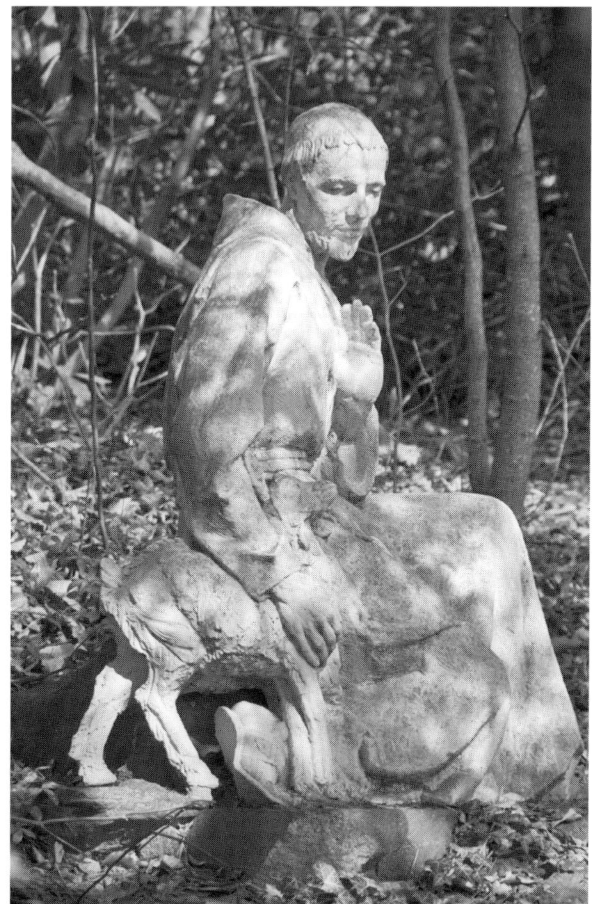

On the grounds of the Kernan Hospital, behind the mansion building, nestled in among the mountain laurel and rhododendrons, is a statue of St. Francis by Henry Berge.

St. Francis is shown seated on a rock, wearing the traditional hooded robe of the order he founded. His feet, protected in open sandals, are just visible below his full-length robe. The rope around his waist, one of the traditional attributes of St. Francis, has three knots, symbolizing the saint's three vows, of poverty, chastity, and obedience. This rope hangs down gracefully between his legs, which are clearly defined beneath the folds of his robe. The short, slender St. Francis is shown with his head shaved and with the beard he is known to have worn in his older years. He embraces a young lamb, pulling it close to his side with his right arm, while the animal's legs remain planted on the ground. With his left hand open and held close to his chest, St. Francis appears to be blessing the animal.

Nearby there are two cast concrete benches for quiet meditation. A small dedication plaque attached to the back of the rock on which St. Francis sits is inscribed, "TRIBUTE OF APPRECIATION / ANNA M. GEARE / FIRST CHAIRMAN OF THE / ARUNDELL CLUB GARDEN SECTION / FOR HER EFFICIENT LEADERSHIP IN / GARDEN WORK." St. Francis is probably best known as the patron saint of animals, but he is also the patron of ecologists and flower growers. Berge has depicted St. Francis, who was born in Assisi and is probably the most beloved of all Catholic saints, as the gentle, humble man that he was, a friend and protector of animals who saw the presence of God in all things.

TITLES
Titan and *Harpie*, 1978

LOCATION
Liberty Elementary School and Recreation Center,
3901 Maine Avenue

SCULPTOR
Paul Daniel (b. 1950)

MEDIUM
Cor-Ten steel, galvanized steel, and stainless steel

DONOR
Baltimore City Percent for Art program

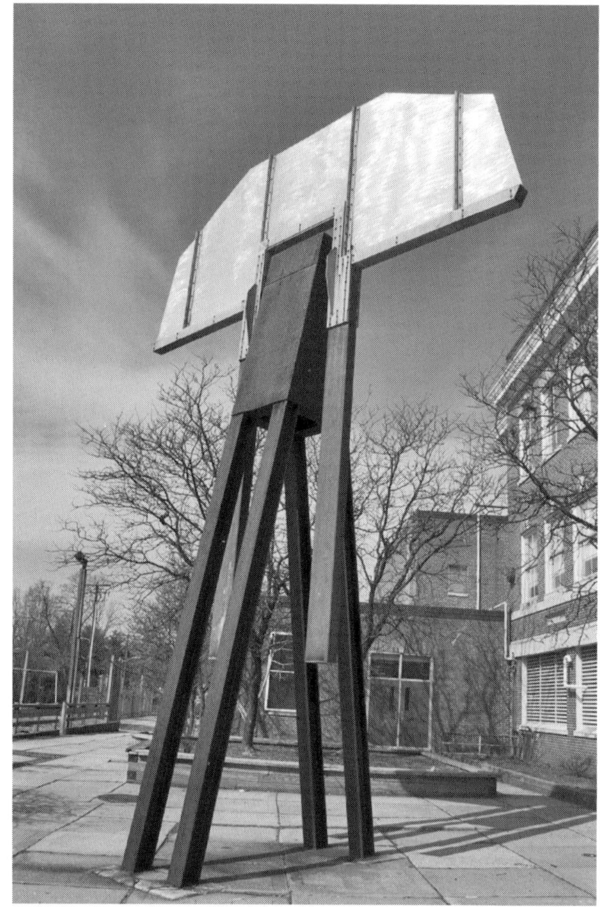

Paul Daniel's first two public art commissions were *Titan*, a monumental, freestanding, abstract sculpture, for the entrance plaza of this elementary school and *Harpie*, a smaller, wall-mounted piece for the adjoining recreation center. The commissions came through Donald B. Ratcliffe and Associates, the architects.

Daniel drew from Greek mythology to title his early sculptures. *Aeolus*, the name of the Greek god of the winds, was the title given to a large wind-driven piece of steel and canvas created in 1975 for temporary placement at the Baltimore-Washington International Airport. Here the title *Titan* makes clear reference to the Greek family of giants who sought to rule the heavens but were overthrown by the family of Zeus. Harpies were the spirits of sudden, sharp gusts of wind that hovered around entrances and sometimes snatched things and people from the earth for Zeus.

The 35-foot-high *Titan,* Daniel's largest piece to date, is made out of three types of steel—Cor-Ten, galvanized, and stainless. The four-footed vertical element that forms an A-frame is made of Cor-Ten steel that has weathered and turned a rich dark brown. A giant, 20-foot horizontal, galvanized frame, or "fin," with five panels of stainless steel is mounted on top of the Cor-Ten "pedestal" and rocks forward and backward, balanced by two pendulous, rectangular tubes that counterweight the fin.

Motion has always been an integral aspect of Daniel's work. *Harpie* is anchored high up on the front wall over the entrance to the recreation center. Like *Titan,*

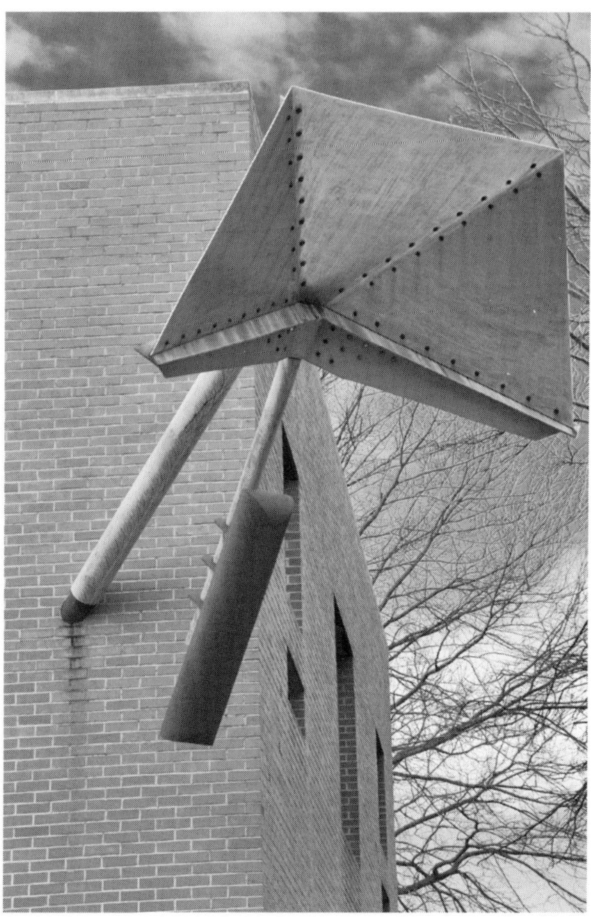

it is made of Cor-Ten, stainless, and galvanized steel and has a moving element. A fin of stainless steel is suspended on a galvanized steel shaft that is mounted on the building. The fin is balanced by a counterweight made of Cor-Ten steel that hangs from the fin and allows it to rock back and forth.

The recreation center faces Maine Avenue. The entrance to the elementary school can more easily be reached from W. Forest Park Avenue.

TITLE
Sea Birds, 1978

LOCATION
Calvin Rodwell Elementary School,
3501 Hillsdale Road

SCULPTOR
Norman Therrien (1935–2007)

MEDIUM
Bronze

DONOR
Baltimore City Percent for Art program

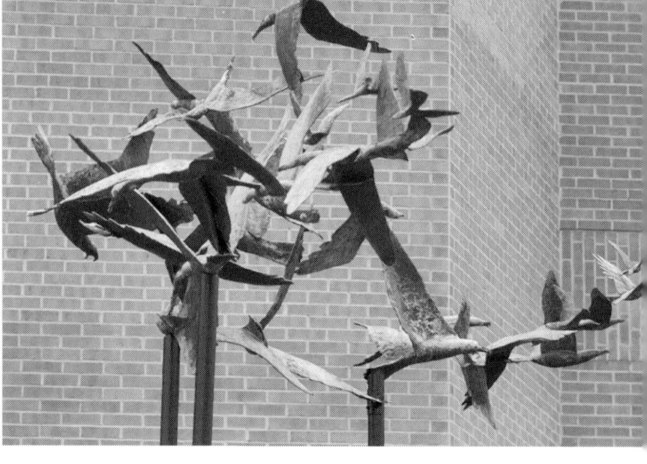

Calvin Rodwell Elementary School was completed in 1978, and Norman Therrien's sculpture was installed that same year.

Sited to the right of the stairs leading up to the main entrance to the school, the piece consists of some thirty birds, in three groups, mounted on three 8-foot steel poles in a configuration that suggests a flock in flight. The birds in each group are welded one to another, creating an expansive horizontal arrangement, and each group is welded to a pole. The birds in each cluster range in size, from very large to very small. Several smaller birds may be welded to one of the larger birds, whose extended wings may be supported by a steel brace to stabilize the wings and to help support more than one of the smaller attached birds.

Therrien had a studio and foundry in East Boothbay, Maine, where he cast this piece himself. He was familiar with the sea birds along the Atlantic coast and had previously made sculptures using cast bronze birds.

Therrien graduated from the Rinehart School of Sculpture at the Maryland Institute in 1963. He lived in Baltimore for many years before relocating to New Orleans. Roger Majorowicz, a colleague and friend of Therrien's, as well as a fellow Rinehart alumnus who had also received commissions through Baltimore's Percent for Art program, helped with the installation of this piece.

TITLE
The Rescue, 1992

LOCATION
Liberty Heights Fire Station,
3906 Liberty Heights Avenue

SCULPTOR
Lisa Kaslow (b. 1953)

MEDIUM
Painted steel

DONOR
Baltimore City Percent for Art program

This 17-foot-long relief sculpture is mounted across an exterior brick wall that extends from the west side of the fire station. Made of steel plate painted brown, the narrative of a series of rescues unfolds in four sections. The relief is a composite of photographic images of fire fighters at work that had appeared in newspapers over time. A plaque added to the wall after the relief was completed names two firefighters from Company 12, one killed in the line of duty on June 1, 1999, and one who received crippling injuries in the line of duty on July 6, 1989. It is stated on the plaque that the sculpture is in their honor, although not originally commissioned with that intent.

On the left is a fireman in his heavy, protective fire-fighting uniform—helmet, boots, jacket, and pants—handing a woman a baby who has been rescued from a burning house. Seen just behind this fireman and partially blocked by him is the Number 12 fire truck with its ladder raised, supporting a fireman who has climbed out to its terminus. The two central panels each depict three three-story row houses with their characteristic stoops. Hovering over the row houses is the fireman on the extended ladder. Nearby, another fireman stands on the rooftop. A third firefighter stands on a tall ladder set on the ground and leaning against a row house. The fourth panel is a fire engine with "E 40" on its front. Stylized, flat, and monochromatic, the relief is more descriptive than emotional.

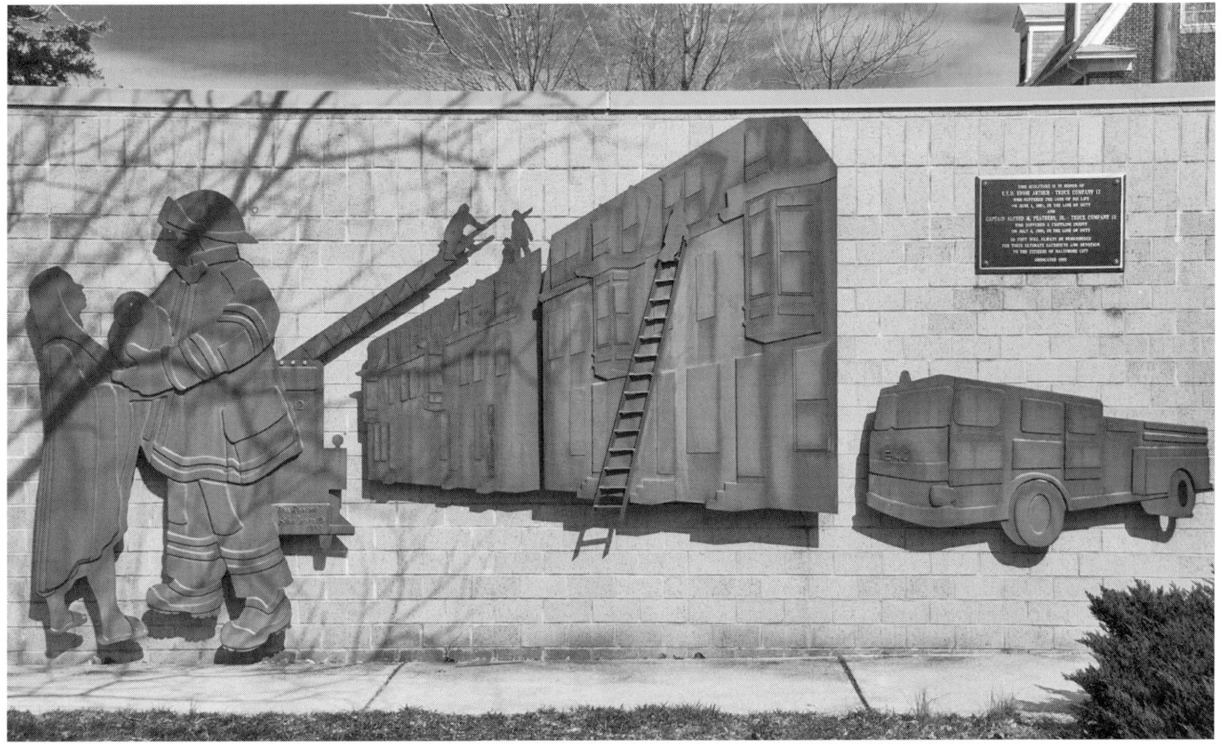

TITLE
Enlightenment, 1999

LOCATION
Dr. Nathan A. Pitts Ashburton Elementary-Middle School, 3935 Hilton Drive

SCULPTOR
William F. Duffy (b. 1953)

MEDIUM
Bronze

DONOR
Baltimore City Percent for Art program

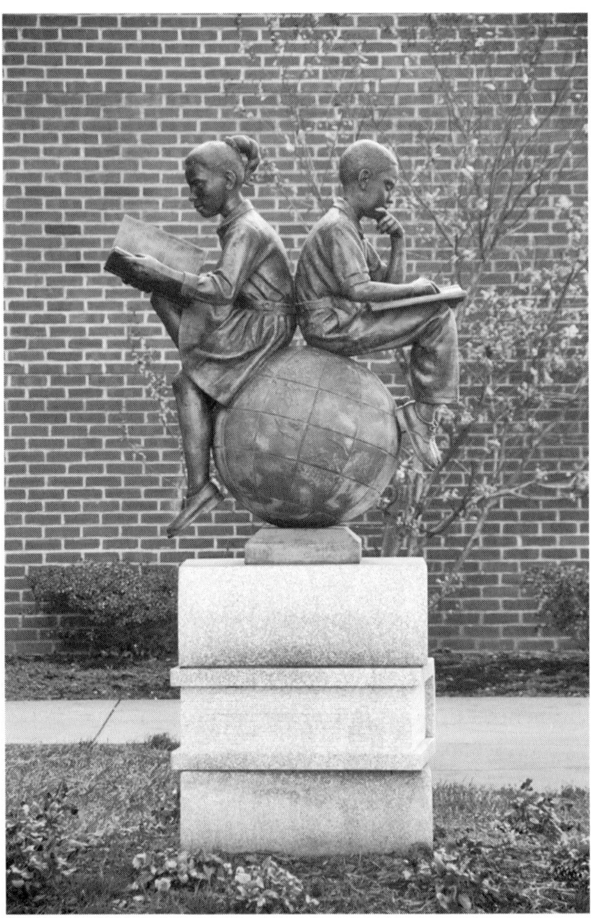

In 1997 Bill Duffy was commissioned to make a work of art for this newly renovated elementary school. He met with a neighborhood committee to discuss what their hopes were for the project. The members of the committee wanted the sculpture to include children who might be students at the school; they wanted it to be worldly, to reflect the idea of reading and learning; and they wanted it to include a reference to the school mascot, an eagle. The committee got everything it asked for.

Sited just beside the walk that leads to the front door of the school, *Enlightenment* depicts two young children, a boy and a girl, both dressed for school, seated back to back on a globe, each reading out of a large book. The two figures and the globe, cast in bronze, are mounted on three very large, stacked granite books. The students are concentrating, with their heads bowed slightly, as they peer into the books, apparently unaware of the eagle that stands on one side of the globe, between and below them. Before or after school, students can explore the continents, which are raised on the globe.

The students at the school got to participate in the creation of their sculpture. Duffy visited the school and took black-and-white photographs of many of them. The boy and girl in the sculpture are not based on two particular students; rather, he drew from the whole series of photographs he had taken.

TITLE
Cold Spring Outcrop, 1983

LOCATION
West Cold Spring Metro Station, Wabash Avenue
at Cold Spring Lane

SCULPTOR
Jim Sanborn (b. 1945)

MEDIUM
Sandstone

DONOR
Maryland Transit Administration

Jim Sanborn's sculpture has always been about elemental geological forces and natural processes that create volcanoes and earthquakes, lightning and tornadoes. Influenced by his study of archaeology and paleontology at Oxford University during his junior year abroad while attending Randolph-Macon College in Ashland, Virginia, he has sought to make visible these invisible forces of nature. He worked with concrete and steel in his early sculpture, an example of which is his *Patapsco River Project* in Cherry Hill Park (R4). On the basis of this early work, Sanborn was chosen by a panel of local arts professionals and practicing artists to create an artwork for one of the first nine metro stations.

Cold Spring Outcrop, or *Wabash Outcrop*, as it has sometimes been called, was one of the first pieces in which Sanborn used sandstone—here large, roughly cut blocks of richly colored stone meticulously stacked. Two separate elements, or "outcrops"—one tall and rectangular, the other lower and triangular—make up this abstract piece. No two blocks are the same size or shape, and there is a surprising range of colors—pink, orange, gold, purple, grey, and brown. The rectangular outcrop, which looks darker and redder, is composed of four vertical stacks of two stones each. The top edge of the upper stone in each stack has been cut at an angle. The triangular outcrop comprises eight stones, five set low to the ground on an angle and three larger stones set on an angle perpendicular to these three. Many of the

larger stones in this outcrop are silver. The title suggests that these stones were uncovered during construction of the new metro station. To encourage this interpretation, Sanborn set his sculpture directly on the ground.

Sanborn is a native of Washington, D.C. He earned his MFA from the Pratt Institute in New York in 1971 and returned to live and work in the D.C. area. While he has been commissioned to create many public monuments across the country, the piece that has received the most attention since it was installed in 1990 is *Kryptos*, his sculpture for the CIA's headquarters in Langley, Virginia, in which he carved an 865-character coded message into an undulating sheet of copper. In 2003 he was given a solo exhibition at the Corcoran Gallery of Art—Atomic Time: Pure Science and Seduction—made up entirely of works related to the development of the first atomic bomb in Los Alamos, New Mexico, in 1945.

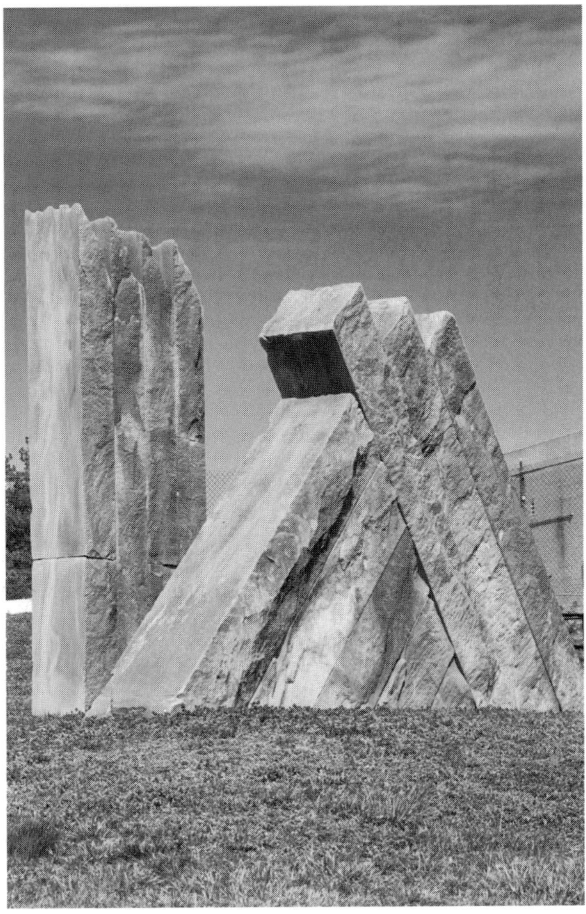

TITLE
Untitled, 1976

LOCATION
George W. F. McMechen Junior Senior School,
4411 Garrison Boulevard

SCULPTOR
William Leizman (b. 1926)

MEDIUM
Mayari-R steel

DONOR
Baltimore City Percent for Art program

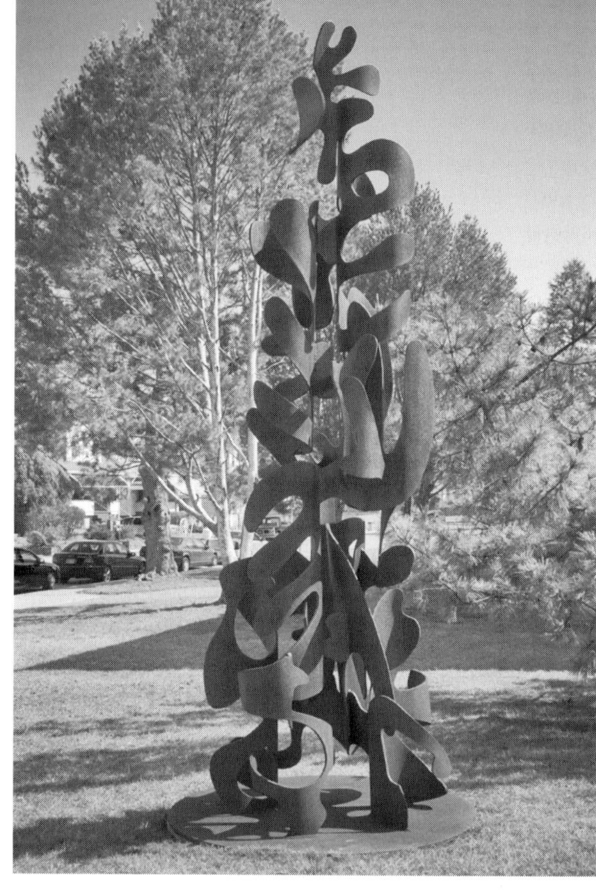

Over a period of eight years, from 1968 to 1976, William Leizman received commissions to create artwork for three public schools and one recreation center through the city's Percent for Art program. This sculpture, which was the last of these, is closely related to his pieces at Rognell Heights Elementary School (Q5) and Cahill Recreation Center (Q3) and foreshadows the last piece he completed for the city, the windscreen at Pennsylvania Station, in 1978 (F5). He created a very consistent body of work.

Leizman's sculptures are abstract, and all made of the weathering steel produced locally at the Bethlehem Steel Company. For each piece, this Mayari-R steel was cut and rolled, and then the pieces were welded or bolted together to create a dramatic verticality or a sweeping horizontal gesture.

This untitled piece has a marked verticality. Narrowing as it rises from a circular base plate, the piece reaches 14½ feet into the air, the cut and rolled sections welded together and stacked around a central axis. The curvilinear edges and cutout shapes create an interesting silhouette against the school and the sky.

The architectural firm Tarter & Kelly built this special-needs school named for George W. F. McMechen (1871–1961), a member of the first class of what is today Morgan State University. McMechen graduated from Morgan in 1895 and attended Yale Law School, graduating in 1899. He established a law practice in Baltimore with W. Ashbie Hawkins in 1904. In 1944 he was appointed to the board of school commissioners, its first African American member.

Leizman's piece is sited near the Fernhill Avenue entrance to the school.

TITLE
Rogers Avenue, 1983

LOCATION
Rogers Avenue Metro Station, Rogers Avenue near Wabash Avenue

SCULPTOR
Greg Moring (b. 1949)

MEDIUM
Cor-Ten steel

DONOR
Maryland Transit Administration

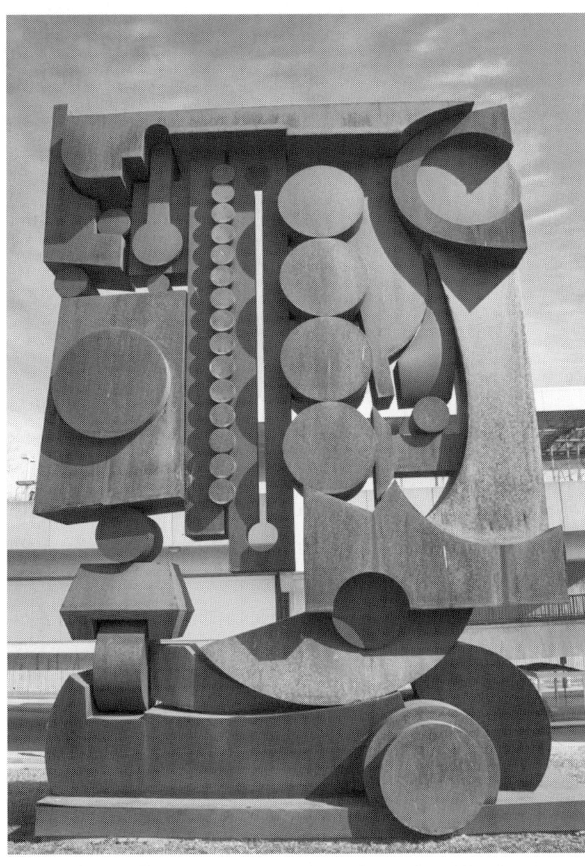

Always fascinated by the logical and visual beauty of machines, Greg Moring used shapes and patterns derived from machinery—gears, bolts, screws, bearings, bushings, seals, levers, fasteners, and drive belts—to design three public sculptures in Baltimore.

Rogers Avenue was the third and last piece in the series. The two earlier pieces are both reliefs. In 1978, using stainless steel, Moring clad an entire wall in the cafeteria at Liberty Elementary School to make it look as if the cover of some huge machine had been removed to reveal its inner workings. In 1981, for Edmondson-Westside High School, he again used the shapes drawn from machine components to suggest another complicated machine that might have worked had it not been spread across 30 feet of exterior wall and exposed for examination (Q6).

For the Rogers Avenue Metro Station, Moring seems to have taken a vertical section of his Edmondson-Westside relief, cut all the pieces out of Cor-Ten instead of the aluminum, and stacked them 19 feet high to make a three-dimensional, architectonic version of the earlier relief. In *Rogers Avenue*, the forms are heavier, more severe, and somewhat more abstracted but have the same "mechanicalness" about them, offering a more complex resolution of the challenge Moring set for himself a few years earlier at Liberty Elementary. The rich, dark brown surface of the Cor-Ten steel heightens the industrial feel of the piece.

TITLE
The Human Dance, 1977

LOCATION
Park West Health System, 3319 W. Belvedere Avenue

SCULPTOR
Nathaniel Mack

MEDIUM
Cor-Ten steel

DONOR
Baltimore City Percent for Art program

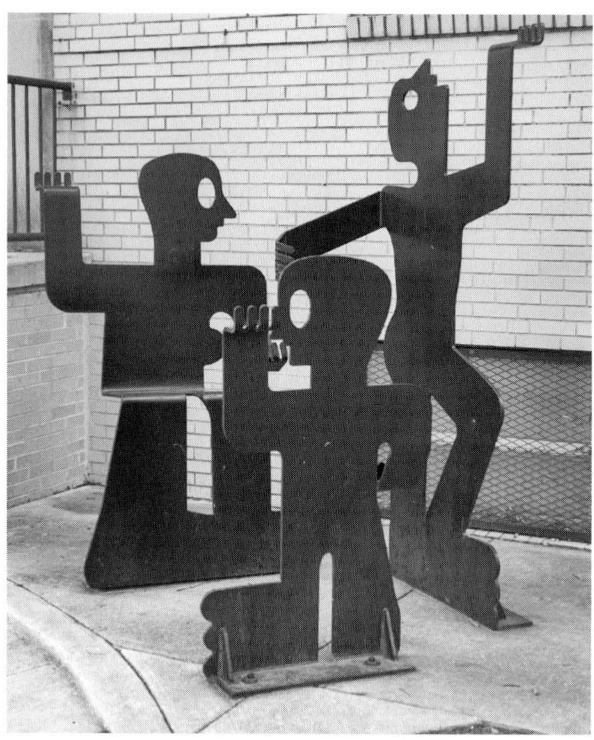

Nathaniel Mack was commissioned in 1976 to make a piece of sculpture for the Pimlico Multi-purpose Center. Now, some thirty years later, the facility is the Park West Health System, and the piece has been moved and reconfigured, and the naturally weathering Cor-Ten steel has been painted black.

Mack cut three very abstracted and stylized figures out of Cor-Ten steel and installed them in three very tight parallel planes close to th street on the sidewalk in front of the building. Originally, the figure of the child was placed between the male and female figures, his raised hand touching the male figure, behind him, and his lowered hand touching the female figure, in front of him. In this configuration, the male's extended arm fit over the shoulder of the female figure, and they were locked together.

Today, the three figures stand separately against the building near the entrance. The male figure stands between the other two figures, with the female figure to his left and the figure of the child to his right. The sense of family has been lessened, but the idea of a dance may have been accentuated.

N12

TITLE
Lions, date unknown

LOCATION
Cylburn Park, 4915 Greenspring Avenue

SCULPTOR
Unknown

MEDIU
Marble

DONOR
City of Baltimore

Four identical statues of lions decorate the grounds of Cylburn Park. Two are at the east entrance to Cylburn Mansion, and two mark the entrance to the perennial gardens. This is one of the pair of lions at the garden entrance.

The Victorian mansion that stands at the center of the park today was begun in 1863 by Jesse Tyson, a Baltimore businessman and importer, rich from the Bare Hills chrome mines inherited from his father. Construction on the home where he and his mother planned to spend their summers was interrupted by the Civil War, and it was not completed until 1869, by which time his mother had died. The house remained unfinished until 1888, when Tyson, then a 61-year-old bachelor, took a bride, the much younger Edyth Johns, a debutante of 19 years. They spent sixteen years together at Cylburn. Tyson died in 1906, and four years later Edyth married Major Bruce Cotton. The Cottons lived at Cylburn until her death in 1942, when the city purchased the 207-acre property from Cotton for a mere $42,300, with the promise that it would be turned into a park, which happened in 1954. Today the mansion serves as the city's horticultural headquarters and home of the Cylburn Arboretum Association.

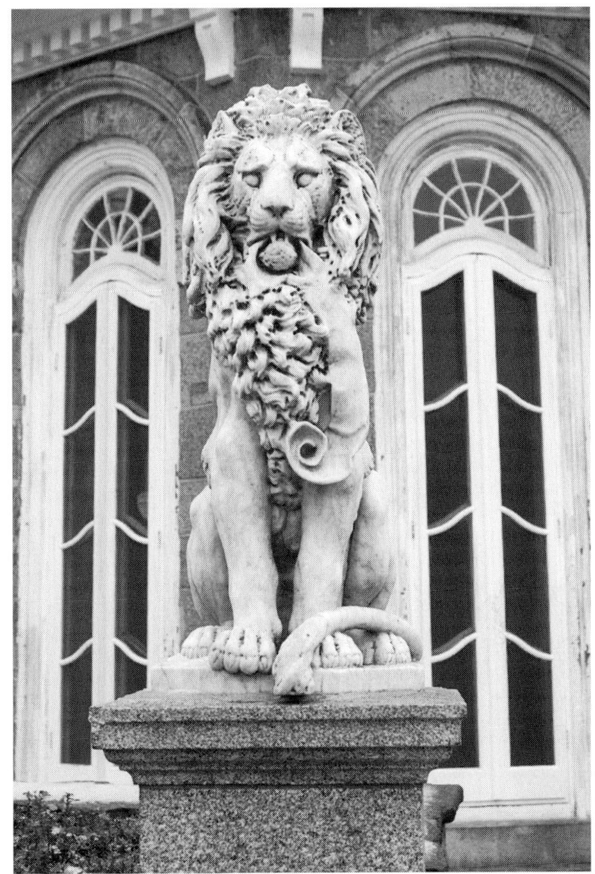

The lions probably date from the end of the construction period and may have been purchased on one of the Tysons' many trips abroad. They sit stiffly upright on their rear haunches, with their front feet placed firmly and their tails wrapped around and over their front left feet. They have a full mange of hair, very curly on the top of the head and down the chest. Each holds an unfurled scroll in its mouth.

TITLE
Lady Baltimore statues, 1880

LOCATION
Cylburn Park, 4915 Greenspring Avenue

SCULPTOR
Herman D. A. Henning (1841–1893)

MEDIUM
Limestone

DONOR
City of Baltimore

These two identical sculptures were originally part of a quartet of ladies that adorned the St. Paul Street Bridge from 1880, when the bridge was built, until 1960, when it was replaced. Three ladies were moved to Cylburn Park in 1974, and the fourth was sent as a gift to Baltimore, Ireland. In 1979 one of the three statues in Cylburn Park was re-sited in a green space along Mount Royal Terrace. The moves were necessitated by the development of the Jones Falls Expressway. (For the complete story of the four ladies, see I17.)

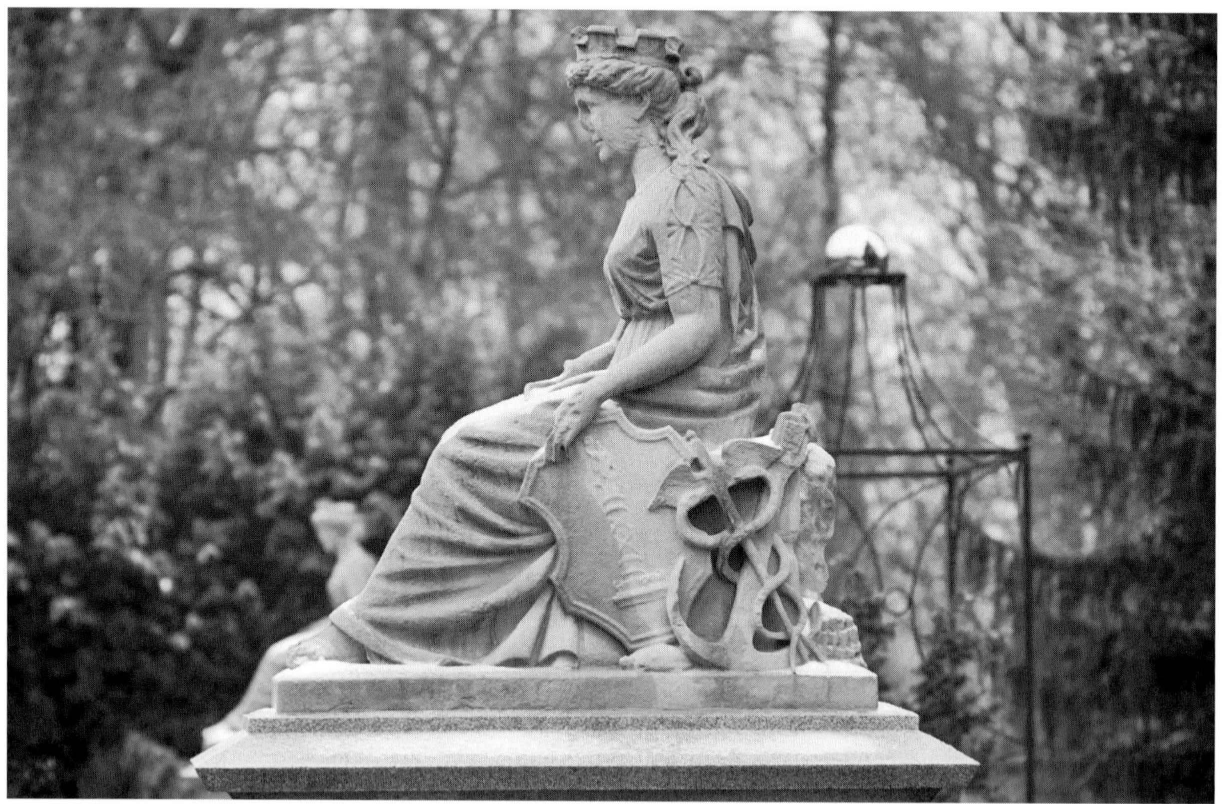

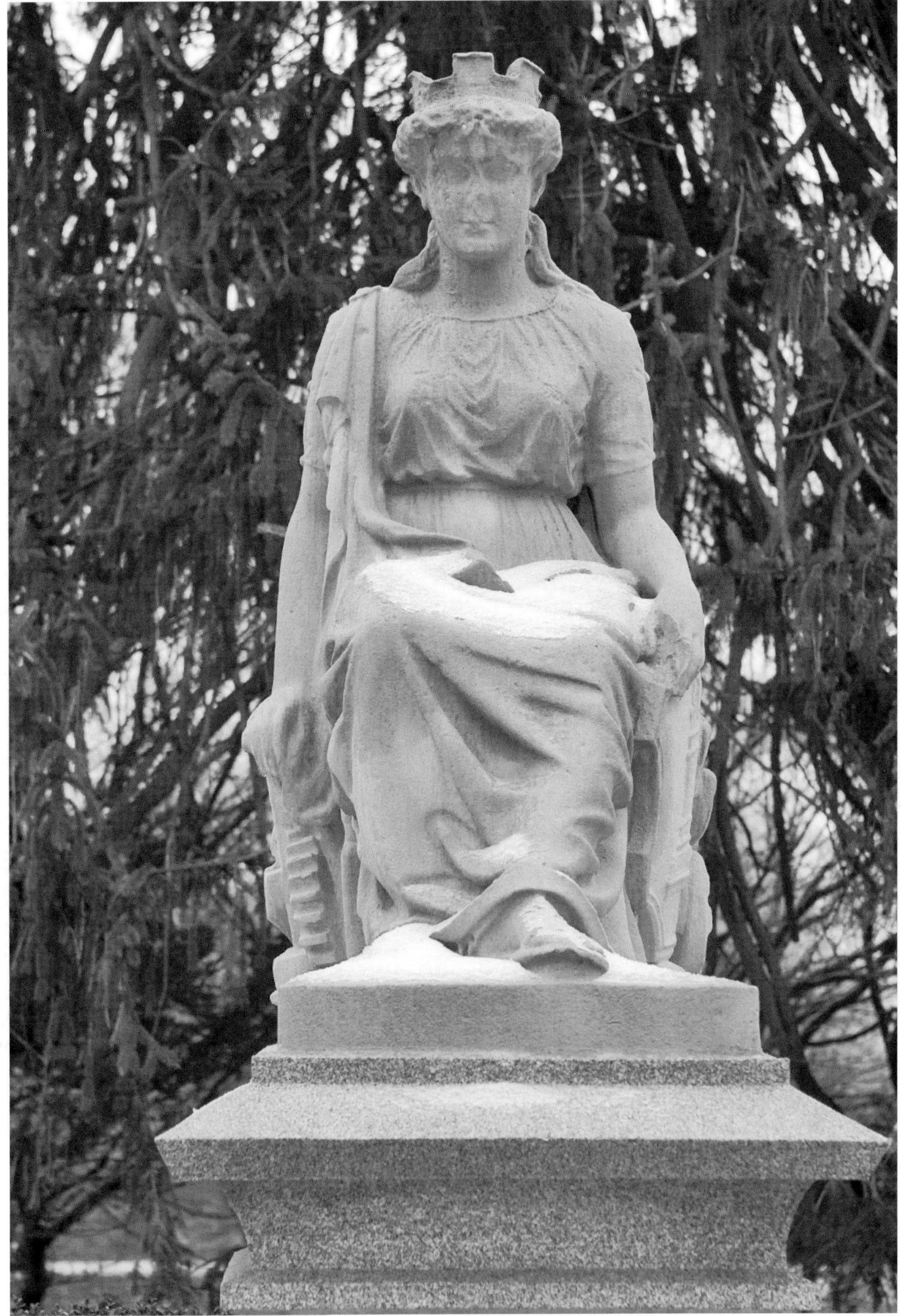

N15

TITLE
Nurturing Nature, 1997

LOCATION
Baltimore Clayworks, 5707 Smith Avenue

SCULPTOR
Supratman "Maman" Rikin (b. 1955)

MEDIA
Cement block, reinforced concrete, high-fired glazed
stoneware tiles, and stoneware

DONOR
Gift of the artist

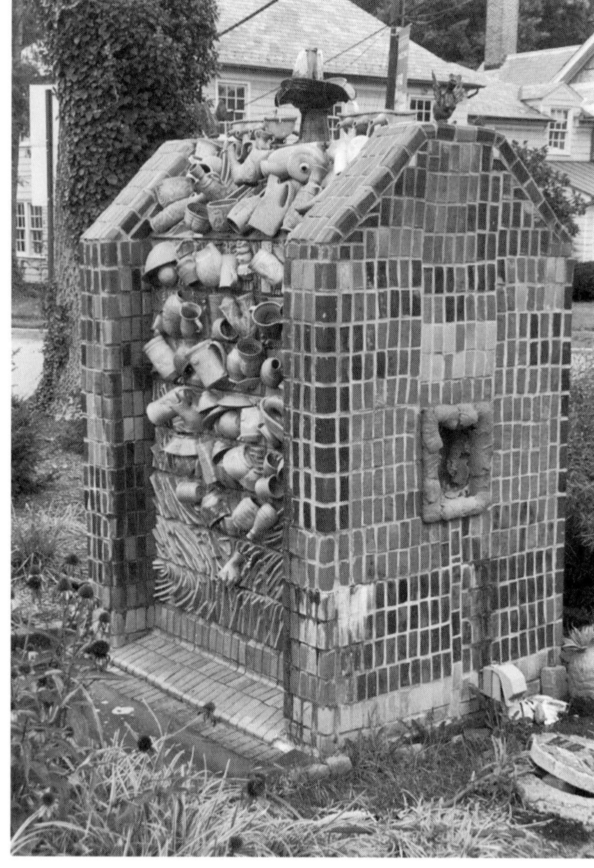

In 1991 Supratman Rikin, better known as Maman, arrived in Baltimore to begin a year-long fellowship at the Baltimore Clayworks. Maman had come to the United States from Indonesia for his education, studying first at the College of the Ozarks, near Branson, Missouri, and then at Pittsburg State University, in Pittsburg, Kansas, before completing an MFA at Southern Illinois University in Carbondale. After graduate school, he came directly to the Clayworks.

Located in Mt. Washington Village, the Baltimore Clayworks is a nonprofit ceramic art center that offers fellowships for visiting artists, teaches classes and conducts workshops, presents exhibitions, rents studio space, and sells clay art. It is an artist-centered community that offers an extraordinarily nurturing environment for visiting artists as well as for member artists and their students. After his fellowship year, Maman remained at the Clayworks for five years as a resident artist.

Grateful to the Clayworks, and in keeping with a tradition of making a work of art to leave behind as a marker of one's residency, Maman created the clay fountain at the corner of Smith Avenue and Greely Road, at the edge of the former Enoch Pratt Library branch site, which the Clayworks purchased when it opened in 1980. Drawing from the architectural forms of his culture, Maman drew from his memory of Buddhist temples like the ones in Bali and Java and set about emulating their structure and surface in his fountain. An 8-foot-high central rectangular cement block is framed at each end with two slightly taller and slightly wider walls covered with high-fired glazed tiles in various shades of blue. The two long facade-like surfaces between the end walls are covered with stoneware tiles to which vessels in various shapes and sizes are attached. Maman had asked every artist in residence at the time to make out of stoneware clay a vessel for collecting or pouring water or a bas-relief. Twenty-five artists contributed vessels and reliefs made specifically for the fountain. These vessel-covered walls, which are a beautiful camel color, are Maman's way of referencing the carvings on the facade of Borobudur, the ninth-century Buddhist monument on Java.

Water flows over these vessel-covered surfaces, over pots of all kinds—mugs, bowls, pitchers, teapots, planters, and jugs, sometimes winged. The system for carrying the water over the walls is simple and straightforward. Having built ponds as a hobby, Maman had had some experience with pumping and circulating water systems. Here the pump is installed underground, from where it pushes the water to the top of the fountain. The water comes out of the dark blue double-spouted vessel at the top and drizzles down over the vessel-covered sides of the fountain. On both sides, the water is directed to a vessel near the ground, held in two hands, where a spout empties water into the pool to be recycled. The TKF Foundation contributed a bench for

relaxing and contemplation and a journal for recording reflections. Jonna Lazarus, of Higgens-Lazarus, supervised the plantings.

Maman's title for his legacy piece at the Clayworks is meant to have multiple references. It refers, of course, to the nurturing effects of water on nature, as well as to the nurturing nature of an artists' collective like the Baltimore Clayworks. The title is also meant to highlight the specific nurturing Maman received during his years in residence, which included legal assistance during the process of becoming a permanent resident of the United States. Today Maman is an associate professor at the Community College of Baltimore County and lives in the Baltimore area.

Across the lawn from the fountain and nearer to the library building is a ceramic *Wart Hog* by Jo Schneider, made in the 1970s. Schneider was one of the first resident artists at the Clayworks in 1980. The *Wart Hog* came with her and has remained.

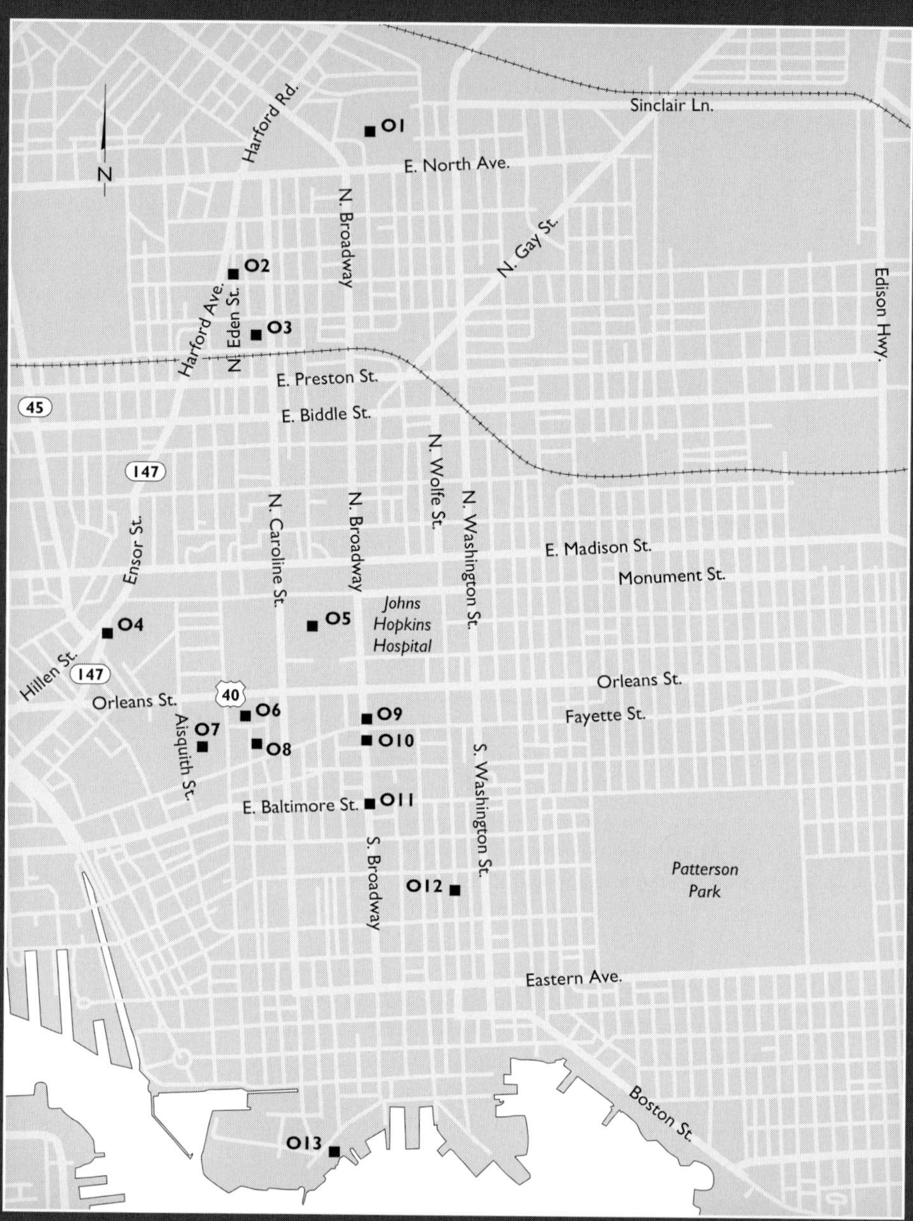

N
Sinclair Ln.
Harford Rd.
E. North Ave.
01
N. Broadway
N. Gay St.
Edison Hwy.
Harford Ave.
02
N. Eden St.
03
45
E. Preston St.
E. Biddle St.
147
N. Wolfe St.
N. Caroline St.
N. Broadway
N. Washington St.
E. Madison St.
Monument St.
Ensor St.
04
Johns Hopkins Hospital
05
Hillen St.
147
Orleans St.
40
Orleans St.
Fayette St.
Alsquith St.
07
06
09
08
010
S. Washington St.
E. Baltimore St.
011
S. Broadway
Patterson Park
012
Eastern Ave.
Boston St.
013

JOHNS HOPKINS HOSPITAL, WASHINGTON HILL, AND ENVIRONS SOUTH

Driving

TITLE
Solar Totem, 1975

LOCATION
Harford Heights Intermediate and Primary School, 1919 N. Broadway

SCULPTOR
Don Drumm (b. 1935)

MEDIUM
Cor-Ten steel

DONOR
Baltimore City Percent for Art program

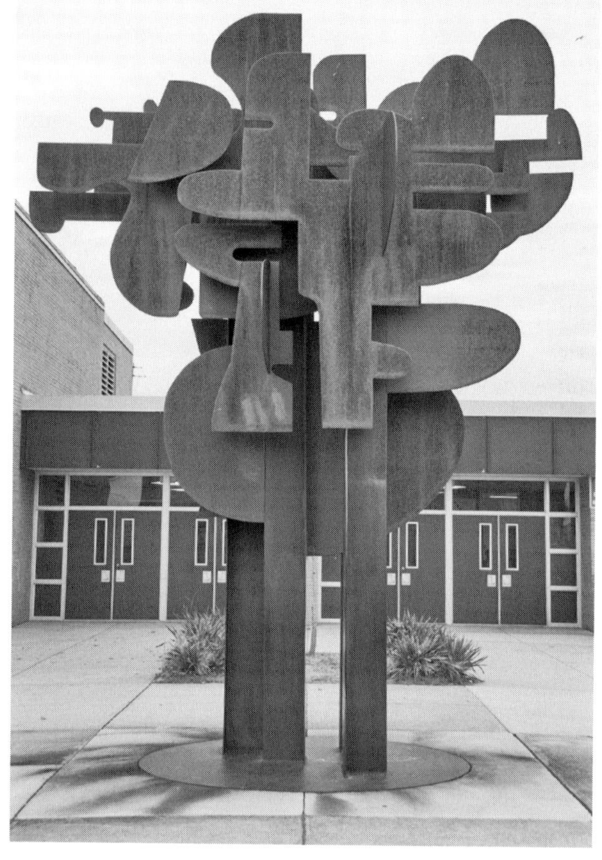

Dalton-Dalton-Little-Newport, an architectural and engineering firm based in Cleveland, Ohio, was hired to complete this new elementary school. The architects knew the work of sculptor Don Drumm, who was based in Akron, Ohio, and invited him to join their project in Baltimore. Drumm was asked to create a sculpture for the entrance plaza and to paint several murals inside, some of which he did with students from Lake Clifton Senior High School. Drumm dedicated the sculpture on the plaza to Martin Luther King.

Rising approximately 22 feet into the air from a circular Cor-Ten base that measures 8 feet in diameter and is embedded in the concrete plaza are four piers cut out of ¼ inch Cor-Ten plate steel. Welded to these four vertical piers is a towering series of curvilinear shapes in two planes that bisect each other. All of Drumm's work is abstract. He gave the title *Solar Totem* to several pieces of sculpture that were vertical and oriented to cast shadows as the sun passed overhead.

Drumm was born in Warren, Ohio. He received his BFA and his MFA from Kent State University in Kent, Ohio. In 1960 he opened his own sculpture studio near Akron, Ohio. In 1971 he expanded his studio to incorporate a gallery, and today he provides gallery facilities to more than five hundred artists and studio space to three resident artists. He was an artist-in-residence at Bowling Green State University, in Ohio, and taught at the Penland School of Crafts in North Carolina. His sculpture can be found on the campuses of Kent State, Bowling Green, and East Tennessee State University in Johnson City, at the Butler Institute of American Art in Youngstown, Ohio, the Akron Art Museum and the Columbus Museum of Art in Ohio, as well as in public places and private collections around Akron. One year after completing this piece, Drumm made a *Solar Totem* for Jack Orr Plaza in Miami, commissioned through the Miami-Dade Country Art in Public Places program.

O2

TITLE
Uni I, 1977

LOCATION
Oliver Multi-Purpose Center, 1601 N. Eden Street

SCULPTOR
Herbert Lee (b. 1949)

MEDIUM
Painted steel

DONOR
Baltimore City Percent for Art program

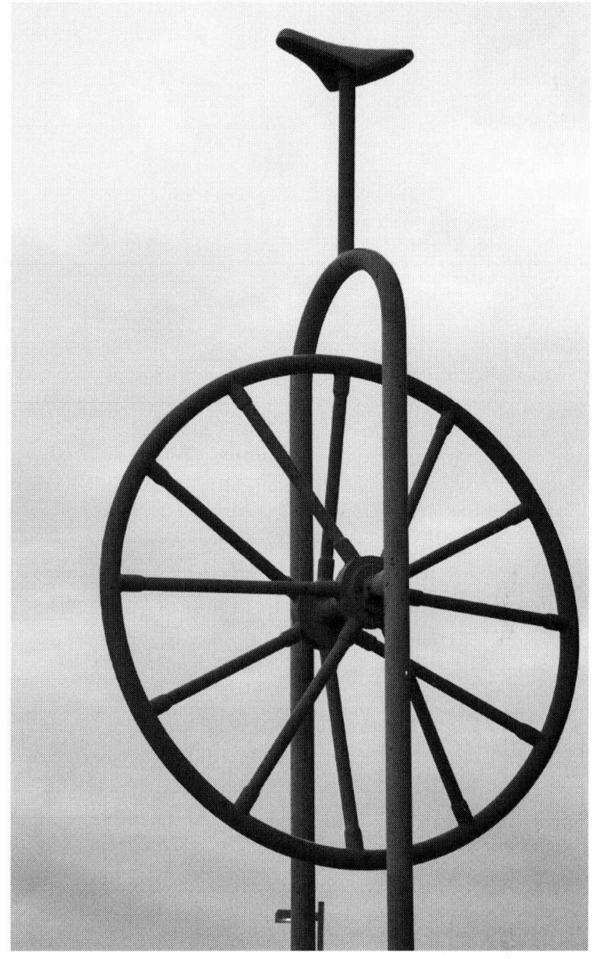

Herbert Lee's unconventional unicycle, which he hoped would become a symbol of unity and community, stands just outside the entrance to this community center. The unusually tall frame to which the seat and the wheel are attached reflects the rounded windows and doorway of the building. Twenty-two feet above the pavement, the yellow seat, which seems to float, is both inviting and intimidating. Something about the large single wheel, painted orange, suggests that riding this unicycle could be difficult for more reasons than its height: there are no peddles. One wonders who might ride this unicycle and with what extraordinary skills.

Lee received an undergraduate degree in art education in 1976 and an MA in studio arts in 1978 from Morgan State University in Baltimore. He was awarded a second Percent for Art commission for a sculpture at Edmondson-Westside High School, which remains his major work in Baltimore (Q7). For many years he divided his time between making art, teaching, and working at the Salvage Depot of the Commission for Historical and Architectural Preservation. Recycling architectural artifacts became his specialty. Today Lee is the project manager for technology wiring and infrastructure for the Baltimore City Public Schools.

03

TITLE
Pegasus, 1971

LOCATION
Dr. Bernard Harris Sr. Elementary School,
1400 N. Caroline Street

SCULPTOR
Roger Majorowicz (b. 1931)

MEDIA
Bronze and stainless steel

DONOR
Baltimore City Percent for Art program

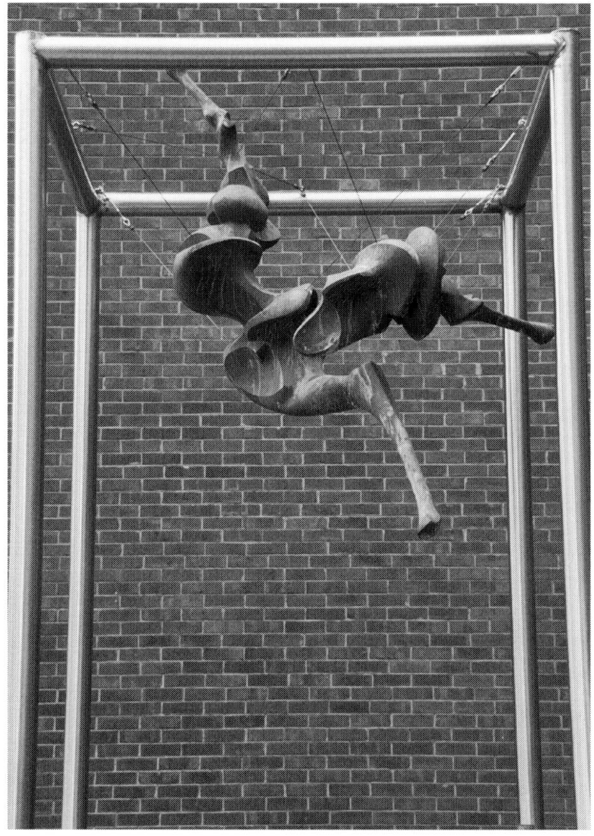

The stories from Greek mythology of Zeus, Athena, Poseidon, Medusa, Perseus, and Pegasus are all tied together in this one small bronze.

Zeus was the supreme ruler of Mount Olympus, where the Greek gods resided. Athena was the goddess of wisdom, war, the arts, industry, and justice, and Poseidon was the god of the sea. Perseus was the son of Zeus and Danae, and Medusa was a lovely young maiden. This particular drama began when Poseidon seduced Medusa in Athena's temple. Furious that her temple had been desecrated, Athena blamed Medusa and turned her into a Gorgon, a horrifying woman with snakes for hair who would turn all who looked at her into stone. King Polydectes wanted to marry Perseus' mother, Danae, against her wishes; to protect his mother, Perseus took up a challenge from the king to cut off Medusa's head and bring it to him, with the promise that if Perseus succeeded, Danae could do as she pleased. With the help of Athena, who gave Perseus Hermes' winged shoes so that he could fly to the land of the Gorgons and a reflective shield so that he would not have to look at Medusa, Perseus was successful. The moment he cut off Medusa's head, a winged horse sprang forth. The horse, Pegasus, who had been fathered by Poseidon, was stabled with Zeus' other steeds on Mount Olympus and given the task of carrying Zeus' thunderbolts. For his faithful service to Zeus, he was transformed into a constellation.

Here, suspended high in the air by stainless steel cables from the stainless steel tubing of a rectangular frame, is an abstract reference to a horse. There is the suggestion of a horse's legs attached to their hip joints and of a horse soaring toward the sky.

04

TITLE
Fireman Saving a Child, 1976

LOCATION
Oldtown Fire Station, 1100 Hillen Street

SCULPTOR
Joseph Sheppard (b. 1930)

MEDIUM
Bronze

DONOR
Baltimore City Percent for Art program

In this large relief, measuring 99 by 76 by 3 inches, Joseph Sheppard has succeeded in creating plenty of action and a real sense of drama.

The bronze relief on the entrance wall of the Oldtown Fire Station, which opened in 1974, depicts a fireman rescuing a young girl from a burning house. The fireman wears a heavy long coat, pants, and boots, as well as a helmet and an oxygen mask, which is attached to a tank strapped on his back. The fireman's ladder, leaning against the window of the burning house, creates a strong diagonal. The fireman descends backwards down the ladder with the young girl in his arms. The window frame, from which flames can be seen leaping, serves to mark one edge of the relief and makes reference to the larger burning house. Clouds of smoke billow out, engulfing the two figures and filling in the background of the relief.

Sheppard signed and dated the relief along its lower edge.

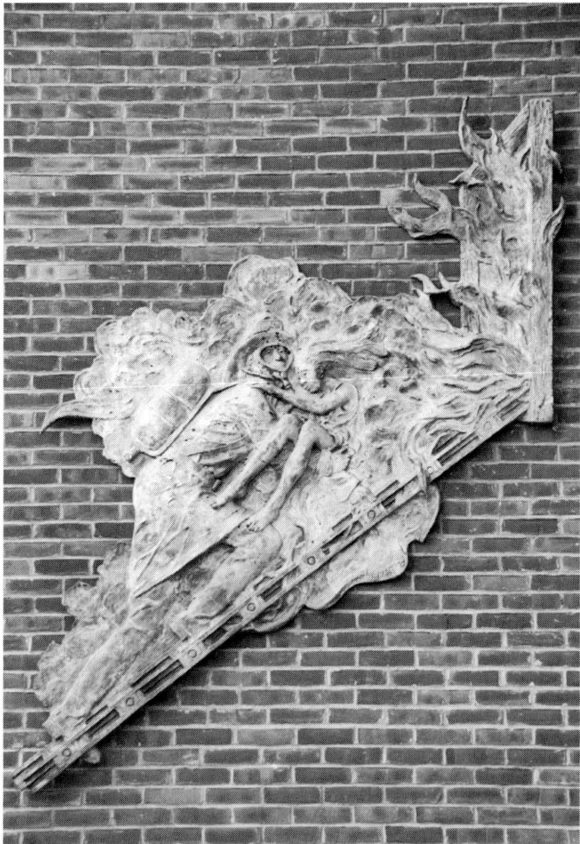

O5

TITLE
Great Ascension, 1983–1984

LOCATION
Johns Hopkins Hospital Outpatient Center,
601 N. Caroline Street

SCULPTOR
Beverly Pepper (b. 1922)

MEDIUM
Painted steel

DONORS
Ryda H. and Robert H. Levi

This large painted steel sculpture was given to the Johns Hopkins Hospital by Mr. and Mrs. Robert H. Levi in 1984 to honor the upcoming centennial of the hospital, celebrated in 1989.

The piece is composed of two triangular forms, both painted white, one long, obtuse triangle, with one angle greater than 90°, and one acute triangle, in which all the angles measure less than 90°. The elongated obtuse triangle rests against the top of the taller, more compact acute triangle. The primary view of the sculpture when it was in its original site, at the hospital's main entrance off Wolfe Street, was from the low end of the long obtuse triangle across its 59-foot length as it rises to rest on the 15-foot-high peak of the acute triangle at the opposite end of the entrance plaza. The soaring steel form energized and activated the space and expressed visually the ideas implied in the title.

Beverly Pepper's stated goal is always to try and relate her work to the lives of the people who will use the space while being mindful of the architectural context. When this work was first installed at the hospital, it was surrounded by brightly colored flowering plants that were changed every season. The white abstract angular sculpture could be seen soaring dramatically from the street toward the hospital entrance, raising spirits and inspiring all who passed there. Today the sculpture has been moved to the other side of the hospital campus, in front of the Outpatient Center.

Pepper is a world-renowned sculptor who was born in New York City and began her artistic career as a painter, studying at the Pratt Institute and the Art Students League in New York City and with Fernand Léger and André L'hote in Paris. It wasn't until 1960 that she began making sculpture. Today her work can be seen in public places across the country and in Europe. One of her earliest major works was a U.S. General Services Administration commission for the San Diego Federal Building in 1975. Current projects include a site-specific sculpture for the Frederik Meijer Gardens and Sculpture Park in Grand Rapids, Michigan, and a fountain for Terni, Italy. Her work has been included in numerous exhibitions, including one-person shows at the Metropolitan Museum in New York City, the Brooklyn Museum of Art, the Albright-Knox Art Gallery in Buffalo, New York, and the San Francisco Museum of Art and in museums and galleries throughout Europe, and she is represented in major public and private collections throughout the world.

In 1975 Robert and Ryda Levi gave the Johns Hopkins University a piece of sculpture, *Centennial,* by David Lee Brown, in honor of the university's centennial, to be celebrated the following year. Robert Levi was a 1937 graduate of the university and later a trustee. *Centennial* stood outdoors for twenty-five years, in the Upper Quad, just outside the Eisenhower Library. In 2002 it was moved inside the library. (For more biographical information on the Levis, see J11.)

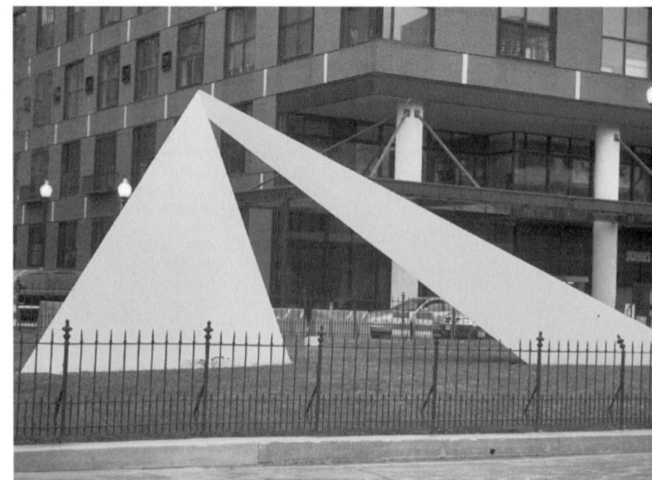

TITLE
Paestum, 1968

LOCATION
Enoch Pratt Free Library, Orleans Street branch,
1303 Orleans Street

SCULPTOR
Roger L. Majorowicz (b. 1931)

MEDIUM
Bronze and stainless steel

DONOR
Baltimore City Percent for Art program

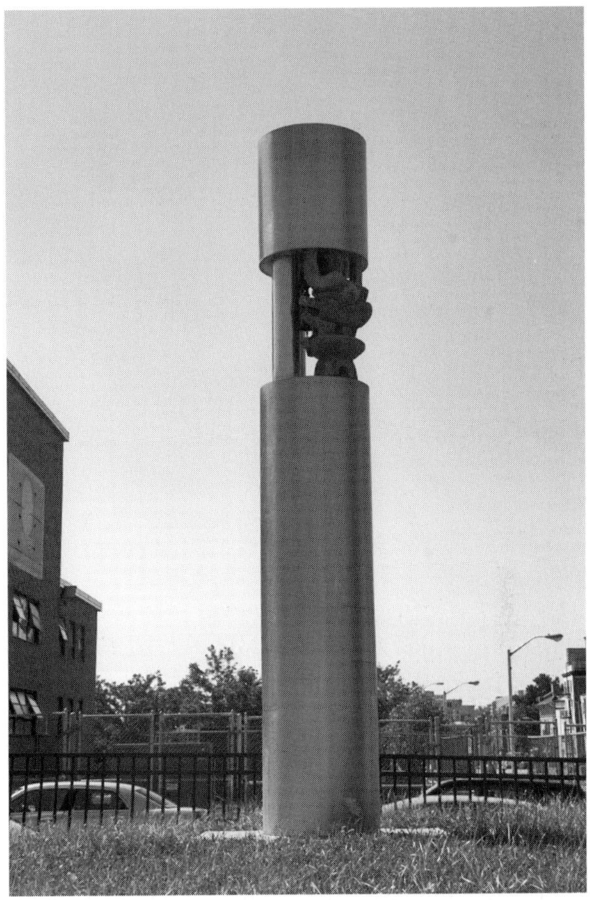

Paestum is an ancient Greco-Roman city in southern Italy, not far from the Amalfi coast. The ruins of Paestum include three of the most beautiful examples of Greek architecture, the temples of Hera, Poseidon, and Athena. Largely what remains of these temples is their columns. This single column by Roger Majorowicz, who lived in Italy for three years, was inspired by the columns of Paestum.

The temples dedicated to Hera, Poseidon, and Athena were all Doric temples. The Doric order of columns is the oldest and the simplest and was used on the Parthenon. Doric columns stand directly on the floor and have a plain capital, a circle topped by a square. Majorowicz's column is 13 feet tall and stands directly on the ground. The stainless steel column is interrupted about two-thirds of the way up by a 2-foot-high opening containing an abstract bronze. The bronze form is meant to represent a caryatid, an architectural element, often in the shape of a female figure, that served as an ornamental support in place of a column or a pilaster.

For sound, installed within this opening was a bell, activated by the wind; however, the clapper was stolen years ago, when the piece was first installed at the Broadway branch of the Pratt Library, at the corner of Broadway and Orleans. Johns Hopkins Hospital negotiated with the city to build a new branch library if the hospital could have the Broadway branch property. Today, Majorowicz's column is no longer part of the library entrance structure but stands across the parking lot at the far corner of the new library property.

O7

TITLE

Untitled, 1940

LOCATION

Pleasant Garden View, 201 Aisquith Street

SCULPTOR

Henry Berge (1908–1998)

MEDIUM

Concrete

DONOR

Housing Authority of Baltimore City

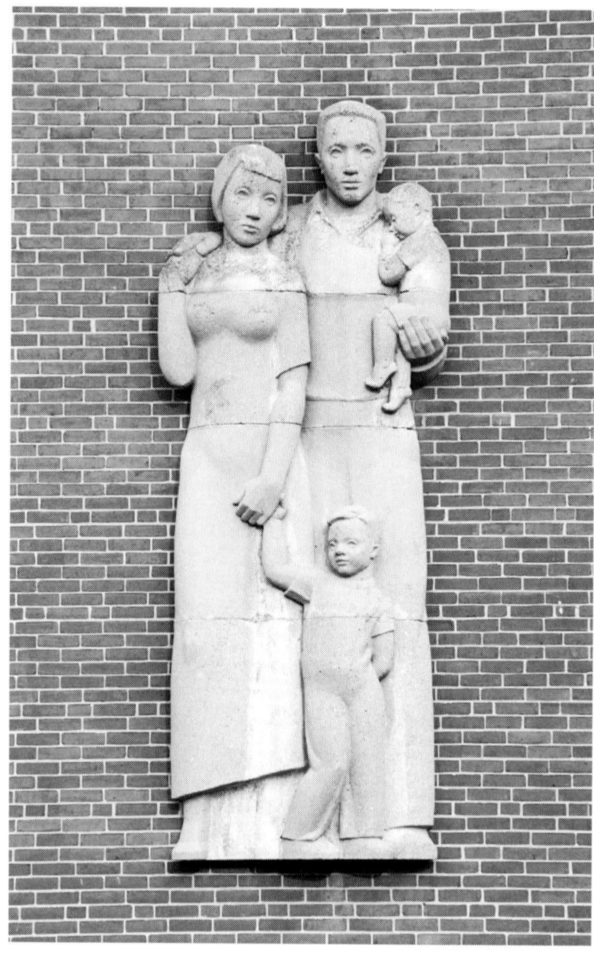

This work was Henry Berge's second commission from Edward C. Minor in 1940, the design chief for Baltimore's Housing Authority. The first commission had been for artwork for McCulloh Homes earlier that year (M1). This commission was for the housing project originally called Lafayette Courts. A third commission would be offered to Berge in 1954 (R3).

Miner wanted a vertical relief for the building, but he did not know how large. Berge made two cutouts of a family grouping, one 10 feet high and one 12 feet, and held them up to the building. Miner approved the larger one, and Berge cast the piece.

Berge created a family grouping comprising a mother, a father, and two children, a toddler and an infant. The mother and father stand very close to each other, the mother slightly in front of her husband. The father's right arm is around her, with his hand resting on her right shoulder. He holds their infant, whose head rests against his left shoulder. The mother touches her husband's hand on her shoulder with her right hand and holds their young son's hand in her left hand. The toddler stands just in front of and between his mother and father. They are all dressed very simply, the mother in a simple long dress, the father in an open-collar shirt and long pants, the young boy in overalls and a short-sleeved shirt, the baby in shorts and a shirt. With very little detailing, Berge has depicted a gentle, loving family of modest means.

O8

TITLE
Untitled, 1940

LOCATION
Frederick Douglass Homes, 1500 E. Lexington Street

SCULPTOR
Reuben Kramer (1909–1999)

MEDIUM
Concrete

DONOR
Housing Authority of Baltimore City

Very early in his career Reuben Kramer received a public commission to create artwork for the Frederick Douglass Homes. Not again until 1979 did Kramer complete a large-scale public commission, this time for a freestanding portrait of Supreme Court Justice Thurgood Marshall (A1).

The history of the commission for the Frederick Douglass Homes involved a partnership between the Housing Authority of Baltimore City and the Baltimore Museum of Art. The Housing Authority wanted to sponsor a competition for a commission for sculptural decoration for a new housing project, and it asked the Baltimore Museum of Art to conduct the competition. The jurors were to be Leslie Cheek Jr., director

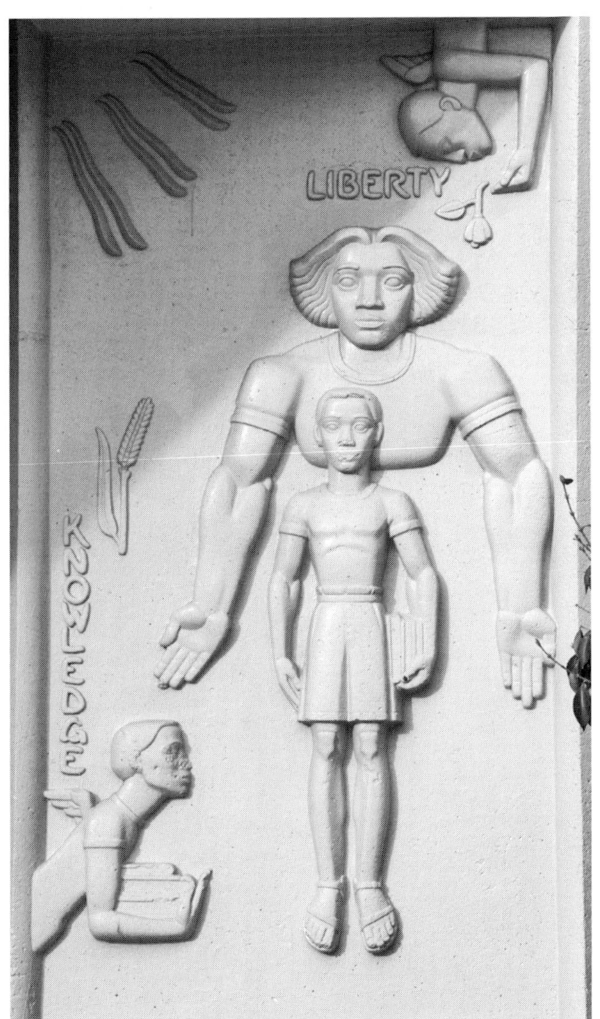

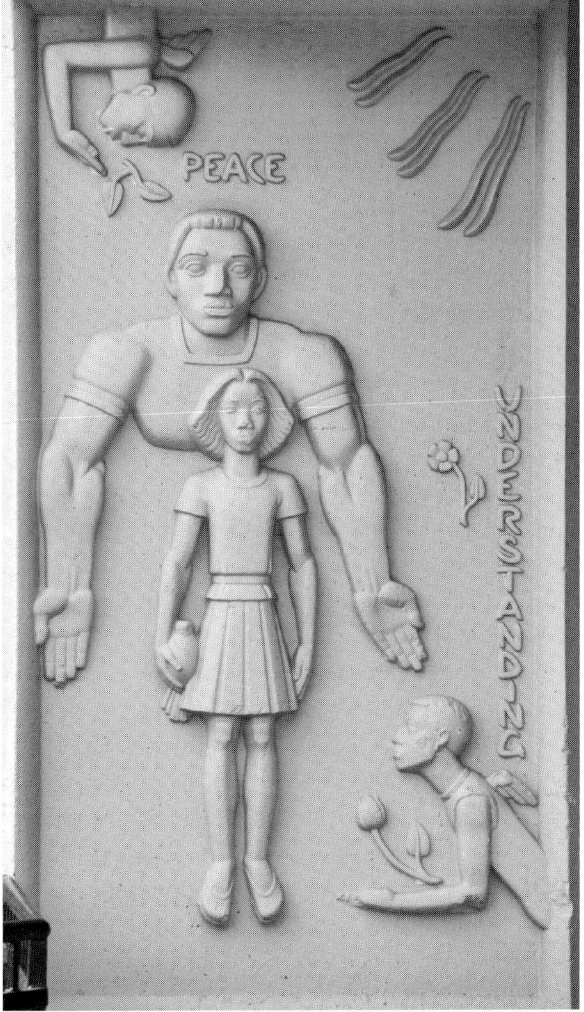

of the museum, John H. Scarff, one of the architects of the housing project, and an out-of-state sculptor to be chosen by Cheek and Scarff. First prize, which was to come in the form of a contract with the Housing Authority, was $1,100. The competition was open to U.S. citizens residing in Maryland who were of legal age. A prospectus of the competition and a blueprint of the buildings were available at the museum. Kramer was announced as the winner on April 26, 1940, at the opening of the museum's outdoor sculpture show.

Kramer designed two relief panels that were cast in concrete and installed on either side of the E. Lexington entrance to the housing project. On the left panel, a man's upper body is represented behind a young girl holding a bird. His arms are extended downward, and the palms of his hands are open, as if presenting the girl. The words "PEACE" and "UNDERSTANDING" appear on the panel. The panel to the right of the entrance has the upper body of a woman behind a young boy holding several books; the woman's arms and palms are positioned similarly to the man's in the opposite panel. The words on this panel are "LIBERTY" and "KNOWLEDGE." Two young boys with wings appear on each panel, in the upper outer corner and the lower inside corner. The imagery is simple, direct, and unembellished.

Two other commissions for sculpture for Baltimore City housing projects were awarded to Henry Berge in 1940 by Edward C. Minor, the design chief at the Housing Authority (M1 and O7). How this commission, awarded competitively, relates to the two commissions awarded directly by Minor is not known.

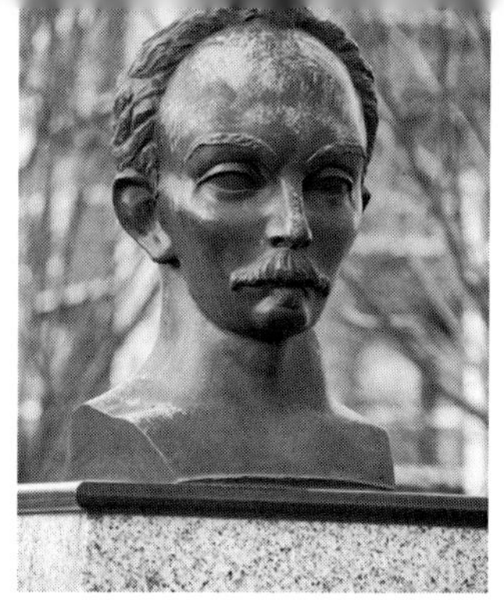

TITLE
JOSÉ MARTÍ MONUMENT, before 1959

LOCATION
Broadway median at Fayette Street

SCULPTOR
Teodoro Ramos Blanco (1902–1972)

MEDIUM
Bronze and granite

DONOR
Cuban American Foundation Pro José Martí Monument

On the granite base of this small bronze monument to José Martí (1853–95), the Cuban poet, essayist, lecturer, and patriot who became the leader of the Cuban struggle for independence, appears the following inscription: "THIS MONUMENT IS DEDICATED / TO THE CITY OF BALTIMORE / BY THE HISPANIC COMMUNITY OF MARYLAND AND / BY THE MEMBERS OF THE BOARD OF / 'THE CUBAN AMERICAN FOUNDATION / PRO JOSÉ MARTÍ MONUMENT, INC.'"

Often called *al apóstol,* "the apostle," Martí was born in Havana of Spanish immigrant parents. He was committed to Cuba's struggle for independence from Spain from a very young age. He published his first newspaper, *La Patria Libre,* in 1869, when he was 16 years old. That same year, he was arrested for denouncing a pro-Spanish classmate and sentenced to six years of hard labor. He was released after two years, only to be exiled to Spain, where at the age 18 he began studies that led to degrees in law and philosophy. During this exile he traveled extensively and became famous throughout the Hispanic world for his political essays and poems and stories of Cuba's future liberation. He returned to Cuba in 1878, only to be exiled again in 1879, an exile that would last the better part of the rest of his life.

Martí had a busy literary career, traveling the world before settling in New York City, where he lived from 1881 to 1895, earning a living as a writer and teacher. In 1892 Martí dedicated himself exclusively to planning and organizing what became Cuba's third war of independence, and he founded the Cuban Revolutionary Party, which raised money for the war. In 1895 he returned to Cuba to fight in the final insurrection against Spain. Just two weeks later, at the battle of Dos Rios, he suffered a fatal bullet wound and died at the young age of 42. Martí is known in Cuba as the father of the Cuban Revolution.

The sculptor of this bust of Martí was Teodoro Ramos Blanco, considered to be one of Cuba's most important artists. He graduated from the Academia San Alejandro, where he studied with Isabel Chapottin. He won international recognition when he received a gold medal at the Seville World's Fair in 1929. Blanco made this bust sometime before Fidel Castro came into power in 1959. Dr. Luis Queral, the chairman of the monument committee, bought the bust from an acquaintance in Miami, who had brought it from Cuba years before. Martí is seen here as a man with an angular face, a receding hairline, heavy eyebrows, and a thick mustache.

The monument was dedicated in the summer of 1998, and its site is reflective of the growing community of immigrants from Cuba, El Salvador, Spain, Mexico, and numerous other Latin countries who have settled along Broadway north from Fells Point. The monument committee felt that Martí could be a role model for all Spanish-speaking members of the community. Soil from all the places Martí lived is contained in a sealed urn, in the monument and the countries are listed on the base, in two columns: "ARGENTINA, BOLIVIA, BRASIL, CHILE, COLOMBIA, COSTA RICA, CUBA, REP. DOMINICANA, ECUADOR, EL SALVADOR, ESPAÑA, GUATEMALA, HONDURAS, KEY WEST, FLA., MEXICO, NEW YORK, N.Y., NICARAGUA, PANAMÁ, PARAGUAY, PERÚ, PUERTO RICO, TAMPA, FLA., URUGUAY, VENEZUELA."

O10

TITLE
Charity, 1865

LOCATION
Thomas Wildey Monument, Broadway median
near Fayette Street

SCULPTOR
Unknown

ARCHITECT
Edward F. Durang

MEDIUM
Marble

DONOR
Fraternal Order of Odd Fellows

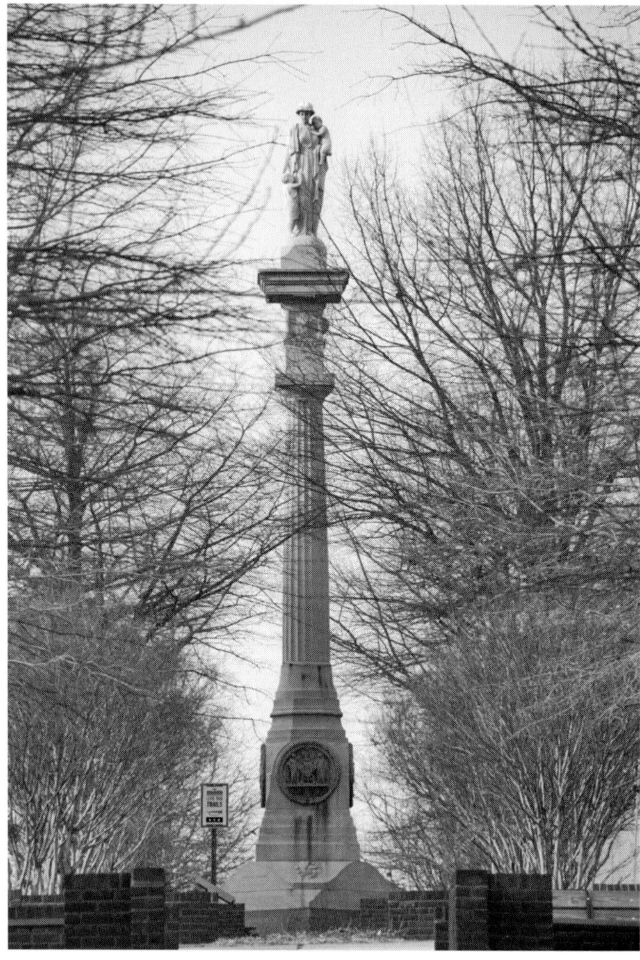

Thomas Wildey (1783–1861) immigrated to the United States from England in 1817 and worked in Baltimore as a maker of coach springs. He is credited with founding the Fraternal Order of Odd Fellows in Baltimore in 1819, and this monument was raised after his death to commemorate that act.

The Order of Odd Fellows is one of the largest and oldest fraternal orders in the United States, deriving from the Odd Fellows in England. The English order came into being during the eighteenth century, at a time when charitable acts were far less common. Today the order is active in twenty-nine countries and has more than 250,000 members. The Odd Fellows' most widely encountered symbol is three linked ovals, containing the letters *F, L,* and *T.* The initials stand for

"Friendship, Love and Truth." Three other important symbols of the Odd Fellows include a heart in a hand, symbolizing charity and good works; a bundle of rods, symbolizing strength in union; and an axe, symbolizing the pioneering spirit of Wildey.

The city gave the Odd Fellows a prominent site at the apex of the hill along Broadway, which offered an unobstructed view of Fells Point. The architect Edward F. Durang designed the square granite base, the marble pedestal, and the beautiful fluted Doric column, which together with the figural group atop the monument measures 52 feet. An inscribed, wreathed bronze tablet appears on each face of the pedestal. The life-size figural group atop the column—a female figure holding an infant in her left arm and looking down on another young child, standing at her side—represents Charity

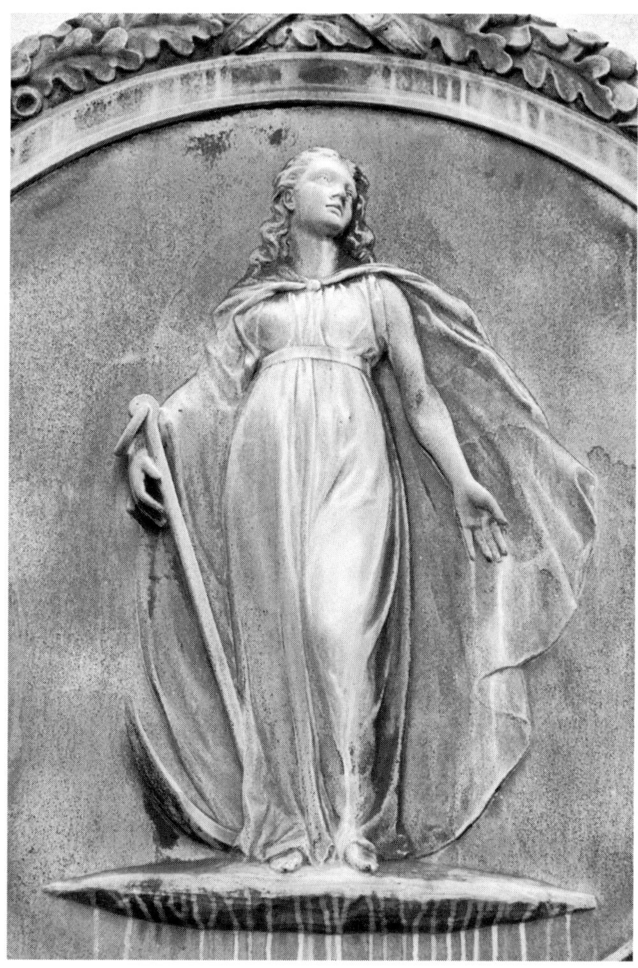

and two orphans, toward whom she is exercising the greatest of virtues. The sculptor is unknown.

Most of the inscriptions on the monument are related to the history of the founding of the order and the raising of the monument. One inscription is meant to inspire and direct its members to service. Carved into the northwest side of the granite base is the inscription, "HE WHO REALIZES THAT THE / TRUE MISSION OF MAN ON EARTH / IS TO RISE ABOVE THE LEVEL OF INDIVI / DUAL INFLUENCE AND TO RECOGNIZE THE FATHERHOOD / OF GOD OVERALL AND THE BROTHERHOOD OF MAN IS NATURE'S TRUE NOBLEMAN." And on one of the four faces of the pedestal appears the following: "AMICITIA AMOR ET VERITAS / WE COMMAND YOU TO VISIT THE SICK, RELIEVE THE DISTRESSED, / BURY THE DEAD AND EDUCATE THE ORPHAN."

The dedication of the monument, on September 20, 1865, was remarkable in that it brought together Odd Fellows from the North and the South for the first time since the end of the Civil War. Jefferson Davis, the former president of the Confederacy, was brought from his prison cell in Baltimore to be in attendance as a special guest of the order. The Odd Fellows had invited President Andrew Jackson as well, but at the last minute he was unable to attend.

Twenty years later, a monument to another Odd Fellow, James L. Ridgely, was raised in Harlem Park (M5). Baltimore remained the home of the national headquarters of the Independent Order of Odd Fellows until 1982, when it was moved to Winston-Salem, North Carolina.

O11

TITLE

LATROBE MONUMENT, 1914

LOCATION

Broadway median at Baltimore Street

SCULPTORS

J. Maxwell Miller (1877–1933) and Edward Berge
(1876–1924)

ARCHITECT

William Gordon Beecher (1877–1963)

MEDIUM

Bronze and granite

DONOR

Baltimore City

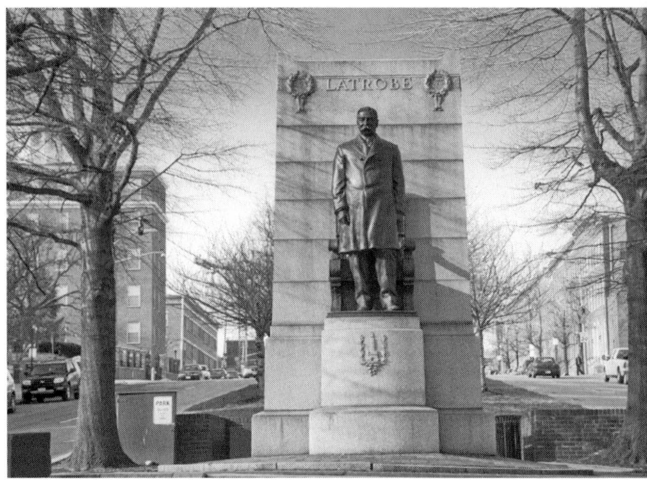

Ferdinand Claiborne Latrobe (1833–1911) served seven times as mayor of Baltimore City; he was elected in 1875, 1878, 1879, 1883, 1887, 1891, and 1893. Those dates appear on this monument, which was erected in "grateful acknowledgement of his eminent services" to the city. Latrobe is depicted in a double-breasted top-coat, standing erect, with his arms at his sides, in front of a large-scale, Renaissance-inspired armchair with elaborately scrolled arms and tooled leather upholstery. The figure and his chair are placed on a tall granite base that stands before a wider granite pier. On the front of the pier, at the top, on either side of his name, appear the dates of his first and last mayoralty elections; the dates of the other five appear across the back and on both sides of the pier, near the top. On the east side of the monument, on the surface between the sabrelike legs of the chair, appear the names of the two sculptors and the architect, William Gordon Beecher, who collaborated on this monument.

Latrobe was born in Baltimore and studied law with his father, John H. B. Latrobe. In 1860 he was admitted to the bar. He was active in Maryland politics all his life. In addition to his years as mayor of Baltimore, he served in the House of Delegates several terms throughout his life, beginning in 1867. He was elected speaker of the House in 1870 and again during a special session in 1901. He was the grandson of Benjamin Henry Latrobe, architect of the Basilica of the Assumption in Baltimore.

Robert M. Graf, who was the model for Berge's monument to Col. George Armistead at Fort McHenry (G17), was the model for this monument to Latrobe.

O12

TITLE
Peely Wheely, 1978

LOCATION
Wolfe Street Academy, 245 S. Wolfe Street

SCULPTOR
James Paulsen (b. 1943)

MEDIA
Direct-welded bronze over steel

DONOR
Baltimore City Percent for Art program

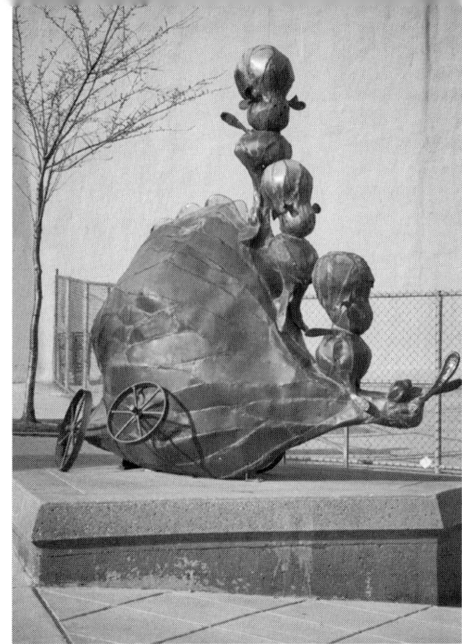

When the Wolf Street Academy opened in 1978, it served children in kindergarten through second grade. Because the audience for this sculpture was so young, James Paulson took his original idea from children's literature, especially the books of Dr. Seuss. He began with the notion of the family dog that walked the children to school each day and then waited outside the school building until the school day was over and the children came out again. The dog morphed into a gentle prehistoric kind of creature large enough to actually transport the children to school on his back.

There is no question that the bronze creature shown arriving at school with three children stacked across his back is friendly. This very awkward and mysterious creature has wheels that appear to aid in his mobility, but clearly his movement would be slow and deliberate. It is hard to imagine how the wheel on the tail could help. The creature seems to struggle for his balance as he teeters on the cement-capped brick base at the front door of the school. Actually the best view of the piece is from that front door—maybe the principal's view.

Paulsen did not title his sculpture. He wanted to leave that task to the students, to whom it really belonged. Just after the dedication of the piece, each student was asked to tell a story—in pictures—explaining where the creature had come from and how it had arrived at the school. Most of them thought the creature had come from the harbor and traveled through the streets of Fells Point, slipping through the narrow covered passages between the houses before arriving at the school. And it was the students who came up with the name *Peely Wheely*.

Paulsen started by constructing a contour armature out of ½ inch steel rods. He then covered the armature with individually cut pieces of ³⁄₃₂ inch bronze (bronze that was less than ⅛ inch thick) that he hammered and shaped over the armature and then welded in place. The technique is very labor intensive; Paulsen spent over a year welding this piece, creating the linear pattern that defines the intricate form of the creature and his passengers. Paulsen even fabricated the wheels, leaving the front one free so that the children could interact with the piece directly by turning it. The piece made a three-second cameo appearance in the movie *Ladder Company 49*, starring John Travolta, which was filmed in Baltimore in 2004.

Paulsen earned a BS from Western Illinois University, an MA in sculpture from Northern Illinois University, and an MFA in sculpture from the University of Delaware. Today he is a professor and head of sculpture at Towson University, where he has been on the faculty since 1969. He has recently completed public art commissions in Scotland, China, and England, where he was a Fulbright Exchange teacher at the University of the West of England in Bristol. His work has been exhibited nationally and internationally and is held in more than forty private collections.

O13

TITLE
Frederick Douglass, 2006

LOCATION
Douglass-Myers Maritime Park and Museum,
1417 Thames Street

SCULPTOR
Marc André Robinson (b. 1972)

MEDIUM
Bronze

DONORS
Living Classrooms Foundation and the Municipal Art
Society of Baltimore City

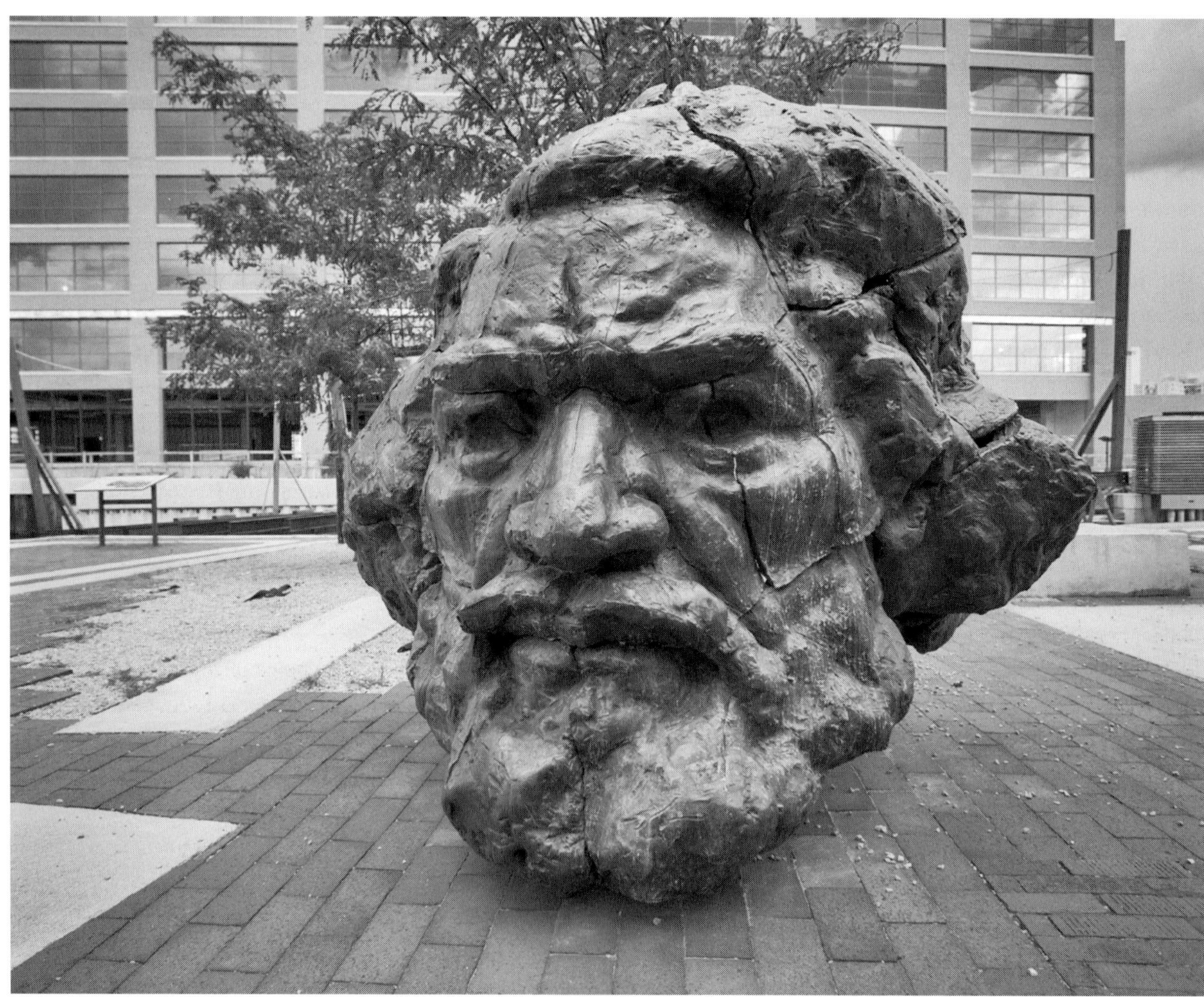

In the summer of 2006, one block away from its East Harbor campus, the Living Classrooms Foundation opened a new campus in Fells Point, the Douglass-Myers Maritime Park and Museum, to celebrate the contributions of the African American community in the development of the city's maritime industry. The new facility is named for Frederick Douglass, who lived in Baltimore and worked in the city shipyards, and Isaac Myers, who led fourteen other free blacks in founding the Chesapeake Marine Railway and Drydock Company, the first African American–owned shipyard in the country.

At the Douglass-Myers Maritime Park, Living Classrooms focuses its public programming and employment training on at-risk youth. It includes an industrial warehouse, a working shipyard, a historic marine railway, hands-on exhibits, and sculpture honoring both Douglass and Myers. Marc André Robinson's sculpture honoring Douglass is a heroic-scale head cast in bronze and installed directly on the red brick entrance plaza, not far from the harbor. It is a very good likeness of Douglass, as good a likeness as James E. Lewis captured more than fifty years earlier in his statue of Douglass for Morgan State University (K8). But that is the only similarity in the two works.

Here, the sculptor focuses only on the physiognomy of Douglass' head and succeeds in revealing Douglass' intellect, his determination, and his humanity. Douglass' furrowed brow, his focused eyes, his set mouth, even the slightest tilt of his head, all contribute to a sense of the man he became. The suggestion that this head may have been dropped and broken into fragments, since sections of bronze are held in place by steel rods, clearly visible from the back, cannot diminish the power of his presence, surely an inspiring one to the youth of Baltimore who come here to learn.

Robinson received his BFA from the Pennsylvania Academy of Fine Arts in Philadelphia in 1998 and his MFA from the Maryland Institute in 2002. A nearby text panel states that his choice of bronze as a material of great permanence was meant to reflect the indelible commitment of Living Classrooms to Baltimore youth.

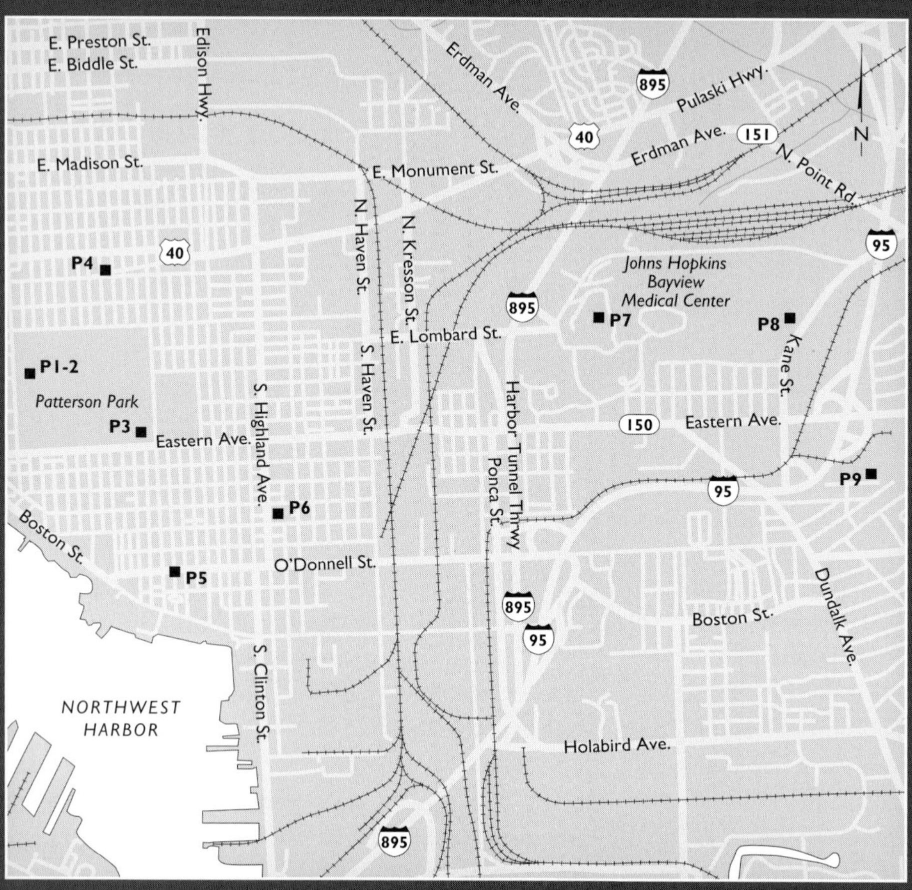

E. Preston St.
E. Biddle St.
Edison Hwy.
Erdman Ave.
895
Pulaski Hwy.
40
Erdman Ave.
151
N. Point Rd
E. Madison St.
E. Monument St.
N
40
P4
N. Haven St.
N. Kresson St.
Johns Hopkins
Bayview
Medical Center
95
895
P7
P8
Kane St.
P1-2
E. Lombard St.
Patterson Park
S. Highland Ave.
S. Haven St.
150
Eastern Ave.
P3
Eastern Ave.
95
P9
P6
Harbor Tunnel Thrwy
Ponca St.
Boston St.
O'Donnell St.
P5
895
95
S. Clinton St.
Boston St.
Dundalk Ave.
NORTHWEST
HARBOR
Holabird Ave.
895

PATTERSON PARK AND CANTON

Driving

P1

TITLE

STAR-SPANGLED BANNER CENTENNIAL MONUMENT, 1914

LOCATION

Patterson Park, Hampstead Hill near the Pagoda

SCULPTOR

J. Maxwell Miller (1877–1933)

MEDIUM

Bronze

DONORS

Students in the public schools of Baltimore

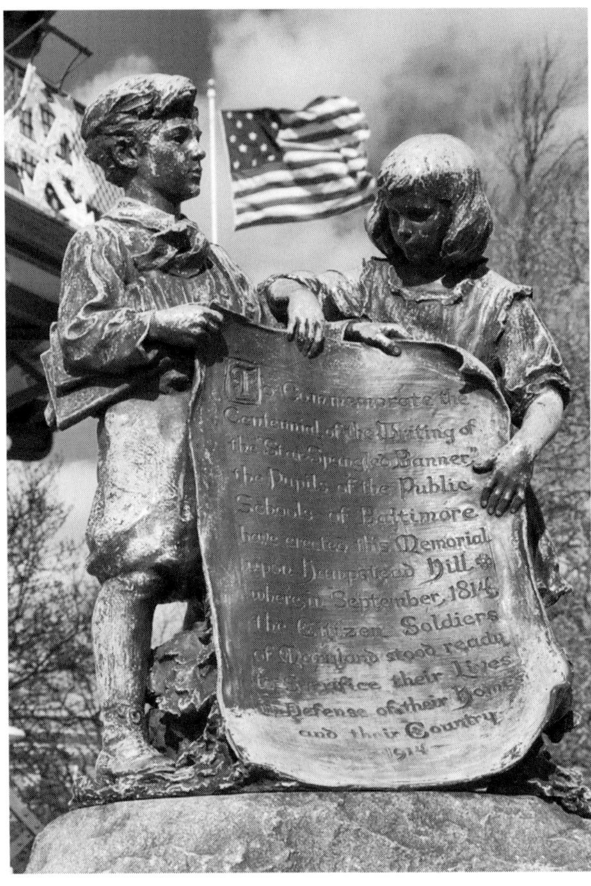

The centennial of Francis Scott Key's writing of the "Star-Spangled Banner" was celebrated throughout Baltimore City. Several pieces of sculpture were commissioned to honor Key's achievement, and this was one of the most charming. Designed by J. Maxwell Miller as the centerpiece on a parade float, it was subsequently installed in Patterson Park, near the Pagoda.

Two 9-year-old schoolchildren, Edna Schooler Campbell and Robert Gimbell, were selected as models for Miller. They were to represent the two schoolchildren who, the apocryphal story went, on their way home from school found a scroll on which the story of how and why the "Star-Spangled Banner" poem was written.

Miller depicted the young boy and girl in charming detail. The boy wears knee-high pants, high top shoes that tie, and a shirt that is full at the waist, and a bow around his collar. With two books and a ruler under his right arm, he holds on to the scroll with both hands. The young girl wears a dress with a bow around the waist, and there are bows on her shoes. She too holds on to the scroll, which unfurls between them, with both hands. This sculpture, which stands on a rough-cut granite boulder, was paid for by money contributed by schoolchildren of the city, including the sculptor's daughter.

Hampstead Hill can be most easily reached from the entrance at S. Patterson Park Avenue and Pratt Street. As stated on the scroll the children are holding,

Hampstead Hill was part of a chain of fortifications where citizen soldiers of Maryland stood ready to sacrifice their lives in defense of their homes and their country. On this ridge stood Rodgers' Bastion—one hundred cannons and twelve thousand men—under the immediate command of Commodore John Rodgers. The British marching on Baltimore are said to have looked up at Hampstead Hill and, seeing Rodgers' Bastion, returned to their ships on the Patapsco River and sailed away. A lone cannon stands near the monument in tribute to Rodgers and his men.

P2

TITLE
Conradin Kreutzer, 1915

LOCATION
Patterson Park, S. Patterson Park Avenue and Gough Street

SCULPTOR
R. P. Golde

MEDIUM
Bronze

DONOR:
United Singers of Baltimore

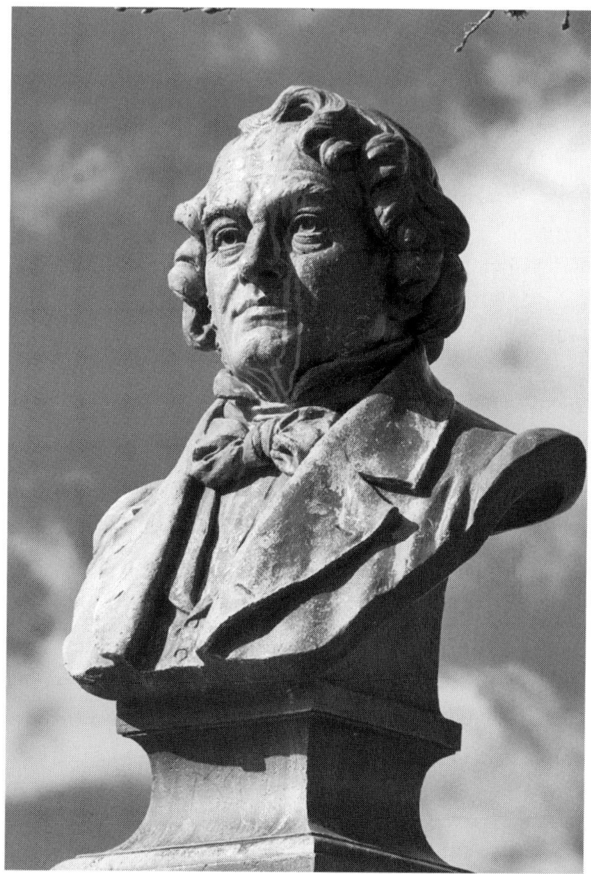

Why, one might ask, is there a bust of Conradin Kreutzer (1780–1849), a famous German composer and conductor, in Patterson Park? The same question could be asked about the bust of Richard Wagner in Druid Hill Park (M11). Interestingly, the answer to both questions is the same. These busts were awarded to the United Singers of Baltimore, who won first prize in National Saengerfests in 1900 and 1915, and both were given to the city.

This bust of Kreutzer was executed by R. P. Golde, who had also created the bust of Wagner. Kreutzer's shoulder-length hair meets his high shirt collar and long, full sideburns. He wears a vest and coat and a bow tied around his neck. He has a heavy brow and a dimple in his chin.

The 1915 Saengerfest, the twenty-fourth such competition, was held in Brooklyn, just as the nineteenth had been in 1900. In Brooklyn's Prospect Park there is a bust of Beethoven that was presented to the city of Brooklyn by the United German Singers of Brooklyn, who won the seventeenth competition in 1894. The monument in Prospect Park has the same format as the two in Baltimore: the head and shoulders of a famous German composer on a tall granite base inscribed with the history of that year's festival. Since the bust in Prospect Park was by a different sculptor, Henry Baerer, there must have been a prototype for the first prize that each sculptor followed and a tradition of presenting the sculpted bust to the winner's city for placement in a park setting.

P3

TITLE

PULASKI MONUMENT, 1942

LOCATION

Patterson Park, Eastern and Linwood avenues

SCULPTOR

Hans Schuler (1874–1951)

ARCHITECT

A. C. Radziszewski

MEDIUM

Bronze

DONOR

Polish-American Citizens' Committee

A bank failure and a world war were among the reasons that the Pulaski Monument was delayed for more than two decades.

Casimir Pulaski (1748–79) was born into an old and distinguished Polish family. Before he reached the age of 20, he and his father, along with other noblemen, raised an army and fought to free their country from the despotism of imperial Russia. After his father died in a Russian prison, Pulaski, by then an outlaw, fled to Paris, where he met Benjamin Franklin, who recommended him to George Washington. Pulaski joined the American forces in the summer of 1777 and so distinguished himself at Brandywine that Washington made him a brigadier general and asked him to organize the Continental army cavalry. Thus, Pulaski became known as the "Father of the American Cavalry." Pulaski recruited the rank and file of his legion in Baltimore. His Maryland Legion carried a crimson banner that is preserved at the Maryland Historical Society today. At the siege of Savannah, on October 9, 1779, Pulaski was shot in his right thigh. He died two days later on a ship bound for Charleston, South Carolina.

A monument to Pulaski was first proposed in 1929. Together, the state and the city were to contribute $15,000, and another $15,000 was to be raised privately by the Polish-American Citizens' Committee. The project faced one setback after another. The first came when a local bank and a Polish building associa-tion failed during the Depression, wiping out most of the funds raised for the monument. Fund-raising began again, and by 1942 Hans Schuler, who had been selected to create the monument, had finished the design of the relief and was ready to have it cast in bronze, when the government commandeered all the metal for defense purposes. By the end of the war, prices for everything, including bronze, had skyrocketed. It was not until the mayor of Baltimore City, Thomas D'Alesandro, and the governor of Maryland, William Preston Lane, each pledged another $10,000 that the monument could be completed. It was dedicated October 14, 1951, after the death of the sculptor in March of that year.

The monument is a heroic bas-relief in bronze set in a 20-foot square frame of granite and brick. A. C. Radziszewski was the architect. In the relief, which is 10 feet tall and 15 feet wide, Schuler depicted Pulaski in uniform, on horseback, sword in hand, leading a cavalry charge at the siege of Savannah. Pulaski's aide-de-camp, Col. Paul Bentalou (1755–1826), a fellow Frenchman who had come to America in 1776 to join the War of Independence and met Pulaski at Brandywine, can be seen just behind him. There is great energy and dynamic movement in the relief. Flags flutter and wheat sheaths sway as Pulaski leads his men into battle. Pulaski is turned in his saddle, looking back to his right, and his horse rears with mouth open as the reins are pulled tight. Pulaski appears to be shouting a command. The five other riders and their horses are all charging, all moving forward. Pulaski and his horse are shown in almost three-quarters relief; the remaining troops are cast in ever-lower relief as they recede into the background.

Bentalou was considered one of the heroes in the siege of Savannah. Even while wounded himself, he carried the mortally wounded Pulaski from the battlefield. He settled in Baltimore after the war.

The monument is signed in the lower right corner of the relief, "Schuler '42."

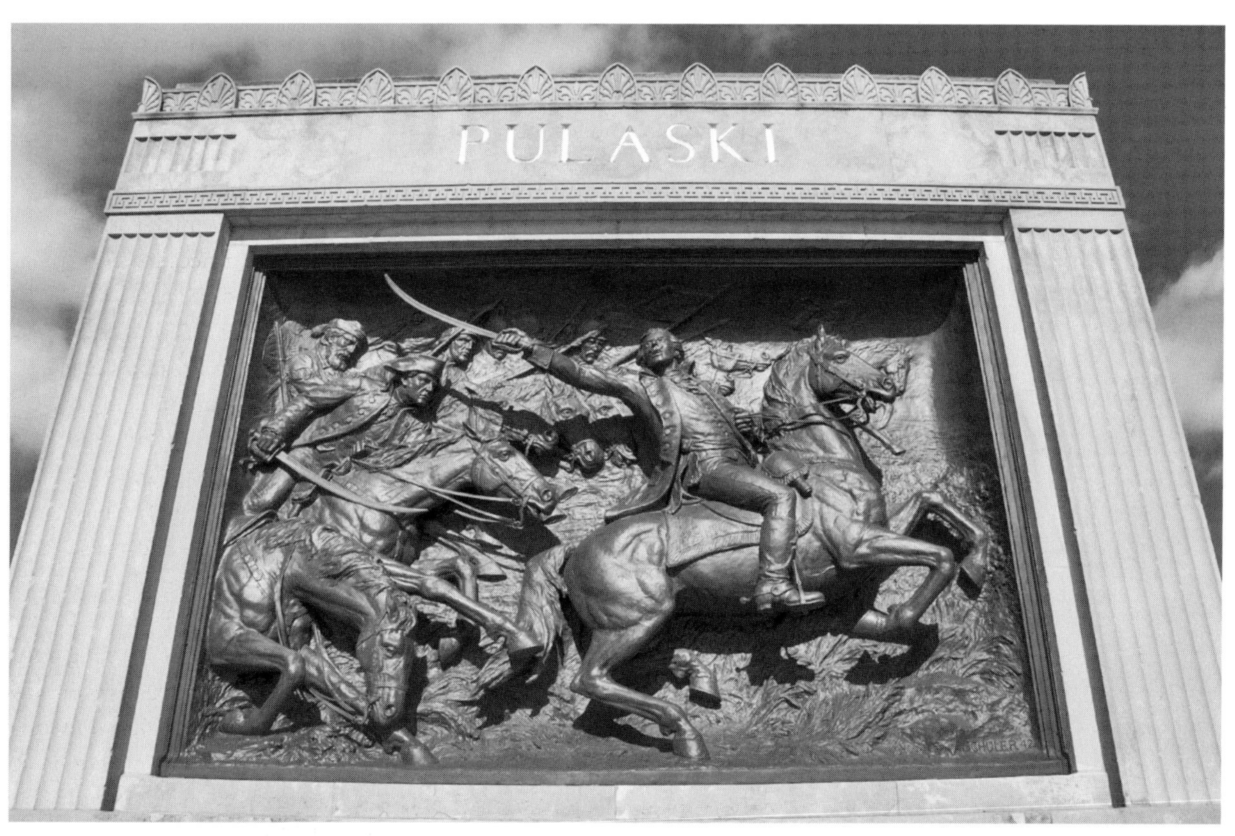
PULASKI

TITLE

SPANISH-AMERICAN WAR MONUMENT *(The Hiker)*,
1943 copy of 1921 original

LOCATION

N. Lakewood Avenue and E. Fayette Street

SCULPTOR

Theodora Alice Ruggles Kitson (1871–1932)

MEDIUM

Bronze

DONOR

State of Maryland

The Hiker is one of the most widely reproduced works of art in the United States. Fifty-two replicas are found throughout the country, from Waltham, Massachusetts, to Arlington, Virginia, to New Orleans, Louisiana, all cast by the Gorham Manufacturing Company in Providence, Rhode Island, between 1921 and 1956, and dedicated to the memory of the volunteer soldiers who died fighting in the Spanish-American War, 1898-1902.

Theodora Alice Ruggles Kitson modeled the original figure of *The Hiker* in 1921. This nickname for the monument derived from the long marches the infantry endured during their years of fighting in Cuba, Puerto Rico, and the Philippines. Kitson had long worked with the Gorham foundry, which came to own the rights to her designs. The foundry continued casting reproductions from her molds and marketing them long after she died. Much later, Dr. John D. Meakin, of the University of Delaware, took advantage of the fact that the replicas of *The Hiker* were sited all over the country. He used samples of bronze from all of them in scientific studies on the corrosion of bronze. The results were published in the *Bulletin of the Association for Preservation Technology* in 1992.

The single male figure stands at rest with his weight on his right foot, his left foot slightly forward. With his arms down, close to his body, he holds a long-barreled rifle horizontally in front of him, the forefinger of his right hand resting on the trigger. His munitions belt is strapped across his body just above his waist, and the straps of his canteen and knapsack crisscross over his chest. He wears knee-high boots laced up the side and an open-necked shirt with the sleeves rolled up above his elbows. His wide-brimmed campaign hat completes a uniform appropriate for assignment in the climates of Cuba, Puerto Rico, and the Philippines. On the back, the letters "US VOL" appear on the knapsack that hangs about waist level, alongside his canteen. On the heel of the left shoe is Kitson's signature, "THEO A. R. KITSON."

The A Greek cross is cut into the front of the rough granite base. Within the outline of the Greek cross appears the dedication to the United Spanish War Veterans. The Baltimore *Hiker* was dedicated in 1943 to those Marylanders who had volunteered for service in the army and navy in 1898 at the request of President William McKinley. A cannon sits nearby, just outside a low wrought-iron fence. The fence was requested by some veterans in 1947 to protect the memorial from vandalism.

Kitson was born in Brookline, Massachusetts. She studied sculpture in Paris under Dagnan-Bouveret and under Henry Hudson Kitson, whom she married in 1893. In 1909, after separating from her husband, she settled in Farmington, Massachusetts, where she maintained a studio until her death. She was one of the most prolific female sculptors in America at the time. Besides *The Hiker*, she is well known for her 1906 memorial in Galesburg, Illinois, dedicated to Mother Bickerdyke, who nursed the wounded during the Civil War, and for her statue in Boston of Tadeusz Kosciuszko, the Polish hero who fought in the American Revolutionary War.

Kitson's hikers should not be confused with those by Allen George Newman (1875–1940). Newman's hiker holds his rifle in his right hand as it rests on his right shoulder. First cast in 1906, Newman's monuments are also dedicated to the memory of the volunteers who died in the Spanish-American War.

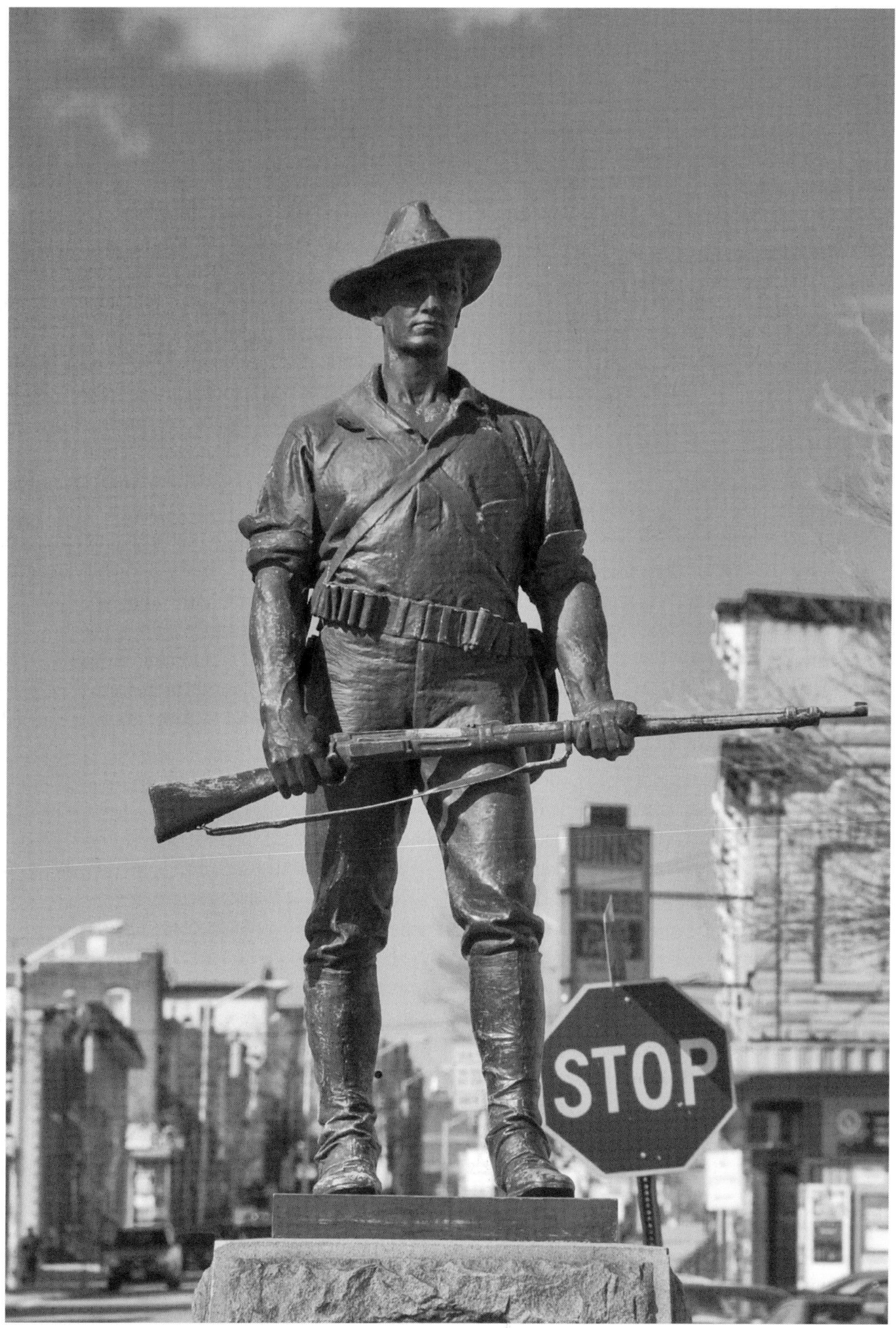STOP

TITLE
Captain John O'Donnell, 1978

LOCATION
Canton Square, O'Donnell Street between
S. Linwood and S. Ellwood streets

SCULPTOR
Tylden Streett (b. 1922)

MEDIUM
Bronze

DONOR
City of Baltimore

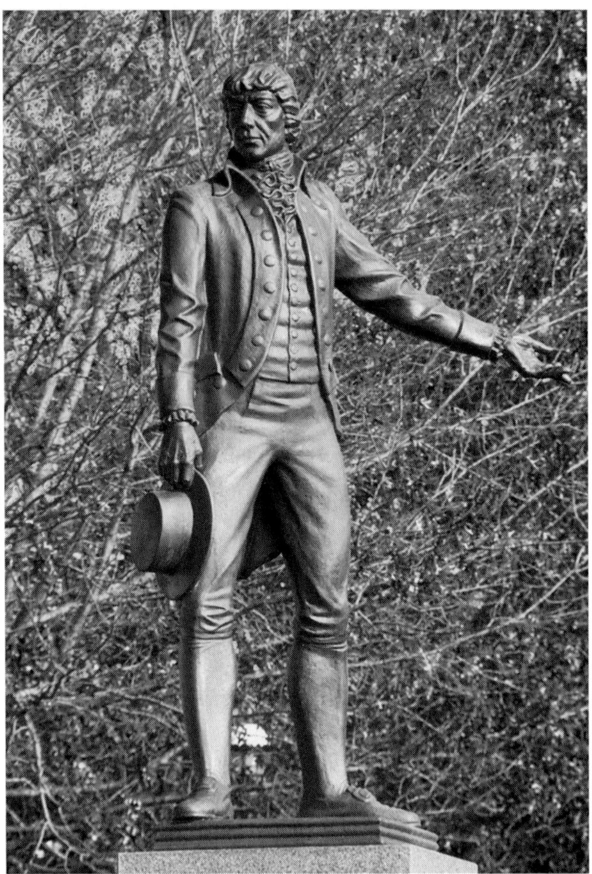

Canton Square is named for Canton, the 2,000-acre waterfront plantation owned by John O'Donnell (1749–1805), which in turn was named for the city in China from which he imported many of his goods.

O'Donnell, an adventurer, was a native of Limerick, Ireland, who in 1785 sailed into Baltimore from China with a valuable cargo of Chinese teas, china, silk, and satin, opening Baltimore's trade with the Far East. Already a wealthy merchant, O'Donnell decided to settle in Baltimore, where he married Darah Chew Elliott, the daughter of a Fells Point sea captain. In addition to the many ships he owned, O'Donnell invested in real estate, building wharves, warehouses, and row houses, as he continued to expand his import business, making many of the long voyages to India and China himself. Although he was a colonel of the militia, he was called Capitan O'Donnell because of the ships he owned and sailed. Ultimately he was elected to the state legislature. When he died, he was one of the wealthiest men in the new country. O'Donnell, his wife, and their two sons are buried in Greenmount Cemetery.

Tylden Streett did not have much to guide him in creating a likeness of Captain O'Donnell. O'Donnell had not wanted images of himself made, so there are no known portraits of him. For his clothing, Streett looked at items of period clothing at the Maryland Historical Society. Streett's 8-foot-high bronze statue of O'Donnell shows him standing with his legs apart, a wide brimmed hat in his right hand, his left hand held out from his side as if presenting Canton to a visitor. O'Donnell looks off in the direction opposite from where his hand is pointing, so that his body slightly turned, making it a more active stance. O'Donnell is depicted wearing a ruffled shirt, knee-high boots with large buckles, and a long coat over his pants. The buttons up the back of the coat are decorative.

The monument was installed in Canton Square in the heart of Canton and dedicated in 1979. Canton was developed in the late nineteenth century out of O'Donnell's plantation by his son, William Patterson, and Peter Cooper.

P6

TITLE
The Quest, 1984

LOCATION
Friendship Academy of Science and Technology,
801 S. Highland Avenue

SCULPTOR
Lisa Kaslow (b. 1953)

MEDIUM
Painted steel

DONOR
Baltimore City Percent for Art program

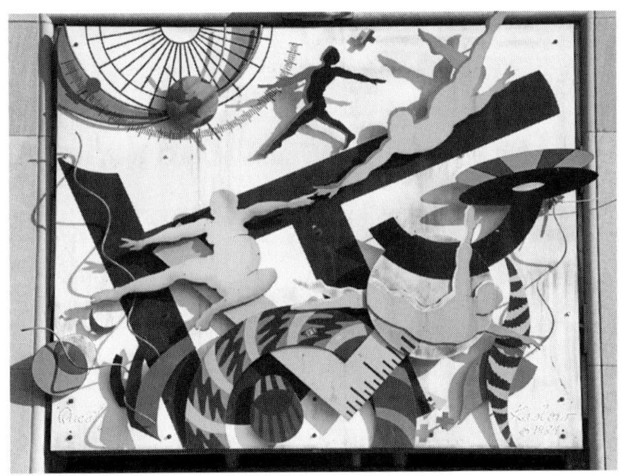

The quest depicted in this work is for knowledge, and the figures and objects included are drawn from Renaissance art, current technology, and popular culture.

After being chosen for this commission by a committee made up of representatives of the Canton community, the board of education, the Civic Design Commission, and the school architect, William Gaudreau of Gaudreau Associates, Lisa Kaslow completed large full-scale drawings, from her approved maquette, of every image to be included in the 8- by 10-foot steel relief. She produced the template drawings with India ink so that the Baltimore-based steel supplier Seaboard Iron and Metal Company could burn cutout steel parts from the templates via an electric eye and pantograph device. Then Kaslow fabricated the bas-relief in her Canton studio. The fabrication process included grinding all the edges, welding mounting studs, and drilling holes to attach the parts to the back plate and mounting system. She then sent the pieces out for sandblasting and base coating with epoxy and baked polyester powder. Through a lengthy process of masking, Kaslow airbrushed the top urethane enamel colors and designs in her studio. She installed the piece herself, directing the crane and crew as they bolted the relief into place.

Kaslow reinterpreted and modernized several iconic images. At the center of the relief is a pregnant pink nude woman reaching out and touching a blue nude male swimmer's hand, offering a new interpretation of Michelangelo's Sistine Chapel ceiling panel showing God reaching his hand out to touch the hand of Adam. As surprising and ambiguous as it is, Kaslow's representation of this scene, like Michelangelo's, is meant to signify nature and the Creation. A third nude figure, reinterpreting Leonardo's idealized man, is the male figure strutting just above the touching hands along the top edge of a T-square. Other objects included in the relief are the sun, the moon, and the earth, in the upper left corner; a magnifying glass enlarging the fourth nude figure, in the lower right corner; a half-circle under a disc, representing the early floppy disc era, near the upper right corner; and a carpenter's square, in the lower middle section, all meant to refer to an active life of learning.

When the school opened in 1984 it was called Canton Junior High School. Today it is an academy of science and technology, one of five new middle-high schools opened in 2008. The imagery of the relief, chosen more than twenty-five years ago, seems even more appropriate today.

P7

TITLE
Archimedean Spiral, 1978

LOCATION
Alpha Building, Johns Hopkins Bayview Medical Center, 5210 Eastern Avenue

SCULPTOR
Paul H. Shepherd

MEDIUM
Aluminum

DONOR
Dr. Robert Shepherd

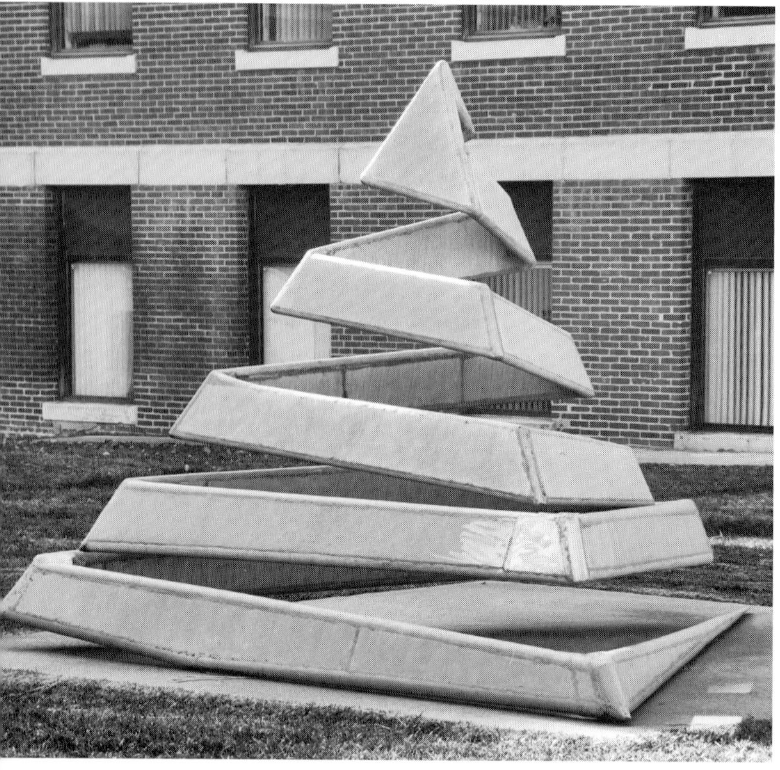

What would the third-century BC Greek mathematician Archimedes think of Paul Shepherd's sculpture? He might be confused on a cloudy day, but he would probably be amused and pleased on a day when the sun was shinning. The pattern of the sculpture reflected on the concrete pad by the sun may be the sculptor's real tribute to Archimedes.

Archimedes described a dynamic spiral whose successive turnings have a constant separation distance. Archimedes' spiral was of course circular and two-dimensional; in Shepherd's work the spiral is triangular and extended into a third dimension. Shepherd's sculpture is constructed out of a band of welded aluminum that turns fourteen times as it wraps 9 feet into the air around a central axis. Shepherd intended for the turnings of his sculpture to have a constant separation distance. And intended or not, the sculpture has a spring to it that allows it to reverberate when touched, not unlike Archimedes' spiral.

Archimedean Spiral looks like a drawing in space. Narrower at the bottom, the aluminum band widens to about 12 inches as it bends repeatedly to reach its full height. The aluminum has no coating and has weathered to a dull grey.

Dr. Robert Shepherd, Paul Shepherd's father, made this gift to the Johns Hopkins Medical Institutions. Originally it sat in the ground-level courtyard of Turner Auditorium, which is part of the Johns Hopkins School of Medicine and Hospital complex in East Baltimore.

Shepherd, who lives in Ellicott City, graduated from the Maryland Institute College of Art in 1974 with a BFA in fine arts.

P8

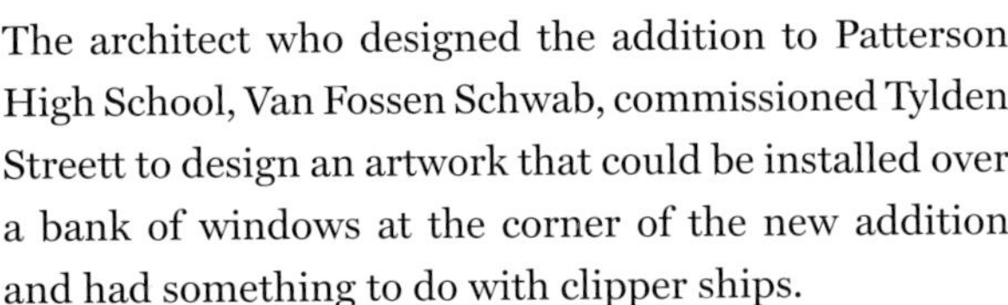

TITLE
Sails, 1978

LOCATION
Patterson High School, 100 Kane Street

SCULPTOR
Tylden Streett (b. 1922)

MEDIUM
Copper

DONOR
Baltimore City Percent for Art program

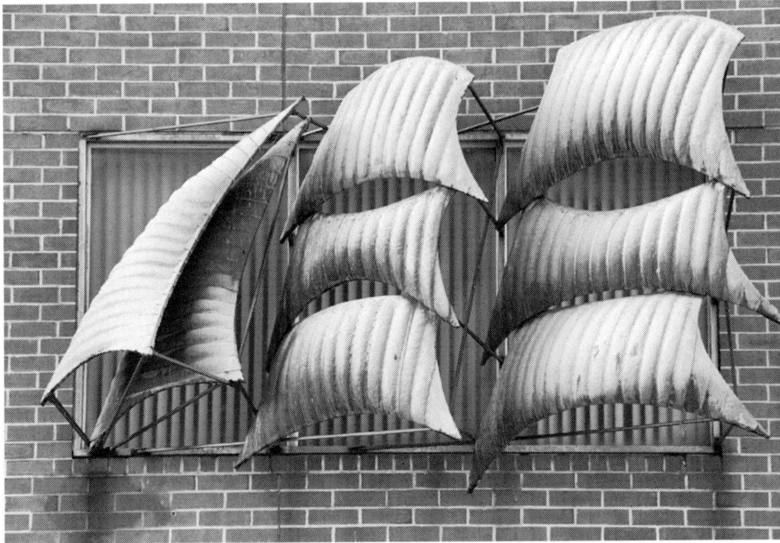

The architect who designed the addition to Patterson High School, Van Fossen Schwab, commissioned Tylden Streett to design an artwork that could be installed over a bank of windows at the corner of the new addition and had something to do with clipper ships.

In addition, Streett received nine specific directives from various city agencies, including the Department of Education and the Civic Design Commission. The artwork (1) had to be protective; (2) had to allow a view through it; (3) had to fit the 6- by 12-foot window frame exactly; (4) could not be of glass; (5) could not be of stained glass; (6) had to be bullet proof; (7) could not be of Cor-Ten steel; (8) had to be pigeon proof; and (9) could not be aluminum. Fortunately, most Percent for Art commissions did not have such specific limitations.

On the entrance sign for Patterson High School, in addition to the name of the school, appears the phrase "Home of the Clippers," and below that is an image of a Baltimore clipper. The school's sports teams were called the Clippers, after a ship from the late eighteenth and early nineteenth centuries that became known as the Baltimore clipper. The Baltimore clipper was a very fast, very maneuverable sailing ship developed in the Chesapeake Bay before the American Revolutionary War and built at Fells Point. It had a V-shaped hull that could cut through the water, multiple masts, a square rig, and a large total sail area. These ships, which "clipped" along at 12 knots or more, were able to sail very close to the wind. They became the vessels of choice for smuggling and for running slaves and opium, when speed was a requirement. Even though they were lightly armed, they were used successfully during the War of 1812 to raid British shipping, which enhanced their reputation.

The idea of a protective window screen made of eight billowing sails took hold, and Streett designed a framework that resembles a ship's rigging. He fabricated the sails out of copper, which he hammered over wooden forms made to create the impression that the sails were filled with air. Then he trimmed the copper so all eight sails would fit and installed them over the windows. Today the sails have weathered to a bluish green.

P9

TITLE
Knowledge, 1976

LOCATION
Southeast Middle School, 6820 Fait Avenue

SCULPTOR
Paul Takacs (1932–2000)

MEDIUM
Cor-Ten steel

DONOR
Baltimore City Percent for Art program

Paul Takacs began this commission with the ideas of learning and letters, and the piece evolved from there. The letters became geometric shapes—triangles, circles, rectangles—which are massed together, stacked vertically and parallel to each other. Fragments of the geometric shapes also appear.

Takacs worked with professional welders at the Culp Welding Company in Silver Spring, Maryland, to fabricate the piece. Made of Cor-Ten steel, it has weathered over time to a rich dark brown. The sculpture stands just to the right of the school entrance.

Takacs was born in Budapest, Hungary, where he attended the Academy of Applied Arts for four years. In 1957 he immigrated to the United States, settling in the Washington, D.C., area, where his family still lives today. Although he first considered himself a painter, he did create several large-scale sculptures early in his career. In the mid-1970s he was working on a large Cor-Ten sculpture for a new Macy's department store in New Rochelle, New York. He believed that publicity in some Maryland newspapers about him and his commission for Macy's brought him to the attention of Robert Patton, the architect for the Southeast Middle School, who offered him this commission.

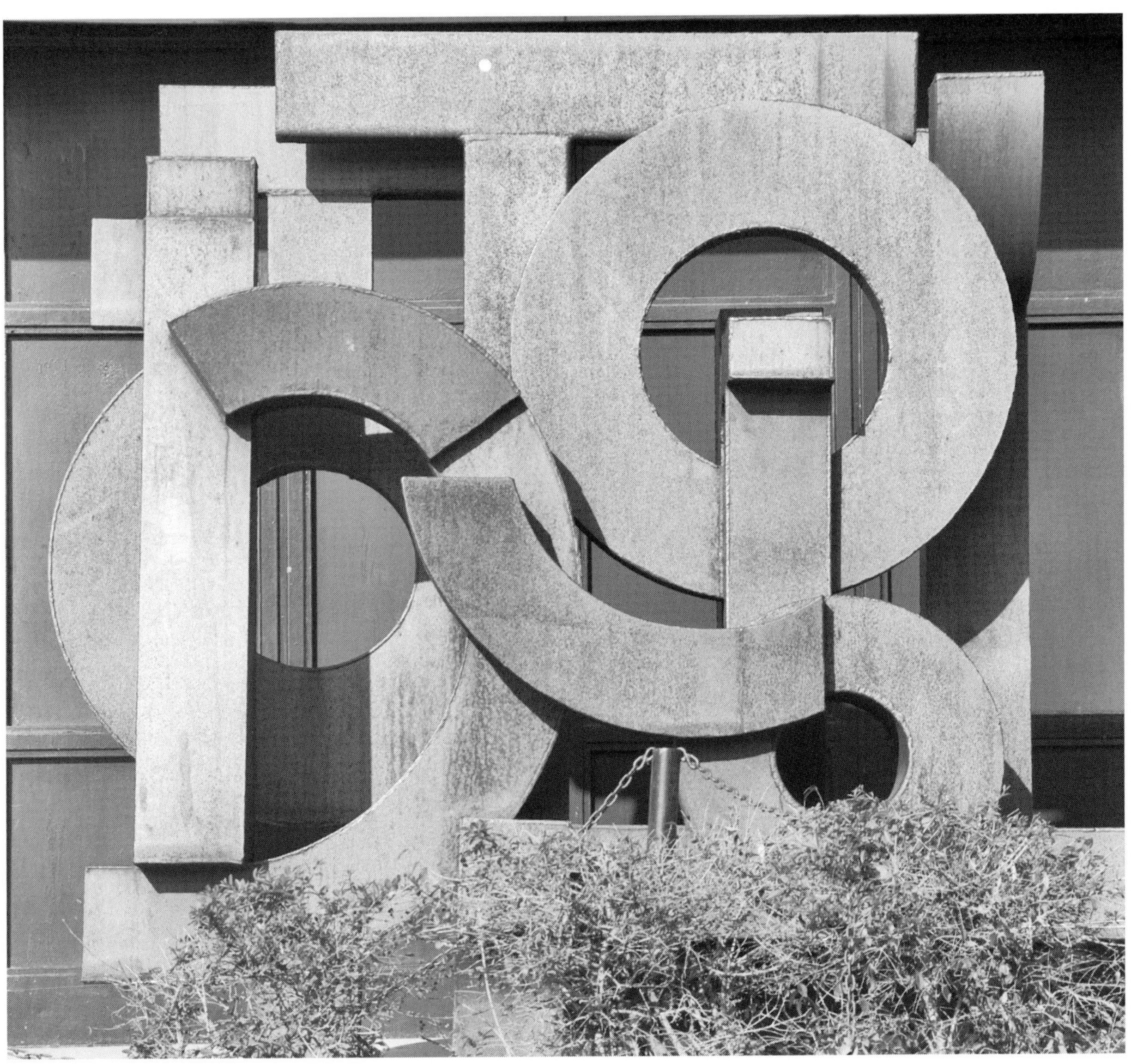

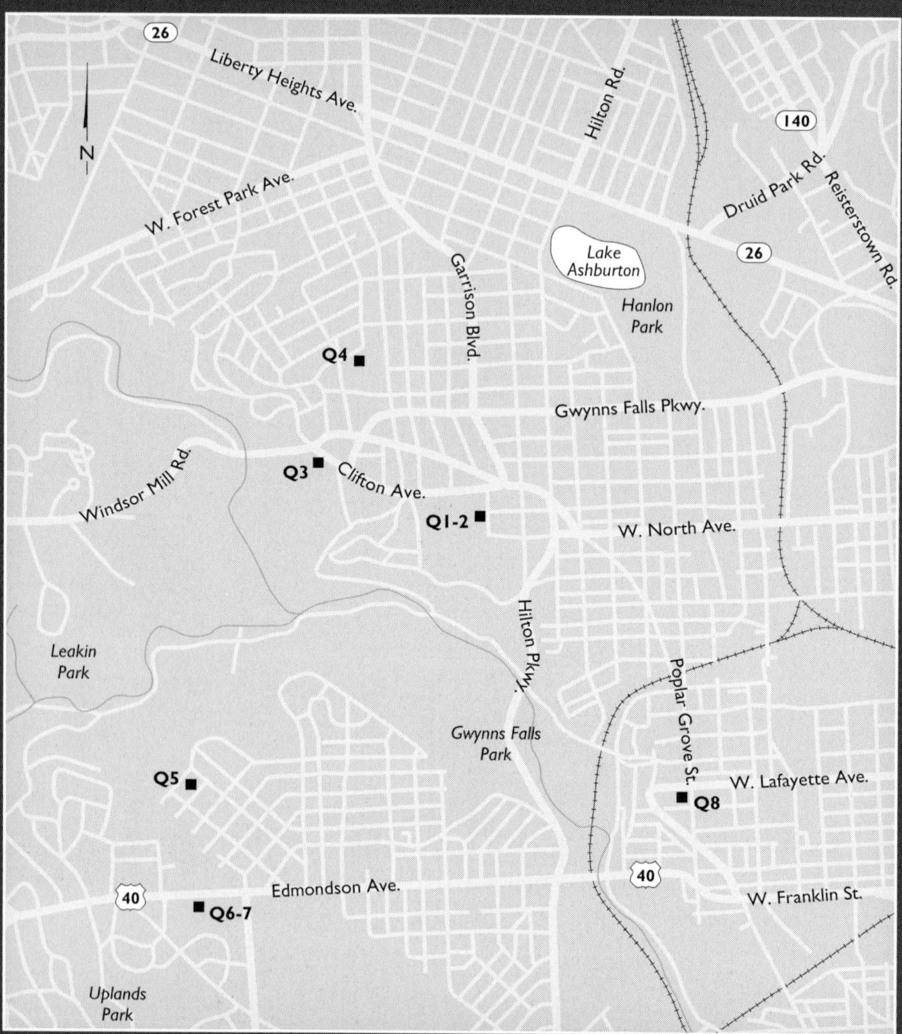

26
Liberty Heights Ave.
Hilton Rd.
140
N
Druid Park Rd.
W. Forest Park Ave.
Reisterstown Rd.
26
Lake
Ashburton
Garrison Blvd.
Hanlon
Park
Q4
Gwynns Falls Pkwy.
Windsor Mill Rd.
Q3
Clifton Ave.
Q1-2
W. North Ave.
Leakin
Park
Hilton Pkwy.
Poplar Grove St.
Gwynns Falls
Park
W. Lafayette Ave.
Q5
Q8
Edmondson Ave.
40
40
W. Franklin St.
Q6-7
Uplands
Park

WEST BALTIMORE

Driving

Q1

TITLE
Turning Point, 1970

LOCATION
The Walbrook Campus, 2000 Edgewood Street

SCULPTOR
Alfredo Halegua (b. 1930)

MEDIUM
Aluminum

DONOR
Baltimore City Percent for Art program

This large aluminum sculpture required the most dramatic installation of any piece in the city. A helicopter was required to lower the 35-foot-long sculpture through the top of the school building into an interior courtyard.

The title, which Alfredo Halegua wanted to reflect the location as a place of learning, underscores the fact that education becomes a turning point in everyone's life. The boomerang shape of the sculpture may also be related to the site: A boomerang is a curved piece of wood designed to return to the person who throws it;

perhaps the sculpture's shape is a reference to the idea that investing in one's education brings rich returns.

Emphatically horizontal and touching down on its circular base in only one place, near the midpoint, *Turning Point* appears perfectly balanced even though the sweeping three-dimensional geometric forms that have been fitted together to conform to the shape of a boomerang reach higher into the air at one end than at the other. The beautifully burnished aluminum surface dramatically reflects the sunlight.

When Halegua began thinking about installing the sculpture, the building was complete. It became obvious that the only way in was through the opening into the courtyard. Using a giant crane turned out to be more costly than using a helicopter, but use of the latter was very restrictive. The helicopter would only be able to hold the piece in the air for five minutes, after which the cables holding the sculpture would have to be released even if the installation was incomplete. The fact that one side of the piece was heavier than the other complicated matters further. The helicopter landed beside the sculpture, which rested on a flatbed truck on the playing fields. The cables were attached, as were two ropes, to help maneuver the piece into place. Installation took 4 minutes and 15 seconds!

Pierre duFayet and Jordi Bonet were also commissioned to create artworks for the school, duFayet for the second courtyard outside the cafeteria (Q2) and Bonet for the entranceway.

Note: This outdoor sculpture is sited in a courtyard within the school for which there is limited access. When school is in session, the sculpture may be viewed between 10:00 a.m. and 5:00 p.m.; visitors must first check in at the school's main office. During the summer months, visitors are advised to call ahead to confirm the hours of operation.

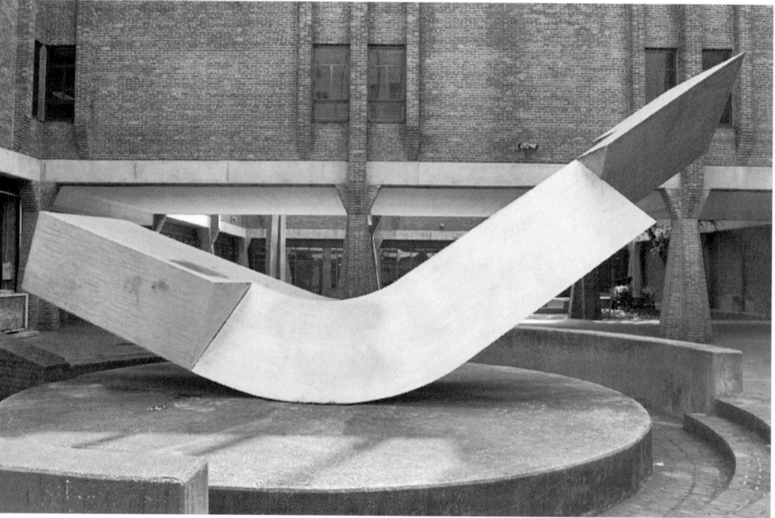

Q2

TITLE
Untitled, 1970

LOCATION
The Walbrook Campus, 2000 Edgewood Street

SCULPTOR
Pierre duFayet (1929–1986)

MEDIA
Aluminum, slate, and epoxy

DONOR
Baltimore City Percent for Art program

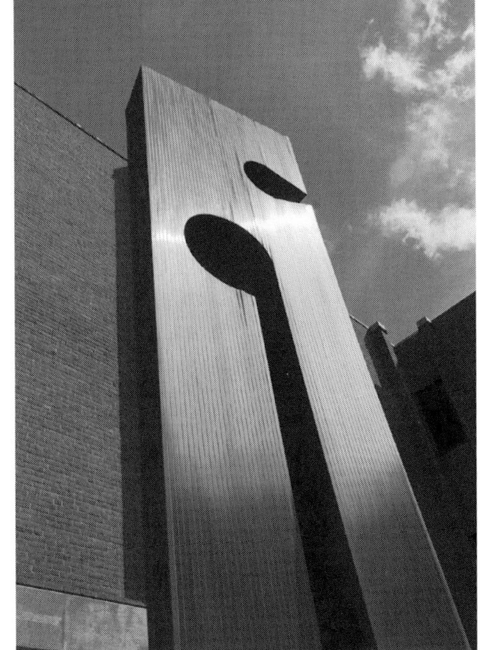

"Not taking advantage of modern techniques is like forever doing watercolors in an age of technology," Pierre duFayet was quoted as saying at the time. Always experimenting with new materials, duFayet chose here to use a mixture of slate and epoxy with aluminum.

In contrast to the more horizontal and exuberant sculpture by Alfredo Halegua in the opposite courtyard (Q1), Pierre duFayet's untitled sculpture is vertical and very controlled. One-inch strips of aluminum were used to face the broad front and back surfaces of a 20-foot-high pier. These aluminum strips accentuate the verticality of the piece and give it a highly reflective silver color. The slate and epoxy mixture, which is dark grey in color and has a nonreflective quality, was applied to the narrower side surfaces. The vertical pier is interrupted in two places: near the top, a small oval cuts in from one edge; and a deep cut leading from the base to above the midpoint culminates in a circular opening wider than the oval opening near the top of the pier. The shape of the long, deep cut led students to christen the piece "The Question Mark." The sculpture stands on a raised mound covered in ceramic tiles that extend across the floor of the courtyard.

DuFayet was born in Paris, France, where he graduated from the Collège Lycée Henri IV and the École Superieure des Arts Appliqués à l'Industrie. In 1956 Du Fayet left Paris for New York, where he worked as an industrial designer and commercial artist. In 1965 he was hired as a designer for the Rouse Company, of Baltimore. The project he worked on for Rouse was the new town of Columbia, for which he designed everything from the typeface for the name Columbia to the 35-foot-high *Tree of Life,* which has since become Columbia's trademark. DuFayet settled in Baltimore and opened a studio in the 500 block of E. Lombard Street. Always experimenting with new materials, such as silicone rubber, fiberglass, and epoxy resins, he received commissions for three new schools in Baltimore. In addition to this commission for Walbrook, he created a mural for the Claremont School that was made out of silicone rubber applied to a fiberglass shell, and for Cecil Elementary School he created three reliefs, sited indoors and out, of stainless steel and epoxy resin.

Note: This outdoor sculpture is sited in a courtyard within the school for which there is limited access. When school is in session, the sculpture may be viewed between 10:00 a.m. and 5:00 p.m.; visitors must first check in at the school's main office. During the summer months, visitors are advised to call ahead to confirm the hours of operation.

Q3

TITLE
Untitled, 1972

LOCATION
Cahill Recreation Center, 4001 Clifton Avenue

SCULPTOR
William Leizman (b. 1926)

MEDIUM
Mayari-R steel

DONOR
Baltimore City Percent for Art program

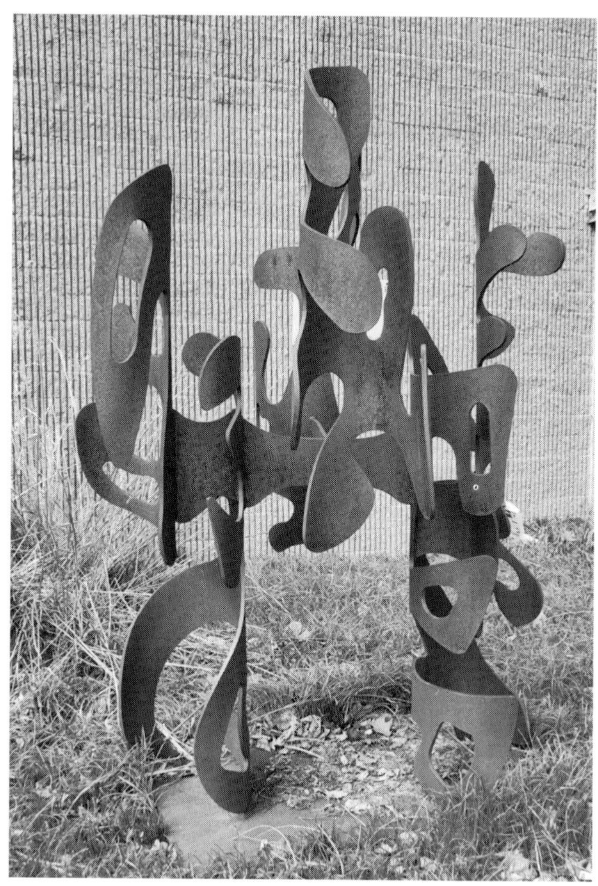

This untitled sculpture was William Leizman's second Percent for Art commission. His first was for Rognell Heights Elementary School in 1968 (Q5).

The abstract sculpture sited near the entrance to the Cahill Recreation Center stands just over 8 feet high. Leizman has used Mayari-R steel, the weathering steel he favored for all his sculptures. Here the steel has developed its typical rusty surface, giving the sculpture a warm chocolate brown color. This predominantly vertical piece is composed of four separate sections. While all four sections were cut and rolled similarly, each is unique. The two taller, lower sections stand parallel to each other and anchor the piece to the base plate. The two upper sections, also parallel to each other, are welded at right angles to the lower sections at their midpoint, creating a sculpture with bilateral symmetry. The curving, amorphously shaped bands of steel that make up each section are as likely to have been left solid in his hands as they are to have been cut out.

Q4

TITLE
Sod Buster, 1975

LOCATION
Windsor Hills Elementary School, 4001 Alto Road

SCULPTOR
Roger Majorowicz (b. 1931)

MEDIUM
Found objects

DONOR
Baltimore City Percent for Art program

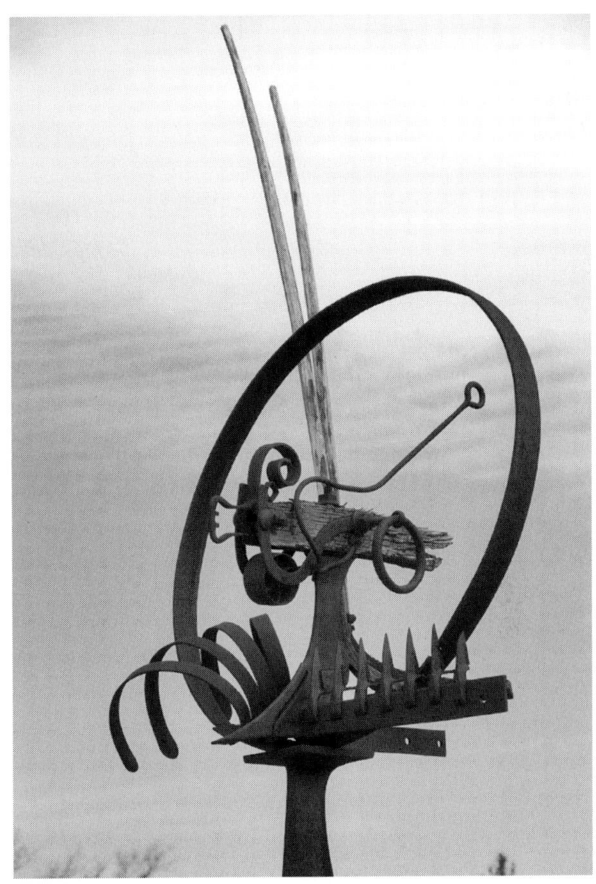

How many found objects can be balanced on the top of an ornamental wrought-iron fence post? *Sod Buster* offers one answer. Made possible with 1 percent of the funding for a new addition to the Windsor Hills Elementary School, the sculpture offers a gentle but warm welcome to the staff and students each day.

Roger Majorowicz found two mangled fence posts in the city of Hollowell, Maine, near what used to be his summer home and studio, where he now lives full time. He straightened them both out and used one for this piece. He submitted a photograph of the finished piece for consideration for this school commission. Since his family was unhappy about losing the piece, he made another piece, *Chanticleer*, out of the second fence post. Today *Chanticleer* stands outside his studio. He says the abstract rooster calls him to work each day.

For the piece that he sent to Baltimore, Majorowicz bolted a short section of I-beam to the top of the fence post and added the following objects: a share from an old walking plow, from which his title derives; a large circle, made of iron that was part of a wheel from a wagon that hauled granite; two (formerly three) wooden shafts, which rise into the air, from an old horse buggy; four short spokes, which turn downward, from a spring-tooth harrow; and a horizontal bar with arrow-shaped pieces projecting upward, from an old mower.

TITLE
Untitled, 1968

LOCATION
Rognell Heights Elementary School,
4300 Sidehill Road

SCULPTOR
William Leizman (b. 1926)

MEDIUM
Mayari-R steel

DONOR
Baltimore City Percent for Art program

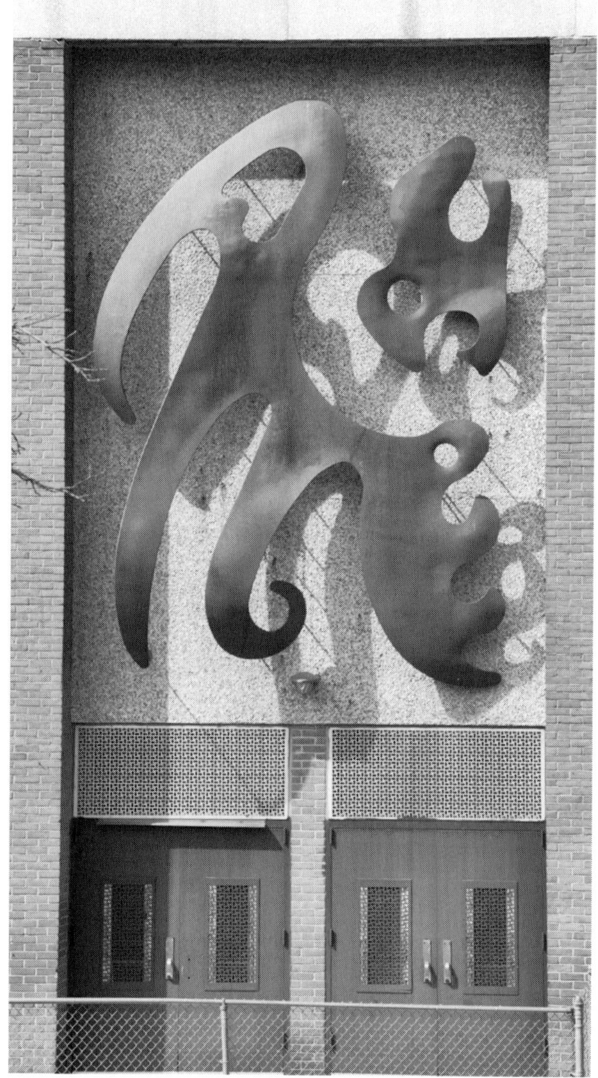

William Leizman was chosen by the architect Charles Pippen to create not one but three artworks for this new school, all reliefs: one for the entrance facade, one for a wall in the lobby, and one for a wall in the cafeteria. This architectural project was one of the earliest to benefit from the city's Percent for Art program.

The huge, 15-foot-high abstract relief mounted on the front of the school, high over two double doors, is now colored a warm chocolate brown. The color and condition of this relief result from Leizman's use of the weathering Mayari-R steel. Broad sheets of this steel were cut and rolled, not folded or welded closed. In broad open sheets the steel can develop a protective coating that appears rich and velvety, as it does here. The undulating relief, in some places 1 foot from the light-colored aggregate wall, in other places 2 feet, casts deep shadows on a sunny day that contribute a heightened dimensionality to the two curvilinear forms, which could be calligraphic markings. The scale of the vertically sweeping forms, the contrast of the dark steel against the light stone wall behind it, and the shadows created by the high relief add up to a very dramatic work of art.

The small relief that Leizman designed for the recreation center around the corner, on Clifton Avenue, is related to the much larger relief on the school facade. It too is composed of two abstract, curvilinear shapes of Mayari-R steel, the larger punctuated by a circular cutout, which are mounted on the wall with threaded rods about 8 inches long. And it too has weathered to a velvety brown.

Q6

TITLE
Westside, 1981

LOCATION
Edmondson-Westside High School,
4501 Edmondson Avenue (U.S. Route 40)

SCULPTOR
Greg Moring (b. 1949)

MEDIUM
Aluminum

DONOR
Baltimore City Percent for Art program

This is the expansive, 50-foot-long, 17-foot-high relief that Greg Moring was designing when he received the commission for the Rogers Avenue Metro Station and from which that piece, *Rogers Avenue* (N10), directly derives.

Here, on the entrance wall to what was originally the Westside Skill Center, once again Moring's inspiration was machinery. The overarching impression is one of conveyer belts on an assembly line, and the rectangular format of the relief reinforces that impression.

On the opposite side of this school building is a relief by Herbert Lee (Q7). Similar in scale and material, the two works differ in interesting ways. Moring designed the abstract, geometric elements to fit together very tightly, and he mounted his relief very close against the brick wall. Lee's piece is more open, in deeper relief, and thus more sculptural, characteristics that led to unforeseen site problems that are obvious today.

This school building, an addition to the 1955 Edmondson High School, was designed for vocational and technical studies by David McCracken, of Basco Associates, who chose Moring and Lee to create the exterior wall reliefs and David English to create a series of prints related to the different vocational skills taught at the school for the interior halls.

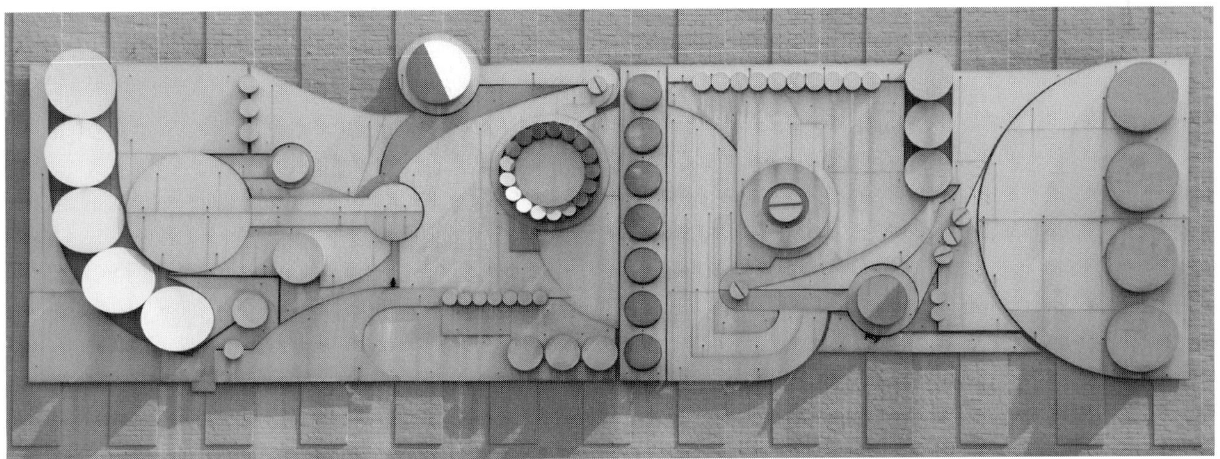

Q7

TITLE
Local #420, 1982

LOCATION
Edmondson-Westside High School,
4501 Edmondson Avenue (U.S. Route 40)

SCULPTOR
Herbert Lee (b. 1949)

MEDIUM
Aluminum

DONOR
Baltimore City Percent for Art program

Even longer than Greg Moring's relief on the opposite wall, Herbert Lee's companion piece for this new high-school building extends 65 feet across the opposite, east wall. Both reliefs are clearly visible from U.S. Route 40 and from the Edmondson Village Shopping Center and the residential area across the street from the school.

Like Moring's piece, Lee's abstract aluminum relief is made up of geometric shapes that repeat across the wall. The circular, oval, and zigzag shapes cast deep shadows on the exposed brick wall and set up a wonderful interplay of positive and negative shapes. This relief, which along with Moring's immediately became a landmark for the neighborhood, had an unexpected problem: birds.

Lee's approach was quite different from Moring's. His relief is made of larger, more sculptural elements spaced in such a way as to leave much of the wall behind it exposed; in addition, it stands further out from the wall, leaving spaces behind as well as around the aluminum shapes. The unexpected result was perfect nesting conditions for birds, exacerbated by a nearby tree. In 1991, after years of nesting birds, the Mayor's Advisory Committee on Art and Culture (today the Baltimore Office of Promotion and The Arts) raised the funding necessary to conserve the piece—to power wash the relief to remove the birds and their nesting materials, to polish the aluminum, to paint the mounting wall, and, finally, to hire Bird Masters of Woburn, Massachusetts, to wrap the piece in a nylon mesh netting designed to keep out the birds. Surprisingly, the mesh is not visible even from a short distance away, and it certainly isn't visible from Route 40. The same mesh was used to wrap the B&O Railroad Building and the sculptural group *Mercury and Commerce* (B4).

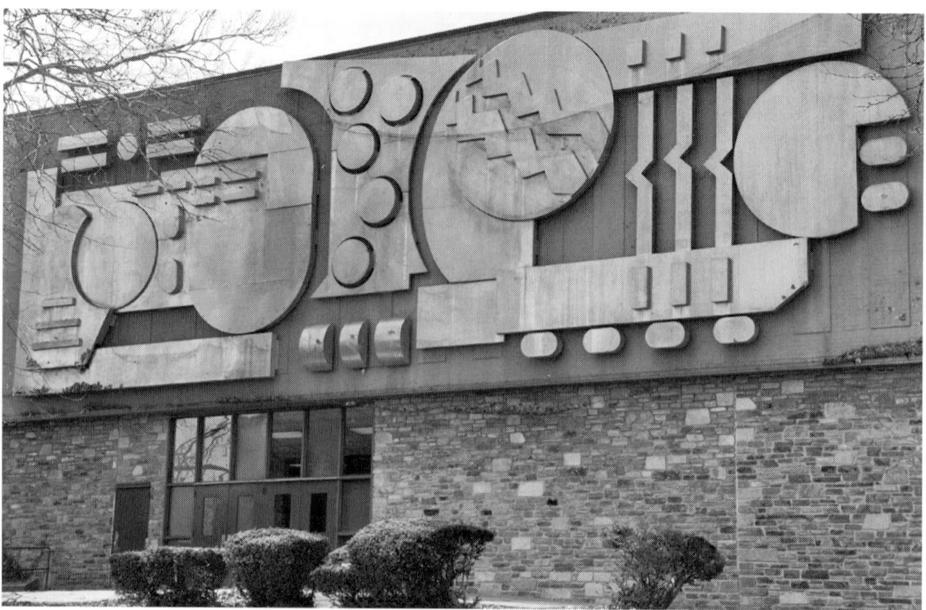

Q8

TITLE
Kinship, 1982

LOCATION
Alexander Hamilton Elementary School,
800 Poplar Grove Street

SCULPTOR
Lisa Kaslow (b. 1953)

MEDIUM
Painted steel rod

DONOR
Baltimore City Percent for Art program

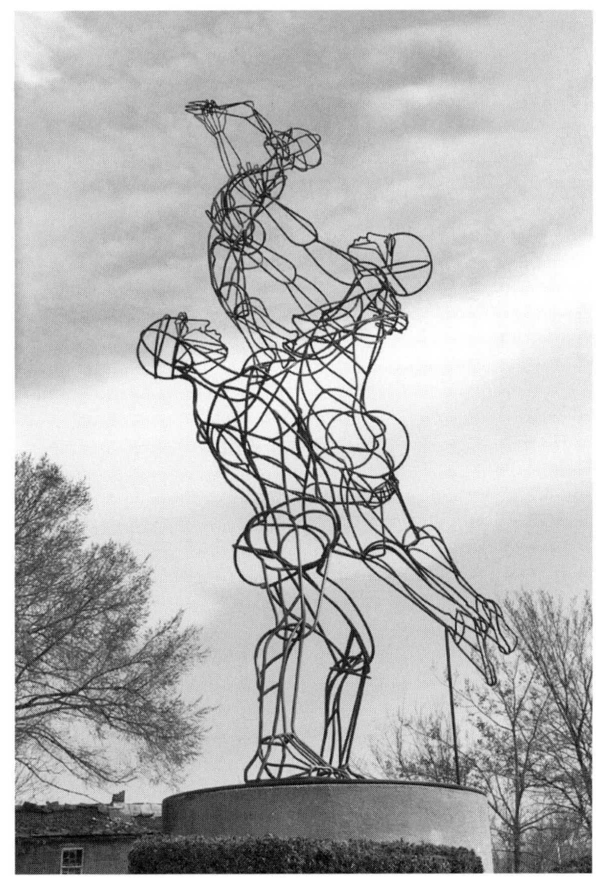

References to family and kinship were frequently voiced during Lisa Kaslow's meeting with community members when she asked what ideas they wanted incorporated into the artwork at their new elementary school.

Kaslow's interpretation of the community's ideas is this 19-foot-high vertical grouping of one definition of family and kinship—a male figure, a female figure, and the figure of a young child. These three figures also serve to represent the whole community of men, women, and children. The male, or father, figure stands with his feet firmly planted far apart on a low circular base as he lifts a female, or mother, figure above him; she in turn lifts a young child above and out in front of her. The figures are made of steel rod of varying dimensions— ½, ¾, and ⅝ inches—all bent by hand, welded together as one continuous piece from top to bottom, and painted black.

Kaslow had been making smaller sculptures out of steel rod of varying dimensions. She had become increasingly interested in the idea of externalizing the internal armature used in figurative sculpture— presenting the exoskeleton of the figure as a different approach to abstraction. This sculpture appears as a line drawing of figures in space.

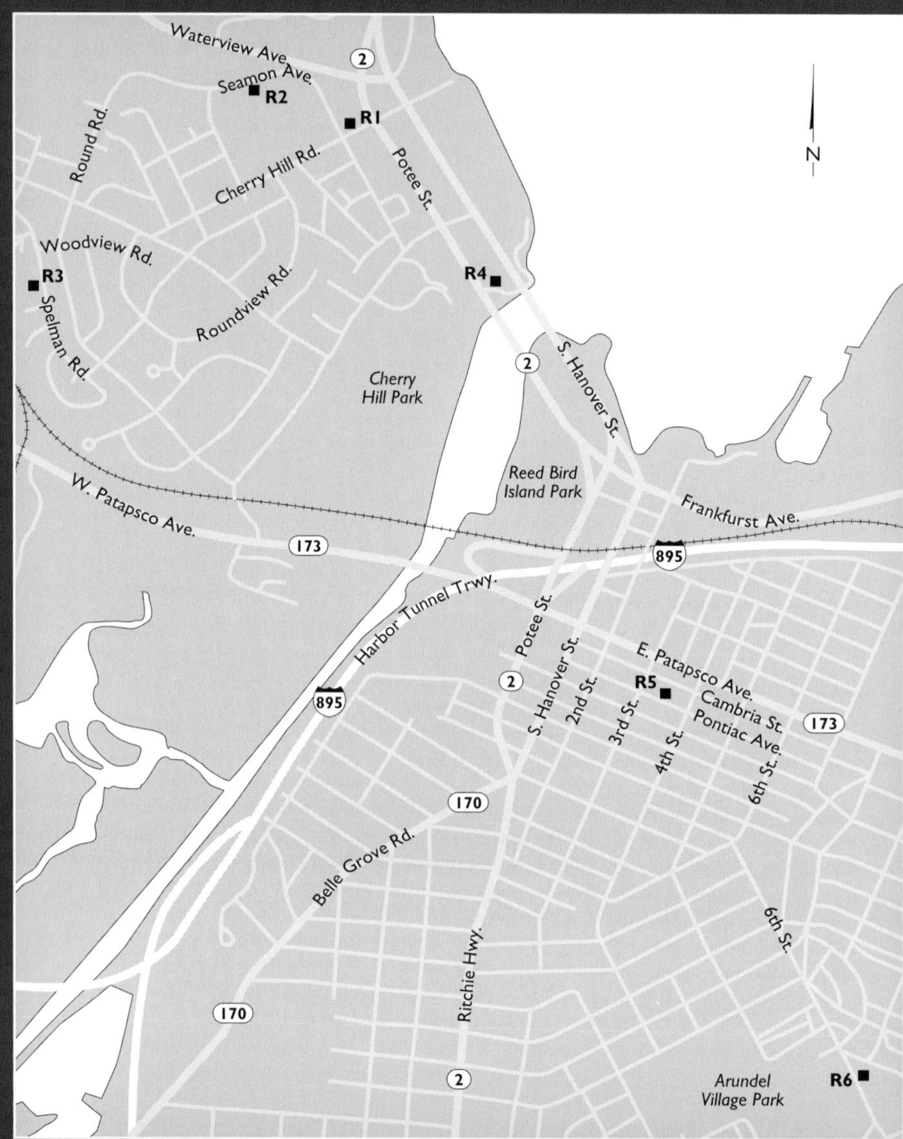

Waterview Ave.
2
Seamon Ave.
R2
R1
Round Rd.
Cherry Hill Rd.
Potee St.
Woodview Rd.
R3
R4
Roundview Rd.
Spelman Rd.
2
S. Hanover St.
Cherry Hill Park
Reed Bird Island Park
Frankfurst Ave.
W. Patapsco Ave.
173
895
Harbor Tunnel Trwy.
895
Potee St.
E. Patapsco Ave.
S. Hanover St.
2nd St.
R5
Cambria St.
Pontiac Ave.
3rd St.
4th St.
6th St.
173
170
Belle Grove Rd.
Ritchie Hwy.
6th St.
170
2
Arundel Village Park
R6
N

CHERRY HILL AND BROOKLYN PARK

Driving

R1

TITLE:
Untitled, 2006

LOCATION
Southern District Police Station,
10 Cherry Hill Road

SCULPTORS
Tim Scofield (b. 1970) and Ledelle Moe (b. 1971)

MEDIUM
Concrete

DONOR
Baltimore City Percent for Art program

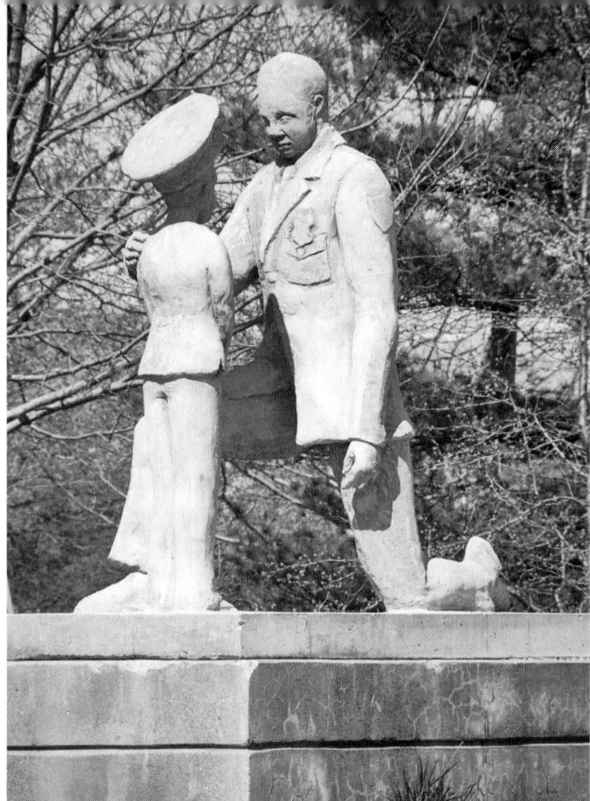

In 1986 the architect Robert J. Nash selected Ronald Anderson (b. 1946) for a public art commission at the police station he had just designed. Anderson cast two concrete figures—a police officer and a young boy. The police officer was shown in uniform, kneeling down in front of the small boy with his right hand on the boy's left shoulder. The policeman was at eye level with the boy and appeared to be talking directly to him. The young boy was wearing the officer's hat, which of course dwarfed the boy.

When the piece was destroyed by a car in 2005, and Anderson was unavailable to take on the job of replacing his original piece, the Baltimore Office of Promotion and The Arts, with a limited insurance settlement, asked Tim Scofield, who was working as the sculpture technician at the Maryland Institute at the time and teaching metal-fabrication workshops, to make a replacement piece. Scofield invited Ledelle Moe, a colleague at the Institute who works in concrete, to collaborate on the project. After meeting with members of the Southern District Community Relations Council, the two artists realized that the police in the Southern District wanted them to re-create the original piece. Scofield and Moe worked from a series of photographs they took of a police officer and his daughter in the positions of the original sculpture. The new piece was installed and dedicated in June 2006.

A project like this is interesting for what it does not reveal about the two artists. A collaboration can result in an almost anonymous work of art, with the artists involved working in ways they might never work if left on their own. A collaboration to make a copy of another artist's work further blurs any evidence of an individual artist's hand at work. That is surely true in this project. For the past decade Scofield, who earned his MFA at Syracuse University before coming to Baltimore in 2000, has been creating kinetic metal sculptures from found objects and fabricated forms. An acrobat or other performer—sometimes Scofield himself—is harnessed onto an arm of one of his flying machines, also called "aerial sculptures," to control the motions of the machine, which might reach 15 feet into the air and rotate 360°. A recent flying machine was exhibited as part of the 2007 Artscape. Moe, who was born in South Africa and earned her MFA from Virginia Commonwealth University in Richmond, creates large-scale installations with human and animal forms that are deeply rooted in the history of her homeland. The surface texture that she created on her recent monumental heads is complex, evocative, and mysterious, suggesting a deep hidden narrative.

R2

TITLE
Untitled, 1969

LOCATION
Southside Academy, 2700 Seaman Avenue

SCULPTOR
James E. Lewis (1923–2007)

MEDIUM
Bronze

DONOR
Baltimore City Percent for Art program

New additions and renovations brought more than extra classrooms and up-to-date electrical systems to the older schools across the city. Beginning in the late 1960s, these construction projects also brought new artwork.

The cornerstone for Cherry Hill Junior High School was laid in 1952. In 1969, when the school was renovated, James Lewis was commissioned to create a work of art for the newly renamed Arnett J. Brown Jr. Middle School. Today, the renamed Southside Academy is a senior high school.

James E. Lewis' untitled bronze abstract relief spreads more than 40 feet across the facade of the school. Centered over the entrance doors, the relief comprises fourteen separate elements. Each of the elements is composed of a basic unit that was then doubled, tripled, or quadrupled in size and varied in design. The abstract shapes are either circles or diamonds, cut out or added. The resulting variation in scale and design animates the space and hints at some hidden language or set of symbols.

In 1965, at the invitation of the American Society of African Culture, Lewis made his first trip to Africa, to deliver a series of lectures at universities, embassies, and cultural centers. For more than a decade thereafter he returned to Africa each year; in 1971 he was invited to join the first archaeological excavation undertaken by the Nigerian government. These trips allowed Lewis to study African culture and ultimately to acquire a sizeable personal collection of African art. He also bought more than two hundred objects for the museum at Morgan State University that today bears his name.

It has been suggested that Lewis' designs on the facade of Southside Academy may be related to Ashanti symbols. The Ashanti people live in Ghana, in West Africa, and their symbols, called Adinkra, can be traced back to the seventeenth century. These symbols, most often used in designs for cloth, were geometric shapes based on the shapes of animals, plants, and other objects. No specific Ashanti symbol can be seen here, but the comparison has merit.

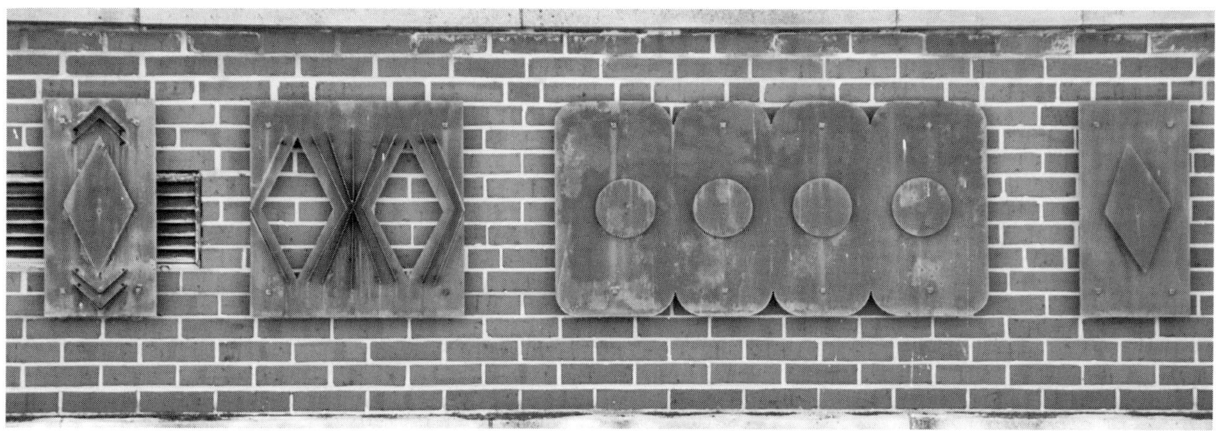

R3

TITLE
Untitled, 1954

LOCATION
Cherry Hill Homes, 2700 Spellman Road

SCULPTOR
Henry Berge (1908–1998)

MEDIUM
Concrete

DONOR
Housing Authority of Baltimore City

Over a period of approximately fifteen years the architect Edward Minor involved Henry Berge in three housing projects. This commission for Cherry Hill Homes was the third. The first two were for the McCulloh Homes (M1) and Lafayette Courts, today Pleasant Garden View (O7).

As with McCulloh Homes and Lafayette Courts, Minor chose the location for the artwork, and together he and Berge came up with a design. Minor always had the final say regarding the design. Minor operated out of the Housing Authority office but may have worked for the federal government. The Housing Authority of Baltimore City built these projects with the assistance of the U.S. Housing Office, and no record can be found of Minor in the city archives.

The relief includes a male figure and two small children, a young girl and an infant boy, arranged across a narrow ledge in a very tight, well-thought-out triangular composition. On the left the young girl, who sits on a small scooter, appears as if she has just twisted around to look back over her shoulder at the other two figures. She is placed just in front of the feet of the male figure, no doubt representing her father. The father figure, shown in profile, sits between the children with his legs extended horizontally across the ledge as he supports himself by leaning on his left hand. On the right the infant boy appears to have just crawled along the ledge to hold onto his father's extended arm as he balances himself with his left hand on a small ball. The father figure holds a book in his right hand, marking his place with one finger as he rests his outstretched arm on his raised knee, as if he has just been interrupted. Berge has captured a very active scene conceived of as taking place during the summer, for the father's sleeves are rolled up and the children, dressed in playclothes, are barefooted.

Like the previous two reliefs for Minor, this one was cast in concrete. This one, however, has been painted white.

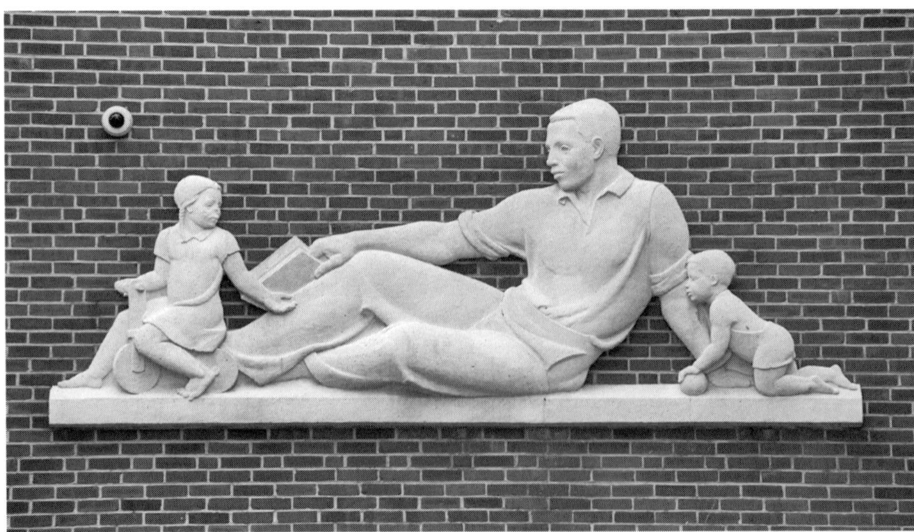

R4

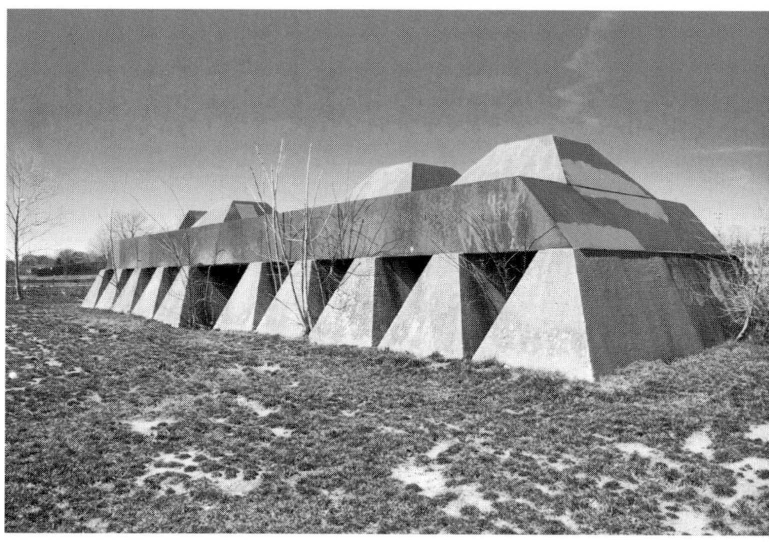

Jim Sanborn's first public sculpture, this piece was created as part of a sculpture symposium sponsored by the city and administered by the Department of Housing and Community Development (HCD) during the summer of 1977. Four artists were commissioned to each create gateway pieces for the city. The only other piece remaining from that symposium is the *Atlantic Blue Roller Column,* by Dominick Cea on Russell Street. (For Cea's piece and for the history of the symposium, see H5.)

This early work reveals the influence of the Mayan culture, the temples of Guatemala in particular, in which Sanborn has always been interested. Abstract and horizontal, the work stands at the far edge of an open field directly fronting the Patapsco River, extending almost 80 feet along the water's edge. Ten pyramidal shapes are aligned symmetrically, five on either side of an opening that contains a pool and allows a view of the river. In the pool there is a grate made of aluminum. Light streams through the open space and is reflected on the grate and in the pool. Resting on top of the flattened pyramids made of concrete is one continuous lintel of weathering steel. The lintel carries four more pyramidal shapes, again symmetrically placed, two on each side of the central opening, and again flattened. In 1977 the concrete was bright white, the steel was a beautiful velvety brown, and the grass was green and lush. The silhouette of the piece was and still is impressive.

HCD assisted the artists at every turn, providing honoraria, materials, equipment, and assistants. For *Patapsco River Project,* Curtis Steel contributed between 12,000 and 15,000 pounds of Mayari-R steel, the city contributed and poured the concrete, and Edward Renneburg & Sons sheared the steel for free. Sanborn estimates that it might have cost him $100,000 to assemble the piece independently.

R5

TITLE
Untitled, 1976

LOCATION
Maree Garnett Farring Elementary School,
300 Pontiac Avenue

SCULPTOR
John Ferguson (b. 1939)

MEDIUM
Cor-Ten steel and stainless steel

DONOR
Baltimore City Percent for Art program

Benjamin Brotman, the architect for the new school, selected John Ferguson for this commission after a limited competition. Ferguson designed and fabricated a relief for the school facade and a related relief for the lobby wall.

This abstract facade relief, like all Ferguson's sculpture, combines curved and angular forms. Here Ferguson combined Cor-Ten steel, which has turned a dark velvety brown, with stainless steel, which is silver and reflective. The dark Cor-Ten and the light stainless steel contrast dramatically as they alternate in this sculpture stretching 15 feet across the red brick wall surface. The undulating form looks like a puzzle, with all its pieces fitting tightly together. The stainless steel shape at the left end, which suggests a bird, and the Cor-Ten shape at the right end which might be a fish, seem to parenthetically enclose the rest of the horizontal design.

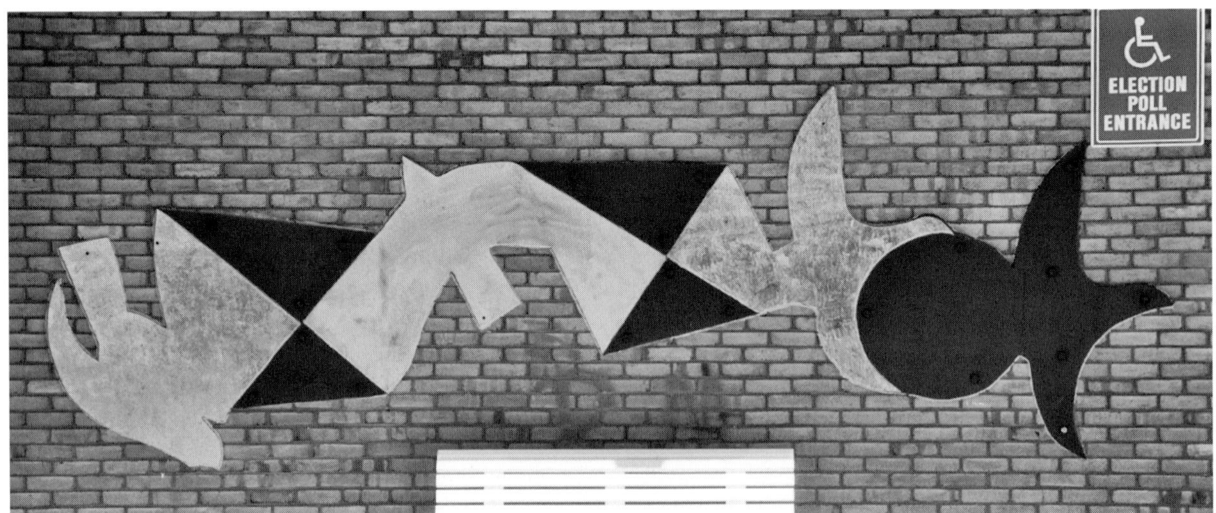

R6

TITLE
A Bird Flying North, 1971

LOCATION
Baybrook Elementary School, 4301 Tenth Street

SCULPTOR
Michio Ihara (b. 1928)

MEDIUM
Aluminum

DONOR
Baltimore City Percent for Art program

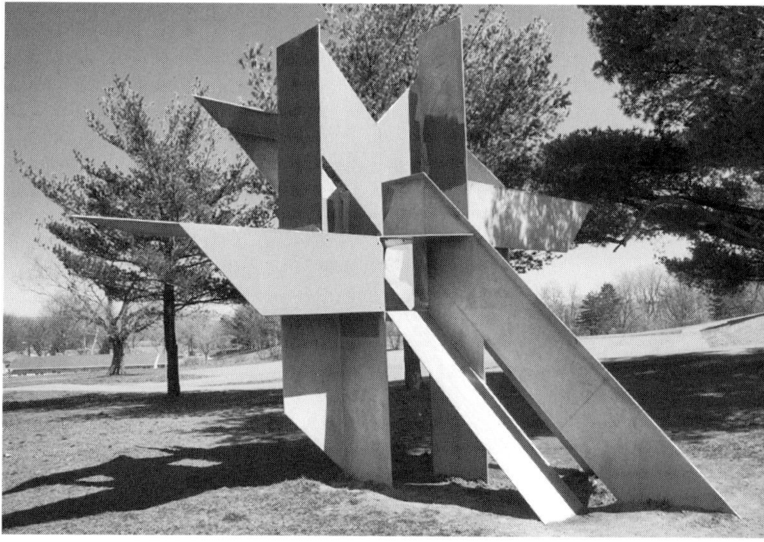

The abstract, modular sculpture at Baybrook Elementary School doubles as a playground climbing structure. Installed near the entrance to the school, it was constructed out of 2-foot-wide sheets of aluminum. Each module was created by cuts made at a 90° or 45° angle. The modules were then welded to a central pylonlike structure, creating many different planes. Two very noticeable "wings" extend outward from two sides of the sculpture, one higher than the other but in about the same plane. The single set of steps up into the structure is not immediately revealed. From high inside the structure one can see the city skyline off in the distance—an accidental yet poetic way of connecting the young students to their city.

Michio Ihara does not like to title his sculpture, but the school wanted a title, so Ihara suggested that the students come up with a title and share it with him. *A Bird Flying North* seemed appropriate to Ihara, who likes aircraft forms and had actually been thinking about incorporating the idea of "taking off" into the piece.

Ihara is a Japanese American, born in Paris, who obtained his American citizenship in 2001. He studied in Tokyo at the University of Fine Arts before coming to the United States in 1961 on a Fulbright Scholarship to study first at the University of Arizona in Tucson and then at the Massachusetts Institute of Technology in Boston. In 1970 he became a permanent resident of Massachusetts, and a fellow at the Center for Advanced Visual Studies at MIT.

Since 1981 he has lived and maintained a studio in Concord, Massachusetts. His work has been commissioned for cities across the country, including New York, Chicago, Boston, Beverly Hills, and many cities in Massachusetts. His sculpture can also be seen in cities across Japan, Korea, and Australia. Ihara received a second commission in Baltimore from Ackerman & Company, an Atlanta-based developer that built the C&P Telephone headquarters building at Pratt and Light streets in 1978. (That sculpture was removed in 2008 by the new owners of the building.) His most recent sculpture in the Baltimore area hangs in the rotunda of the newly renovated St. Joseph Medical Center, on Osler Drive in Towson. Unlike his two earlier pieces in Baltimore, which are stationary, his suspended sculpture at St. Joseph Medical Center and most of his other public sculptures are kinetic and wind activated.

Epilogue

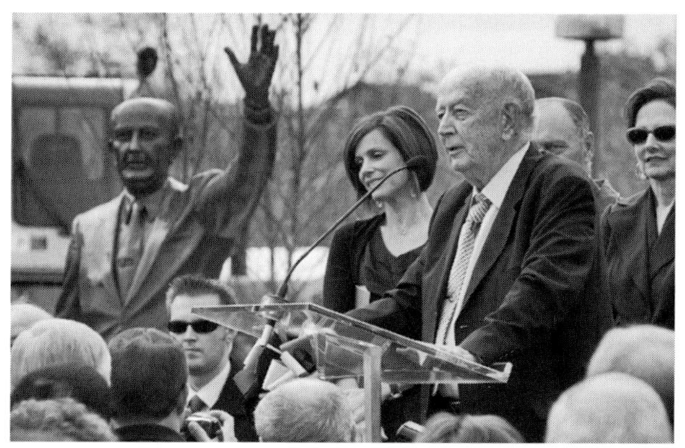

IN JANUARY 2009, ONE MORE HIGHLY visible piece of public sculpture was installed and dedicated in the Inner Harbor, joining the other sculptures included in the first tour in this guide. This newest piece of sculpture is Rodney Carroll's standing portrait of William Donald Schaefer, who served as a member of the city council from 1955 to 1971; mayor of Baltimore from 1971 to 1987; governor of Maryland from 1987 to 1995; and state comptroller from 1999 to 2007.

Planning for the statue began three years earlier. Edwin F. Hale Sr., chairman and CEO of 1st Mariner Bancorp, originally spearheaded this project. Hale wanted the portrait statue to be the centerpiece of the plaza area between the two Harborplace pavil-ions so that it would be visible from Pratt Street. The Public Art Commission refused to grant permission for the statue to be sited there, and Hale pulled out of the project.

By then too many people were excited about the possibility of a statue of Schaefer being installed somewhere in the Inner Harbor, and planning continued. Willard Hackerman, CEO and president of Whiting-Turner Contracting and a longtime friend of Schaefer's, stepped forward with his wife, Lillian Patz Hackerman, offering to fund the project and essentially leaving every design decision relating to the sculpture and its site to the artist. Carroll then chose this site, just south of the Light Street pavilion, and asked the landscape architect Carol Macht, of Hord Coplan Macht, to design a garden to surround the statue.

Carroll made a trip to the Maryland State Archives, where he found hundreds of photographs and videos that thoroughly documented not only Schaefer's tenure as city councilman, mayor, governor, and comptroller but also his typical stance, his gait, his gestures, and many other subtleties that Carroll has included in his sculpture. Early in the process of modeling the statue, Carroll invited Schaefer to visit his studio, where he got the full measure of the man, literally. Carroll then asked to borrow many personal items from Schaefer to use as guides in his design: a suit, a shirt, a pair of his shoes, his watch, and a favorite tie clasp showing the seal of Baltimore with its image of the Battle Monument. Carroll's careful attention to all the details of the man is impressive and contributes to the statue's excellent resemblance.

Surely one of the most challenging questions facing the artist was from what point in time, across the long span of his career, to depict Schaefer. In the end, Carroll chose to present a composite of the man over his entire career. Schaefer's figure and face, as well as his shirt and tie, are drawn from the 1980s, when Schaefer was at the height of his career as mayor. To this figure Carroll added a haircut and one of Schaefer's suits from the 1990s and a pair of shoes from 2005. The shoes turn up at the toes, just as they always have on Schaefer. Carroll chose a gesture he had seen over and over again in pictures and on videos of Schaefer walking into a crowd: his hand raised in a warm greeting. The raised hand also gave the sculptor an excuse to add a sense of movement to the sculpture, depicting a slight turning motion to the left. The definition of the back of the suit jacket underscores this contrapposto movement. In his other hand Schaefer holds an action memo, something for which he became well known. His staff had these memos printed, and each one had a number. The number on the one in the statue, 11221, represents Schaefer's birth date—November 2, 1921—and the statue was dedicated on his birthday. Schaefer's department heads would receive real memos noting things that needed their immediate attention. The message was, "Do it now." Schaefer became famous for beginning his cabinet meetings by asking, "What have you done to help someone today?" Both these quotes, along with his signature, appear on the memo in his right hand.

Carroll wanted his statue of Schaefer to stand close to the ground, not to be raised high above visitors on a tall pedestal. The two white, five-sided slabs of marble—a direct reference to the historic marble steps of Baltimore and to the five-sided Fort McHenry—achieve that goal. Schaefer is presented here as a man of the people, moving among them with ease, welcoming people to Baltimore, the city he loved and served for so many years. It should be noted that while he was a city councilman he introduced the ordinance setting aside 1 percent of the cost of city construction projects for the inclusion of artworks; it became law in 1964. Baltimore was only the second city in the country to enact such legislation, through which some three hundred works of art have been commissioned, among them the sixty-six pieces found outdoors today and included in this guide. For the introduction of that ordinance alone, Schaefer might deserve a statue that could be included in this guide. But he achieved so much more for the city, as mayor and as governor. Under his leadership, there were successful urban revitalization projects like Ridgely's Delight and Otterbein; the creation of Harborplace, which was the city's major redevelopment project of the late 1970s; and the push to build two stadiums near each other downtown and near the Inner Harbor. Schaefer's statue looks out over the Inner Harbor, his major contribution to Baltimore's renaissance, much as the statue of another mayor, Thomas D'Alesandro, overlooks Charles Center, where the renaissance of downtown Baltimore began under his leadership in the late 1950s—leadership that Schaefer continued so ably.

Acknowledgments

First and foremost, I must thank Kathleen Kotarba, the executive director of the Commission for Historical and Architectural Preservation (CHAP), who got me involved in researching Baltimore's history of monument making. Kathleen hired me to conduct the Baltimore segment of a national program known as Save Outdoor Sculpture!—or SOS!—sponsored by the Smithsonian Institution's Museum of American Art, to survey all the outdoor sculpture in the country. From September 1991 through August 1992, when I surveyed all the sculpture in Baltimore, and over the next few years, as I completed the research required on each public artwork, I got completely hooked. Leading up to the symposium that Kathleen and I planned to celebrate the end of our segment of this national program, I gave a series of neighborhood sculpture tours and found that I enjoyed that experience more than I had ever imagined. As a result, I have been conducting research on these monuments, giving tours, and lecturing about Baltimore's outdoor sculpture ever since.

I next want to thank my editor, Robert J. Brugger, who began asking me if I would consider putting my research on monument making in Baltimore into book form as soon as my survey work was completed. His patience over the intervening years and his guidance and encouragement over the past four years will always be remembered and very much appreciated. I would also like to thank my copyeditor, Joanne Allen, for her thoughtful suggestions and thorough review of the text.

I must acknowledge the authors of previous publications on Baltimore's sculpture that have proved invaluable to my research, which are fully cited in the preface to this book: William S. Rusk, Wilbur H. Hunter, John Dorsey, Leslie Freudenheim, and Henry and Carolyn Naylor. I would also like to acknowledge Harold A. Williams, editor of the *Sunday Sun* and the *Sun Magazine* from 1954 to 1979, who gave me his collection of newspaper clippings on Baltimore's monuments, almost fifty years in the making, and I thank Genya Hopkins for suggesting to Mr. Williams that I be the recipient.

I am grateful to many others for their involvement and assistance. Linda DePalma, a sculptor herself, helped me conduct the year-long survey in 1991–92 and has read and offered editorial advice on more than a few entries in this guidebook. Her advice on those entries aided me in my approach to all the others. Lydia Kenselear, at the Maryland Institute College of Art, handled way too many requests from me in my search for Rinehart graduates who had made sculpture for the city. Others who helped me locate sculptors include Kim Domanski and Gary Kachadourian, at the Baltimore Office of Promotion and The Arts; Norman Carlberg, who was the director of the Rinehart School of Sculpture from 1961 until his retirement in 1996; James Adajian, a 1978 Rinehart graduate who helped me reach several of his contemporaries; and Rebecca Hoffberger, the founding director of the American Visionary Art Museum, who visited with me and answered many follow-up e-mails about the outdoor sculpture sited around her museum, including contact information for the artists. Deborah Bedwell, director of the

Baltimore Clayworks, told me the history of the fountain on the Mt. Washington campus and helped me reach its sculptor.

Melanie Harwood, the registrar at the Baltimore Museum of Art, and her staff members, Francis Klapthar and George Chang, were very helpful with the early history on the outdoor sculpture at their museum. Linda Baldwin, the librarian at the BMA, was always accommodating when I needed materials, and the conservator Ann Boulton never failed to answer my e-mails. She was especially helpful in discussions about the great lions out in front of the museum. Jay Fisher, deputy director at the BMA, very kindly reviewed my entries on the museum's outdoor sculpture. Jennifer Gibson, an administrator for General Services Administration's Art in Architecture Program, helped me pull together information on the program's four outdoor pieces in Baltimore. Fred Lazarus, president of the Maryland Institute, and Robert Alholm, director of its physical plant, provided answers to my many questions about the sculpture sited around the Institute. Douglas Frost, formerly the vice president for development at MICA, who is currently writing a history of that institution, also answered myriad questions about Rinehart graduates and their work that can be found in many other sites throughout the city. Several residents of Homeland, including Judy Smith, Yvonne Lenz, Paul Robie, and Lynn L. Petersons, manager of the Homeland Association, helped me uncover the very early history of that community, which included the purchase of Edward Berge's *Wildflower*, sited permanently on Springlake Way. Mary Porter, a landscape architect in the Department of Recreation and Parks, answered all my questions about sculpture sited in the city's parks. Steve Stenersen, president and CEO of U.S. Lacrosse, discussed the early history of the sculpture in front of his museum, at the edge of the Johns Hopkins University campus. Jeanne Willoz-Egnor, director of collections management at the Mariners' Museum in Newport News, Virginia, shared information on a small bronze statue of Columbus in her museum and the associated Schiaffino family history.

Nancy McCall, archivist for the Johns Hopkins Medical Institutions, and Jackie O'Regan, the curator for cultural properties at the Johns Hopkins University, both provided information on public sculpture under their respective purviews. Margaret Burri, librarian for history and curator of manuscripts, was always helpful when I needed access to material in the Milton S. Eisenhower Library, Special Collections. James Abbott, director and curator at Evergreen Museum and Library, helped me with my description of the great chair on the Latrobe Monument. Bea Julian, the librarian at the DuSable Museum of African American History, shared photographs of the live casting process used by René Townsend for her piece at the DuSable Museum and for her sculpture at MICA. Barbara Kellner, manager of the Columbia Archives, provided very valuable information on Pierre duFayet, a sculptor who worked for the Rouse Company and who created sculptures for Columbia, Maryland, as well as for several public schools in Baltimore. Mary Klein, the archivist for the Episcopal Diocese of Maryland, assisted with information about the Victory Cross, as did Thomas S. Doyle, at the Hilgartner Stone Company. James Dilts shared the research he had completed on the B&O Railroad office building that opened in 1906 with the heroic sculptural group *Mercury and Commerce* above the entrance. I must also thank Alan Shapiro, a classics professor at Johns Hopkins University; Beth Cohen, an editor for the *American Journal of Archaeology;* Michele H. Bogart, a professor of art history at the State University of New York at Stony Brook; and John P. Maranto, Curator of Archives and Small Objects at the B&O Railroad Museum in Baltimore for their participation in discussions on the questionable identification of *Commerce* on the B&O Railroad building. And for assistance with the translation of the Latin inscriptions on several Baltimore monuments, I must thank my good friend Carol Strickland, an art historian and independent scholar in New York. For another war monument, the Watson Monument, which is dedicated to those Baltimoreans who served and died in the Mexican War, I must thank Calvin Buikema, former superintendent of parks, for sharing information on the recently installed antique cannonballs on that monument's base and for many other revealing conversations about the city's monuments.

Several architects discussed their building projects that had included sculpture. This proved invaluable, especially in cases of sculptors who had died and whom I had never interviewed. Charles Brickbower and I had a long e-mail conversation about his 1969 Mercantile building in Hopkins Plaza, for which Antoni Milkowski's *Diamond #II-III* had been planned and installed. Walter Schamu and James Wollon were very helpful in finding now-retired architects who had designed buildings with associated Percent for Art monies. James Wollen also put me in touch with Peter Kurtze, who helped me identify the stone portraits of Buckler and Fenhagen at City College. James Pettit shed new light on his collaboration with Art Benson on *Nut and Bolt* for the Mount Royal Elementary/Middle School.

A very special thanks is reserved for the contemporary sculptors who gave of their time to be interviewed for this guide. What they shared with me during those conversations, sometimes held standing in front of the sculpture under discussion, led to a better understanding of their earliest ideas and challenges and to a heightened appreciation of the work, insights that I have tried to weave into discussions of their work. This book has really been written for all the sculptors who made artwork for the city, to whom we owe a continuing debt of gratitude. I hope this guide reminds people of public sculpture too often overlooked or taken for granted and sparks a renewed interest in and appreciation of the work of art and the slice of Baltimore history it reveals.

I owe a huge debt of gratitude to Edwin Remsberg, who joined me in this endeavor and crisscrossed the city for two years to photograph the sculpture presented here. His participation was valuable for more than the visual images; he alerted me to sculptures he found that were not on my list and challenged me in the most positive way about what I was including and what I was not. I enjoyed those conversations enormously, for they helped clarify my goals.

The publication of this guide was made possible in part by funding from The Middendorf Foundation and the Friends of the JHU Press, for which I am deeply grateful.

Finally, I would like to thank my husband, who not only gave up his office in our small New York apartment for the four years I spent working on this guide but accompanied me on more than one occasion to look at sculpture. Our two sons, Mark and Andrew, also drove me around from time to time to look at sculpture, outings I will long remember and treasure.

Appendix 1

TIME LINE

The date in the left-hand column indicates the year the sculpture appeared in Baltimore. A date in parenthesis after the title is the earlier or later completion date or the date of the original after which Baltimore's copy was made. Pieces no longer on view outdoors and thus not included in this book are noted by an asterisk (*). Works that are badly damaged and still on view but not included in this book are indicated by a dagger (†). And works commissioned through the Percent for Art program are noted by a double dagger (‡).

1817 *Moses* and *Christ*, by Antonio Capellano [B6]

1818 *Angel of Truth*, by Antonio Capellano [B10]

1825 *Lady Baltimore*, on the Battle Monument, by Antonio Capellano [D1]

1829 *George Washington*, on the Washington Monument, by Enrico Causici [C1]

1857 *George Washington*, by Edward Sheffield Bartholomew [M9]

1865 *Thomas Wildey Monument*, by an unknown sculptor [O10]

1879 Calvert Street Bridge *Lions*, by Herman D. A. Henning [I20]

1880 *Lady Baltimore* statues on the St. Paul Street Bridge, by Herman D. A. Henning [I17, N13–N14]

1885 *War, Peace, Force,* and *Order* (1846), by Antoine-Louis Barye [C2–C3, C10–C11]

Seated Lion (1846), by Antoine-Louis Barye [C4]

Military Courage (1879), by Paul Dubois [C6]

James L. Ridgely Monument, by an unknown sculptor [M5]

1887 Roger B. Taney Monument (1872), by William Henry Rinehart [C7]

1888 *Lions* (date unknown), by an unknown sculptor [N12]

1890 George Peabody Monument (1869), by William Wetmore Storey [C12]

Untitled, by John Monroe [M7]

1892 Columbus Monument, by Achille Canessa [M10]

1893 William Wallace Monument (1869), by D. W. Stevenson [M8]

1901 *Goddess of Liberty,* on the Maryland Line Monument, by A. L. Van den Bergen (Berghen) [I4]

Wagner, by R. P. Golde (1900) [M11]

1903 John Eager Howard Monument, by Emmanuel Frémiet [C8]

Confederate Soldiers and Sailors Monument (1902), by F. Wellington Ruckstuhl [I12]

Lt. Col. William H. Watson Monument (1902), by Edward Berge [I16]

1904 Severn Teakle Wallis Monument, by Laurent Honoré Marqueste [C14]

1906 *Mercury and Commerce,* by John Evans [B4]

1907 *William T. Walters,* by William Henry Rinehart [C17]

1908 Cecilius Calvert Monument, by Albert Weinert [D2]

1909 Union Soldiers and Sailors Monument, by Adolph Alexander Weinman [J1]

1911 John Mifflin Hood Monument, by Richard E. Brooks [D3]

Francis Scott Key Monument, by Marius Jean Antonin Mercié [I19]

1912 *Francis Scott Key,* by Hans Schuler [C9]

1914 Col. George Armistead Monument, by Edward Berge [G17]

Latrobe Monument, by J. Maxwell Miller and Edward Berge [O11]

Star-Spangled Banner Centennial Monument, by J. Maxwell Miller [P1]

* Star-Spangled Banner Centennial Memorial, by Hans Schuler

1915 Fallsway Fountain, by Hans Schuler [F2]

Conradin Kreutzer, by R. P. Golde [P2]

1916 *On the Trail* (1902), by Edward Berge [K13]

1917 Major General Samuel Smith Monument, by Hans Schuler [G2]

1918 Confederate Women's Monument (1915–17), by J. Maxwell Miller [J25]

1920 World War I Memorial, by J. Maxwell Miller [K5]

1921 Edgar Allan Poe Monument (1916), by Moses J. Ezekiel [F3]

Servicemen's Memorial, by Edward Berge [K15]

1922 Francis Scott Key Monument, by Charles Henry Niehaus [G18]

Chapin A. Harris Monument, by Edward Berge [J3]

1924 Boy and Turtle Fountain (1916), by Henri Crenier [C5]

Lafayette Monument, by Andrew O'Connor [C15]

Wildflower (1923), by Edward Berge [L13]

1925 *To the Glory of Maryland* (1923), by Hans Schuler [I21]

1926 *Sea Urchin* (1922), by Edward Berge [J20]

1927 *Aquatic Sea Horses*, by Edmond Romulus Amateis [D8]

1929 *To the Fine Arts*, by Adolph Alexander Weinman [J7]

Lions, by Adolph Alexander Weinman [J8]

1930 * *The Thinker* (1880), by Auguste Rodin

1931 *Untitled*, by Benjamin T. Kurtz [D5]

1935 Johns Hopkins Monument, by Hans Schuler [J13]

1936 Luther Monument, by Hans Schuler [K10]

1937 *St. Francis of Assisi*, by Henry Berge [N2]

1939 Lizette Woodworth Reese Monument, by Grace Hill Turnbull [K3]

1940 *Recreation* and *Education*, by Henry Berge [M1]

Untitled, by Henry Berge [O7]

Untitled, by Reuben Kramer [O8]

1942 Sidney Lanier Monument (1941), by Hans Schuler [J27]

1943 Spanish-American War Monument (The Hiker) (1921), by Theodora Alice Ruggles Kitson [P4]

1948 Lee and Jackson Monument, by Laura Gardin Fraser [J2]

Discus Thrower (1902), by an unknown sculptor after Myron of Eleutherai [J4]

Seated Mercury (19th century), by an unknown sculptor [J5]

Athena Parthenos (1902), by an unknown sculptor after Phidias [L8]

Apollo Belvedere (1902), by an unknown sculptor after Leochares [L9]

Lions (ca. 1857), by an unknown sculptor [M13]

1951 Pulaski Monument (1942), by Hans Schuler [P3]

1954 *Untitled*, by Henry Berge [R3]

1955 *Isaiah Bowman*, by Laura Gardin Fraser [J16]

1956 *King Penguin*, by Grace Hill Turnbull [A6]

William Henry Welch, by Sidney Waugh [J14]

Daniel Coit Gilman, by Sidney Waugh [J15]

1956 *Frederick Douglass*, by James E. Lewis [K8]

1959 *Sea Urchin*, by Henry Berge after Edward Berge [C16]

1960 *Simon Bolivar* (1948), by Felix G. W. de Weldon [L7]

1962 *Naïad* (1932), by Grace Hill Turnbull [C13]

1964 *Discus Thrower*, by Joe Brown [J21]

Runner, by Joe Brown [J22]

1966 *Boy with Goose* (1851), by an unknown sculptor after Boethus [M14]

1967 *James Cardinal Gibbons*, by Betti Richard [B7]

‡ *Untitled*, by Peter van Rossum [H8]

‡ *Untitled*, by Thomas F. Hoffmaster [I18]

*‡ *The Wishbone House*, by Colin Greenly

1968 *No. 9*, by John Ferguson [L4]

‡ *Linear Growth Structure*, by E. Clifton Boudman [M17]

‡ *Paestum*, by Roger Majorowicz [O6]

‡ *Untitled*, by William Leizman [Q5]

*‡ *Untitled*, by Pierre duFayet

1969 *Diamond #II-III*, by Antoni Milkowski [B1]

‡ *Children's Round Square*, by Alfredo Halegua [H9]

The Boy Scout (1937), by R. Tait McKenzie [J29]

‡ *Untitled*, by Earl F. Hofmann [K1]

‡ *Untitled*, by Harry Bertoia [K12]

‡ *Form in Space*, by Harry Hilson [K17]

‡ *Winged Victory*, by Harry Hilson [K18]

‡ *Untitled*, by James E. Lewis [R2]

* *Untitled*, by Stan Edmister

*‡ *Untitled*, by Harry Hilson

1970 *Energy*, by Francesco Somaini [H1]

‡ *Turning Point*, by Alfredo Halegua [Q1]

‡ *Untitled*, by Pierre duFayet [Q2]

*‡ *Untitled*, by Joel Perlman

*‡ *Untitled*, by Joel Perlman

1971 ‡ *Untitled*, by Fernanda Zopf [L15]

‡ *Pegasus*, by Roger Majorowicz [O3]

‡ *A Bird Flying North*, by Michio Ihara [R6]

1972 Negro Soldier's Monument (1971), by James E. Lewis [D6]

‡ *Untitled Crab*, by Edmund Whiting [G1]

‡ *Colossus I*, by Alfredo Halegua [I1]

Give Peace a Chance, by Theodore C. Scuris [J17]

‡ *Untitled*, by William Leizman [Q3]

1973 ‡ *Fire Chariot*, by Roger Majorowicz [E3]

Catch the Wind If You Can, by Jeffrey Johnson [I15]

1974   *No. 10*, by John Ferguson [L1]

    * *Untitled*, by J. Arthur Benson

    *‡ *Untitled*, by James E. Lewis

1975   ‡ *Untitled*, by Fernanda Zopf [M4]

    ‡ *Solar Totem*, by Don Drumm [O1]

    ‡ *Sod Buster*, by Roger Majorowicz [Q4]

    * *Centennial*, by David Lee Brown

    †‡ Forum Fountain, by Stafford Rolph

1976   *Untitled*, by Hiroshi Mikami [A12]

    Untitled, by Gerald Höweler [A14]

    Amanogawa (1977), by Robert DuBourg [D9]

    Baltimore (1977), by William Bennett [D10]

    ‡ *Caterpillar*, by Norman Carlberg [F6]

    ‡ *Untitled*, by Fernanda Zopf [H7]

    Untitled, by John Parker [I11]

    On Point, by John Ferguson [L2]

    Boy with Fish (date unknown), by an unknown sculptor [L12]

    ‡ *Untitled*, by William Leizman [N9]

    ‡ *Fireman Saving a Child*, by Joseph Sheppard [O4]

    ‡ *Knowledge*, by Paul Takacs [P9]

    ‡ *Untitled*, by John Ferguson [R5]

    *‡ *Lady Madonna with Child*, by Stan Edmister

    *‡ *#31*, by Andrew Mezensky

    * *Untitled*, by Jacquin P. Smolens

1977   *Easy Landing*, by Kenneth Snelson [A7]

    Atlantic Blue Roller Column, by Dominick Cea [H5]

    ‡ *Steel Henge*, by Alton Parker Balder [H10]

    Guardian Lions (mid-19th century), by an unknown sculptor after Antonio Canova [J6]

    ‡ *The Human Dance*, by Nathaniel Mack [N11]

    ‡ *Uni I*, by Herbert Lee [O2]

    Patapsco River Project, by Jim Sanborn [R4]

    * *Points on a Line*, by Greg Moring

1978   *Baltimore Federal* (1977), by George Sugarman [A2]

    Untitled, by William Leizman [F5]

    ‡ *Untitled*, by David von Schlegell [G14]

    ‡ *Untitled*, by Judith Chodak Goldberg [J28]

    ‡ *Boanerges*, by Mary Ann Mears [K16]

    ‡ *Titan* and ‡*Harpie*, by Paul Daniel [N3–N4]

    ‡ *Sea Birds*, by Norman Therrien [N5]

    ‡ *Peely Wheely*, by James Paulsen [O12]

    Archimedean Spiral, by Paul H. Shepherd [P7]

    ‡ *Sails*, by Tylden Streett [P8]

    * *Reclining Connected Forms (Conception)* (1973), by Henry Moore

    †‡ *Untitled*, by Norman Carlberg

    * *Untitled*, by Michio Ihara

1979   *Thurgood Marshall*, by Reuben Kramer [A1]

    Red Buoyant (1978), by Mary Ann Mears [A4]

    ‡ *Samurai Rocker*, by Richard D. Gottlieb [F7]

    ‡ *Seal*, by Frayda Shalowitz [F7]

    ‡ *Citisphere*, by Robert G. Fergerson [K6]

    ‡ *OM*, by Oliver Patrick Scott [M3]

    Captain John O'Donnell (1978), by Tylden Streett [P5]

    *‡ *Brio*, by Mary Ann Mears

1980   *Under Sky / One Family*, by Mark di Suvero [A8]

    Janet and Alan Wurtzburger Sculpture Garden [J10]

    ‡ *The Guide*, by Ayokunle Odeleye [K4]

    ‡ *The Of Course Culture Horse*, by Stan Edmister [L14]

1981   *Chorale*, by Isaac Witkin [E5]

    Host of the Ellipse, by Ronald Bladen [E6]

    Fanned Arena (1979), by Lila Katzen [J18]

    ‡ *Westside*, by Greg Moring [Q6]

1982   *Untitled*, by Greg Moring [A13]

    ‡ *Nut and Bolt*, by J. Arthur Benson [I13]

    Violins Violence Silence, by Bruce Nauman [J9]

    ‡ *The Immortals*, by Tylden Streett [K2]

    ‡ *The Learning Tree*, by Patrick F. McGuire [M6]

    ‡ *Local #420*, by Herbert Lee [Q7]

    ‡ *Kinship*, by Lisa Kaslow [Q8]

1983   Bufano Sculpture Garden [J23]

    Billie Holiday (1983–2009), by James Earl Reid [M2]

    Cold Spring Outcrop, by Jim Sanborn [N8]

    Rogers Avenue, by Greg Moring [N10]

    * *Two Friends*, by Jo Schneider

1984   Columbus Monument, by Mauro Bigarani [A10]

    Great Ascension (1983–84), by Beverly Pepper [O5]

    ‡ *The Quest*, by Lisa Kaslow [P6]

    * *Home Run*, by Greg Moring

1985   *John Eager Howard*, by David L. Gerlach [E2]

    Pearlstone Park, by Scott Burton [I3]

A single date following the sculptor's name is the year the work was both completed and first installed. When the date is followed by a second date in parentheses, then the first date is the year the work was first installed and the date in parentheses is the earlier or later completion date or the date of the original after which Baltimore's copy was made.

A2   *Baltimore Federal,* by George Sugarman, 1977: From the entrance to the Edward A. Garmatz Federal Building and U.S. Courthouse, 101 W. Lombard Street, to the edge of the property, 2000

A3   *Fan Figure,* by Greg Moring, 1987: From the streetscape at Liberty and Pratt streets to the streetscape further east on Pratt Street, 1994 (during expansion of the Convention Center)

A6   *King Penguin,* by Grace Hill Turnbull, 1956: From the corner of Rash Field to outside the World Trade Center, 1978, to a garden outside the Harbor Cruises Pavilion on Light Street, date unknown

A12   *Untitled,* by Hiroshi Mikami, 1976: From Shot Tower Park to Commerce Street Park, between 1989 and 1995 (during construction of the Metro station at Shot Tower Park)

A14   *Untitled,* by Gerald Höweler, 1976: From Shot Tower Park to Commerce Street Park, between 1989 and 1995

C2–C3,

C10–C11   *War, Peace, Force,* and *Order,* by Antoine-Louis Barye, 1885 (1846): From the west square to the ends of the balustrades in Mount Vernon Place, 1916

C14   Severn Teakle Wallis Monument, by Laurent Honoré Marqueste, 1904: From the south square of Mount Vernon Place to the east square, 1920

D3   John Mifflin Hood Monument, by Richard E. Brooks, 1911: From Baltimore and Liberty streets (Hopkins Place) to Preston Gardens, 1963

D6   Negro Soldier's Monument, by James E. Lewis, 1972 (1971): From Courthouse Square (Calvert Street) to War Memorial Plaza, 2007

F2   *Fallsway Fountain,* by Hans Schuler, 1915: From the original terminus of The Fallsway to E. Biddle and Guilford streets, 1967

F3   Edgar Allan Poe Monument, by Moses J. Ezekiel, 1921 (1916): From Wyman Park to the University of Baltimore School of Law at 1415 Maryland Avenue, 1983

F5   *Untitled,* by William Leizman, 1978: From the Charles Street entrance to Penn Station to the east side of the station, 2004

G2   Major General Samuel Smith Monument, by Hans Schuler, 1917: From Wyman Park to a park named for Smith at the corner of Light and Pratt streets, 1953; to Federal Hill, 1970

G14   *Untitled,* by David von Schlegell, 1978: From the entrance plaza of Southern High School to behind the school that is now Digital Harbor High School, 2002

G18   Francis Scott Key Monument, by Charles Henry Niehaus, 1922: From the center of the road leading into Fort McHenry to the southwest on the park grounds nearer the water, 1962

H1   *Energy,* by Francesco Somaini, 1970: From Center Plaza in Charles Center to the entrance to the Baltimore RESCO plant, 1985; to behind Baltimore RESCO (today Wheelabrator Baltimore), ca. 1995

H5   *Atlantic Blue Roller Column,* by Dominick Cea, 1977: From the median on Russell Street at Washington Boulevard to further south in the same median, 1992

I11   *Untitled,* by John Parker, 1976: From Howard Street to Preston Street to Mount Royal Avenue and Lafayette Street, dates unknown

I15   *Catch the Wind If You Can,* by Jeffrey Johnson, 1973: From in front of the Fox Building, on Mount Royal Avenue, to the Commons, 120 McMechen Street, ca. 1992

I16   Lt. Col. William H. Watson Monument, by Edward Berge, 1903 (1902): From the median at Mount Royal Avenue and Lanvale Street to Mount Royal Terrace, 1930

I17,

N13–N14   *Lady Baltimore* statues, by Herman D. A. Henning, 1880: From the St. Paul Street Bridge (along with a fourth lady not included in this volume) into storage in Druid Hill Park, 1960; these three moved to Cylburn Park (while the fourth sent to Baltimore, Ireland, on a permanent goodwill to Baltimore, Ireland, on a permanent goodwill mission), 1974; one of the three (I17) moved to a green space along Mount Royal Terrace, 1979

I20 Calvert Street Bridge *Lions,* by Herman D. A. Henning, 1879: From the bridge into storage in Druid Hill Park, 1957; three installed in Lanvale Park, 1976, and one too badly damaged to be re-sited

J1 Union Soldiers and Sailors Monument, by Adolph Alexander Weinman, 1909: From Druid Hill Park to Wyman Park, 1959

J3 Chapin A. Harris Monument, by Edward Berge, 1922: From North Avenue and Linden Street to the edge of Wyman Park, 1939

J13 Johns Hopkins Monument, by Hans Schuler, 1935: From the center of Charles Street opposite the entrance to Johns Hopkins University to Charles and 33rd streets, on a small piece of land given to the city by the university, 1955

J17 *Give Peace a Chance,* by Theodore C. Scuris, 1972: From the eastern end of Wyman Quadrangle, Johns Hopkins University, to the southeastern side of Shriver Hall, 2001

J20 *Sea Urchin,* by Edward Berge, 1926 (1922): From Mount Vernon Place to Johns Hopkins University's Decker Garden, 1959

J29 *The Boy Scout,* by R. Tait McKenzie, 1969 (1937): From a garden beside the entrance to the Morris and John D. Schapiro Scout Service Center, 701 Wyman Park Drive, to a newly designed plaza in front of the building, 2001

K3 Lizette Woodworth Reece Monument, by Grace Hill Turnbull, 1939: From Eastern High School to Lake Clifton High School, 1985; back to what is today Johns Hopkins at Eastern, on a piece of land given to the city by the university, 2009

K5 World War I Memorial, by J. Maxwell Miller, 1920: From City College on Howard Street to the new City College on 33rd Street, 1928

K10 Luther Monument, by Hans Schuler, 1936: From Druid Hill Park to Hillen Road and 31st Street, overlooking Lake Montebello, 1959

K15 Servicemen's Memorial, by Edward Berge, 1921: From Glenmore Avenue and Belair Road to Herring Run Park, near Parkside Drive, ca. 1925; to Belair Road and Shannon Drive, also in Herring Run Park, 1933

L1 *No. 10,* by John Ferguson, 1974: From an interior courtyard of the centrally located commercial area of the Village of Cross Keys to the main entrance of the development, early 1980s

M7 *Untitled,* by John Monroe, 1890: From the facade of the Old Post Office on Fayette Street to the lawn of the headquarters of the Department of Recreation and Parks, 2600 Madison Avenue, 1932

M9 *George Washington,* by Edward Sheffield Bartholomew, 1857: From the facade of the Noah Walker Building on E. Baltimore Street to Druid Hill Park, 1885

M14 *Boy with Goose,* 1851 copy of a 2nd-century BC sculpture by Boethus: From the grounds of Druid Hill Park, where it was installed in 1966, into the Children's Zoo in the Baltimore Zoo, after 1992

M15 *John Daniel II Gorilla,* by Valerie Harrisse Walter, 1927: From the office of the director of the Baltimore Zoo, to whom it was gifted in 1948, to outdoors on the grounds of the zoo, 1995; to the Chimpanzee Forest, ca. 2008

M16 *Untitled,* by Peter Otfinoski, 1995–97: From the Baltimore Marine Center in the Inner Harbor to the William S. Baer School, 2004

N11 *The Human Dance,* by Nathaniel Mack, 1977: From the sidewalk in front of Parkwest Multi-Purpose Service Center to close to the building, beside the entrance, after 1992

O5 *Great Ascension,* by Beverly Pepper, 1983-84: From the Wolfe Street entrance to Johns Hopkins Hospital to the North Caroline Street entrance to the Outpatient Building, 2004

O6 *Paestum,* by Roger Majorowicz, 1968: From the second Broadway branch of the Enoch Pratt Free Library, at the intersection of Broadway and Orleans Street, to the Orleans Street branch, at 1303 Orleans Street, 2007

P7 *Archimedean Spiral,* by Paul H. Shepherd, 1978: From Johns Hopkins Hospital's Turner Auditorium Plaza to the Johns Hopkins Bayview Research Campus on Eastern Avenue, between 1988 and 1992

Appendix 3

TITLE: *The Thinker*, 1880
SCULPTOR: Auguste Rodin (1840–1917)
MEDIUM: Bronze
DONOR: Baltimore Museum of Art
ORIGINAL LOCATION: Front entrance stairway of the Baltimore Museum of Art, Art Museum Drive
DISPOSITION: Given to the Baltimore Museum of Art by Jacob Epstein in 1930 and immediately installed outdoors; moved indoors in 1971 after conservation on conservator's recommendation.

TITLE: Star-Spangled Banner Centennial Memorial, 1914
SCULPTOR: Hans Schuler (1874–1951)
MEDIUM: Bronze
DONOR: National Star-Spangled Banner Centennial Commission
ORIGINAL LOCATION: Niche on the facade of City Hall
DISPOSITION: Moved to an interior location at City Hall.

TITLE: *The Wishbone House*, 1967
SCULPTOR: Colin Greenly (b. 1928)
MEDIUM: Concrete
DONOR: Baltimore City Percent for Art program
ORIGINAL LOCATION: Play lot near Warwick and Baltimore streets
DISPOSITION: Moved to Calvert and 22nd streets before it disappeared.

TITLE: *Untitled*, 1968
SCULPTOR: Pierre duFayet (1929–1986)
MEDIUM: Stainless steel and resin
DONOR: Baltimore City Percent for Art program
ORIGINAL LOCATION: Cecil Elementary School, 2000 Cecil Avenue
DISPOSITION: Whereabouts unknown.

TITLE: *Untitled*, 1969
SCULPTOR: Stan Edmister (1938–2007)
MEDIUM: Painted steel
DONOR: On loan from the artist
ORIGINAL LOCATION: In front of the Mount Royal Station building of the Maryland Institute College of Art
DISPOSITION: When the artist left Baltimore, he terminated the loan and took the piece with him.

TITLE: *Untitled*, 1969
SCULPTOR: Harry Hilson (1935–2004)
MEDIUM: Fiberglass resin and steel
DONOR: Baltimore City Percent for Art program
ORIGINAL LOCATION: Woodholme Elementary School, 7300 Moyer Avenue.
DISPOSITION: Whereabouts unknown.

TITLES: *Untitled* and *Untitled*, 1970
SCULPTOR: Joel Perlman (b. 1943)
MEDIUM: Painted steel
DONOR: Baltimore City Percent for Art program
ORIGINAL LOCATION: Southwestern High School, 200 Font Hill Avenue
DISPOSITION: The City sold Southwestern School to the SEED School of Maryland. It is being transformed into a boarding school and is not open to the public at this time.

TITLE: *Reclining Connected Forms (Conception)*, 1973
SCULPTOR: Henry Moore (1898–1986)
MEDIUM: Travertine marble
DONOR: United States Fidelity & Guaranty Company (USF&G)
ORIGINAL LOCATION: USF&G Building Plaza
DISPOSITION: Purchased by USF&G for the plaza of its new building in the Inner Harbor in 1978, it was given to the Maryland Institute and moved to the Convention Center in 1980, where it was on loan for a decade before being sold at auction at Sotheby's in New York in the early 1990s.

TITLE: *Untitled*, 1974
SCULPTOR: J. Arthur Benson (b. 1933)
MEDIUM: Cor-Ten steel, stainless steel, and aluminum
DONOR: Gift of the artist
ORIGINAL LOCATION: Southwest corner of Mount Royal Avenue and Dolphin Street
DISPOSITION: Deteriorated over time and removed by the artist.

TITLE: *Untitled*, 1974
SCULPTOR: James E. Lewis (1923–2007)
MEDIUM: Bronze
DONOR: Baltimore City Percent for Art program
LOCATION: Walter P. Carter Elementary School, 820 E. 43rd Street
DISPOSITION: Badly damaged by vandalism.

TITLE: *Centennial*, 1975
SCULPTOR: David Lee Brown (b. 1939)
MEDIUM: Stainless steel
DONORS: Ryda H. and Robert H. Levi
ORIGINAL LOCATION: Upper quadrangle, Johns Hopkins University, 3400 N. Charles Street
DISPOSITION: Moved inside the Milton S. Eisenhower Library at Johns Hopkins University.

TITLE: *Forum Fountain*, 1975
SCULPTOR: Stafford Rolph (1936–1997)
MEDIUM: Concrete
DONOR: Baltimore City Percent for Art program
LOCATION: Paul L. Dunbar Senior High School, 1400
Orleans Street
DISPOSITION: Badly damaged by vandalism, awaiting
restoration.

TITLE: *Lady Madonna with Child*, 1976
SCULPTOR: Stan Edmister (1938–2007)
MEDIUM: Painted steel
DONOR: Baltimore City Percent for Art program
Original location: David E. Weglein School, 200
S. Central Avenue
DISPOSITION: It was removed after the city sold the school build-
ing to the Culinary Art Institute in 1989 and stored in Druid
Hill Park. Years of neglect led to its deterioration.

TITLE: *#31*, 1976
SCULPTOR: Andrew Mezensky (b. 1945)
MEDIUM: Found objects
DONOR: Baltimore City Percent for Art program
ORIGINAL LOCATION: Harriet Tubman Elementary School, 1807
Harlem Avenue
DISPOSITION: Whereabouts unknown.

TITLE: *Untitled*, 1976
SCULPTOR: Jacquin P. Smolens (b. 1930)
MEDIUM: Wood
DONOR: Inner Harbor Management Corporation
ORIGINAL LOCATION: Inner Harbor, east of the Science Center
DISPOSITION: The playground sculpture was removed.

TITLE: *Points on a Line*, 1977
SCULPTOR: Greg Moring (b. 1949)
MEDIUM: Painted steel, stainless steel, and aluminum
DONOR: 1977 City-sponsored sculpture symposium
ORIGINAL LOCATION: On the grounds of the Baltimore City
Hospitals, 4940 Eastern Avenue (today Johns Hopkins
Bayview Medical Center)
DISPOSITION: Removed in 1984 for planned expansion of the
newly renamed Francis Scott Key Medical Center and
stored in Druid Hill Park until another site could be found.
Years of neglect led to its deterioration and eventual
destruction.

TITLE: *Untitled*, 1978
SCULPTOR: Norman Carlberg (b. 1928)
MEDIUM: Fiberglass
DONOR: Baltimore City Percent for Art program
LOCATION: Friendship Academy of Engineering and Technology
(formerly Northern Parkway Junior High School), 2500 E.
Northern Parkway
DISPOSITION: Badly damaged by ill-conceived maintenance,
awaiting restoration.

TITLE: *Untitled*, 1978
SCULPTOR: Michio Ihara (b. 1928)
Medium: Stainless steel
DONOR: C&P Telephone Company
ORIGINAL LOCATION: C&P Telephone Building (today Verizon)
at Pratt and Light streets
DISPOSITION: Removed by new owners in 2008 to allow for
reconfiguration of the entrance.

TITLE: *Brio*, 1979
SCULPTOR: Mary Ann Mears (b. 1946)
MEDIUM: Painted steel
DONOR: Baltimore City Percent for Art program
ORIGINAL LOCATION: Fort Worthington Recreation Center,
2701 E. Oliver Street
DISPOSITION: Whereabouts unknown.

TITLE: *Two Friends*, 1983
SCULPTOR: Jo Schneider
MEDIUM: Slate and steel
DONORS: Gift of Betty Cooke and William Steinmetz
in memory of their son Daniel (1955–82)
ORIGINAL LOCATION: Friends School of Baltimore,
5001 N. Charles Street
DISPOSITION: Damaged beyond repair and removed
by the school.

TITLE: *Home Run*, 1984
SCULPTOR: Greg Moring (B. 1949)
MEDIUM: Painted steel
DONOR: On loan from the artist
ORIGINAL LOCATION: 33rd Street opposite Memorial Stadium
DISPOSITION: Sold to an out-of-town collector.

TITLE: *Untitled*, 1986
SCULPTOR: Ronald Anderson (b. 1946)
MEDIUM: Concrete
DONOR: Baltimore City Percent for Art program
LOCATION: Southern District Police Station,
10 Cherry Hill Road
DISPOSITION: Badly damaged by a car. Removed and replaced
(P1).

TITLES: *The Right Light and The Briefing*, 1987
SCULPTOR: Seward Johnson (b. 1930)
MEDIUM: Bronze
DONOR: Baltimore City Percent for Art program
ORIGINAL LOCATION: Outside the Convention Center,
1 W. Pratt Street
DISPOSITION: Moved indoors to the Charles Street lobby
and the Sharpe Street lobby, respectively, of the
Convention Center.

TITLE: *Boy Releasing a Bird,* 1989
SCULPTOR: William F. Duffy (b. 1953)
MEDIUM: Painted steel
DONOR: Baltimore City Percent for Art program
ORIGINAL LOCATION: Carrie Murray Outdoor Education Center,
1901 Ridgetop Road
DISPOSITION: The center expanded into the plaza area where the
sculpture was sited. Its whereabouts is unknown.

TITLE: *Untitled,* 1991
SCULPTOR: Jeffrey Schiff (b. 1953)
MEDIUM: Bronze
DONORS: Market Center Development Corporation
and City of Baltimore, Municipal Art Society of Baltimore,
and National Endowment for the Arts
ORIGINAL LOCATION: Center Plaza, Liberty and Lexington streets,
at the entrance to what was formerly the BGE Building
DISPOSITION: In storage awaiting resiting. BGE sold the building, and the new owners had other plans for the
front of the building.

Note: *La Chiffonière* (1973–78) by Jean Dubuffet (1901–85)
arrived in Baltimore in July 1978 on loan from the Pace
Gallery in New York. The lead agency in arranging this loan
was the Department of Housing and Community Development. The sculpture was sited in front of the Baltimore
World Trade Center on Pratt Street while efforts were
made to raise the funds to acquire the piece for the city.
In January 1979, after six months and an inability to raise
the necessary funds, HCD arranged for the sculpture to be
returned to the Pace Gallery. Today it can be seen at the
Embarcadero Center in San Francisco.

For Further Reading

Arnett, Earl, Robert J. Brugger, and Edward C. Papenfuse. *Maryland: A New Guide to the Old Line State.* Baltimore: Johns Hopkins University Press, 1999.

Bach, Penny Balkin. *Public Art in Philadelphia.* Philadelphia: Temple University Press, 1992.

Beardsley, John. *Gardens of Revelation: Environments by Visionary Artists.* New York: Abbeville, 2003.

Bogart, Michele H. *Public Sculpture and the Civic Ideal in New York City, 1890–1930.* Chicago: University of Chicago Press, 1989.

Brugger, Robert J. *Maryland: A Middle Temperament, 1634–1980.* Baltimore: Johns Hopkins University Press, 1988.

Causey, Andrew. *Sculpture Since 1945.* Oxford and New York: Oxford University Press, 1998.

Chapelle, Suzanne Ellery Greene. *Baltimore: An Illustrated History.* Sun Valley, CA: American Historical Press, 2000.

Dorsey, John. *Architect John Russell Pope's Baltimore.* Baltimore: Baltimore Museum of Art, 2004.

———. Introduction to *Public Monuments and Sculpture of Baltimore: An Introduction to the Collection,* by Henry Naylor and Carolyn Naylor. Bethesda, MD: Writer's Center, 1987.

———. *Mount Vernon Place.* Baltimore: Maclay & Associates, 1983.

———. *Mr. Peabody's Library: The Building, The Collection, The Neighborhood.* Baltimore: Enoch Pratt Free Library, 1978.

Dorsey, John, and James Dilts. *The Architecture of Baltimore.* Centreville, MD: Tidewater, 1981.

Freudenheim, Leslie M. *Baltimore's Public Art, 1960–1980.* Baltimore: Maryland Institute College of Art, 1980.

Gayle, Margot, and Michele Cohen. *The Art Commission and the Municipal Art Society Guide to Manhattan's Outdoor Sculpture.* New York: Prentice Hall, 1988.

Goode, James M. *Washington Sculpture: A Cultural History of Outdoor Sculpture in the Nation's Capital.* Baltimore: Johns Hopkins University Press, 2009.

Heartney, Eleanor, et al. *GSA Art in Architecture: Selected Artworks 1997–2008.* Washington, DC: U.S. General Services Administration, 2008.

Johnston, William R., and Simon Kelly. *Untamed: The Art of Antoine-Louis Barye.* Baltimore: Walters Art Museum, 2006.

Kelly, Jacques. *Bygone Baltimore.* Norfolk, VA: Donning, 1982.

Lacy, Suzanne, ed. *Mapping the Terrain: New Genre Public Art.* Seattle: Bay, 1995.

Lanier, Sidney. *Poems of Sidney Lanier.* Edited by Mary Day Lanier. Athens: University of Georgia Press, 1981.

Reese, Lizette Woodworth. *Selected Poems of Lizette Woodworth Reese.* New York: George H. Doran, 1926.

Richardson, Brenda. *Scott Burton.* Baltimore: Baltimore Museum of Art, 1986.

Ross, Marvin Chauncey, and Anna Wells Rutledge. *A Catalogue of the Work of William Henry Rinehart, Maryland Sculptor, 1825–1874.* Baltimore: John D. Lucas, 1948.

Rusk, William Sener. *Art in Baltimore: Monuments and Memorials.* Rev. ed. Baltimore: Norman, Remington, 1929.

Ryon, Roderick N. *West Baltimore Neighborhoods: Sketches of Their History, 1840–1960.* Baltimore: University of Baltimore, 1993.

Senie, Harriet F., and Sally Webster, eds. *Critical Issues in Public Art: Content, Context, and Controversy.* New York: HarperCollins, 1992.

Shivers, Frank R., Jr. *Walking in Baltimore: An Intimate Guide to the Old City.* Baltimore: Johns Hopkins University Press, 1995.

Stockett, Letitia. *Baltimore: A Not Too Serious History.* Baltimore: Johns Hopkins University Press, 1997. Originally published by Grace Gore Norman, Baltimore, 1928; limited illustrated edition, 1936.

Thalacker, Donald W. *The Place of Art in the World of Architecture.* New York: Chelsea House, 1980.

Trulove, James Grayson, ed. *Bones of the Earth, Spirit of the Land: The Sculpture of John Van Alstine.* Washington, DC: Editions Ariel, 2000.

Turnbull, Grace. *Chips from My Chisel: An Autobiography.* Rindge, NH: R. R. Smith, 1953.

This index lists sculptors and their works that were commissioned for, purchased for, or gifted to the City of Baltimore between 1817 and 2009 for placement outdoors. A general index follows.

Takacs, Paul: biography of, 344; *Knowledge*, 344–45
Therrien, Norman: biography of, 302; *Sea Birds*, 302
Townsend, René A.: biography of, 172; *Untitled*, 172–73
Turnbull, Grace Hill, 9; biography of, 23; instrumental in keeping *Boy and Turtle Fountain* in Baltimore, 63; *King Penguin*, 23; Lizette Woodworth Reese Monument, 234; *The Naïad*, 73

Van Alstine, John, 9; biography of, 256; *Implement XXV/River Arch*, 256
Van den Bergen (Berghen): biography of, 170; *Goddess of Liberty* on Maryland Line Monument, 170–71
Von Schlegell, David, 7; *Untitled*, 141, 374

Walter, Bart, 8; *Friends*, 265; *Otter Rocks*, *Mountain Silverback Gorilla*, *Polar Bear* and other sculptures at or soon to be at the Maryland Zoo, 288
Walter, Valerie Harrisse, 9; *John Daniel II Gorilla*, 291
Waugh, Sidney: biography of, 212-13; *William Henry Welch* and *Daniel Coit Gilman*, 212–13
Weinert, Albert: biography of, 84; Cecilius Calvert Monument, 84–85
Weinman, Adolph Alexander, 6; biography of, 196; *To the Fine Arts* and *Lions*, 204; Union Soldiers and Sailors Monument, 196–97
Whiting, Edmund, *Untitled Crab*, 126
Wilson, Ben: biography of, 134-35; Meditation/Wedding Chapel, 134
Witkin, Isaac, 19; biography of, 109; *Chorale*, 109

Zopf, Fernanda: biography of, 160; *Untitled* (1971), 271; *Untitled* (1975), 278; *Untitled* (1976), 120

Baltimore city fire stations, 106, 241, 303, 319

Baltimore City Fraternal Order of Police, 8, 99

Baltimore City Fraternal Order of Police Memorial (F. Streett), tour entry, 99

Baltimore city parks: Bedford Square, 261; Billie Holiday Plaza, 275; Canton Square, 340; Cherry Hill Park, 361; Clifton Park, 210, 246; Commerce Street Park, 7, 8, 20, 30–32; Cylburn, 188, 309, 310; Druid Hill Park, 8, 281–91; Federal Hill Park, 127, 145; Harlem Park, 279; Herring Run, viii, 248; Howard's Park, 105; Lanvale Street Park, 4; Patterson Park, 334, 335, 336–37; Preston Gardens, 86–87; Shot Tower Park, 8, 30–31, 97–99; Wyman Park, 116, 196, 198, 200, 204

Baltimore City Percent for Art program: *Bird Flying North, A* (Ihara), 363; *Bird in a Tree* (Duffy) 298; *Boanerges* (Mears), 249; *Caterpillar* (Carlberg), 121; *Children's Round Square* (Halegua), 162; *Citisphere* (Fergerson), 237; *Colossus I* (Halegua), 166; *Dogs and Cats* (Peterson), 152; *Double Gamut* (DePalma and Daniel), 52; *Enlightenment* (Duffy), 304; *Fire Chariot* (Majorowicz), 106; *Form in Space* (Hilson), 250; *Guide, The* (Odeleye), 235; *Harpie* (Daniel), 300; *The Human Dance* (Mack), 308; *The Immortals* (T. Streett), 233; *Inertia Study* (Hess), 238–39; *Kinship* (Kaslow), 355; *Knowledge* (Takacs), 344–45; *Knowledge + Love = Brotherhood* (Kaslow), 247; *Learning Tree, The* (McGuire), 280; *Linear Growth Structure* (Boudman), 294; *Local #420* (Lee), 354; *Nut and Bolt* (J. A. Benson), 183; *Of Course Culture Horse* (Edmister), 270; *OM* (Scott), 277; *Paestum* (Majorowicz), 321; *Peely Wheely* (Paulsen), 329; *Pegasus* (Majorowicz), 318; *The Quest* (Kaslow), 341; *The Rescue* (Kaslow), 303; *Sails* (T. Streett), 343; *Samurai Rocker* (Gottlieb), 122–23; *Sea Birds* (Therrien), 302; *Seal* (Shalowitz), 122; *Sod Buster* (Majorowicz), 351; *Solar Totem* (Drum), 316; *Steel Henge* (Balder), 163; *Titan* (Daniel), 300; *Triaxial Link* (Niebauer), 22; *Turning Point* (Halegua), 348; *Uni I* (Lee), 317; *Untitled* (Bertoia), 245; *Untitled* (duFayet), 349; *Untitled* (Ferguson), 362; *Untitled* (Goldberg), 228; *Untitled* (Greenamyer), 241; *Untitled* (Hoffmaster), 189; *Untitled* (Hofmann), 232; *Untitled* (Leizman, 1968), 353; *Untitled* (Leizman, 1972), 350; *Untitled* (Leizman, 1976), 306; *Untitled* (Lewis), 359; *Untitled* (McCarty), 144; *Untitled* (Scofield and Moe), 358; *Untitled* (van Rossum), 161; *Untitled* (von Schlegell), 141; *Untitled* (Zopf, 1971), 271; *Untitled* (Zopf, 1975), 278; *Untitled* (Zopf, 1976), 160; *Untitled Crab* (Whiting), 126; *Westside* (Moring), 353; *Winged Victory* (Hilson), 251; *Winged Youth* (Carroll), 244. *See also* Percent for Art legislation

Baltimore city public schools: Alexander Hamilton Elementary, 355; Baybrook Elementary, 363; Brehms Lane Elementary, 247; Calvin Rodwell Elementary, 302; Charles Carroll Barrister Elementary, 160; City College, 235, 236, 237; Cold Stream Park Elementary, 232; Dallas F. Nicholas Sr. Elementary, 121; Diggs-Johnson Middle, 161; Digital Harbor High (formerly Southern High), 7, 141, 374; Dr. Bernard Harris Sr. Elementary, 318; Dr. Nathan A. Pitts Ashburton Elementary, 304; Edmondson-Westside High, 20, 353, 354; Eutaw-Mashburn Elementary, 189; Federal Hill Elementary, 126; Francis Scott Key Elementary, 144; Friendship Academy of Science and Technology (formerly Canton Junior High), 341; George W. F. McMechen Junior Senior, 306; Govans Elementary, 270; Guilford Elementary, 271; Harford Heights Intermediate and Primary, 316; John Eager Howard, 280; Lake Clifton Campus (formerly Lake Clifton High), 7, 245; Liberty Elementary, 300; Maree Garnett Farring Elementary, 362; Margaret Brent Elementary, 122; Mergenthaler High, 230; Montebello Elementary, 244; Mount Royal Elementary/Middle, 183; Northeast Middle, 249; Patterson High, 343; Rognell Heights Elementary, 352; Roland Park Elementary/Middle, 20, 258; Southeast Middle, 344; Southside Academy (formerly Arnett J. Brown Jr. Middle), 359; Steuart Hill Elementary, 162; Vivien T. Thomas Medical Arts Academy (formerly Francis M. Wood Senior High), 163; Walbrook Campus (formerly Walbrook High), 348, 349; Waverly Elementary, 233; William H. Pinderhughes Elementary, 278; William S. Baer School, 292–93; Windsor Hills Elementary, 351; Wolfe Street Academy, 329; Woodholme Elementary, 250–51

Baltimore Clayworks, as site of *Nurturing Nature* (Rikin), 312–13

Baltimore Community Foundation, 10

Baltimore Convention Center: as site of *Fan Figure* (Moring), 20; as former site of *The Right Light* (Johnson) and *The Briefing* (Johnson), 377

Baltimore Development Corporation, 20

Baltimore Federal (Sugarman), 7; tour entry, 18–19

Baltimore Gas & Electric Company (BG&E, BGE), 9; assistance to H. Berge on his restoration of *Angel of Truth* (Capellano), 54–55; commissioned *Energy* (Somaini) and gifted it to Baltimore RESCO (today Wheelabrator Baltimore), 150–51

Baltimore Marine Center, 292

Baltimore Museum of Art (BMA), vii, 4, 6; competition for relief at Frederick Douglass Homes, 323–24; drawings by di Suvero for *Under Sky/One Family*, 25; early history in Mount Vernon Place, 63

Huber, Frederick R., 77, 218
Hughes, Patrick, 140
Human Dance, The (Mack), tour entry, 308
Hunter, Wilbur Harvey, vii

IBM Building, 7; as site of *Red Buoyant* (Mears), 21
Immortals, The (T. Streett), tour entry, 233
Inertia Study (Hess), tour entry, 238–39
Inner Harbor, vii; Tour A, 14–35
Inner Harbor Promenade: as site of *Easy Landing* (Snelson), 24; as site of *King Penguin* (Turnbull), 23
International Sculpture Symposium of Baltimore, 8; history of, 30–31; tour entries for Bennett's piece, 98; DuBourg's piece, 97; Höweler's piece, 33; Mikami's piece, 30
Isaiah Bowman (Fraser), tour entry, 214
Italian American Organization United of Maryland, 27
Italian United Society of Baltimore, 286

Jackson, Thomas J. "Stonewall," monument to, 198–99
James Cardinal Gibbons (Richard), tour entry, 48–49
James L. Ridgely Monument (Unknown), tour entry, 279
Janet and Alan Wurtzburger Sculpture Garden, tour entry, 207
John Daniel II Gorilla (V. H. Walter), tour entry, 291
John Eager Howard (Gerlach), 7, 68; tour entry, 105
John Eager Howard Monument (Frémiet), 4; tour entry, 67
John F. Steadman Fire House, as site of *Fire Chariot* (Majorowicz), 106
John Mifflin Hood Monument (Brooks), tour entry, 86–87
Johns Hopkins Bayview Medical Center (formerly City Hospitals): as former site of Moring's *Points on a Line*, 31, 377; as site of *Archimedean Spiral* (Shepherd), 342
Johns Hopkins at Eastern (formerly Eastern High School), 9; as site of Lizette Woodworth Reese Monument (Turnbull), 234
Johns Hopkins Hospital, 9; as site of *Great Ascension* (Pepper), 320
Johns Hopkins Monument (Schuler), tour entry, 210–11
Johns Hopkins University, the (JHU), vii, 8; Bufano Sculpture Garden, 221; Decker Garden sculpture (Berge, E.), 218; donation of land for BMA, 204; Levering Hall sculpture (Kline), 217; Matin Center sculpture (Hartmann), 209; Olin Hall sculpture (Katzen), 216; Shriver Hall sculpture (Waugh and Fraser), 212–13; Sidney Lanier Monument (Schuler), 226–27; Space Telescope Science Institute, 132; White Athletic Center sculpture (Brown), 219–20. See also Hopkins, Johns; Johns Hopkins at Eastern; Johns Hopkins Bayview; Johns Hopkins Hospital; Johns Hopkins Monument

Jones Falls Expressway, 115, 188, 192, 197, 374–75
José Martí Monument (Blanco), tour entry, 325

Katyn Memorial. *See* National Katyn Memorial
Kawasaki, gift from the city of, 21
Keeler, Cardinal William H., 50
Kernan Hospital, as site of *St. Francis of Assisi* (H. Berge), 299
Key, Francis Scott: Mercié monument on Eutaw Place, 190–91; Niehaus monument at Fort McHenry, 146–47; relation to Roger B. Taney, 65; Schuler relief in Mount Vernon, 69; Star-Spangled Banner Centennial Monument (Miller), 334; writing of the "Star-Spangled Banner," 69, 146, 190. *See also* Battle Monument; Fort McHenry; War of 1812
King Penguin (Turnbull), tour entry, 23
Kinship (Kaslow), tour entry, 355
Klutch, Charles E., 204
Knott Foundation, Marion I. & Henry J., 259
Knowledge + Love = Brotherhood (Kaslow), tour entry, 247

Lacrosse Museum and National Hall of Fame, 9; as site of *Dehontshihgwa'es* (Hartmann), 222
Lady Baltimore (Capellano), tour entry, 82
Lady Baltimore statues (Henning): from St. Paul Street Bridge, 4; tour entries, 188, 310
Lafayette, Marquis de, 68. *See also* Lafayette Monument
Lafayette Courts. *See* Pleasant Garden View
Lafayette Monument, 5, 6; tour entry, 75–76
landscape architects: Joseph Hibbard, 208; Mahan Rykiel Associates, 50, 93; George E. Patton, 207. *See also* architects and architectural firms
Lanier, Sidney, 226–27
Latrobe, Ferdinand Claiborne (Baltimore mayor), 328. *See also* Latrobe Monument
Latrobe Monument (J. M. Miller and E. Berge), tour entry, 328
Lazarus, Fred, 94
Lazzarini, Francesco, 1
Learning Tree, The (McGuire), tour entry, 280
Lee, Robert E. *See* Lee and Jackson Monument
Lee and Jackson Monument (Fraser), 181; monument of Lee and a soldier in Dallas, Texas, 199; tour entry, 198–99
Leo Castelli Gallery, 205
Levi, Ryda H., and Robert H., 8, 9; gifts of: *Centennial* (D. Brown), 320, 376; *Great Ascension* (Pepper), 320; sculpture garden at BMA, 208; *Whirligig*, 129. *See also* Levi Sculpture Garden at the BMA
Levi Sculpture Garden at the BMA, tour entry, 208
Liberty Heights Fire Station, as site of *The Rescue* (Kaslow), 303